TimeOut

Naples

Capri, Sorrento & the Amalfi Coast

timeout.com/naples

Penguin Books

PENGUIN BOOKS

Published by the Penguin Group
Penguin Books Ltd, 80 Strand, London WC2R ORL, England
Penguin Books USA Inc., 375 Hudson Street, New York, New York 10014, USA
Penguin Books Australia Ltd, 250 Camberwell Road, Camberwell, Victoria 3124, Australia
Penguin Books Canada Ltd, 10 Alcorn Avenue, Toronto, Ontario, Canada M4V 3B2
Penguin Books (NZ) Ltd, cnr Rosedale and Airborne Roads, Albany, Auckland, New Zealand

Penguin Books Ltd, Registered Offices: Harmondsworth, Middlesex, England

First published 2000
Second edition 2002
10 9 8 7 6 5 4 3 2 1

Colour reprographics by Icon, Crowne House, 56-58 Southwark Street, London SE1 1UN
Printed and bound by Cayfosa-Quebecor, Ctra. de Caldes, Km 3 08 130 Sta, Perpètua de Mogoda, Barcelona, Spain

Edited and designed by
Time Out Guides Limited
Universal House
251 Tottenham Court Road
London W1T 7AB
Tel + 44 (0)20 7813 3000
Fax + 44 (0)20 7813 6001
Email guides@timeout.com
www.timeout.com

Editorial

Editor Anne Hanley
Deputy Editors Phil Harriss, Cath Phillips
Listings Researcher Fulvia Angelini
Proofreader Simon Coppock
Indexer Anna Raikes

Editorial Director Peter Fiennes
Series Editor Ruth Jarvis
Deputy Series Editor Jonathan Cox
Guides Co-ordinator Anna Norman

Design

Group Art Director John Oakey
Art Director Mandy Martin
Art Editor Scott Moore
Senior Designer Lucy Grant
Designers Benjamin de Lotz, Sarah Edwards
Scanning/Imaging Dan Conway
Ad Make-up Glen Impey
Picture Editor Kerri Littlefield
Deputy Picture Editor Kit Burnet
Picture Librarian Sarah Roberts

Advertising

Group Commercial Director Lesley Gill
Sales Director Mark Phillips
International Sales Co-ordinator Ross Canadé
Advertising Sales Manager (Italy) Margherita Tedone
Advertising Assistant Sabrina Ancilleri

Administration

Chairman Tony Elliott
Managing Director Mike Hardwick
Group Financial Director Kevin Ellis
Marketing Director Christine Cort
Marketing Manager Mandy Martinez
US Publicity & Marketing Associate Rosella Albanese
Group General Manager Nichola Coulthard
Production Manager Mark Lamond
Production Controller Samantha Furniss
Accountant Sarah Bostock

Features in this guide were written and researched by: Introduction Anne Hanley. **History** Anne Hanley. **Naples at War** Simon Pocock. **Naples Today** Stefano de Stefano. **Painting in Naples** Victoria Primhak. **Architecture** Victoria Primhak. **Accommodation** Michele Mastronardi. **Sightseeing** Simon Pocock (*Port-side* Victoria Primhak, *Neo-Gothic in Naples* Victoria Primhak, *Campi Flegrei* Mark Walters). **Restaurants** Adrienne Harrison. **Cafés, Bars & Gelaterie** Chris Rose, Adrienne Harrison. **Shops & Services** Julia Church, Adrienne Harrison. **Children** Simon Pocock. **Contemporary Art** Victoria Primhak. **Film** Chris Rose. **Gay & Lesbian** Michele Mastronardi. **Nightlife & Music** Chris Rose. **Performing Arts** Chris Rose, Jonathan Barry. **Sport & Fitness** Simon Pocock. **Around Naples: Introduction** Anne Hanley. **Capri** Lee Marshall. **Ischia** Victoria Primhak, Anne Hanley. **Procida** Victoria Primhak. **Pompeii & Vesuvius** Mark Walters. **Sorrento & Around** Chris Rose, Anne Hanley. **The Amalfi Coast** Lee Marshall. **Further Afield** Mark Walters. **Directory** Fergal Kavanagh, Tricia Reynolds, Chris Rose (*Glossary* Anne Hanley).

The Editor wishes to thank: Marcella Scotto and Nonna Paola, Simon Pocock for his dedication beyond the call of duty and the indefatigable Fulvia Angelini. Special thanks to Lee and Clara Marshall.

Maps by LS International, via Sanremo 17, 20133 Milan, Italy; lsinigaglia@geomaker.com.

Photography by Adam Eastland except: pages 15, 21, 23, 31 Corbis; pages 7, 8, 13, 17, 83 AKG London; pages 10, 11, 18 Hulton Archive; page 26 Associated Press; page 28 Art Archive; page 169 Allsport; page 182 Anne Hanley.

The following images were supplied by the featured establishments: pages 150, 151.

Contents

Introduction

Step off a train at Naples' Stazione Centrale and you may wonder whether you've made a terrible mistake. There are few European cities – even this far south into the Mediterranean – that can quite match Naples' otherness. It's a breathtaking swirl, a multicoloured kasbah of perpetual, deafening motion amid the crumbling vestiges of very faded grandeur. It's threatening and mesmerising, alienating and entrancing.

It's not, exactly, that Naples is un-European: the city's architecture and culture is very definitely in the southern European mould, with Spanish influences and lashings of the baroque style that was so fashionable in the 18th century when this urbane, cultured city was in its glorious heyday. For, yes, despite the traffic chaos, the crumbling masonry and evident harsh poverty, this paradoxical city is unquestionably urbane and cultured, even now.

It's an urbanity that seeps out in little things: an exhaustive disquisition on Renaissance building styles from the shabbily dressed porter of a decrepit palazzo; the innate gentility of a taxi driver as he explains that he is leaving you far from your destination to save you paying extra for negotiating the centre's labyrinthine one-way system. (The former may have made up every fact; the latter may merely be inventing excuses to time his home-coming with the pasta being placed on the table. But it's all done with a panache that – if you let it – will win your heart.)

The culture contained in this city simply stuns. There's the Teatro San Carlo of course, which continues to churn out top-rate opera despite limping from financial crisis to financial crisis. And there are the great collections: the artefacts ripped untimely from Pompeii and Herculaneum and now in the Museo Archeologico Nazionale; the stupendous works in the Galleria di Capodimonte; the lashings of paintings to be found in any number of churches that are artworks in themselves.

But after many decades of inexorable slide towards mere survival, Naples has pulled itself up by its bootstraps in the past ten years and made a commendable – and, all signs suggest, successful – effort to reinject a little life into an artistic scene that had seemed moribund. While other Italian cities polish up their treasures, putting them on display in ever more spectacular ways, Naples is going one step further and creating new ones. Modern sculptures appear in ancient squares; new metro stations are transformed into contemporary masterpieces, drawing favourable criticism from an art world that until recently didn't even have Naples on its radar screen.

So, with all this going on, why is it that the majority of visitors to the province of Naples and its surrounding region of Campania get no closer to the city's throbbing heart than its airport or a nervous hop from one platform to the other in its crowded railway station?

The answer is: there's too much else to see and do. Close at hand are resorts such as Capri, Sorrento and the glorious Amalfi Coast towns – some of the most chic, most beautiful and most visited on the Med. And, as if that weren't enough, there are archaeological wonders such as Pompeii and Herculaneum to sate visitors' cravings for the odd bit of ancient history to punctuate the swimming and sunbathing. Such a concentration of attractions is unrivalled anywhere.

Which inevitably leads many to shun a city with a reputation for poverty and crime, however unjustified this latter may be (well... as long as you don't flash your Rolex too ostentatiously). But shunning Naples is a terrible mistake. Overwhelming as the experience is, this city is the jewel in the crown of the Campania experience.

You'll need to brace yourself, of course. You'll need to suspend your Anglo-Saxon preconceptions and hang-ups and throw yourself wholeheartedly into the seething mass, accepting your role as 'o straniero ('the foreigner'). The experience will be unforgettable.

You'll be welcomed warmly by locals not made blasé by generations of holiday-resort status; every one will want to share their city's splendours and reveal its secrets to you; some people will test you too, checking that you have your wits about you and aren't easily ripped off. Don't take offence: remember, this is a city where for centuries only the very fittest (and a tiny number of the richest) survived.

Immerse yourself and revel in *napoletanità*.

ABOUT TIME OUT GUIDES

This is the second edition of the *Time Out Naples Guide*, one of the expanding series of Time Out guides produced by the people behind London and New York's definitive listings magazines. This edition has been completely updated and all listings checked by a team of Naples-based writers and experts.

THE LIE OF THE LAND

Naples is bustling and chaotic, so for ease of use we have divided many chapters by district. Within easy reach of the city are the islands of Capri, Ischia and little-known Procida, as well as resorts such as Sorrento and the Amalfi Coast, and archeological wonders like Pompeii and Herculaneum. All of these destinations are covered exhaustively in this guide.

ESSENTIAL INFORMATION

For all the practical information you might need for visiting the area – including transport systems, emergency numbers and useful websites – turn to the Directory chapter at the back of this guide. It starts on page 280. Each chapter of the Around Naples section has its own local transport instructions and hotel and restaurant listings.

THE LOWDOWN ON THE LISTINGS

We have tried to make this book as easy to use and as useful as possible. Websites, phone numbers, transport information, opening times and admission prices are all included.

However, southern Italian owners and managers are notoriously apt to change their arrangements at any time. Smaller shops, bars and restaurants rarely keep strictly to their 'official' opening times; many may decide to pull down the shutters and take holidays without warning. Before you go out of your way, we'd strongly advise you to phone ahead to check opening times and other particulars.

Arts programmes are often finalised at the last moment; opening times of museums and galleries can change abruptly, though often for the better with late-night openings, especially during the summer months. A trip to the local tourist office (*see p293* and under Tourist information in each chapter of the Around Naples section) on arrival is always a good idea.

While every effort has been made to ensure the accuracy of the information contained in this guide, the publishers cannot accept responsibility for any errors it may contain.

There is an online version of this guide, as well as weekly events listings for 35 international cities, at **www.timeout.com**

PRICES AND PAYMENT

In the listings, we have noted which of the following credit cards are accepted: American Express (AmEx), Diners Club (DC), MasterCard (MC) and Visa (V). Other cards may be taken.

For every restaurant we have given average prices for a full meal; they are guidelines, however, not gospel. Hotel prices have a tendency to rise unjustifiably during the high season. If prices vary wildly from those we've quoted, ask whether there's a good reason. If there isn't, go elsewhere. Then please let us know. We aim to give the best and most up-to-date advice, so we want to know if you've been badly treated or overcharged.

We have given adult ticket prices for museums, galleries and archeological sites. EU citizens and those from countries with reciprocal agreements aged 60-plus or under 18 should be admitted free to publicly owned sights.

TELEPHONE NUMBERS

To phone Naples from outside Italy, first dial the international code, followed by 39 (the code for Italy), then 081 (the area code for Naples) and finally the (usually seven-digit) number. When within Italy, all telephone numbers now require that the area code is dialled as part of the number, whether you are within the relevant area or not. For more details on phone codes and charges, *see p292*.

MAPS

At the back of this guide (and within the Around Naples section) you'll find maps of Naples and the towns and islands featured, as well as plans of major archaeological sites. In chapters referring to the city of Naples itself, grid references to maps on pages 310 to 313 are given after each listing.

LET US KNOW WHAT YOU THINK

We hope you enjoy the *Time Out Naples Guide*, and we'd like to know what you think of it. We welcome your tips for places to include in future editions and take notice of your criticism of our choices. There's a reader's reply card at the back of this book – or you can email us on naplesguide@timeout.com.

In Context

History

From Greek trading post to 'most beautiful crown'.

When the first Greeks washed up on Ischia – which they named Pithekoussai – the hill where Rome would later be founded was barely settled. It was the eighth century BC and adventurers from the island of Euboea set up a trading station near what is now Lacco Ameno (*see p196*). The lively volcanic activity on the island didn't suit all the newcomers, some of whom decamped rapidly to Cuma (*see p101*) on the mainland, and got down to the crucial business of improving trade networks around the Mediterranean basin.

Infinitely more sophisticated and organised than the tribes that had long populated the lush hinterland and sparser mountain region beyond, the Greeks soon made Cuma the area's most powerful city. The addition of a Sibyl – a prophesying voice of the gods – in her cave deep inside the town added to its allure (*see p8* **Rushing streams of sound**). Confident in their control of the area, the Cuman Greeks spread down the coast, founding Parthenope (near Pizzofalcone; *see p67*) in c680 BC,

Dikaiarchia (Pozzuoli; *see p98*) in c530 BC and Neapolis ('New Town') in 470 BC; the original Greek plan can still be made out in the grid-pattern streets in central Naples.

Yet as the Cuman Greeks were extending their sphere of influence, so were the people that would prove the first real challenge to their power: the Etruscans. Based in what is now Tuscany, the highly advanced Etruscans spread slowly southwards from the ninth or eighth centuries BC, establishing their southern capital at Capua in about 600 BC. They rapidly absorbed the extraordinary culture imported into the region by the Greeks, adding their own particular twists to it. Conflict was inevitable between two such dynamic peoples, and battles were fought at Cuma in 524 and 474 BC, both won by the Greeks but both exhausting the strength of the rivals, and leaving them prey to the encroaching Samnite hill people.

Shepherds and fighters, the Samnites took Capua in 424 BC and Cuma in 421 BC. Into this scenario stepped another tribe with a mounting

Rushing streams of sound

'There is a cleft in the flank of the Euboean Rock forming a vast cavern. A hundred mouthways and a hundred broad tunnels lead into it, and through them the Sibyl's answer comes forth in a hundred rushing streams of sound.'
Virgil, *The Aeneid*, Book 6

Traditionally depicted as a hag prone to fits of frenzied prophesying, the Sibyl (pictured in calmer mood) was a spokeswoman for the god Apollo. The Cuman Sibyl was by no means Apollo's only mouthpiece – indeed, there were Sibyls in many important centres of Apollo-worship – but she was his best known and, legend relates, his most canny.

In the fifth century BC, the Greek god Apollo hardly featured in the Roman pantheon. So it was hardly surprising that when the Cuman Sibyl offered to sell Rome's King Tarquinius Superbus nine books of Sibylline prophesy at a high price, he rejected her offer. The Sibyl, however, didn't let up. She threw three of her books into the fire and offered the remaining six for the same high price. She was refused. She threw a further three into the fire and offered the remaining three at the same price.

By this time, the superstitious Tarquin was thoroughly unnerved by the holy woman's calm determination. He forked out for the remaining three, which were kept on the Capitoline hill in Rome for consultation in

moments of greatest need. Thus Apollo became a key figure in Roman mythology... and the Sibyl got her original asking price.

lust for land and power: the Romans. Around 340 BC the Romans began bringing the Samnites to heel. By 328 BC they had turned on Neapolis itself, laying siege to the city; it held out for two years before handing itself over to the conquerors.

ROMAN RULERS, GREEK FASHIONS

The city's flourishing trade suffered a setback as it was forced to supply ships and men for Roman naval battles. Its assimilation into greater Rome laid a damper on its economy that remained for centuries.

Neapolis continued to grow in population and culture, however, clinging proudly to its Greek identity and language. As all things Hellenic became fashionable in Republican Rome, wealthy Roman offspring were dispatched to the southern city for their education, while their parents enjoyed the balmy climate in holiday villas along the coast from Cuma to Sorrento. To make

communications easier, the Appian Way (via Appia), the first major Roman highway, was begun in 312 BC.

The idyll suffered the occasional brutal interruption: in the Second Punic War (218-201 BC), the Romans battled Hannibal's Carthaginian forces back and forth across the plains of the Neapolis hinterland; during the Roman Civil War (88-82 BC), Sulla occupied Neapolis, massacring a large proportion of its inhabitants during his triumphal march on Rome, where he was to rule as dictator from 82 to 79 BC; and in 73 BC, runaway slave Spartacus established the headquarters of his slaves' army on the slopes of Mount Vesuvius, from where he set out on his rampages up and down the Italian peninsula.

But Neapolis pulled itself up by its bootstraps, and by the time the Roman Empire was established in 27 BC, it was once again a centre of learning, attracting writers, teachers and holidaymakers. Virgil lived in the city for many years, composing his Georgics, and is buried here; the sybaritic General Lucullus built a home where Castel dell'Ovo now stands.

If the city flourished under the Empire, not so the surrounding region – Campania – where agriculture was hit hard by imports of cheaper grain and oil from Rome's new possessions in Africa and Spain. In the largely abandoned areas around the Volturno estuary to the north of the city and Paestum to the south, malaria was rife. When Vesuvius erupted in AD 79, burying surrounding towns beneath lava and ash, Pompeii was already little more than a ghost town.

'Wealthy Roman offspring were dispatched to the southern city for their education.'

As the Empire declined, so did Naples and Campania, which from the early fifth century was prey to Goth and Vandal attackers. The latter razed Capua in AD 456 and the former won and lost Naples itself several times during the fifth century, despite works to strengthen the walls in 440. It was in Naples that the Western Roman Empire truly came to an end, when the last emperor, Romulus Augustulus, imprisoned by the Goth King Odoacer, died in AD 476.

THE DUCHY OF NAPLES

Over in Byzantium (Constantinople), the Eastern emperor Justinian was keen to reassert his power over Italy. In the 530s he dispatched his prize general, Belisarius, to do the job.

In 536, Naples' walls held Belisarius out for three weeks. Then one of the general's men spotted a water conduit leading into the city, and a handful of crack fighters crawled inside. Attacked from within and without, Naples fell and many Neapolitans were slaughtered.

The Byzantines harried the increasingly demoralised Goths until 553 when the last Goth ruler was killed. The following year, Naples became a Byzantine-controlled duchy, with dukes, magistrates and military leaders appointed by the Eastern emperor's Italian representative, the Exarch of Ravenna. (By 645, this tight rein was loosened, and a Neapolitan by the name of Basilio became the first native duke of the city, with the blessing of the emperor himself.)

With its population of 40,000, Naples was flourishing once again, its importance growing in inverse proportion to that of declining Capua. But marauding foreigners would continue to threaten the area.

In 568, the Germanic *longobardi* (Lombards) swept across the Alps, taking northern Italy without too much of a struggle and moving swiftly down the peninsula. Their sieges of Naples – in 581, 592 and 599 – were unsuccessful, though much of Campania, including Capua and, in 625, Salerno, fell to them. At the same time, Naples was beset from the sea by Saracens, a generic term for the mainly north African Arab tribes that raided and traded across the Mediterranean. In the ninth century came the Franks, who were allies of the Pope (generally speaking) but sworn enemies of the Neapolitans.

Uninterested in territorial aggrandisement itself, the little duchy was content to ensure its own independence by playing its conflicting allies (Byzantium and the Pope in Rome) and foes (Lombards, Franks and Saracens) off against each other, sealing secret pacts, and balancing loyalty against distance, coherent policy against tactical advantage.

In the early 800s, Duke Sergio I used Saracens to fight his battles against the Lombards, in return for which he helped the Saracens snatch Messina from Byzantium, to which Naples was, in theory, allied. In 849, however, it was Sergio's fleet that inflicted a crippling defeat on Rome-bent Saracens in a naval battle off Ostia (an event commemorated later by Raphael in frescos in the Vatican). Thirty years later, Duke Sergio II employed Saracens from the *ribat* – a thriving, semi-tolerated, makeshift trading post located beneath Naples' city walls – to capture a troublesome bishop.

While Naples played its Machiavellian games to keep all the wolves from the door, inside the walls the city was growing in beauty and wealth. Churches were built, schools were founded; artists and goldsmiths worked furiously to decorate the proud duchy. In the mid-tenth century, with Saracens attacking from the sea and disgruntled Byzantines besieging from the landward side, Duke John III still found time to dispatch monks to libraries around Christendom to copy manuscripts sacred and profane to enrich his own splendid collection. Industry and trade flourished; Neapolitan textiles were sought-after all around the Mediterranean basin.

Beyond Naples and the lands directly under its control, things started to look up for the Lombard-dominated territories after the Germanic overlords converted to Roman-style Christianity in the seventh century. Firmly settled in their southern dominions, the Lombards themselves embarked on a bout of building and learning, especially in their capital at Benevento (*see p273*) in the hills to

Hannibal has his sights set on Naples in the Second Punic War. *See p8.*

the north-east of Naples. By the eighth century, however, divisions were appearing in the united Lombard front, as Salerno grew in importance and wealth. In 849, the Lombard centres of Benevento and Salerno split, severely weakening the Lombard position. Capua, too, became a separate Lombard principality in the tenth century.

> ### 'Based north of Naples, the Normans grew wealthier and increasingly power-hungry.'

Not many miles from Salerno, Amalfi had emerged as a law unto itself, resisting Lombard encroachments, slipping away from the control of the Duchy of Naples (though highly active in the duchy's mercantile activities) and continuing to swear fealty to Byzantium, which became an invaluable trading partner for this growing sea power.

THE NORMAN CONQUEST

This fragmented state of affairs was soon to come to an end. In a final show of strength in 1027, the Lombard Prince Pandolf IV of Capua seized power in Naples, helped by Neapolitan barons keen to oust the reigning Duke Sergio IV. Holed up in Gaeta, Sergio turned to an unruly band of Normans who had strayed into southern Italy shortly before. He married his sister to their leader, Rainulf Drengot, and made him Count of Aversa. The combined Neapolitan and Norman force drove the Lombards out of Naples.

With Aversa – a small town to the north of Naples – as their power base, the Normans grew in number as more compatriots arrived from France, grew wealthier thanks to their mercenary activities, and became increasingly power-hungry. In 1062 they took Capua, in 1073 Amalfi. In 1077 Lombard Salerno fell to Robert *le Guiscard* ('the Crafty') – a member of the powerful Hauteville (Altavilla) family – who made the city his mainland capital. At this time Salerno was a boom-town famous throughout Christendom for its extraordinary medical school (*see p268*).

The Normans besieged Naples for two years to no avail. Robert turned his sights on Byzantium, but died in his bid to oust the Byzantine emperor. His brother Roger focused on southern Italy, most of which was firmly under Norman control by 1130, when his son was crowned Roger II, King of Sicily.

The Norman monarch demanded that Duke Sergio VII of Naples recognise him as sovereign. Sergio obliged, then retracted, joining an anti-Norman League that scored numerous bloody victories against the French interlopers. Having identified Naples as the centre of opposition, Roger laid siege after siege to the city, but he was driven back by weather and disease and the unhealthy exhalations from the volcanic areas surrounding it.

Sergio, having made another of his temporary pledges to support Roger, died fighting for the Normans in October 1137. The Neapolitan people turned to the anti-Norman Pope Innocent II for help, holding out against the Norman king for a further two years. When

Innocent was taken prisoner by the Normans, however, Naples was left with little choice; in August 1139, a delegation swore fealty to the Sicilian crown in Benevento.

Despite the lengthy struggle, the capitulation was not an unpopular one. When Roger visited Naples in autumn 1140, 30,000 people turned out to greet him with joy. Within walls over 4.5 kilometres (2.8 miles) long, Roger was impressed by great houses and lavish churches. Outside the walls, trade flourished in two separate ports.

But with its incorporation into the Kingdom of Sicily, Naples moved backstage and was overshadowed by Palermo. A model of stability and efficiency, the Norman kingdom was also highly centralised, leaving little scope for independent action by its constituent parts. The Neapolitan nobility – for centuries a thorn in the side of the ruling dukes – swore fealty to the Norman crown in exchange for feudal land and privileges.

The Norman conquest coincided with a period of high agricultural production in the Campanian countryside, and with explosive growth in the shipping trade, though this boom was thanks mainly to canny immigrants from Amalfi, Pisa and Genoa, rather than to Neapolitan activity as such. Relative peace and prosperity meant a livelier market for the city's artisans. This general well-being, which ended, coincidentally, with the Norman line, may explain Naples' loyalty to Roger's vacillating grandson Tancred when his throne was contested by the more dynamic Henry Hohenstaufen of Swabia, the son of Holy Roman Emperor Frederick Barbarossa and son-in-law of Roger.

After Tancred's death in 1194, Henry became king of Sicily and punished Naples by ripping down its walls. However, Henry, too, was to die three years later, leaving a three-year-old heir, Frederick. Still smarting from its punishment, Naples entered into the dynastic struggles of the German emperors, wholeheartedly backing the claims of Otto IV of Brunswick over those of the baby king Frederick II. The city decided to recognise Otto as sovereign, sticking by him through papal excommunications and various routs on the battlefield.

It was a wonder, then, that the victorious Frederick, when he was safely on the thrones of the Holy Roman Empire and southern Italy in 1214, decided to invest so much in Naples

and treat it with such munificence. Though his brilliant, learned and artistically astonishing court remained in Palermo, he rebuilt Naples' walls and fortifications, and made the city an intellectual centre of his Italian kingdom. Naples' new university – the Studium – was established to promote Ghibelline (pro-empire) teachings in contrast to the Guelph (pro-papacy) ones of the great university at Bologna.'

Nothing, however, could erase Naples' historic hatred of the Hohenstaufen family. In 1251, after the death of Frederick II, the city rose up against attempts by his son Conrad to assert control. With the backing of Pope Innocent IV, it declared itself a free commune, resisting sieges laid by Conrad's Italian representative, his illegitimate brother Manfred. In 1253, however, imperial forces managed to break through.

When the emperor died the following year, the commune was re-established briefly. In 1258, Manfred became king of Naples but the Neapolitans seized the first possible opportunity to offload their Hohenstaufen sovereign. Charles of Anjou had hardly completed his invasion of Sicily in 1265 when the city rushed to pledge its loyalty to the newly arrived French dynasty.

ANJOU AND ARAGON

The Anjous, to set themselves apart from their predecessors, moved the capital of their Italian kingdom from Palermo to Naples, though the realm continued to be called the Regno di Sicilia. New buildings went up, and merchants and craftsmen from all around Mediterranean Europe flocked to the booming city. Charles I (who reigned from 1265 to 1282) had the Castel Nuovo (see p59) built, and a new, wealthy and well-planned quarter grew around it.

In Sicily, things did not go so smoothly for the Angevin kings. Resentful at the removal of the capital from its soil, as well as at harsh taxes imposed by the newcomers, Sicilian barons began plotting with Peter III, King of Aragon, to overthrow Charles. The rebellion went into top gear on Easter Monday 1282, when some rowdy French soldiers were killed after vespers outside a Palermo church; over the following night, in a riot that became known as the *Vespri siciliani*, 2,000 French people were killed.

The ensuing Vesper Wars dragged on until 1302, raging through Sicily, and up and down the southern mainland, until Charles finally acknowledged that Sicily was lost and was reduced to ruling the southern Italian mainland.

Naples thrived as the Angevins sought to make the city a fitting capital for their dynasty. Under the third Angevin king, Robert (reigned 1309-43), the Castel Sant'Elmo (*see p87*) was built. However, the city's growing wealth and population caused lasting harm to the area around it. Naples' port expanded exponentially, sounding the death knell for one-time naval powers such as Amalfi, Gaeta and Salerno. And while the agricultural regions immediately surrounding the city capitalised on the food demands of the growing populace, the foothills of the Apennines became increasingly poor and more depopulated, and malaria flourished in the marshy districts around the mouth of the Volturno, and in the Sele valley south of Salerno.

Naples' relationship with its French rulers was loyal, though never unquestioningly so. When Andrew of Hungary, husband of the beautiful and highly intelligent Queen Joan I (reigned 1343-81) was murdered in 1345, the Neapolitan people caught and wreaked their vengeance on his suspected murderers. King Louis I of Hungary suspected, however, that Joan might have had something to do with his brother's demise, and invaded Naples in 1348. Joan remedied the situation by fleeing to her county of Provence, and selling her city of Avignon to the Pope in return for absolution for any misdemeanours she might have committed. In 1352, she returned to Naples to a rapturous welcome. Thirty years later, when Joan backed the anti-Pope Clement VII, her own people rose up to overthrow her in favour of her cousin Charles III of Durres (reigned 1381-86), a champion of Pope Urban VI.

When Charles' son Ladislas (reigned 1386-1414) died, the Neapolitans defended his sister, the promiscuous Joan II (reigned 1414-35), against her second husband Jacques de Bourbon, who tried to wrest power from her. They also backed Joan's designated heir, her cousin René of Anjou (Good King René of Provence) against the claims of Alfonso 'the Magnanimous' of Aragon (King Alfonso V of Sicily), whom she had previously adopted then disinherited.

But Alfonso was more than a match for René, whom he drove out of Naples shortly after Joan's death. Southern Italy was one kingdom again, and a long period of Spanish control had begun.

With his leech-like crowd of Catalan followers, Alfonso (reigned 1442-58) failed to ingratiate himself with his Neapolitan

subjects, despite his lenient treatment of a city that had fought tooth and nail to prevent him taking the Neapolitan crown. His illegitimate son Ferdinand (or Ferrante) I (reigned 1458-94) won some hearts when he ejected the overbearing freebooters and championed the arts and trades of the expanding city.

Naples' powerful barons, however, continued to oppose the Aragonese presence; some persuaded France's King Charles VIII to occupy the city in 1494. But the Neapolitan people rose up against French domination, reinstating King Ferrante's grandson, Ferdinando II (or Ferrandino).

On Ferrandino's premature death the following year, the people pressed for the crown to be given to his young widow Joan, sister of Spain's King Ferdinand 'The Catholic'. The barons, on the other hand, conspired to place Ferrandino's uncle Frederick (reigned 1496-1501) on the throne. This solution enraged both France and Spain, which marched together on Naples in 1501.

THE VICEROYS

When the French arrived first, Frederick hoped to salvage something for himself by agreeing to hand over Naples and part of his realm to King Charles VIII. But when the great Spanish General Consalvo di Cordoba appeared at the city walls in 1503, the people of Naples welcomed him in, and Spain's King Ferdinand added the Neapolitan crown (reigned 1503-16 as Ferdinand III) to his already impressive list of titles.

Ferdinand visited his new acquisition during 1506, conferring privileges on both the nobles and the *piazza* – the people – and leaving behind him the first of a long succession of viceroys who would be feared, hated and generally mistrusted over the next two and a half centuries.

With the arrival of the viceroys, the Neapolitans' say in the running of their own affairs diminished greatly. The parliament, in which nobles and the people were represented, served almost exclusively to rubber-stamp inaptly named *donativi* – not in fact donations but crippling taxes. Even the barons were deprived of their near-omnipotence. During his term of office, Pedro di Toledo (viceroy from 1532 to 1553) had no qualms about imprisoning or even executing nobles who until then had enjoyed total impunity.

And though violent Neapolitan protests halted various attempts to introduce the Spanish Inquisition, and the city reaped some benefit from the viceroys – especially from Toledo, who was responsible for vast redevelopment to improve living standards

Bourbon rulers made 18th-century Naples a city worthy of its age. *See p15.*

in the city, building the Quartieri spagnoli (*see p77*) – on the whole, Spanish rule did little to improve Naples' lot.

In the very early days, the city did profit from the extraordinary economic boom resulting from the Spanish conquest of the New World. Nevertheless, the ensuing hyper-inflation-fuelled slump hit hard in a city with no strong trade infrastructure (trade having long been dominated by transient merchants from Genoa, Amalfi and Pisa). The slump was accentuated by short-term administrators who had little interest in stamping out the endemic corruption in the realm's bureaucracy, and by chronic crime levels in the unpoliced countryside (which regularly failed to produce enough food to feed the population).

> ### 'At the beginning of the 17th century, Naples was Europe's biggest city, with a population of 300,000.'

Yet it was on this depressed part of its dominions that Spain depended to finance its European wars. Taxes were levied on just about every commodity or transaction: on flour and bread, on tobacco, on rents, on hemp and on imported metals. Even ransoms paid to free Neapolitans from Turkish pirates were subject to tax. But the levy most certain to set the city aflame was the one on fruit and vegetables.

It was this tax that sparked the worst uprising to hit Spanish-controlled Naples when it was reintroduced in 1646. In 1647, Neapolitans rallied behind a 27-year-old

fisherman from Amalfi called Tommaso Aniello (known as Masaniello), who headed an increasingly bloody revolt between 7 July and his assassination on 16 July. Masaniello was pro-king but anti-levy. His task of leading the undisciplined mob was rendered all the more difficult by a vacillating viceroy, the Duke of Arcos. Arcos promised to suspend the tax but didn't, armed the people then sent his troops to gun them down, and pledged greater clout in parliament to the *piazza* (masses) while stationing troops to cover the retreat of the barons' henchmen after they had murdered Masaniello.

A disaffected aristocrat, the Prince of Massa, led the revolt after Masaniello's death. Then France, taking advantage of the chaos, dispatched Henry, Duke of Guise, to steer the revolution in its favour. But by April 1648 the Neapolitans had grown tired of the upheaval. Endlessly optimistic, they settled for a new viceroy – the Count of Oñate – and a promise of more reasonable taxes in the future.

At the beginning of the 17th century, Naples was Europe's biggest city, with a population of over 300,000. The plague that ravaged the area for six months in 1656 left three-quarters of the population dead. But the rest of Europe, sinking deeper into dynastic struggles and wars of succession, had little time to worry about the devastation caused by disease in this poverty-stricken outpost.

SPANISH SUCCESSION, POLISH SUCCESSION

The end of the Spanish Habsburg line, in the person of the childless Charles II (Charles V of Naples, reigned 1665-1700), left various crowns up for grabs. England, France and Holland agreed that Spain and the Spanish Netherlands should pass to the Austrian Habsburg, Archduke Charles (younger son of the Holy Roman Emperor, Leopold I), with Naples and Sicily passing to France. Charles II rejected this arrangement, having been persuaded by his Bourbon brother-in-law, King Louis XIV of France, that a Bourbon would keep Spanish dominions intact.

On Charles' death in 1700, Louis' grandson Philip of Anjou became Philip V of Spain, sparking a continental conflict that would last from 1701 to 1714. When France backed Philip and invaded the Spanish Netherlands, Britain, Holland and Austria formed an anti-French alliance. But when Archduke Charles unexpectedly became Holy Roman Emperor Charles VI in 1711 after the death of his older brother, the allies balked at fighting to enhance his power still further.

Sick of the succession of Spanish viceroys, and hoping for their own independent monarch in the shape of a minor Habsburg, Neapolitan nobles sought Austrian victory in the War of Spanish Succession. The Neapolitan people, as much at loggerheads with their nobles as ever, were happy to support Spain's new Bourbon king, and Philip V was given a tumultuous welcome when he visited the city in 1702.

In 1707, however, Austrian forces occupied southern Italy, and Naples once again found itself with a series of Habsburg-appointed viceroys at its helm.

Succession in Poland caused the next major European shake-up (1733-5), pitting Russia and Habsburg-controlled Austria (in favour of Augustus III) against the Franco-Spanish Bourbon alliance (which backed Stanislav I, father-in-law of France's Louis XV).

'THE MOST BEAUTIFUL CROWN'

When the War of Polish Succession broke out, the squat, ugly but very likeable Spanish Infante Don Carlos (Charles), younger son of Philip V and the scheming Elisabetta Farnese, was in Florence, amusing himself (according to the British envoy of the time, Horace Mann) by shooting the eyes out of birds in the Gobelins tapestries in the Pitti Palace and whisking courtiers' wigs off with strategically placed hooks and lines.

Elisabetta had sent her teenage son with a 40,000-strong army to occupy her family's dominions in Parma and Piacenza. He was also to take over Tuscany on the death of Gian Gastone Medici, the last of his line and a Farnese relation. But when the Bourbons entered hostilities with Austria, Elisabetta set her sights

Maria Carolina

Maria Carolina, one of the 16 children of Empress Maria Theresa of Austria, was a highly educated, highly strung 16-year-old when she was dispatched to Naples to marry King Ferdinand IV in 1768.

Though she was aware, in theory, what awaited her in her new home – Ferdinand's childishness bordering on derangement was no secret in European court circles – she was still taken aback. But with admirable poise – and a shrewd knack for convincing her unsophisticated spouse to do what she thought best – she remained the power behind the southern Italian throne until 1811, perhaps by dint of sticking to her redoubtable mother's dictum: 'in your heart and in the uprightness of your mind be an Austrian; in all that is unimportant, appear to be a Neapolitan.'

Maria Carolina's real hold on power began in 1777 when, after the birth of a male heir (she was to have 11 children), she was given a place on Naples' Council of State. She was then able to oust her arch-enemy, Bernardo Tanucci, the liberal minister who had been responsible – among other more positive things – for her husband's utter lack of education, and who resented her hold over Ferdinand.

higher. Shortly after his 18th birthday, she ordered her son to mobilise his army, and take 'the most beautiful crown in Italy'.

> **'With the Age of Enlightenment in full swing, Charles III transformed Naples into a city worthy of the times.'**

Charles' procession south was good-natured and largely unimpeded. Austria failed to reinforce its embittered, over-taxed city of Naples and Charles entered the city in triumph in May 1734. In July 1735, having expelled the Austrians from the whole of southern Italy, he was crowned Charles III of the Kingdom of Sicily. Though the Peace of Vienna (1738) obliged Charles to cede Parma, Piacenza and most of Tuscany to Austria, he was confirmed as king of an independent southern Italian realm. Finally, Naples was a capital again,

She enthusiastically promoted John Acton, a French-born minor British aristocrat who would be navy minister, foreign minister and then prime minister of her husband's realm until 1806.

Whether the cold, dignified but striking Acton was the queen's lover or not remains a point of debate. He was certainly her firm favourite and wasn't loath to exploit his position to encourage her pro-British and anti-French sympathies. If the queen was able to control her husband and courtiers, she had no such knack with her chief minister; Acton's jealousy or uprightness prompted him to act as self-appointed guardian of the queen's behaviour, holding her in thrall and banishing from court anyone whom he perceived the queen taking too great a liking to.

It was another Englishman who brought Maria Carolina's career of plotting and politicking to an end in 1811. Ill and hysterical, the ageing queen found herself at loggerheads with Lord William Bentinck, the British ambassador to court in Palermo and virtual dictator of Sicily. The two loathed each other at first sight; the liberal Whig Bentinck considered the queen behind any number of reactionary schemes. Having forced King Ferdinand to abdicate in favour of his son, Bentinck then forced him to pack his wife Maria Carolina back to Austria where she died, still plotting a return to Naples, three years later. 'At least she strove to attain something outside herself,' wrote historian Harold Acton in *The Bourbons of Naples*. 'Even her failure had a certain lurid magnificence.'

with a monarch it could call its own. It welcomed the Spanish newcomer with open arms, and Charles reciprocated.

With the Age of Enlightenment in full swing, the king (supported, from 1737, by his wife Maria Amelia of Saxony, upon whom Charles doted) transformed his capital into a city worthy of the times.

No opera lover, he built Europe's finest theatre, the San Carlo (*see p61*); no scholar, he established the Biblioteca Nazionale. Under Charles' rule, the excavation of Herculaneum and Pompeii got under way. The 16th-century Palazzo Reale was extended and refurbished. To pursue his passion for hunting, Charles had magnificent palaces built at Portici, Capodimonte and Caserta. To house the city's poor, he commissioned the Albergo dei Poveri (*see p81*), the largest edifice in southern Europe.

The death of the Austrian emperor in 1740 plunged Europe into war again. Unwillingly, Charles was prevailed upon to back the Franco-Spanish-Prussian alliance contesting the accession of the late emperor's daughter

Maria Teresa to the Austrian throne. Once the redoubtable empress had secured her crown (and Naples had been forced to capitulate in humiliating fashion to her British allies, who threatened to bombard the city from the sea in 1742), Charles could settle back down to the business of running his kingdom, or of choosing very competent men to do so for him.

In 1759, Charles abdicated and returned to Spain, to succeed his father as King Charles III. He left his eight-year-old heir Ferdinand under the jealous tutorship of his most trusted adviser, the honest and highly competent Tuscan lawyer Bernardo Tanucci. Tanucci had been instrumental in seeking to introduce bureaucratic and fiscal reforms into Charles' shambolic state. The continued power of the feudal barons limited his success there, however. Even more resounding was his failure to provide Ferdinand with an education worthy of a monarch.

When the highly educated, highly cultured and very strong-willed Maria Carolina (*see above* **Maria Carolina**), daughter of the

Austrian empress, arrived in Naples to marry the young king in 1768, she was shocked. He played with toys, talked coarse local dialect, enjoyed rough games with low-class youths, and abhorred anything to do with books or learning. Ferdinand was, however, terribly impressed by his intelligent young wife, whose orders – especially in matters of state – he soon accepted unquestioningly.

With the birth of her first son in 1777, Maria Carolina entered the Council of State, as stipulated in her wedding contract. From this position of strength, she was able to engineer the downfall of her arch-enemy Tanucci.

In 1778, she adopted as her favourite John Acton, a wandering British naval hero, who may have become her lover. Born in France, Acton had made vast improvements to the Tuscan navy before being summoned to modernise Naples' neglected fleet.

In Spain, King Charles was furious that a subject of his enemy Britain should be gaining influence in his former realm. Indeed, Acton was apt to pass classified information from the queen's lips to the British ambassador, Sir William Hamilton, and he steered Naples into an iron-clad alliance with Britain. He also served Naples faithfully, however, displaying exceptional honesty and organisational powers in the midst of ministers known for their inefficiency and graft.

> ## 'Acton, the queen's favourite, steered Naples into an iron-clad alliance with Britain.'

He may also have attenuated the worst excesses of the queen's hysteria following the outbreak of the French Revolution. For the reactionary Maria Carolina, the masses seizing power was shock enough; the masses' execution of her sister Marie Antoinette in 1793 was beyond the pale.

Naples entered enthusiastically into the anti-French alliance. A Neapolitan army of 60,000 troops occupied French-held Rome on 27 November 1798, with the triumphant King Ferdinand at its head. But Karl Mack, the Austrian general who led the Neapolitan forces, proved to be a bungling fool. When France's General Championnet marched back into Rome 11 days later, the Neapolitans fled, with the French on their heels.

EXILE AND RESTORATION

In Naples, news of the defeat was greeted by the fiercely royalist masses with ferocious attacks on those Neapolitan liberals who had championed French ideals of liberty and equality. The massacre ended only as the French entered the city, and the Repubblica Partenopea was declared in January 1799.

The royal family, accompanied by Acton, fled to Sicily on board Admiral Horatio Nelson's ship the *Vanguard* (*see p17* **Naples and the hero of the Nile**). In Naples, efforts – confused and mostly bungled – by Republican leaders to introduce pro-equality reforms failed totally to impress the poor, who swiftly took advantage of the early withdrawal of the French military to rise up and force liberals to take refuge in the city's forts.

Further south, the queen's envoy Cardinal Fabrizio Ruffo led his raggle-taggle Christian Army of the Holy Faith up the boot of Italy, in a bloody campaign to oust the French and their sympathisers. In June, the Republican leaders agreed to a capitulation, the terms of which were promptly ignored by Nelson and King Ferdinand. Over 200 executions – including that of royalist-turned-rebel Admiral Francesco Caracciolo and aristocratic child prodigy Eleonora Fonseca di Pimental – were carried out.

Naples was a minor player on the more vast European chessboard, and easily sacrificed by allies in general disagreement over how to cope with the vast Revolutionary and then Napoleonic armies descending on them. When France beat Austria at Marengo in 1800, becoming the dominant European power on land and debilitating Naples' chief ally, the kingdom bartered its independence for those parts of Tuscany that still belonged to the Neapolitan crown. Only Britain – still Europe's greatest sea power – stood by the little kingdom; but with French troops poised in Rome, this friendship was more a red flag to a bull than a guarantee against invasion.

In 1805, Austria suffered another crippling defeat on the battlefield at Austerlitz and French forces under Joseph Bonaparte occupied Austria's ally Naples on 14 January 1806. The royals fled to Sicily once again, and Joseph was declared king of Naples, to be replaced on the throne by Napoleon's brother-in-law Joaquin Murat (*see p18* **King Joaquin**) in 1808 when Joseph was crowned king of Spain.

Try as they might, the Napoleonic rulers failed to win the hearts of the fiercely royalist southern Italians. The reforms introduced under French rule were numerous and, on the face of it, very much to the advantage of the people: feudalism was abolished and land redistribution begun; absolute power was wrested from the hands of the Neapolitan aristocracy and the towns of Campania gained in status and importance.

Naples and the Hero of the Nile

Captain Horatio Nelson sailed into Naples harbour in 1793, seeking reinforcements for the British naval units defending Toulon against French Revolutionary forces (among which, incidentally, was a young officer called Napoleon Bonaparte).

The captain was greeted by Britain's ambassador to Naples, Sir William Hamilton. In his *Life of Nelson*, Robert Southey wrote: 'Sir William, after his first interview with him, told Lady Hamilton he was about to introduce a little man to her who could not boast of being very handsome, but such a man as, he believed, would one day astonish the world.' The introduction took place, in all likelihood, at the Hamiltons' house in vico Santa Maria a Cappella Vecchia (*see p92*).

Nelson returned to Naples in 1798, not as a little-known young naval captain, but as the victor of the Battle of the Nile. At the time, Nelson wrote to his wife Frances Nisbet: 'Up flew [Lady Hamilton], and exclaiming, "Oh God, is it possible?" she fell into my arm more dead than alive. Tears, however, soon set matters to rights.'

Nelson was swept by the Hamiltons – and by Emma Hamilton in particular – into a social and courtly whirl of a kind he had never known. He was chosen by the royal family to evacuate them when French forces occupied Naples in 1799. But in exile in Palermo, it became clear that things were not as they should be in the Hamilton-Nelson household. So blatant was the affair that had blossomed between the Hero of the Nile and the beautiful blacksmith's daughter who had captured the (much older) heart of the erudite William Hamilton, that living arrangements in Palazzo Palagonia began to excite gossip, much of it far from favourable.

'Poor Nelson was to be pitied – never was man so mystified and deluded,' wrote Pryse Lockhart Gordon in his *Personal Memoirs* after a dinner with the trio. Lord and Lady Elgin reported their disgust at the slavish attendance Nelson danced on Emma.

Irked by the rumours, the Admiralty in London ordered Nelson to quit Palermo to defend Minorca. He refused – justifying himself on strategic grounds that later proved correct – and remained on hand to carry the Hamiltons back to Naples when the Repubblica Partenopea (*see p16*) collapsed in 1799.

There, egged on by Emma, Nelson was persuaded to ignore a truce that had been signed by the leader of the royal forces promising the Repubblica's leaders safe passage out of Naples. Instead, they were imprisoned on Nelson's orders and one, Francesco Caracciolo, underwent a summary trial and execution on board Nelson's own ship.

Nelson's refusal to relocate to Minorca still rankled in the Admiralty, which ordered the Hero of the Nile home to an office job in 1800. London had not, however, banked on the triumphal progress that Nelson – accompanied the whole way by the Hamiltons – would make overland across Europe. He was given rapturous welcomes everywhere the party stopped. The people of London turned out in droves to greet him.

Luckily for Nelson's superiors, there were still more battles to be fought, and the problem of what to do with this hot potato was solved by dispatching him to the Baltic. Emma was pregnant with his daughter Horatia when he left.

Nelson was back in Britain just long enough to stand by Emma at the deathbed of the by-then very disgruntled William Hamilton, who had only begun to question his marital arrangements shortly before he died in 1803. Then the admiral set sail for the Mediterranean – and death at the Battle of Trafalgar in 1805.

King Joaquin

An innkeeper's son, Joaquin Murat (1767-1815) studied for the Church before opting for something more military and joining a cavalry regiment in 1787, in time to throw his lot behind Revolutionaries and France's rising star Napoleon Bonaparte. Napoleon's right-hand-man in Italy, Egypt and the coup d'état of 1799, Murat sealed what looked like a life-long symbiosis when he married Caroline Bonaparte, becoming his commander's brother-in-law.

But Joaquin grew increasingly discontent with advancing in the great man's shadow. In Spain in early 1808, his attempts to snatch the unoccupied throne caused uprisings; Napoleon gave that crown to his biddable brother Joseph (previously Naples' ruler) and packed Joaquin (or Gioacchino to the Italians) off to play at being monarch in Naples.

There's no denying that Murat did good in Naples. Besides giving the city an Orto botanico (botanical garden; *see p82*) to be proud of, he crushed the arrogant, all-powerful landowners, made cotton-growing into a major money-spinner, encouraged manufacturing industry by attracting foreign investment and took effective steps to stamp out endemic local banditry.

But he never endeared himself to the local populace, underestimating, perhaps, their extreme reactionary royalism. His own lavish court was an affront to a people that had been perfectly happy with its now-exiled Bourbon monarchs. And his ambitions drove a wedge between him and his protector Napoleon.

Any qualms that Murat might have had about sticking by his brother-in-law were confirmed in 1812 when he was given the task of leading the shattered French army in its retreat after the disastrous Russian campaign. Despite frequent strongly worded reminders from Napoleon that Naples was a mere vassal of the French empire, Murat

began secret negotiations with France's enemies Britain and Austria. Naples helped oust France from Italy. But Murat was betrayed by his so-called allies who opted to reinstate the Bourbon Ferdinand IV rather than keep him on Naples' throne. Perhaps realising how weak his position was, Murat had also encouraged secret pro-Unification societies such as the Carbonari (*see p19*). But his desperate appeals for Italian unification and independence – preferably with him leading the new nation – fell on deaf ears, especially among the reactionary Neapolitan masses.

Ousted from Naples in 1815, Murat and 30-odd supporters made one final pathetic attempt to reassert control over southern Italy. The bid was to prove fatal: Murat was captured in Pizzo Calabro on 8 October 1815 and executed five days later.

Though their weak-willed ex-monarch Ferdinand dithered in Palermo – thoroughly under the thumb of British ambassador Lord William Bentinck, who first forced Ferdinand to promulgate a democratic constitution, and then to send his by now fanatically scheming wife Maria Carolina into exile in Austria in 1811 – the Neapolitan masses remained doggedly hostile to the French, rising up against them on innumerable occasions in

minor protests up and down the mainland provinces. They were also singularly unimpressed by Murat's efforts to create a united Italy when Napoleon's star waned.

During ten years of French rule, Naples' rightful monarch spent much of his time hunting contentedly in the Palermo hinterland, while the British – the only power that could have reinstated him in his capital – exploited Sicily as their Mediterranean power-base.

At the Council of Vienna in 1816, Europe's victorious conservative monarchies confirmed Ferdinand as Naples' ruler; to mark the event, he adopted the new title of King Ferdinand I of the Kingdom of the Two Sicilies. The old king received a rapturous welcome when he returned. But he and his successors were to misjudge the changing nature of the times; the enthusiasm would soon wane.

Ferdinand responded to the demands of the shadowy Carbonari liberal reform movement by promulgating a parliamentary constitution in 1820. However, he then stood by contentedly as his reactionary ally Austria sent troops into his kingdom to squash these dangerous signs of anti-absolutism.

Ferdinand died in 1825. His successor Francesco I had shown early signs of liberal leanings, but these disappeared very shortly after he took the throne.

Ferdinand II, who became king in 1830, successfully brought Naples' huge public debt under control, helped Naples' numerous poor on the orders of his first wife (the saintly Maria Cristina of Savoy), and initiated a series of important public works projects, including the completion of the Portici railway (*see p211*), the first on the Italian peninsula, which opened in 1839. But the king was as totally committed to absolutism as his predecessors. Liberal movements were watched by an efficient spy network, and revolts were ruthlessly put down, often before they even began.

> **'Naples' faint glory evaporated, and Rome was designated capital of the newly united realm.'**

In 1847-8, when the city of Naples joined the more openly rebellious Sicily in demanding a constitution, Ferdinand granted it, but then played moderate and extreme liberal camps off against each other until he could justify dissolving the bickering parliament in 1849.

NAPLES AND UNIFICATION

Ferdinand II's son Francesco II (reigned 1859-60) came to the throne in mid-Risorgimento, as Piedmontese troops fought to oust the Austrians from northern Italy. Each victory for these Italian unification forces was greeted with joy in Naples, but the new king could still not see that he was digging his own grave with his harsh repression of liberalism. It was becoming clearer – even to the masses who had backed the Bourbons through thick and thin – that Italian unification could only bring change for the better.

With unification troops having taken Sicily and much of the southern mainland, Francesco agreed to the definitive introduction of a constitution in June 1860. It was too little, too late. The city's residents turned out en masse to welcome unification General Giuseppe Garibaldi, with an enthusiasm boosted by the fact that he had established his credentials as a royalist, rather than as a republican. When Garibaldi entered Naples on 7 September 1860, banners hanging from every window showed the cross of the Piedmontese royal family, the Savoys.

On 21 October the city voted overwhelmingly in favour of joining a united Italy ruled by Victor Emanuel II of Savoy.

It was to be ten years before the Unification of Italy was complete – with the capture of Rome. For Naples, integration into the national fabric meant that any faint glory that still clung to the once-flourishing capital evaporated. It was Rome that the Unification leaders aspired to, and Rome was designated capital of the newly united realm. Despite some housing reforms after a devastating cholera epidemic in 1884, on the whole Naples languished in growing neglect and poverty.

TWENTIETH-CENTURY DEVASTATION

Naples' importance – as a port, and as the gateway from southern to northern Europe – was only fully recognised once again during World War II (*see p21* **Naples at War**); this time, it was much to the city's detriment. Aerial bombardments ripped out much of the city's historic centre and waterfront; its fantastic state archive, perhaps the richest in Europe, was destroyed by German occupiers.

The Germans were ejected in an uprising known as *Le Quattro giornate napoletane* (the four days of Naples) in which, between 27 and 30 September 1943, Naples' citizens paved the way for the arrival of the Anglo-American forces. When the Allies entered the city's blackened shell, they found Neapolitans barely eking out the most pitiful of livings.

Yet the injection of Allied food and funds – coupled with Allied reliance on underworld figures to get things done – served more to fuel the black market and crime than to put the city back on its feet. Reconstruction was carried out in an unregulated, lawless fashion; in the early 1970s, an official enquiry found that almost none of the post-war buildings in the Naples area – a large majority of them horrendous eyesores – had planning permission. Beset by local government corruption, high crime and unemployment rates, and decaying urban infrastructure, Naples had entered one of its worst dark ages.

Key events

8th century BC Euboean Greeks arrive in Ischia; establish colony at Cuma.
c470 BC Greeks establish Neapolis.
326 BC Rome conquers Neapolis.
AD 79 Vesuvius erupts, destroying Pompeii and Herculaneum.
536 Byzantine commander Belisarius takes Naples; city swears fealty to Eastern Empire.
625 Lombards take Salerno.
763 Naples' Stephen II pledges loyalty to Pope, but still feigns loyalty to Eastern Empire.
8th century Naples' population 40,000; dukes found libraries and schools.
849 Lombard cities of Salerno and Benevento fight, ending Lombard unity in Campania.
1027 Lombards overrun Naples; ejected in 1030 with help of Norman mercenaries.
1059 Normans offer tribute to Pope Nicholas II; southern Italy becomes a Norman-controlled feudal territory allied to the Pope.
1060s-1070s Normans take Capua (1062), Amalfi (1073) and Salerno (1077).
1077-1130 Salerno is Norman capital of mainland south, famed for medical school.
1135-37 Naples' Sergio VII declares then denies allegiance to Norman King Roger II.
1137 Sergio dies. Neapolitans resist Roger with support of Pope Innocent II.
1139 Normans imprison Innocent. Naples falls; incorporated into Kingdom of Sicily.
1140 Population 30,000.
1194 Last Norman, Tancred, dies; Roger's son-in-law Holy Roman Emperor Henry IV, a Hohenstaufen, crowned King Henry I of Sicily.
1224 University established in Naples.
1251 Neapolitans set up free commune, fight off the Hohenstaufen Conrad IV, who takes control of the city in 1253.
1258-66 Last Hohenstaufen, Manfred, rules; Neapolitans offer fealty to Charles of Anjou.
1265 Angevins invade southern Italy; Manfred beaten at Benevento.
1442 Male Anjou line dies out; Alfonso V 'the Magnanimous' of Aragon takes over Naples.
1458 Alfonso's illegitimate son crowned Ferdinand (Ferrante) I.
1494 Charles VIII of France invades Naples and is crowned king. Much-loved Ferdinand II (Ferrandino), who lost Naples to the French, regains crown.
1501 Aragonese rule ends with ousting of King Frederick by forces of France and Spain.
1503 Neapolitans welcome Spanish troops; for 200 years kingdom ruled by viceroys.

1622 Spanish economy in tatters; Naples taxed heavily to pay for costly wars.
1647 Fisherman Tommaso Aniello (Masaniello) leads revolt against tax on fruit.
1656 Plague kills three-quarters of Naples' 350,000 inhabitants; economy devastated.
1701-14 Spanish War of Succession; Naples supports Bourbon King Philip V of Spain.
1707 Austria occupies Naples; 27 years of viceroys follow.
1734 Charles Bourbon, a son of Spain's Philip V, expels Austrians from Naples.
1735 Charles conquers all southern Italy; crowned Charles III of Kingdom of Sicily.
1759 Charles abdicates to become king of Spain; eight-year-old son becomes King Ferdinand IV of Naples under regency.
1768 Weak Ferdinand marries Maria Carolina of Austria, who ousts reformers (1777) and champions Briton Sir John Acton, who gradually takes over running of the kingdom.
1798 Naples occupies French-run republic in Rome. French retake Rome, march on Naples.
1799 Royal family flees on Nelson's ship; pro-French Neapolitan intellectuals declare a republic but working classes remain royalist; rebels defeated and Ferdinand returns.
1806 Napoleon sends invasion force under brother Joseph; court flees again; Joseph proclaimed king of Naples.
1816 Royal family returns to Naples; Ferdinand resumes absolutist rule.
1820 Uprising engineered by Carbonari group forces Ferdinand to grant constitution.
1821 Ferdinand allows Austrian troops to invade and squash constitutional government.
1848 Sicilian rebellion forces Ferdinand II to grant constitution; parliament closed 1849.
1860 Naples joins united Kingdom of Italy.
1884 Cholera epidemic sparks housing and infrastructure reforms.
1943 Naples heavily bombed by Allies; captured by Germans after Italian capitulation; *Quattro giornate* uprising against Germans, who destroy infrastructure as they withdraw.
1946 Neapolitan Enrico de Nicola becomes first president of Italian Republic.
1971 Public Works Ministry report says most post-war buildings in Naples area are illegal.
1980 Earthquake in Campania kills 3,000.
1993 Left-winger Antonio Bassolino elected mayor; sparks 'Neapolitan Renaissance'.
2002 Naples' revamp continues with opening of new art-laden metro stations.

Naples at War

The devastation of World War II has had a lasting effect.

On 28 May 1993, after a brief but poignant ceremony, the clock hands on the graceful campanile of Sant'Eligio (*see p66*) began to turn once more. They had stood still since 5.39pm on 28 May 1943 when the Italian munitions ship *Caterina Costa* caught fire and exploded while loading troops and arms bound for the North African front.

The force of the explosion hurled debris as far as Capodimonte. More than 500 people lost their lives; thousands more were injured. The tragedy – coming, as it did, shortly before the collapse of the Rome–Berlin axis, the fall of Mussolini from power and the end of the Italian military adventure – was etched indelibly in the minds of the city's populace. But it was just one in a long series of tragedies that made life in this desperately poor, desperately battle-weary city even harsher than before.

Despite untold deprivations, a threat from Nazi occupiers to deport the city's young male population caused dampened spirits to flare up in what became known as *Le Quattro giornate napoletane* (the four days of Naples). In a series of spontaneous uprisings – mainly centred on the Vomero district – from 27 to 30 September 1943, the population kept the

German garrison so busy that it was unable to concentrate on rebuffing the advancing Allies and was forced to retreat from the city, leaving behind a trail of blown-up buildings.

When Anglo-American forces entered Naples on 1 October they found a city on its knees. Over the years Allied air raids had claimed more than 20,000 lives. Transport networks, utilities and thousands of buildings had been destroyed. Retreating German troops had sabotaged what was left in the scorched-earth policy they implemented throughout the region.

'It is astonishing to witness the struggles of this city so shattered, so starved, so deprived of all those things that justify a city's existence, to adapt itself to a collapse into conditions which must resemble life in the Dark Ages,' wrote Norman Lewis in his wartime diary, published as *Naples '44*.

The arrival of the Allies was greeted with relief. Neapolitans welcomed their liberation from bombs and starvation. Before long, however, the city's million-odd population was swelled by the influx of 100,000 Allied soldiers. Then there were the remnants of Mussolini's disbanded forces, unable to return to their homes in German-occupied northern Italy and exiled in Naples. Hopes for a quick return to peacetime normality faded fast as the city struggled on through more air raids – German this time. Malnutrition and outbreaks of typhoid and other serious diseases were the rule rather than the exception. To cap it all, Vesuvius erupted in spring 1944.

There were lighter moments during the Allied occupation of Naples, as recorded by Lewis in *Naples '44* and Curzio Malaparte in *La Pelle* (Skin): both relate how the sadly reduced contents of the city's aquarium appeared on plates at a dinner staged to welcome American General Mark Clark; both spread the city's unfortunate reputation for kleptomania, with accounts of entire military vehicles disappearing, piece by piece, overnight.

But Malaparte, and John Horne Burns in *The Gallery*, in particular, also provide heart-wrenching snapshots of the prevailing sense of despair. Under their pens the city shed its Olde Worlde ruffianesque image for a grimier, sleazier portrait of ragged *scugnizzi* (street urchins) and *segnurine* (girls forced into prostitution). It was an image subsequently exported around the post-war western world by Allied ex-servicemen. For 50 years this was to be the Neapolitan stereotype, reproducing itself with such tedious monotony that, until very recently, Naples seemed trapped in an air-bubble dated 1943.

THE LEGACY OF WORLD WAR II

If Naples' 'renaissance' (*see p25*) has erased this image to a large extent, much of the devastation wreaked by World War II is still visible today, directly or indirectly.

The port area, the railway station in piazza Garibaldi, the industrial infrastructure in the eastern suburbs of the city around San Giovanni a Teduccio and the steelworks in Bagnoli were all badly damaged, hamstringing post-war recovery. Some buildings along the via Marina waterfront are still awaiting demolition or redevelopment. The Palazzo Reale (*see p60*), Palazzo Maddaloni (*see p81*) and Palazzo Doria D'Angri (*see p81*) were struck by bombs; in piazza Trieste e Trento many *palazzi* still bear the scars of shrapnel or shell-bursts. Many churches were damaged, most of them spending many years boarded-up before restoration work got under way; others disappeared completely, their names now long lost. Santa Chiara (*see p69*) took a direct hit on 4 August 1943; the resulting fire raged out of control for six days (though, in a rare happy ending, the subsequent rebuilding arguably improved on what had been destroyed).

Thousands of residential buildings were levelled, to be replaced by cheap modern constructions. There are few streets without their ugly modern block, standing out inelegantly between the stately old *palazzi*.

But the war left other, less visible, more insidious traces, including a system of institutionalised corruption that was a direct legacy of the Allied occupation. An acute shortage of food and other prime necessities had fostered a thriving black market; indeed, with so few legitimate goods to sell, there was virtually no other market to speak of. On to the black market went thousands of tonnes of the Fifth Army supplies then being shipped through the hastily repaired port of Naples. An estimated 40 per cent of throughput went AWOL.

'According to the Psychological Warfare Bureau,' Lewis wrote, '65 per cent of the per capita income of Neapolitans derives from transactions in stolen Allied supplies.' Allied indifference to (and in some cases collaboration with) the local wheeler-dealers led to the creation of a system-within-a-system. From it arose a new political and business class, its well-being dependent on the art of turning a blind eye.

The whole topsy-turvy system came of age in the late 1950s and '60s with the unauthorised transformation of large tracts of splendid countryside on the Vomero hill into cheap second-rate housing estates. It was not until *Mani pulite* anti-corruption enquiries in the mid 1990s that any serious attempt was made to arrest the decline. It remains to be seen if the process can be reversed.

Perhaps unsurprisingly, Neapolitans were struck by a severe attack of mass amnesia as ex-combatants – both those who had stuck with Mussolini and those who had gone over to the Allied side in 1943 – trickled home from POW camps, German labour camps and military service under the Nazi occupiers in northern Italy. Only by erasing bad wartime memories could national reconciliation be achieved.

But along with the bad memories, many of the inspirational moments were also deleted. Rather than becoming a monument to the courage of a downtrodden city, the hallowed ground around the old Collana stadium in the Vomero district where a motley assortment of deserters and students had taken on the pride of the German armed forces during the *Quattro giornate* was ploughed up and sold off to make way for swathes of ugly residential development. There's something ironic, therefore, about the fact that 60 years on, a large inscription proudly attributing the construction of the central post office (*see p77*) to 'Year XIV of the Fascist Era' has been spruced up and returned to its original and rightful place.

Wartime images: the return of Italian prisoners of war (above) and the arrival of Allied troops (below)...

...meanwhile, Neapolitans (above) had to contend with a city shattered by bomb damage and crushing poverty.

City in tumult: general strike in Naples.

Naples Today

After a decade of renewal, can the city keep up the pace?

The closing years of the 20th century were hopeful, hectic ones for Naples; the very first years of the 21st are proving to be equally action-packed, with the unveiling of art-filled new metro stations (*see p149* **Art goes underground**), a revolution getting under way at the port (*see p64* **Port-side**) and more facelifts for key Centro storico hubs such as piazza Dante.

Yet despite these tangible steps forward – the effect of ten unprecedented years of efficient, honest government – Naples' image remains largely unchanged. *Napolitanità* continues to be a metaphor for Italianness: lively, gesticulating people, a sun-kissed climate, pizza, spaghetti, and *O' Sole Mio* being belted out on every street corner. Naples' colourful, carefree image is a veneer that has done the city more harm than good. Content to live up to their reputations, Neapolitans

(and successive administrations until the 1990s) allowed the city's crippling underlying problems to go unheeded.

Naples' unique combination of outstanding beauty and overtones of mythology made it a tourist magnet from Roman times to the 19th century. But even as Grand Tourists flocked to the Bay of Naples, the city was digging its own grave. The difficult heritage of chronic overcrowding, and the patent failure of the Bourbon monarchs to provide their capital with productive infrastructure at a time when the rest of Europe was industrialising rapidly, would weigh on Naples into the 21st century.

Moreover, not even the genuinely glamorous characteristics that drew the Grand Tourists to Naples could conceal the creeping damage caused by extreme poverty and the lack of basic amenities for the massive, poverty-stricken population of the city's slums.

Rather than improving with time, this state of affairs grew steadily worse, even as the rest of Italy was pulling itself up by its bootstraps after the end of World War II. In the post-war period it became progressively harder to maintain the illusion that there was anything at all picturesque about Naples' anomalous underbelly. Those heart-warming folklore characters were shown up for what they really were: a mask for an enormous social problem that was waiting to explode.

Naples today is still not one but two cities. There's a thriving cultural and artistic scene: the San Carlo opera house (*see p164* **San Carlo**) limps from one economic crisis to another, but it remains one of Italy's – nay, Europe's – most prestigious. The Neapolitan theatre tradition (*see p166*) continues to flourish, helped recently by a programme that granted abandoned publicly owned space in the suburbs to experimental theatre companies. And the so-called 'Vesuwave' of rock, jazz and home-grown cinema is still rolling along.

But in the dreary suburbs and mean streets of the Naples that no tourist would venture into, there's an equally thriving 'sub-proletariat'. Among this underclass, unemployment (26.4 per cent in the province of Naples in 2001) and school truancy (20.54 per cent of 7- to 13-year-olds at the start of the 2001-02 academic year) go hand in hand with a deep-rooted culture based on violence and crime. In 2001 murders fell to their lowest level in ten years, but 80 people still met violent ends.

CRIME AND THE CAMORRA

At the beginning of the 21st century, Naples' organised crime outfits – known by their old Spanish name of *La Camorra* – are growing ever more insidious and becoming ever more uncontrollable. From 1945 until the early 1970s, Naples' hoods were content to exert control over contraband cigarettes and the wholesale fruit and vegetable market. Then gang boss Raffaele Cutolo and his *Nuova Camorra Organizzata* stepped on to the scene, prompting clans not under his control to band together as the *Nuova Famiglia Unita* in a bloody feud against him. Cutolo upped the stakes, deciding to enter the booming narcotics market. He also extended his racketeering tentacles over the vast sums of reconstruction money pouring into the region after 27 November 1980, when an earthquake devastated the Naples area, killing almost 3,000 and leaving many more homeless.

Admirable efforts by police and prosecutors put an end to the feud. But what remained after the demise of the powerful Camorra groups was a host of tiny, but nonetheless bloodthirsty,

families prepared to fight to the death (literally) in order to control rackets in their own high-risk neighbourhoods in the Neapolitan hinterland.

The Naples of racketeering and gang warfare and the Naples of high art and culture sit together uncomfortably, harbouring mutual ill-feeling and contempt, and rendering the job of governing the city a difficult one. Not that many post-war city governments have tried: the occupants of Palazzo San Giacomo (*see p57*) from the 1950s until the 1990s did far more damage than much-needed good to the poor, beleaguered city.

SPECULATION AND CORRUPTION

In no field has this been more true than construction, where property speculation has proved as serious a problem as organised crime. Between 1950 and 1970, successive mayors encouraged property speculators to do what millennia of earthquakes and eruptions had failed to achieve: devastate one of the world's most spectacular locations. High- and low-rise cement blocks mushroomed around the shores of the bay. With his battle cry of 'housing for all', 1950s mayor Achille Lauro sanctioned the razing of delightful 19th-century and art deco *palazzi* that were dotted around the Vomero (*see p85*) and Posillipo hillsides (*see p95*) in order to make way for the blanket development of apartment-block monstrosities.

> **'At the beginning of the 21st century, Naples' organised crime outfits are growing ever more insidious and ever more uncontrollable.'**

The rot stopped briefly in the late 1970s, when an administration led by Communist mayor Maurizio Valenzi took steps towards halting the decline. He swept aside the privileges and spoils system that had been introduced by former councils, but fell in the bitter recriminations of post-earthquake reconstruction.

Valenzi's demise left Naples politically adrift. Between 1983 and 1993, ten mayors succeeded one another as the city sank further into decline. Public services ground to a halt: a mere 300 decrepit buses served a city of some two million people, and rubbish collection was left in the incapable hands of companies that were suspected of strong Camorra links.

In 1992, *Mani pulite* ('clean hands') anti-corruption inquiries began around the country, swiftly bringing down an entire generation of politicians not averse to the odd backhander. In Naples, where corruption – and the consequent public frustration at its devastating results – was rife, ministers, ex-ministers and councillors with power bases in the city soon found themselves swept up and out in the vortex.

THE RENAISSANCE

It was while *Mani pulite* was in full swing that Neapolitans took a decisive step in the right direction. In 1993, former Communist Antonio Bassolino was elected mayor at the head of a centre-left alliance (he narrowly fought off a challenge from Alessandra Mussolini, the grand-daughter of *Il Duce*). The city's fortunes at last began to change.

Dynamic and determined, Bassolino enjoyed overwhelming support from a large middle ground of the population who were sick of struggling to survive in a metropolis where nothing functioned and where any attempts to improve their lot met with hostility or amused disbelief. He began a rapid clean-up of the sadly unkempt, utterly traffic-choked city centre. Importantly, he did so as world leaders (and the international media) descended on Naples for the 1994 Group of Seven (G7) summit. Prepared to find nothing but poverty and decay, these visitors instead discovered a resplendent city centre that was pulsating with art and life. The renaissance that the oft-disappointed Neapolitans were cautiously beginning to think was within their grasp began to be trumpeted around the world.

The immediate results of the Neapolitan renaissance are clear to see in the much-restored Centro storico (*see p67*), the range of cultural events, and the newly found pride of Neapolitans in their city. Bassolino romped back into office in 1997 with a personal mandate of 73 per cent. Yet his second-term performance was less dramatic. This may have been partly because he had exhausted his stock of superficial conjuring tricks and turned his attention wholly (and with some success) to the less flashy but more pressing problems of crime and a disastrous economy.

Whatever the reasons, Bassolino's support dropped to 56 per cent when he was elected president of the Campania regional government in 2000, forcing him to bow to the conflicting and often petty interests of the small parties in his governing alliance. This kind of political in-fighting is precisely what Naples and its surrounding region don't need.

Into Bassolino's shoes in City Hall stepped Rosa Russo Jervolino, Naples' first-ever woman mayor. A strong-willed lady with a grating voice, Russo has had the enviable task of cutting the ribbon for many schemes initiated by her predecessor, including the art metro stations and *piazze* overhauled by such high-

Mayor **Rosa Russo Jervolino**.

profile architects as Gae Aulenti (who was also responsible for Paris's Quai d'Orsay).

She has also inherited slower-moving projects such as revamps for former industrial zones in San Giovanni in the eastern suburbs and Bagnoli in the west. More than a year into her mandate, she had made little progress in breaking down the acrimony that surrounds these projects. Moreover, Russo and her centre-left administration (too much of its time eaten up in bickering between allies) had yet to produce convincing policies to exorcise the spectres of unemployment and decay – a top priority in a city where a flourishing crime sector is only too happy to step in when the legal economy can't feed hungry mouths.

THE UNCERTAIN WAY FORWARD

Although the city looks spectacularly better today than it did in 1993, and although Neapolitans can still delight in their new-found civic pride, the underlying problems remain immense. Under Bassolino's dynamic leadership, Naples showed it was ready and willing to be reborn. The sparkling, vital metropolis – from its ancient core in the Centro storico to its hyper-technological offshoot in the Centro Direzionale (*see p103*) – has taken the first, crucial steps out of its centuries-old morass. Its future – encouragingly – is in the hands of a very determined woman.

Caravaggio's **Flagellation**.

Painting in Naples

History and nature have left their mark on Naples' art.

The vicissitudes in Naples' fortunes and history – coupled with the extraordinary violence of the nature that surrounds it – have left their mark on Neapolitan painting. From the arrival of the Angevin dynasty in the 12th century to the unification of Italy in the 19th, great artworks were commissioned and then lost (the most notable example being Giotto's frescos in the Castel Nuovo; *see p59*) as tastes and rulers changed.

For much of the city's history, the Church and the monastic orders were the foremost patrons of art. Down the centuries, the paintings in Neapolitan churches have been neglected, painted over, destroyed, bombed, stolen or damaged by earthquakes. In some cases only what was buried or hidden for centuries underground or beneath layers of paint has survived. Only in recent decades has there been a gradual restoration of what remains of Neapolitan religious art in situ. The hidden glories of the medieval city, for centuries overwhelmed by the dramatic baroque art so typical of Neapolitan churches, have been brought to light.

Foreign rulers, too, had a hand in encouraging Naples' artistic output. In the 17th century, for example, Spanish viceroys developed an immense lust for local works – though many of these left Naples with their owners. During his four-year term, Count Olivares amassed sufficient paintings and antique sculpture to fill 40 ships on his return to Spain; much of his collection now graces the Prado in Madrid.

> **'Naples and the Campania region are home to some of the world's greatest examples of classical art.'**

Naples' great families put together private collections over generations, many of which were broken up as noble fortunes declined in the 19th century. In a few lucky cases, they were left to the State (and can now be found in Museo di Capodimonte and the Certosa di San Martino) or religious institutions (*see* Pinacoteca Girolamini and Pio Monte della Misericordia, *both p75*).

CLASSICAL ART

Naples and the Campania region are home to some of the world's greatest examples of classical art. Much of it – including mosaics

Where to see...

(see p98; these works were in storage at the time of writing).

Caravaggio
Seven Acts of Mercy: Pio Monte della Misericordia (*see p75*).
Flagellation: Museo di Capodimonte (*see p84*).

Pietro Cavallini
Scenes from the Lives of Christ and John the Baptist: San Domenico Maggiore (*see p69*).
Last Judgement and *Bible Scenes*: Santa Maria Donnaregina (*see p76*).

Donatello
Tomb of Cardinal Rinaldo Brancaccio: Sant'Angelo a Nilo-Cappella Brancaccio (*see p69*).

Artemisia Gentileschi
Judith and Holofernes and *Annunciation*: Museo di Capodimonte (*see p84*).
San Gennaro Tames Animals in the Amphitheatre, *Adoration of the Magi* and *Saints Procolo and Nicea*: Duomo di Pozzuoli

Masaccio
Crucifixion (*pictured*): Museo di Capodimonte (*see p84*).

Michelangelo
Cartoon of Three Soldiers: Museo di Capodimonte (*see p84*).

Raphael
Farnese family portraits and *Cartoon of Moses*: Museo di Capodimonte (*see p84*).

Rembrandt
Judith and Holophernes and *Nathan and David*: Museo di Capodimonte (*see p84*).

Titian
Portrait of Pierluigi Farnese: Palazzo Reale (*see p60*).
Farnese family portraits, *Danaë* and *Mary Magdalen*: Museo di Capodimonte (*see p84*).

from Pompeii and marble and bronze statues from Herculaneum – can be seen in the Museo Archeologico Nazionale (*see p79*).

But there's plenty still in (or near) situ. The frescoed slabs from the Tomba del Tuffatore (480 BC), now in the museum in Paestum (*see p271*), are the only surviving examples of classical Greek painting in Magna Grecia. The detail of two male lovers intent on their conversation in the banquet scene, and the image of the diver – symbolic of the sudden passage from life to death – have come to symbolise Greek culture.

The heights of Roman figurative art can be seen in the wall paintings in Pompeii (at Villa dei Misteri and Casa dei Vettii; *see p216*), with their warm, intense tonalities, dominated by the russet-brown colour known as Pompeian red.

BIRTH OF A LOCAL TRADITION

It is difficult, however, to spot a truly local tradition in these classical examples. Only with the coming of Christianity did Campanian art really take off, in the frescos and mosaics decorating the catacombs of the city. The paintings in the catacombs of San Gennaro (*see p83*) date back to the second century AD, when Christianity was a clandestine cult; they mix classical decoration with Christian symbolism. The lack of a gold background, the use of classical elements and the figures collocated in the banquet scene, differentiate the local early Christian art from the Byzantine tradition, although gradually the Byzantine influence and classical tradition mingled.

Outside the city, late classical elements, mixed with Byzantine iconography and elements introduced by the Lombards (*see p9*), continued to influence religious painting; the late 11th-century frescos in Sant'Angelo in Formis near Caserta (*see p276*) show the maturity of the local artists in realistic, figurative art.

The domination of Naples by foreign powers was inevitably reflected in art. The arrival of the Anjou dynasty in the 13th century (*see p11*) led to an initial decline in local art as artists and architects were imported first from France and then from other parts of Italy to make Naples a centre of artistic fervour. **Pietro Cavallini** was brought from Rome; his refined use of colour and calm naturalism can be seen in the frescos (1309) that decorate the Brancaccio chapel in San Domenico (*see p69*) and the church of Donnaregina Vecchia (*see p76*).

Giotto arrived from Florence and worked as court painter from 1328 to 1334, decorating Castel Capuano (*see p71*), Castel Nuovo (*see p59*) and Santa Chiara (*see p69*). Though only traces of his own work remain, Giotto

influenced many local painters. His Neapolitan pupil **Roberto di Oderisio** (active 1340-70) continued Giotto's experimentation with space and perspective in the fresco cycle of Old Testament stories in Santa Maria Incoronata (1340-43; *see p57*). In the same church, Oderisio offers a fascinating glimpse of Angevin court life in *The Sacraments* and *The Triumph of the Church* (1352-54) with their scenes of fashionably dressed Neapolitan nobles.

Power struggles in the late 14th century halted the innovations in Neapolitan art. Few examples remain from the period, in which the late Gothic style prevailed; the most notable are fascinating frescos in San Giovanni a Carbonara (*see p71*) by **Leonardo da Besozzo** and **Perinetto da Benevento**.

The Renaissance swept into Naples around 1450, with the advent of Alfonso 'the Magnanimous' of Aragon (*see p12*), who brought Aragonese/Catalan culture to the city.

Niccolò Antonio Colantonio (active in Naples 1440-70), the most important Neapolitan painter of the 15th century, was to fuse the Flemish and Burgundian traditions left over from the last of the Anjous with the new Renaissance spirit. His extraordinary capacity for reproducing Flemish painting in its microscopic detail can be seen in the *St Jerome in his Study* (1445) in Capodimonte. During his artistic development, Colantonio was the first to bring the spatial innovations of Piero della Francesca to Naples, in the representation of *San Vincenzo Ferrer* for the church of San Pietro Martire (1462; *see p65*).

In the early 16th century, Naples' Spanish viceroys were little more than transient bureaucrats, uninterested in commissioning artworks. The task of patronising the arts fell to the new monastic orders that arrived in the city from the 1530s. In new monasteries, and refurbished older ones, emotional and tortured Mannerism dominated. The Mannerist style of the Sienese **Marco Pino** (c1525-c1587) can be seen in the brilliance of the twisted figure of Christ in San Domenico (1564; *see p69*); however, his paintings for Santi Severino and Sossio (1571-77; *see p63*) were tempered by his knowledge of Spanish figurative painting.

THE GOLDEN AGE OF NAPLES

Counter-Reformation fervour and immense sums spent on building and decorating churches and monasteries provided a fertile climate for the golden century of Neapolitan art. Religious commissions were a counterpoint to a troubled period scourged by earthquake, volcanic eruption, epidemics, famine and riot, and subject to a repressive regime under the Spanish viceroys.

Strangely, few of the founders of the so-called Neapolitan School were Neapolitan. Michelangelo Merisi da **Caravaggio** (c1571-1610), the most influential, fled to Naples after killing a rival tennis player in Rome in 1606 and remained for little more than a year. His theatrical intensity, stark naturalism and vivid contrasts struck a chord with the local passionate temperament. His flesh-and-blood *Flagellation* (in Capodimonte) and *Seven Acts of Mercy* for the Pio Monte della Misericordia (*see p75*) revolutionised the tired Mannerist tradition. He paved the way for the enthusiastic reception of new painters.

> **'Caravaggio's theatrical intensity, stark naturalism and vivid contrasts struck a chord with the local passionate temperament.'**

Caravaggio's follower **Jose/Jusepe/Giuseppe de Ribera** (c1588-1652; *see below* **Gang warfare**) was born near Valencia. With Greek-born **Belisario Corenzio** and Neapolitan **Battistello Caracciolo**, he formed a tyrannical cabal: only with the group's consent could other artists work on religious commissions in the city. Ribera's malice was boundless – he deliberately ruined Massimo Stanzione's *Dead Christ* at the entrance of San Martino under the pretext of cleaning it. Ribera's taste for vivid narrative was sometimes grotesque, as in the *Drunken Silenus* (Capodimonte), but he gradually developed an extreme pictorial elegance with refined colours, which can be seen in the *Pietà* (1637) in the Certosa di San Martino. In contrast, from the 1630s there was a move towards a neo-Venetian painterliness and Bolognese classicism, which can be seen in the intimate works of **Massimo Stanzione** (c1585-1656), who was to decorate the most important Neapolitan churches, including the Certosa di San Martino, Gesù Nuovo (*see p68*) and San Paolo Maggiore (*see p76*).

Artemisia Gentileschi (1593-1652/3), who lived in Naples from 1630 until her death, experimented with dramatic chiaroscuro effects. Her *Judith and Holofernes* (Museo di Capodimonte) had a great impact on Neapolitan painting. (The victim of a well-publicised rape, Artemisia was wont to dwell on the subject of female vengeance.) In later life, she adopted Bolognese classicism in her religious works; this is visible in three large altarpieces made for the cathedral at Pozzuoli (*see p98*; in storage at the time of writing).

Bernardo Cavallino (1616-56), the major Neapolitan painter of the 1640s, represented the transition from lucid Caravaggesque naturalism to more refined painterliness in delicate, intimate work, influenced by Gentileschi and Stanzione. **Giovanni Lanfranco** (1582-1647), after initial success in Rome, had been eclipsed by the leading artists of the papal court and jumped at the chance to work for the Jesuits in Naples in 1634. He was the most successful fresco painter in Naples for the next 15 years; his warm colours and chiaroscuro contrasts can be seen in the Gesù Nuovo, the Certosa di San Martino, Santissimi Apostoli (*see p76*) and the Cappella del Tesoro.

The flourishing, passionate atmosphere of the city affected its artists: naturalistic still-life paintings by **Giovanni Recco** (c1615-c1660) and **Paolo Porpora** (1617-c1680) were juicier and fleshier; larger-than-life **Salvatore Rosa** (1615-73) – artist, poet, actor and musician – painted romantic battle-pieces, *banditti* and the poetic landscapes that were particularly popular in 18th-century England.

The terrible plague of 1656 raged for six months, exterminating nearly half the population and many artists, including Stanzione. **Micco Spadaro** (1609-75) chronicled the event in his precise *Piazza Mercatello in Naples during the Plague of 1656* (now in San Martino).

Those Neapolitan artists who survived the plague embraced the baroque wholeheartedly. **Mattia Preti** (1613-99) brought new life to the city in his four-year stay, by his use of light

Gang warfare

Jusepe de Ribera's rags-to-riches success story was the result of ruthless career-mongering. A poor painter's apprentice, at the age of 18 Ribera set out from his native Spain for Italy, where legend has it that he begged and wheedled a living on the streets.

In 1615 he was painting in Rome, fired with enthusiasm for Caravaggio, following whose footsteps he moved to Naples. A marriage to the daughter of painter and art dealer Giovanni Battista Azzolini proved a shrewd move. His sensational style and bold originality quickly caught on among the Spanish viceroys and religious orders; his sadistic martyrdoms became the last word in religious taste. But that did not sate Ribera's immense ambition. A grasping selfishness and as the basis of composition. His extraordinary versatility in the use of colour, light and shadow is best seen in the *Stories of the Life of San Pietro Celestino and Santa Caterina di Alessandria*, painted for the vault of the nave of San Pietro a Maiella (*see p76*).

Local boy **Luca Giordano** (1634-1705), moving from airy, baroque visions to iridescent rococo, dominated the scene for nearly 50 years. Nicknamed *Luca fa presto* ('Luca does it quickly'), he was one of the most prolific painters of all time; in his seventies he completed his frescos in the Certosa di San Martino in just a few days. **Francesco Solimena** (1657-1747) merged naturalism and the influence of Preti and Lanfranco.

The Certosa di San Martino is a magnificent example of Neapolitan baroque splendour. Artists vied for commissions from the fabulously rich but famously stingy Carthusian monks. With works by Caracciolo, Stanzione, Ribera, Lanfranco and Giordano, the chapel forms a unique gallery of 17th-century Neapolitan painting.

LANDSCAPE PAINTING

Landscape painting reached the height of its popularity in the 18th century, when the taste for the picturesque, the classical and the sublime made the spectacular scenery around Naples, the bay islands and the classical sites a must for the Grand Tourist. The most popular image was the panoramic or bird's-eye view of Naples from the sea. Vibrant, lustrous portraits of the city painted in 1700 by **Gasper Van Wittel** (1652/3-1736) – a few of which remain in the Certosa di San Martino – revolutionised landscape painting, with their synthesis of naturalism and the Dutch School. The warm Neapolitan light and local colour inspired him to combine reality and humanity in scenes like *Largo di Palazzo* and *Galleys in the Port*.

With the growth of Romanticism, increasing numbers of foreign painters were drawn to lyrical, emotional Naples. Vesuvius fast became a favourite theme, personifying the heroic and diabolic in a blend of the picturesque and the sublime. Frenchman **Pierre-Jacques Volaire** (1729-1802) captured this spirit in his dramatic *Eruption of Vesuvius with the Bridge of the Maddalena*, now in Capodimonte.

Not all collectors wished to experience such strong emotions. A market grew for sentimental standardised images of Naples in gouache. The situation improved in the 19th century, with landscape artists expressing their individual, contemplative interpretations of the Bay of Naples.

Dutchman **Antonio Pitloo** (1791-1837) infused his real-life landscapes (some now in the Certosa di San Martino) with natural colour and life, inspiring the Posillipo school. **Giacinto Gigante** (1806-76), many of whose works are now in Capodimonte, was the unchallenged leader of this school, where impressions of an idyllic landscape are expressed in delicate, romantic fashion. **Filippo Palizzi** (1818-99) continued to experiment with landscape painting, contrasting natural colours, light and vague contours (in the Certosa di San Martino).

jealousy made him the leader of a vicious, tyrannical cabal. Fellow painters Belisario Corenzio and Battistello Caracciolo abetted 'Lo Spagnoletto' in a cycle of intrigue, terror and violence against anyone who dared to set themselves up in competition.

The plum job at the time was the decoration of the Cappello del Tesoro in the Duomo. One by one, the cabal's competitors for the commission were removed: Guido Reni's assistant was badly wounded; Domenichino (a sensitive soul) was hounded out of the city in a state of collapse, terrorised by threatening letters, unable to eat for fear of poison and unable to sleep for fear of daggers in the dark.

When Ribera could not frighten his enemies away, he resorted to dirty tricks. He persuaded the monks of the Certosa di

San Martino to let him 'clean' Massimo Stanzione's *Dead Christ* for the entrance, then destroyed it with acid. With Caracciolo's death in 1641, the reign of terror of Ribera's gang came to an end. Ribera, highly respected despite his thuggery, died in 1652.

Once the Roman forum, now **piazza San Gaetano**.

Architecture

Ancient remains, baroque gems and the stunningly modern.

In 1645, British diarist John Evelyn travelled to Naples and enthused: 'the building of the city is for size the most magnificent of any in Europe, the streets exceedingly large, well-paved, sweet and clean'.

But, he noted, the poor slept in grottos, warehouses, or on the streets.

When Evelyn visited, the residents of one of Europe's most populous cities were crammed into a tiny walled area. Regulations introduced by Spanish viceroy Pedro di Toledo (*see p12*) in the mid-16th century strictly limited building outside the city walls. Unable to build out, Neapolitans built up, using the area's tough volcanic tufa stone and incorporating inherited architectural elements. What green there had been – sweeping convent gardens and orchards – was rapidly built over.

Naples' *palazzi* were 'open' structures upon which each successive era and architect left a mark. By the 18th century, low-ceilinged top storeys had been added to *palazzi*, then decorated according to the latest fashion. Inside, courtyards, windows, façades and arches were altered in the name of 'modernity'; from the end of the 19th century, jutting-out loos were tacked on to corners in tiny towers or on loggias. As late as the 1960s, jerry-built

extensions and flats – invisible from street level – were crammed on to historic rooftops. Today, Naples remains a city of architectural contrasts: huge portals to *palazzi* dominate dark, narrow alleys. Tall, freshly restored *palazzi* stand cheek-by-jowl with ramshackle neighbours. And great crowds still elbow their way up lanes and alleys once trodden by their ancient forebears, dodging the inevitable scooters.

GREEK CAMPANIA AND CAMPANIA FELIX

The temples in **Paestum** (*see p271*) and the sanctuary of the Sybil in **Cuma** (*see p101*) testify to the thriving Greek communities in Campania. Nothing remains of the original settlement of Paleopolis, but the chequerboard plan of Neapolis (the new city founded by the Greeks around the seventh century BC) can still be seen clearly from the belvedere of **San Martino** (*see p89*). The Roman *decumani* (main roads) – now **via Anticaglia**, **via dei Tribunali** and **Spaccanapoli** (*see p67*) – intersected north-south by *cardines*, followed the original Greek layout. The Greek *agorà* (marketplace, later the Roman forum) stood by today's **piazza San Gaetano**.

Small sections of the Greek walls can be seen just a metre below the current street level in **piazza Bellini** (see p72).

Centuries of construction have hidden the remains of the Roman city from view. They're still there, though: there's a fascinating glimpse of market life beneath the church of **San Lorenzo Maggiore** (see p74) and the **Duomo** (see p73), while an area of Roman baths has been incorporated into the museum behind the church of **Santa Chiara** (see p69).

> **'Today, Naples remains a city of architectural contrasts. Tall, freshly restored *palazzi* stand cheek by jowl with ramshackle neighbours.'**

Some of what didn't end up underground found its way into later buildings: two columns and marble bases from a temple to Castor and Pollux can be seen in the late 16th-century façade of **San Paolo Maggiore** (see p76).

The kind of prosperous town planning that passing centuries obscured in the city is very much in evidence at **Pompeii** (see p216) and **Herculaneum** (see p211). But the *Campania Felix* of the Romans is dotted with other smaller reminders of the extent to which this region, with its mild climate and spectacular landscape, was beloved and adorned in ancient times: there are sumptuous homes in **Capri** (Tiberius' **Villa Jovis**, see p180), **Castellammare di Stabia** (see p220) and near **Sorrento** (see p225); temples at **Baia** (see p99); and a four-tier amphitheatre in **Capua Vetere** (see p278), a model for the Colosseum in Rome.

A NEW CULT: CHRISTIANITY

When Emperor Constantine embraced the cult of Christianity in AD 313, its followers came out of their hidey-holes and built places of worship near the burial sites of their early saints. Taking the Roman *basilica* (a meeting place with columned porticos outside) as their model, the Christians turned them inside out, putting the columns in the interior to form side aisles. Paleo-Christian basilicas can still be seen above the catacombs of **San Gennaro Extra Moenia** (see p83), and in the fourth-century **Santa Restituta**, incorporated into the **Duomo** in the 13th century.

During the early Middle Ages the real stratification of the city began, with new constructions going up above the Greek and Roman ones around the *agorà*/forum in **piazza San Gaetano**. These, in their turn, made way

for later buildings; nothing remains of the civic architecture of the period. Further south, the early Middle Ages are better represented: the religious architecture along the Amalfi coast, in **Ravello** (see p259) and in **Salerno** (see p268) is a harmonious mix of Byzantine and Romanesque styles. Near Caserta (see p276), the tenth-century basilica of **Sant' Angelo in Formis** has 11th-century mosaics of clear Byzantine influence.

NORMANS AND ANGEVINS

In the 11th century, the Normans made Palermo the capital of their southern Italian kingdom, and Naples became a quiet political backwater. But the city expanded west towards **Castel dell'Ovo** (see p56) when Roger II made the castle his fortified Neapolitan citadel, and inland to **Castel Capuano** (see p71) after Roger's son William built the new castle in the late 12th century.

Charles of Anjou made Naples a capital once again in 1266, summoning French architects to transform it into a worthy home for his court. The walls were pushed out further to the east, and around what is now piazza Mercato a rash of civic buildings sprang up (only to be sacrificed to an urban renewal project in the late 19th century).

There were more public buildings, as well as noble *palazzi*, built outside the walls around the **Castel Nuovo** (see p59) when that castle, designed by Pierre de Charles, went up in 1279 below the hill of Pizzofalcone; of the original Angevin structure, only the Cappella Palatina remains. The church of the **Incoronata** (see p57) is the sole survivor of the Angevin civic buildings nearby. It owes its strange, two-nave design to the fact that it served originally as a court.

The Angevin period also saw a flurry of church building, mostly – though not exclusively – concentrated in the old centre. The church of **Sant'Eligio** (see p66), with its pointed-arch portal, is a rare example of French Gothic in Naples. Local influences soon began to fuse with the French imports, producing such gems as **San Lorenzo** (see p74), where the choir is clearly of French inspiration but the nave the work of Neapolitan masons. The luminous southern Gothic church of **Santa Maria Donnaregina** (see p76), spread over two floors (with three naves below and the frescoed choir for the nuns above), has remained largely untouched since the 13th century, although the façade was reworked by Ferdinando Sanfelice. Gothic simplicity can still be seen in the **Duomo** and the convent complex of **Santa Chiara** (see p69). Elsewhere, baroque makeovers changed the

Angevin churches beyond recognition; **San Domenico** (*see p69*) is a good example. The **Certosa di San Martino** (*see p89*), built by Francesco de Vito and Tino da Camaino in 1325-68, was dramatically reworked later by Cosimo Fanzago.

Outside Naples, Angevin rule brought particular prosperity to Ravello. The 13th-century **Villa Rufolo** (*see p261*), its magnificent two-storey courtyard surrounded by the kind of Arab-inspired loggias and arches so common on the Amalfi coast, is a stunning example of the noble homes of the period.

RENAISSANCE CAMPANIA

The Renaissance swept into Naples in the 15th century with Alfonso of Aragon's humanist court, peopled by artists and architects from Catalonia. The moment of transition is exquisitely documented in the anonymous *Tavola Strozzi* (1474), now in the **Certosa di San Martino** museum. The walls were enlarged yet again, and provided with towers and gates; the fortress of the **Carmine** (*see p65*) marked the city's eastern limit, while the Nuovo and Ovo castles marked the western limit.

The new king chose **Castel Nuovo** (*see p59*) as his home, sending for the Majorcan Guillermo Sagrera in 1449 to oversee alterations. Sagrera produced a trapezoid plan with five huge towers, inspired by similar buildings in Provence and Catalonia. He designed the **Sala dei Baroni** with its magnificent 28-metre (93-foot) high vaulted ceiling. But the crowning glory of the early Renaissance in Naples was the **Arco di Trionfo**, a double arch flanked by Corinthian columns, celebrating the virtues and power of the Aragon dynasty, between the two high towers of the entrance to the Castel Nuovo. Its style is clearly Tuscan, showing just how quickly Sagrera's Catalan–Majorcan manner became interwoven with Italian influences.

The same Tuscan flavour was popular with Neapolitan nobles: **Palazzo Maddaloni** (*see p81*), for example, has a Renaissance portal and a smooth rusticated yellow and grey tufa façade (contrasting oddly with late Gothic elements such as the low arches in the courtyard, the vestibule and arch behind); the diamond-pointed rustication of the façade of the church of **Gesù Nuovo** (*see p68*) was originally the façade of a palace. The Tuscan influence reached its apex in the **Palazzo Gravina** and the Brunelleschi-style chapels in the church of **Sant'Anna dei Lombardi** (*see p78*) next door. The Tuscan Renaissance form of the ideal city was in reality little different from the Greek *polis*, encompassing the same elements in town-planning.

Time to reflect at **piazza Dante**. *See p35*.

THE VICE REGNO

The arrival of troops from the recently united Kingdom of Spain in 1503 was to change the face of the city. The fortifications of Castel Nuovo were beefed up, a task that took 30 years; a new city wall with polygonal bastions was built around the city, from via Foria to Castel Sant'Elmo, and then along the seafront to the east to protect Naples from the continuing threat of attack from the sea.

> **'The highly decorative flourishes of the baroque appealed to the Neapolitan imagination.'**

In 1540, the most avid builder of all the Spanish viceroys, Pedro de Toledo, commissioned a new palace, complete with formal gardens, more or less where today's Palazzo Reale stands. To cope with a chronic lack of housing (Naples' population had almost doubled to 220,000 inhabitants in 50 years), he extended the walls to increase the city area by one third. Illegal shanty towns that had spread west (towards Pizzofalcone) and north (from via Monteoliveto up the hill towards Sant'Elmo) of the new palace were razed to make way for new quarters. An impressive thoroughfare, **via Toledo** (*see p77*), was created to link the old and new parts of town, and noble palaces sprang up along it. Immediately to the west of via Toledo, a network of intersecting streets sprawling up the hill known as the

Quartieri spagnoli (*see p77*) was built to house Spanish troops; as demand for housing grew, the original single-storey dwellings rose to four or five floors.

THE BAROQUE

The highly decorative flourishes of the baroque appealed to the Neapolitan imagination, and few employed them more extensively than Cosimo Fanzago (1591-1678), the city's most prolific church architect, who dedicated 33 years to revamping the Certosa di San Martino. The extraordinary **guglia di San Gennaro** (*see p68*) epitomises his decorative exuberance; the gruesome bronze skulls on the façade of the church **Santa Maria del Purgatorio ad Arco** (*see p76*) show him in glummer Counter-Reformation mood.

The advent of the Bourbon dynasty in 1734 produced a rash of imposing civic buildings that gave Naples a veneer of modernity but failed to impose any true order on its architectural chaos.

Fernando Fuga (1699-1781), Giovanni Antonio Medrano (born 1703) and Luigi Vanvitelli (1700-73) designed the immense, official palaces of the kings; Domenico Antonio Vaccaro (1678-1745) and Ferdinando Sanfelice (1675-1748) were responsible for many of the city's private and religious buildings.

Only one-fifth of Fuga's over-ambitious design for his **Albergo dei Poveri** (*see p81*) poorhouse was ever completed, but even so it was Europe's largest civic construction. Medrano designed the **San Carlo** opera house (*see p61*) that made Naples one of Europe's musical capitals, and the **Palazzo Reale** at Capodimonte (*see p84*) to house Charles III's spectacular art collection. Vanvitelli gave the city the imposing Foro Carolino, today **piazza Dante** (*see p78*).

But it was the Bourbon love of the countryside (and its potential for hunting activities) that allowed these architects their most grandiose scope. Medrano began work on **Reggia** at Portici (*see p211*), later to be replaced by both Fuga and Vanvitelli; the royal palace sparked a building boom along the coast south of Naples, where noble families constructed luxurious homes on the so-called **Miglio d'Oro** (*see p211*) near Charles' favourite palazzo.

Vanvitelli's crowning glory – and perhaps the finest product of the Neapolitan baroque – was the **Reggia** at Caserta (*see p276*), its internal vistas, ceremonial staircase and octagonal vestibule ensconced in a garden where fountains and waterfalls feature as fully fledged architectural elements. Sanfelice devoted his talents to nobles' city palaces. His work was an organic but lively blend of decorative stucco and stonework that was imitated all over the city. His staircases in **Palazzo Sanfelice** (*see p81*), **Palazzo Serra di Cassano** (*see p56*) and **Palazzo dello Spagnuolo** (*see p81*) are simply spectacular. Vaccaro's touch is best seen in the cloister of **Santa Chiara**, a splendid tiled garden in shades of blue and yellow.

THE CLEAN-UP CAMPAIGN

In the 19th century, urban renewal projects – originally designed to impose some order on Naples' haphazard urban development – degenerated into wholesale destruction of poorer, more dilapidated but nonetheless historic areas of the old city centre.

Early in the century, the city's French rulers introduced neo-classical touches in **piazza del Plebiscito** (*see p61*). This style was continued by Ferdinand I, on his restoration, in the church of **San Francesco di Paolo** (*see p61*), which was designed by Pietro Bianchi. Nobles fled the crowded centre, building seafront palaces along the **Riviera di Chiaia** (*see p92*). The simple two-floor **Villa Floridiana** (*see p90*), with its English-style irregular garden design, was built for Lucia Migliaccio, the morganatic wife of King Ferdinand.

But the *Consiglio Edilizio* (building council), set up with the best intentions in 1839, soon became a vehicle for rampant speculation.

Ultra-modern **Centro Direzionale**. *See p36.*

Clearance of the city's historic slums started in via Duomo, radiating out to the bay. An entire nave of the basilica of **San Giorgio Maggiore** (*see p70*) was destroyed. Plans to hack a road through the 15th-century **Palazzo Cuomo** (*see p68*), with its rusticated façade, sparked a protest campaign; philanthropist Prince Gaetano Filangieri financed the reconstruction of the façade 20 metres (66 feet) further back, designing the interior to house his art collection.

The eclectic, revivalist style of British architect Lamont Young (*see p88* **Neo-Gothic in Naples**) dictated the fashion in the late 19th century. His creations range from the neo-Gothic **Palazzina Grifeo** to the pseudo-Tudor **Castello Aselmeyer**, both situated off corso Vittorio Emanuele. Young's sense of the weird and wonderful caught on. Neo-medieval and Chinese-style villas can still be seen along via Posillipo, while art nouveau decoration flourished in buildings for the new, prosperous professional classes in **Vomero** (*see p85*) and via dei Mille.

A cholera epidemic in 1884 gave unscrupulous speculators further scope. With the excuse of making Naples a healthier city, the *Società per il Risanamento*, owned by northern bankers, created straight 'clean' streets by ruthlessly razing not only insalubrious slums, but 57 historic *fondaci* (merchants' yards, shops and lodgings) and medieval and Renaissance buildings. (Before destruction, the slums were recorded for posterity by painter Vincenzo Migliaro; his works can be seen in the Certosa di San Martino.)

'World War II bomb sites gave way to a haphazard concrete jungle of devastating ugliness.'

Between the two world wars, Naples was endowed with its fair share of the rational design favoured by the country's Fascist regime. The **Palazzo delle Poste** (*see p77*) with its curved façade lightened by rectangular steel windows is a good example, as is the **Mostra d'Oltremare** (*see p103*), a mixture of now uncared-for gardens, water features and exhibition spaces.

THE FINAL BLOW

Allied bombs did immense damage to Naples' Centro storico during World War II. Ironically, painstaking post-bombardment restoration work gave the city such gems as the church of **Santa Chiara**, rebuilt to its original specifications without later baroque trappings.

Elsewhere in the city, however, bomb sites gave way to a haphazard concrete jungle of devastating ugliness. Naples' sole skyscraper – standing out like a sore thumb just off piazza Municipio – was permitted by Mayor Achille Lauro in the 1950s. The havoc wreaked by construction magnate Mario Otieri inspired Francesco Rosi's searing indictment of the treatment meted out to Naples in his film *Le Mani sulla città* (*Hands on the City*, 1963).

Unregulated and unchecked, the concrete sprawl spread beyond the city limits, making the fortunes of ruthless property-developers. The 18th-century villas in Portici were engulfed by modern apartment blocks (blithely built within spitting distance of an active volcano, Vesuvius). Huge council-housing estates, built in the 1970s outside Naples to house the city centre's very poor, became crime-ridden no-hope ghettos. The most futuristic complex of all – named Le Vele ('the sails') after the sail-like shape of the buildings – is now being demolished. A concrete eyesore hacked out of the cliffs on the Amalfi coast (the never-completed Hotel Fuente) was finally demolished in 1999; the shell of an abandoned cement factory still haunts the coastline past Castellammare di Stabia.

Naples was wounded still further by the 1980 earthquake, which did unimaginable damage to the fabric of the city – many historic buildings are still shored up with iron chains.

HOPE FOR THE FUTURE

So tight was space in the 1980s that an ambitious project got under way to extend the city eastwards; but the **Centro Direzionale** (*see p103*), designed by Japanese architect Kenzo Tange, was unappealingly isolated on marshy land near the city's prison and a derelict industrial area. Now housing offices, law courts and homes, it has yet to be completed.

Sustainable town planning is the buzzword for 21st-century Naples. The wall that separated piazza Municipio from the port was demolished in May 2000. Abandoned industrial buildings and warehouses on the seafront are being converted (*see p64* **Port-side**). Funds have been made available for restoration in the Centro storico, and the underground railway is being extended and embellished (*see p149* **Art goes underground**).

An ambitious project to convert the abandoned steelworks at **Bagnoli** into a science park, leisure park and marina (*see p94* **Science city**) is limping slowly forwards. But true to tradition, progress continues to be hampered by continual flouting of building regulations; and chronic air pollution still threatens Naples' historic buildings.

Accommodation

Accommodation 38

Features

Accommodation

Chaotic bustle or elegant isolation... Naples' hotels cater for all tastes.

Urban planning has never been a strong point in Naples; as a result, the city has developed in a haphazard fashion, each *quartiere* acquiring its own distinctive architectural and social flavour. This reflects on the type of accommodation offered in different areas of the city.

The foreshore from via Partenope in the Santa Lucia district (*see p61*) along the Chiaia seafront (*see p91*) to Mergellina (*see p93*) is safe, has splendid views and is well connected by public transport to everything you're likely to want in Naples (though it does suffer somewhat from a surfeit of hotels and, therefore, their occupants). It's handy for the hydrofoil dock (Mergellina) and the ferry port, if you're planning on making quick getaways to the islands. The swishest four-stars and the more pleasant *pensioni* are concentrated here.

There are remarkably few hotels in the Centro storico (*see p67*), but there's no denying that this is the best place to be if you're seeking full immersion in Naples' culture and nightlife... not to mention countless everyday instances of true *napoletanità*, a concept that has to be experienced to be believed. If you have a sense of adventure and time on your hands, ask porters and bar staff for B&B tips: you may be lucky and find yourself in an inexpensive antique-filled room in a historic palazzo. *See also p42* **Bed and breakfast**.

After a full day of sweaty trudging, you might want to retire to the less chaotic, more residential Vomero (*see p85*). Situated on a hill above the centre, it has easy, efficient access to all of the downtown area by means of three funicular railways, the new ultramodern metro with its sculptures and modern art (*see p149* **Art goes underground**) and a variety of buses (best avoided at rush hour).

The area around Stazione Centrale/piazza Garibaldi (*see p62*) is very noisy by day and very dodgy by night. If you're staying in cheap accommodation in that area, there's a good chance that your fellow guests will be renting rooms by the hour; you'll certainly see an interesting cross-section of humanity.

Public transport has improved greatly of late but, nevertheless, think very carefully about where you want to be and what you plan to do before booking accommodation. A more central, expensive hotel could save on taxis in the long run.

PRACTICALITIES

Many hotels, especially upper range ones, offer special deals for weekend stays, in low season and for large groups: check websites and ask when booking. Prices quoted below include breakfast unless otherwise stated.

If you are travelling with children, most hotels will put another bed in the room – for which they should charge no more than 35 per cent extra. If you want a single room and are put in a double, you should be charged no more than the highest single rate, or 65 per cent of the price of a double.

High season is from June to September, and at Christmas and New Year. If you're travelling in May, you will need to book months in advance: the Maggio dei Monumenti (*see p53*) attracts visitors in their thousands as the doors of churches, historical sites and private chapels that are usually firmly closed to the public are thrown open.

Italian hotels are classified according to a star system (running from one star for a cheap *pensione* to five stars for high-end facilities). Naples has no five-star accommodation, even though its top four-star hotels are truly luxurious. If you're considering the other end of the market, you'll have no trouble at all finding budget accommodation.

Standards vary wildly, however, from the clean-and-simple to the cockroaches-and-louche-neighbours. It's a good idea, therefore, to ask to see the room before checking in: you don't want to have to argue with a desk clerk who's already taken possession of your passport and credit card.

For destinations outside Naples, see individual chapters in the **Around Naples** section. For booking agencies, *see p283*.

Royal Naples

Note that all seafront hotels along via Partenope have been included in the **Chiaia to Posillipo** section that begins on *p46*.

Upper range

Jolly Hotel

Via Medina 70 (081 410 5111/fax 081 551 8010/ www.jollyhotels.it). Bus C25, C55, C57. **Rates** €127-€146 single; €146-€177 double. **Credit** AmEx, DC, MC, V. **Map** p311 2C.

Clock the view from the restaurant at the **Paradiso**. *See p47.*

Atmospheric **Suite Esedra**. *See p42.*

Built in the wake of World War II by a property developer apparently devoid of any aesthetic sense, the Jolly is one of Naples' worst eyesores: it rises incongruously above the city centre like a monument to 20th-century capitalism, a green neon sign completing the horrible effect. From inside, however, it's another story. The rooms are small and rather impersonal, but they do have all the comforts that you'd expect of a hotel in this class, and the views from the top floors are breathtaking. The Jolly is well located for the major shopping streets and the Centro storico, and its restaurant is not at all bad.
Hotel services *Bar. Restaurant.* **Room services** *Air-conditioning. Minibar. TV: satellite.*

Mercure Angioino
Via Depretis 123 (081 552 9500/fax 081 552 9509/ www.accorhotel.com). Bus C25, C55. **Rates** €152 single; €180 double. **Credit** AmEx, DC, MC, V. **Map** p313 2C.
The modern, comfortable Mercure is situated close to the ferry port: a good option for getaways to the islands and the Amalfi Coast.
Hotel services *Bar. Disabled: adapted rooms. No-smoking rooms.* **Room services** *Air-conditioning. Minibar. TV.*

Miramare
Via Nazario Sauro 24 (081 764 7589/fax 081 764 0775/www.hotelmiramare.com). Bus C25. **Rates** €140-€179 single; €206-€244 double; €260-€282 double with sea view. **Credit** AmEx, DC, MC, V. **Map** p313 2A.
The Hotel Miramare was founded in 1944 in an aristocratic art deco villa. Small and nicely kept with a welcoming atmosphere, the hotel sprang to fame in the 1950s when its restaurant/piano bar, the

Shaker Club, drew top-name Italian and international singing stars for live performances. Breakfast is served on the roof-garden terrace with breathtaking views over the bay. Guests get a 10% discount at nearby restaurants La Cantinella (*see p111*) and Il Posto Accanto. Special deals at weekends (minimum two nights) and in January, February, August and over Christmas.
Hotel services *Bar. Restaurant. Solarium.*
Room services *Air-conditioning. Jacuzzi (some rooms). TV.*

Moderate

Chiaia Hotel de Charme
Via Chiaia 216 (081 415 555/fax 081 422 344/ www.hotelchiaia.it). Bus C22. **Rates** €93 single; €109 double for single use; €124 double. **Credit** AmEx, DC, MC, V. **Map** p313 1A.
If you hanker after a touch of aristocratic class, this is the perfect place. The hotel is part of Marchese Lecaldano's newly restored home, two minutes from the Palazzo Reale (*see p60*). Most rooms have their original furniture and are named after ancestors of the marquis who lived in them. You may not be charged for Sunday night if you book a four night-plus stay in low season. Staff are very professional.
Hotel services *Babysitting. Disabled: adapted rooms (2). Internet access. Limousine service. Reading room. Tours.* **Room services** *Air-conditioning. Dataport. Hairdryer. Jacuzzi (7 rooms). Minibar. Safe. TV.*

Upper range

Executive
Via del Cerriglio 10 (tel/fax 081 552 0611/081 552 8363/081 552 3980). Bus CD, CS, C25. **Rates** €93-€114 single; €130-€155 double; €207-€238 junior suite. **Credit** AmEx, DC, MC, V. **Map** p311 1C.
Hidden away in a tiny side street off a busy thoroughfare, the Executive's simple entrance gives on to an oasis of comfort and peace (as long as you keep the double-glazing firmly shut). The rooms are comfortable if somewhat anonymously modern. The port, Centro storico and Centro Direzionale business district are all close at hand.
Hotel services *Babysitting. Bar. Garage. Roof garden. Sauna. Solarium.* **Room services** *Air-conditioning. Minibar. Safe. TV: satellite.*

Starhotel Terminus
Piazza Garibaldi 91 (081 779 3111/fax 081 206 689). Metro Piazza Garibaldi/bus CD, CS, C30, C40, C55. **Rates** €127-€159 single; €160-€218 double. **Credit** AmEx, DC, MC, V. **Map** p310 2B.
Right opposite the Stazione Centrale, this modern hotel attracts a mostly business clientele. Despite its 200-plus rooms, it manages to feel cosy and relaxed. There are two fairly acceptable restaurants and a

Bed and breakfast

B&Bs are a new arrival on the Neapolitan hospitality scene, and there is not, to date, a huge range of options. The term generally signifies rooms rented by licensed individuals in private apartments, often sharing a bathroom with the family.

When booking, try to ascertain very precisely what's on offer. At worst, you could find yourself in a poky room far from the centre with over-inquisitive hosts. At best – and the best can be very good indeed – you may get lucky in a room with frescoed ceilings in a Centro storico palazzo of the kind usually only visible to the public in Maggio dei Monumenti openings (*see p53*), with charming hosts who make your stay into something really special.

The tourist office in piazza dei Martiri (*see p293*) has a list of room-renters. The following agencies will also fix you up with well-vetted places to stay.

Associazione Bed & Breakfast

Cupa Camaldoli 18, Vomero Alto (no phone/ www.tightrope.it/bbnaples/index.htm). Bus C44 from piazza Medaglie d'Oro. **Rates** from €30 per person. **No credit cards.** **Map** off p312 1C.

Contactable by email or in person only, this association has three types of accommodation available in various parts of town: rooms with shared bathrooms, rooms with private bathrooms, and flats. All hosts are carefully selected by the association itself.

My Home Your Home

Via Duomo 276 (081 282 520/081 203 209/outside opening hours 348 731 9244/fax 081 289 780/ www.myhomeyourhome.it). Bus R1, R2. **Open** 10am-2pm, 3.30-6.30pm Mon-Fri. **Credit** AmEx, MC, V. **Map** p310 2C.

This agency rents rooms, flats and villas in and around Naples, with rates fluctuating wildly according to the kind of accommodation you're after.

Rent a Bed

Vico Sergente Maggiore 16 (tel/fax 081 417 721/www.rentabed.com). Funicular Centrale to Augusteo/bus R2. **Open** 9.30am-1pm, 3-6pm Mon-Fri. **Rates** €21-€40 per person in double rooms & apartments. **Credit** MC, V. **Map** p313 1A.

This agency started out renting rooms around the city, but has expanded its activity into B&B and apartment rentals. A large choice is on offer, both in Naples and around the region, including accommodation on the Amalfi Coast, Capri and other islands, plus farmhouses in the Neapolitan hinterland. Contact by email if possible (via the website).

---

roof garden with a view of Vesuvius. The major drawback is the location: piazza Garibaldi is no place to be out after dark.

Hotel services *Beauty salon. Conference rooms. Restaurants. Sauna. Turkish bath.* **Room services** *Air-conditioning. Minibar. TV.*

Suite Esedra

Via Cantani 12 (081 553 7087/fax 081 287 451/ www.sea-hotels.com). Bus CD, CS, C55. **Rates** €83-€114 single; €114-€155 double; €181-€310 suite. **Credit** AmEx, DC, MC, V. **Map** p311 1B.

Opened in 1997 on the wave of Naples' rebirth as a tourist attraction, the Suite Esedra makes up for in atmosphere what it lacks in history. The cosy, well-equipped rooms are individually decorated with astronomy motifs; the Venus suite, with its private rooftop plunge pool, is a delight. Handy for the Centro storico, the port and the railway station, the Suite Esedra has only one drawback: it's just off the thundering, smog-filled and definitely insalubrious corso Umberto I.

Hotel services *Bar. Garage. Roof garden. Sauna. Solarium.* **Room services** *Air-conditioning. TV.*

Moderate

Cavour

Piazza Garibaldi 32 (081 283 122/fax 081 287 488/ www.hotelcavournapoli.it). Metro Piazza Garibaldi/ bus CD, CS, C30, C40, C55. **Rates** €73-€78 single; €104-€130 double. **Credit** AmEx, DC, MC, V. **Map** p310 2B.

This comfortable, long-established hotel has been refurbished tastefully and would be quite justified in edging up its prices were it not for the location: piazza Garibaldi is definitely an insalubrious spot, especially after dark.

Hotel services *Bar. Restaurants.* **Room services** *Air-conditioning. TV.*

Europeo

Via Mezzocannone 109 (tel/fax 081 551 7254/ www.sea-hotels.com). Bus E1, CD, C58. **Rates** €62 single; €93 double. **Credit** AmEx, DC, MC, V. **Map** p311 1C.

Cheap and rather basic, the Europeo has modern rooms with air-conditioning – a rarity in this price range – and is conveniently located near the

Luxurious **Excelsior**. See p46.

university district and the Centro storico. The hotel doesn't serve breakfast. You can book online.
Hotel services *Garage.* **Room services** *Air-conditioning. TV: satellite.*

Centro storico

Upper range

Caravaggio
Piazza Riario Sforza 157 (081 211 0066/fax 081 442 1578/www.caravaggiohotel.it). Bus CS. **Rates** €83-€103 single; €130-€150 double; €170-€202 suite. **Credit** AmEx, DC, MC, V. **Map** p311 1C.
Located bang next to the Duomo (*see p73*), in the heart of the Centro storico, this four-star hotel combines the beauty of its 17th-century premises with all mod cons, plus an ideal location within walking distance of most of the churches and monuments of the centre.
Hotel services *Bar. Computer. Fax. Internet access.* **Room services** *Air-conditioning. Dataport. Telephone. TV: satellite.*

Moderate

Neapolis
Via Francesco del Giudice 13 (081 442 0815/fax 081 442 0819/www.hotelneapolis.com). Metro Dante/bus CD, E1, 47. **Rates** €65-€75 single; €100-€115 double; €115-€135 triple; €135-€145 quad. **Credit** AmEx, DC, MC, V. **Map** p311 1C.
Near to buzzing piazza Bellini and the Centro storico nightlife, this hotel has all the traditional services, plus a PC with free internet access in all rooms. The

hotel also provides special software with which you can design your own itinerary of the city. An additional bed is provided free of charge for families of four in triple rooms.
Hotel services *Bus to airport/station. Laundry service. Safe. Tours.* **Room services** *Air-conditioning. Computer with internet access. Minibar. Radio. Telephone. TV.*

Toledo & Sanità

Upper range

Mediterraneo
Via Ponte di Tappia 25 (081 551 2240/fax 081 252 0079/www.italyhotel.com/napoli/mediterraneo). Bus C25, C55, C57. **Rates** €135 single; €181 double; €465 suite. **Credit** AmEx, DC, MC, V. **Map** p311 2C.
Centrally located and good value, the Mediterraneo is impersonal and business-like, a drawback somewhat compensated for by the bustling atmosphere once you step outside the front door.
Hotel services *Bar. Restaurant.* **Room services** *Air-conditioning. Minibar. TV.*

Oriente
Via A Diaz 44 (081 551 2133/fax 081 551 4916/ www.oriente.it). Bus CS, C57, R1, R3, R4, 24. **Rates** €155-€175 single; €220-€238 double; €357 suite. **Credit** AmEx, DC, MC, V. **Map** p311 1C.
Situated just a short walk from the shops in via Toledo, and not far from the Centro storico, the Oriente has a very modern marble façade that makes it look severe and cold. Once inside, the decor is welcoming, however, with a touch of personality and style. The surrounding area is off the beaten

Grand Hotel Parker's: a favourite with Brits since the 19th century.

nightlife track, making it dreary or pleasantly tranquil, depending on your point of view.
Hotel services *Bar. Garage. Laundry service. Limousine service. Restaurant.* **Room services** *Air-conditioning. Dataport. Minibar. TV: satellite.*

Moderate

Toledo

Via Montecalvario 15 (081 406 871/fax 081 406 800/www.sea-hotels.com/www.hoteltoledo.com). Bus CS, C57, R1, R3, R4, 24. **Rates** €80 single; €120 double. **Credit** AmEx, MC, V. **Map** p312 2A.
Neapolitans shudder at the very idea of staying in the Quartieri spagnoli (*see p77*), but this area's reputation for crime far outstrips reality and (as long as you don't parade your diamond tiara about after dark) you're unlikely to see anything but the pulsating, colourful side of life here. The three-floor 17th-century palazzo that houses the Toledo has been completely restructured and elegantly furnished. The pedestrianised shopping precinct of via Toledo is just a few steps away.
Hotel services *Babysitting. Bar. Garden. Restaurant. Solarium.* **Room services** *TV.*

Capodimonte

Upper range

Villa Capodimonte

Via Moiariello 66 (081 459 000/fax 081 299 344/ www.villacapodimonte.it). Bus 110, 137. **Rates** €144.61 single; €196.25 double; €237.57 suite. **Credit** AmEx, DC, MC, V. **Map** p310 1C.
If the hectic pace and hellish traffic down in the centre bewilder you, the Villa Capodimonte will

seem an oasis of perfect peace. Built in 1995, on Capodimonte hill (*see p83*), the hotel has glorious views over the bay, a small manicured park and rooms with terraces or gardens.
Hotel services *Bar. Garage. Roof garden.* **Room services** *Air-conditioning. Minibar. TV: satellite.*

Vomero

Deluxe

Grand Hotel Parker's

Corso Vittorio Emanuele 135 (081 761 2474/081 663 527/www.grandhotelparkers.com). Funicular Chiaia to corso Vittorio Emanuele/bus C28, C27. **Rates** €198-€223 single; €223-€273.50 double; €488-€976.50 suite. **Credit** AmEx, DC, MC, V. **Map** p313 1B.
A mecca for 19th-century British travellers, Parker's was closed for many years. A recent restoration has returned it to its original grandeur: crystal chandeliers, period furniture, antique paintings and statues abound. It also houses a library of antique volumes. The rooms are tastefully furnished and comfortably equipped. The two restaurants, one on the roof garden, serve good international food. Specify when booking if you want a room with a view.
Hotel services *Bar. Car rental. Conference rooms. Garage. Restaurants. Solarium.* **Room services** *Air-conditioning. Dataport. Minibar. TV: satellite.*

Hotel San Francesco al Monte

Corso Vittorio Emanuele 328 (081 251 2461/ fax 081 251 2485/www.hotelsanfrancesco.it). Funicular Centrale to corso Vittorio Emanuele/ bus C16. **Rates** €130-€170 single; €210-€260 double; €270-€310 junior suite; €330-€385 suite. **Credit** AmEx, DC, MC, V. **Map** p313 1A.

Heaven awaits at the **Paradiso**, overlooking the Bay of Naples.

Closed and left to decay for decades, this 16th-century Franciscan convent has finally been restored to its original splendour and reopened as a hotel in 2002. All the beautifully furnished rooms – once the monks' cells – have views over the bay. A sun roof and panoramic terraces add to its charm and the big back garden climbing up the Vomero hill offers breathtaking views and an open-air restaurant. A free hotel bus runs to and from the centre of town every 30 minutes.

Hotel services *Babysitting. Car rental. Conference rooms. Laundry service. Tours.* **Room services** *Air-conditioning. Dataport. Hairdryer. Jacuzzi (some rooms). Minibar. Radio. Room service. Safe. Telephone. TV: satellite.*

Upper range

Britannique

Corso Vittorio Emanuele 133 (081 761 4145/ fax 081 660 457/www.hotelbritannique.it). Funicular Chiaia to corso Vittorio Emanuele/ metro Piazza Amedeo/bus C28, C16. **Rates** €78-€119 single; €135-€176 double. **Credit** AmEx, DC, MC, V. **Map** p313 1B.

Built as a private villa at the end of the 19th century, this palazzo was bought by a Swiss company when tourism became a major industry in Naples. It was converted into a hotel for an international (and in particular British) crowd relaxing after their strenuous tours of the Amalfi Coast, Capri and Pompeii. Its understated elegance has the air of a long-gone colonial era and it's a very far cry from characterless chain hotels. There's a 10% discount for all bookings made online.

Hotel services *Bar. Garden. Restaurant.* **Room services** *Air-conditioning. Minibar. TV.*

Budget

Margherita

Via Cimarosa 29 (tel/fax 081 556 7044). Funicular Montesanto to via Morghen, Centrale to piazzetta Fuga or Chiaia to via Cimarosa/bus C28, C31, C32, C36. Closed 2wks Aug. **Rates** €32 single without bath; €58 double without bath. **Credit** MC, V. **Map** p312 2B.

The Margherita is very basic and has rather dreary rooms, but it's in a very safe part of town, near the Certosa di San Martino (*see p89*), and just a short funicular ride away from the centre of the action. No services to mention.

Deluxe

Excelsior

Via Partenope 48 (081 764 0111/fax 081 764 9743/ www.excelsior.it). Bus C25, 140. **Rates** €248 single; €300 double; €465-€1,034 suite. **Credit** AmEx, DC, MC, V. **Map** p313 2A.

A landmark in the Neapolitan *dolce vita*, the Excelsior has seen royals, film stars and jet setters of all ilks walk its luxuriously decorated halls and corridors. Its fascination remains, helped by its enviable position overlooking the bay, with Vesuvius in the background and the Borgo Marinaro right opposite. Every room is different, though all share a fin-de-siècle atmosphere. The top-floor restaurant, La Terrazza, enjoys breathtaking views. The bar on the ground floor is open to non-residents.

Hotel services *Babysitting. Bar. Business services. Car rental. Disabled: adapted rooms. Garage.*

Laundry & dry-cleaning service. Limousine service.
Moorage for boats (extra charge). No-smoking
rooms. Restaurants. Solarium. **Room services**
Air-conditioning. Dataport. Minibar. Room service
(24hrs). TV: pay/satellite.

Santa Lucia

Via Partenope 46 (081 764 0666/fax 081 764 8580/
www.santalucia.it). Bus C25, 140. **Rates** €209.99-
€289.99 double; €319.99 double with sea
view; €359.99-€389.99 junior suite; €469.99-
€1,599.99 senior suite. **Credit** AmEx, DC, MC, V.
Map p313 2A.

The long-running Santa Lucia was renovated in
1998. Situated opposite the Castel dell'Ovo (see p56)
and the Borgo Marinaro with its many bars and
restaurants, the hotel enjoys marvellous views of the
bay. It's elegantly furnished, the atmosphere is relaxing and the staff are very professional.
Hotel services Bar. Restaurant. **Room services**
Air-conditioning. Jacuzzi. Minibar.

Vesuvio

Via Partenope 45 (081 764 0044/fax 081 764 4483/
www.vesuvio.it). Bus C25, 140. **Rates** €285 single;
€336 double; €465-€1,292 suite. **Credit** AmEx, DC,
MC, V. **Map** p313 2A.

Built in 1882, when the Santa Lucia seafront was
created in a huge redevelopment, the Vesuvio was
completely destroyed during World War II and
rebuilt in 1950 with the addition of two extra floors.
On the top floor is the restaurant, which is famous
for its view. The hotel's luxury and comfort are legendary and have attracted royalty and world leaders
down the years, the latest being Bill Clinton, who
stayed here during the 1994 G7 summit.
Hotel services Babysitting. Bar. Business services.
Disabled: adapted rooms. Laundry & dry-cleaning

service. Limousine service. No-smoking rooms.
Room services Air-conditioning. Dataport.
TV: pay/satellite.

Upper range

Majestic

Largo Vasto a Chiaia 68 (081 416 500/fax 081
410 145/www.majestic.it). Metro Piazza Amedeo/
bus C28, C22, C25. **Rates** €145 single; €184 double;
€300 suite. **Credit** AmEx, DC, MC, V. **Map** p313 1B.
The Majestic is perfectly located in a quiet side street
in the heart of the smart via dei Mille shopping area.
The Villa Comunale (see p92) and the seafront are
a stroll away. Its rooms are furnished with a sober
elegance; some, on the upper floors have sea views.
Hotel services Babysitting. Bar. Disabled: adapted
rooms. Garage. No-smoking rooms. Restaurant.
Room services Air-conditioning. Minibar. TV.

Paradiso

Via Catullo 11 (081 761 4161/fax 081 761 3449/
www.bestwestern.it). Bus C21. **Rates** €108 single;
€176 double. **Credit** AmEx, DC, MC, V. **Map** p314.
The beautiful – indeed, aptly named – Paradiso is
situated high on the hill of Posillipo, away from the
hustle of the city. From this idyllic perch, you can
watch the traffic hell below and heave a sigh of relief
that you're not in it. The rooms are airy and bright.
Hotel services Bar. Restaurant.

Royal Continental

Via Partenope 38-44 (081 245 2068/081 764
4636/081 764 4800/fax 081 764 5707/081 764
4661/www.hotelroyal.it). Bus C25, 140. **Rates** €145
single; €255 double; €360 suite. **Credit** AmEx, DC,
MC, V. **Map** p313 2A.

Canada: elegant, inexpensive and on the seafront.

You won't find marble staircases or chandeliers in this simple, modern hotel (it was built 30 years ago, and a wing was added more recently) in Chiaia. But it's functional and perfectly comfortable, and much favoured by busy business people who may or may not take time out to appreciate its wonderful location and view.
Hotel services *Bar. Pool. Restaurant. Roof garden.*
Room services *Air-conditioning. Minibar. TV.*

Moderate

Canada

Via Mergellina 43 (081 680 952/fax 081 681 594/ tel & fax 081 682 018/www.sea-hotels.com). Metro Mergellina/bus R3, 140. **Rates** €114 single; €150 double. **Credit** AmEx, DC, MC, V. **Map** p313 2C.
The Canada is slap bang on the Mergellina seafront by the Chalets (*see p93*), an area of pavement cafés and *pizzerie* that buzzes through the summer. Conveniently located near the Mergellina hydrofoil port for quick transfers to the islands, the hotel's rooms are furnished with unpretentious elegance.
Hotel services *Bar.* **Room services**
Air-conditioning. TV.

Parteno

Via Partenope 1 (081 245 2095/fax 081 247 1303/ www.parteno.it). Bus C24, C25, C28, R3, 140/ tram 1, 4. **Rates** €96-€107 single; €117-€133 double; €160 double with sea view. **Credit** AmEx, MC, V. **Map** p313 2A.
Though this is officially a hotel, the Parteno has a cosy, warm, B&B ambience – you'll feel like the personal guests of the charming owners. The few rooms – each named after a flower – are stylishly furnished;

some have windows or balconies with a view towards Capri. It's a 15-minute walk from the main port and hydrofoil port at Molo Beverello and five minutes from the designer boutiques on via Calabritto and piazza dei Martiri (*see p91*).
Room services *Air-conditioning. Minibar. TV.*

Pinto-Storey

Via G Martucci 72 (081 681 260/fax 081 667 536/ www.pintostorey.it). Metro Piazza Amedeo/bus C24, C25, C27, C28. **Rates** €78-€83 single; €99-€120 double. **Credit** AmEx, MC, V. **Map** p313 1B.
With its charming art deco entrance and convenient location near the via dei Mille shopping area, the Pinto-Storey is an ideal hotel in this price range, especially if you're seeking to avoid the hustle and bustle of the Centro storico. The rooms, all recently restored, are very pleasant.
Room services *Air-conditioning (extra charge). Minibar. TV.*

Splendid

Via A Manzoni 96 (081 645 462/fax 081 714 6431/ www.hotelsplendid.it). Bus C21, C27, C31. **Rates** €100 single; €130 double; €140 double with sea view. **Credit** AmEx, DC, MC, V. **Map** p314.
On the top of Posillipo hill (*see p95*), far from the smoke of the exhaust pipes, the Splendid looks away from the centre, towards Pozzuoli, the Campi Flegrei and Capo Miseno (*see p97*), from where Pliny wrote his terrifying account of the eruption of Vesuvius in 79 BC. Unless anodised aluminium is your thing, you might find the interior decor a little disappointing, but the rooms are pleasant nonetheless. It's a bit of a hike to the centre.
Hotel services *Bar. Garage. Restaurant.*
Room services *Air-conditioning.*

Budget

Crispi
Via F Crispi 104 (tel/fax 081 668 048). Metro Piazza Amedeo/bus C24, C25, C28. **Rates** €52 single; €88 double. **Credit** MC, V. **Map** p313 1B.
A flophouse until not so long ago, the Crispi has cleaned up its act somewhat, though the rooms remain glum. But it's very central and quite cheap, and there are lots of good restaurants and bars in the area – Chiaia – which is one of the safest in Naples. Not a service in sight.

Le Fontane al Mare
Via N Tommaseo 14 (081 764 3811/fax 081 764 3470). Bus C12, C18, C19, C24, C25, C28, 140. **Rates** €50 single without bath; €60 single with bath; €65 double without bath; €87 double with bath. **Credit** AmEx, DC, MC, V. **Map** p313 2A.
One of the cheapest places to stay along the Chiaia seafront. Very central, it has a small terrace with a beautiful view. Decent enough for the price.
Hotel services *Bar.*

Ostello Mergellina (Youth Hostel)
Salita della Grotta a Piedigrotta 23 (081 761 2346/ 081 761 1215/fax 081 761 2391). Metro Mergellina/bus C12, C16, C18. **Rates** €13.50 per person in dorm; €16 double. **No credit cards.** **Map** p313 2C.
Very clean, and centrally located in the Chiaia area. The rooms have been recently refurbished with light wood furniture, and the reception areas are spacious and welcoming. Double rooms are also available. Booking is obligatory in July and August. The restaurant serves full evening meals for €8.
Hotel services *Bar. Payphone. Restaurant.*

Ruggiero
Via Martucci 72 (081 663 536/fax 081 761 2460). Funicular Chiaia to piazza Amedeo/metro Piazza Amedeo/bus C24, C25, C28. **Rates** €60 single without bath; €70 single with bath; €80 double without bath; €90 double with bath. **Credit** DC, MC, V. **Map** p313 1B.
If you're not too fussy about appearances, but are looking for a cheap roof and a bed in a very central location, this is the place for you. The whole centre is reachable on foot from here.
Hotel services *Bar. Restaurant.*
Room services *TV.*

Campi Flegrei

See also p50 **Campsites.**

Budget

Agriturismo Il Casolare di Tobia
Contrada Coste di Baia, via Selvatico 12, Bacoli (081 523 5193/http://sibilla.net/ilcasolare). Bus SEPSA 1 from piazza Garibaldi to Bacoli. **Closed** 2wks Dec-Jan; 2wks Aug. **Rates** €33.57 single; €46.48-€51.65 double. **No credit cards. Map** p314.

Parteno: for a personal touch. *See p48.*

Hotel Cavour: nicely refurbished. *See p42.*

Campsites

There are no camping facilities within easy reach of the city centre: most are located in beautiful green spots, mostly in the Campi Flegrei area (*see p97*) in western Naples. The ones listed below are well organised. They are also handy for the sea, but don't expect an azure, inviting Mediterranean.

Averno

Via Montenuovo Licola Patria 85, Arco Felice Lucrino, Pozzuoli (081 804 2666/fax 081 804 2570) Bus SEPSA 1 from piazza Garibaldi. **Rates** €6.50 per person; €6.50 per camper van or tent pitch; €2.50 per car. **Credit** AmEx, MC, V. **Map** p314.
Big and well equipped, this campsite in the Campi Flegrei is a fair hike from Naples but only 2km (1.25 miles) from the beach.
Services *Bar. Disco. Gym. Jacuzzi. Pool. Restaurant. Sauna. Tennis court.*

Vulcano Solfatara

Via Solfatara 161, Pozzuoli (081 526 7413/ www.solfatara.it). Metro Pozzuoli/ bus SEPSA 1 from piazza Garibaldi. **Closed** Nov-Mar. **Rates** €7-€8.70 per person; €4.10-€6 per tent pitch; €7-€8.70 per camper van. **Credit** AmEx, DC, MC, V. **Map** p314.
Just 800m (933yds) from the Pozzuoli metro stop, this is the most convenient campsite for visiting Naples and surrounding areas. It's less than an hour into town on the metro, and handily placed for the ferry port at Pozzuoli. Moreover, it's right on the fringes of the bubbling, hissing Solfatara crater (*see p91*). There are bungalows for rent too: one for four people costs from €36.90 to €92.20 for a deluxe model in high season.
Services *Bar. Pool. Restaurant.*

A 19th-century farmhouse in a volcanic crater (inactive, thankfully, for the last 10,000 years), Il Casolare di Tobia is nothing if not bucolic. Surrounded by vineyards and the gardens in which vegetables used in the *agriturismo*'s excellent and well-known restaurant (*see p114*) are grown. Only four rooms are available, each with two or four beds, as well as communal cooking facilities for breakfast and an open terrace with a view over the fields. Children aged up to two stay for free; there are discounts for groups.

Elsewhere

Upper range

Holiday Inn

Via Centro Direzionale, Isola E6, Centro Direzionale (081 225 0111/fax 081 562 8074/www.hotel-invest.com). Metro Piazza Garibaldi/bus C30, C40, C58, C61, C81, 191. **Rates** €185-€195 single; €205-€236 double; €246 suite. **Credit** AmEx, DC, MC, V. **Map** p310 2A.
Located in the Centro Direzionale business area , this hotel – part of the international chain – is handy for Capodichino airport and the main railway station but very far removed (in spirit, though not geographically) from the city's sights. As a result, it attracts mostly people doing business in the Centro Direzionale. It's not a nice place for strolling around, especially at night. Like the district, the Holiday Inn is strong on mod cons and weak on atmosphere.
Hotel services *Bar. Disabled: adapted rooms. Gym. Jacuzzi. Restaurant. Sauna.* **Room services** *Air-conditioning. Dataport. TV.*

Good-value **Le Fontane al Mare**. See p49.

Sightseeing

Introduction

Step into your role in Naples' great living theatre.

Sightseeing

Il lupo, says an old Italian proverb, *perde il pelo ma non il vizio* ('wolves can change their coats but not their bad habits'). Only the most stubborn observer could refuse to acknowledge the tangible signs of the facelift that Naples has been undergoing during the past ten years or so. Redevelopment schemes, pedestrianisation, improved road, rail and air links: the list goes on, as does the restoration work. But has this reversed the city's decline or simply put it on hold? Will political in-fighting erode this delicate process and return the city to its traditional paralysis? The future of Naples hangs, as usual, in the balance. In the meantime, thankfully, Naples' unique treasures are still there for all to see.

The origins of Naples' very endearing peculiarities become clear only by considering the history of this strikingly beautiful city, with its bay, distant mountain ranges and volcano on the horizon. The place has attracted intense competition over the centuries, both from outside (a succession of foreign rulers have left ample traces) and, more importantly, from within.

For centuries the capital of what one European royal (*see p14*) described as Italy's 'most beautiful crown', Naples has all the artistic and architectural glories befitting a city of such importance. Its museums and churches are among the world's finest, and will keep any visitor busy and culturally satisfied no matter how long he or she stays. Don't, however, become so immersed in the culture that you miss the city's most outstanding feature: its people.

Competition for living space, employment, power and personal attention has always been intense among the city's overcrowded inhabitants. Moreover, a succession of lackadaisical, corrupt foreign governors (*see chapter* **History**) taught Neapolitans to shift for themselves; sloth and extravagance at high levels was countered with a frantic struggle for survival behind the scenes.

That sense of struggle still makes Naples what it is; each Neapolitan is a player in a living theatre. Observe the daily drama of city life as it unfolds and you too will be assigned a role: that of *'o straniero* (the foreigner). You may be offered all forms of Mediterranean hospitality (although your role demands that you normally refuse). Never forget that behind the scenes, real life in Naples can be hard.

A densely populated city of over a million inhabitants, Naples has its fair share of petty crime. Be wary, without being frightened. Avoid flashy jewellery and carry the minimum amount of cash necessary. Keep a low profile: large backpacks are the best indicators of hapless visitors/easy prey. Avoid deserted alleys. Bag-snatchers generally whip by on scooters. If you fall victim to them, don't go in for heroics; you may find that keeping calm will unnerve the thieves, most of whom are kids who specialise in picking on panicky Neapolitan ladies in furs. Remember that if you're prepared for the worst, you can safely expect the best. *See also* **Safety & security** and **Emergencies** *in chapter* **Directory**.

PALAZZI

Naples' *palazzi* (and their inner courtyards and gardens) are the city's best-kept secrets. Nearly all are in private hands, carved up into flats. Though most of those mentioned here have memorable exteriors, and some have wonderful courtyards (usually visible by walking confidently through the door off the street), chances of visiting their interiors are rare and should be grasped unhesitatingly if they arise; the *piano nobile* (main floor) of even the dowdiest building often contains a *salone* with a beautifully frescoed ceiling. If you're here in May, watch out for one-off *Maggio dei Monumenti* (*see p53*) openings.

CHURCHES

Naples is awash with churches, be they bustling places of worship, deconsecrated buildings used for non-religious purposes, or firmly boarded up for *restauro* (which can be active or dormant, begun recently, after the floods in 2001, the earthquake in 1980 or in the wake of World War II). Over 50 per cent of the city's churches fall into the boarded-up category.

The 17th-century Counter-Reformation was the golden period for Neapolitan churches, vast numbers of which owe their current appearance to baroque treatment administered at that time. Many churches, however, hide much older interiors.

Though churches are best visited in sober attire, all but the most indecent extremes of exposure are generally tolerated from tourists. To avoid giving offence, use common sense: don't visit during mass unless there are empty

Naples' people are its most outstanding feature.

side aisles where you can blend quietly into the shadows. Most priests are only too happy to talk about their churches; don't expect exhaustive historical knowledge, though.

MUSEUMS AND GALLERIES

Naples boasts some of the world's finest museums: the **Museo Nazionale Archeologico** (*see p79*) is second to none, while the art collections at the **Museo di Capodimonte** (*see p84*) and the **Certosa-Museo di San Martino** (*see p89*) are spectacular. Due to insufficient staffing levels (and union touchiness), even museums of this calibre will close some rooms on a rotating basis. Be prepared to make more than one trip to any given museum if you want to see it all.

ANCIENT SITES

Buried and built over by space-starved citizens down the ages, what remains of Greek and Roman Naples is almost exclusively underground. Comparatively little has been excavated; still less is open to the public. That said, there are glimpses beneath the churches of **Santa Chiara** (*see p69*), **San Lorenzo** (*see p74*), **Santa Maria in Purgatorio ad Arco** (*see p76*) and the **Duomo** (*see p73*). Thanks to the unflagging commitment of the **Napoli Sotterranea** association (081 296 944/368 354 0585/www.lanapolisotterranea.it), other sites should be visitable in the not-too-distant future.

OPENING TIMES

Traditionally, Monday is lock-out day in Naples, but the situation has improved since the four 'biggies' (Palazzo Reale, Museo Nazionale, Museo di Capodimonte and the Certosa-Museo di San Martino) began staggering their closing days.

Though every effort has been made to get opening times right in this guide, they can change without warning; these changes are often for the better, including late-night summer openings for major galleries and sites. Ask at tourist information offices for latest updates, or phone ahead.

Churches are a case apart. As flocks – rather than tourists – are churches' main concern, visiting times are more fluid, often depending on the prior engagements or whims of a single priest and a dwindling band of ageing volunteers. Accordingly, some churches now actively discourage sightseeing on Sundays. Far from grumbling about their unpredictable time-keeping, we should probably be thankful they are there at all.

Maggio dei Monumenti (Monuments in May) is a special treat for tourists, who should seriously consider planning their visit at this time – though finding out what's on and when can be difficult: city hall, which organises the event, is remarkably loath (or quite unable) to provide programme information. Try the **EPT** (*see* **Directory: Tourist information**) instead. Even the most secretive of properties usually open their doors for at least one Sunday, and there are walks, talks and even guided snorkling trips too.

TICKETS AND ADMISSION

We've given the prices of full adult tickets. At state-owned sites, EU citizens under 18 and over 65 are admitted free; some places offer further reductions for groups, full-time students and so on. Keep a range of ID with you at all times: you never know when you might qualify for cheaper tickets. Ticket prices at sites not owned by the state – including many smaller museums and galleries – vary, but rarely exceed €3.

In spring 2002 the city council introduced the **Napoli Artecard** (information tollfree 800 600 601/www.napoliartecard.com), a pass costing €13 (€8 for 18-25 years old). Valid for 60 hours (though this may be revised upwards), it allows free entrance to two (all for 18-25s) of the participating sights (Museo Nazionale Archeologico, Capodimonte, San Martino, Sant'Elmo, Castel Nuovo and Palazzo Reale; sights in the Campi Flegrei were due to be added, *see p97*) and a 50 per cent discount at the others, plus free use of city transport and of a dedicated shuttle bus between participating museums. It can be purchased at the airport, at train and metro stations, at participating museums, at some newsstands and travel agencies, or through the website.

Ticket sales and the bookshops at Capodimonte, the Museo Nazionale Archeologico, Castel Sant'Elmo, the Certosa-Museo di San Martino, Villa Pignatelli and the Museo Nazionale della Ceramica Duca di Martina are operated by a private company called Pierreci. For information, consult the website www.pierreci.it. For details in English, or to book guided group visits in advance, phone 848 800 288 from landlines within Italy, or 06 3996 7150/081 741 0067 from cellphones or (putting 00 39 first) from abroad.

PUBLIC TRANSPORT

Traffic makes bus travel in Naples extremely problematic; you're likely to spend more time stuck in traffic jams than if you'd walked. There's a dedicated bus lane along corso Umberto, making bus travel to destinations between the San Carlo opera house and the Stazione Centrale viable. The bus is also indispensable when travelling to Mergellina and Posillipo (leave from Santa Lucia or the Riviera di Chiaia).

Naples' trams – feted in song and poetry – are definitely worth a trip. They run now along the shoreline from piazza Mercato through to piazza Vittoria in the Chiaia district. As this guide went to press, however, they stopped short of the delightful trundle along the revamped **Villa Comunale** (*see p92*), on account of work on the new express tramway out to **Fuorigrotta** (*see p104*).

The funicular railways inspired a famous ditty (*Funicolì, funicolà*), but these extraordinary machines will only take you to the Vomero and back. Kids love them.

Naples also has a growing **Metropolitana** (underground). The Piazza Cavour stop serves the Sanità district and the northern part of the Centro storico; Montesanto station is best for via Toledo and the southern part of the Centro storico; Piazza Amedeo station serves the Chiaia district; Mergellina station is ten minutes' walk from the port where hydrofoils leave for the islands.

The new **Metropolitana Collinare** deserves a special mention. Since a limited service was first run in 1993, it has gradually been adding stations; the latest, Dante, opened in spring 2002. Some of the new stations have transformed their surrounding areas (*see p194* **Art goes underground**). The line, which includes some ingenious bits of civil engineering, currently runs from piazza Dante through piazza Vanvitelli to the suburb of Secondigliano (though there's little to warrant getting off once you've reached this destination).

Three light railways serve outlying suburbs and towns: the **Circumvesuviana** goes east past Pompeii and towards Sorrento; the **Cumana** and **Circumflegreo** west through Fuorigrotta to the Campi Flegrei (*see p97*).

A single ticket, allowing up to three trips on all metropolitan transport – including one trip only on the underground railways and funiculars – costs 77¢ and is valid for 90 minutes. A 24-hour ticket for unlimited travel on all metropolitan public transport costs €2.32. Tickets must be bought at a newsstand or *tabacchi* shop before boarding a bus.

For **travel information** on city bus services phone 800 639 5250 (8.30am-6pm Mon-Fri; from within Naples only), or 081 763 2177 after office hours and at weekends; alternatively, consult the website www.anm.it.

Underground railways and funiculars are run by a separate consortium (Metronapoli); for information ring 800 568 866 (7.30am-7.30pm Mon-Sat) or consult the website www.metro.na.it. Information on light railways and country bus services can best be found in *trasporti* links on the the city council site www.comune.napoli.it.

For more information on public transport, *see p54* **Tickets and admission**; *p104* **Useful bus routes**; and *chapter* **Directory: Getting Around**.

Royal Naples & Monte Echia

Naples' history began on the grave of a broken-hearted mermaid.

For many centuries – until the very recent creation of the Centro Direzionale (*see p103*) – the government and administration of Naples were carried out in an area to the west of the port, near the island of Megaris. It was on the island, where the imposing bulk of the **Castel dell'Ovo** now stands, that Naples' history began more than 2,500 years ago.

Legend recounts that passing sailors happened upon the washed-up body of the siren Parthenope. Jilted by Ulysses, the heart-broken mermaid had decided to drown herself. The ancient mariners duly buried her body on the rock and thus it was that the original settlement of Parthenope or Paleopolis ('old town') was established.

History – or more specifically archaeology – may not confirm the legend, but it does confirm the location. For the island of Megaris and Monte Echia that towers above it were settled as a trading colony in 680 BC by Greeks from nearby Cuma (*see p101*). Two hundred years later, the settlers moved slightly further inland to found Neapolis ('new town'). There are two focal points to this very old 'new' area, which is a mishmash of local government offices, historical sites, exclusive shops and dramatically low-rent housing: **piazza del Municipio** and **piazza del Plebiscito**.

Monte Echia

Rising to the south-west behind piazza del Plebiscito is Monte Echia, the remains of the crater rim of an extinct volcano (the island of Megaris is another chunk) and the site of ancient Paleopolis.

In the first century BC, the Roman general Lucullus owned an extensive villa here, surrounded by an estate that stretched from the top of the hill down to the shoreline and along as far as Mergellina.

It's a 20-minute walk from piazza del Plebiscito up via Egiziaca a Pizzofalcone and salita Echia to the scruffy public gardens on top of Monte Echia. From the gardens' terrace, note the sinister observation posts of the modern police headquarters and bask in a rather obstructed though still glorious view of one of the cradles of Western civilisation. On the northern side of the hill (also reachable by lift, free of charge, from the eastern end of via Chiaia), the Pizzofalcone district contains more military and police establishments, including the **Nunziatella** military academy with its baroque church, as well as the melancholy **Palazzo Serra di Cassano**.

Pizzofalcone is also home to the early 17th-century churches of **Santa Maria degli Angeli** (open 7.30-11.30am, 5-7pm Mon-Sat; 8.30am-1.30pm, 6-7.30pm Sun) and **Santa Maria Egiziaca a Pizzofalcone** (open 9-10am, 5-7.30pm Mon-Sat; 9am-1pm, 5-7.30pm Sun). The former has an enormous dome, not immediately visible from the road, while its interior features a splendid barrel-vaulted

Strangely deserted: the **Castel dell'Ovo**. *See p56.*

ceiling and two delicate marble reliefs by Tito Angelini in the first chapel on the right. The latter has a most unusual convex façade.

From Monte Echia, the Rampa di Pizzofalcone zigzags down towards the **Castel dell'Ovo**. On the seafront, via Partenope and via Sauro skirt the Santa Lucia district (*see p61*), then pass by Pietro Bernini and Michelangelo Naccherino's **Fontana dell' Immacolatella** (1601) and back to piazza del Plebiscito (*see p61*). Savour Naples' briny side as you inhale the seafood smells wafting from the extractor fans of the waterfront restaurants and admire the yachts packed into the marina at the island of Megaris.

Castel dell'Ovo

Via Partenope (081 246 4111). Bus 140, C24, C25, C28, R3/tram 1. **Open** 9am-6pm Mon-Sat; 9am-1.30pm Sun. **Admission** free. **Map** p313 2A.

The castle you see today is the result of 1,000 years of military occupation that began in Norman times. It was given its present appearance by the Aragonese in the 16th century. Prior to that, in the Middle Ages, a monastic community lived here; even earlier, it was part of the vast estate of Roman general Lucullus. When the poet Virgil stayed here in the first century BC, local legend says he buried an egg (*uovo*) in the ground, predicting that when the egg broke some disaster would happen – hence the name of the castle.

After crossing the bridge, pass through the main portal and either climb straight on up to the right, or bear left out along to the far end of the *mole*

(breakwater), where the gun emplacements used to stand – a strangely deserted spot with Naples so close and yet completely hidden from view by the castle. From here you can munch your *panino* in peace as you gaze out across the dark blue waters of the Bay. Some of the rooms leading off the long climb up the ramp inside the castle itself are offices, while others are exhibition areas; yet others are currently being excavated and restored, and for the moment are only visible through glass.

La Nunziatella

Via Generale Parisi 16 (081 764 1451/081 764 1520/www.esercito.difesa.it/professio/nunziatella/index.htm). Bus C22. **Open** 9am-10am Sun for mass; by appointment at other times. **Map** p313 2A.

This pocket-sized baroque jewel belongs to the adjacent prestigious military academy that was founded by the Bourbon royal family in 1787. It took its name from the existing church of the Annunziata, designed by Ferdinando Sanfelice in 1737. Notice the unusual tiled flooring and striking 18th-century marble altar by Giuseppe Sammartino.

Palazzo Serra di Cassano

Via Monte di Dio 14 (081 245 2150/fax 081 764 2654/www.iisf.it). Bus C22. **Open** by appointment only. **Map** p313 1A.

You'll find it hard to get a proper view of the trim façade of this immaculately kept *palazzo*, hemmed in as it is by other buildings. One of the high points in Ferdinando Sanfelice's (*see p35*) career as an architect in the early 18th century, it has a no-nonsense double stairway leading up to the apartments in cool grey volcanic stone with a beautifully cut

Volcanic stone and marble balustrades at the **Palazzo Serra di Cassano**.

marble-pillared balustrade. The apartments feature some fine frescos and original furniture. The main entrance to the building, in via Egiziaca, was closed in 1799 by the Prince of Cassano in mourning for the death of his son Gennaro, one of the leaders of the short-lived Parthenopean Republic (*see p16*). Gennaro was beheaded in piazza del Plebiscito, and the entrance, which at the time enjoyed an unobstructed view of the Royal Palace, remained closed until bicentenary celebrations in 1999. The palazzo is now the headquarters of the Italian Institute for Philosophical Studies.

Royal Naples

Recently made into a traffic-free zone, the vast neo-classical **piazza del Plebiscito** is dominated by the church of **San Francesco di Paola** and the **Palazzo Reale**.

Adjoining piazza del Plebiscito to the north-east, piazza Trieste e Trento is home to Naples' most elegant watering hole, the **Gambrinus** café (*see p124*), from where guided tours to the underground 16th-century **Acquedotto di Carmignano** depart.

Also in the square is the church of **San Ferdinando** (open 8am-noon Mon-Fri; 8am-noon, 5.30-6.30pm Sat; 9.30am-1pm Sun) with frescoed scenes from the lives of illustrious Jesuits on its ceiling and some fine 19th-century marblework by Tito Angelini and the Vaccaros in the chapel in the left-hand transept.

Leading west out of the square is via Chiaia, a street of high-density clothes shops that vary enormously in price and quality. Amorous athlete and supreme self-publicist Giacomo Casanova and the infinitely more serious German poet Johann Wolfgang von Goethe both stayed at the imposing **Palazzo Cellamare** (No.149; not open to the public) in the 18th century (though not at the same time).

Via Toledo leads north from the square. Another shoppers' paradise, it has now been pedestrianised (*see chapter* **Via Toledo & La Sanità**). A couple of hundred metres along the road on the right is the entrance to the magnificent **Galleria Umberto**.

Heading east out of piazza Trieste e Trento, the via San Carlo leads past the illustrious **Teatro San Carlo** opera house, the gardens of the Palazzo Reale, and into the heavily congested **piazza Municipio**.

At the northern end of the piazza, the early 19th-century **Palazzo San Giacomo** was built to house the massive bureaucracy of the Bourbon monarchs. Today, it's the headquarters of Naples city council, and a magnet for all kinds of protesters. An easily missed door on the right of the palazzo leads to the charmingly royalist 16th-century church

The Angevin **Castel Nuovo**. *See p59.*

of **San Giacomo degli Spagnoli** (open 7.30-11am Tue-Sat; 11am-2pm Sun); behind the altar, the tomb (1570) of Spanish viceroy Don Pedro di Toledo (*see p12*) sits amid the crumbling, fraying remains of a very theatrical chapel; ask the sacristan for the keys – if you can find him.

Via Medina is the new home to the impressive **fontana di Nettuno** (fountain of Neptune), brought here in 2001 from its previous site in nearby piazza Bovio (which was cluttered beyond recognition as this guide was being prepared, with a building site for the new underground railway). Almost opposite the fountain stands the deconsecrated church of **Santa Maria Incoronata**. Regrettably closed

The rambling fishermen's quarter of **Pallonetto**. See p61

to the public as this guide went to press (with no reopening date set), the church was adapted from a court house in the second half of the 14th century to commemorate the coronation of Angevin Queen Joan. It was reputedly much loved by Petrarch, Boccaccio and Giotto; restored frescos inside by Giotto's pupil Roberto Oderisi show scenes from the coronation in 1352. The porticoed colonnade has pillars with Ionic capitals.

On the opposite side of the street, the **Pietà dei Turchini** church (open 7.15am-noon, 5-7.30pm Mon-Fri; 8.30am-11.30am, 5-7.30pm Sat; 9.30am-1.30pm Sun) started life as a poorhouse where children were dressed in turquoise shifts. The imposing police headquarters at the end of the street on the left dates from the Fascist period.

On the southern side of piazza Municipio rise the towers of the **Castel Nuovo**. Beyond it is the port, which at the time of writing was undergoing massive redevelopment (*see p64* **Port-side**). Ferries for Sicily, Sardinia, North Africa and the islands leave from the Stazione Marittima (1936). From here a tram heads west past the military harbour and public gardens, and through the breathtakingly smoggy Galleria della Vittoria tunnel; hop out at the end by the offices of *Il Mattino*, Naples' daily paper, and head into the Santa Lucia district (*see p61*).

Acquedotto Carmignano

Vico Sant'Anna di Palazzo 52 (081 400 256/ www.lanapolisotterranea.it). Bus 24, C22, C82, R2, R3. **Open** *Guided tours only (from Bar Gambrinus, via Chiaia 1-2)* 9pm Thur; 10am, noon, 6pm Sat; 10am, 11am, noon, 6pm Sun.* **Admission** €7. **No credit cards. Map** p313 1A.

Naples' historic infrastructure extends for miles beneath the city centre at a depth of 40m (130ft) and more. A maze of water ducts and cisterns tunnelled into the rock during the 16th and 17th centuries, the Carmignano drainage system was developed as part of the expansion of the city under the Spanish viceroys. It can be visited on hour-long tours. The tunnels were in use until the disastrous cholera epidemic of 1884, and again as air-raid shelters in World War II. The volcanic tufa rock that was extracted was used to build the houses above. Excavation is still in progress. Not for the claustrophobic. Booking is not necessary.

Castel Nuovo (Maschio Angioino)

Piazza Municipio (081 795 2003). Bus C25, E3, R1, R2, R3/tram 1. **Open** *June-Mar* 9am-7pm Mon-Sat. *Apr, May* 9am-7pm Mon-Sat; 9am-2pm Sun. Ticket office closes 1hr earlier.* **Admission** €5. **No credit cards. Map** p311 2C.

Called *nuovo* (new) to distinguish it from the older Castel dell'Ovo, this castle is better known locally as the Maschio Angioino (Angevin stronghold). It was built in 1279 by Charles of Anjou and used by

subsequent Angevin monarchs as a royal residence and fortress. It also became a centre of arts and literature, attracting such illustrious characters as Petrarch, Boccaccio (some of his best tales in the *Decameron* are set in a very realistic Naples) and Giotto, who, in around 1330, frescoed the main hall and chapel of the castle.

Unfortunately, little of Giotto's work remains. The castle's current appearance is the result of radical alterations carried out by Aragonese monarchs in the mid-15th century; the splendid triumphal arch was added for the entry of Alfonso I 'the Magnanimous' of Aragon into the city in 1443, a scene that is depicted in the relief above the portal.

In the back left-hand corner of the courtyard, stairs lead up to the Sala dei Baroni, probably named after the mutinous barons murdered here by King Ferrante in 1486. Giotto's frescos have disappeared; not so the unusual umbrella-vaulted ceiling that now looks down upon the lively proceedings of Naples city council meetings.

The plain yet elegant Cappella Palatina, also shorn of its Giottos (except for tiny traces in the embrasure of the right-hand apsidal window), is the only section that still remains from the Angevin period. An ambitious restoration project – well under way as this guide went to press – includes the addition of a lift to the top of the north-eastern tower (which has three floors from the original Angevin structure, and a terrace walkway on top). The dungeons are also

Dropping names

Acton (street)
Named after Ferdinando Acton, son of John Acton (*see p16*) – unloved by Neapolitans for his role in the bloody repression after the short-lived Parthenopean Republic in 1799.

Maschio Angioino (castle)
Literally 'Angevin male'... but *maschio* can also mean 'stronghold'.

Pallonetto (district)
Probably refers to the one-time presence of a covered area used for ball (*pallone*) games.

Pietà dei Turchini (church)
The church was originally part of a poorhouse (*pietà* means 'pity'); its name refers to the colour (*turchino* = deep blue) of uniforms worn by the children.

Rua Catalana (street)
Though this street is now associated with blacksmiths and metalworkers, its name recalls Catalonian merchants who traded here well before Boccaccio set one of his *Decameron* tales in the district in the 14th century.

Palazzo Reale: overwhelms by size.

to be opened to the public: one room features glass-covered tombs containing bones (probably the barons'); the other room, known as *Fossa del Coccodrillo*, is believed to be where a gigantic crocodile would emerge from a drain (now covered with a grating) to devour prisoners.

In the far left-hand corner of the inner courtyard, a large area has been given imaginative glass flooring to enable visitors to examine some very recent finds. These include the foundations and cemetery areas (replete with skeletons) of a convent that long pre-dates the building of the castle itself.

The first and second floors host the *museo civico* and art gallery, containing works of dubious quality but much local colour. Also housed here is the fine bronze door commissioned in 1475 by the Aragonese to commemorate their victory over the Angevins; the embedded cannonball probably dates from a sea battle off Genoa in 1495 when the door was being removed to France. There are fine views over the bay from the terrace walkways.

Galleria Umberto

From piazza Trieste e Trento to via Toledo. Bus 24, C22, C82, R2, R3. **Open** 24hrs daily. **Map** p313 1A.
This steel and glass-covered cross-shaped arcade was completed in 1890, and is generally compared favourably to its slightly older counterpart, the Galleria Vittorio Emanuele II in Milan. (Unlike its Milanese twin, the mosaic bull under the central dome in Naples has no testicles.) The somewhat sleazy air of the place tends to distract attention from the elaborate neo-Renaissance decorations and fine engineering. During a World War II air raid, all the glass was blown out of the massive dome.

Palazzo Reale

Piazza del Plebiscito (081 794 4021). Bus 24, C22, C82, R2, R3. **Open** 9am-8pm Mon, Tue, Thur-Sun; ticket office closes 1hr earlier. **Admission** €4.
No credit cards. Map p313 1A.
Work on the Royal Palace was started in 1600, under the rule of the Spanish viceroys, by Neapolitan architect Domenico Fontana. The bulk of the palazzo was completed in two years, although a number of features (such as the magnificent staircase) were still being added 50 years later. The Bourbon monarchs had the building extended eastwards in the mid-18th century, when niches were added to the façade. Under French rule in the early 19th century, the interior took on its current neo-classical appearance. The hanging gardens were created midway through the 19th century, while the statues of Naples' kings date from the late 19th century.

Don't miss the badly marked ticket office to the left of the main entrance. Access to the 30 royal apartments is from the top of the staircase. The apartments overwhelm more by size and number than by content. There's an unremarkable collection of paintings (some interesting for their portrayal of Neapolitan rulers and customs), frescos, tapestries, chandeliers and furniture from the 17th to the 19th centuries; the gilt-and-stucco ceilings are impressive; and the Teatrino di Corte (1768) is a gloriously ornate private theatre. In contrast, the hanging gardens were in a sad state of dilapidation as this guide went to press. Experts are seeking the original plans in order to restore them to their 17th-century glory.

The Palazzo Reale houses the Biblioteca Nazionale (national library) with its impressive reading rooms, collections of manuscripts and musty books, some dating to the fifth century. There's also a poorly signposted tourist office (081 252 5711; open 9am-3.20pm Mon-Fri) on the first floor (take the lift), stocked with excellent handouts in all languages for a number of sites in Naples, though not for the palazzo itself. Note that the Palazzo Reale is open until 11pm on Saturday at certain times of the year; consult tourist information offices for details.

Piazza del Plebiscito

Bus 24, C22, C82, R2, R3. **Map** p313 1A.

The semicircular colonnade with Doric columns adorning this stately piazza was begun in 1809 under French ruler Joaquin Murat; the church of San Francesco di Paola (*see below*) was added later by the restored Bourbon monarchy in thanks for the end of the French occupation. The bronze equestrian statues of Bourbon kings Charles III and Ferdinand I are by Antonio Canova.

Until 1994 the piazza was a grimy oil-streaked expanse of tarmac used as a bus depot and car park. One of the most splendid *piazze* in Italy, if not Europe, has now been restored to its former glory, including a spanking new surface completely relaid with local volcanic cobblestones. This is traditionally the site for large inner-city events: concerts, political rallies, New Year's Eve raves and so on. The cool porticoed colonnade is a great haven for anyone suffering from agoraphobia or sunstroke; were it not for swarms of kids on silencer-less scooters, it would be almost peaceful.

San Francesco di Paola

Piazza del Plebiscito (081 764 5133). Bus 24, C22, C82, R2, R3. **Open** 8am-noon, 3.30-6pm Mon-Sat; 8am-1pm Sun. **Map** p313 1A.

One of Naples' neo-classical rarities, San Francesco is surprisingly unpopular with the locals. This plain yet majestic imitation of the Pantheon in Rome was erected in 1817 by King Ferdinand in thanks for the repossession of his kingdom after the period of French rule. It was named after a saint who, conveniently, came from the town of Paola in Calabria, near to whom Joaquin Murat – Napoleon's brother-in-law and Naples' king from 1808 to 1815; *see p18* **King Joaquin** – had been shot by Ferdinand's police after an ill-fated attempt to lead a national Italian uprising. The apex of the cool grey dome stands 53m (185ft) above the ground.

Teatro San Carlo

Via San Carlo 98F (081 797 2412/fax 081 797 2306/www.teatrosancarlo.it). Bus 24, C22, C82, R2, R3. **Open** *Box office, see p164.* **Map** p313 1A.

The original San Carlo theatre was built in 1737 in just eight months to a design by Giovanni Medrano, who was also responsible for the royal palaces in Capodimonte (*see p84*) and Portici (*see p211*). Burnt down in 1816, it was rebuilt in less than a year. Now second in prestige only to Milan's La Scala, the San Carlo has lavish interior decor, replete with acres of red velvet and intricate gilded stucco moulding, plus an unusual revolving clock in the vault of the proscenium arch. A century and a half ago, foreign tourists complained of the noise level during performances; in the boxes, the local aristocracy would chat, consume meals and play cards. Tours of the theatre had been suspended indefinitely as this guide went to press. Check the website or phone for the latest information; alternatively, break out your smartest clothes and catch a performance.

Santa Lucia

Via Chiatamone and via Santa Lucia wind through Santa Lucia, with the rambling backstreets of the old fishermen's quarter, the **Pallonetto**, rising up towards Pizzofalcone (*see p55*) above.

To the left of the altar in the tiny church of **Santa Maria della Catena** at via Santa Lucia 102 (open 8-11am Mon, Tue, Thur-Sat; 9am-noon Sun) is the tomb of Francesco Caracciolo, one of the leaders of the Parthenopean Republic (*see p16*); Caracciolo was hanged on orders from a certain Admiral Nelson (*see p17* **The Hero of the Nile**).

The church of **Santa Lucia** (open 7am-noon, 5-7pm Mon-Sat; 8am-1pm, 5-7pm Sun) was rebuilt after its 19th-century predecessor was bombed in World War II; a church has stood on the site since the ninth century or earlier.

Piazza del Plebiscito: almost peaceful.

Sightseeing

The Port & University

Redevelopment fever grips the goldsmiths' quarter and the docks.

Sailing times are clearly indicated for a quick getaway.

Traffic is carried into Naples from the eastern approach by means of two busy, congested thoroughfares running roughly parallel to the main harbour area. The long, straight four-lane corso Umberto I – driven through the poorest part of the city in 1884 to act as a cholera break – and the via Marina constitute a traffic-snarled link between the motorway exits, the functional 1960s **Stazione Centrale** (railway station), the port area and the University district.

Corso Umberto & the Università

Corso Umberto I (also known as *il Rettifilo*) runs from piazza Garibaldi to piazza Bovio. The former is a vast, rectangular and decidedly sleazy car and bus interchange – not to mention home to the Stazione Centrale train station – with an early 20th-century monument to Giuseppe Garibaldi (*see p19*). At the time of writing, piazza Bovio was a construction site for a new underground station; usually it's home to the fine **Fontana di Nettuno** (*see

p57), built in the late 16th century by a number of artists, including Domenico Fontana and Pietro Bernini, and placed here in 1889.

At first glance, corso Umberto seems little more than an endless array of tacky clothes shops and street vendors, but there's plenty to see along the way: from the university area at the piazza Bovio end of the street, to the ill-famed **Forcella** district and the extraordinarily colourful street market around the **Porta Nolana** by the station.

The Università di Napoli Federico II was founded in 1224. Its faculties (including law, which has 40,000 registered students) are now scattered around the city, but the nucleus is still in the area north of piazza Bovio. Also here is the headquarters of the 16th-century Università Orientale, so-called because its first students came from China. Around the two universities is a host of churches and splendid *palazzi*, some of them, alas, quite derelict. In via Monteoliveto, north-west of piazza Bovio, **Palazzo Gravina** (No.3; open during university term) is now the architecture faculty;

its 16th-century façade was restored after being burnt down by Swiss troops trying to flush out Italian patriots in 1848. Next to the hideously busy crossroads overlooked by the Questura (police station), via **Santa Maria La Nova** leads to the church of the same name (closed indefinitely for restoration). Its Renaissance façade matches that of Palazzo Gravina; its cloister can be seen at No.43.

Via Santa Maria La Nova continues to piazzetta Monticelli, where the petite early 15th-century **Palazzo Penna** (No.11; not open to the public) is one of Naples' few surviving houses from that era.

In largo San Giovanni Maggiore, the small chapel of **San Giovanni Pappacoda** has a splendid early 15th-century ogival portal, a rare example of Gothic decoration in Naples; it's now deconsecrated and only open for university functions. Opposite stands **Palazzo Giusso** (No.30; open during university term), seat of the Università Orientale. The church of **San Giovanni Maggiore** (No.29; closed indefinitely for restoration) was built over the ruins of a pagan temple in the fourth century, but rebuilt in the 17th and 18th centuries.

The main entrance to the Università di Napoli is on corso Umberto, but a side entrance in via Mezzocannone gives easier access to the fascinating **Musei Inter-dipartimentali** (Interdepartmental Museums). Through the university buildings in via Paladino, the church of **Gesù Vecchio** (No.38; open 7am-noon, 4-6pm Mon-Sat; 7am-noon Sun) dates from the late 16th century.

In piazza Grande Archivio, the **Archivio di Stato** (No.5) was once the convent of the adjoining church of **Santi Severino e Sossio** (which is closed indefinitely for restoration). Towards the station, the church of **San Pietro ad Aram** stands guard over the notorious Forcella district.

More than any other downtown area, the district of **Forcella** lives up to the stereotype of lowlife Naples: racketeering, rip-off joints, petty crime, legendary cases of gangland honour and solidarity, but above all a long history of crushing poverty and neglect. Here, unwanted children, or those their parents could not afford to care for, ended up in the infamous wheel of the foundling hospital beside the church of **Santissima Annunziata**, and women were saved from the streets in the convent of **Santa Maria Egiziaca** (via Egiziaca a Forcella 31, now the Ascalesi Hospital). Even today, there's often a sense of uneasy tension.

Dropping names

Forcella (district)
Reference to the Y-shaped fork in the road here; a glance at the map shows that Y-junctions are the leitmotif of the whole area.
Mezzocannone (street)
Not named after a piece of artillery but after a short (*mezzo*, 'half') drinking-fountain (*cannone* comes from *canna*, 'pipe'), which used to stand in the street.

From piazza Bovio to piazza Mercato, street names recall past trades:
Armieri Armourers
Canestrari Basket-weavers
Casciari Housebuilders
Chiavettieri Key-makers
Giubbonari Jacket-makers
Lanzieri Lancers (lance-makers)
Orefice Goldsmith
Scoppettieri Fusiliers (rifle-makers)
Speziaria Vecchia Old spice stores
Zabatteria Reminiscent of Venetian dialect, referring to immigrant cobblers from northern Italy

Musei Inter-dipartimentali

Via Mezzocannone 8 (081 253 7516/ www.musei.unina.it). Bus 14, CD, E1, R2. **Open** 9am-1.30pm, 3-5pm Mon; 9am-1.30pm Tue-Fri; 9am-1pm Sat, Sun. **Admission** *all museums* €1.50, €3 family ticket; *single museum* 70¢. **No credit cards. Map** p311 1C.
These four delightful little museums – known collectively as the Naples University Interdepartmental Museums – can be found in and around the large rambling area that makes up the Università di Napoli Federico II. Although the main entrance is on corso Umberto, the easiest access to the museums, despite the chaotic signposting, is actually from via Mezzocannone. The four museums (in order of appearance) are: the splendid Mineralogy and Geology Museum; the refurbished Anthropology Museum (on the first floor across the courtyard); upstairs to the Zoology Museum (kids love this one); and then down and out of the building across to the magnificent, newly restored ex-Basilian convent and cloisters that house the Palaeontology Museum (largo San Marcellino).

San Pietro ad Aram

Corso Umberto I 292 (081 286 411). Metro Garibaldi/bus R2/tram 1. **Open** *Church* 7-10.30am, 5-7pm Mon-Wed, Fri, Sat; 7-10.30am Thur; 7am-1pm, 5-7pm Sun. *Crypt* closed indefinitely for restoration. **Map** p311 1B.
In the first century AD, the sea reached almost to where the Stazione Centrale now stands, lapping against what would later become the huge estates

Sightseeing

of the convent of San Pietro ad Aram. It was here, according to local tradition, that St Peter was driven ashore by a storm that prevented him from reaching his intended destination of Pozzuoli (*see p98*) in AD 44. Undaunted, Peter seized the opportunity to convert Asprenus (who became the first bishop of Naples) and Candida, both of whom were canonised. The first reliable written sources speak of a church on this spot in 877. However, the so-called altar of St Peter that stands immediately to the left inside the church's vestibule dates back no further than the 12th century. The church we see today was constructed in the second half of the 17th century on top of the early Christian basilica that is now incorporated into the crypt, along with some catacombs.

Port-side

Although it has been hankered after and promised for decades, the makeover of Naples' port has only just begun.

The wall dividing the docks from the city has come down. From the port-side road, nothing (save the serried ranks of tourists' coaches and milling hordes waiting for island-bound boats) comes between you and the glorious sea. Manoeuvring towards the jetty on an early-morning or late-evening ferry (not a closed hydrofoil if you want the best view) now provides a jaw-dropping opportunity to see Naples as it once was.

Ignore the shabby blocks to your right; block out the high-rise Jolly Hotel; and look up the hill with its vineyards (yes, really) to San Martino (*see p89*) above the Quartieri spagnoli (*see p77*), magically illuminated at night – or just enjoy a great view of the Castel Nuovo (*see p59*).

The port of Naples extends from the depressed eastern suburb of San Giovanni a Teduccio to Santa Lucia in a huge mass of dry and wet docks, abandoned warehouses and factories, constituting what has euphemistically been called 'industrial archaeology'. Ambitious plans are afoot to revamp it all. So far, a warehouse on the Immacolatella Vecchia dock has become an exhibition space, and the huge *piazzale* in front of the port's main building (the Stazione Marittima, a typical example of Fascist bombast) is occasionally spruced up for Naples' traditional all-night New Year's Eve party and for concerts in the Estate a Napoli festival.

The ferry port facilities on the western Molo Beverello dock – once a decidedly seedy place where it paid to keep a firm grip on your bags, while watching the boats come and go with little indication of provenance or destination – have been given a lopsided facelift. Ticket-sellers remain surly and there's still no waiting-room or even many seats on which to await your boat. But on the upside, sailing times are now clearly indicated and the place is unquestionably cleaner. Moreover, there are a couple of clean, fairly priced bars; order a drink at a table and you can stay there until your boat comes in... a relief in the pouring rain or steaming summer sun.

Santissima Annunziata

*Via dell'Annunziata 34 (081 207 455). Metro
Garibaldi/bus R2/tram 1.* **Open** *Wheel* 9am-1pm
Mon-Sat. *Church* closed for restoration. **Admission**
free. **Map** p311 1B.

The church owes its current appearance to a design
by Carlo Vanvitelli in the mid 18th century. However,
the whole Annunziata complex, including the
church, dates back to the 14th century. The complex
includes the fine courtyard and fountain, the revolving wheel for the acceptance of foundlings, and the
adjoining orphanage (now a hospital) set up for their
care. At 67m (235ft), the church dome is one of the
highest in the city. The main entrance to the old hospital is from via Annunziata, next to the church.
Dominated by a large bell tower with a majolica
clock (by the same hand as the tiled courtyard in
Santa Chiara – *see p69*), the entrance features a
splendid and much underrated carved marble portal
(c1500) by Malvito; in the apex, a loving yet unsen-
timental Madonna gathers children under her cloak.
The fine wooden doors (by Belverte and Da Nola)
are also from the early 16th century.

Foundling wheels are by no means unique to
Naples. In preference to abortion, mothers would
place unwanted newborn babies here and, at least
in Naples, there was never a shortage of childless or
good Christian couples waiting to adopt them. In the
latter case, the children would be given the surname
'Esposito', meaning 'laid before' God's mercy. This
particular wheel remained in use until the 1980s.
The *ruota* is not a tourist attraction for Neapolitans.
It's a reminder of very recent, very harsh times; don't
mistake the stoicism with which this symbol is
borne for indifference.

Neapolitans hanker after port redevelopment.

On the waterfront

On the southern side of corso Umberto, via
Nolana leads to **Porta Nolana**. Just before
this graceful 15th-century city gate (the
Circumvesuviana railway station is beyond),
the whole world explodes into a seething
mass of colour and smells as you enter via
Supramuro, the entire length of which is
occupied by the most vibrant and chaotic street
market in Europe. Open Monday to Saturday
(mornings only), it has fresh produce and
fish spilling out of shops and on to pavement
stalls, as well as shops dealing in specialist
merchandise such as leather or fabrics.

Via Marina (also known simply as *La
Marina*) cuts along the port past piazza del
Mercato. Now a massive car park, the piazza
still lives up to its name with shops selling
cheap toys, cheap garden furniture, cheap
mattresses, cheap clothes and cheap underwear.
The southern prospect over the sea is
obstructed by a hideous modern construction;
there is little to indicate that this was the site
of the public burning, hanging and beheading

of wrong-doers down the ages, including
King Corradino of Swabia in 1268 and the
leaders of the Parthenopean Republic (*see
p16*) in 1799 (executions took place beside
the easternmost obelisk).

The names of the Parthenopean leaders
are listed in sombre fashion just inside the
church of **Santa Maria del Carmine** in the
adjacent piazza of the same name. Traffic
streams to and from the motorway exit past
the two remaining piers of the 14th-century
Porta del Carmine gate (white with black
piperno stone highlights) and the two towers
from the same period – all that's left of the
fifth castle in Naples' medieval defence system.
The rest was demolished in 1906.

Naples' waterfront was subjected to heavy
bombardment during World War II (*see p21*
Naples at War); only two splendid and
little-known churches – **Sant'Eligio** and
San Giovanni a Mare – remain amid the
post-war juxtaposition of derelict, ramshackle
structures and brand new office blocks.

Off via Marina in via Porta di Massa, the
Faculty of Letters occupies the ex-convent of
San Pietro Martire (open during university
term), with its fine cloisters and church. Built
in the late 13th century as a bulwark against

portside vice, the church was remodelled in the 18th century. The area south of corso Umberto, between piazza Bovio and piazza Nicola Amore, is known as **I quattro palazzi**, after its four fine fin-de-siècle buildings. Within this area, the **Borgo degli orefici** (goldsmiths' district) still features an age-old community of silversmiths and goldsmiths, and *orefice* (goldsmith) features often in street names.

Via Marina continues past the container port. Further west, opposite the 16th-century church of **Santa Maria di Portosalvo** (closed indefinitely), the **Immacolatella** quayside area – between the 18th-century Capitaneria di Porto (harbour master's office) and the Stazione Marittima – has been earmarked for redevelopment (*see p64* **Port-side**). At the time of writing, work has gone little further than the creation of a gigantic car park and a coach terminal. What will become of **Dolcezze Siciliane** (*see p125*), the tiny portside shop selling delicious Sicilian specialities straight off the Palermo ferry, is anybody's guess.

San Giovanni a Mare

Via San Giovanni 8 (081 264 752). Bus 14, CD, R2/tram 1. **Open** 9am-noon daily; afternoons by appointment. **Map** p311 1B.
So-called because the sea (*il mare*) used to wash up against its walls, this 12th-century building is the only surviving Norman church in Naples. The foundations of the original apse can now be viewed through glass at the junction of the nave and the transept (a 13th-century addition). The first side altar on the left – the one with an unusual cambered arch – contains a small photographic exhibition of restoration work recently carried out.

Sant'Eligio

Via Sant'Eligio (081 553 8429). Bus 14, R2, CD/ tram 1. **Open** 8.30am-12.30pm Mon-Wed; 8.30am-12.30pm, 5-7pm Thur-Sat; 9.30am-2pm Sun. **Map** p311 1B.
This extraordinary 13th-century church was badly damaged in 1943. Subsequent restoration work enabled the uncovering of much of the original

building. Sant'Eligio was the first church built in Naples by the Angevin monarchs (*see p11*). The fine archway and bell tower are from the 15th century; the clock may date from the 16th century.

Santa Maria del Carmine

Piazza del Carmine 2 (081 201 196). Bus 14, CD, R2/tram 1. **Open** 6.30am-12.30pm, 5-7.30pm Mon-Sat; 6.30am-2pm, 5-7.30pm Sun. **Map** p311 1B.
Part of a large complex, including a convent (visits by appointment only) and social centre for drug addicts, the Carmine has a colourful past and present. A pre-12th century church was rebuilt in the 13th century thanks to the mother of Corradino of Swabia, who had been executed some years previously in the adjacent piazza Mercato. In return for a cash injection, she was allowed to bury her son's ashes in the church. They are believed to be under, or in, the pedestal of the monument to Corradino in the transept, erected in 1847. One thing is sure: they aren't in the statue itself. SS agents sent by Hitler in 1943 searched in vain for the remains of that earlier German leader who failed to conquer Italy. Opposite the monument is the pulpit from where Tommaso Aniello (aka Masaniello; *see p13*) delivered a fiery speech in 1647, calling on the people to rise up against the Spanish occupiers. He was later murdered in the convent and buried in an unidentified tomb here. Many notables from the failed 1799 revolution (*see p16*) also lie here.

Tradition has it that during a siege in 1439, a cannonball pierced the wall of the church and headed straight for the 14th-century wooden crucifix in a tabernacle under the transept arch. The head miraculously ducked, the eyes closed and the hair (which had previously been brushed back) all fell on to one side. Impressed, King Alfonso ordered the shooting to stop, but his brother Pietro continued, only to be mortally wounded in the head a few minutes later. On conquering the city, Alfonso went to pay his respects to the image. Popular devotion focuses, however, on the 14th-century image of the Madonna della Bruna, behind the main altar, which has been associated with many miraculous events. Crowds flock to the church on 16 July, when the magnificent bell tower, built between the 15th and 17th centuries, is lit up in a blaze of fireworks.

Centro Storico

Naples' historic centre stands on ancient Greek foundations.

The streets in the Centro storico make up a regular grid plan that betrays ancient origins: three *decumani* (main roads) run dead straight from east to west, intersected from north to south by *cardines*. It was in this area that the Angevins concentrated their initial construction fervour when they made Naples the capital of their realm in the 13th century (*see p12*); huge churches soared above lowly houses.

The main street here – the ancient *decumanus inferior* at the heart of Greek and Roman Neapolis – is known as Spaccanapoli and today incorporates *vie* Benedetto Croce, San Biagio dei Librai and Vicaria Vecchia. By day, its route is traversed by bands of high-school kids traipsing about outside an important city *liceo* (high school) in what looks like mass truancy, while flocks of tourists clamber amid stalls selling joss-sticks, second-hand books and fancy religious articles, necks craning upwards towards the dusty detail of decrepit *palazzi*. By night, the sounds and smells of southern Italian nightlife waft out of ventilator shafts. Around Christmas the crush gets unbearable as locals flock to via San Gregorio Armeno to purchase figures for their nativity cribs.

Spaccanapoli

Spaccanapoli, the ancient *decumanus inferior*, is the name given to a series of streets that make up the long, straight dividing line through the heart of old Naples. (Its length is best appreciated from the Certosa di San Martino, *see p89*.) Most of Spaccanapoli is now a pedestrian precinct, packed with tourists and students to-ing and fro-ing between historical sights, schools and university departments. Its daytime inhabitants determine the nature of the shops: bookshops and bookbinders, musical instrument shops (especially in via San Sebastiano running up towards the Conservatory of San Pietro a Maiella), jewellers' shops, as well as vendors of religious articles, pictures and frames, fried food and souvenirs.

Towards the western end of Spaccanapoli, piazza del Gesù has a towering rococo obelisk, the **Guglia dell'Immacolata** (1747-50) and elegant *palazzi*, including the **Palazzo Pignatelli di Monteleone** (closed to the public; calata Trinità Maggiore 53), where Edgar Degas was a frequent visitor. The piazza

is overlooked by the unusual façade of the church of the **Gesù Nuovo** and the lopped-off bell tower of **Santa Chiara**.

The short stretch of Spaccanapoli called via Benedetto Croce, after the Neapolitan philosopher and historian (1866-1952), is crammed with prestigious *palazzi*. Croce's own home, **Palazzo Filomarino** (No.12) has two 14th-century arches walled into the left-hand staircase, while the portico in the courtyard is from the 16th century (the *portiere* is fierce but won't bite if you go in). The **Palazzo Carafa della Spina** (No.45) has an unusually high doorway from the late 16th century; a pair of weather-beaten marble lions sit patiently in the smog (their blackened mouths were used to snuff out torches), and unusually lively fauns frolic above the portal.

Sightseeing

Neapolis surfaces in the Centro storico.

Work on the elaborate obelisk, the **Guglia di San Domenico**, in piazza San Domenico, was started in 1658 in thanks for the end of a plague epidemic, but only completed 99 years later. The piazza itself is dominated by several fine 16th- and 17th-century *palazzi* (none of which is open to the public), including the red-ochre **Palazzo Corigliano** (No.12), now owned by the university, **Palazzo Casacalenda** (No.16) and **Palazzo Sangro** (No.9), in addition to the church of **San Domenico Maggiore** itself.

Before becoming via San Biagio dei Librai, Spaccanapoli crosses piazzetta Nilo, which contains the little church of **San Angelo a Nilo**. The statue in the small square of the same name portrays the Nile Reclining. It dates from Roman times when worship of the Nile was commonly practised by the Egyptian community that lived in this area.

Further down via San Biagio is **Palazzo Marigliano** (No.39), with a well-preserved façade from 1513, and a fine coat of arms; steps at the back of the courtyard lead to a small but recently restored 'invisible' garden (open 10am-2pm Mon-Fri). At No.114, the **Monte di Pietà** chapel (open 9am-7pm Sat; 9am-2pm Sun) has statues of Safety and Charity by Pietro Bernini in the façade, and a 17th-century frescoed ceiling by Belisario Corenzio. The massive bulk of the church of **San Giorgio Maggiore** stands where Spaccanapoli crosses via Duomo. To the north on via Duomo is the **Museo Civico Filangieri**.

Spaccanapoli becomes via Vicaria Vecchia. The pretty church of **Sant'Agrippino** (No.86; currently being repaired following flood damage in autumn 2001) was almost totally destroyed during World War II, but its delicate, original 13th-century arches in the apse have been salvaged, and much of the furnishings of the utterly derelict church of **Santa Maria a Piazza** (via Forcella 12) opposite have been moved here, including the 13th-century crucifix. There's also a fine carved wooden door from the late 15th century (now inside the church).

In a litter-strewn pit at the centre of nearby piazza Calenda you'll find a chunk of ancient Greek city wall.

Gesù Nuovo

Piazza del Gesù 2 (081 551 8613). Metro Montesanto or Dante/bus E1, R1. **Open** 7am-12.30pm, 4-7pm Mon-Sat; 7am-2pm, 4-7pm Sun. **Map** p311 1C.

The façade of this extraordinary church is not that of a church at all. The diamond-shaped ashlar work dates back to a 1470 palazzo that only at the end of the 16th century was transformed by architect Giuseppe Valeriani into a church for the Jesuit order. The portals, windows and external decorations date from this period. Inside is a stupefying barrel-vaulted

The ashlar façade of **Gesù Nuovo**.

ceiling, and a dome that has been rebuilt several times. The inner façade has a large fresco (1725) by Francesco Solimena, while the ceilings and walls are a veritable treasure trove of frescos and paintings, including works by Luca Giordano and Giuseppe Ribera, with marble statues by Cosimo Fanzaga.

A large, busy room on the right-hand side of the church is dedicated to Giuseppe Moscati, a doctor who died in 1947 and was fast-tracked to canonisation in 1977 on a wave of grass-roots support that shows no sign of abating. A biochemist, Moscati turned down important academic posts to look after Naples' penniless sick. The ex-votos covering the chapel walls give an indication of local faith in the good doctor's miracle-working abilities; there are more tales of his prowess on the Jesuit website (www.gesuiti.it/moscati).

Museo Civico Filangieri

Via Duomo 288A (081 203 211). Bus E1, R2. **Open** closed indefinitely for restoration as this guide went to press. **Map** p310 2C.

The museum was founded in 1882 by Prince Gaetano Filangieri with the aim of creating a place where students of industrial design could observe and copy outstanding examples from the fine and applied arts. It contains more than 3,000 items, ranging from suits of armour and weapons to paintings and sculptures from the 14th to the 19th centuries, majolica and chinaware, coins and crib figures. The glass-ceilinged main hall, the Sala Agata, with its

Sightseeing

mezzanine wooden-balustraded walkway, is a fine exhibit in itself. Fifteenth-century Palazzo Cuomo, which houses this museum, was dismantled in the late 19th century and rebuilt 20m (70ft) further back to allow for road-widening.

Sant'Angelo a Nilo

Piazzetta Nilo (081 420 1222). Metro Montesanto or Dante/bus E1. **Open** 10am-noon, 2-4pm Mon-Fri. **Map** p311 1C.

Also known as the Cappella Brancaccio on account of its association with the family of that name, this church contains the fine marble tomb (1426) of Cardinal Rinaldo Brancaccio in a chapel to the right of the altar; it was made in Pisa, and Donatello had a hand in its creation. The fine bas-relief portraying the Assumption on the front of the tomb, the cardinal's head and the right-hand caryatid are the only works by the Tuscan artist in Naples, although it is unlikely he actually came here. There's a delicate bell tower, but it's difficult to see.

Santa Chiara

Via Benedetto Croce (church 081 552 6280/ museum 081 552 1597/www.oltreilchiostro.org). Metro Dante or Montesanto/bus E1. **Open** *Church* 8am-12.30pm, 4.30-7.30pm daily. *Museum & cloister* 9.30am-1pm, 2.30-5.30pm Mon-Sat; 9.30-1pm Sun. **Admission** *Church* free. *Museum & cloister* €4. **Credit** AmEx, MC, V. **Map** p311 1C.

The church and convent of Santa Chiara was built for Robert of Anjou's wife, Sancia, in the early 14th century, and has always been a favourite with local aristocracy. Its original Gothic features were hidden by baroque restructuring in the mid 18th century. A direct hit in an air raid in August 1943 started a fire that raged out of control for six days, destroying everything but the four walls of the main church. During the 1950s a rose window, the portal, the chapel arches and high mullion windows, exterior flying buttresses and some altars and shrines were salvaged or faithfully copied, and the church was rebuilt along its original Gothic lines. Of the impressive bell tower, set aside from the church, only the base is original. To the left of the church, a door leads into the tiled cloister, a haven of baroque peace. Beyond the cloister, a museum has bits and pieces salvaged from the bomb attack, including some superb 14th-century friezes, bas-reliefs and busts, plus an archaeological area revealing a gymnasium and baths from the old Roman city.

San Domenico Maggiore

Vico San Domenico Maggiore 18/piazza San Domenico Maggiore 8A (081 459 298). Metro Dante/bus E1. **Open** 8.30am-noon, 4.30-7pm daily. **Map** p311 1C.

This large castellated building is somewhat reminiscent of a bouncy castle. An extraordinary rear entrance leads up from the piazza by means of a curved double flight of marble steps under the main altar, but the basilica is best entered from the side street, vico San Domenico.

The porticoed entrance with pointed arch dates back to the late 13th century when the church was built, incorporating the pre-existing church of Sant'Angelo a Morfisa (right of the altar, closed to the public). The church has been much altered over the ages. The chapels include some fine works of art: marble tombstones from the 13th century (first chapel on right); 14th-century frescos by the great and unjustly neglected Roman artist Pietro Cavallino (second on right); and a couple of fine paintings by Mattia Preti (fourth on right). The Neapolitan headquarters of the Dominican order, the monastery hosted the hermeticist philosopher Giordano Bruno (burnt at the stake for heresy in Rome in 1600), who studied here, and St Thomas Aquinas, who stayed in the latter part of the 13th century and to whom the sixth chapel on the right is dedicated. In that chapel is a 13th-century icon in a glass case over the altar, which is reputed to have spoken temptingly to Thomas, offering him anything he wanted in return for the nice things the saint had written about Him. At which the unacquisitive Thomas scored heavenly brownie points by replying, 'Nothing, if not You' (in Latin, of course). The large, luminous sacristy has a fine fresco by Francesco Solimena on the ceiling and a bizarre collection of coffins; their contents include the decapitated body of a victim of the infamous barons' conspiracy of 1486.

Dropping names

Banchi Nuovi (street)
Merchants from all over Italy and Europe had traditionally set up *banchi* (stalls) in this street, especially under the Aragonese and Spanish viceroyalty. A flood wrecked the area in 1569, after which new (*nuovi*) stalls had to be built.

Carbonara (street, church)
Area outside the city walls where rubbish was burnt (*carbone* means 'charcoal').

Crocelle ai Mannesi (piazza)
Mannesi were woodcutters, many of whom set up workshops in the area around San Giorgio Maggiore to make large wooden floats for religious processions. *Crocelle* is a reference to the large red crosses worn by a local order of monks as they tended to the sick.

Librai (street)
Booksellers.

Nilo (piazzetta, street)
In Graeco-Roman times, there was a thriving community of merchants from Alexandria in Egypt here.

Scassacocchi (street)
'Coach-breakers' or scrapyard.

San Giorgio Maggiore

Via Duomo 237A (081 287 932). Bus E1, R1.
Open 8.30am-noon, 5-7pm Mon-Sat; 8.30am-1pm
Sun. **Map** p311 1C.

The original basilica was built in the fourth century
by St Severus (364-410) in an area of Naples occupied by families driven out of their homes around
Vesuvius by the AD 79 eruption. Severus's relics are
now behind the altar; his splendid marble throne is
on the right of the main aisle. The vestibule – with
its three Byzantine-Roman arches, at the entrance
in piazzetta Crocelle ai Mannesi – was the apse of
the original basilica, and the only bit of it to have
survived an earthquake in 1640. Subsequently,

architect Cosimo Fanzago rotated the floorplan by
180°, placing the 17th-century apse and main altar
at the opposite end of the church.

The city walls

Considering the sprawling chaos of 21st-
century Naples, it is hard to imagine the city
neatly confined within its walls from its Greek
beginnings until the middle of the 17th century.
But those city limits, around what is now
the Centro storico, remained substantially
unchanged for 2,000 years. When the Norman
King Roger visited Naples in 1140, he admired

Bloody miracles

Naples has been called the *Urbs Sanguinum*
('city of blood') and with good reason. Of the
countless manifestations of God's Will and
Power in the city, liquefaction of congealed
saintly blood is definitely a favourite. And
though most of the city's inhabitants are
extremely sceptical about such phenomena,
they also have a great affection for them.
'It's not true,' they'll tell you, 'but I believe it.'

The most illustrious bloody miracle involves
the city's patron **San Gennaro** (St Januarius)
who met his glorious end in 305 during the
persecutions of Diocletian. Legend provides
a number of versions of his attempted
execution – from death by wild beasts in
the Pozzuoli amphitheatre (*see p98*), to
incineration in a fiery furnace (as portrayed
by Giuseppe Ribera in the Duomo, *see p73*),
to being dragged in chains from Nola to
Pozzuoli (a good 40 kilometres/25 miles).
Gennaro survived these ordeals, however, to
be beheaded in the Solfatara (*see p99*).

His blood was scooped up by a far-sighted
old woman and eventually brought to the
catacombs of San Gennaro (*see p83*).
About a century later (though official records
date only as far back as 1389) the dark
brown desiccated blood liquefied, to a
rapturous reception.

Gennaro's blood bubbles into action in its
purpose-built chapel in the Duomo three
times a year: on the Saturday before the first
Sunday in May, on 19 September (his feast
day), and on 16 December, egged on by
hysterical crowds. The time taken for the
blood to liquefy (usually between two minutes
and an hour) at the September session is
considered a portent of what lies in store
for Naples, its citizens and football team
over the following 12 months.

But though he's the best known, San
Gennaro is certainly not the only saint whose
Neapolitan remains perform such tricks.

Santa Patrizia (St Patricia), possibly
the niece of a Byzantine emperor, fled
unwanted male attentions in her native
country and died, young and unblemished,
in Naples some time between the fourth
and eighth centuries. For centuries, her
body (and a phial of blood said to have
spurted miraculously from her well-dead gum
when a molar was extracted) was kept in
a now-derelict church in the city bearing
her name; in the 19th century it was
moved to its present home in San Gregorio
Armeno (*see p75*).

The phial of blood 'liquefies' every Tuesday
morning, on 25 August, and any time when
a sufficiently ardent group of believers
gathers around her tomb. But even those
scientists who are prepared to suspend their
disbelief over the San Gennaro phenomenon
scoff at the slight change of colour that takes
place – possibly brought about by warmth of
hands – in the substance purporting to be
Patrizia's dried blood.

San Giovanni Battista's (St John the
Baptist) blood froths into action in the same
church on 29 August and sometimes on
24 June; the last reported liquefaction of
San Pantaleone's vital juices – also kept in
San Gregorio Armeno – goes back to 1950,
as does that of **San Luigi Gonzaga** in the
Gesù Vecchio (*see p63*).

The blood of **San Lorenzo** (St Lawrence) –
fittingly, in San Lorenzo (*see p75*) – is
currently in a perpetually liquid state.
Santo Stefano's blood – with Patrizia's in San
Gregorio Armeno – seems to have given up
liquefying altogether.

San Domenico Maggiore. *See p69.*

its 4.5 kilometres (three miles) of impregnable walls. During the early 15th century, the Aragonese King Ferdinand I had them extended for a few hundred extra metres. In the 16th century, Spanish viceroy Don Pedro de Toledo beefed up defences still further by stringing walls or ditches between the city's five castles: Castello del Carmine (now demolished), Castel Capuano (*see p71*), Castel Sant'Elmo (*see p87*), Castel Nuovo (*see p59*) and Castel dell'Ovo (*see p56*).

A few minutes' walk from the eastern end of Spaccanapoli, the impressive **Porta Capuana** gate, with its carved marble triumphal arch and dark towers, dates from 1484. The stretch of wall dates from Ferdinand's extension of the fortifications.

In nearby piazza de Nicola, **Castel Capuano** (closed to the public) owes its Renaissance appearance to modifications carried out in the early 16th century, when it was changed from palace to law court; in fact, it was built in the late 12th century. The façade of this irregularly shaped building contains striking decorative elements in white plaster, contrasting with the severe black piperno stone. Between castle and gate is the early 16th-century church of **Santa Caterina a Formello** (open 8.30am-7.30pm Mon-Sat; 8.30am-1pm Sun).

Heading north-east from the church, via Carbonara was so called because it was where rubbish was burnt; ten minutes up the street on

the right is the rambling yet visually pleasing complex of **San Giovanni a Carbonara**, with its carved treasures.

San Giovanni a Carbonara

Via Carbonara 5 (081 295 873). Metro Cavour or Museo/bus 110, E1. **Open** 9.30am-1pm Mon-Sat. **Map** p310 2B.

This 14th-century church stands at the top of a dramatic flight of steps (1707), by Ferdinando Sanfelice (*see p35*), above the modern church of the same name. At the head of the staircase, the chapel of Santa Monica (closed indefinitely for restoration) has a marble Gothic portal. The entrance to the church is to the left of this portal. The church's sculptures are numerous and magnificent. The monument and tomb of King Ladislas (1428) behind the main altar is 18m (63ft) high, and shows Renaissance touches in its mainly Gothic design. The round chapel behind the altar has a complex majolica-tiled floor, 15th-century frescos portraying the lives of the hermits, and the tomb of Gianni Caracciolo (1433), the much-hated lover of King Ladislas' sister and successor, Queen Joan II. The whole complex suffered severely in the air raids of August 1943.

Via dei Tribunali

Via dei Tribunali was the *decumanus maior* of Greek Neapolis. Nowadays, pandemonium reigns supreme at all times. The street has maintained its distinctly commercial flavour intact since ancient times, and is lined with small shops and street markets. The traffic can be infuriating.

At the eastern end of via dei Tribunali, piazza Riario Sforza is home to the monumental **Guglia di San Gennaro**, inaugurated in 1660 after the city had been saved from an eruption of Vesuvius in 1631 by the prompt intervention of its patron saint. Opposite, the 17th-century church of the **Pio Monte della Misericordia** contains Caravaggio's spellbinding *Seven Acts of Mercy* (1607). In the church's *pinacoteca* (gallery) next door is a small collection, including works by Giuseppe Ribera and Luca Giordano.

To reach the main entrance of the **Duomo** requires a detour north along via Duomo.

Via dei Tribunali continues up the hill past the white façade of the early 17th-century church of the **Girolamini** (closed indefinitely for restoration), attached to the **Pinacoteca** of the same name. Opposite, grimy yet timeless plaster statues look down from above the portal of the derelict church of **Santa Maria della Colonna** (No.283; closed indefinitely for restoration); they have stood there for nearly 200 years. Beyond, the medieval church of **San Lorenzo Maggiore** stands above an archaeological site.

Sightseeing

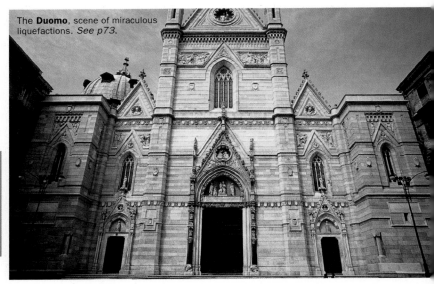

The **Duomo**, scene of miraculous liquefactions. *See p73.*

Off to the left in **via San Gregorio Armeno** is the church of the same name, preceded (before passing beneath the arch) by its convent and cloisters. This street is famous for its Christmas nativity scenes and for selling the necessary accessories for this special Neapolitan artform (*see p139*). Even in midsummer, the shops pour their unseasonal wares out on to the narrow street.

Back on via dei Tribunali, the imposing church of **San Paolo Maggiore** stands on piazza San Gaetano, which was the *agorà* (later the forum) of the ancient city. Beside the church is the entrance to the fourth-century BC underground **Acqueduct**.

At No.339 is a palazzo (not open to the public) built in the 13th century for Philip of Anjou; it has its original, sturdy four-span portico and a 13th-century portal. Opposite is the church of **Santa Maria dell'Anima ad Arco**. The baroque **Santa Maria Maggiore** (closed indefinitely for restoration) has a pretty Romanesque bell tower known as the Pietrasanta, probably left from an earlier church. The adjacent **Cappella Pontano** is a Renaissance work from 1492, though the interior is the result of a baroque makeover.

Beyond the small and rather bare 17th-century church of the **Croce di Lucca** (which is currently closed for restoration), vico San Domenico Maggiore then via Francesco de Sanctis lead to the extraordinary funerary chapel, **Cappella Sansevero**.

Back on via dei Tribunali, the splendid church of **San Pietro a Maiella** stands next to the **Conservatorio**, illustrious producer over the years of such musicians as Scarlatti and Pergolesi.

At the centre of piazza Bellini are scant remains of fourth-century BC Greek city walls – and much 21st-century rubbish.

Acqueduct

Piazza San Gaetano 68 (081 296 944/368 354 0585/www.napolisotterranea.org). Metro Dante or Montesanto/bus E1. **Open** *guided tours every 2hrs noon-4pm Mon-Fri; 10am-6pm Sat, Sun.* **Admission** *Acqueduct €6.71. Acqueduct & Roman theatre €9.30.* **No credit cards. Map** p311 1C.

Situated 35m (123ft) below street-level, these tunnels, aqueducts and chambers date back to the fourth century BC and the dawn of the Greek city of Neapolis. They were gradually incorporated into the city's labyrinthine water supply system, remaining in use until the cholera epidemic of 1884. The guided tour covers about 1km (half a mile) of the almost 450km (225 miles) of tunnels, and lasts about 90 minutes. The Association that runs the site also conducts tours (by appointment only, admission €2.60 each) of the recently excavated Roman theatre around the corner in via Cinque Santi, and the nearby church of Santa Maria del Purgatorio ad Arco (*see p76*).

Cappella Sansevero

Via Francesco de Sanctis 19 (081 551 8470). Metro Dante or Montesanto/bus E1. **Open** *Nov-Apr 10am-4.40pm Mon, Wed-Sat; 10am-1pm Sun; May-*

Sightseeing

Oct 10am-6.40pm Mon, Wed-Sat; 10am-1pm Sun.
Admission €5. **No credit cards. Map** p311 1C.
The funerary chapel of the Di Sangro family was
built in 1590, but took on its current appearance in
1749-66 thanks to the eccentric prince of Sansevero,
Raimondo di Sangro, who hired the most important
sculptors of his day to decorate it. The high altar is
carved in accordance with the 'picture hewn out of
stone' criteria of the day; the statues have high-
sounding titles: *Domination of Self-will, The
Pleasures of Marriage, Shyness.* The *Veiled Christ*
(1753) by Giuseppe Sammartino is uncanny in its
realism; so impressed was neo-classical sculptor
Antonio Canova that he tried to purchase the statue
during one of his visits. The extraordinary figures
in the crypt are not just uncanny: they're downright
macabre. Obsessed with embalming, the pseudo-
scientist prince carried out experiments on his
defunct domestics, injecting their bodies with chemical substances to preserve their inner organs. Local
lore has it that they were not always dead when this
operation took place.

Duomo

*Via Duomo 147 (081 449 097/www.duomodi
napoli.com). Bus E1, R2.* **Open** *Church* 8am-
12.30pm, 4.30-7pm Mon-Sat; 8am-1.30pm, 5-7.30pm
Sun. Archaeological area & baptistry 9am-noon,
4.30-6.30pm Mon-Sat; 8.30am-1pm Sun.* **Admission**
Church free. *Archaeological area & baptistry* €3.
No credit cards. Map p310 2C.
Naples' cathedral dates back to the fourth century
with the founding of the basilica of Santa Restituta.
At the end of the fifth century the cathedral of Santa
Stefania was constructed perpendicular to the orig-

inal basilica, while the current Duomo was built
over Santa Stefania at the end of the 13th century,
incorporating Santa Restituta as a side chapel. The
disappointing 19th-century façade (the three portals are from 1407) remains hidden from view in a
rather unprepossessing lay-by, and little prepares
the visitor for the splendours within. The gloom of
the 100m-long (328ft) Latin-cross interior fails to
conceal the fine gilt coffered ceiling (1621) and the
paintings between the windows and arches, by
Luca Giordano and his school.

The large chapel on the right is the Cappella di
San Gennaro, also known as Il Tesoro. It contains
a large number of bronze and silver statues of saints
associated with Naples' patron saint, Gennaro;
many of them are normally kept in the sacristy
(closed to the public) and only put on display here
during May and September. The most famous of
these, a 14th-century French silver bust, is kept in
a strongbox behind the altar, together with two
phials containing Gennaro's congealed blood; the
head of the bust contains his skull bones. It is here
that the blood liquefies on Gennaro's feast day, 19
September (*see p70* **Bloody miracles**). The chapel
has a magnificent gilded bronze gate by Cosimo
Fanzago (1668), and fine frescos by Domenichino
(1631-43) showing miraculous episodes from the
saint's life. San Gennaro emerges unscathed from a
fiery furnace in a painting (1647) by Giuseppe Ribera
above the right-hand altar.

Back in the main church, to the right of the high
altar, the chapel of Sant'Aspreno and the Minutolo
family chapel have original Gothic decorations. In
the magnificent marble late 16th-century *succorpo*

San Paolo Maggiore. *See p76.*

or *confessio* by Tommaso Malvito, beneath the altar, is a fine statue of a kneeling Cardinal Carafa and an altar with urn containing more of San Gennaro's bones. On the left side of the nave is the entrance to the fourth-century church of Santa Restituta, Naples' oldest remaining basilica, to the archaeological area and to the baptistry. The painting on the ceiling of Santa Restituta is attributed to Luca Giordano.

In the archaeological area are Greek and Roman walls and columns, early Christian mosaics, part of the original Santa Stefania cathedral and sections of Greek and Roman roads. On the baptistry ceiling you can see outstanding mosaic decorations dating back to the fifth century.

Pinacoteca Girolamini

Via Duomo 142 (081 449 139). Bus E1, R2.
Open 9.30am-12.50pm Mon-Sat. **Admission** free.
Map p310 2C.
A flight of steps leads up to the right from the entrance and into another world: a splendid cloister encompassing a veritable forest of medlar and lemon trees. The small art gallery is one of Naples' most rewarding. The last two rooms (four and five) are the best, with Battista Carracciolo's superb chiaroscuro *Baptism of Christ* and other works by the same artist, plus Andrea Vaccaro's *Adoration of the Shepherds*, Luca Giordano's stirring *Mourning the Death of Christ*, and five paintings bearing all the typical grotesque features of Giuseppe Ribera's school. Along the side walls are works by Neapolitan stalwarts Paolo De Matteis and Francesco Solimena. The 60,000-volume library is renowned but closed to all but the most insistent of scholars.

Pio Monte della Misericordia

Via dei Tribunali 253 (081 446 944). Metro Dante or Montesanto/bus E1. **Open** *Church* 9am-1pm Mon-Sat. *Gallery* closed for restoration, though visits can be arranged by appointment 9am-1pm Thur, Sat. **Admission** free. **Map** p311 1C.
The slow-moving restoration work on the whole building makes planning a visit to this splendidly musty old art gallery extremely hazardous. If you strike lucky, you will see pieces of 19th-century furniture and fine paintings, including delicate, satiny oil paintings by the 18th-century Francesco De Mura in the entrance, a *St Anthony* by Giuseppe Ribera, and a *St Agnes* by Massimo Stanzione in the Sala del Coretto; there's a rather ugly self-portrait of Luca Giordano in the second antechamber. The attendant will provide you with a glossy catalogue of the main works of art, and leave you free to roam around on your own.

San Gregorio Armeno

Via San Gregorio Armeno 1 (081 552 0186). Metro Dante or Montesanto/bus E1. **Open** 9am-noon Mon, Wed-Fri; 9am-12.45pm Tue; 9am-12.30pm Sat, Sun.
Map p311 1C.
Built on the site of a Roman temple to the fertility goddess Ceres, the 16th-century church of San Gregorio owes its unflagging popularity to the cult

of St Patricia (*see p70* **Bloody miracles**), whose relics are conserved here and whose blood obligingly liquefies not only on her feast day (25 August), when impressive celebrations are held, but regularly each Tuesday (hence the extended opening time). Patricia might well have been Naples' patron saint had the closed order of nuns that brought her relics from her native Constantinople in the eighth century not kept them shrouded in secrecy in their convent (the nuns also brought relics of San Gregorio, but somehow these never attracted so much attention). After many years when only women were allowed a glimpse, Patricia's remains are now on view to all and sundry in a chapel to the right of the altar.

The church is preceded by an unusual vestibule with pillars, while the interior is a veritable treasure trove of Neapolitan baroque. There are paintings and frescos by Luca Gordano and Paolo de Matteis, and a fine 17th-century marble altar by Dionisio Lazzari. To reach the adjacent convent and cloisters, continue up via San Gregorio, under the arch, and turn left into via Maffei; press the intercom at the first gate on the left. Still visible by the entrance are the bronze drums through which supplies were passed to the nuns. The cloisters, with their orange trees and pretty fountain, are a haven of peace and quiet (despite the primary school run by the sisters) and have a view over the church's majolica-tiled dome.

San Lorenzo Maggiore (church)

Via dei Tribunali 316 (081 454 948). Metro Dante or Montesanto/bus E1. **Open** 8am-noon, 5-7pm daily. **Map** p311 1C.
Returned more or less to its original 13th-century appearance by post-war restoration work, the vast, stern interior of this much-frequented church is in stark contrast to the tiddly baroque façade (1742) which was designed by Ferdinando Sanfelice (*see p35*). It was here that Boccaccio fell in love with Fiammetta (as recounted in the *Decameron*); Petrarch stayed in the adjoining convent. The convent was also the headquarters of the Parthenopean government in 1799 (*see p16*).

Some traces of the 17th- and 18th-century baroque treatment have remained inside, most noticeably in the third chapel on the right. A splendid Gothic triumphal arch leads into the delicate ribbed cross-vaulted apse. On the high altar is an early 16th-century relief sculpture of Naples by Giovanni da Nola. Sections of the original mosaic flooring are preserved under glass in the transept. The left-hand transept chapel has two paintings by Caravaggio's follower Mattia Preti.

San Lorenzo Maggiore (archaeological site)

Via dei Tribunali 316 (081 211 0860/ www.sanlorenzomaggiorenapoli.it). Metro Dante or Montesanto/bus E1. **Open** 9am-5pm Mon-Sat; 9am-1pm Sun. **Closed** 1wk Aug. **Admission** €4. **No credit cards**. **Map** p311 1C.

Undoubtedly one of the most extraordinary archae-ological sites in the whole Naples region. Right at the heart of the most densely populated city in Europe, you can stand in silence and feel that you have been whisked back in time to Graeco-Roman Neapolis. In this confined area under San Lorenzo, excavation work is still in progress. What has been dug up to date are the streets of ancient Naples as they were 2,000 years ago: a butcher's shop, a dyer's, a baker's and a beautiful porticoed arcade.

Santa Maria del Purgatorio ad Arco

Via dei Tribunali 39 (church 081 292 622/
Hypogeum 081 296 944/368 354 0585). Metro
Dante or Montesanto/bus E1. **Open** *Church* 9am-
1pm Mon-Sat. *Hypogeum* by appointment only.
Admission *Church* free. *Hypogeum* €2.60.
No credit cards. Map p311 1C.
The three bronze skulls (a fourth was stolen in the 1950s) outside its railings, and its popular name *cap'e morte* ('death's head'), are clues as to why this 17th-century church has such a hold on Neapolitans. Especially during wartime, womenfolk would adopt and look after skulls, transferring on to them the love and care they felt for their menfolk missing in action. They would shower them with presents of perfume and pillows. During peacetime the process degenerated into a mere expedient for obtaining favours through divine intercession; delays by the chosen soul could result in its earthly remains being smashed and loyalties being shifted elsewhere. Accordingly, the Church has now officially banned the practice, though it is said to live on.

Inside, you'll see a winged skull and crossbones behind the main altar. As well as several baroque paintings, there's a circular *Madonna and Child* attributed (by some) to Giotto. Beneath the church is a hypogeum (underground chamber), which con-tains a pile of dusty bones. Barely visible through a grating from here is another area containing a pile of bones and skulls.

San Paolo Maggiore

Via dei Tribunali (081 454 048). Metro Dante or
Montesanto/bus E1. **Open** *Church* 9am-noon Mon-
Sat. *Crypt* 9am-noon, 5-7pm daily. **Map** p311 1C.
This lofty magniloquent church, dating from the end of the 16th century, stands on the site of a Roman temple to Castor and Pollux. In front of the façade are two tall, white fluted pillars from the temple. The interior is notable for the colossal size of its Latin-cross interior, while the sacristy has fine frescos by Francesco de Maria. The adjoining ex-convent in via San Paolo 14 is now an archive containing legal documents from the 15th century onwards.

San Pietro a Maiella

Piazza Luigi Miraglia 393 (081 459 008).
Metro Dante or Montesanto/bus R1, R4. **Open**
7.30am-noon, 5.30-7pm Mon-Sat; 8.30am-1pm Sun.
Map p311 1C.
Approached from via dei Tribunali, San Pietro looks for all the world like an English country

church, with its cusp-shaped spire, made in tufa stone. Dating from the beginning of the 14th cen-tury, the interior still bears many of its original Angevin features. There's a range of round and pointed arches, which are in stark contrast to the elaborate coffered ceiling adorned with paintings (1656-61) by Mattia Preti, and the lavish works of art, including a fine *Madonna Appearing to Celestinus V* by Massimo Stanzione in the fourth chapel on the right. The church is generally closed on August afternoons.

The decumanus superior

The third ancient *decumanus* runs parallel with, and to the north of, via dei Tribunali, starting opposite the church of San Giovanni a Carbonara (*see p71*) at via Santa Sofia. It passes the towering church of the **Santissimi Apostoli** (open 8am-1pm, 4.15-8pm Mon-Sat; 9am-1.30pm Sun), believed to have been built over a Roman temple to Mercury. The street then changes name to via dei Santissimi Apostoli, passing the baroque church of **Santa Maria Donnaregina**; behind the church, up vico Donnaregina, stands the eponymous 14th-century church. The *decumanus* then becomes via dell'Anticaglia; the two Roman brick archways used to join a large theatre on the south of the street to baths on the north.

Santa Maria Donnaregina

Vico Donnaregina 26 (tel/fax 081 299 101).
Bus E1. **Open** by appointment only; fax a request.
Map p310 2C.
A 17th-century portal leads through a dainty porti-coed cloister from the same period. On the left is a door to the deconsecrated 14th-century church. The bare interior has fan-vaults that, like the walls, still bear traces of 14th-century Giotto-style frescos. Tino da Camaino's magnificent marble tomb of Queen Mary of Hungary (1323) is against the left-hand wall. From the altar steps, looking up and back, the nuns' choir with its coffered ceiling and stunning 14th-century frescos by Pietro Cavallino is visible above. Depicting Bible scenes, saints and contemporary nobles, the frescos are the most complete of their age in Naples. The church was abandoned for about 250 years from the 1600s to the 1850s, eclipsed by the 17th-century church next door; this probably saved it from a baroque makeover and the inevitable destruction of the frescos.

From 1924 to 1925 the rear wall of the newer build-ing, which had gobbled up the apse of the old church, was placed on rollers and moved 5m (16ft) back, creating the space between the two churches and revealing the frescoed wall. The old church is home to Naples University's architectural restora-tion department, and is unofficially open for visits from around 9am to 12.30pm from January to June. To be sure of getting inside, however, fax the num-ber given above at least a week in advance.

Via Toledo & La Sanità

A perfect cameo of all that is Naples.

The Centro storico (*see p67*) is bordered along two of its sides by major thoroughfares – via Toledo and via Foria – converging at the **Museo Nazionale Archeologico**. Via Toledo is now pedestrianised for much of its length.

Generally considered to be the main street of a city that has no real centre as such, it is a perfect cameo of all that is Naples. A few flashy shops and banks mask the forlorn urban reality of the Quartieri spagnoli, while an astonishing assortment of characters from bankers to beggars stroll or struggle their way along the *palazzo*-lined route, which seems to enshrine life. Beyond the unspeakably traffic-clogged via Foria lie the Sanità, Miracoli and Vergini districts, throwbacks to a Naples that was.

Via Toledo & the Quartieri spagnoli

Via Toledo was created in the early 16th century by Spanish viceroy, Don Pedro de Toledo (*see p12*), but was rechristened via Roma when Naples became part of the newly formed Italian republic in 1860. A recent return to its original name has led to confusion and you may hear it called both.

Forming a link between the Quartieri spagnoli and the old city to the east, the via Toledo was lined with *palazzi* so elegant that it was lauded as one of Europe's most impressive streets by Grand Tourists. Where the homes of nobles and rich bankers once dazzled visitors, clothing retailers now hold sway. The *palazzi* (*see p81* **Faded grandeur**) are still there, though, visible above the shopfronts and from *cortili* (courtyards) behind impressive portals leading off via Toledo.

Transformed into a pedestrian area on the occasion of the 1994 G7 summit, the southern stretch of via Toledo is *the* place to experience the *struscio*, that particularly southern Italian phenomenon in which vast crowds of well-dressed people stroll and strut back and forth along the main drag. Neapolitans of all ages flock here to relax and unwind, chatting and chatting up, seeing and being seen. The pace of the thing is extremely slow; steer clear of via Toledo in the evening if you are in a hurry.

The pedestrian area terminates at the junction with via Diaz. East along via Diaz, modern piazza Matteotti is dominated by the vast, semicircular and resoundingly fascist façade of the 1930s **Palazzo delle Poste** (post office), while towering over the square from behind the modern **Questura** (police headquarters) is the 33-storey **Jolly Hotel** (*see p38*), one of the most unpopular eyesores ever to receive planning permission from the now-discredited city council of the 1950s.

North of the post office in piazza Monteoliveto, the 15th-century church of **Sant'Anna dei Lombardi** was originally part of a much larger convent complex. Some of the complex has today been incorporated into the adjacent Carabinieri (police) station, scene of controversial investigations ranging from the one that resulted in the execution of the leaders of the Parthenopean Republic in 1799 (*see p16*) to the *Mani pulite* anti-corruption enquiries of the early 1990s.

Further north still, the grim 20th-century façade of the church of **Spirito Santo** (open 9-11.30am Mon-Sat; 10am-noon Sun) masks a vast, cool, grey and white interior, and one of the largest domes in the city.

Dropping names

Cisterna dell'Olio (street)
'Oil tank'. Olive oil was stored in the house at No.6.
Guantai (street)
'Glove makers'. The glove trade was, and still is, important in Naples.
Lammatari (street)
Neapolitan for 'starch-makers'. Starch was used by bakers, tailors and washerwomen.
Pignasecca (street and market)
Dry pine-cone (*see p134* **La Pignasecca**).
Ponte di Tappia (street)
Refers to a private footbridge (*ponte*) built across the street in the latter part of the 16th century by a Spanish nobleman called Tappia.
Vergini (district)
Once contained a cemetery for members of a pre-Christian male sect dedicated to the minor Greek divinity Eunostos. This closed order observed rules of chastity and temperance.

Cramped, poor and fascinating: the **Quartieri spagnoli**.

The rigidly regular streets on the slope west of via Toledo constitute the **Quartieri spagnoli**, built during Don Pedro de Toledo's flourish of urban development in the 16th century to house Spanish occupying troops. Cramped from the start, the Quartieri gradually became home to some of the poorest of Naples' poor; ground floors which were scarcely fit for Spanish horses 400 years ago became the damp, exhaust-filled dwellings of wretched human beings. They still are, and the Quartieri boasts some unenviable records: Europe's highest rates of unemployment and respiratory disease are just two. Yet there's something fascinating about this warren of streets… for the visitor. Residents (and city councils) would rather see the back of this glaring manifestation of urban decay.

One exception to this rule is the delightful via Pignasecca, which is home to a chaotic street market (*see p134* **La Pignasecca**). With the market in full swing, crowds of people streaming towards the city centre by the nearby funicular railway and underground stations, and ambulances screaming around Pellegrini hospital, the swirling inferno that engulfs the street is both loud and mesmerising.

Sant'Anna dei Lombardi

Piazza Monteoliveto 14 (081 551 3333). Metro Montesanto/bus E1, R1, R4. **Open** 9am-12.30pm Tue-Sat. **Map** p311 1C.

The church dates from the early 15th century, though it was refurbished in the 17th. Inside are several Renaissance sculptures, including an extraordinary group of terracotta statues entitled *Mourning the Death of Christ* by Guido Mazzoni (1492). The sacristy has a fine ceiling frescoed by Florentine artist Giorgio Vasari in 1544; the unusual inlaid wooden panels along the walls are from the same period.

Piazza Dante

At the point where via Toledo becomes via Enrico Pessina, **piazza Dante** is dominated by the crescent-shaped **Convitto Nazionale**, originally a state-funded boarding school for poor children from outside Naples. Designed in the mid-18th century by Luigi Vanvitelli, the Convitto has 26 statues representing the virtues of Charles III. True to its origins, it now houses several state schools. At the Convitto's northern end is the **Port'Alba** arch, built in the early 17th century and rebuilt 150 years later. After a long period as a building site, the piazza was restored – much to everyone's relief – to undreamed-of heights of elegance for the opening in 2002 of its underground station (*see also p149* **Art goes underground**).

The **Museo Nazionale Archeologico**, home to some of Italy's most outstanding treasures, is further north on the smoggy, noisy

via Pessina. En route, in via Bellini, stands the **Accademia delle Belle Arti** (Fine Arts Academy, not open to the public), with its mid 19th-century façade in tufa stone. From the northern end of via Bellini, the rather sleazy and generally unloved **Galleria Principe di Napoli** leads to piazza Museo.

Beyond the museum on via Santa Teresa degli Scalzi stands the church of **Santa Teresa degli Scalzi** (No.43; open noon-1pm Tue, Thur, Fri; 10.30am-1.30pm Sun), which was built in the 17th century and reworked in the 18th century. The church is largely neglected, its fickle congregation having decamped to the Gesù Nuovo (*see p68*), which has a chapel dedicated to the 'miraculous doctor' Giuseppe Moscati. Unlike the church, the old people's centre and school for the blind attached to St Teresa's are alive and kicking.

Piazza Cavour, with its busy underground station and scruffy public gardens, leads east out of piazza Museo. The recently restored **Porta San Gennaro**, with a 17th-century fresco by Mattia Preti, was part of the 15th-century walls.

Museo Nazionale Archeologico

Piazza Museo 19 (081 564 8941/ www.archeona.arti.beniculturali.it). Metro Cavour or Museo/bus 47, CS, E1. **Open** *Museum* 9am-7.30pm Mon, Wed-Sun; ticket office closes 1hr earlier.

Gabinetto segreto Guided tours only every 30mins 9.30am-1.30pm, 2.30-6.30pm Mon, Wed-Sun. **Admission** €6.50 (*see also p53*). **No credit cards.** **Map** p310 2C.

Built in the early 17th century as the seat of Naples University, the *palazzo* that now houses the Museo Nazionale was chosen in 1777 by King Ferdinand I as the perfect home for the immense Farnese collection of ancient artefacts inherited from his grandmother, Elisabetta Farnese. Plunder from digs at Pompeii (*see p216*), Stabiae (*see p220*) and Herculaneum (*see p211*) was added to the collection, making the Museo Nazionale one of the world's largest and most fascinating archaeological museums. On-going restorations mean that exhibits are often out not where they're meant to be.

The museum is distributed over four floors. The basement (Rooms 17-23) contains the Egyptian section, which includes Egyptian objects imported into Italy during the Roman period and unearthed in excavations in the Campania region and Rome. There's a large collection of obelisks, busts, funerary statues, jewellery, sarcophagi from the Hellenic and Ptolemaic periods, and the obligatory mummy, once part of the Borgia collection.

On the meandering ground floor is the Farnese collection (the Farnese paintings are in Capodimonte; *see p84*), most of which was filched from ancient sites in Rome by the powerful Parma-based Farnese family during the 16th century, when Alessandro Farnese ruled as Pope Paul III (1534-49). In Room 1 on the right of the entrance hall are the *Tirannicidi*, the tyrant-killers Armodios and Aristogitones, who did away with the cruel Athenian rulers Hippia and

Ancient porn in the **Museo Archeologico**.

Hipparchos in 514 BC; the pair is a Roman copy of the fifth-century BC Greek original. In the same room is a Roman copy of Polycletus' *Doriforo*. Elsewhere on this floor is a series of busts and statues (see the two fine heads of Caracalla in the un-numbered gallery leading off the entrance hall into

Room 8), some of which are simply enormous. There's the powerful *Ercole Farnese* (Farnese Hercules; between Rooms 11 and 12) and the recently restored *Toro Farnese* (Farnese Bull; Room 16), a large marble group from the early third century AD found in the Baths of Caracalla in Rome. In Room 8, the graceful Roman copy of a Greek *Venere* (Venus) *Callipige* glances daintily backwards at her reflection in the water as she slips off her clothes.

Room 10 contains the tiny, delicate *Tazza Farnese,* a small dish made in Egypt during the Ptolemaic period and consisting of four layers of sardonyx agate. Its transparent beauty is renowned; examine it from both sides. The mezzanine floor houses the mosaic collection, including the large scene depicting the battle between Alexander the Great and Darius from the House of the Faun in Pompeii (Room 61). Also here is the **Gabinetto segreto** (*see below*), a collection of ancient pornography.

The first floor, centred around the Sala Meridiana, contains artefacts from Pompeii, Herculaneum, and other southern Italian sites, as well as the pre- and proto-historical sections. The vast, echoing Sala Meridiana is 54m (189ft) long and 20m (70ft) high. On its walls are paintings on archaeological themes from the Farnese collection. On its floor is a line marking a zodiacal Meridian; around noon, an oval bead of light snakes in through a hole high in the top right-hand corner of the room striking the Meridian in the appropriate zodiacal sign.

To the left as you enter the Sala, Rooms 85-89 contain glassware, silver and pottery from Pompeii, while Rooms 66-78 have friezes and frescos from Herculaneum and Stabiae.

To the right as you enter the Sala, the first entrance leads to Rooms 114-117, with artefacts from the Villa dei Papiri in Herculaneum; note the lovely bronze Hermes in the centre of Room 117. The second series of rooms on the right (130-140) contains vases, bowls and funerary offerings from Greek and Roman Paestum, and from other sites around Magna Graecia (ancient southern Italy).

The pre- and proto-history section is reached from the third corridor on the right. The rather complex layout here features, on the upper mezzanine floor, Palaeolithic, Neolithic and Early Bronze Age finds from the Campania region (Rooms 148 and 149), including stone artefacts dating back to 100,000 BC. The lower mezzanine floor (Rooms 145 and 146) houses finds from the Middle and Late Bronze Ages. The main section (Rooms 124-127) is arranged according to place not time, and includes Palaeolithic bones and flints (300,000 BC) found on Capri (Room 127); the Iron Age is represented best, with eighth- and ninth-century funerary relics from a number of necropoli from Capua to Ischia.

The Gabinetto segreto (off-limits to children under 11) features some of the erotic works of art uncovered at Pompeii and Herculaneum. The recently rubbed-down collection of explicit paintings and sculptures includes a vast range of phallus talismans – winged ones, jingling ones with bells, others with

Faded grandeur

Via Toledo's *palazzi* once drew gasps of admiration from Grand Tourists. Nowadays, few people give them a second look as they browse in the big-name fashion emporia that line the street.

Palazzo Berio (No.256) was designed by Luigi Vanvitelli in 1772, **Palazzo Barbaja** (No.205) was home to the composer Gioacchino Rossini between 1815 and 1822, **Palazzo Zevallos di Stigliano** (No.184 – now a bank) has a portal by Cosimo Fanzago, while the grim square bulk of the headquarters of the **Banco di Napoli** (No.178) is every inch a product of the Fascist 1930s. The neo-classical **Palazzo Buono** (No.340) is now occupied by the Rinascente department store. From the balcony of

Palazzo Doria d'Angri (No.29 – it still bears scars from a World War II bomb), Giuseppe Garibaldi proclaimed the annexation of the Kingdom of the Two Sicilies to the newly formed Kingdom of Italy in September 1860 (*see p19*). Near **Palazzo d'Angri** across a side street off via Toledo, **Palazzo Carafa di Maddaloni** (via Maddaloni 6), built in 1582, is a good example of just how dilapidated Neapolitan *palazzi* can get: an earthquake in 1980 damaged the frescoed *salone*, which has remained closed ever since; traces of its baroque glory can be seen in the frescoed barrel-vaulted ceiling of the entrance and the cross-vaults of the right-hand staircase (just walk into the entrance... if you can get past the porter).

hats on. One item approaches the subject in pre-Freudian manner, depicting a frantic struggle between the member and its owner. The high (or low) point of the collection is a sculpted Pan, caught in the act with a nanny-goat. The collection has attracted controversy over the ages, and was only reopened to queues of giggling tourists in 2000.

La Sanità & beyond

The image of traffic-clogged via Foria was given a boost in 2001 with the opening of the Museo underground station. Behind its rather drab red-ochre exterior, the station opens up to reveal a veritable feast of hi-tech architecture and art (*see p149* **Art goes underground**). The ongoing facelift of piazza Cavour – including a pedestrian link from the station to the Museo Nazionale Archeologico (*see p79*) – is in stark contrast to the other end of the road where a planned facelift for the Albergo dei Poveri has generated massive publicity and massively unrealistic completion deadlines.

Nestling between via Foria (which follows the line of the old city walls), via Santa Teresa degli Scalzi and the hill of Capodimonte is an area made up of three districts: **La Sanità** ('healthy', because it was outside the city walls), **I Miracoli** (because of the miracles wrought around saintly inmates of the catacombs) and **Le Vergini** (named after a pre-Christian no-sex-please Greek religious group). Now densely populated and unquestionably *folkloristico* (dearly loved Neapolitan comedian Totò, see *p151*, was born here in via Antesaecula 109; there's a plaque above the greengrocer's), the area is honeycombed with underground burial

places: from the early Christian **catacombe di San Gaudioso** under the church of **Santa Maria della Sanità** and the **catacombe di San Severo** under the church of the same name, to the comparatively recent **cimitero delle Fontanelle**.

The area also contains two gems (visible from outside) by 18th-century architect Ferdinando Sanfelice: **Palazzo Sanfelice** (via Sanità 2 and 6), now sadly dilapidated, was the architect's own home; and the truly magnificent 'flying' staircase in **Palazzo dello Spagnuolo** (via dei Vergini 19), which has recently been restored to its former glory. Further east, pine tree-lined piazza Miracoli is home to the 17th-century church of **Santa Maria dei Miracoli** (open 8.15-11.30am, 5-8pm Mon-Sat; 8am-1pm Sun).

Beyond Porta San Gennaro, traffic crawls relentlessly along via Foria, past the **Orto botanico** (botanical gardens), to piazza Carlo III, which is dominated by the fearful bulk of the **Albergo dei Poveri** (closed to the public), the largest public building in Europe. Vast as it is (the façade measures 354 metres/1,239 feet; the building covers 103,000 square metres/360,500 square feet), the Albergo is only one-fifth the size of Ferdinando Fuga's original design, commissioned by Charles III to house Naples' destitute and homeless. Construction began in 1751 and was completed in 1829. In 2000, a project to repair serious damage from the earthquake of 1980 and general decay got under way, and is due for completion in 2006.

Via Santi Giovanni e Paolo runs north-east out of the eastern end of piazza Carlo III. The great tenor Enrico Caruso (1873-1921) was born

Sightseeing

at No.6. A dingy plaque on the wall introduces this as the house 'where the world first heard his voice'. Naples itself heard very little more of it; slated by Neapolitan critics early in his career he never came back.

Catacombe di San Gaudioso/ Santa Maria alla Sanità

Via della Sanità 124 (081 544 1305/ www.cib.na.cnr.it/vergini/index.html). Metro Cavour or Museo/bus C51, C52. **Open** *Church* 8.30am-12.30pm, 5-8pm Mon-Sat; 8.30am-1.30pm Sun. *Catacombs* Guided tours 9.30am, 10.15am, 11am, 11.45am, 12.30pm daily, plus 5.10pm, 5.50pm, 6.30pm Sat. **Admission** €3. **No credit cards.** **Map** p312 1A.

Tunnelled out of the Capodimonte hillside in Roman times for use as water cisterns, the subterranean labyrinth of the San Gaudioso catacombs was a burial site from the fifth century AD onwards, as indeed was the whole of this part of Naples, which until the 18th century was outside the city walls (*extra moenia*). For public health reasons, burial within the walls of the crowded city was forbidden. The burial here of St Gaudiosus – a North African bishop and hermit – in 452 made the site an important shrine. There are patches of mosaic (from the fifth and sixth centuries) and frescos (some from the fifth, others from the 17th and 18th centuries) in the damp and musty caves. A fascinating range of burial techniques is demonstrated. Note the method used from 1620 to 1650: the corpse was walled upright in a niche with its head cemented into the rear wall; after the body fluids had drained away, the headless body was buried (a job carried out by convicts) and the skull was removed, to be repositioned over a frescoed portrait of the illustrious deceased. The remains of St Gaudiosus and the skulls were transferred to the nearby Cimitero delle Fontanelle (*see below*) during the cholera epidemic of 1974.

In the 17th century, Dominican friars who had previously tended the chapel of San Gaudioso in the catacombs built the Greek-cross-plan basilica of Santa Maria della Sanità above. There's a fine *Madonna and Child with Saints Hyacinth, Rosa of Lima and Agnes* by Luca Giordano over the entrance to the vestry. From the transept, steps lead down to the Cappella di San Gaudioso, which dates from the fifth century but was rebuilt in the tenth and 15th centuries. The hour-long guided tours leave from the basilica; departure times may vary. Phone ahead to request an English-speaking guide.

Catacombe di San Severo

Piazzetta San Severo a Capodimonte 81 (081 544 1305). Metro Cavour or Museo/bus C51, C52. **Open** *Church* 9.30-11.30am, 5.30-7.30pm Mon-Fri; 5.30-7.30pm Sat; 9.30-11.30am Sun. *Catacombs* by appointment only. **Admission** donation expected. **Map** p310 1C.

The church here today was built in 1573, but stands on the site of a monastery complex around a much earlier church founded by Naples' first bishop,

Severus. When Severus's saintly body was moved to San Giorgio Maggiore (*see p70*) in the ninth century, the site lost importance. On the left side of the nave, steps lead down to a tiny cubicle containing all that is left of the original catacombs. A wall fresco from the late fourth century depicts St Peter and St Paul – the earliest representation of these apostles found in Naples – alongside the city's own San Gennaro and San Severo.

Cimitero delle Fontanelle

Via delle Fontanelle 154 (081 296 944). Metro Cavour or Museo/bus C51. **Closed to the public.** **Map** p312 1A.

Note that although this extraordinary site has been closed to the public since the 1970s, plans were afoot as this guide went to press to lease management of the site to the Napoli Sotterranea association (*see p53*) which would arrange guided tours. All enquiries should be addressed to the association.

This enormous trapezoidal cavern with side galleries – once a quarry for tufa building stone – acquired importance during the cholera epidemic of 1835, when the authorities decided to move all the city's dead here from their resting places in and around the city. This process was repeated during the outbreak of 1974, when more bones were brought here from the catacombs of San Gaudioso (*see above*). About 40,000 skulls and bones were subsequently stacked up around the cavern. The place is far from ghoulish: it has all the peace and tranquillity of a cemetery, though some outlandish lighting effects are created as sun filters down through the vegetation-covered air shafts, dancing over the mournful statues and piles of dusty bones.

The Cimitero underwent a popularity boom after World War II. Parents of boys killed in action would 'adopt' skulls in memory of their sons; for Neapolitans, the place evokes painful memories.

Orto botanico (Botanical Gardens)

Via Foria 223 (081 449 759/www.orto botanico.unina.it). Metro Cavour or Museo/ bus 14, 15, 47, CD, CS, C51. **Open** by appointment 9am-2pm Mon-Fri. **Admission** free. **Map** p310 1B.

A steep double flight of steps leads up out of the smog and into a shady park lined with a sturdy mixture of plane trees palms and riotous vegetation. Despite the constant roar of the traffic, and the proximity of one end to the vast rat-infested remains of the Albergo dei Poveri, this garden is a veritable haven of peace. Founded in 1807 by Joseph Bonaparte (*see p16*), it now belongs to Naples University's science department.

There's a fine array of palms, aquatic plants, cacti, ferns and shrubs from all around the world. In the centre of the park is the *castello*, which pre-dates the park by about 150 years. On the *castello*'s first floor is a dainty, well-kept museum containing fossilised plants and leaves, and plant artefacts from non-industrialised civilisations. The greenhouses and their collections are not open to the public.

Capodimonte

A magnificent art collection in a magnificently green setting.

Titian's *Danaë* in the **Museo di Capodimonte**. *See p84*.

Fly in to Naples on a clear day and you can't miss the vast red-tiled bulk of the **Palazzo Reale di Capodimonte** below you just before landing. Dominating what had been an unimportant hill north of the centre, the palace and surrounding park was created by King Charles III, who saw its hunting potential in the 18th century. It remains a verdant haven; beneath it lie the fascinating **Catacombe di San Gennaro**, as little known as the palace is famous.

South-west of the park on via Capodimonte, the pseudo-classical 20th-century church of the **Madre del Buon Consiglio** (open 8am-12.30pm, 4.30pm-7pm Mon-Sat; 8am-1pm, 5-7pm Sun) is a bombastic imitation of St Peter's in Rome. The **Osservatorio astronomico**, south-east of the park, bears witness to progress made during the Bourbon Restoration (*see p19*).

On the road that curves downhill from Capodimonte's Porta Grande are the **Ponti Rossi**, the well-preserved remains of an aqueduct built during the reign of the Emperor Claudius (AD 41-54) to bring Naples fresh water the mountains near Avellino. It was through this aqueduct that Byzantine forces led by the eastern emperor's redoubtable General Belisarius breached the city walls in 536, thanks to some spot-on military espionage (*see p9*).

Catacombe di San Gennaro

Via Capodimonte 16 (081 741 1071). Bus 24, 110, R4. **Open** guided tours only 9.30am, 10.15am, 11am, 11.45am daily; afternoon tours for groups by appointment only. **Admission** €5. **No credit cards. Map** p310 1C.

From a pleasant garden (entrance to the left of the church) overlooking the Sanità district (*see p81*), steps lead down into the two-level catacombs, which contain fascinating – if dilapidated – frescos from as far back as the second century AD. This was a burial rather than a hiding place; early Neapolitan Christians were persecuted in a much less systematic way than their counterparts in Rome. When the body of San Gennaro (St Januarius) was brought here from **Pozzuoli** (*see p98*) in the fifth century, the catacombs became an important pilgrimage centre. On the upper level, there are some fine frescoed arcosolium tombs (sarcophagi in arched, frescoed niches) in the main ambulatory, with fifth-century mosaics and frescos from the second century in the vestibule, one possibly portraying Adam and Eve. The tour is about 45 minutes. The lower level has an eighth-century baptismal tub and a chapel dedicated to Sant'Agrippino (which was closed indefinitely as this guide went to press). The early Christian basilica of San Gennaro Extra-moenia above the catacombs has also been closed for years and is currently used as a storeroom by the nearby hospital.

Museo di Capodimonte

Porta Grande via Capodimonte; Porta Piccola via Miano 2 (081 749 9111/www.beniculturali.it). Bus 24, 110, R4. **Open** *Park* 8am-1hr before sunset daily. *Museum* 8.30am-7.30pm Tue-Sun. **Admission** *Park* free. *Museum* €7.50. **No credit cards. Map** p310 1C.
When construction work began in 1738 on the palace that now houses one of Italy's richest and artistically richest museums, King Charles III envisaged no more than a hunting lodge. Seduced by plans for something far grander – and hard-pushed to find space for the vast collection he had inherited from his mother, Elisabetta Farnese (*see p14*) – a monumental three-storey *palazzo reale* (royal palace) went up at the heart of a magnificent park covering 7sq km (2.5sq miles). Though it was 100 years before the finishing touches were put to the palace, the Farnese collection was moved there in 1759; acquisitions by Charles and later Bourbon monarchs enriched the gallery; sections dedicated to porcelain and weaponry were added in the late 19th century.

Many of Capodimonte's finest pieces were filched by French occupiers in the late 18th century, but later returned. The palace was variously a receptacle for the royal collections, the main seat of the court, and a royal summer holiday home. Recently restored, the second-floor gallery is truly stunning.

The main entrance to the palace is a regal affair (if you ignore the kids playing football outside and the planes thundering overhead). Inside, cool cavernous porticos on the ground floor hide bars, shops, and access to the extensive prints and drawings section. The Farnese collection, with its natural extension the Bourbon collection, is upstairs, as are the smaller Borgia, porcelain and contemporary collections, and the armoury. There's information about the individual works of art (in English) in each room.

Italian art makes up the bulk of the Farnese collection. It starts in Room 2 with ground-breaking portraits by Raphael (of the future Pope Paul III when he was still Cardinal Alessandro Farnese) and by Titian (of Paul III with hat, without hat, and with younger Farneses; the Cardinal Alessandro in the fourth Titian portrait is one of the children pictured with Paul III). Titian's masterpiece, *Danaë*, is in Room 11. Danaë, daughter of King Argos, is being seduced by Jupiter in the form of golden rain; the courtesan who modelled for the painting was probably the lover of a Farnese cardinal. El Greco's *El Soplon*, a version of a work mentioned by Pliny, is in the same room.

Umbrian and Tuscan schools are represented by Masaccio (the 15th-century *Crucifixion* from a now-dismantled altarpiece in Room 3 is one of the few additions to the collection since Unification in 1861) and an early work by Botticelli, the *Madonna with Child and Two Angels* (Room 6). Sixteenth- and 17th-century works from the Farnese family's native Emilia region are plentiful. There are several works by Correggio, including the *Mystic Marriage of St Catherine* (1517) in Room 12; Parmigianino's *Antea* (Room 12) with her virginal look and odd attire is a byword for Mannerism; Annibale Carracci's *Mystic Marriage of St Catherine* is in Room 19 and his allegorical *Hercules at the Crossroads* is in Room 20; Guido Reni's *Atlanta and Hippomenes* is in Room 22.

The 15th-century Veneto tradition is represented above all by Giovanni Bellini's *Transfiguration* (Room 8; note the blend of religious mysticism and realistic rural Veneto setting), and Andrea Mantegna's *Portrait of Young Francesco Gonzaga* (Room 8) and *St Euphemia* (Room 7). Not to be overlooked in this galaxy of Italian talent are Brueghel's two enigmatic pieces *The Parable of the Blind* and *The Misanthrope* in Room 17.

Also on the first floor are the Royal Apartments, including Queen Maria Amalia's boudoir (packed with Capodimonte porcelain), the magnificent ballroom, the dainty Pompeian drawing room, and a range of French furniture and paintings.

The newly refurbished second floor features works made in Naples from the 13th to 19th centuries. All the greats are here: Simone Martini's *St Ludovic of Toulouse* (Room 65) was originally intended for the church of **San Lorenzo** (*see p74*); Caravaggio's powerful *Flagellation* (Room 78) influenced generations of Neapolitan painters; Massimo Stanzione's *Moses' Sacrifice* is in Room 89, his *Madonna and Child* in Room 93; Giuseppe Ribera's *St Jerome and the Angel* and the complex allegorical *Drunken Silenus* are in Rooms 90 and 91; Pietro Cavallino's *St Cecilia in Ecstasy* is in Room 94; Luca Giordano's *Madonna of the Canopy* is in Room 103; Francesco Solimena's *Aeneas and Dido* (Room 104) inspired his friend Alessandro Scarlatti to set the classical subject to music in 1696. A third-floor attic houses modern and contemporary paintings.

The area immediately around the palace pulsates with locals, especially on sunny Sundays; the rest of the enormous park is strangely deserted. Laid out in the mid-18th century to a design by Ferdinando Sanfelice (*see p35*), the park has five tree-lined avenues radiating from a hub near the palace. There are smaller buildings dotted about, including the Reale Fabbrica delle Porcellane (royal porcelain factory). Work in the factory came to an abrupt standstill in 1759, as Charles shifted the whole operation to his native Spain when he left Naples to take that crown; the factory is now a craft school.

Osservatorio astronomico

Salita Moiariello 16 (081 557 5111/www.na.astro.it). Bus 24, 110, R4. **Open** guided tours only, once a mth (usually Thur pm); book well in advance by phone 8-10am Mon-Fri. **Admission** free. **Map** p310 1C.
This magnificent neo-classical building dates from 1819, and was commissioned by King Ferdinand I soon after his restoration to the throne (*see p19*). The first observatory in Italy and one of the first in Europe, it contains a fine collection of equipment, historical and modern, some of which may be used during the tour. It also has a superb setting on the Miradois hill overlooking the entire Bay of Naples (150m/525ft above sea level).

Vomero

Castle and monastery stand guard over high-rise developments.

Landscape paintings of Naples have long since featured **Castel Sant'Elmo** and the **San Martino** monastery, standing guard over the city on a high bluff over the Centro storico and Chiaia foreshore. The Vomero, the hill on which these two remarkable monuments still stand, was once portrayed as a green blur dotted with sheep and clumps of trees. Unfortunately, much of Greater Vomero – the backdrop to this romantic idyll – now lies buried under an unseemly slag heap of cheap high-rise housing projects; little thought was given to civic amenities, and only recently has the new Collinare underground railway (*see p54*) brought some of these bleak outposts closer to the city centre.

Gone for good, then, are the days when parents would take the funicular up to what was essentially a hilltop village on Sunday mornings for a picnic in the country. Post-war reconstruction put an end to that, while in the 1970s the *tangenziale* inner-city ring road was built, over and under much of the hill. Since then the rest of the slopes have been enveloped by building projects such as the new hospital – the Secondo Policlinico – and development of the older Cardarelli and Monaldi hospitals, all of which are vital to healthcare for the whole of southern Italy. These in turn have attracted more housing projects.

Three of Naples' four funicular railways lead up to the Vomero. At the heart of the district is **piazza Vanvitelli**, a round space where the tree-lined via Scarlatti (recently pedestrianised, its *struscio* on summer evenings rivalling that in via Toledo, *see p77*) meets via Bernini (traffic hell). With its elegant café tables spilling out on to pavements peopled by well-heeled residents, piazza Vanvitelli epitomises the pan-European middle-class air of the Vomero that can alienate as much as captivate. The temperature is a degree or two lower up

Standing guard: **Castel Sant'Elmo** dominates the Vomero hill. *See p87.*

Church, gallery, museum and view: the satisfying **Certosa-Museo di San Martino**. *See p89*.

here than down the hill; the streets are noticeably cleaner. On summer evenings the square fills to bursting point with a vast crowd of teenagers (and would-be teenagers) whiling away their time in aimless chatter and endless pose-striking.

Before the funiculars were built in the late 19th and early 20th centuries, getting to the Vomero involved scaling the long flights of steps from the city centre. The steps are still there; they're a pleasant way to make the journey down from the Vomero without suffering its traffic (though this is not an advisable route at night).

To reach the westernmost flight – the Calata di San Francesco – cut through the cool, dreamy **Parco della Floridiana** from its top gate (stopping to take in the magnificent views from its belvedere and to visit its **Museo Nazionale della Ceramica Duca di Martina**), then exit on to via Aniello Falcone from the bottom gate.

Heading west along via Falcone, the Calata descends sharply to the left, shortly after passing a splendid art nouveau *palazzo* on the right. Cut across the corso Vittorio Emanuele and carry on down via Arco Mirelli to get to the Chiaia seafront. (A short hike east on corso

Vittorio, on the other hand, will take you to Castel Aselmeyer in the lower reaches of the Parco Grifeo, home to some of the extraordinary creations of English architect Lamont Young; *see p88* **Neo-Gothic in Naples**.)

To the west of the imposing **Castel Sant'Elmo** – part of the city's 16th-century defence system – the **Gradini di Petraio** steps start in via Caccavello and cut down past the austere baroque church of **San Carlo alle Mortelle** (open Sept-July 8.30am-noon, 5.30-8pm daily; Aug 5.30-8pm daily); *mortella* is the dialect word for myrtle, which used to flourish hereabouts. The path then continues through the **Quartieri spagnoli** (*see p77*).

The Castel Sant'Elmo towers above the recently revamped **Certosa-Museo di San Martino**. From the square in front of the museum, the staircase known as via Pedamentina a San Martino leads towards the Centro storico (*see p67*).

All three stairways cross the winding, traffic-snarled corso Vittorio Emanuele, which opened areas formerly occupied by terraced gardens and vineyards to construction when it was built in the mid-19th century. Today, the corso provides access to a handful of patches of

welcome inner-city green that have recently
been rescued from decay and ruin or are in the
process of being so. The via Pedamentina steps
emerge closest to all of them.

Heading north along corso Vittorio Emanuele
from the foot of the steps, via Cupa Vecchia on
the left leads to the small **Parco Viviani** (open
8am to 1hr before dusk daily).

Almost opposite the steps on the other side
of the corso, vico Trinità delle Monache leads
down to a far more ambitious city council
project: the **Parco dei Quartieri spagnoli**
(open 9am-5pm Tue-Sat; 9am-2pm Sun). The
project involves the redevelopment of a one-
time military hospital (which started its life in
the 17th century as the Trinità delle Monache
convent) and the surrounding area.

The original three-phase plan foresaw the
demolition of some of the uglier modern
eyesores, and the creation of a garden and
park overlooking the old city. There'll be a
natural history museum, a sports complex and
concert areas. Phase one – a garden – was
completed in 2000. There have been problems,
not least the re-routing of many main sewers and
drains. Given the dilapidated condition of the

fine older buildings in the area, the council's
extremely scant budget will be stretched to the
limit to finish stages two and three; plans to
complete the project by 2003 will clearly have
to be redrawn .

Further south, on the right behind the old
convent of Santa Lucia al Monte (which is
currently being converted into a hotel), one
of the Vomero's original hillside olive groves
and vineyards has recently been replanted
(fax 081 764 3737, studiomorra@libero.it;
open by appointment only); wine, olive oil and
honey are produced.

Castel Sant'Elmo

*Via Tito Angelini 22 (081 578 4030). Funicular
Montesanto to via Morghen, Centrale to piazzetta
Fuga or Chiaia to via Cimarosa/bus V1.* **Open**
9am-7.30pm Tue-Sun (ticket office closes 1hr earlier).
Admission €1 (*see also p54*). **No credit cards.**
Map p312 2B.

The site where Castel Sant'Elmo stands was occupied in the tenth century by a small church called St
Erasmus, corrupted over the centuries to 'Elmo'. A
castle has stood here since 1329, when King Robert
of Anjou modified the pre-existing Norman watchtower using artists, architects and workmen who
were subsequently employed on the construction of

the adjacent monastery of San Martino. It acquired its six-pointed star shape in the mid 16th century during an extensive reorganisation of the city's defences. In 1587, the ammunition warehouse was struck by lightning; the castle was badly damaged and 150 people died.

Over the years, the castle's dungeons have held many illustrious inmates, including heroes of the 1799 Parthenopean Republic. They continued to serve as a military prison until the mid 1970s. Despite being close to the centre, spacious and airy, the castle has never been a popular R&R destination for Neapolitans. Its unmistakable bulk has, however, long provided a focal point for pictorial cityscapes, including the extraordinary *Tavola Strozzi*, which is housed in the Certosa-Museo di San Martino next door (*see p89*).

Entry to the castle is by a new gateway in via Angelini, about 90m (300ft) on the right before reaching largo San Martino. The ground floor is closed, although glimpses of its gloomy interior (including the prisons) may occasionally be snatched through glass panels on the first floor. This, too, is normally closed except during important exhibitions, which allow this magnificently restored area to be shown to its full advantage.

Piazza d'Armi, as the top floor is called, is in fact the castle's roof, and is best reached by lift; the 360° view over Naples from here is the best, least impeded and arguably most breathtaking of anywhere in the city. The walkway around the battlements is splendid. A gently sloping path inside the castle leads you back down across the drawbridge, passing under the coat of arms of Charles V.

Neo-Gothic in Naples

Lamont Young (1851-1929), born in Naples to English parents, brought an eclectic neo-Gothic picturesque English style of architecture to late 19th-century Naples. A true eccentric, Young was an engineer, entrepreneur, architect and inventor; he drew up an elaborate, utopian plan for an integrated train, tram and bus system in 1880 (Neapolitans are still waiting for their metro to be completed today).

But his greatest gift to the city was a series of stylistically eccentric buildings at Naples' fashionable heart. Young's father had bought up land below Villa Floridiana (*see p90*) in the mid 19th century from the Grifeo family, heirs of the Duchess of Floridia. This area on the slopes of Vomero – known as **Parco Grifeo** – was to become the in place for the new Neapolitan nouveau riche.

Young's first design, the neo-Gothic **Castello Grifeo** (1875), was freely inspired by Walter Scott's Castle of Abbotsford, built in 1820. The fake cracks in the crenellated watchtower were designed that way, an echo of the picturesque follies so popular in late Victorian England. His next design, for **Palazzina Grifeo** (situated next door at Parco Grifeo 39), was in rigidly symmetrical neo-Renaissance style, though it has been radically altered since. A Swiss chalet (1893-94, no longer standing) was built in the garden of the pre-existing Pompeian-style Villa Lucia.

Young's **Castello Aselmeyer**, incongruously perched above corso Vittorio Emanuele, incorporated Tudor elements (bow windows, loggias) so dear to the English upper-middle class, with Gothic picturesque elements; the two towers on the corso were the entrance to the lift that rose to the castle itself.

For some years before World War I, Young's interests veered from organising 'package Grand Tourists' to industry. In 1914, he bought a slice of land sloping up the ramps from via Chiatamone to Monte Echia (*see p55*) where he was to build his final dream, **Castello Lamont** – an elaborate design of square and round towers, wooden bow windows and wrought-iron decorations. The building, sadly abandoned for many years, is now a burned-out shell inhabited only by stray cats.

None of Young's creations is open to the public, though the edifices in Parco Grifeo can be seen by walking down from Villa Lucia – from where the views over the bay are stunning – to corso Vittorio Emanuele along the very picturesque corso Parco Grifeo.

Castello Aselmeyer
Corso Vittorio Emanuele 166. Funicular Centrale to corso Vittorio Emanuele/bus C16.

Castello Grifeo
Parco Grifeo 37. Funicular Chiaia to corso Vittorio Emanuele/bus C28 (ask to be set down at Parco Grifeo).

Castello Lamont
The burned-out shell of Young's home can be seen from the Rampa Lamont Young (now gated), which runs from Monte Echia down to via Chiatamone (map p313 2A). Steer clear of the area at night.

The **Certosa-Museo di San Martino** has priceless architectural and artistic assets.

Certosa-Museo di San Martino

Largo San Martino 5 (081 558 5942/081 558 6408). Funicular Montesanto to via Morghen, Centrale to piazzetta Fuga or Chiaia to via Cimarosa/bus V1. **Open** 8.30am-7.30pm Tue-Sat; 9am-7.30pm Sun. Box office closes 1hr earlier. **Admission** (includes Castel Sant'Elmo) €6 (*see also p54*). **Credit** (bookshop only) MC, V. **Map** p312 2A.

With its church, art gallery, museum and extraordinary collection of Nativity scenes – plus the splendid architectural surroundings, gorgeous cloister and terraced gardens with striking views – the San Martino monastery is one of Naples' most satisfying attractions. The Carthusian monastery was founded in 1325, although its present appearance is the result of much reworking at the end of the 16th century. Under the priors' spiritual and, above all, economic management, it gradually became renowned for its priceless architectural and artistic assets. Like most monasteries, San Martino was dissolved under French rule (1806-15); the monks moved back in only briefly before the *certosa* (charterhouse) was wrested from them once again in the wake of Italian Unification in 1861. A long period of neglect was arrested after the war and a lengthy multi-phase restoration programme has been going on ever since.

To the left after the ticket office, the church's late 17th-century façade is by Cosimo Fanzago; it conceals remnants of the Gothic original, such as the pointed arches and cross-vaulted ceiling in the pronaos (projecting vestibule), which has frescos (1651-6) by Micco Spadaro depicting the persecution of Carthusians in England in the reign of Henry VIII.

The church's interior contains as complete (and well labelled) a selection of Neapolitan painting and sculpture as you could hope for. Massimo Stanzione's *Deposition* (1638) dominates the inner façade, flanked by two fine portraits by Giuseppe Ribera (*see p30* **Gang warfare**), who is also responsible for the 12 paintings of prophets (1638-43) tucked into the spandrels of the arches. The delicate 18th-century marble altar balustrade is by Giuseppe Sammartino. The walls and side chapels feature paintings by the Vaccaros, Francesco Solimena and Stanzione. In the vaulted ceiling are frescos (1637-40) by Giovanni Lanfranco: *Ascension with Angels, Apostles and Saints*. Bonaventura Presti used material already prepared by Fanzago for his intricate inlaid marble floor (1664). Don't miss the rooms surrounding the church: the choir features Ribera's *Communion of the Apostles*, Guido Reni's *Adoration of the Shepherds* (1642) and Battista Caracciolo's *Washing of Feet* (1622); the sacristy has some exquisite marquetry (on the recently restored cupboards are 56 panels showing biblical scenes). In the Cappella del Tesoro are Ribera's *Pietà* and frescos by Luca Giordano, while both the parlatorio and the chapter room (where there are several works by Battista Caracciolo) are essential viewing.

A long passageway leads left out of the small Chiostro dei Procuratori into the Chiostro grande (great cloister) – one of Italy's finest. This bright, sunny area was created in the 16th century by Giovanni Antonio Dosio, although the work was completed by Cosimo Fanzago who added the small monks' graveyard (note the fine balustrade and skulls) and the busts and statues above the cool Tuscan-Doric pillared portico.

The Pinacoteca (art gallery) is beautifully laid out on two floors in the northern, eastern and southern wings of the main cloister, recently reopened to the public in all its splendour. The main bulk of works from the 17th and 18th centuries, originally made for the monastery, is now housed in the prior's quarters in the southern wing (Rooms 17-23) and includes works by Ribera (*Sts Jerome and Sebastian*),

Dropping names

Arenella (piazza)
'Arena' refers to sand or silt. After heavy rain, both substances would be washed down from the hills above Naples and would get deposited in this area, near the Vomero.

Case Puntellate (street)
'Houses supported by scaffolding'. This is one of the oldest parts of rural Vomero; the rickety old country houses have long since gone and have been replaced by modern blocks.

Medaglie d'Oro (piazza)
Commemorates recipients of the Italian gold (*oro*) medal for valour in World War I. Five streets running into the piazza bear recipients' names.

Mortelle (church)
'Myrtle' in Neapolitan dialect. Myrtle grew in abundance where San Carlo alle Mortelle now stands. Further along corso Vittorio Emanuele, the area now known as Cariati (near the Centrale funicular station) was called Celse, a reference to the mulberry trees that grew here.

Petraio (steps)
Neapolitan for 'stonemason'. These steps passed through quarries.

San Giacomo dei Capri (street)
The original road running north out of the Vomero and still cobbled. It refers to the one-time presence of a community of monks from the monastery of San Giacomo on Capri.

Lanfranco (*Our Lady of the Rosary*) and Stanzione (*Baptism of Christ*); Spadaro was responsible for the frescoed ceilings in Rooms 14, 15 and 16. Room 8 contains a remarkable sculptured group of the *Madonna and Child with the Infant John the Baptist* by Pietro Bernini (father of the more famous Gianlorenzo).

The *certosa*, the Carthusian order and the history of Naples, are constant themes in the works in the Pinacoteca. In Room 23 are portraits of priors. There are splendid maps (such as the vast one of the city from 1775 by Duca di Noja in Room 45) and landscape paintings (with work ranging from the anonymous *Tavola Strozzi* with its detailed depiction of 15th-century Naples in Room 32, and Didier Barra's bird's-eye view of Naples at the end of the 16th century, to a fine series of late 17th-century paintings by Gaspar Van Wittel in Room 40). On the first floor are 19th-century paintings by local artists. And if the art's all too much for you, take a look at the breathtaking views to be had from every window and balcony.

There's a section devoted to the art of Nativity scenes, including a massive *presepe* (crib) with particularly rare pieces (currently being restored, though open for viewing on special occasions). You'll also find sections dedicated to theatre, to ships and shipping, and in the former pharmacy, to porcelain and glassware.

Downstairs in the creepy Gothic basements (rarely open) are sculptures and coats of arms from the Middle Ages to the 18th century.

From the front terrace and well-kept gardens there's yet another superlative view over the bay.

Parco della Floridiana/Museo Nazionale della Ceramica Duca di Martina

Via Cimarosa 77 (081 578 1776). Funicular Montesanto to via Morghen, Centrale to piazzetta Fuga or Chiaia to via Cimarosa/bus E4, V1. **Open** *Park* 8.30am-1hr before sunset daily. **Museum** *guided tours only* 9.30am, 11am, 12.30am Tue-Sun. **Admission** €2.50 (*see also p54*). **No credit cards. Map** p313 1B.

In 1815, King Ferdinand returned to Naples after a ten-year period of French rule, bringing his second wife, with whom he had contracted a morganatic marriage. Lucia Migliaccio, Duchess of Floridia, was given this splendid villa and garden. The park is a favourite spot for Vomero walkers and joggers; its network of paths, lawns and spinneys makes the Vomero a bit different from the rest of the city. The view from the terrace at the bottom of the garden is memorable. In the 1920s, the villa and garden were purchased by the State; the park was opened to the public and the villa was turned into the Museo di Ceramica Duca di Martina.

The first floor is dedicated to European ceramics: there's an early 18th-century picture frame from Sicily in Room 2; some fine local biscuit pieces, two dishes from the royal dinner service showing costumes of the realm, and the fine *Capodimonte Declaration* by Gricci in Room 5; some splendid Meissen porcelain in Room 6; pieces by Ginori (including *Three Putti with a Goat*) in Room 9; china from Vincennes/Sèvres and Saint-Cloud in Room 10; and an interesting Meissen clock-cum-inkstand in Room 11.

The ground floor has majolica from the Middle Ages onwards: near the entrance in Room 18 is a set of vases showing biblical scenes; Room 21 has an interesting walking stick with a glass top (look inside and you will see a portrait of King Ferdinand's second wife; wits joked that this was the only way he could get the little-loved lady into the court). In Room 22 is a reliquary casket from Limoges. In the basement are oriental ceramics: China's Ming (1368-1644) and Qing (1644-1911) dynasties are represented, and there's a Tang (618-906) drummer on horseback in Room 24. The Meiping vase in the shape of a phoenix is rare. Japanese porcelain is represented by many items from the Edo period (1615-1867), including a pair of fine octagonal dishes in Room 34.

Chiaia to Posillipo

A classic seafront stroll from designer shops to rarefied residences.

Romantic **Chiaia** and pine-wooded **Posillipo**.

Compared to the hustle and bustle of the Centro storico, the quieter western districts conjure up images of Goethe's romantic Chiaia foreshore with the pine-wooded Posillipo hill in the background. Little remains of the German poet's idyll, though Mergellina harbour still has its fishing community, and some of the narrowest and oldest *vicoli* (alleys) in the city can be found between piazza Amedeo and the Villa Comunale. The area is definitely more aloof – from the designer shops and elegant Liberty *palazzi* round via dei Mille, to the rarefied, snooty air on via Petrarca. The long seafront stroll from Santa Lucia (*see p61*) round to Mergellina is a classic.

Chiaia

On the northern fringe of Chiaia, piazza Amedeo is a cosy, tree-lined, cobbled square overlooked by some splendid art deco *palazzi*. At No.14, **Palazzo Regina Margherita** (not open to the public) has a faded majolica-tiled façade with mullioned windows. South from piazza Amedeo, via Ascensione – or its parallel via

Bausan – is where playwright Eduardo de Filippo (*see p162*) was born: controversy still rages over the exact location. In nearby piazzetta Ascensione, the church of the **Ascensione** (open 8-11am, 5-8pm Mon-Sat; 8am-1.45pm Sun) is a Cosimo Fanzago creation from the mid 17th century.

Heading east out of the square, via Colonna is home to the church of **Santa Teresa a Chiaia** (open 7.30-10.45am Mon-Sat; 7.30am-1.30pm, 5.30-7pm Sun), also designed by Fanzago (1650). It has a striking three-storey façade; inside are several works by Luca Giordano. With its gracious double flight of curved steps and semicircular forecourt, this church is much loved by its well-heeled parishioners.

Via Colonna becomes via dei Mille and then via Filangieri, where Naples' most exclusive clothes shops are located. At the southern end of this elite drag, **piazza dei Martiri** is dominated by four stone lions guarding an obelisk celebrating Victory. This monument was constructed in the mid 19th century in honour of the martyrs of the 1799 revolution; one lion is dead, another is turning to dislodge

Now open daily, the **Villa Comunale** has a magnificent bandstand...

a sword from its wither, while the third looks pretty much OK and the fourth is definitely on the prowl. The piazza is flanked by two splendid *palazzi* (both closed to the public): **Palazzo Partanna** (No.58 – only the portal remains from the original 1746 construction; the rest is 19th-century neo-classical) and **Palazzo Calabritto** (No.30 – with a fluted column portal by Luigi Vanvitelli).

Leading out of the piazza, the narrow vico Santa Maria a Cappella Vecchia was once home to British Ambassador Sir William Hamilton, his wife Emma and her soul-mate Admiral Horatio Nelson (*see p17* **Naples & the Hero of the Nile**). An archway dated 1506 leads into the courtyard of what was a Benedictine abbey until 1788, after which it was rented out to a string of notables including the Hamiltons. Under a second archway (No.31) is the house where Admiral Nelson was introduced to Emma in 1793.

Via Morelli leads into the uninspiring-looking via Chiatamone, the nearest road to the coast until the late 19th century, when the parallel via Partenope and its luxury hotels were built. Via Chiatamone attracted the best and worst of Neapolitan tourism; in 1770, Giacomo Casanova visited a club in the anonymous 17th-century palazzo (now Nos.26-30) to drum up custom for a smart new brothel on Posillipo hill run by Irish madame Sarah Goudar.

To the west, the once-picturesque **Riviera di Chiaia** is now synonymous with tyres thrashing over cobbles, threatening the lives of anyone rash enough to attempt the hazardous crossing to the sole park in this area, the **Villa Comunale**, home of the **Acquario**. Percy Shelley and his wife Mary stayed at No.250 (the original building was demolished in the 1950s) from 1818 to 1819. During this period they took a child to the church of **San Giuseppe a Chiaia** (open 5-8pm Mon-Sat; 8.30am-1.30pm Sun) to be christened; the child's identity remains a mystery to this day. **Villa Pignatelli** (No.200) was built for Ferdinand Acton, son of King Ferdinand I's prime minister, John Acton (*see p16*).

A detour north from the Riviera di Chiaia along via **Santa Maria in Portico** leads to the church of the same name (open 8-11am, 5-7.30pm daily); there's a life-size Nativity scene (1647) to the left of the altar.

Stazione Zoologica (Acquario)

Villa Comunale (081 583 3111). Bus 140, 152, C28, R3/tram 1. **Open** closed as this guide went to press; due to reopen late 2002. **Admission** €1.55. **No credit cards. Map** p313 1B.

One of Europe's oldest aquariums, the Stazione Zoologica was founded by German naturalist Anton Dohrn in 1872. The ground floor of this two-storey building still contains its original 24 tanks, housing sea creatures from the Bay of Naples: coral, jellyfish, turtles, seahorses, an octopus or two, lobsters and starfish. Water for the tanks is brought directly from 300m (350yds) out in the bay, though, thankfully for the inmates, it's filtered and left to decant.

Villa Comunale

Riviera di Chiaia/via Caracciolo (no phone). Bus 140, 152, C28, R3/tram 1. **Open** *May-Oct* 7am-midnight daily. *Nov-Apr* 7am-10pm daily. **Admission** free. **Map** p313 1B.

Swathes of historical buildings were demolished to make way for this park designed by Luigi Vanvitelli. It was inaugurated in 1781 as the *Giardini reali* (royal gardens) and was originally only open to the public once a year, on the feast of Mary's nativity (8 September). It quickly became known as the *Tuglieria*, a typically Neapolitan tongue-in-cheek comparison to the Tuileries in Paris. The *Toro Farnese* – now in the Museo Nazionale (*see p79*) stood here until 1825, when it was replaced by a large bowl found in Paestum (*see p271*). Now surrounded by four lions, the bowl is the centrepiece of the Fontana delle Paparelle. The Villa was restored for the G7 conference in 1994, when the then US President, Bill Clinton, jogged along the newly laid paving. There's a magnificent bandstand, built in 1887, plus the small-is-beautiful Stazione Zoologica (aquarium, *see p92*).

Villa Pignatelli

Riviera di Chiaia 200 (081 669 675). Bus 140, 152, C28, R3. **Open** 9am-2pm Tue-Sun. **Admission** €2.07 (*see also p53*). **No credit cards. Map** p313 1B. Built in 1826 for Ferdinand Acton, the son of Naples' prime minister, Sir John Acton, Villa Pignatelli is a mishmash of styles, with a neo-Doric portico and a neo-Palladian vestibule. The Rothschild family bought and enlarged it in 1841; it passed to the Pignatellis in 1867 and to the Italian State in 1952. On the ground floor are magnificent rooms including the ballroom, dining room, library and series of 'coloured rooms'; the Green Room contains a priceless collection of porcelain and majolica artefacts from the 17th to the 19th centuries. On the first floor is the Banco di Napoli collection. Room 1 has works by 19th-century sculptor Vincenzo Gemito, including charming terracotta and bronze busts of street urchins and working-class women. Room 2 has the collection's finest piece, Francesco Guarino's intense *St George* (17th century). There are some outstanding 18th- and 19th-century landscapes in Room 6.

The villa also holds occasional temporary exhibitions. The lawns of the English-style garden are a magnet for mothers and babysitters with children.

Mergellina & Piedigrotta

Further west, the Riviera forks: north of largo Torretta lies the densely populated district of Torretta; towards the sea are the elegant *palazzi* of viale Antonio Gramsci, thus renamed in the 1970s after the founder of the Italian Communist Party, though still known as viale Elena. Straight ahead, the traffic-hellish via Piedigrotta leads to the extraordinary, late-Liberty (art nouveau) Mergellina railway station.

Before the railway bridge is **Santa Maria di Piedigrotta** (open 7am-noon, 5-8pm Mon-Sat; 7am-2pm, 5-8pm Sun); a church has stood since the 13th century on this spot, which is associated with apparitions of Mary. This church is still the fulcrum of the feast-day celebrations of Mary's nativity on 8 September,

Sightseeing

...and tree-lined stretches for joggers and strollers.

although the song festival that accompanied the religious event has fizzled out. The pavement beneath the railway bridge is life-threateningly unpleasant, but leads to the very rewarding **Parco Virgiliano**.

Via Mergellina skirts the bay to the area known as the **Chalets** – no, not Klosters but a ramshackle assortment of jerry-built ice-cream parlours and late-night dives. In largo Barbaia (from where Naples' shortest funicular ascends to the hillside suburbs above), via Orazio climbs up Posillipo hill to Naples' most exclusive residential areas, which have little to offer but fine views and a smug sense of wealth. Back on the bayfront, the church of **Santa Maria del Parto** (via Mergellina 21; open 5.30-8pm Mon-Sat; 9.30am-1pm, 6-8pm Sun) stands at the head of a long flight of steps (spare yourself the climb by taking the lift at number 9B). The church was built by 15th-century poet Iacopo Sannazzaro (his tomb is behind the altar); its lights guided fishermen home. In the first side chapel on the right, the painting *St Michael Vanquishing the Devil* recalls a 16th-century episode in which ambitious prelate Diomede Carafa was sorely tempted by a local beauty, Vittoria D'Avalos. When she declared her love for him, he illustrated his quandary by commissioning this work; the realistic faces of the archangel and the serpent are those of Diomede and Vittoria respectively. Via Mergellina becomes via Posillipo at largo

Science city

Standing on the site of the decommissioned Bagnoli steelworks, **Città della Scienza** is the jewel in the crown of a massive and much-publicised redevelopment project. From a pre-existing nucleus of kid-friendly scientific attractions, the Città reopened – massively extended and improved – in November 2001.

The main exhibition hall is located inside a vast industrial warehouse, tastefully refurbished and restored to the peak of its industrial pride. Inside is a mega-assortment of hands-on games, experiments and interactive video booths, with plenty for kids and parents to do.

No avenue of science has been left unexplored, with special attention lavished on properties of the physical world – from experiments with hydraulics ('bubbles' in kiddie-speak), light and mirrors, to energy displacement and a hair-raising demonstration of the effects of static electricity. One stand features some excellent slow-motion footage of objects and liquids caught in the act of breaking and spilling: you have to reassemble the order of video frames to score a 'well done'.

Another section caters for toddlers: plenty of beanbags and cushions, with games and activities that rely less on reading ability and more on touching, feeling and smelling.

The most popular item for older kids is the avatar computer puppet called Bip. Bip appears on a number of mysterious screens around the hall and is remote-controlled by the extremely helpful and friendly young staff (some of whom speak English) who keep him in two-way communication with his young audience via video-cameras and microphones placed strategically near the screens. A virtual Punch and Judy show.

Exhaustive (alas, at times exhausting) written explanations (in English) are provided for all the exhibits.

Also inside is the **Planetarium** (regular showings throughout the day, admission €1.50). For a commentary in English, contact the Città in advance, although knowledge of Italian is not essential to appreciate this trip across the Neapolitan sky.

Set spectacularly opposite the island of Nisida (*see p96*), the Città della Scienza has snack bars, with a restaurant (due to open soon after this guide went to press) in the large tiled area around the main hall. There's also a splendid walkway along the waterfront with views over the bay. Across the road, plans are still afoot to resurrect the pre-existing nature park (pets, farm animals and gardens), which in its previous manifestation held much promise but little else.

The Città della Scienza is part of a more ambitious plan to transform the whole town of Bagnoli into a hi-tech science park interspersed with light industry; at the time of writing, most building activity had ground to a halt while political institutions wrangled over issues regarding the sharing of investment and benefits. In the meantime, the quality of access roads and parking facilities leaves much to be desired.

Città della Scienza

Via Coroglio 104, Posillipo (081 372 3728/ www.cittadellascienza.it). Metro Bagnoli, then bus C9, C10 to Città della Scienza/bus 140 to Capo Posillipo then F9. **Open** 9am-5pm Tue-Sat; 10am-7pm Sun. **Admission** €7; €6 under-18s; free under-4s. **Credit** AmEx, DC, MC, V. **Map** p314.

Tyres thrash over cobbles on the **Riviera di Chiaia**. *See p92.*

Sermoneta, where there is a fountain (1635)
by Carlo Fanzago, Cosimo's son, named after
the now-buried River Sebeto that flowed
through Naples in ancient times, perhaps
beneath today's via Toledo.

Parco Virgiliano

*Salita della Grotta 20 (081 669 390). Metro
Mergellina/bus C16, C24.* **Open** *9am-1hr before
sunset daily.* **Admission** *free.* **Map** *313 2C.*
To do justice to this splendidly peaceful spot you
will need to climb an extremely long flight of steps.
For your pains, you'll get a view into the *Crypta
Neapolitana*, a first-century AD road tunnel (closed).
Stories abound of the atrocious conditions in this
primitive borehole as cart-drivers fought to control
their vehicles in the choking dust. (Conditions in the
modern tunnel beneath haven't improved greatly.)
At the top of the stairs stands what is controversially known as Virgil's Tomb, looking much like a
large dovecote. Virgil did live in Naples. He died,
however, in Brindisi. Whether he was brought back
here for burial is an issue that has spawned thousands of polemical volumes.

Posillipo

Via Orazio becomes via Petrarca and then
merges with via Manzoni; shortly before this
junction, on the left, a narrow road – confusingly
named via Petrarca – forks downhill and allows
wonderful views over the Bay of Pozzuoli
and the former steelworks at **Bagnoli**. This
is a preserve of courting couples; newspaper
obscures the condensation-soaked windows of
many a quivering car. A right turn (uphill) into
via Manzoni at the juction, on the other hand,
leads to a Spanish watchtower, the **Torre
Ranieri** (1530). This was one of a chain of
towers, many of which still stand along the
coast; its signals could be seen from Baia.

From largo Sermoneta, cobbled via Posillipo
clatters gradually away from the bathing
establishments that nestle along the shoreline,
passing the decrepit **Palazzo Donn'Anna** in
the piazza of the same name. Shortly after the
municipal bus depot on the right, the moody
grey faux-Egyptian **Mausoleo** war memorial
(open 7am-noon Tue-Sun) overlooks the road
from its position in a peaceful shady garden
dominated by massive pine trees.

A dearth of safe bathing in Naples proper is
partially offset by facilities (though definitely
not suitable for young kids and non-swimmers)
available at the end of three charming, winding
lanes leading down from via Posillipo. No buses
ply these routes so it's a long haul back up
again. All are best out of high season.

Via Russo passes the presidential summer
residence **Villa Roseberry** (closed to the
public except on rare, crowded occasions during
the Maggio dei Monumenti; *see p53*). Via
Marechiaro starts where via Posillipo meets via
Boccaccio; it winds down to a tiny car park
surrounded by fish restaurants. The Calata del
Ponticello a Marechiaro leads round to the right
to a romantic spot overlooking a pebbly beach.

Discesa la Gaiola leads off left from Discesa
Coroglio. Shortly before reaching **Villa
Pausilypon** and the **Grotta di Seiano**, a
pathway on the left descends to the pleasant
cove of La Gaiola, with a small shingle beach
and a long quay to swim off; there are no
restaurants here, so bring picnic provisions.

Via Posillipo itself continues on through a
cutting in the headland before becoming
Discesa Coroglio, dropping sharply down
towards the alternative entrance to the Grotta
di Seiano and the vast sprawling ex-industrial
site of the Bagnoli steelworks, now occupied in

Faux-Egypt at the **Mausoleo**. *See p95.*

part by the **Città della Scienza** (*see p94* **Science city**). In the distance, the attractive-looking island of **Nisida** is home to a NATO naval support base and a reformatory, and is thus very much closed to the public.

Grotta di Seiano

Discesa la Gaiola 36 or Discesa Coroglio (081 230 1030/guided tours 081 795 2003). Bus 140 to Capo Posillipo, then F9. **Open** closed at time of writing; contact the tourist office (*see p293*) for latest information. **Admission** free. **Map** p314.

This tunnel was built in the first century AD by the architect Cocceius, who was also responsible for the Grotta di Cocceio (*see p100*) running between Cuma and Lago Averno, and for the Crypta Neapolitana (*see p95*) between Piedigrotta and Fuorigrotta. The tunnel stretches for 800m (933yds) along the coast; its galleries provide fine views over the sea off Capo Posillipo. The Grotta was closed as this guide went to press, but there were plans to begin guided visits; phone the number above for information.

Palazzo Donn'Anna

Piazza Donn'Anna 9 (no phone). Bus 140. **Map** p314.

This rambling, partly derelict building has a long, sad history. The reputed site of Queen Joan II's (*see p12*) perverse and cruel amorous pursuits in the 15th century, the original building was demolished in 1642 to make way for the present palazzo, designed by Cosimo Fanzago for an aristocratic couple who married in 1636. The husband, a Spanish diplomat, was recalled to Spain after only two years, abandoning his wife; she died soon after. The palazzo is private property, although a polite word at the gatehouse should gain you admission to the porticoed terrace; the view across the bay is fantastic.

Villa Pausilypon

Discesa Coroglio 36 (081 230 1030/guided tours 081 795 2003). Bus 140 to Capo Posillipo, then F9. **Open** closed at time of writing; contact the tourist office (*see p293*) for latest information. **Admission** free. **Map** p314.

This Roman villa belonged to Emperor Augustus (63 BC-AD 19). Apart from the remains of the villa itself, there's a theatre that is used for occasional open-air concerts. No decision on reopening the villa had been taken as this guide went to press; if and when it reopens, it will be visitable on guided tours booked at the number given above.

Dropping names

Belledonne (street)
'Beautiful women'. Not thought to be a reference to the oldest profession, but to the presence here of beauty parlours or perfume sellers. (Things haven't changed much since then.)

Chiaia (district, street)
Neapolitan dialect for 'beach', similar to Spanish *playa*.

Mergellina (district)
Of unclear origin, maybe (1) diminutive of *mergus* (merganser), a sea-bird common here, or (2) diminutive of Latin *margo*, sometimes meaning 'beach' or 'strand'.

Piedigrotta (district)
'At the foot of the tunnel' linking this district to Fuorigrotta ('outside the tunnel'; *see p104*)

and the Campi Flegrei (*see p97*). The Roman tunnel is still visible from the Parco Virgiliano (*see p95*).

Pilastri (piazza)
The hard-to-find remains of two black 'pillars' still stand by what was a 19th-century roadside public-health checkpoint for merchants coming from malaria-ridden Agnano into Naples.

Posillipo (district, street)
From the Greek *pausilypon* ('break from pain'), the name given by Roman self-made man Vedius Pollius to his villa on Capo Posillipo (*see p95*).

Vetriera (street)
'Glass-making'. There were still six factories in Naples at the beginning of the 19th century.

Campi Flegrei

Cities under water, cities underground and volcanic activity all over.

Sightseeing

The atmospheric **Castello di Baia**. *See p100.*

An area steeped in myth and history, the Campi Flegrei (Phlegrean Fields) west of Naples are a continual source of fascination. This is a land of bubbling, steaming volcanic activity, the reputed home of the Sibyl (a Greek prophetess; *see p8* **Rushing streams of sound**) and the entrance to the Underworld. Here Roman emperors and aristocrats built fabulous summer palaces, and 18th-century aesthetes such as Sir William Hamilton (*see p16*) were enthralled by the landscape.

Much of the aura of mystery of the Campi Flegrei has now evaporated, however, destroyed by *abusivismo edilizio* – building without planning permission – that has carpeted broad swathes of the countryside with cement. The classical ring to the place names can be deceptive: Arco Felice (happy arch), named after the old Roman arch spanning the road from Pozzuoli to Cuma, is a traffic nightmare; **Lago di Averno** (Virgil's Lake Avernus) and Lago Lucrino (the Lucrine lake famed for its oyster beds in antiquity) have unseemly litter-strewn perimeters.

Some areas have been spared: two volcanic craters (Monte Nuovo and **Astroni**) have been transformed into nature reserves; **Pozzuoli** has been spruced up and gentrified, with its extensive underground Roman remains – the Rione Terra – about to be opened to the public as this guide went to press; **Baia** has added a new wing to the spectacular museum within its castle walls and increased opportunities for visiting the underwater remains of the ancient town; while **Cuma** – long known as mainly a Greek site – has now opened up parts of its Roman heritage to the public.

TICKETS AND TRANSPORT

As this guide went to press, the highly successful Artecard cumulative museum/transport ticket (*see p54*) was due to be extended – at no extra cost – to cover Baia's castello, archeological site and underwater city, the Rione Terra in Pozzuoli (*see above*) and Cuma. A dedicated shuttle bus service for these sites and special ferry services were to be included in the price of the ticket.

Getting there

By bus

The Campi Flegri area is notoriously difficult to reach by public transport, though the M1 and 152 buses from piazza Garibaldi by Naples' Stazione Centrale pass by Solfatara and the church of San Gennaro. As of summer 2002 there were plans to introduce a dedicated shuttle bus service between the Campi Flegrei's main sights, linked to the Artecard cumulative ticket (*see p54 and p87*).

By car

Take the *tangenziale* ring road westwards out of Naples (direction Pozzuoli) and peel off at the appropriate exit (for Astroni and Solfatara take exit 11 at Agnano). All sites listed are within half an hour's drive of the centre if traffic isn't too dire.

By train

The Cumana railway (081 551 3328) runs three to four trains per hour to coastal sites in the Campi Flegrei. For Baia, get off at Lucrino and take the shuttle bus to the old station in Baia, from where two bus lines depart to Cuma (CD or CS). For Pozzuoli (amphitheatre and Solfatara) take the Metropolitana to Pozzuoli-Solfatara, then there's a one-kilometre walk uphill to the volcano; for Astroni, pick up a bus outside the Campi Flegrei Metro station.

Astroni

Astroni is one of the natural wonders of the Campi Flegrei: an entire volcanic crater carpeted with Mediterranean vegetation. Tapped by the Romans for its geothermal waters (the baths have never been discovered)

The reconstructed nymphaeum in Baia's **Castello**. *See p100*.

and used by Naples' various dynasties from the 15th to 19th centuries as a hunting area, Astroni is now a World Wide Fund for Nature (WWF) reserve. A gentle pedestrianised road winds down from the entrance at the lip of the crater towards the lakes on the crater floor, through holm oak woodland that changes to deciduous at the bottom. A shady picnic site has been laid out and hides have been erected by the lakeside, but the whole area is so densely vegetated that birdwatching here requires a good pair of ears rather than binoculars.

Riserva degli Astroni

Oasi WWF, Agnano (081 588 3720/www.astroni.it). **Open** 9.30am-4.30pm daily; ticket office closes 2pm. **Admission** €5 (free for WWF members). **Map** p314.

Pozzuoli

As this guide went to press, swathes of Roman Puteoli were due to be opened to the public in the Rione Terra archeological site. Contact the Naples tourist office for details. *See also p97* **Tickets and transport**.

Greeks from Cuma founded Dikaiarchia in c530 BC as a bulwark against encroaching Etruscans and Samnites (*see p7*). The Romans renamed it Puteoli and made it a colony in 194 BC. Extensive Roman remains can be seen throughout what was a thriving entrepôt port.

The seafaring tradition is still strong. Pozzuoli is the closest mainland harbour to the islands of Procida (*see p204*) and Ischia (*see p191*), and its ferry port does brisk business. Neapolitans come here in droves to dine on freshly caught fish and *frutti di mare* (seafood) at considerably lower prices than in Naples. Down near the port is the ancient fish and meat market, the **macellum**, commonly known as the Serapeo (Temple of Serapis). Its columns are visibly perforated by molluscs, showing that the macellum has spent much of its existence submerged in seawater. This is due to a rising and sinking phenomenon called Bradyseism, caused by what's going on a couple of kilometres below the earth's surface.

Located north-east of the port, the 40,000-seater **Anfiteatro Flavio** (Flavian amphitheatre) was the ancient world's third largest, after the Colosseum in Rome and Capua's amphitheatre (*see p278*). Rising above – both literally and figuratively – the congested roads, railtracks and ugly modern apartment blocks that surround it, the amphitheatre was built mostly during Vespasian's rule (AD 70-79), though work may have started under Nero. The impressive *carceres* (cells) in the underground area below the arena indicate that the amphitheatre was used for *venationes*,

Riserva degli Astroni, a natural wonder. See p98.

contests involving exotic animals, shipped in through Puteoli's port from one of the Empire's distant provinces. The large *fossa* (ditch) cutting across the arena may have contained the stage setting, which was raised or lowered depending on the backdrop required. The impressive underground cells are visitable, while the *cavea* (stalls) and the arena are back in use again for slightly more sedate, musical forms of entertainment from June to September (information from the site ticket office or 081 526 6639/azienturismopozzuoli@libero.it).

For a taste of just how 'burning' the Campi Flegrei still are, take a walk across the dormant volcanic crater of the **Solfatara** to the east of the town centre. From an eerie lunar landscape, hissing wisps of sulphurous steam rise up; here and there mud bubbles. The entrances to a foul-smelling *sudatorium* (built in the 19th century and now partially closed) on the north-eastern side of the crater form weird saunas.

The ancient Romans called it the Forum Vulcani and visited it with the same morbid fascination as its modern-day tourists (though the signposting is probably better today; there's a restaurant and campsite as well).

On the via San Gennaro 200 metres (230 yards) south of Solfatara, the 16th-century church, the **Santuario di San Gennaro**, marks the spot where Naples' patron saint was decapitated. The deed was done, legend has it, near the second column on the right; the congealed blood on a stone, kept in the first chapel on the right, turns a bright healthy red

on the days when a phial-full of San Gennaro's blood liquefies in Naples' Duomo (*see p70* **Bloody miracles**).

Anfiteatro Flavio

Via Terracciano 75 (081 526 6007). **Open** 9am-1hr before sunset daily. **Admission** (includes Cuma and the museum and site of Baiae) €4. **No credit cards.** **Map** p314.

Santuario di San Gennaro

Via San Gennaro Agnano 10 (081 526 1114). **Open** 8am-noon, 4.30-8pm Mon-Sat; 8am-1pm, 4.30-8pm Sun. **Admission** free. **Map** p314.

Solfatara

Via Solfatara 161 (081 526 2341/www.solfatara.it). **Open** 8.30am-1hr before sunset daily. **Admission** €4.60. **No credit cards.** **Map** p314.

Baia

From well before Christ until well into the 18th century, Baia (possibly named after Baios, a companion of Ulysses who, according to legend, was buried here) was one of Italy's prime holiday resorts (*see p100* **Baths, banquets and buggery**), combining all those essential ingredients of sea air, health-giving mineral springs and glorious scenery.

Modern Baia consists mostly of unattractive strip development along the main coast road, with arrays of bars, restaurants and *gelaterie* servicing the through traffic to the area's summer resorts of Bacoli and Miseno.

In Roman times, movers and shakers built splendid villas here. Much of ancient Baiae now lies under the sea (the **città sommersa** can be seen from the Associazione Aliseo's glass-bottomed boat; *see p101*), but there's still a certain opulence about the site and its natural setting. Emperor Caligula (reigned AD 37-41) built a causeway of boats and ships across the stretch of water from Baiae to Puteoli (now Pozzuoli). According to a second-century account by Suetonius, 'Caligula is generally supposed to have built the bridge as an improvement on Xerxes' famous bridging of the much narrower Hellespont. Others believed that he planned this huge engineering feat to terrify the Germans and Britons into submission.'

The **Parco Archeologico** is arranged in terraces overlooking the bay. Up at the top, the view from the Villa dell'Ambulatio gives a good idea of the layout. At the end of the *ambulatio* is the *balneum* (bathroom), a jewel of stuccoed artistry. The level below contains a *nymphaeum* (*see p297* **Glossary**) or perhaps a miniature theatre; further down on the lowest terrace stands the Tempio di Mercurio (Temple of Mercury), a large *natatio* (swimming pool) with an imposing dome (50-27 BC) that pre-dates the cupola of the Pantheon in Rome.

Housing some of the archaeological finds from the area is the **Museo Archeologico dei Campi Flegrei**, in the atmospheric Castello di Baia, built late in the 15th century on the ruins of a Roman fort to improve the area's defences; the castle was given its present appearance from 1538 to 1550. There's a reconstructed *sacellum* (shrine) used for the cult of the emperors, represented here in flattering statues of Vespasian and Titus; the bronze equestrian statue of the unpopular Domitian was reworked to depict his successor Nerva after he had been deposed. On the upper level is a reconstruction of a *nymphaeum* that was excavated in the 1980s but lies, together with much of Baiae, under six metres (20 feet) of water. The statues, though, have been brought to the surface, and include a headless Odysseus plying Polyphemus (statue not found) with wine, a favourite theme of Roman sculptors. The rest of this castle (few English panels) is given over to a new display of archaeological finds from all over the Phlegrean fields.

North of Baia, the **Lago di Averno** (Lake Avernus) was where Virgil led Dante down into the Underworld, but the *sommo poeta* might think twice about getting his feet wet in its decidedly uninviting waters today. The sulphurous belching from beneath the surface of this crater lake was once said to be potent enough to stop passing birds dead in mid-flap. On the north-western shore, the **Grotta di Cocceio** (closed to the public) leads to a wide, dead-straight tunnel that runs to the Sibyl's cave in Cuma (*see p8* **Rushing streams of sound**). In antiquity, Averno was an inner harbour, connected by canals to the sea via the **Lago di Lucrino**, where stubs of Roman walls and arches – evidence of grandiose engineering schemes of 2,000 years ago – can still be seen.

Baths, banquets and buggery

By Julius Caesar's time, the Phlegrean Fields had already acquired a dubious reputation back in the capital. For Cicero, the very word 'Baiae' conjured up visions of feasting, orgies and adultery. More than a century later Martial sharply observed that women arrived at Baiae looking like chaste Penelopes and left behaving like Helens, an opinion pretty much confirmed by Ovid, a poet not usually given to muck-raking.

But it was narrator *per excellenza* Petronius, Nero's Arbiter of Taste, who was to immortalise ancient life in the Phlegraean Fields with his *Satyricon*, telling of a sumptuous dinner party held by nouveau-riche Trimalchio, probably in his villa at Cumae. It was a banquet of gargantuan proportions, with such delicacies as dormice rolled in honey, and peahen's eggs stuffed with warblers rolled up in spiced yolk of egg. Not surprisingly, several of his over-plied guests were unable to find their way back home through the warren of unlit streets near Trimalchio's villa.

When the Senate enjoyed its late summer recess, down came Rome's VIPs to sample this good life around Baiae. Real estate was pricey here, but as a home-owner in the area you might gain privileged access to imperial ears, so the investment could reap a series of favours. An impressive array of Roman emperors holidayed nearby, no doubt taking advantage of excellent spa facilities: Caligula, Claudius, Domitian, Hadrian, Antoninus Pius and Commodus. Nero too was a distinguished visitor: it was in the bay of Baiae that his henchmen comically bungled an assassination attempt on his mother, Agrippina. Arranging a convincing shipwreck on a flat-calm sea was never going to be easy.

Sibylline instructions were issued at **Cuma.**

Città sommersa (underwater city)

Associazione Aliseo, piazza della Repubblica 42, Baia (081 526 5780). **Tours** *Mid Mar-early Nov* noon, 4pm Sat; 10.30am, noon, 4pm Sun. **Tickets** €7.70; €6.20 6-12s. **No credit cards. Map** p314. The Association, which also arranges scuba-diving trips to Baiae and other underwater sites, organises weekday boat trips for large groups by appointment. Tickets are sold on board the boat, which is moored in Baia harbour. Evening trips are an on-off thing: phone before venturing out to Baia. There are also occasional night tours at 9pm on Saturday and Sunday from mid June to mid September.

Museo Archeologico dei Campi Flegrei

Via Castello 39, Bacoli (081 523 3797). **Open** 9am-1hr before sunset Tue-Sun. **Admission** (includes the site of Baiae, Cuma and the amphitheatre in Pozzuoli) €4. **No credit cards. Map** p314.

Parco Archeologico e Monumentale di Baia

Via Fusaro 75, Baia (081 868 7592). **Open** 9am-1hr before sunset Tue-Sun. **Admission** (includes the museum of Baia, Cuma and the amphitheatre in Pozzuoli) €4. **No credit cards. Map** p314.

Cuma

With ample supplies of fresh water and rich agricultural land, not to mention sweeping views along the coast, it's not hard to see what made Euboean Greeks settle around the **Acropoli di Cuma** (Acropolis of Cumae) in the eighth century BC.

Little is known about the history of the Greek colony of Cumae, but archaeological remains point to a flourishing settlement that was to have a considerable influence in Italy throughout the classical period. The settlement had extensive trading contacts with the Etruscans (*see p7*).

The Romans expanded the site, building a forum to the east and linking Cuma by a series of impressive tunnels to the Lago di Averno, an important inland harbour for the Roman fleet.

Virgil recounts (in Book VI of the *Aeneid*) the fascination exerted by the cave of the Sibyl, a prophetess (*see p8* **Rushing streams of sound**). With its eerie light shafts (the *centum ostia* – 100 mouths – as the poet called them) in a long, echo-filled gallery, the fascination remains today. It was here that the Trojan Aeneas received his Sibylline instructions to descend to the Underworld beneath Lake Avernus (*see p100*).

Apollo, the god of light and divination, was worshipped here, as the nature of the temple on the lower level of the Acropolis shows. On the highest level – and it's worth trekking up to the top for the sweeping views through the oak woods along the way – is the Tempio di Giove (Temple of Jupiter), built in the third century BC but manhandled by Roman refurbishers in Imperial times.

South of Cuma, the Acherusia Palus of antiquity, now **Lago Fusaro**, has a *cascina* (lodge) designed in 1782 by Carlo Vanvitelli, joined by a causeway to terra firma. Beyond Lake Fusaro is **Capo Miseno** (Misenum) from where Pliny the Younger watched Vesuvius erupt in AD 79.

Acropoli di Cuma

Via Montecuma (081 854 3060). **Open** 9am-1hr before sunset daily. **Admission** (includes the museum and site of Baiae, and the amphitheatre in Pozzuoli) €4. **No credit cards. Map** p314.

Elsewhere

Naples' unprepossessing suburbs harbour a few gems.

The serene sanctuary of **Eremo Santissimo Salvatore a Camaldoli**.

There is little left of the quaint rustic charm of the outskirts of Naples, buried, as they are, under the cement of post-war reconstruction. The hallmark of these areas is an overwhelming sense of isolation from history, architecture or environmental awareness. Not much remains to lure the visitor… with a few exceptions.

North-west

The opening in recent years of the Collinare railway (*see p54*) – a considerable feat of engineering – has improved access to the city centre from the north-western suburbs, encouraging more construction in what was once Naples' green lung. What is left of the countryside has now been preserved in the park around the **Eremo** (hermitage) **di Camaldoli**, and in the new **Parco Urbano Viale del Poggio**.

Eremo Santissimo Salvatore a Camaldoli

Via dell'Eremo 87 (081 587 2519/eremo. camaldoli@libero.it). Bus C44 from piazza

Medaglie d'Oro. **Open** for mass only 5pm Thur; 8.45am, 11.30am, 6pm Sun. **Admission** free. **Map** off p312 1C.

The chapel built here in 493 by St Gaudosius was replaced in 1585 by the current church and monastery. The monks' cells were little houses, each with its own garden. The belvedere affords a high (458m/1,600ft above sea level), hazy view over the Bay of Naples. Occupied by monks of the Camaldolese order until 1998 (by which time only three were left), the site was taken over by the Sisters of St Bridget; as this guide went to press, a long-running, meticulous restoration of the buildings, gardens and walkways is nearly complete. The thriving religious community caters above all for bona fide Christians, offering weekend retreats, prayer meetings, simple accommodation and refreshments; mass is held daily (at midday).

Visitors are always welcome, though the estate is not actually officially open to the public. A courtesy phone call beforehand is recommended in order to avoid disappointment.

Parco Urbano dei Camaldoli

Via Rai (no phone). Bus C44 from piazza Medaglie d'Oro. **Open** 7am-sunset daily. **Map** off p312 1C.

Founded in 1995, the park is intended to halt the uncontrolled expansion of urban development on the upper reaches of the Vomero hill. A network of paths on both sides of via Rai leads through chestnut-wooded, orchid-strewn slopes. There are breathtaking views over the Bay of Naples.

Parco Urbano Viale Del Poggio

Viale del Poggio 60 (no phone). Metro Colli Aminei/bus C38, R4. **Open** 7am-sunset. **Map** off p312 1C.
Another brand-new inner-city park, this unusual site was opened in 2000 and has rapidly become a local favourite. The park clings to the hillside in an exposed position above the city ring road, affording little protection against sun or heavy rain (a notice at the entrance states the park may close during thunderstorms). Admire the fierce view over the palace at Capodimonte and out across the bay. There are plenty of play facilities, well-maintained grass, a lake and lots of seating, all of which makes it an excellent place for kids and frazzled parents.

North-east

Naples' defunct residents are laid to rest in a vast cemetery area north-east of the centre, towards Capodichino airport. On via Santa Maria del Pianto, the **Cimitero Monumentale** (open 8am-5pm daily) has imposing older graves; the newer **Cimitero Nuovo** (open 8am-5pm daily) is opposite. On busy days the area outside the graveyards hosts an animated cut-flower market, which is watched over carefully by the Polizia Mortuaria; flower vendors have been known to gather up one day's floral tributes from graves for resale the following day.

There's a rather more dignified resting-place near the piazza at the top of via Nuova del Campo; the **'British' Cemetery** (open 9am-5pm Mon-Fri; 9am-1pm Sat, Sun) is in fact international and interdenominational.

Prior to 1898, foreigners were buried in the **Cimitero degli inglesi** nearer the centre of town in piazza Santa Maria della Fede (map p310 2B). When the cemetery was closed, the remains of its inmates were either repatriated or dumped in a common burial ground, and the area was reborn as the **Parco ex-cimitero degli inglesi**. The larger tombs have been left, however. With its shady trees and friendly gardens, this is a corner of a foreign field which will be forever England.

Centro Direzionale

Just north of the tracks leading into Stazione Centrale (and highly visible from trains to Naples), the gleaming Centro Direzionale district rose in the late 1980s from the ashes of a hideous industrial site. The first fruits of

a decades-long administrative battle over redevelopment of derelict eastern Naples, the Centro Direzionale is an incomplete version of a design by Japanese architect Kenzo Tange.

The district is dominated by the towering twin mirror-glass blocks of the Enel electricity board. Many state and corporate bodies – the regional government, Telecom Italia, the state railways – have relocated here. The central criminal court was to have been rehoused in the infamous Tower Block A, which, however, went up in flames in mysterious circumstances in August 1990; the charred remains are being slowly rebuilt, though the work of the criminal judiciary continues to be hampered by other mysterious fires that have plagued its offices.

The central avenue of the district could have been lined up with Vesuvius for a magnificent view, but the volcano is barely visible between the towers, and there's little to take your mind off the barren litter-strewn expanse of wind-swept concrete.

The gleaming **Centro Direzionale**.

Fuorigrotta

So-called because of its position outside (*fuori*) the two tunnels into the Mergellina area, the eastern suburb of Fuorigrotta was developed under Fascism in the 1920 and '30s. A downmarket residential district, it has wide, regular streets that are rather soulless.

Piazzale Tecchio lies at the heart of Fuorigrotta, which is best reached by taking the metro to Campi Flegrei or the Cumana railway to Mostra. The piazza was given a facelift for the soccer World Cup in 1990. The gigantic 82,000-seater **Stadio San Paolo**

(1959) dominates the scene. On Sundays in season, it's a deafening swirl of sky-blue shirts and scarves, though the halcyon days of Maradona & Co are a very distant memory (*see p168* **Calcio & Napoli**).

Beyond, the **Mostra d'Oltremare** was built in 1939-40 to show off 'achievements' in Italy's African colonies. Heavily bombed during World War II, it was extensively rebuilt as a trade exhibition space in 1952. It is officially open for shows and exhibitions only, although the quiet pine tree-lined area is accessible at any time. The **Edenlandia** funfair (*see p146*) is at the far end of the Mostra area.

Useful bus routes

Circular routes

There are four **R** routes plied by the pride of the city's new bus fleet; large and cumbersome, these buses can be guaranteed to block even the widest of streets. All four routes intersect in the via Medina/piazza Municipio area.

R1 From piazza Medaglie d'Oro (*see p90*) to the Museo Nazionale Archeologico (*see p79*), piazza Dante, piazza Carità/via Toledo (*see p77*), piazza Municipio (*see p57*) and back.

R2 From the Stazione Centrale train station along corso Umberto (*see p62*) to piazza Municipio and back.

R3 From Mergellina (*see p93*), along the Riviera di Chiaia (*see p92*) and the Villa Comunale to piazza Municipio, piazza Carità/via Toledo and back.

R4 From the Cardarelli hospital in the north-western suburbs, past the palace at Capodimonte (*see p84*), piazza Carità/via Toledo to piazza Municipio and back.

A-to-B routes

C16 Regular, reliable service running from Mergellina (*see p93*) along corso Vittorio Emanuele to piazza Mazzini and via Salvator Rosa (Vomero; *see p85*).

C18 The only direct bus running from piazza Vittoria along the seafront, through the Fuorigrotta tunnels (*see p104*) and into the heart of Maradonaland (*see p168* **Calcio & Napoli**).

C21 Posh route starting from piazza Sannazzaro in Mergellina and running up the hill to Capo Posillipo (*see p95*) along via Orazio and via Petrarca.

C24 Reliable service for the well-heeled, running from Mergellina through piazza Amedeo (*see p91*), along via Colonna and the Villa Comunale (*see p93*) to piazza Vittoria.

C25 Pleasant tourist round-trip from piazza Amedeo along the Villa Comunale and seafront, past Castel dell'Ovo (*see p56*) into piazza Municipio, touching the end of corso Umberto at piazza Bovio; back via the San Carlo opera house (*see p61*) and piazza Trieste e Trento.

C27 Important but crowded route running from piazza Amedeo up via Tasso to via Manzoni, and right along snobs' alley to Capo Posillipo itself (*see p95*).

C28 Running into the heart of Vomero from piazza Vittoria, taking in the smart shopping street of via dei Mille, via Tasso and via Aniello Falcone along the way.

140 The only bus that runs up via Posillipo from Mergellina, this route starts at Santa Lucia opposite the Castel dell'Ovo.

Shuttle routes

E1 Skirts most sides of the Centro storico from its departure point in piazza Gesù Nuovo (*see p68*). Most of its stops are within easy walking distance of each other, however; the bus is useful mostly for overladen shoppers.

Eat, Drink, Shop

Restaurants

You won't go hungry in this city of food lovers.

Food comes high on the list of life's priorities for your average Neapolitan, and conversation tends to revolve around it to a large degree. Where can you find the best *parmigiana di melanzane*? Is seafood and pasta better *macchiato* (with a touch of tomato) or *in bianco* (without)? How far can you push *al dente* before pasta becomes positively crunchy? Excerpts from mind-blowing gastronomic experiences can be overheard on public transport; what from afar appears to be a heated argument may turn out to be a discussion over the perfect pizza texture or the best way to prepare your coffee.

Such a demanding audience makes it difficult to eat badly in Naples; the number of eateries where the food is exquisite is extensive. At first glance an establishment may appear rundown and cramped, but what it lacks in co-ordinated decoration, it is quite likely to make up for in food quality. Don't fall for the pastel tablecloths and matching napkins of the tourist trap; most of Naples' best eating experiences can be had in spit-and-sawdust *trattorie* and *osterie* (the terms are more or less interchangeable) rather than in the plusher restaurants.

HOW TO ORDER

Ordering in a Neapolitan restaurant is a pantomime, but if you don't let the palaver fluster you, it can be immensely entertaining. Although restaurants are by law obliged to produce a menu, many fail to do so. If a list of dishes is forthcoming, its contents may bear little relation to what is being prepared in the kitchen, especially in smaller *trattorie*. Don't let this put you off; it only means that the chefs, in their tiny kitchens, are using the best, freshest ingredients available at market stalls that day. Menus may be in dialect (*see p120* **The menu**) or may list dishes named after a former chef or the owner's beloved Mamma. You can overcome these difficulties by looking around at what others are eating – don't feel embarrassed, staring is a favourite local pastime – and pointing out what you fancy.

The *menu turistico* is best avoided; the *menu del giorno*, on the other hand, is likely to be fresh and tasty. It is perfectly acceptable to order a *primo* (pasta course) but no *secondo* (main course). On the whole, portions tend to be abundant. If you're not up to a full main course, replace it with *contorni* (cooked vegetables such

as peppers, aubergines, spinach and courgettes), *antipasti misti di mare* (seafood hors d'oeuvre) or an *insalata verde* (fresh green salad).

VEGETARIANS

In the southern Italian culinary mind, meat does not include ham or *pancetta* (bacon). Vegetarians should double-check by asking *c'è la pancetta?* ('is there bacon in it?') when they are told that dishes such as *pasta e fagioli* (pasta and bean soup) or *pasta patata e provola* (pasta with potatoes and smoked cheese) are valid veggie options. For fish eaters, Naples is heaven, but to avoid a hellish bill, get your host to weigh the fish and quote you a price before it goes in the oven.

PIZZA

A truly historic delicacy dating back to the 16th century, the Neapolitan pizza is in a class of its own, soaring way above the thin, crisp, dry Roman variety or the thick doughy American type. Naples credits itself as being the birthplace of the pizza and Neapolitans, through their zeal to maintain their supremacy as producers of the dish, have elevated pizza from its origins as the simplest food of the poorest of the poor to the status of a gourmet art form.

The best Restaurants

For a romantic evening
D'Angelo Santa Caterina. *See p117.*

For a hearty appetite
Il Casolare da Tobia. *See p114.*

For dining al fresco
La Vela. *See p120.*

For hungry archaeologists
Féfé. *See p114.*

For serious fish fanatics
Dora. *See p119.*

For something completely different
La Stanza del Gusto. *See p111.*

For a touch of history
Simposium. *See p115.*

It's worth queuing to dine at the faultless **Osteria da Tonino**. *See p119*.

The Neapolitan pizza is a truly balanced creation; a fairly soft, thinnish base, and medium amounts of topping contained within a thick doughy rim. To count as the genuine article, a Neapolitan pizza must be cooked in a wood-fuelled oven.

Many of Naples' best *pizze* are made in spit-and-sawdust places where staff have never heard of a *prenotazione* (reservation) and where queues can be huge. Don't be put off: the turnover is usually remarkably quick. Don't neglect, however, to single out the head waiter and book your place in the queue: if you don't make your presence known, you may be there all night. *See also p113* **Top toppings**.

WINE BARS

Wine culture in southern Italy dates back to Roman times and beyond; in the south, however, wine is always accompanied by food. Traditionally, both oil and wine were bought in *vini e olii* (wine and oil) outlets, but only the most hardened of drinkers would actually spend time in these places. You'll still find a couple of tiny tables squashed between barrels of oil and *vino sfuso* (wine from the barrel) in some shops; others, on the other hand, have become fully fledged restaurants.

Neapolitans may have been slow to jump on the wine-bar bandwagon, but they are making up for lost time. New wine bars are mushrooming all over the city, all with fairly extensive menus to accompany your wine. Wine lists often appear extensive, but to avoid disappointment and time wasting, it is worth asking which are out of stock before you make your choice. (*Sono tutti disponibili?* 'Are they all available?') Local producers can be slow in delivering, so stocks are depleted around October and November. *See also p108* **Selecting local wine**.

SNACKS

Neapolitans are street animals and as a result spend time snacking on the hoof. As in any large city, there are snack bars where you could munch off the floor and snack bars where you wouldn't let your dog eat.

The food served in bars is incredibly cheap, with pizzas ranging from €1.50 to €2.50 each and fried foods at 15¢ or 25¢ a piece. Some places have seats and there is rarely an extra charge for these. Generally, snack bars in Naples are fairly hygienic and, as long as the hot snacks haven't been sitting around for too long in a warm display cabinet, you should have no problems. It's worth persisting at the busier bars, where the turnover of food is brisk.

The pavement fried-food stalls (*friggitorie*), where bits and pieces are plunged into oil – some of it smelling like Castrol GTX – in a large wok-like frying pan on wheels are, in general, best avoided. The ones listed below, however, are reliable.

Selecting local wine

Campania is one of the rising stars of the Italian wine firmament. A clutch of energetic young producers is finally doing justice to grapes like Aglianico – a red that can hold its own with Tuscany's Sangiovese or Piedmont's Nebbiolo – and rediscovering interesting local varieties such as Piedirosso and Gragnano. Producers from the Cilento and Amalfi coast are also creating some worthwhile new wines, but these can be hard to come by, so grab the opportunity should it arise. Unfortunately, many less scrupulous producers have jumped on to the Falanghina and Aglianico bandwagon, with wines ranging from mediocre to downright awful. Things are further complicated by the tendency of some producers to bottle their very best wines as humble old *vino da tavola*, thus bypassing the ploddingly restrictive DOC regulations. As a result, the names of wineries and individual crus are always a safer guide to quality than the official classifications.

Reds

Aglianico del Taburno
This full-bodied red ranges from bog-standard to palate-blowing. Cantina del Taburno and Ocone are the best-known producers, but La Rivolta in the Cilento also does a tasty version.

Costa d'Amalfi Furore Rosso
A Piedirosso and Aglianico blend, this delicious full-bodied red from the Amalfi Coast matures well. The Gran Furor (Marisa Cuomo) label is by far the best.

Falerno del Massico
Both this and its white equivalent (*see below*) were known to the Romans, and were drunk on special occasions in ancient Pompeii. They are still going strong today. The best producers are Villa Matilde and Moio.

Gragnano
A slightly fizzy, dry wine that should be drunk young. Grotta del Sole – which specialises in rare local varieties like this one – is the best producer.

Montevetrano
In the hinterland of Salerno, photographer Silvia Imparato has been making one of Campania's most impressive reds for years. It's a blend of Cabernet Sauvignon and Merlot, with a little Aglianico thrown in.

Per'e Palummo
The 'foot of the dove' is a red grape native to Ischia, where it makes for a surprisingly complex wine. Look out for D'Ambra and Pietratorcia (which uses the grape in its Ischia Rosso blend).

Piedirosso
Drink this light and very pleasant wine while it's still young: two years old at the most. Ocone and Grotta del Sole are both good producers.

Taurasi
Produced around the little village of Taurasi near Avellino, this 100 per cent Aglianico is serious competition for the Brunello of the north. Look for the Mastroberardino, Feudi di San Gregorio and Caggiano labels.

Stalls selling *o muss'e o per 'e puorc* (pig's muzzle and trotters with salt and lemon: a traditional Neapolitan speciality) in the Pignasecca area (*see p134* **La Pignasecca**) are generally clean. But if this dish isn't your idea of a tasty stomach-filler, try something from one of the enormous mobile sandwich stalls that sell an excellent range of doorstopper sandwiches; these, too, are usually clean.

On the seafront along via Caracciolo (map p313 2B) is a line of stalls selling fresh, hot and tasty *taralli* (crunchy pastry/biscuit rings with pepper and almonds) and *treccine* (the long, plaited version). Unfortunately for vegetarians, they contain animal fat.

From November to February, chestnut roasters, with their old-fashioned coal braziers, will sell you piping-hot, fragrant roasted chestnuts to warm you up.

WHAT TO DRINK

The house wine served in most restaurants – especially in *osterie* and *vini e olii* (bottle shops with tables) – is local and good. The red is a safer bet than the white between November and April. Order *un bicchiere di rosso/bianco* (a glass of red/white) or *un quarto* (a quarter-litre carafe) to start, giving you the option of ordering more, or opting for a bottled variety. *See also above* **Selecting local wine**.

Many *osterie* and restaurants do not serve coffee (or if they do it is likely to be limited to espresso). They do, however, serve post-prandial shots of traditional *digestivi* to facilitate digestion: try the *limoncello* (a sweet infusion of lemon peel in alcohol), *nocillo* (a hazelnut variety) or *basilico* (made with basil). These are often made in-house and can be surprisingly potent.

Vigna Camarato
Produced by Villa Matilde, this single cru Aglianico has been attracting serious praise from Italy's wine critics. Try the 1997 or '98.

Whites

Biancolella
An Ischian grape that the D'Ambra winery does great things with. Look out for its Tenuta Frassitelli cru. Pietratorcia blends it with Fiano to produce the superb, barrel-aged Scheria Bianco cru.

Coda de Volpe
A pleasant, light, easy-quaffing white. Ocone is the best producer.

Costa d'Amalfi Furore Bianco
This blend of Biancolella (known locally as Biancazita) and Falanghina from the Amalfi Coast really works. Try the Apicella label, or the Fior d'Uva cru turned out in tiny quantities by Gran Furor (Marisa Cuomo).

Falanghina
The name means 'little stick'; in ancient times it was the first vine to be trained over a support. Probably the most popular of the Campanian whites, it's fresh and fruity. Try Grotta del Sole, Villa Matilde, Mustilli, Ocone, Feudi di San Gregorio or Moio.

Falerno
Dry but fruity. As with the red of the same name, Villa Matilde leads the field.

Fiano di Avellino
Another ancient, perfumed, full-bodied white that's worth trying. Again, Feudi di San Gregorio is one of the best producers, closely followed by Terredora and Mastroberardino. A case apart is the fragrant Kratos produced in the Cilento by one-man-band Luigi Maffini; his Kleos and Cenito reds are also worth hunting down.

Greco di Tufo
One of the few whites that can be drunk more than a year after bottling, but still best young. There are many inferior types about; for the best, seek out the Feudi di San Gregorio version.

THE BILL AND PRICES

All restaurants charge *coperto* (cover charge), which is generally between €1.50 and €2.50 per person. When the bill arrives, check it carefully (particularly if there was any confusion over your order) and calmly query anything that is unclear. It is customary, though by no means obligatory, to leave a tip (usually around ten per cent), which is a particularly good investment if you intend to return to the restaurant. In theory, restaurants are obliged to issue a receipt; in practice, this is often overlooked.

Average restaurant prices given below are for one person consuming a *primo, secondo* and a *contorno*, plus a dessert or *antipasto* and a quarter-litre carafe of house wine. For *pizzerie*, the price covers a pizza, a beer and one pre-pizza snack.

Royal Naples

Restaurants

Amici Miei

Via Monte di Dio 78 (081 764 4981/081 764 6063).
Bus C22, C25, R2. **Meals served** *Sept-June* 1-3pm, 8-11.30pm Tue-Sat; 1-3pm Sun. *July* 1-3pm, 8-11.30pm Mon-Fri. Closed Aug. **Average** €35. **Credit** AmEx, DC, MC, V. **Map** p313 1A.
To appreciate this family-run restaurant and its excellent cuisine fully, build up an appetite beforehand. Try the palate-blowing *paccheri Amici Miei* (pasta with an aubergine and gorgonzola sauce). There's no fish, but there is excellent chargrilled meat (the lamb is particularly tasty), vegetables and cheeses. Delicious *dolci* are made in the kitchen, including *crema pasticciera* served with brandied chestnuts, and chocolate mousse. There's also a

Eat, Drink, Shop

timeout.com

The online guide to the world's greatest cities

Family-run **Amici Miei** is a class act. *See p109.*

good choice of quality southern wines at very reasonable prices; try the Primitivo di Manduria (red) or the Vigna Caracci (white).

Bersagliera

*Borgo Marinaro 10-11 (081 764 6016/
www.labersagliera.it). Bus C25.* **Meals served**
noon-3.30pm, 7.30pm-midnight Mon, Wed-Sun.
Closed 2wks Jan. **Average** €35. **Credit** AmEx,
DC, MC, V. **Map** p313 2A.

The famous neighbour of Zi Teresa (*see p112*), this restaurant is slightly more sophisticated in terms of decor and clientele. The cuisine, majoring in fish-based dishes, is generally of a high standard. The *taglierini alla Bersagliera* (fine ribbon pasta with baby octopus, black olives and tomato) is strongly recommended.

La Cantinella

*Via Cuma 42 (081 764 8684/www.lacantinella.it).
Bus C25.* **Meals served** *May-Aug* 12.30-3pm,
7.30-11.30pm Mon-Sat. *Sept-Apr* 12.30-3pm, 7.30-
11.30pm Mon-Sat; 7.30-11.30pm Sun. Closed 2wks
Aug. **Average** €65. **Credit** AmEx, DC, MC, V.
Map p313 2A.

There's no denying that this holy of holies among Neapolitan restaurants serves some wonderful food, including *pesce spada affumicato* (smoked swordfish) or *penne con calamaro e cavolo* (pasta with squid and white cabbage). But in a misguided attempt to internationalise the menu, rich sauces are often added, overpowering the subtle flavour of seafood dishes in particular. The service is professional and the wine list is international, if somewhat pricey.

Ciro

*Borgo Marinaro 29-30 (081 764 6006/fax 081
764 6989). Bus C25.* **Meals served** 12.30-3.30pm,

7.30pm-midnight Mon, Tue, Thur-Sun. **Average**
€40. **Credit** AmEx, DC, MC, V. **Map** p313 2A.

In a lovely setting below the Castel dell'Ovo (*see p56*), Ciro offers delightful service and old-fashioned charm. The quality of the food can be inconsistent, though: fish-based dishes, such as *'mpepata di cozze* (steamed mussels with pepper and lemon), are generally tasty; meat is less of a forte. Prices are on the high side, but the view is hard to beat.

La Mattonella

*Via Nicotera 13 (081 416 541). Bus C22, C25,
R2.* **Meals served** *July, Aug* 12.30-3.30pm,
8pm-midnight Mon-Sat. *Sept-June* 12.30-3.30pm,
8pm-midnight Mon-Sat; 12.30-3.30pm Sun. Closed
3wks Aug. **Average** €20. **No credit cards.**
Map p313 1A.

This tiny *osteria* takes its name from the strange collection of tiles (*mattonelle*) that decorates its walls. The antipasti are great (tiny mozzarella balls and aubergine and cheese rolls), as is the spaghetti with *calamaretti* (baby squid). Good *vino locale* is served in ceramic jugs from Vietri on the Amalfi Coast.

La Stanza del Gusto

*Vicoletto Sant'Arpino 21 (081 401 578/
off.gastr.partenopee@libero.it). Bus 140, C9,
C18, C22, C25.* **Meals served** 8-11.30pm Tue-Sat.
Closed 3wks Aug. **Average** €35. **Credit** MC, V.
Map p313 1A.

Just off the hustle and bustle of the via Chiaia retail frenzy, this little gem is hidden at the top of a tiny flight of stairs. The à la carte menu changes regularly and presents such delicacies as *caramelle con pesce spada e zaffirano* (pasta with swordfish and saffron) or *pasta corta con salsiccia e finocchio* (pasta with sausage and fennel). Try the *agnello con*

Eat, Drink, Shop

Step up to **La Stanza del Gusto**. See p111.

zenzero (lamb with ginger) as a main course and the delicious *mousse di caffè e cioccolato con spumo di ricotta* (coffee and chocolate mousse with ricotta cheese sauce) for dessert. There's an extensive international wine list and friendly but professional service. The *menu degustazione* (€50 including wine) is unique: you select a theme (seafood, mushrooms or lamb, for example) and owner Mario Avalone will personally select seasonal ingredients and come up with a customised menu and accompanying wine; several days' advance booking is required for this.

Transatlantico

Via Luculliana 15, Borgo Marinaro (081 764 8842/ www.ristorante-transatlantico.com). Bus C25. **Meals served** 12.30-3.30pm, 7-11pm Mon, Wed-Sun. Closed 4wks Jan, Feb. **Average** €40. **Credit** AmEx, DC, MC, V. **Map** p313 2A.
Modern and chic, this fairly recent addition to the Borgo attracts nouveau-riche speedboat owners who moor their vessels outside. The service is excellent and the food competent, if pricey, ranging from pizzas (should you fancy the location but not the full bill) to *antipasti misti di mare* and seafood dishes. *Calamaro a la brace* (grilled squid) is recommended. The wine list contains very different qualities of white Falanghina wine with similar names, so check the label and go for the Grotta del Sole.

Trattoria San Ferdinando

Via Nardones 117 (081 421 964). Bus C22, C25, R2. **Meals served** 12.30-3.30pm Mon-Thur;

12.30-3.30pm, 8-11.30pm Fri, Sat. Closed 3wks Aug. **Average** €20. **Credit** AmEx, DC, MC, V. **Map** p313 1A.
The menu changes daily but there is always a choice of seafood, veggie or meat pasta dishes. Firm favourites are *pasta e fagioli* (pasta and beans), *pasta e calamaretti/seppioline* (pasta with baby squid or cuttlefish). There's a good selection of *contorni* and the *secondi* aren't bad either. The grilled squid is particularly flavoursome as is the *scarola* (cooked endive with olives and capers).

Zi Teresa

Borgo Marinaro 1 (081 764 2565/www.ziteresa.com). Bus C25. **Meals served** 1-3.30pm, 8-11.30pm Tue-Sat; 1-4pm Sun. Closed lunch 1wk Aug. **Average** €35. **Credit** AmEx, DC, MC, V. **Map** p313 2A.
With humble beginnings in 1916 as a little *osteria* selling beans and mussels, Zi Teresa – now run by Teresa's grandchildren – is a favourite for christening, first communion and anniversary parties, so expect large groups and a good deal of noise. The food is consistently good; try *pasta fagioli e cozze* (pasta with beans and mussels) or *tubetti con fiore di zucca* (pasta with courgette flowers). All the *dolci* are made on the premises, and you can taste it: the tiramisù is particularly good. The tables overlooking the port are by far the most pleasant. Book them well in advance, especially for Sunday lunch.

Pizzerie

Brandi

Salita Sant'Anna di Palazzo 1 (081 416 928/ www.brandi.it). Bus C22, C25, R2. **Meals served** 12.30-3.30pm, 7pm-midnight daily. Closed 1wk Aug. **Average** €20. **Credit** AmEx, DC, MC, V. **Map** p313 1A.
A wide range of politicians, including former US President Bill Clinton, has consumed *pizze* here. Brandi claims to be the place where the pizza margherita was invented (for Italy's Queen Margherita, in 1889), but there are many contenders for that distinction. The pizza is consistently good, and there's a fair restaurant menu too, for which you'll pay around €40. Booking recommended.

Da Ettore

Via Santa Lucia 56 (081 764 0498). Bus C25. **Meals served** 12.30-3pm, 7.30-11.30pm Mon-Sat. Closed Aug. **Average** €20. **Credit** MC, V. **Map** p313 2A.
Although Da Ettore is also a restaurant, it is renowned for its wonderful pizzas and for its *pagniottiello*, a sort of pizza-bread bap stuffed with delicious fillings. The *fiorilli* (deep-fried courgette flowers) are great when available, but the *vino locale* is rough: better to opt for a bottled wine. Ettore doesn't take evening bookings, so get there early or be prepared to queue.

I Re di Napoli

Piazza Trieste e Trento 7-8 (081 423 013). Funicular Centrale to Augusteo/bus C25.

Meals served noon-4pm, 7.30pm-midnight
daily. **Average** €15. **Credit** AmEx, MC, V.
Map p313 1A.
One of three sister *pizzerie* (*see below* and *p117*), the
Re di Napoli serves a wide choice of *pizze*; stick to
the classic varieties, and you won't go wrong. Also
interesting is the pizza DOC, a hot pizza base topped
with fresh mini-mozzarella and tomatoes.

I Re di Napoli

Via Partenope 29-30 (081 764 7775). Bus C25.
Meals served 12.30-4pm, 7.30pm-1am daily.
Closed lunch 2wks Aug. **Average** €10. **Credit**
AmEx, DC, MC, V. **Map** p313 2A.
There's a lovely view of the Castel dell'Ovo (*see p56*).

Port & University

Restaurants

Taverna Dell'Arte

*Rampe San Giovanni Maggiore 1A (081 552 7558).
Bus C25, R1, R2.* **Meals served** 8pm-midnight
Mon-Sat. Closed 3wks Aug. **Average** €30. **Credit**
MC, V. **Map** p311 1C.
Dell'Arte has that perfect combination of homely
atmosphere, good food and wine, and attentive service. The menu is limited, but ingredients are used
imaginatively and quality is consistently high. Try
the *paccheri ai carciofi* (large tube pasta with an artichoke, pine nut and black olive sauce), *calamaro con
patate* (squid cooked with potatoes and a little
tomato) or *tagliatelli con funghi porcini* (pasta with
porcini mushrooms). Basil sorbet is served between
courses to refresh the palate. This place is popular,
so booking is usually essential.

Pizzerie

Da Michele

*Via Sersale 1 (081 553 9204). Metro Piazza
Garibaldi/bus R2.* **Meals served** 10am-11pm Mon-
Sat. Closed 2wks Aug. **Average** €5. **No credit
cards**. **Map** p311 1B.
This traditional eatery is seriously minimalist:
large marble tables; only two types of pizza
(margherita or marinara); beer and water. Friendly,
fast service and enormous, truly delicious *pizze* at
unbelievably low prices. Take a number at the door
before joining the inevitable queue.

Centro storico

Restaurants

Bellini

*Via Santa Maria di Costantinopoli 79-80
(081 459 774). Metro Dante/bus C57, R1, R4.*
Meals served *July-Sept* 12.30-3.30pm, 7.30-11pm
Mon-Sat. *Oct-June* 12.30-3.30pm, 7.30-11pm Mon-Sat;
12.30-3.30pm Sun. Closed 1wk Aug. **Average** €25.
Credit MC, V. **Map** p311 1C.

Top toppings

You can ask for just about any combination
of pizza toppings you like, though your
request may be received with contempt if
it mixes ingredients that, in the waiter's
opinion, couldn't possibly go together.
Most locals opt for the margherita, on
the grounds that you cannot improve on
perfection. Traditional pizzas include...
Caprese or **margherita al filetto**: with
fresh cherry tomatoes and mozzarella.
This can also be topped with a few leaves
of rocket (*rucola* or *rughetta*) after cooking.
Capricciosa: with tomato, black olives,
artichokes and ham.
Margherita: with tomato, mozzarella,
basil and oil.
Marinara: with tomato, oregano, garlic
and oil.
Prosciutto crudo e rucola in bianco: with
parma ham, mozzarella and fresh rocket.
Ripieno (known elsewhere as *calzone*):
a pizza folded pasty-style, stuffed with
mozzarella, ricotta and salami, and topped
with a little tomato and basil.
Ripieno fritto: a deep-fried version of
the *ripieno* also containing pieces of pig
fat (*cicoli*) in the filling, for those on good
terms with their liver.
Salsiccia e friarielli: with loads of
mozzarella, sausage and *friarielli*, a
sort of spinach only found in this area.

Bellini majors in enormous portions of pasta with seafood: dishes that are a first and second course in one. For something particularly good, try the delicious *linguine ai frutti di mare* (pasta with a mixture of fresh seafood) and *linguine con astice* (pasta with langoustine).

Cantina della Sapienza

Via della Sapienza 40 (081 459 078). Metro Piazza Cavour/bus C57, R4. **Meals served** noon-3.30pm Mon-Sat. Closed Aug. **Average** €15. **No credit cards**. **Map** p311 1C.

The nearest thing to Neapolitan home cooking you'll

Dining out of town

The remarkably high standard of food in Naples' restaurants is due in large part to the extreme freshness of locally grown ingredients used. So take a trip to the places where the raw materials come from – the stretch of land between Lucrino and Capo Miseno – and it stands to reason that the gastronomic experience should be even more extraordinary.

Vegetable plots, orchards and vineyards (Per'e Palummo and Falanghina) abound in this area in the Campi Flegrei (*see p97*) west of the city where the volcanic soil is extraordinarily fertile. The coastal waters around here teem with seafood.

And there is a plethora of restaurants in this district. Many, sadly, are over-publicised and overrated. However, there are also some real gems, serving food fresh out of the garden prepared with a passion for gastronomic tradition.

Caronte

Via Lago d'Averno 2, Lago d'Averno (081 804 1429). Cumana rail to Lucrino/Monte di Procida bus from piazza Garibaldi or piazza Municipio, get off at Lucrino. **Meals served** 1-4pm, 7pm-midnight Tue-Sun. Closed 1wk Aug, 2wks Dec. **Average** €18. **No credit cards**. **Map** p314.

Situated on Lago d'Averna (*see p99*), the aptly named Caronte (Charon – the boatman who rowed souls across to the Underworld) is a family-run snack-bar-turned-restaurant that provides not only a breathtaking view across the lake, but great grub to accompany it. The antipasti servings are copious and tasty. Try the cannelloni or *fagioli con seppie* (beans and cuttlefish). Fish dishes are also good and the *crostone* (toasted sandwiches) with *salsiccia* and *friarielli* (*see p121* **The menu**) or *provola* cheese are excellent and a meal in themselves. Give desserts a miss. The *vino* is home-produced and palatable.

Il Casolare da Tobia

Via Selvatico 12 (081 523 5193/ www.sibilla.net/ilcasolare). Cumana rail to Lucrino then take the Torregàveta bus

and get off at first stop; bus SEPSA 1 from piazza Garibaldi to Bacoli. **Average** €25. **No credit cards**. **Map** p314.

This unique eatery, a ten-minute walk from the dramatic Castello di Baia (*see p100*), is situated on the side of a richly cultivated volcanic crater and – though just five minutes from the sea – gives the impression of being in the heart of hilly countryside. The food complements the atmosphere and is truly incredible value for money. Using lots of organically-grown produce from their own vegetable garden, owners Tobia and Elisabetta create veritable banquets based on traditional recipes and varying with the seasons. Excellent *vino locale* (Falanghina and Per'e Palummo) is served. It's not great for vegetarians, however, as animal fats and ham are used in most recipes. Don't wear stilettos for the short, steep path down to the restaurant. There's accommodation too (*see p50*).

Féfé

Via Miseno 137, Case Vecchie, Bacoli (081 523 3011). Monte di Procida bus from piazza Garibaldi or piazza Municipio, get off at last stop. **Meals served** June-Sept 8.30-11pm Mon-Fri; 1-5pm, 8.30-11pm Sat, Sun. Oct-Apr 8-11.30pm Tue-Fri; 1-5pm, 8-11.30pm Sat; 1-5pm Sun. May 8.30-11pm Tue-Fri; 1-5pm, 8.30-11pm Sat, Sun. Closed 2wks Dec. **Average** €25. **Credit** MC, V. **Map** p314.

Situated on the picturesque port where Roman fleets once moored, this tiny restaurant serves delicious but relatively pricey dishes made from fresh, traditional ingredients. An aperitif, the ingredients of which remain a mystery, is served as you arrive. The *pasta zucchini e cozze* (own-made pasta with mussels and courgettes) and *pezzogna al forno con patate* (blue-spotted bream baked with potatoes) are both most appetising. Féfé attracts the alternative bourgeoisie of Naples and you'll find everyone seems to know everyone else. The best tables are outside, but be prepared to queue as this is a popular spot.

find in a restaurant. The menu changes every day, but favourites include *pasta alla siciliana* (with aubergines, tomato and mozzarella) and *pasta al ragù* (with meat and tomato sauce). The *parmigiano di melanzane* (baked aubergine with mozzarella and tomato) is top-notch. Friendly family service, fine desserts and good *vino locale* (red).

La Cantina del Sole (aka Il Corpo di Napoli)

Via Paladino 3 (081 552 7312). Metro Dante/ bus R2. **Meals served** 7pm-midnight Tue-Sat; 1-3.30pm, 7pm-midnight Sun. Closed Aug. **Average** €35. **Credit** MC, V. **Map** p311 1C.
This little restaurant offers an incredible array of dishes, with many recipes dating back to the 17th and 18th centuries. The *genovesi al sugo di agnello* (pasta with onion and lamb sauce) is hearty. For something light but flavourful, try the *spaghetti alla maccheronata* (fresh tomatoes, lashings of basil and a sprinkling of pecorino cheese – no oil or garlic).

Mimì alla Ferrovia

Via Alfonso d'Aragona 19-21 (081 553 8525). Metro Piazza Garibaldi/bus R2. **Meals served** noon-4pm, 7.30pm-midnight Mon-Sat. Closed 2wks Aug. **Average** €30. **Credit** AmEx, DC, MC, V. **Map** p311 1B.
Excellent, fresh, no-nonsense fish dishes, at fair prices for this quality of cooking. The *calamarata* (pasta rings with clams, prawns, mussels and fresh tomatoes) is exceptional. The service is friendly and there's lots of atmosphere, but expect to wait, as bookings are rarely accepted.

Simposium

Via B Croce 38 (081 551 8510/ www.gastronomiastorica.it). Metro Dante or Montesanto/bus C25, R1, R2. **Meals served** 9pm-midnight Fri; 1-4pm, 9pm-midnight Sat; 1-4pm Sun. **Average** €20. **No credit cards**. **Map** p311 1C.
Evening meals here are by appointment only. Moved by his passion for the Neapolitan cuisine of the past, Giovanni Serritelli organises meals cooked with original period recipes, accompanied by appropriate music and entertainment. Meals are served at a communal – and conversation-inspiring – banqueting table, presided over by Giovanni himself. Special banquets and cultural events should be booked by Thursday. Simposium opens for lunch every day in July and August.

Pizzerie

Lombardi a Santa Chiara

Via B Croce 59 (081 552 0780). Metro Dante/ bus C25, R1, R2. **Meals served** 1-3pm, 8-11.30pm Tue-Sun. Closed 3wks Aug. **Average** €20. **Credit** AmEx, MC, V. **Map** p311 1C.
One of Naples' best-established *pizzerie*, Lombardi offers good service, excellent pizza and a decent wine list – but very long queues, especially at weekends.

D'Angelo Santa Caterina. *See p117.*

There also a selection of scrumptious *dolci* and a very good restaurant menu. It's recommended that you book in advance.

Di Matteo

Via dei Tribunali 94 (081 455 262). Metro Dante/bus R1, R2. **Meals served** 10am-midnight Mon-Sat. Closed 2wks Aug. **Average** €10. **No credit cards. Map** p311 1C.
A highly popular pizzeria in the heart of the old city. The decor is unimpressive, but the pizzas are fabulous. This is one of the few places where the *ripieno fritto* (*see p113* **Top toppings**) is to be recommended. Delicious deep-fried bits and pieces – *frittura* – can be nibbled to keep hunger at bay while you're in the street waiting for your turn.

Trianon da Ciro

Via Colletta 46 (081 553 9426). Metro Piazza Garibaldi/bus R2. **Meals served** 10.30am-3.30pm, 6.30-11.30pm daily. **Average** €8. **No credit cards. Map** p311 1B.
This is a traditional pizzeria with absolutely no frills. There are long marble tables and a fairly limited choice of *pizze*, all of which are, however, truly delicious. To accompany them, there's Coca-Cola, beer and water. That's it. You may be expected to write your own order.

Wine bars

Berevino

Via San Sebastiano 62 (081 290 313). Metro Dante or Montesanto/bus C57, R1, R4. **Open** 4-8pm Mon; 11am-8pm Tue; 11am-2am Wed; 4pm-2am Thur-Sat; 8pm-2am Sun. Closed 3wks Aug. **Credit** MC, V. **Map** p311 1C.

This wine bar/shop serves a delicious selection of munchies to accompany your choice of wine from its fairly extensive, though not international, wine list. Big on Campanian wines.

Snacks

Ciao Pizza
Via B Croce 42 (081 551 0109). Metro Dante/ bus R1, R4. **Open** 9am-midnight Mon-Fri; 6pm-3am Sat; 5.30pm-1.30am Sun. Closed 2wks Aug. **No credit cards. Map** p311 1C.
Tasty, energy-boosting traditional pizza triangles. **Branch:** via San Carlo 3 (081 421 616).

Friggitoria-Pizzeria Giuliano
Calata Trinità Maggiore 33 (081 551 0986). Bus R1, R4. **Open** 10am-11pm Mon-Sat. Closed 3wks Aug. **No credit cards. Map** p311 1C.
Probably the best *pizzette* (snack-sized pizza) in town. Both the *ripieno* and the margherita are exceptional. Potato croquettes and *zeppole* (deep-fried dough balls) are crisp and fresh.

Toledo & Sanità

Restaurants

La Vecchia Cantina
Via San Nicola alla Carità 13-14 (081 552 0226). Metro Dante or Montesanto/bus C57, R1, R4. **Meals served** noon-3.30pm, 8-11pm Mon, Wed-Sat; noon-3.30pm Sun. Closed 2wks Aug. **Average** €15. **Credit** AmEx, DC, MC, V. **Map** p312 2A.
This little *osteria* serves delicious, traditional food at unbeatable prices. The Cantina is located next to the fish market; its grilled squid and swordfish are good as is the *linguine con polipetti* (pasta with baby octopus). Excellent *vino locale* (red).

Pizzerie

Ciro a Santa Brigida
Via Santa Brigida 71 (081 552 4072). Funicular Centrale to Augusteo/bus C25, R2. **Meals served** 12.30-3.30pm, 7.30pm-midnight Mon-Sat. Closed 2wks Aug. **Average** €20. **Credit** AmEx, DC, MC, V. **Map** p313 1A.
Although fundamentally a restaurant, *pizze* is what Ciro does best. If you've experienced the usual pizza varieties once too often, try the *pizza ai frutti di mare* (seafood pizza) for a change. Lovely old-fashioned service and a good wine list.

I Re di Napoli
Piazza Dante 16 (081 544 7230). Metro Dante/ bus C57, R1, R4. **Meals served** noon-1am daily. Closed 1wk Aug. **Average** €15. **Credit** AmEx, DC, MC, V. **Map** p312 2A.
This branch of a group of three pizzerias (*see p112* and *p113*) is a handy pitstop before, after or during a visit to the Museo Nazionale Archeologico (*see p78*).

Snacks

Friggitoria Fiorenzano
Piazza Montesanto 6 (081 551 2788). Funicular Montesanto to Montesanto/metro Montesanto. **Open** 8am-10pm Mon-Sat. Closed 2wks Aug. **No credit cards. Map** p312 2A.
A great selection of tasty snacks. Try the deep-fried artichokes (only in season). The owners also have a pizzeria next door.

Lo Sfizietto
Corner of vico Basilico Puoto & via Pignasecca (no phone). Funicular Montesanto to Montesanto/ metro Montesanto. **Open** 10am-10pm daily. Closed 3wks Aug. **No credit cards. Map** p312 2A.
Traditional *pizzette*, oven-baked and fried *calzone*, and an array of fried snacks.

Vomero

Restaurants

D'Angelo Santa Caterina
Via Aniello Falcone 203 (081 578 9772). Bus C28. **Meals served** 7.30-10.30pm Mon, Wed-Sat; 1-3.30pm, 7.30-10.30pm Sun. Closed 2wks Aug. **Average** €60. **Credit** AmEx, DC, MC, V. **Map** p313 1C.
Set in peaceful bougainvillea- and jasmine-filled surroundings, with amazing views over the city, this restaurant is ideal for a romantic dinner or an extra-special lunch. Service is friendly but professional and the food is abundant and excellent. The antipasti – comprising delicacies such as deep-fried baby squid, marinated sardines and octopus, sautéed prawns or smoked swordfish – are a meal in themselves. The varied wine list is reasonably priced for a restaurant of this calibre.

La Cantina di Sica
Via Bernini 17 (081 556 7520). Funicular Chiaia to via Cimarosa, Centrale to piazza Fuga/bus C28, C31, C32, V1. **Meals served** 1-4pm, 8pm-midnight daily. Closed 1wk Aug. **Average** €25. **Credit** AmEx, MC, V. **Map** p312 2B.
This recently refurbished restaurant serves good, traditional dishes such as *pasta patata e provola* (pasta, potato and smoked cheese) or *pasta alla siciliana* (pasta with aubergines, tomato and mozzarella) at slightly higher prices than your average trattoria. There's an interesting choice of delicious *contorni*; try the *parmigiano di peperoni* (layers of cooked peppers and white sauce). The *vino locale* is fair but pricey at €9 a carafe, so it's probably worth going for a bottled wine.

Osteria Donna Teresa
Via Kerbaker 58 (081 556 7070). Funicular Chiaia to via Cimarosa, Centrale to piazza Fuga/bus C28, C31, C32, V1. **Meals served** 12.30-3pm, 7.30-11pm Mon-Sat. Closed Aug. **Average** €13. **No credit cards. Map** p312 2B.

A small selection of exemplary home cooking is offered. Try *polpette* (meatballs) in tomato sauce or *salsicce al sugo* (sausages with tomato sauce). The very insistent owner will probably force you into eating at least two courses. Good *vino locale* (red).

Pizzerie

Acunzo

Via Cimarosa 60/62 (081 578 5362). Funicular Centrale to piazza Fuga or Chiaia to via Cimarosa/ bus C28, C31, C32, V1. **Meals served** 1-3pm, 7.30-11pm Mon-Sat. Closed Aug. **Average** €15. **Credit** MC, V. **Map** p312 2B.

All the usual pizzas are here, but also some unusual specialities such as *calzone* stuffed with pasta or beans. Avoid the house wine.

Angolo del Paradiso

Via Kerbaker 152 (081 556 7146). Funicular Centrale to piazza Fuga or Chiaia to via Cimarosa/ bus C28, C31, C32, V1. **Meals served** 12.30-3pm, 7.30-midnight Tue-Sun. Closed 2wks Aug. **Average** €9. **No credit cards.** **Map** p312 2B.

In addition to a fair restaurant menu, staff at Angolo serve top-notch traditional pizzas at low prices. For something different, try the *cinque gusti* (five small slices with different toppings).

Pizzeria Cilea

Via Cilea 43 (081 556 3291). Bus 181, C31, C32. **Meals served** 1-4pm, 7-11.30pm Mon-Sat; 7.30-11.30pm Sun. Closed 2wks Aug. **Average** €10. **No credit cards.** **Map** p312 2C.

Delicious *pizze* and *frittura* at exceptional prices: the Cilea does a mean *ripieno* and an excellent *margherita al filetto*; the *contorni* are also very good. It's tiny and very popular, so be prepared to queue (not advisable for groups of more than four).

Wine bars

Bocca d'Oro

Piazzetta Durante 1 (081 229 2010). Funicular Centrale to piazza Fuga or Chiaia to via Cimarosa/ bus C28, C31, C32, V1. **Open** 12.30-4pm, 8.30pm-2am daily; 8.30pm-midnight Mon, Sun. Closed 2wks Aug. **No credit cards.** **Map** p312 2B.

This *vineria* has a good wine list and excellent food to accompany it. Take, for instance, the delicious *rotelli alle noci* (ravioli with ricotta in a walnut sauce). It also does a nice line in *bistecca fiorentina* (T-bone steak) and serves assorted cheeses and salamis.

Snacks

Friggitoria Vomero

Via Cimarosa 44 (081 578 3130). Funicular Chiaia to via Cimarosa, Centrale to piazza Fuga/ bus C28, C31, C32, V1. **Open** 9am-2pm, 5-10pm Mon-Fri; 5pm-midnight Sat. Closed Aug. **No credit cards.** **Map** p312 2B.

Enjoy fantastic fish at **Dora**. *See p119.*

Wonderful freshly fried *graffe* (light doughnuts), just right for breakfast, are available from 9.30am. Other fried delights are ready from 10am: mini-potato croquettes, *zeppole* (deep-fried dough balls), courgettes, courgette flowers and aubergine fried in batter. Great for a cheap, tasty filler on your way to Castel Sant'Elmo (*see p87*).

Chiaia to Posillipo

Restaurants

Donna Margherita

Vico II Alabardieri 4-6, Chiaia (081 400 129). Bus C22, C25. **Meals served** 12.30-3pm, 8pm-12.30am daily. **Average** €17. **Credit** AmEx, DC, MC, V. **Map** p313 1A.

Large portions of reasonable pasta at fair prices, and the pizzas are good too. There's a very pleasant garden for summer and a gazebo for winter.

Don Salvatore

Via Mergellina 5, Mergellina (081 681 817/ www.donsalvatore.it). Bus 140, C16, C24, R3. **Meals served** 12.30-3.30pm, 7.30pm-midnight Mon, Tue, Thur-Sun. **Average** €60. **Credit** AmEx, DC, MC, V. **Map** p313 2C.

Highlights here are the delicious fish and meat dishes, and superb antipasti. Try the *cecinielle* (a tiny transparent fish fried in patties with batter), *polpo ai carciofi* (octopus with artichokes) or *calamaretti con uva passa* (baby squid with sultanas and pine nuts). The hospitable owner Tonino Aversano is a passionate wine expert; he'll help you choose the perfect bottle to complement your meal from the exceptional, continually updated wine list. Recent additions worth trying include Fiano di Maffini and Aglianico del Taburno La Rivolta.

Dora

Via Ferdinando Palasciano 30, Chiaia (081 680 519). Bus 140, C9, C18, C24, C25, C28. **Meals served** 12.30-3pm, 8pm-midnight Mon-Sat. Closed 2wks Aug. **Average** €50. **Credit** DC, MC, V. **Map** p313 1B.

The best fish money can buy in one of the tiniest restaurants in the city; if you don't book, you'll never get in. Try the oysters, *pezzogna* (blue-spotted bream), or the *zuppa di pesce* (fish soup). The char-grilled prawns are exceptional.

Giuseppone a Mare

Via F Russo 13, Posillipo (081 769 1384/081 575 6002). Bus 140, then 10mins walk. **Meals served** noon-3.30pm, 7.30-11.30pm Tue-Sat; 1-3.30pm Sun. Closed 2wks Aug. **Average** €50. **Credit** AmEx, DC, MC, V. **Map** p314.

With a stunning picture-postcard view over the bay, Giuseppone is a legend. It's a luxurious restaurant with fittingly attentive service and carefully prepared food. The antipasti are flavoursome, the *fusilli marinari* (own-made pasta with baby squid, prawns and shellfish) superb.

Osteria Castello

Via Santa Teresa a Chiaia 38, Chiaia (081 400 486). Funicular Chiaia to Parco Margherita/metro Piazza Amedeo/bus C24, C25, C26, C27, C28. **Meals served** *June-Aug* 8-11.30pm Mon-Sat. *Sept-May* 8-11.30pm Mon-Fri; 1-3.30pm, 8-11.30pm Sat. Closed 3wks Aug. **Average** €30. **Credit** AmEx, DC, MC, V. **Map** p313 1B.

This lively *osteria* attracts all sorts, making it a great place for people-watching. The *pappardelle ai frutti di mare* (long, wide ribbon pasta with seafood) is excellent (when in season) and the *fagotto alla fiamma* (sausage-like meat with cheese and a cream sauce, flambé) is extremely tasty. There's plenty of choice for vegetarians – try *funghi pleos* (pleos mushrooms) or *radicchio alla brace* (barbecued radicchio). The menu is far from clear, but don't hesitate to ask the head waiter, Alfredo, to explain.

Osteria da Tonino

Via Santa Teresa a Chiaia 47, Chiaia (081 421 533). Funicular Chiaia to Parco Margherita/metro Piazza Amedeo/bus C24, C25, C26, C27, C28. **Meals served** *Oct-May* 12.30-4pm Mon-Wed; 12.30-4pm, 8-11pm Thur-Sat. *June, July, Sept* 12.30-4pm Mon-Sat. Closed Aug. **Average** €18 lunch; €25 dinner. **No credit cards**. **Map** p313 1B.

This is one of the busiest *osterie* in town, but dinner is an experience worth queuing for. Owner Tonino (now only working at lunchtimes) will enthral you with his banter; his wife's cooking will delight your senses. Try *seppie in umido* (cuttlefish stewed in a little tomato) or *provola alla pizzaiola* (cheese with a tomato and basil sauce). The *pasta ragù e ricotta* (meat, tomato and ricotta cheese) cannot be faulted.

Trattoria dell'Oca

Via Santa Teresa a Chiaia 11, Chiaia (081 414 865/081 421 533). Funicular Chiaia to Parco Margherita/metro Piazza Amedeo/bus C24, C25, C26, C27, C28. **Meals served** 1-3pm, 8-11.30pm Mon-Sat. Closed 3wks Aug. **Average** €20. **Credit** AmEx, DC, MC, V. **Map** p313 1B.

The decor is slightly more northern European than in most Neapolitan *osterie*, but this one serves good traditional fare nonetheless. *Caprino con speck* (soft cheese and smoked ham) makes an interesting *antipasto*; *penne alla scarpariello* (pasta with fresh tomatoes, pecorino cheese, basil and a touch of chilli) and *tagliata alle erbe* (thinly sliced beef grilled with herbs and olive oil) are very tasty, and the service is friendly and efficient.

Vadinchenia

Via Pontano 21, Chiaia (081 660 265/081 421 533). Funicular Chiaia to Parco Margherita/metro Piazza Amedeo/bus C24, C25, C26, C27, C28. **Meals served** 8pm-midnight Mon-Sat. Closed Aug. **Average** €45. **Credit** AmEx, DC, MC, V. **Map** p313 1B.

Silvana and Saverio have taken the best ingredients from various parts of Italy and combined them to palate-blowing effect. Favourite dishes include *cavatelli* (a small nut-shaped pasta) in a gorgonzola and pistachio sauce, served in a bowl formed of melted parmesan cheese and beautifully flavoured stuffed squid. *Pecorino con miele e pistacchio* (cheese with honey and pistachio) makes an unusual alternative to a traditional dessert. The forte of the excellent wine list is in local wines. Avoid Saturday if you want specially attentive service. The

Wine bar **Barrique**. *See p120.*

August closing can be extended into late July and early September. Booking is essential.

La Vela
Porticciolo di Marechiaro, Posillipo (081 769 2313). Bus 140 to Posillipo then 10mins walk. **Meals served** *May-Sept* 1-11.30pm daily. *Oct-Apr* 1-11.30pm Mon, Tue, Thur-Sun. **Average** €30. **Credit** AmEx, MC, V. **Map** p314.
It's a fair hike from the centre to this restaurant, down the little alleyways and steps of the Marechiaro towards the sea. Turn right where the steps divide and La Vela is right on the seafront. It serves good seafood (try the *sauté di vongole*, sautéd clams) and has a breathtaking view over the tiny port and the bay beyond.

Pizzerie

Ciro a Mergellina
Via Mergellina 18-21, Mergellina (081 681 780/ http://ciroamergellina.com). Metro Mergellina/ bus 140, C24, R3. **Meals served** *Oct-May* 1-4pm, 7.30pm-1am Tue-Sun. *June-Sept* 1-4pm, 7.30pm-1am daily. **Average** €25. **Credit** AmEx, DC, MC, V. **Map** p313 2C.

The decor is basic, but the setting – next to the port in Mergellina – is pretty. Ciro is primarily a restaurant, where you can expect to pay around €45 for a meal that's good but unexceptional, but it's the pizzas that are the big draw. Try the *pizza ai frutti di mare*: it's what the chef does best.

Da Pasqualino
Piazza Sannazzaro 77-79, Mergellina (081 681 524). Metro Mergellina/bus 140, C16, C24, R3. **Meals served** noon-4pm, 7pm-midnight Mon, Wed-Sun. **Average** €10. **Credit** AmEx, DC, MC, V. **Map** p313 2C.
This is one of the best *pizzerie* in the piazza and incredibly good value for money, so queues tend to be long. Excellent *frittura*: deep-fried mozzarella, potato croquettes and aubergines. There's a fair restaurant menu, and the *vino locale* isn't at all bad.

Wine bars

Barrique
Piazzetta Ascensione 9, Chiaia (081 662 721). Metro Piazza Amedeo/bus C24, C25, C26, C27, C28. **Open** 7.30pm-1am Tue-Sun. Closed 2wks Aug. **Credit** MC, V. **Map** p313 1B.

Eat, Drink, Shop

The menu

Antipasti
Alici marinate: sardines marinated in garlic, chilli and parsley.
Antipasti di mare: a selection of (usually) cold, cooked seafood such as octopus, squid, clams, smoked swordfish, salmon and marinated sardines.
Antipasti misti (or **di terra**): a selection of salamis, hams, cheeses and olives.
Bruschetta: toast with chopped tomatoes, garlic, basil and oil, or, occasionally, aubergine or olive paste.
Funghi trifolati: cooked diced button mushrooms with garlic, chilli and parsley.
Involtini di peperoni: cooked peppers, rolled and filled with cheese and breadcrumbs.
Mozzarella e prosciutto: mozzarella and parma ham.
Prosciutto e fichi: parma ham and figs.
Prosciutto e melone: parma ham and cantaloupe melon.
Saute di vongole: sautéd clams.

Pasta
Alla Barese: with broccoli.
Alla Genovese: thick onion and ham sauce.
Alla puttanesca, alla bella donna: with tomato, capers, black olives and a touch of chilli.

Alla Santa Lucia, alla bella Napoli, alla pescatora: with seafood and shellfish.
Alla Siciliana: with tomato, aubergine, basil and mozzarella.
Alla Sorrentina: with tomato and mozzarella.
Alle vongole: with clams (specify *in bianco* if you don't want your clams cooked in tomato sauce).
Al sugo: simple tomato and basil sauce.
Con fagioli e cozze: with beans and mussels.
E ceci: with chickpeas.
Provola e patata: with smoky cheese and potato.
Ragù e ricotta (**alla mammà**): tomato and meat sauce blended with soft ricotta cheese.

Carne (meat)
Carne alla pizzaiola: meat served with a tomato and basil sauce.
Carne al ragù: slow-cooked beef served in a tomato sauce.
Gattò di patata: a shepherd's pie-like dish with mozzarella and ham.
Involtino: a small roll of beef (or aubergine – *involtini di melanzane*) stuffed with ham and cheese.
Polpette: meatballs, usually served in a thick tomato sauce.

Nicely done out in terracotta, Barrique features low lighting and relaxed jazz music. There's an interesting variety of Italian wines from around Naples and other areas; a choice of well-flavoured salami, olives, cheeses and ham to nibble with your wine; and a couple of pasta dishes that change daily.

Enoteca Belledonne

Vico Belledonne a Chiaia 18, Chiaia (081 403 162).
Bus C16, C22, C24, C25, C28, R3. **Open** *Oct-May* 9am-2pm, 4.30-9.30pm Mon-Thur; 9am-2pm, 4.30pm-2am Fri, Sat. *June-Sept* 9am-2pm, 4.30-9.30pm Mon-Sat. Closed 3wks Aug. **Credit** DC, MC, V. **Map** p313 1B.

This little wine bar tends to get jam-packed and spill into the alleyway outside at weekends (a few tables remain inside). It's a little quieter during the week. There's an amazing choice of Italian wines, with bottles divided by region on racks around the walls. Wine by the glass is of a decent standard and is sold at low prices. Staff are happy to help out with packaging your bottled purchases for shipment home. A few light snacks are available at weekends.

Vinarium

Vico Santa Maria Cappella Vecchia 7, Chiaia
(081 764 4114). Bus C9, C18, C24, C25, C28, R3/

tram 1. **Open** *Sept-June* 1.30pm-2am Mon-Sat.
July noon-4pm Mon-Sat. Closed Aug. **Credit** AmEx, DC, MC, V. **Map** p313 1A.

A fair range of wines at reasonable prices. Vinarium is noisy and very busy at the weekends, so be prepared to queue. Rather run-of-the-mill risottos and toasted sandwiches are served.

Snacks

La Focaccia Express

Vico Belledonne a Chiaia 31, Chiaia (081 412 277).
Bus C22, C25. **Open** 10am-2am Mon-Sat; 6pm-3am Sun. Closed 3wks Aug. **No credit cards.**
Map p313 1B.

This place serves the most delicious choice of pizza slices (*pizza al taglio*) and focaccia imaginable. Try the *peperoni e patata* (peppers and potato), *ricotta e salsiccia* (ricotta and sausage) or *margherita al filetto* (with cherry tomatoes and mozzarella). To be sure of a really fresh slice, watch the oven and buy what has just come out. A phenomenal range of beers (over 50, the owner claims) and wine by the glass and bottle are in stock. The TV is usually on; if you're a football fan this is a good place to get involved in a match.

Pesce & frutti di mare (fish & seafood)

Calamaro ripieno: stuffed squid.
Mazzancolle: very large prawns.
'Mpepata di cozze: mussels steamed with pepper and served with lemon.
Mussillo marinato: marinated cod-like fish.
Pignatiello: seafood soup served with fingers of toasted bread.
Polipo affucate/affogato: literally 'drowned octopus', cooked in an earthenware dish with a little water and tomato.
Purpietielle/purpo/polpo/polipo: octopus.
Seppie in umido: similar to polipo affucate/affogato (*see above*) but with cuttlefish.
Totano: similar to squid, often cooked with potatoes.

Contorni (vegetables)

Carciofi alla giudea: artichokes cooked with olives and capers.
Fagiolini all'agro: cooked green beans with garlic and lemon.
Friarielli: spinach-like greens, unique to the Naples area.
Melanzane a funghetto: diced aubergines cooked in tomato and basil.
Melanzane alla brace: sliced char-grilled aubergines, dressed with garlic, chilli, parsley.

Peperoncini verdi: tiny sweet green peppers cooked in tomato and basil.
Peperoni in padella: pan-fried peppers (often with capers and black olives).
Scarola 'mbuttit'/'mbuttonat': stuffed endive (usually with capers, pine nuts and olives).

Formaggi (cheese and things done with it)

Caprese: fresh mozzarella, tomatoes and basil.
Mozzarella in carrozza: deep-fried, traditionally on a small square of bread, but nowadays in breadcrumbs.
Provola: similar to mozzarella but with a smoky taste.
Provola alla pizzaiola: smoky cheese cooked in a tomato and basil sauce.

Methods of cooking

All'acqua pazza (fish): baked with garlic, parsley and a touch of tomato.
Al sale (fish): cooked under a huge pile of sea salt.
Con pomodoro al filetto: cooked with fresh cherry tomatoes.
In bianco: without tomato.
Macchiato: with a touch of tomato.

Eat, Drink, Shop

Cafés, Bars & Gelaterie

Caffè and cakes is an unforgettable ritual in Italy's coffee capital.

Naples regards itself as Italy's coffee capital, though why this should be so is a hotly debated topic. Being a port where cargo ships from coffee-producing countries docked must certainly have played a significant part. Developing a better way of brewing the drink – in the little topsy-turvy stove-top coffeemaker still known as a *napoletana* – also gave the city a claim to the title.

Whatever the reason, Neapolitans were already hooked by the mid 17th century when coffee houses became the meeting places of the aristocratic, the monied and the intellectual elites, providing forums for political debate and learned discussion. Of these historic *caffè letterari*, only **Gambrinus** (*see p124*) remains, although its intellectual clientele has long since been edged out by fur coats and tourists. For something more reminiscent of the days of yore, make for quieter watering holes on piazza Bellini or piazza San Domenico.

CAFFÈ ETIQUETTE

Coffees consumed in the rarefied atmosphere of such elegant salons are few these days: most are downed in one while standing at the bar. Drinkers rarely pause even for a break in conversation, which can make the average Neapolitan coffee bar seem like a British pub at closing time. Don't be afraid to elbow your way in to get closer to the bar.

Unless you're being served at a table, drinks should usually be paid for at the till before ordering at the counter. Take your receipt and slap it down, along with a 10¢ or 20¢ coin to speed up service. Don't expect the bar staff to ask what you'd like: you may wait all day. Instead, summon up all the assertiveness (though not rudeness) you can muster and say *due cappuccini* or *due caffè* ('please' or 'could I possibly have' are unnecessary).

If you are at a table, the waiter will bring the bill with your drinks. You may be expected to pay immediately; it is customary (although not necessary) to leave a few coins as a tip. Table prices are about double normal bar prices, or sometimes more.

CAFFÈ PRACTICALITIES

The terms *bar* and *caffè* are interchangeable. All bars sell hot and cold drinks, alcoholic drinks and sweet snacks. Some have more to offer: a *bar-tabaccheria* also sells cigarettes, bus tickets and phone cards, while a *bar-pasticceria* offers cakes, pastries and often ice-cream, though this last can also be found in a *bar-gelateria*.

The *bar-lotteria* has the wherewithal for playing Italy's various lotteries and football pools; most will have a copy of the lottery bible, *La Smorfia*, a manual for converting dreams into winning numbers. Alternatively, look out for the sign saying 'Totocalcio' and ask for a *schedina* (coupon) if you fancy a flutter on the football.

CAFFÈ COMPLEXITIES

Neapolitans expect their coffee very strong and very sweet. If you don't want your coffee to come already sugared, ask for it *amaro*. To retain your dignity, don't even think of asking for a 'moccacino' or any of the other concoctions served in Anglo-Saxon coffee houses. With all the coffee variations (listed below) on offer, you probably won't be tempted to anyway.

Brasiliano: espresso topped with frothy milk and cocoa, sometimes with a dash of alcohol.
Caffè: a short, very strong espresso; known as a *ristretto* ('concentrated') further north, this tooth-enamel-removing strength is the norm for the south.
Caffè alla nocciola: an espresso with sweet hazelnut froth added; there is also a chocolate variety.
Caffè corretto (literally 'corrected'): an espresso with a dash of alcohol added, usually grappa but you can decide what you want (whisky, rum, cognac, Bailey's).
Caffè d'orzo: a barley-based coffee substitute prepared espresso-style.
Caffè freddo: iced coffee, usually very sweet; only sold in the warm months.
Caffè Hag: decaf espresso (this one's not always available).
Caffè latte: a milkier version of the cappuccino without cocoa.
Caffè lungo: a slightly less concentrated version of the standard *caffè*.
Caffè macchiato: an espresso with a touch of milk.
Cappuccino (or **cappuccio**): usually more coffee than milk; specify without sugar (*amaro* or *senza zucchero*) or without cocoa (*senza cacao*) or very hot (*molto caldo*), as there is a tendency to serve it lukewarm to allow customers to drink up quickly and get on their

Bar Mexico: for the best espresso in town. See p125

The cake ritual

Cakes are a ritual in Naples and locals will cross the city to purchase the right ones for special occasions... even if it's only Sunday lunch with the mother-in-law. Those listed below are Neapolitan favourites.

Babà (stress the second syllable): a much lighter version of what you may recognise as a rum baba; it was, apparently, invented by French chefs in Poland before being brought south; in Neapolitan dialect *tu si 'nu babà* can be roughly translated as 'you're gorgeous'.

Chiacchiere: icing sugar-covered tongues of lightly fried flour and egg mixture; eaten by Neapolitans at Carnevale in the run-up to Lent; occasionally they are served with heavy *sanguinaccio*, a chocolate sauce that was originally made from a mixture of pig's blood and cocoa, though this concoction is now (mercifully) illegal.

Pastiera: a deep flan filled with a mixture of ricotta cheese and softened cereals flavoured with orange-blossom water; formerly an Easter cake, it can now be found year round.

Raffioli: sponge and marzipan covered in white icing; a soft and sugar-heavy treat around Christmas time.

Rococò: a teeth-challengingly hard almond biscuit made at Christmas.

Sfogliatella: sweet, lightly spicy ricotta cheese in either puff pastry (*riccia*) or shortcrust pastry (*frolla*). Omnipresent, and usually excellent.

Torrone: a light, chocolate-based nougat eaten around All Souls' Day (1 November).

Torta caprese: a moist, heavy cake made with chocolate and hazelnuts and dusted with icing sugar.

Zeppole di San Giuseppe: fried or baked choux pastry filled with custard and topped with bitter wild cherries, sold around the feast of St Joseph (Father's Day in Italy) on 19 March.

Eat, Drink, Shop

way. Cappuccinos are served for breakfast only: no self-respecting Neapolitan would be seen dead drinking this after midday.

Cappuccino freddo: a cold cappuccino, often made with sweet iced coffee.

Latte macchiato: hot milk served with a dash of coffee.

PASTICCERIE

Neapolitans take their cakes seriously, and will happily cross from one side of the city to the other to obtain the perfect cake. *Dolci* are a must for special occasions, including Sunday lunch, and consequently long queues form at top *pasticcerie* on Sunday mornings, so be prepared for a wait. If you decide to eat your cake seated at a table at a *bar-pasticceria*, feel free to avoid any misunderstanding or disappointment by accompanying the waiter to the counter and pointing out the pastry you want.

GELATERIE

See p127 **The ice-cream challenge**.

Royal Naples & Monte Echia

Cafés & bars

Bar del Professore

Piazza Trieste e Trento 46 (081 403 041). Funicular Centrale to Augusteo/bus 24, C22, C25, C57. **Open** 7.30am-midnight daily. **No credit cards.** **Map** p313 1A.

This slightly downmarket neighbour to Gambrinus (*see below*) has a few tables outside at which to consume an excellent espresso (if the thundering traffic doesn't put you off). Specialities include *caffè alla nocciola* (hazelnut coffee) and *caffè al cioccolato* (chocolate coffee). It's often packed.

Gambrinus

Via Chiaia 1-2 (081 417 582). Funicular Centrale to Augusteo/bus 24, C22, C25, C57. **Open** 8am-1.30am daily. **Credit** AmEx, MC, V. **Map** p313 1A.

Naples' most famous café is ideally situated to provide a rest after sightseeing or shopping, or an *aperitivo* before the opera. Established over a century ago, Gambrinus still retains much of its original decor. Some rooms favoured by left-wing intellectuals were closed down by Fascist authorities in the 1930s and have only recently reopened. Now home to more fur coats than anti-Fascists, the place is still a worthwhile stop. Expect to be looked down upon by the snooty waiters if you're not suited and booted.

Pasticcerie

Pintauro

Via Toledo 275 (081 417 339). Funicular Centrale to Augusteo/bus 24, C22, C25, C57. **Open** 9.15am-8pm Mon-Sat. Closed Aug. **No credit cards.** **Map** p313 1A.

This tiny, very basic *pasticceria* serves a traditional but limited selection of delicious *dolci* from its no-nonsense marble counter. The *sfogliatelle* and *babà* are excellent, if somewhat oily. The service has no frills either, with surliness a feature.

Gelaterie

Gelateria della Scimmia

Piazza Trieste e Trento 54 (081 410 322). Funicular Centrale to Augusteo/bus 24, C22, C25, C57. **Open** *May-Aug* 7.30am-midnight daily. *Sept-Apr* 7.30am-12.30am daily. **No credit cards. Map** p313 1A.
You'll find the same scrummy ice-cream as at its counterpart in piazza Carità (*see p126*), but this more central branch also has a bar and *pasticceria*.

Port & University

Pasticcerie

Attanasio

Vico Ferrovia 2-3 (081 285 675). Metro Piazza Garibaldi/bus R2. **Open** 6.30am-8pm Tue-Sun. Closed July (maybe). **No credit cards. Map** p310 2B.
It's a bit out of the way, but Attanasio is worth tracking down as it makes the finest *sfogliatelle* in the city and, therefore, the world: fluffy, sweet and spicy ricotta cheese wrapped in light flaky pastry, hot out of the oven. Near the railway station, this is perfect for last-minute stocking up as you depart.

Dolcezze Siciliane

Piazzale Immacolatella Vecchia (081 552 1990). Bus 24, R3, C25. **Open** 7.30am-7.30pm Tue-Sat; 7.30am-2pm Sun. Closed 2wks July & Aug. **No credit cards. Map** p311 2C.

Enjoy super *sfogliatelle* at **Attanasio**.

Fresh *dolci* from Palermo delivered daily. The shop is inside the port; enter from piazza Municipio, turn left and keep walking – it's worth the effort.

Centro storico

Cafés & bars

Luise a San Domenico

Piazza San Domenico Maggiore 5/8 (081 552 8740). Metro Museo or Piazza Cavour/bus CS, E1, R2. **Open** *Mar-Oct* 8am-midnight Mon-Fri; 8am-3am Sat, Sun. *Nov-Feb* 7.30am-9pm Mon-Fri; 7.30am-2am Sat, Sun. **Credit** AmEx, MC, V. **Map** p311 1C.
There's a good choice of sweet and savoury foods, lots of tables inside and out, friendly service and daily newspapers to read make this the best bar on this lively piazza. Customers include everyone from local buskers and beggars to students and the area's many arty types.

Pasticcerie

Scaturchio

Piazza San Domenico Maggiore 19 (081 551 7031/081 551 6944). Metro Museo or Piazza Cavour/bus CS, E1, R2. **Open** 7.30am-8.30pm daily. Closed 2wks Aug. **Credit** AmEx, DC, MC, V. **Map** p311 1C.
Right on bustling piazza San Domenico Maggiore, Scaturchio is the place for delicious *sfogliatelle*, *millefoglie* and *sachertorten*. Watch the world walking along Spaccanapoli from the tables on the square, or nip around to the kitchens behind where the owner will explain the finer details of Neapolitan pastry-making.

Toledo & Sanità

See also p157 **Intra Moenia**.

Cafés & bars

Bar Mexico

Piazza Dante 86 (081 549 9330). Metro Dante/bus 24, R1, R4. **Open** 7.30am-8.30pm Mon-Sat. Closed 2wks Aug. **No credit cards. Map** p311 1C.
Arguably the best espresso in Naples, but beware – it comes served with sugar already added, making it fairly treacly stuff. The Mexico also sells a wide range of excellent, freshly roasted coffee; try the Harem or Moana blend. The *frappe di caffè* (iced coffee whisked up to pure froth) is a real treat.

Caffè dell'Epoca

Via Costantinopoli 82 (081 402 794). Metro Dante or Museo/bus 24, R1, R4. **Open** 7.30am-10pm Mon-Sat; 7.30am-2pm Sun. **No credit cards. Map** p311 1C.
Established in 1886, the Epoca serves a serious espresso, plus good *cornetti* (croissants) and other breakfast pastries. The decor is uninspiring, but as

Eat, Drink, Shop

Acquafrescai

In those not-so-distant days when Naples' drinking water was decidedly insalubrious, Neapolitans headed for the streetside stall of their nearest *acquafrescaio* (fresh-water seller) for a refreshing glass of mineral water. Most of these stalls have disappeared, but a few, including some magnificent 19th-century examples, remain. These days they sell much more than cholera-free water.

Perhaps the most tempting thirst-quencher on a steamy day is the fizzing *spremuta di limone*: the stall-holder takes a few huge, fresh lemons, squeezes them with an old-fashioned mechanical press, then adds a dash of fizzy water and – on request and advisedly – a teaspoon of bicarbonate of soda (sugar may also be offered, but it's best without). The bicarbonate makes the liquid fizz ferociously; you have to drink the mixture down in one. (It is a fine hangover cure.)

Look out for the splendid old marble-and-brass counter in **piazza Teodoro Monticelli** (map p311 1C); it's often closed due to the owner's advanced age, but opens more frequently in the summer. Next to the Pizzeria Sorbillo on **via Tribunale** (map p311 1C) is a marble-topped counter run by an extremely friendly old lady. There are slightly more

modern zinc-topped counters on **piazza Trieste e Trento**, next to the newspaper kiosk (map p313 1A; *pictured*), **via Monteoliveto** (map p311 1C), **via Chiaia** (map p313 1A; next to the Teatro Sannazzaro), **via Concezione a Montecalvario** (map p312 2A; the narrow street leading up to the Quartieri Spagnoli after the Rinascente department store) and the **Riviera di Chiaia** (map p313 2C; at the point where the road forks into two after the Villa Comunale).

the café is near the School of Fine Art, it often exhibits students' work. There are a couple of tables outside during the summer months.

Gelaterie

Gelateria della Scimmia

Piazza Carità 4 (081 552 0272). Funicular Centrale to Augusteo/metro Montesanto/bus R1, E3. **Open** *Apr-Sept* 10am-midnight daily. *Oct-Mar* 10am-9.30pm Mon, Tue, Thur, Fri; 10am-midnight Sat, Sun. **No credit cards. Map** p312 2A.
One of the city's oldest and most renowned *gelaterie*. It's sparsely furnished and often busy. Look out for the interesting chocolate-coated banana on a stick.

Vomero

Cafés & bars

La Caffettiera

Piazza Vanvitelli 10 (081 578 2592). Funicular Chiaia to Cimarosa or Centrale to Vomero/metro Vanvitelli/bus V1. **Open** 7am-midnight Mon-Fri, Sun; 7am-1.30am Sat. Closed 2wks Aug. **Credit** MC, V. **Map** p312 2B.

Like its sister café in piazza dei Martiri (*see p127*), this stylish Vomero hangout is striving for old-world charm yet gets nouveau-riche elegance. There are tables outdoors, and a tinkly pianist plays in the rear room on occasion.

Carraturo

Via Bernini 9 (081 229 8320). Funicular Chiaia to Cimarosa or Centrale to Vomero/metro Vanvitelli/bus V1. **Open** 7am-midnight Mon-Fri, Sun; 7am-1.30pm Sat. **Credit** AmEx, DC, MC, V. **Map** p312 2B.
Carraturo serves great coffee and the best selection of cakes in the centre of Vomero. It's less pretentious than the neighbouring Caffettiera (*see above*), but there's nowhere to sit down.

Pasticcerie

Bellavia

Via L Giordano 158 (081 578 9684). Metro Collana/bus V1. **Open** 8am-9pm Tue-Sat; 7.30am-9.30pm Sun. Closed Aug. **Credit** AmEx, DC, MC, V. **Map** p312 2B.
Specialises in Sicilian cakes, including superlative *cannoli* (no easy thing to find in Naples) as well as impressive birthday cakes.

Gelaterie

Otranto

*Via Scarlatti 78 (081 558 7498). Metro Vanvitelli/
bus V1.* **Open** *May-Sept* 10am-midnight Mon, Tue,
Thur-Sun; *Oct-Apr* 10am-10pm Mon, Tue, Thur-Sun.
No credit cards. Map p312 2B.
Don't let the sparse atmosphere and minimal furnishings put you off: ice-cream experts have this
place down as one of the finest in the city. Worth
checking out, even if you happen to be in Naples in
the middle of winter.

Chiaia to Posillipo

Cafés & bars

Bar Guida

*Via dei Mille 46, Chiaia (081 426 570). Metro
Piazza Amedeo/bus C24, C25.* **Open** 7.30am-9pm
Mon-Sat. Closed 2wks Aug. **No credit cards.
Map** p313 1B.
Located slap in the middle of this swish part of
town, Guida offers a good range of drinks and light
lunches (get the staff to make up a sandwich by
choosing from what's on offer in the food cabinet).
There are a few seats where you can rest your
weary feet after hitting the shops.

Caffè Amadeus

*Piazza Amedeo 5, Chiaia (081 761 3023). Metro
Piazza Amedeo/bus C24, C25.* **Open** 7am-3am daily.
Credit AmEx, MC, V. **Map** p313 1B.
There's not much space inside, but from the tables
in the piazza you can observe the youth of Naples
indulging in their customary evening pastimes of
posing on Vespas, chatting, and insouciantly causing major traffic congestion.

La Caffettiera

*Piazza dei Martiri 30, Chiaia (081 764 4243). Bus
C25.* **Open** *May-Oct* 8am-midnight daily. *Nov-Apr*
8am-10pm Mon-Fri; 7am-midnight Sat; 8am-11pm
Sun. Closed 2wks Aug. **Credit** MC, V. **Map** p313 1A.
La Caffettiera has the service and decor of the coffee houses of the past; it's only the atmosphere that's
not quite right. There are tables outside in a lovely
piazza surrounded by designer shops, and customers who appear either to have just jumped off a
yacht or to be about to clinch a mega-bucks deal.
The blue-rinse contingent lurks inside. Not cheap.

The ice-cream challenge

Far from being a relaxing treat, procuring
an ice-cream in Naples inevitably involves
immense amounts of exhausting decision-
making: just as well that the end result
makes it all worthwhile.

First, select your product. Where a *gelateria*
boasts *produzione proprio*, it means the
ice-cream is made right there on the
premises (the claim is usually true); this is
generally the best quality ice-cream, although
standards obviously depend on the *gelateria*
in question. *Produzione artigianale* means
the ice-cream is home-made (in other words,
not mass-produced), though not necessarily
on the premises.

Second, there's the question of the nature
and size of your ice-cream vehicle: *coppetta*
(tub), *cono* (cone) and *brioches* (buns) usually
begin at €1, then rise to accommodate ever-
larger quantities. Even your basic €1 cone,
however, always entitles you to two flavours.

Last but not least, there are the flavours,
and most *gelaterie* offer a bewildering choice.
The flavours break down into *crema* (creamy
ones) and *frutta* (fruit). Here are some of
the most popular among the former.
Caffè: coffee, often combined with hazelnut.
Fior di latte: cream.
Nocciola: hazelnut.

Stracciatella: plain ice-cream with fragments
of crunchy chocolate.
Zabaglione: ultra-creamy, very sweet ice-
cream made with eggs and Marsala wine.

The classic combination for fruit ice-creams
is *fragola e limone* (strawberry and lemon),
but there's nothing stopping you branching
out into more exotic flavours, such as *fichi
d'india* (prickly pear), *limoncello* or liquorice
if you fancy something different.

To make the choice even more difficult,
most *gelaterie* also offer a vast selection of
sorbetti (sorbets) and *semifreddi* (a halfway
house between mousse and ice-cream), both
of which can be served with or without *panna*
(sweetened whipped cream).

Another traditional summer treat is *granita
di limone*, a rough-cut version of sorbet found
both in *gelaterie* and on stalls scattered
around the city during the warmer months.
Some stalls also serve *grattacheccha*, an
even rougher sorbet, with ice scraped on
demand off a large chunk and doused with
flavoured syrup or lemon juice. Though they
may not always look very salubrious, these
streetside stalls are generally perfectly clean.
If in doubt, frequent the ones mobbed by
locals: Neapolitans are as fussy about food
hygiene as they are about flavour.

Eat, Drink, Shop

You can't beat the *babà* at **Remy Gelo**.

Cimmino's delicious selection of cakes and pastries (try the *mimosa* or *torta al cioccolato bianco*) can be consumed at pavement tables opposite the bar, which are pleasant when not engulfed by fumes from rush-hour traffic. A popular place with local lawyers and yuppies, who take their *aperitivi* here.

Moccia
Via San Pasquale a Chiaia 21-22, Chiaia (081 411 348). Bus C25. **Open** 8am-9pm Mon, Wed-Sun. Closed 2wks Aug. **Credit** AmEx, DC, MC, V. **Map** p313 1B.
One of the most famous cake shops in the city, with prices to match its reputation. Try the *fungo al cioccolato*, a mushroom-shaped choux pastry filled with chocolate, or a slice of the excellent *pastiera*.

Gelaterie

Chalet Ciro
Via Caracciolo, Mergellina (081 669 928). Metro Mergellina/bus 140, C24, R3. **Open** 6.45am-2am Mon, Tue, Thur-Sun. **No credit cards.** **Map** p313 2C.
One of the greats of Neapolitan ice-cream: locals will take the trip right across the city just to eat here. After making your choice from the apparently infinite selection, sit outside and watch the boats coming and going in the port of Mergellina.

Gelateria Bilancione
Via Posillipo 238B, Posillipo (081 769 1923). Bus 140. **Open** *Mar-July, Sept, Oct* 7am-1am Tue-Sun. *Aug* 5pm-1am Tue-Sun. *Nov-Feb* 7am-11pm Tue-Fri; 7am-1am Sat, Sun. **No credit cards.** **Map** p314.
This is one of Naples' most traditional *gelaterie*. The fantastically flavoured ice-creams and mouthwatering sorbets ensure the place is always packed, and there are spectacular views across Naples from the benches opposite the shop.

Remy Gelo
Via Galiani 29, Mergellina (081 667 304). Metro Mergellina/bus R3. **Open** *Apr-Sept* 9am-midnight daily. *Oct-Mar* 9am-midnight Tue-Sun. **No credit cards.** **Map** p313 2C.
One of the most renowned of Naples' *gelaterie*, though experts reckon it has lost ground to Ciro and Bilancione (for both, *see above*). Remy offers a huge range of ice-creams, sorbets, *semifreddi* (ice-cream cakes) served in different-sized tubs, pots and cones, all made on the premises. There's also a delicious *babà* filled with ice-cream.

La Torteria
Via Filangieri 75, Chiaia (081 405 221). Bus C25. **Open** 7am-10.30pm daily. Closed 1wk Aug. **Credit** AmEx, MC, V. **Map** p313 1A.
Produced in limited quantities by a family company in the area, one of the specialities served at La Torteria is unusual fruit flavours packed into the peel or shell of the fruit itself. Like the artistic cakes, the ice-cream walnuts, apples and mandarins look beautiful and taste even better.

Chalet Primavera
Largo Barbaia 1, Mergellina (081 681 705). Metro Mergellina/bus 140, C24, R3. **Open** 8.30am-1am daily. **No credit cards.** **Map** p313 2C.
One of the several 'chalets' along this stretch of the seafront. Twenty years ago these places were the height of Neapolitan chic; now they're deliciously tacky. Admire the stunning views across the bay, surreally interrupted by large portly families, courting teens, kids hanging out of cars, the old rusty boats in the small port, the roar of traffic at weekends. An experience of the essence of Napoli.

Pinterré
Via Partenope 12, Chiaia (081 764 9822). Bus C25. **Open** 9am-3pm Mon-Thur, Sun; 9am-5pm Fri, Sat. Closed 2wks Aug. **Credit** MC, V. **Map** p313 2A.
This large pavement café is packed full of Naples' idle rich (or aspirers to the label), especially in summer. Its excellent sea view is spoiled only by a busy road between customers and the seafront. Pinterré is an ideal spot for people-watching and scrutinising the latest in designer gear and affectations. Snacks are fresh and include pizza and good *dolci*.

Pasticcerie

Bar Cimmino
Via Filangieri 12-13, Chiaia (081 418 303). Bus C25. **Open** *Oct-Apr* 7am-10.30pm daily. *May-Sept* 7am-10.30pm Mon-Thur; 7am-1am Fri-Sun. Closed Aug (maybe: phone to check). **No credit cards.** **Map** p313 1A.

Shops & Services

Small is *bellissima* in this city bursting with intriguing stores and exuberant street markets.

Famous **Salumeria Rognoni**. *See p135.*

Anton Chekhov, driven to a rare burst of *joie de vivre* by Naples' retail scene, enthused, 'and the shops? Enough to make your head spin! Splendid!' The city is still a shopper's paradise, with a mixture of energy and chaos that makes it exciting and infuriating in equal measure.

It's just as well that most stores still close for lunch or you could literally shop till you drop. There's something to please every taste and budget. Neapolitans, being the fussbudgets that they are, ensure that quality is high.

You'll get better value for money and more choice in little shops and markets than in major department stores. And you'll pay for the address in Chiaia: the very same item will cost a lot less in either via Toledo or the Centro storico where bargains abound year-round (but peak during the sales in January, February and August).

WHEN THE GOING GETS TOUGH, THE TOUGH GO SHOPPING

Don't be fazed by window-shopping motorcyclists who mount the pavement and pull up next to you for a peep at the sales. Unless you relish the challenge of elbowing your way through the *passeggiata* crowd, avoid shopping between 6pm and 8pm. Don't carry your wallet or other valuables in your bag where nimble fingers will find them. Be warned, too, that UK and US sizes listed on labels don't always correspond, so try before you buy.

For a touch of old world elegance, take a turn around the Galleria Umberto and up via Toledo, via San Biagio dei Librai and the streets around piazza dei Martiri. Bumping and jostling are all part of the shopping experience, so throw yourself bodily into it and enjoy. For less atmosphere, but a decidedly more restful

Via Costantinopoli: packed with antique shops. *See p131*.

shopping experience, head for via Chiaia, or the area around piazza Vanvitelli and via Scarlatti in the Vomero district. Wherever you go there'll be bootleggers, their wares displayed on the pavement or on stalls, willing to bargain over their music, bags, clothes and sunglasses.

BROWSERS BEWARE!
Naples has three types of shop assistant: the talking clam, the store detective and the lady on the phone who won't deign to notice you. Whichever you encounter, expect a lot of huffing and puffing as you work your way around, fingering the merchandise. *Sto solo dando un'occhiata* will alert staff to the fact that you're just looking. Which may be all you can do in some shops where trying on tops and jumpers is not permitted. Ask to be shown the display items on the shelves (*potrebbe farmi vedere quello?* – 'could you show me that?') or risk incurring the shop assistant's wrath. In the Centro storico, any attempts to speak Neapolitan will be greeted with unreserved enthusiasm; a simple *grazi asseje* (pronounced 'gratzeeyah sighyah') will warm the cockles of even the surliest shop-keeping heart.

OPENING HOURS
Take a well-earned break when the majority of shops close for lunch from about 1.30pm to 4.30pm. Some clothes and food shops now open on Sunday mornings, particularly around Montesanto and the Centro storico. Some food

shops still close on Thursday afternoon in winter (November to April) and on Saturday afternoon in summer. The majority of non-food shops are closed on Monday mornings and on Saturday afternoons during summer (May to October). Neapolitans abandon the city in August, so don't be surprised to find many shops closed for the whole month.

QUICK-CHANGE ARTISTS
If the name over the door doesn't correspond with the address given in this chapter, check inside. Chances are it's the same business trading under a different name.

Antiquarian books & prints

See also p136 **Arte e Gioielli**.

Bowinkel
Piazza dei Martiri 24, Chiaia (081 764 4344). Bus C25, C28/tram 1, 4. **Open** 9am-1.30pm, 4-7.30pm Mon-Fri; 9am-1.30pm Sat. Closed Aug. **Credit** AmEx, DC, MC, V. **Map** p313 1A.
Naples' most respected dealer in period water-colours, prints and photographs. Delivers abroad.

Colonnese
Via San Pietro a Maiella 33, Centro storico (081 459 858/www.colonnese.it). Funicular Montesanto to Montesanto/metro Dante or Montesanto/bus R1, R2, R3. **Open** 9am-1.30pm, 4-7.30pm Mon-Fri; 9am-1.30pm Sat. Closed 1wk Aug. **Credit** AmEx, DC, MC, V. **Map** p311 1C.

Passionate publishers and collectors of books on the arts, holistic medicine, magic and history for adults and children. New, as well as old and rare publications, photographs and prints vie for space in this bookworm's paradise. Look out for the distinctive Neapolitan tarot and playing cards. Ask about literary tours and cultural events.

Antiques

You'll find antiques shops all over Naples, but the best known are in via Costantinopoli in the Centro storico and around piazza Martiri in Chiaia (*see also p138* **Markets**).

Campobasso

Via Carlo Poerio 17, Chiaia (081 764 0770). Bus C25, C28/tram 1, 4. **Open** 10am-1.30pm, 4.30-8pm Mon-Sat. Closed Aug. **Credit** AmEx, DC, MC, V. **Map** p313 1A.
Campobasso specialises in Neapolitan religious artefacts dating back to the 17th century. Gems include portraits of the Virgin embroidered with precious stones, waxen cherubs reclining in beds of filigree flowers under glass domes, votive offerings and saints' relics.

Mario Giordano

Via Costantinopoli 100-100A, Centro storico (081 210 946). Metro Dante/bus R1, R2, R3. **Open** 9am-1.30pm, 4-7.30pm Mon-Fri; 9am-1.30pm Sat. **Credit** AmEx, DC, MC, V. **Map** p311 1C.
A very fairly priced range of interesting antique furniture and ceramics, prints and exquisite reproductions of antique Neapolitan furniture made from recycled wood is kept here. Ask Mario about the monthly antiques market he organises at the Maschio Angioino (*see p59*).

Artist supplies, stationery & photocopying

Cartolerie (stationery shops) abound throughout the city and many also provide a photocopying and faxing service.

Gambardella

Largo Corpo di Napoli 3, Centro storico (081 552 1333/nilocarta@tin.it). Bus E1. **Open** 9am-7pm Mon-Fri; 9am-1.30pm Sat. Closed 3wks Aug. **Credit** AmEx, DC, MC, V. **Map** p311 1C.
An insane paper chase of a shop containing over 480 paper creations, many of them created in-house. The place is floor to ceiling with wrapping paper, boxes, cards, stationery and ribbons, mostly handmade.

E Graphe

Piazza Miraglia 391, Centro storico (081 446 266/egraphe@tin.it). Metro Dante/bus R1, R3. **Open** 9am-2pm, 4-7.30pm Mon-Fri; 9am-1pm Sat. Closed Aug. **Credit** AmEx, DC, MC, V. **Map** p313 1C.
Designs in recycled paper. There's a wonderful selection of coloured inks in quaint little wax-sealed

bottles, and calligraphy pens. Have a look at the unusual Italian parking signs. Graphe also has a photocopying and faxing service.

Penna & Carta 1989

Largo Vasto a Chiaia 86, Chiaia (081 418 724/www.pec-it.com). Bus C25/tram 1, 4. **Open** 10am-1.30pm, 4.30-8pm Mon-Sat. Closed Aug. **Credit** AmEx, DC, MC, V. **Map** p313 1B.
As well as a beautiful selection of top-quality stationery and accessories, and a truly wonderful line in fountain pens, this shop also sells pretty hand-blown glass pens.

Books

You'll find the best range of antiquarian (*see also p130* **Antiquarian books**) and second-hand bookshops in the Centro storico, between *vie* Costantinopoli and San Biagio dei Librai, and around Port'Alba (*see p78*). A growing number of bookshops stock novels, art, history and travel books in English and other languages. The café bookshops in piazza Bellini in the Centro storico are worth browsing for Neapolitan imprints and memorabilia. **Eva Luna**, in the same piazza, has a fine selection of women's, gay and Neapolitan publications, as well as antiques and stationery.

Libreria Feltrinelli

Piazza dei Martiri/via Santa Caterina a Chiaia 23, Chiaia (081 240 5411). Bus C25, C28/tram 4. **Open** 10am-10pm Mon-Fri; 10am-11pm Sat; 10am-2pm, 4-9pm Sun. **Credit** AmEx, DC, MC, V. **Map** p313 1A.
Naples' biggest bookshop has three floors of stationery, music, videos – and books. On the lower level there's a wide selection of novels in English, along with some of the latest publications on Neapolitan history and culture. Recharge your batteries in the café on the same floor. Theatre and concert bookings on the first floor.
Branch: via San Tommaso d'Aquino 70, Toledo (081 552 1436/fax 081 552 4468).

Bowinkle for prints. *See p130.*

Eat, Drink, Shop

Me**eting**

furniture

antiques accessories antique prints pictures furniture

Via Chiatamone, 5/F

80121 Napoli

tel. 081 7643410

fax 081 7649529

80121 Napoli

Universal Books

Corso Umberto 22, Port & University (081 252 0069). Bus 105, C55, R2. **Open** 9am-1pm, 4-7pm Mon-Fri; 9am-noon Sat. Closed 2wks Aug. **Credit** DC, MC, V. **Map** p311 1C.

Step through the courtyard to escape the madding crowd and peruse Universal's selection of literature and non-fiction in English.

Department stores

Coin

Via Scarlatti 88/100, Vomero (081 578 0111). Funicular Montesanto to via Morghen, Centrale to piazzetta Fuga or Chiaia to via Cimarosa/ bus C36. **Open** *Sept-June* 10am-1.45pm, 4.20-8pm Mon-Sat. *July, Aug* 10am-1.45pm, 4-8pm Mon-Fri; 10am-1.45pm Sat. **Credit** AmEx, DC, MC, V. **Map** p312 2B.

There's a good household and furnishings department at this store, which also hosts regular music, art and film events.

La Rinascente

Via Toledo 340, Toledo (081 411 511). Funicular Centrale to Augusteo/metro Diaz/bus R1, R2, R4. **Open** 9am-8pm Mon-Sat; 10am-2pm, 5-8pm Sun. **Credit** AmEx, DC, MC, V. **Map** p312 2A.

Known for its wide choice of underwear and perfumes, La Rinascente also sells clothes and household goods.

Upim

Via Nisco 11, Chiaia (081 417 520). Funicular Chiaia to Parco Margherita/metro Piazza Amedeo/bus C25. **Open** 9am-1pm, 4-8pm Mon-Sat; 10am-1.30pm, 4.30-8pm Sun. **Credit** AmEx, DC, MC, V. **Map** p313 1B.

You'll discover plenty of cheap clothes, cosmetics, underwear, toys and household goods here, but don't expect service with a smile.

Fashion

Every second shop in Naples is a purveyor of fashion, or so it seems. While Neapolitan outposts of large chains are springing up, most stores still reflect the individual tastes of the owner. Explore the Centro storico, via Toledo, the Chiaia district (*see p91*) and the shops around via Scarlatti. But don't forget the markets (*see p138*).

Boutiques

Eddie Monetti

Menswear: via dei Mille 45, Chiaia (081 407 064). Funicular Chiaia to Parco Margherita/metro Piazza Amedeo/bus C25. **Map** p313 1B.
Womenswear: piazzetta Santa Caterina 8, Chiaia (081 403 229). Bus C25/Tram 1, 4. **Map** p313 1A. *Both* **Open** 9.30am-1.30pm, 4.30-8pm Mon-Sat. Closed 2wks Aug. **Credit** AmEx, DC, MC, V.

Eddy Monetti is not only an institution... it's the first word in quality and timeless style. Neapolitans, who in general wouldn't be caught dead in anything not bought new this season, still wear their Monetti trousers bought 30 years ago.

Fusaro

Via Toledo 280, Toledo (081 420 7014). Funicular Centrale to Augusteo/bus C25. **Open** 10am-1.30pm, 3.30-8pm Mon-Sat. Closed 3wks Aug. **Credit** AmEx, DC, MC, V. **Map** p313 1A.

Collars, cuffs, buttons and fronts. Fusaro's top-quality shirts come at reasonable prices.
Branch: via Toledo 327, Toledo (081 412 996).

Garlic

Via Toledo 111, Toledo (081 5524 4966/ www.mediatour.it/napoli/garlic). Funicular Montesanto to Montesanto/metro Montesanto/ bus 24, 105, R1. **Open** 9.30am-8pm Mon-Sat. Closed 2wks Aug. **Credit** AmEx, DC, MC, V. **Map** p312 2A.

Garlic's idiosyncratic range of clothes, shoes and accessories is aimed at those who are stylish, original or very adventurous. Check downstairs for sales.

Marinella

Riviera di Chiaia 287A, Chiaia (081 245 1182/ www.marinellanapoli.it). Bus C28/tram 1, 4. **Open** 6.30am-1.30pm, 4-8pm Mon-Sat. Closed 2wks Aug. **Credit** AmEx, DC, MC, V. **Map** p313 1B.

For more than 80 years, the Marinella family has been providing that extra-special sartorial something for the man who has everything. The firm is most famous for its ready-to-wear and made-to-measure ties, but you'll also find a selection of its own and imported watches, men's scents, jewellery, clothing and shoes.

Maxi Ho

Via Nisco 20, Chiaia (081 414 721). Funicular Chiaia to Parco Margherita/metro Piazza Amedeo/bus C25. **Open** 10am-1.30pm, 4.30-8pm Mon-Sat. Closed 1wk Aug. **Credit** AmEx, DC, MC, V. **Map** p313 1B.

A collection of designer clothes and shoes that veers towards the avant-garde and includes Dolce & Gabbana and Prada.

Melinoi

Via B Croce 34, Centro storico (081 552 1204). Bus 137, E1, R1, R3/Metro Dante. **Open** *Sept-June* 10am-2pm, 4.30pm-8pm Mon-Sat; 10am-2pm Sun. *July* 10am-2pm, 4.30pm-8pm Mon-Sat. Closed 2wks Aug. **Credit** AmEx, DC, MC, V. **Map** p311 1C.

For individual, stylish and less conventional clothing, check out Melinoi's range of Italian, French and Spanish labels. Individuality comes at a price, mind.

Nardiello

Via Scarlatti 195/197/201, Vomero (081 578 3184). Funicular Montesanto to via Morghen, Centrale to piazzetta Fuga or Chiaia to via Cimarosa/metro Vanitelli/bus C36. **Open** 9.30am-1.30pm, 4-8pm Mon-Sat. **Credit** AmEx, DC, MC, V. **Map** p312 2B.

La Pignasecca

The wrath of God – or rather that of a less-than-chaste priest – is responsible for the total absence of pine trees in the once heavily forested Pignasecca (literally, 'dry pine cone'). According to legend, a bishop canoodling with his mistress beneath the pines was robbed of his mitre by a passing magpie. The bird proudly displayed the bauble in its nest at the top of the highest tree. In a fit of pique, the furious prelate excommunicated all the birds in the Pignasecca. When the decree was hammered into the offending tree, it promptly fell, unleashing a domino effect throughout the forest.

Today you won't find a single pine in La Pignasecca. You will, however, find everything else under the sun in one of the city's oldest markets: the best and cheapest fish, vegetables, deli goods, cut-price perfume, fashion, linen and kitchenware.

Begin your tour in piazzetta Montesanto, with its noisy vendors joking in dialect, its bustle and colour: this is the essence of Naples. Get there in the morning and you'll be greeted by a man with a portable music stall and a barking dog. Cars, Vespas and ambulances scream by, but don't let them put you off: these folk have been driving since they were weaned. If it's hot, ask Antonio for a *spremuta* (freshly squeezed fruit juice) at one of the city's oldest *acquafrescaio* stalls (*see p126* **Acquafrescai**) tucked away behind the banana and veg stands.

The crowd will carry you ineluctably along via Portamedina to **Scaturchio** (No.24), where you can enjoy a coffee and cake with pyjama-clad patients from the hospital across the road. Don't forget to look up when you pass the slipper shop at No.18: the balcony decorated with dried fruit and vegetables belongs to the banana lady in piazzetta Montesanto.

Shimmering **Pescheria Azzurra**.

If you blink, you'll miss the delightful and aptly named **Il Buco** (the hole) lingerie shop a few doors up. Unless it's Monday, the **Pescheria Azzurra** (No.4) will be shimmering with exotic fish, the like of which you've only ever seen in a Pompeian mosaic, the enormous head of a swordfish taking pride of place. If you can tear yourself away from the *vongole* (clams), you'll find yourself in piazzetta Pignasecca, the stall-packed home

---

A bit off the beaten tourist track up in the Vomero district (*see p85*) Nardiello specialises in Canali, Trussardi and other Italian men's labels, both casual and classic.

Branch: Centro Direzionale ISE/3 (081 562 7153).

Designer labels

Naples has all the designer emporia you'd expect in a major Italian city with the usual price tags.. Shops are clustered around piazza

dei Martiri (bus C25, C28/tram 1, 4; map p313 1A). You'll find both **Ferragamo Uomo** and **Ferragamo Donna** in the piazza. Tiny via Calabritto is home to a veritable galaxy of fashion stars **Armani**, **Cacharel**, **Gucci**, **Louis Vuitton Italia** and **Versace**. **Max Mara** and **Valentino** are just down the road in via Filangieri. Most designer shops offer tax-free services to non-EU tourists. The majority are open from 10am-1.30pm and 4-8pm Monday to Saturday. All are closed for two weeks in to **Pane** (No.35), a tiny shop bursting at the seams with freshly baked cakes celebrating saint days and speciality breads of the region. Try a piece of the enormous *Montevergine* in *bianco* (white), *nero* (wholemeal) and *bionda* (mixed); the pointy-ended *sfilatino* (a cousin of the baguette and a remnant of French domination); and *freselle*, a dried bread that looks like a sliced bagel (sprinkle with water and cover with your favourite sandwich fillings). Chances are **Music Romano** (*see p141*) is competing with the traffic and the barking vendors by means of its selection of Neapolitan CDs. To the left of Romano's is via Forno Vecchio, an alley worth exploring for its hole-in-the-wall jewellery shops. Moving towards via Pignasecca brings you to **Salumeria Rognoni** (No.38), famous for nutbread and cheeses. If you can't squeeze in the door, duck down via Pasquale Scura to **Antiche Delizie** at No.14 (*see p137*).

Back among the chaotic tumble of stalls and shops on via Pignasecca, pop into **Profumeria Pantera Rosa** (No.39) for some good deals in big-name brands. Across the road, take note of the triperies and their vendors, all of whom are a whiter shade of pale. At **Egidio** (No.34) fill your bags with lingerie and nighties, then struggle upstairs for exquisitely embroidered bed- and table-linen at bargain-basement prices. For kids' shoes, cross the road to **Giusi Baby** (No.58), which has something for even the fussiest. **Spina** (*see p140*), the last word in kitchenware, is at No.62.

By now, you're loaded with booty and in desperate need of chocolate, so nip into piazza Carità, turn right into via Liberio and press your nose up against the glass at **Dolce Idea di Bottone Gennaro** (No.2; *see p138*). Or if it's ice-cream you're craving, try Naples' most celebrated *gelato* at **La Scimmia** (*see p126*) in piazza Carità.

La Pignasecca

Via Pignasecca and surrounding streets, Toledo. Funicular Montesanto to Montesanto/metro Montesanto/bus 24, 105, R1. **Open** 8am-1pm daily. **Map** p312 2A.

Egidio

Via Pignasecca 34 (081 551 8640). **Open** 8.30am-2pm, 3.45-8pm Mon-Sat. Closed 2wks Aug. **No credit cards**.

Giusi Baby

Via Pignasecca 58 (081 552 9175). **Open** 9am-2pm, 4-8pm Mon-Sat. Closed Aug. **Credit** AmEx, MC, V.

Pane

Via Pignasecca 35 (081 552 0299). **Open** 8am-1.30pm, 4-7.30pm Tue, Wed, Fri; 8am-1.30pm Thur; 10am-1.30pm Sat. Closed Aug. **No credit cards**.

Pescheria Azzurra

Via Portamedina 4 (081 551 3733). **Open** *Sept-July* 8am-1.30pm, 4-7.30pm Tue, Wed, Fri, Sat; 10am-1.30pm Thur, Sun. *Aug* 8am-1.30pm Tue-Sun. **No credit cards**.

Profumeria Pantera Rosa

Via Pignasecca 39 (081 551 9591). **Open** 9am-1.30pm, 4-8pm Mon-Sat. Closed 2wks Aug. **Credit** AmEx, MC, V.

Salumeria Rognoni

Via Pignasecca 38 (081 552 0834). **Open** 8.30am-2pm, 4.30-8pm Mon-Wed, Fri, Sat; 8am-1.30pm Thur. Closed 1wk Aug. **No credit cards**.

Scaturchio

Via Portamedina 24 (081 551 3850). **Open** 7am-2pm Mon; 7am-7.30pm Tue-Sat; 7am-7.30pm Sun. Closed 2wks Aug. **No credit cards**.

August apart from Gucci, which remains open throughout. And all will happily take just about every credit card you care to flash at them.

Mid-range fashion

Carla G

Via Vittoria Colonna 15, Chiaia (081 400 005). Metro Piazza Amedeo/bus C25. **Open** 10am-1.30pm, 4.30-8pm Mon-Sat. Closed 3wks Aug. **Credit** AmEx, DC, MC, V. **Map** p313 1B.

On the main Chiaia retail strip, Carlo G has all the latest women's fashion, offering good-quality at very fair prices.
Branch: via Merliani 43/44, Vomero (081 558 6423).

Diagonale

Via Chiaia 218, Chiaia (081 411 914). Bus C25, R2. **Open** 10am-2pm, 4.30-8pm Mon-Sat. **Credit** AmEx, MC, V. **Map** p313 1A.
An interesting range of clothes and fashion accessories geared to please women of all ages. Staff are unusually helpful.

Eat, Drink, Shop

Timeless **Arte in Oro**.

Kids' clothes

From baby's first public appearance, no expense is spared. If prices in the well-heeled parts of town shock you, don't despair: you'll find the big names and quality copies at the markets (*see p138* **Markets**) and in Pignasecca (*see p134* **La Pignasecca**).

Canestrelli

Via Chiaia 131, Chiaia (081 401 954). Bus C25/tram 1, 4. **Open** 10am-1.30pm, 4.30-8pm Mon-Sat. Closed 2wks Aug. **Credit** AmEx, DC, MC, V. **Map** p313 1A.
Stockists of traditional handmade clothing for babies and children.

Pupi Stellari

Via Carlo Poerio 54C, Chiaia (081 764 2515). Bus C25, C28/tram 1, 4. **Open** 10am-1.30pm, 4.30-7.30pm Mon-Sat. Closed Aug. **Credit** AmEx, DC, MC, V. **Map** p313 1B. *
A great collection of fun, well-made and comfortable clothes for kids. Good reductions in the sales.

Fashion accessories

Jewellery & watches

Not known for understatement in their tastes, the Neapolitan passion for the baroque extends to their baubles as well. Don't leave without seeing the city's famous cameos (*see also p213* for cameo factories in Torre del Greco) and ornate 18th-century Bourbon jewellery.

For the best deals in antique and modern jewellery, wander around the Spaccanapoli area (*see p67*) of the Centro storico. For a wider selection at varying prices, try the Borgo degli Orefici (*see p66*), which has been the centre of goldsmithing since the Middle Ages.

Arte e Gioielli

Via Loggia di Genova 6, Port & University (081 201 694). Bus 105, C55, R2/tram 1, 4. **Open** 9.30am-6pm Mon-Fri; 9.30am-1pm Sat. Closed 2wks Aug. **Credit** AmEx, DC, MC, V. **Map** p311 1C.
A delightful collection of mostly Neapolitan antique jewellery can be found here, as well as prints, furniture, clocks and tableware at fair prices.

Arte in Oro

Via B Croce 20, Centro storico (081 551 6980). Metro Dante/bus E1, R1, R2, R3, R4. **Open** 10am-1.30pm, 4.30-7.30pm Mon-Sat. Closed 3wks Aug. **No credit cards. Map** p311 1C.
The Marciano brothers create exquisite copies of classical Roman jewellery in a shop that doesn't seem to have changed since it opened at the beginning of the last century. Unique jewellery and antique items at affordable prices.

Gallotta

Via Chiaia 139, Chiaia (081 421 164/www.gallotta.com). Bus C25/tram 1, 4. **Open** 9am-1.30pm, 4.30-8pm Mon-Sat. Closed Aug. **Credit** AmEx, DC, MC, V. **Map** p313 1A.
Exclusive pieces – at exclusive prices – produced by Neapolitan craftsworkers.

De Nobili

Via Filangieri 16B, Chiaia (081 421 685/www.denobili.com. Bus C25/tram 1, 4. **Open** 10am-1.30pm, 4.30-8pm Mon-Sat. Closed Aug. **Credit** AmEx, DC, MC, V. **Map** p313 1A.
This shop pays homage to the goldsmiths of the past with its exclusive and limited-edition pieces in gold, precious stones and coral. They will make individual pieces on request.

Leather & shoes

Nobody wears a pair of shoes for more than a season in Naples, with the cannier shopper buying his or her footwear and other leather goods from the Pignasecca, Poggioreale or other local markets (*see p138* **Markets** and *p134* **La Pignasecca**).

Famà

Via Toledo 9, Toledo (081 552 5567). Funicular Montesanto to Montesanto/metro Montesanto /bus 24, 105, R1. **Open** 9am-8pm Mon-Sat; 10am-1pm, 5.30-8.30pm Sun. **Credit** AmEx, DC, MC, V. **Map** p312 2A.
Situated in a street of bargain bag shops, Famà sells mostly locally made leather luggage, handbags and wallets at bargain prices. The friendly staff can be bargained down.

Fratelli Tramontano

Via Chiaia 142-143, Royal (081 668 572). Funicular Centrale to Augusteo/bus C25, R2. **Open** 10am-1.30pm, 4-8pm Mon-Sat. Closed 2wks Aug. **Credit** AmEx, DC, MC, V. **Map** p313 1A.

Traditional Neapolitan craftsmanship manifests itself in the superb-quality handmade shoes and bags displayed here.

Parlato

Via San Pasquale a Chiaia 27, Chiaia (081 406 677/www.parlatopelletterie.it). Bus C28/tram 1,4. **Open** 9.30am-1.30pm, 4.30-8pm Mon-Sat. Closed 2wks Aug. **Credit** AmEx, DC, MC, V. **Map** p313 1B.

The Parlato family has been in the leather trade for generations. Excellent quality, original designs: jackets, handbags, purses, belts and bags are sold at accessible prices.

Yien

Via Alabardieri 40/43, Chiaia (081 412 770/ www.spaldingbros.com). Bus C25. **Open** 10am-2pm, 4-8pm Mon-Sat. Closed 3wks Aug. **Credit** AmEx, DC, MC, V. **Map** p313 1A.

If Italian design is beginning to look a touch production line to you, step into Yien for a more individual approach to shoes, clothes, jewellery and fashion accessories.

Food & drink

If you're a foodie, you've come to the right town. Neapolitans shop daily and stick to whatever is in season, which may be why everything looks and tastes so good. The best place to shop for regional delicacies is Pignasecca market (*see p134* **La Pignasecca**). You can get bread rolls, with fillings of your choice, made up on the spot in *salumerie*. Stop for a fresh fruit juice at one of the many *acquafrescaio* stalls (*see p126* **Acquafrescai**). Don't get caught foodless and hungry on Thursday afternoons when most food shops are closed.

Antiche Delizie

Via Pasquale Scura 14, Toledo (081 551 3088). Funicular Montesanto to Montesanto/metro Montesanto/bus 24, 105, R1. **Open** 7.30am-8.30pm Mon-Sat. **Credit** AmEx, DC, MC, V. **Map** p312 2A.

Home of the best mozzarella in town and a mouth-watering selection of meats, cheeses and preserves. Try the aubergine antipasti, *caprignetti* (soft goat's cheese in herbs) and cheeses with *tartufo* (truffles). There's also a good range of local wines to choose from and pasta dishes (made in-house) to take away. It's not cheap, but it's friendly and well run.

Start your **Pignasecca** experience in **piazza Montesanto**. *See p134.*

Markets

See also p134 **La Pignasecca**.
Naples' markets provide high-octane shopping opportunities for bargain hunters who enjoy a challenge and a bit of atmosphere. Neapolitans are passionate market shoppers and don't let obstacles – ie other people – get in the way once they spot the longed-for bargain. Stick out your elbows, watch your wallet and be prepared to fight for what you want. Leave your credit cards somewhere safe: you won't need them.

Bancarelle a San Pasquale
Via San Pasquale, via Carducci & via Imbriani, Chiaia. Bus C25/tram 1, 4. **Open** 8am-2pm Mon-Wed, Fri, Sat. Closed Aug. **Map** p313 1B.
Fruit, vegetables, spices and fish are sold between via San Pasquale and via Carducci. Clothes, underwear and jewellery stalls are in nearby via Imbriani.

Fiera Antiquaria Napoletana
Villa Comunale, Chiaia. Bus C25/tram 1, 4. **Open** from 7am last Sun of the month and occasional Sat. Closed Aug. **Map** p313 1-2B.
Attractive as much for its setting along the graciously decadent Riviera di Chiaia, as for its clutter of furniture, paintings, prints (usually fakes), beautiful antique nativity figures, jewellery and junk.

Mercatino di Antignano
Between via Mario Fiore and piazza degli Artisti, Vomero. Metro Medaglio D'Oro/bus R1. **Open** 8am-1pm Mon-Sat. Closed Aug. **Map** p312 2B.

A great place to go gift shopping for kitchenware, bags, clothes, jewellery, shoes, towels and linen. New, end-of-line and second-hand wares are sold. There's also a good produce market.

Mercatino di Poggioreale
Via M di Caramanico, off via Nuova Poggioreale. Bus C61, C62/tram 1, 4. **Open** 8am-2pm Mon, Fri, Sat (mostly men's clothes), Sun. Closed Aug. **Map** p310 1A.
Famous for its mind-boggling range of shoes, as well as adult and children's clothes, household goods and fabrics. Stock is all-encompassing, from top of the range to tat and tragic seconds, so check everything carefully.

Mercatino di Posillipo
Viale Virgilio, Posillipo. Bus C27. **Open** 8am-2pm Thur. Closed Aug. **Map** p314.
Clothes, shoes and bags. Get there early or you'll miss the bargains.

Mercatino di Resina
Via Pugliano, Ercolano. Circumvesuviana rail to Ercolano. **Open** 8am-1pm daily. Closed Aug. **Map** p209.
This market in Ercolano south of Naples rivals the flea market of Paris, but is on a human scale. Anything from ancient theatre costumes to leather jackets and finely embroidered linen nighties of the belle époque can be snapped up. Combine a trip here with a visit to the ancient site of Herculaneum (*see p211*), right next door to the market.

Enoteca Dante
Piazza Dante 18, Centro storico (081 549 9689). Funicular Montesanto to Montesanto/metro Dante or Montesanto/bus 24, 105, R1. **Open** 9am-8.30pm Mon-Sat. Closed 2wks Aug. **Credit** AmEx, DC, MC, V. **Map** p311 1C.
The Annunziata family have been specialists in fine regional wines for over 40 years. Ask to see their range of local Aglianico, Greco di Tufo, Falanghina and Lacrima Cristi. You'll also find a wide array of wine, liqueurs and champagne from other parts of Italy and around the world.

Cakes & confectionery

See also p124 **The cake ritual**.
In Naples, purchases are still wrapped as if they were gifts, and most especially so in confectionery and cake shops. Chocoholics will find everything they need at the following unmissable locations.

Dolce Idea
Via Solitaria 7/8, Royal (081 764 2832). Bus R2. **Open** 9am-2.30pm, 3.30-8pm Mon-Sat. Closed mid July-Aug. **Credit** AmEx, DC, MC, V. **Map** p313 1A.
Mouth-watering traditional Neapolitan chocolates. Make an appointment to see how the workshop operates. Also open on Sunday mornings in winter. **Branches**: via San Liborio 2, Toledo (081 420 3090); via Bonito 2B, Vomero (081 556 0563).

Gay Odin
Via Toledo 214, Toledo (081 400 063). Funicular Centrale to Augusteo/bus C25, R2. **Open** 9.30am-8pm Mon-Sat; 10am-2pm Sun. Closed 1wk Aug. **Credit** AmEx, DC, MC, V. **Map** p313 1A.

Eat, Drink, Shop

his fresh pasta and exquisite almond *taralli* biscuits, a traditional Neapolitan speciality.
Branches: via Foria 212, Sanità (081 451 166); piazza degli Artisti 6/7, Vomero (081 578 2382).

Healthfood

Tropical Fruits

Via Montesanto 6, Montesanto (081 580 1006). Funicular Montesanto to Montesanto/metro Montesanto/bus 24, 105, R1. **Open** 8am-2pm, 4.30-8pm Mon-Sat. Closed 2 wks Aug. **Credit** AmEx, MC, V. **Map** p312 2A.
When you just can't face another bowl of pasta, turn to Tropical Fruits for a refreshing range of international foods, pre-packaged healthfoods, organic vegetables and supplements.

Gifts

You won't have any trouble finding distinctively Neapolitan pressies in a city with such a rich cultural history and such a strong sense of self.

Drogheria Santa Chiara

Via Benedetto Croce 50, Centro storico (081 551 6444). Bus E1, R1. **Open** *Sept-May* 10am-2pm, 4.30-8pm Mon-Sat; 11am-1.30pm Sun. *June, July* 10am-2pm, 4.30-8pm Mon-Fri; 10am-2pm Sat. Closed Aug. **Credit** AmEx, DC, MC, V. **Map** p311 1C.
Great gift ideas with a local flavour, from hand-painted ceramics to handmade candles, *limoncello* and grappa, preserves and chocolate-coated figs. There's also a delicious selection of sugar-free nibbles. The friendly staff speak English and French.

Napoli Mania

Via Toledo 312-313, Toledo (081 414 120/ www.napolimania.com). Funicular Centrale to Augusteo/bus C25, R2. **Open** *Jan-Apr, June-Nov* 10am-1.45pm, 4.30-8pm Mon-Sat. *May, Dec* 10am-1.45pm, 4.30-8pm daily. **Credit** AmEx, DC, MC, V. **Map** p313 1A.
These souvenirs are unique and witty, with watches, ceramics, gadgets and T-shirts (featuring *bons mots* in Neapolitan dialect) created by the owners. There's also a branch at the airport.

Ceramics

The Naples area is famous for its hand-painted Capodimonte porcelain. Further south, around the town of Vietri sul Mare (*see p265*) at the southern tip of the Amalfi Coast, beautiful ceramics are made, much of which reflect centuries of domination by the north African Saracens, the Spanish and the French. Neapolitan tile work (majolica) rivals that of the Middle East and is still evident on the cupolas and in the churches of Campania (*see p69* **Santa Chiara** and *p240* **The Amalfi Coast**).

Imelda-heaven at **Poggioreale**.

Mercato delle Pulci (Flea Market)

Via de Roberto, Poggioreale. Bus 191, C61, C62/tram 1, 4. **Open** 8am-1pm Sun. Closed Aug. **Map** p310 1A.
Arrive early for the best deals in old and antique ceramics, furniture, bric-a-brac, tools and pure unadulterated trash. Scour the flea market and then stroll up to il mercatino di Poggioreale (*see above*) for more bargain hunting.

Everything in this hyper-elegant temple to things chocolatey is simply heavenly... if you can handle the snooty service. Try the chocolate-coated coffee beans and the flaky, milk-chocolate *foresta*. For a memorable aftertaste sample the chocolate with chilli. If you want to see how its's all done, ring the factory for an appointment (Oct-May only).
Branches: via Toledo 427, Toledo (081 421 867); via Vittoria Colonna 15B, Chiaia (081 418 282).
Factory: via Vetriera 12, Chiaia (081 417 843).

Leopoldo

Via V Colonna 46, Chiaia (081 416 161). Funicular Chiaia to Parco Margherita/metro Piazza Amedeo/bus C25, C28. **Open** 8.30am-2pm, 4.15-8.30pm Tue-Sat; 8.30am-2pm Sun. Closed 3wks Aug. **No credit cards**. **Map** p313 1A.
Reward yourself after a hard hour's shopping by hoeing into Leopoldo's sweets and cakes. Take away

Musical **via San Sebastiano**. *See p141.*

La Bottega della Ceramica

Via Carlo Poerio 40, Chiaia (081 764 2626). Bus C25/tram 1, 4. **Open** 9.30am-1.30pm, 4.30-8pm Mon-Sat. Closed Aug. **Credit** AmEx, DC, MC, V. **Map** p313 1B.
Exquisite handmade ceramics from the south of Italy, sold at very reasonable prices.

Decumanus

Via B Croce 30/31, Centro storico (081 551 8095). Metro Dante/bus E1, R1, R3, R4. **Open** 9.30am-1.30pm, 4-8pm Mon-Sat; 10am-2pm Sun. Closed 2wks Aug. **Credit** AmEx, DC, MC, V. **Map** p311 1C.
Reproductions of Capodimonte porcelain, period ceramics and the type of souvenir that Grand Tourists might have taken home.

Homeware

Croff

Via A Diaz 32/40, Toledo (081 552 3983). Funicular Centrale to Augusteo/metro Diaz/bus R1, R2, R4. **Open** 9.30am-1pm, 4-7.30pm Mon-Sat. **Credit** AmEx, DC, MC, V. **Map** p311 1C.
Household goods and furnishings, ranging from twee to trendy, at competitive prices.
Branch: Galleria Vanvitelli, Vomero (081 5789 698).

Spina

Via Pignasecca 62, Toledo (081 552 4818). Funicular Montesanto to Montesanto/metro Montesanto/bus 24, 105, R1. **Open** 10am-2pm, 4-8pm Mon-Sat. Closed 3wks Aug. **Credit** AmEx, DC, MC, V. **Map** p312 2A.
This shop has teapots, pots, pans and kettles, but most of all coffee pots in every shape, size and colour. So you can pick up a traditional Neapolitan coffee pot for recreating your holiday coffee experiences back home.

Nativity figures & religious kitsch

For centuries, via San Gregorio Armeno has been home to the Christmas crib. Believer or not, you'll find something to please your eye and your pocket, from figurines of priests and politicians roasting in hell to miniature food and animals and sublimely crafted angels.
The street is one long pedestrian gridlock for weeks before Christmas. For a less crowded selection of Madonnas with electric halos and backlit views of Christ levitating over the Bay of Naples, take a stroll round the corner to via San Biagio dei Librai.

Marco Ferrigno

Via San Gregorio Armeno 10 (no phone). Bus E1. **Open** 9.30am-1.30pm, 4-8pm Mon-Sat. Closed 3wks Aug. **Credit** MC, V. **Map** p311 1C.
Don't leave without sticking your nose round Marco's door. His terracotta figures of Neapolitan peasants, biblical characters and street markets are sought by collectors all over the world. The shop is like a fairy grotto.

Health & beauty

Most Neapolitan chemists stock a wide range of homeopathic medicine and can give you informed advice. Look for *omeopatico* signs. Healthfood and exquisitely packaged herbal remedies, essential oils and beauty products can be found in *erboristerie*.

Il Chiostro Erboristeria

Via Santa Chiara 5, Centro storico (081 552 7938). Bus E1, R1. **Open** 10.30am-2pm, 4-8pm Mon-Fri; 10.30am-2pm Sat. Closed 3wks Aug. **No credit cards**. **Map** p311 1C.
Everything for the health-conscious, from herbal remedies to healthfood, can be found in this tiny shop next to the church of Santa Chiara.

Helianthus

Galleria Vanvitelli 34/35, Vomero (081 578 2953). Funicular Chiaia to via Cimarosa, Centrale to piazza Fuga/metro Vanvitelli/bus C36. **Open** 9.30am-1.30pm, 4.30-8pm Mon-Sat. Closed 2wks Aug. **No credit cards**. **Map** p312 2B.
A large choice of natural remedies, healthfood and beauty products. The staff are very helpful.

Officina Profumo – Farmaceutica di Santa Maria Novella
Via Santa Caterina a Chiaia 20, Chiaia (081 407 176). Bus C28/tram 1, 4. **Open** 10am-1.30pm, 4.30-8pm Mon-Sat. Closed 2wks Aug. **Credit** AmEx, DC, MC, V. **Map** p313 1B.
The Officina remains faithful to the original recipes of its monkish founders and everything is beautifully packaged. Let your nose do the choosing. Try the *Acqua di Santa Maria Novella* cologne to combat shopping fatigue.

Perfumes & cosmetics

Profumerie sell cosmetics, toiletries and perfumes (*see also p134* **La Pignasecca**).

Fusco Profumeria
Corso Novara 1H, Port & University (081 283 421). Metro Piazza Garibaldi/bus 14, 110, 125, R2/tram 1. **Open** 10am-2pm, 4-8pm Mon-Fri; 10am-2pm Sat. Closed 2wks Aug. **Credit** AmEx, DC, MC, V. **Map** p310 2B.
Naples' largest range of cut-price perfumes and cosmetics is kept at Fusco. At these prices, it's not worth bothering with airport duty free.
Branch: piazza Amedeo 7, Chiaia (081 682 610).

Music

Centuries of colonisation have left their mark on Neapolitans, who have both an exaggerated sense of pride and a huge chip on the shoulder. Nowhere is this more evident than in music, with its Arab, Spanish and French influences. The contemporary music scene is the result of a resurgence of interest in local culture. *See also p156.* The delicate Neapolitan mandolin, the *ciaramella* horn and other traditional instruments can be bought in shops on via San Sebastiano in the Centro storico.

Fonoteca
Via Cisterna dell'Olio 19, Toledo (081 551 2842/fonoteca@iol.it). Bus 149, R1, R3. **Open** *Sept-June* 9am-9pm Mon-Sat; 10am-2pm Sun. *July, Aug* 9am-9pm Mon-Sat. Closed 3wks Aug. **Credit** AmEx, DC, MC, V. **Map** p311 1C.
You may not find the top ten chart albums, but there's an eclectic range that repays browsing. Staff are always happy to let you listen before buying. For second-hand CDs and LPs, take a couple of steps down the road to No.14 (081 542 2006). The Vomero branch of Fonoteca has new and second-hand CDs, as well as a large selection of vinyl.
Branch: via Morghen 31C/D, Vomero (081 556 0338).

Music Romano
Piazzetta Pignasecca 18, Toledo (081 552 2343). Funicular Montesanto to Montesanto/metro Montesanto/bus 24, 105, R1. **Open** 8am-2pm, 4-8pm Mon-Sat. Closed 2wks Aug. **Credit** AmEx, DC, MC, V. **Map** p311 1C.

Don't be misled by the name. The Romanos specialise in Neapolitan music, from folk to classical and the latest contemporary artists.

Supermarkets

CRAI
Via San Tommaso d'Aquino 29/31, Toledo (081 551 7205). Funicular Centrale to Augusteo/metro Diaz/bus R1, R2, R4. **Open** 8am-8pm Mon-Sat. **Credit** AmEx, DC, MC, V. **Map** p313 1A.
If you're having a bad hair day and can't face negotiating in another language, slope along to CRAI where you can get everything you want off the shelf.

Services

Beauticians

Since time imperial, the mud and the waters of the region's volcanic spas have been smoothing brows and calming nerves. Getting plucked, pedicured and pampered is *de rigueur* for any Neapolitan, male or female. Apart from the local beauty shops, natural spa treatments can be had along the coast and on Ischia (*see p191*).

Dibi Centre
Via Pontano 27, Chiaia (081 681 638). Bus C24. **Open** 9am-7pm Mon-Fri; 9am-1pm Sat. Closed 3wks Aug. **Credit** AmEx, DC, MC, V. **Map** p313 1B.
Waxing, pedicures, facials, seaweed wraps and, for the all-year-round tan, sunbeds.

Liliana
Via dei Mille 16, Chiaia (081 406 971). Bus C25. **Open** 9am-7pm Mon-Sat. Closed Aug. **Credit** MC, V. **Map** p313 1B.
Every type of beauty treatment imaginable.

Hairdressers

Italian hairdressers are closed on Mondays. An appointment is generally not needed, but be prepared to spend a lot of time watching the world go by.

Jean Louis David
Via E Toti 7, Toledo (081 551 6849). Funicular Montesanto to Montesanto/metro Montesanto/bus 24, 105, R1. **Open** 9am-6pm Tue-Sat. **Credit** AmEx, DC, MC, V. **Map** p312 2A.
Speedy, stylish, hassle-free and reliable haircuts for women and men. Choose a style and colour from the JLD catalogues. Shampoo, cut and dry from €25 (there's 20% discount for students). English spoken.
Branch: corso Arnaldo Lucci 135, Port & University (081 282 654).

Manolo Tranchesi
Via V Colonna 14, Chiaia (081 421 678). Funicular Chiaia to Parco Margherita/metro Piazza Amedeo/bus 25. **Open** 9.30am-6.30pm Tue-Sat. Closed 2wks Aug. **Credit** AmEx, DC, MC, V. **Map** p313 1B.

Eat, Drink, Shop

Manolo will keep you entertained in English and a few other languages, too. Shampoo, cut and dry from €36. Women only.

Mimmo Ilardi

Via D'Ayala 17, Chiaia (081 406 527). Bus 25.
Open 8.30am-5pm Tue-Sat. Closed 2wks Aug.
No credit cards. Map p313 1B.
A men-only barber where you can get a shave, a beard trim, a manicure or a haircut. Shampoo, cut and dry costs €18.

Laundry & dry-cleaning

My Beautiful Laundrette & Internet Café

Via Montesanto 2, Toledo (081 542 2162/ mybeautifullaundrette@yahoo.it). Funicular Montesanto to Montesanto/metro Montesanto/bus 24, 105, R1. **Open** 10am-8.30pm Mon-Sat. Closed 2wks Aug. **No credit cards. Map** p312 2A.
Check your email while your smalls take a spin, or leave your washing with the manager and go sight-seeing instead.

Paduano

Via San Pasquale a Chiaia 1, Chiaia (081 404 467). Bus C25/tram 1, 4. **Open** 9am-1.30pm, 4.30-7pm Mon-Fri; 9am-1.30pm Sat. Closed 3wks Aug.
No credit cards. Map p313 1B.
Quick and reliable.

Opticians

There's plenty of choice and you'll pay less for glasses in Naples than further north. Most opticians can make up your prescription glasses in one hour. Cheap ready-made glasses are available from most opticians, and some supermarkets and department tores. Most opticians will replace lost glasses screws for free.

Luigi Buono

Via Toledo 16, Toledo (081 552 4391). Funicular Centrale to Augusteo/bus 25, R2. **Open** 10am-1pm, 4.30-8pm Mon-Sat. Closed 2wks Aug. **Credit** AmEx, DC, MC, V. **Map** p313 1A.
Helpful and friendly, staff here do free eye-tests and a quick glasses replacement service.

Sacco Ottica

Via D Capitelli 35-37, Centro storico (081 551 2552). Bus 24, 149, E1, R1. **Open** 9.30am-1.30pm, 4-7.30pm Mon-Sat. Closed 2wks Aug. **Credit** AmEx, MC, V. **Map** p311 1C.
Your prescription can be made up in one hour by the friendly staff at Sacco Ottica.

Pharmacies

See also **Directory: Health.** Note that the chemists' – indicated by green crosses outside the shop – listed below are only open one Saturday in every two.

Cristiano

Riviera di Chiaia 77, Chiaia (081 681 544). Bus C28/tram 1, 4. **Open** 9am-1pm, 4-8pm Mon-Sat. Closed Aug. **Credit** AmEx, DC, MC, V. **Map** p313 1B.
Service here is very helpful and professional from staff who are patient with foreigners.

Farmacia d'Atri

Piazza Municipio 15, Royal (081 552 4237). Bus C25, R2, R3, V10/tram 1, 4. **Open** 9am-1pm, 4-8.30pm Mon-Sat. Closed Aug. **Credit** MC, V. **Map** p311 2C.
Staff speak English.

Photo developers

Maurizio di Cesare

Via D Capitelli 19, Toledo (081 551 3114). Bus 24, 149, E1, R1. **Open** 10am-1.30pm, 4-7.30pm Mon-Fri; 9am-1pm Sat. Closed 1wk Aug. **Credit** AmEx, DC, MC, V. **Map** p312 2A.
Well-organised and friendly service with photos developed in one hour.

Ticket agents

See also p131 **Feltrinelli.**

Box Office Associazione Culturale

Galleria Umberto I 17, Royal (081 551 9188/fax 081 551 0297/boxoffice@boxofficeclub.it). Funicular Centrale to Augusteo/bus 149, R2. **Open** 9.30am-1.30pm, 3.30-7pm Mon-Fri; 9.30am-1pm, 4.40-7.30pm Sat. **No credit cards. Map** p313 1A.
A conveniently central place to pick up tickets for just about everything that happens in Naples.

Concerteria

Via Schipa 23, Chiaia (081 761 1221/ www.concerteria.it). Bus C28/Cumana rail to corso Vittorio Emanuele. **Open** 10am-1.30pm, 4.30-7.30pm Mon-Fri; 10am-1.30pm Sat. Closed 3wks Aug. **Credit** MC, V. **Map** p313 1C.
Information about, and tickets for, anything and everything that's going on.

Travel agents

Air Spes

Via G Oberdan 18-20, Toledo (081 551 2343). Funicular Centrale to Augusteo/metro Toledo/ bus C57, E2, R1, R3. **Open** 9.15am-1pm, 4-7pm Mon-Fri; 9.15am-1pm Sat. Closed 1wk Aug. **Credit** AmEx, DC, MC, V. **Map** p313 1A.
Olimpia and her English-speaking team make train, ferry, hotel and flight bookings.

Partenotour

Piazza dei Martiri 23, Chiaia (081 764 6565). Bus C25, C28/tram 1, 4. **Open** 9am-1.15pm, 4-7.30pm Mon-Fri; 9am-1pm Sat. Closed 1wk Aug. **Credit** AmEx, DC, MC, V. **Map** p313 1A.
Train, ferry, hotel and flight bookings. Credit cards are accepted for ticket bookings only.

Eat, Drink, Shop

Arts & Entertainment

Children

There's little in the way of green, but plenty of beaches.

When *palazzi* and churches pall, take to the islands...

Arts & Entertainment

The attention that is lavished on Neapolitan *bambini* may be nature's attempt to compensate for the lack of facilities that other Western children would take for granted; space to run around in, above all, is at a premium. This makes Naples a difficult city for children... and for the parents and schools whose job it is to look after them.

Like much of the adult population, Neapolitan children live in and on the streets, bringing a new meaning to the concept of street wisdom. It's not unusual to see two or three children riding (without helmets, naturally) on the back of *mamma*'s scooter, young children smoking nonchalantly, children abusing all and sundry in atrocious language (just be grateful you don't understand) and children roaming the streets in carefree truancy during school hours.

Anyone visiting Naples with children will certainly feel the city's scarcity of kiddy facilities, especially when offspring refuse point-blank to go near another church or museum.

But there are a few public parks, most noticeably the traditional **Villa Comunale** and the **Villa Floridiana** (for both, *see p93*). Alternatively, try one of the newly opened stretches of green in the outskirts, such as **Parco Camaldoli** (*see p102*) or **Parco del Poggio** (*see p103*). But you'll have to trek out to this last one if you're after shiny new facilities such as swings and roundabouts.

When trees and grass get boring, the jetties and breakwaters around the port area and Mergellina harbour provide long breezy walks and the opportunity to watch the ferries and hydrofoils steam in and out.

There is also the occasional child-heaven in the area, such as the splendid **Città della Scienza** (*see p94* **Science city**) in Bagnoli, recently extended and reopened to much fanfare and a considerable amount of whole-hearted praise: multilingual staff help keep kids busy. Closer to the centre, there's the ageing but dependable **Edenlandia** funfair.

But choose carefully, and you'll find 'adult' attractions in the city and beyond that are just as likely to captivate your kids. The four university museums (*see p63* **Musei inter-dipartimentali**) are packed with fascinating rocks, fossils and stuffed animals, while the nativity crib section of the **Certosa di San Martino** (*see p89*) is a sight to behold. For any child with even a passing interest in medieval fortifications, the **Castel dell'Ovo** (*see p56*) and **Castel Sant'Elmo** (*see p87*) allow room for martial manoeuvres. The dungeons of **Castel Nuovo** (*see p59*) are pleasantly grim.

Catacombs (*see p82* and *p83*) may appeal to older children's sense of the macabre; the underground sites on Napoli Sotterranea excursions (*see p53*) are pleasantly spooky, though the otherwise excellent guides tend to be oddly impervious to children's requirements.

Yes, most of Naples' transport system is a nightmare with kids in tow, but the funicular railways (*see p54*) are fascinating; take the Montesanto funicular and watch the winding gear at the top through glass panels.

OUTSIDE THE CENTRE

The volcanic activity of the Naples area is sure to thrill your offspring. Walk them across the hissing lunar landscape at **Solfatara** (*see p99*), drag them up **Vesuvius** (*see p222*) to peer into the crater, or take a trip to Ischia to see steam gushing from between the rocks on the beach at **Sant'Angelo** (*see p201*).

Pompeii (*see p216*) and other ancient sites can be brought alive with a bit of imaginative role play, while the **Pietrarsa railway museum** (*see p211*) is a true delight, however slight your appreciation of trains might be.

ONCE MORE UNTO THE BEACH

When all this has palled, there's always the beach. City authorities insist that the water along the Naples seafront is getting cleaner. That's as may be. But after even a cursory examination you will probably want to put quite a distance between the city and your bathing activities. The shingly **Posillipo** beaches (*see p95*) are close to the centre but are generally unsuitable for toddlers. **Torre**

Go for it!

Neapolitan children get away with any amount of what your mummy and daddy would consider terrible behaviour. Learn to act like them, and maybe you will too.

● Eating spaghetti with a fork? Dead simple: pick up your fork as if it were a hammer. Choose a FEW strands of spaghetti and turn the tip of the fork round on the plate till the strands are all wound round. Put in mouth. If at first you don't succeed, whinge loudly until your parent cuts them up, then use a spoon.

● Not even the hottest, most exhausted or most laden-down Neapolitan granny will accept a seat offered to her on a crowded bus if she can give it to you instead. Don't stand on ceremony: grab it.

● No one in Naples will ever tell you to keep quiet anywhere: they'll admire your healthy lungs. Let rip!

● Mickey Mouse/Charlie Brown/Snoopy: never heard of them? Wise up to these evergreen Neapolitan favourites before you get here. When your parents demand that you stop reading comics and go to see another church you can refuse, saying that you're indulging in a little cultural research.

● Your parents may decide to do things the Neapolitan way and let you stay up until 11pm every night. Offer to put your parents to bed for a change.

● No one will look disapproving if you're taken to smart restaurants: even if you misbehave dreadfully, everyone will think you're a little sweetie.

Arts & Entertainment

The beaches on the islands may be short, rocky and/or crowded, but the water will be cleaner than in the city, and the boat ride is guaranteed to be seriously entertaining.

See p191 for the best beaches on Ischia, *p205* for the Lido on Procida and for various recommendations in the Capri chapter *see p173*. Alternatively, try the beaches on the coast around Sorrento (*see p225*) or along the Amalfi Coast (*see p240*).

SHOPPING

Most main shopping areas have toy shops, but wares tend to be of the unimaginative moulded plastic type. **Feltrinelli** (*see p130*) has the only stock of children's reading material in English. For kids' clothes, *see p136*.

Edenlandia

Viale Kennedy, Fuorigrotta (081 239 4800/ www.edenlandia.it). Metro to Campi Flegrei, then C2 or C3 bus to Edenlandia/Cumana railway to Edenlandia. **Open** *Apr, May* 2-8pm Tue-Fri; 10.30am-midnight Sat, Sun. *June, Sept* 5pm-midnight Mon-Fri; 10.30am-midnight Sat, Sun. *July, Aug* 5pm-midnight Mon-Sat; 10.30am-midnight Sun. *Oct-Mar* 10.30am-midnight Sat, Sun. **Admission** €2.58; day pass to most attractions €8.26. **Credit** AmEx, DC, MC, V. **Map** p314.

Edenlandia is a traditional funfair – it's ageing but the kids won't notice – with a good Big Dipper, Ghost Train, Dodgems and Canoe Chute. Recent additions include a 3D-cinema with regular showings, a 40m (131ft) high Katapult Tower (both extra at €2.60) and a flight simulator (€1.60). The site has snack bars, a pizzeria (good) and a restaurant. Opening times should be checked in advance as they tend to change unannounced. There's also a zoo – slated for closure as this guide went to press – and a busy kids' theatre, with occasional performances in English (*see p165* **Le Nuvole**).

...and/or the beach.

Gaveta at the end of the Cumana railway and **Licosa** at the end of the Circumflegrea branch of the same railway line have sandy stretches, albeit rather insalubrious ones. Alternatively, head out of town.

Grin and bear it!

Children are public property in Naples, as you will soon find out. Don't be shy: it won't work. Every Neapolitan mother and grandmother feels it her right and duty to baby you. The younger and/or blonder you are, the more attention they will lavish on you. Kids, this is what you can expect:

● Old ladies will pinch your cheeks, but don't worry, they don't mean any harm: it's only because they like the look of you.

● Alarmed-looking mummies will come running if they see you tearing about and getting sweaty. They think perspiring is bad for you. Unfortunately, they'll look even more worried if you sit down nicely and stop

sweating: there's only one thing worse than sweat, they believe, and that's letting sweat dry off on you. Best to smile sweetly and play where they can't see you.

● Even on sweltering spring days, Neapolitan mummies will be terribly upset if they see you without your winter coat on; in Naples, children aren't allowed to remove their winter things until it's officially summer. But talk loudly in English and they will soon cotton on – they'll think you're just an odd foreigner who doesn't understand about keeping warm.

● You'll have the bumpiest ride of your life if you're in a buggy or pushchair; maybe it's time to learn to walk.

Contemporary Art

Art is mushrooming in Naples' underground.

Since 1993, under mayors Antonio Bassolino (now head of the regional council) and his successor Rosa Russo Jervolino, the city council and associated institutions have been taking a decided interest in contemporary art. During his two terms of office, Bassolino commissioned works for the *piazze* of Naples, including Jannis Kounellis' **windmill** in largo Ponte di Tappia, the controversial **fountain** by Ernesto Tatafiore in via Scarlatti and temporary installations by artists such as Mimmo Palladino and Mario Merz that loom large in piazza del Plebiscito (*see p61*) during New Year's festivities.

And though Naples – unlike Italy's other major cities – still has no museum of modern and contemporary art, things seem about to change. There's a limited contemporary collection (including Andy Warhol's take on Vesuvius) hidden away on the top floor of the **Museo di Capodimonte** (*see p84*), but plans to flesh this out in a dedicated gallery elsewhere in the city have languished in the pipeline for over 30 years. A huge warehouse on the refurbished Immacolatella dock (*see p64* **Portside**) in the port was given a new lease of life in 2002 as a gallery space for temporary exhibitions and installations; it may yet become the long-awaited gallery. In the meantime, the best time to enjoy large-scale shows of contemporary art in Naples is from May to late September. For three years from 2002, a programme of one-off exhibitions in **Castel Sant'Elmo** (*see p87*) will include such treats as a jaw-dropping exhibition of huge Italian works from the Stein Collection.

UNDERGROUND

Year-round, on the other hand, contemporary art has gone underground in the most ambitious state-sponsored project in Italy. The startling new metro line (*see p149* **Art goes underground**) has become a free gallery of everything and everyone from the local art scene in the past 20 years. The erratic itineraries installed in the new metro stations were conceived by architects Gae Aulenti, Alessandro Mendini and Domenico Orlacchi, and by art critic Achille Bonito Oliva.

NAPLES (NEAR HOXTON)

In response to this gauntlet thrown down by the public sector, Naples' enterprising private collectors and galleries have been slow to

Art outside and in at...

respond. But a tiny new gallery – **404 arte contemporanea**, promoting young artists – has just opened in the seedy area behind the station, light-years away from the fashionable galleries in the Centro storico or the Riviera di Chiaia. Owner Francesco Annarumma was the first to give a one-woman show to up-and-coming British artist Nicola Chamberlain. Moreover, Naples is home to one of the hottest new talents on the international scene: 27-year-old Piero Golia, initially sponsored by **Studio Morra**. Golia has already shown in the 1-20 Gallery in New York.

As in days of yore, both the city and the extraordinary violence of nature in the Naples area continue to inspire contemporary artists. Local gallery-owners in the 1970s rocked the art world by sponsoring avant-garde movements such as Fluxus. The huge earthquake that killed 3,000 people in 1980 hit the headlines across the world and sparked off one of the most fascinating and varied shows of

...Salvator Rosa metro station.

contemporary art ever to be staged around a single event: the **Terrae Motus** exhibition, commissioned by the **Fondazione Amelio** and now housed permanently in the **Reggia** in Caserta (*see p276*) including works by Warhol, Beuys, Twombly, Haring and Mapplethorpe. The tradition of private artistic initiative continues with the **Fondazione Morra**, which has set up the **Istituto di Scienze delle Comunicazione Visive**, where artists' workshops, experimental cinema workshops, visual poems and exhibitions are organised.

The city remains a fount of inspiration to international artists. Mimmo Scognamiglio has commissioned a cycle of laboratories/shows by internationally renowned artists (including Andrew Gormley, Max Neuman and Marina Numez) inspired by and dedicated to the esoteric 18th-century Neapolitan noble inventor-scientist Raimondo de Sangro (*see p73*).

Foreign cultural institutes such as the **Goethe Institut** and the French **Centre Grenoble** sponsor visiting artists and arrange exhibitions: watch the local press for details. Shows by young local artists are also organised in deconsecrated churches, cafés and clubs; for details keep an eye on posters in the streets of the Centro storico and check the local press.

In the summer months, many gallery owners transfer to the islands of Capri (*see p173*), Ischia (*see p191*) and Procida (*see p204*), and open temporary summer exhibitions for the season; again, the local press and free handouts in tourist offices have details.

A useful website for up-to-date listings (in Italian only) of exhibitions in the area is www.exibart.com.

Galleries

Archivio Fotografico Parisio

Gallery: Porticato San Francesco di Paola 10/ Photo archive: piazza Carolina 10, Royal (081 764 5122/archivioparisio@libero.it). Bus R2, R3. **Open** *Gallery* 9.30am-1.30pm Tue-Sat. *Archive* 9.30am-6.30pm Tue-Fri. Closed Aug. **No credit cards. Map** p313 1A.
This fascinating historical archive and permanent exhibition of 20th-century Neapolitan photography backs on to the columns of piazza del Plebiscito. The gallery also sells photos and books.

404 arte contemporanea

Via Ferrara 4, nr Centro Direzionale (081 554 6139/info@adrart.it). Metro Piazza Garibaldi/bus R2/tram 1. **Open** 5.30-8pm Tue-Fri. Closed Aug. **No credit cards. Map** p310 2B.
This tiny exhibition space hosts up-and-coming international and local artists. Chat to owner Francesco Annarumma for the lowdown on who's who and what's what in the local arts scene.

Framart Studio

Via Nuova San Rocco 62, Capodimonte (081 741 4672/framartstudio@tin.it). Bus 160. **Open** 9.30am-1pm, 3.30-7pm Tue-Fri; by appointment Sat, Sun & Aug. **No credit cards. Map** off p310 1A.
Near Capodimonte, this well-established gallery holds three or four collective exhibitions a year of avant-garde and historic avant-garde art by different international artists. It also organises lively debates with art critics.

Galleria Scognamiglio

Via M d'Ayala 6, Chiaia (081 400 871/ mimscogn@tin.it). Metro Piazza Amedeo/bus C24. **Open** 11am-1pm, 4.30-7pm Mon-Fri; 11am-1pm Sat. Closed Aug. **No credit cards. Map** p313 1B.
This gallery near piazza Amedeo holds personal exhibitions by Italian and foreign artists. Mimmo Scognamiglio personally commissions works.

Istituto di Scienze delle Comunicazioni Visive

Via Vergine 19, Sanità (081 454 064/ studiomorra@libero.it). Metro Piazza Cavour/ bus 201. **Open** 10.30am-1pm, 4-7pm Mon-Fri. Closed Aug. **No credit cards. Map** p310 2C.
This large exhibition space shows the work of established contemporary artists such as Hermann Nitsch in one of the most remarkable buildings in the centre, Palazzo dello Spagnuolo. Workshops run by artists are held here regularly.

Studio Morra

Via Calabritto 20, Chiaia (081 764 3737/ studiomorra@libero.it). Bus R3/tram 1. **Open** 10.30am-7pm Mon-Fri; by appointment Sat. Closed mid July-Aug. **No credit cards. Map** p313 1A.
This central exhibition space is the place to come for work by up-and-coming artists.

Studio Trisorio

Riviera di Chiaia 215, Chiaia (081 414 306/ info@studiotrisorio.com). Bus R3. **Open** 11am-1pm, 4.30-7.30pm Mon-Fri; 11am-1pm Sat. Closed Aug. **No credit cards. Map** p313 1B.
One of the most active and well-established galleries of international contemporary art in Naples.

Art goes underground

Contemporary art in Naples has moved underground – quite literally – to a new metro line running from piazza Dante (*see p78*) to Cilea in the Vomero district (*see p85*).

In piazza **Dante**, where a late 19th-century statue of the 13th-century poet bears down incongruously over a new station of the same name, Dante's *Divine Comedy* – an epic tale of a descent into the Underworld – is the inspiration for the works of art specially commissioned for the glass-and-steel station. There are two paintings by Carlo Alfano on the mezzanine level, followed by works on Dantean themes by four more artists: Joseph Kossuth's neon quotation is on the first level; the escalator descends to Jannis Kounellis' powerful and disturbing 25-metre (82-foot) metal panel that depicts shoes and clothing trapped under broken sections of railway lines, echoing the commuters' fleeting glimpse of the work as they rush past; two versions of Michelangelo Pistoletto's *Europe* (the outline in black reversed and superimposed over a red original) are situated above the escalators that lead down yet further into the depths to face a monumental mosaic by Nicola De Maria, before descending to the platforms.

The next stop, **Museo** – true to its name – houses reproductions of pieces in the Museo Nazionale Archeologico (*see p79*) overhead. A striking bronze horse's head and a cast of the famous *Farnese Hercules* statue from Rome's Baths of Caracalla are on the mezzanine level.

There's a dramatic rush forward to the 21st century at the next two stations, which have specially commissioned works by contemporary Neapolitan artists and futuristic designs interacting with the city.

Work at **Materdei** station – situated in an undistinguished, slightly down-at-heel early 20th-century square – has been accompanied by some urban renewal above ground, including a much-needed pedestrian zone where kids' playground sculptures were designed by Belgian Alex Mocika. Below, the station's mosaics are by Fulvia Mendini and the bronze sculptures by Nino Longobardi.

But the most dramatic stop is **Salvator Rosa**, which has two entrances in the run-down, heavily polluted, traffic-choked road linking downtown Naples with Vomero (*see p85*). The entrances are covered with two steel-and-glass spires – a postmodern echo of the spires in piazza San Domenico (*see p68*) and piazza del Gesù (*see p67*) – while an external escalator links the station with piazza Leonardo. The station entrance has been given an artistic facelift with coloured mosaics by Gianni Pisani and playful sculptures by Mimmo Paladino and Salvatore Paladino. Inside, there's a mix of sculptures, panels and installations: note the fibreglass and papier-mâché cars by Perino & Vele.

In **Cilea**, the final stop on the art tube, figurative art is an integral part of the architecture. At each stage of the down escalator, a huge panel draws the gaze upwards to Marisa Albanese's sculptures of helmeted fighters (perhaps hinting at the rush-hour crush?) and Anna Sargenti's disturbing, challenging story of an extreme tango in the ruins of a ghost underground, as well as other offerings.

Film

Movies galore... but mostly dubbed.

Like most Italians, Neapolitans are generally cine-literate, and cinema-going is an enormously popular pastime. This means that there is a good choice of films, and ticket prices are reasonable. But for many, film-going is a social occasion in which the film isn't necessarily the most important thing; be prepared for a fair amount of chatter, not to mention the chirrup of mobile phones. Most films are still shown with an interval (the film is hastily stopped for five minutes while the projectionist nips out for a cigarette).

Look out for *seconda visione* – films that you may have missed first time round getting a second run. Showings in the afternoon and early evening cost less than later on in the evening. Many cinemas also run their own cineforum: usually a weekday evening in which both new and old films are shown at knockdown prices to audiences holding season tickets. At some, there's an animated post-screening debate.

THE CURSE OF THE DUBBER

Neapolitans share the national Italian distaste for subtitles. Any British or American films you see here will almost certainly be dubbed. Naples has two cinemas showing films in VO (*versione originale*, also called *lingua originale*): the **Abadir** (*see below*) on Tuesday and the **Amedeo** (*see p152*) on Thursday. Watch out, too, for the very occasional non-dubbed film in summer, festival (*see p152*) or cineforum programmes.

THE MULTIPLEX PLAGUE

The multiplex plague has hit the city over the past couple of years, in the shape of a few 15-screen mega-venues in the hinterland between Naples and Caserta. This has already resulted in some closures. How other small neighbourhood cinemas in the city will cope remains to be seen.

Cinemas

At 4.30pm and 6.30pm showings during the week, tickets are reduced to €6.20. None of the cinemas listed below takes credit cards.

Abadir

Via Paisiello 35, Vomero (081 578 9447).
Metro Collana/bus V1. **Tickets** €7. **Seats** 500.
Map p312 2C.

This otherwise unremarkable cinema is worth noting for its Tuesday night English-language films – mostly current big-budget Hollywood stuff, but a few more interesting movies too. The evening shows are always packed, so get there early.

Academy Astra

Via Mezzocanone 109, Port & University (081 552 0713). Bus CD, CS, R2. **Tickets** €7. **Seats** 472.
Map p311 1C.

The Astra is something of a Neapolitan institution, offering a selection of interesting European films (which are, however, rarely shown in the original language). Look out for the €3 second-run showings on Mondays. Stop in the bar outside afterwards for a spot of intellectual banter with earnest cinephiles.

Agorà

Via Guantai Nuovi 4-6, Toledo (081 552 4893).
Bus E2, E3, R1, R4. **Tickets** €7. **Seats** 249.
Map p311 2C.

The centrally located Agorà was a porn cinema up until a few years ago when its owners obviously decided that even European art-house cinema had more money-making potential than tits'n'bums. Second-run films (€3) are shown on a Monday night.

Massimo Troisi (right) in **Il Postino**.

Naples on screen

Naples and the surrounding area have provided the backdrop to a vast range of very different films, from Billy Wilder's *Avanti* to Anthony Minghella's *The Talented Mr Ripley* and the fourth and fifth *Star Wars* instalments (in which the Reggia in Caserta – *see p276* – was Queen Amidala's palace).

But Naples generates its own films too, many of which have an important place in the annals of Italian cinema history. By the time the pizza-making Sofia Loren shimmied and winked her way into cinema history in Vittorio de Sica's *L'Oro di Napoli* (1954; pictured), Naples had already established itself with films such as *Napoli milionaria* (1950) from the winning team of playwright Eduardo de Filippo and Totò, aka The Prince of Laughter. La Loren moved elsewhere. Totò, on the other hand, knocked out five films a year – including some of Italy's best-loved comedy classics – until the 1970s.

In general, however, the '70s was an unhappy decade for Naples' home-grown cinema, though Mario Merola's tear-jerking *Il Zappatore* has recently found favour with revisionist film critics. The 1980s, on the other hand, saw the emergence of the stuttering, dialect-prone comedian and actor Massimo Troisi, whose anxious, melancholic and bitingly witty persona in films such as *Ricomincio da tre* (1981) and *Non ci resta che piangere* (1984) dealt with the fate of southerners in a north-centred economy. Troisi was Naples' Woody Allen: able to raise a – somewhat bitter – laugh without lapsing into southern stereotype. At the end of making one of his best films, the Oscar-nominated *Il Postino*, Troisi died in 1994 at the age of just 41.

His rejuvenating legacy lived on, however. In the 1990s a new scene arose around directors Mario Martone, Pappi Corsicato and Antonio Capuano. Martone drew on his background as a theatre director to produce intense, finely acted psychological dramas played out against the backdrop of some of the city's toughest suburbs in *L'Amore molesto* (1995) and *Teatro di guerra* (1998). Corsicato, on the other hand, is Naples' answer to Pedro Almodóvar. His *Libera* (1993) consists of three overlapping, garishly coloured, tackily dressed tales of sex-change parents, housewife porn stars and sentimental wedding singers. It's hilarious stuff, but despite promising beginnings, Corsicato has been slow to follow through.

Capuano has also delved into the darkest recesses of the city for his morally complex, hard-hitting films *Vito e gli altri* (1991), *Pianese Nunzio, 14 anni a maggio* (1996) and *Luna Rossa* (2001) – intriguingly shot stories of complicated lives overshadowed by poverty, corruption and organised crime.

● For a full Naples filmography, *see p296*.

Choose from four screens and a mix of films at the **Modernissimo**.

Amedeo

*Via Martucci 69, Chiaia (081 680 266). Metro
Piazza Amedeo/bus C24, C25.* **Tickets** €6.70.
Seats 323. **Map** p313 1B.

An unusually long, thin space (get there early to get
a decent seat), the Amedeo shows current films –
though usually Hollywood blockbusters only – in
English on Thursday nights.

Galleria Toledo

*Via Concezione a Montecalvario 36B, Quartieri
spagnoli (081 425 824/www.galleriatoledo.com).
Metro Montesanto/bus E2.* **Tickets** €6. **Seats** 300.
Map p312 2A.

Located in the heart of lively Quartieri spagnoli (*see
p77*), the Galleria Toledo is best known as an avant-
garde theatre space. It occasionally runs well-
curated short seasons of films by particular directors
(usually in *lingua originale*).

Modernissimo

*Via Cisterna dell'Olio 59, Centro storico (081 551
1247). Metro Dante/bus 24, R1, R4.* **Tickets** €7.20.
Seats *Sala 1* 450; *Sala 2* 100; *Sala 3* 100; *Sala 4* 25.
Map p311 1C.

Located on the edge of the Centro storico, four
screens offer choices ranging from children's cinema
(with childcare included) on a Sunday afternoon to
showings of restored classics, the occasional block-
buster, and the kind of oddities that will only ever
be seen by a handful of cine-enthusiasts in the
living room-sized Sala 4.

Festivals & summer programmes

Artecinema

*Teatro Mercadante, piazza Municipio 1, Royal
(081 414 306). Bus C25, E3, R1, R2, R3/tram 1.*
Date late Oct. **Admission** free. **Map** p311 2C.

Organised by the well-established Studio Trisorio
gallery (*see p148*), this is an annual three-day
marathon of films about art and artists. There's
always something fascinating (and in the original
language), but it's worth checking the programme
to make sure you don't end up sitting through a
three-hour documentary in Swahili.

Castel Nuovo (Maschio Angioino)

*Piazza Municipio, Royal (081 795 2003). Bus 24,
C22, C25, C57/tram 1.* **Tickets** €6. **Date** July.
No credit cards. Map p311 2C.

This festival offers an interesting collection of recent
and older films – usually dubbed, unfortunately –
in a beautiful open-air space to the side of the
Angevin castle (*see p59*). Films are often followed
by live music.

CortoCircuito

*Venues vary (information 081 410 4401/
www.cortocircuito.it).* **Date** Dec. **Admission** free.

Billed as a festival of short audiovisual communication, CortoCircuito is mostly a celebration of short
films, but also includes adverts, music videos and
video art from all over the world. Quality ranges
from brilliant to abominable, and subtitles and
translations are haphazard. But the great thing
about short films is that if you hate one, there'll be
another along in a few minutes.

Villa Pignatelli

*Riviera di Chiaia 200, Chiaia (information 081 425
037). Bus C28, R3.* **Date** July & Aug. **Tickets** €3.
No credit cards. Map p313 1B.

The Galleria Toledo (*see above*) runs a series of
lovingly curated double bills of new and old films
from around the world (usually in the original language) in this sumptuous villa (*see p92*). Some are
much-loved classics, others utter obscurities and
there are occasional connected musical events.

Gay & Lesbian

Naples' gay scene has far to go; but at least it's got a bookshop.

Despite their po-facedly Catholic façade, Neapolitans have always been tolerant towards minorities, be they religious, racial or sexual. Indeed, the *femminiello* (a very camp gay) has been an integral part of traditional Neapolitan theatre culture since the 17th century and is considered cute rather than contemptible. Terms for gay – from the Neapolitan dialect *ricchione*, to the nationally used *frocio*, *finocchio* and *checca* – are rarely meant as insults. The same tolerance informs official attitudes; police raids in gay pubs, discos or cruising areas are virtually unheard of.

A gay 'scene' in Naples is a relatively new concept. Until the recent past, very few people would admit to being gay, preferring instead to get on with things behind a 'respectable' heterosexual veneer. The term 'scene', however, does not fully encapsulate the wealth of gay experiences you may come across in a city such as Naples. If you're on the ball, you'll discover opportunities in the most unlikely places: just keep your gaydar tuned in.

Gay men who are turned on by construction workers, taxi drivers or uniforms stand a good chance of scoring here. Don't let butch appearances put you off; this is fertile hunting ground as long as you stick to the rules (he's always 'the man'). Whatever you do, don't be too obvious. Allusion is your best tactic: it gives both parties a chance to pull out with no risk or loss of face.

Cruising

Centro Direzionale
Map p310 2A.
Around the Holiday Inn hotel; after midnight and only by car. Dangerous.

Via Brin
Map p311 1A.
After midnight, only by car. Dangerous.

Villa Comunale
Map p310 1A-B.
After midnight, on foot or by car. The park has been fenced, making viale Dohrn (off piazza della Repubblica) the only remaining cruising area. Fairly safe.

If a male gay scene is a new concept in Naples, the lesbian scene is an even more recent phenomenon. Unshackled by the preconceptions of more established gay communities, and launching straight into a post-feminist social environment, Naples' lesbians have been quick to find their own identity. Male and female gays share meeting places and events; most of Naples' gay clubs are managed by lesbians. So new is the lesbian scene that terms for the various stereotypes – *bubù* (lipstick lesbian), *severa* (tough), *totora* (butch) – are all neologisms.

Gay venues are still few and far between. On the other hand, any time and anywhere is good for cruising, so keep your eyes peeled.

Bars & clubs

Most places are straight venues, functioning as gay meeting places one day a week. They don't usually charge an entrance fee, but you are obliged to have at least one drink. Any drinks you have are marked on a slip you receive at the entrance and are paid for on leaving. In the summer, the crowds migrate from the stuffy, packed winter nests to open-air places on the cooler hills that surround the city, or to Capri.

Port & University

Bar B-Discobar
Via Giovanni Manna 14 (081 287 681/338 840 7769). Bus CS, R2. **Open** 8.30pm-3am Sat. Closed mid Aug-mid Sept. **No credit cards.** **Map** p311 1C.
A disco, a darkroom area, sauna (*see p155*), video room and a 'labyrint', as the sign says. There are two bars, one with sofas to facilitate socialising. You'll need Ariadne's thread not to lose your way in this intricate three-level maze of small grottos and narrow corridors. Search hard enough, and you may find your Theseus… or your Minotaur. You must spend a minimum €13 on drinks. All types and ages.

Centro storico

Intramoenia Caffè Letterario
Piazza Bellini 70 (081 290 720). Metro Dante/ bus CD. **Open** 10am-2am daily. **No credit cards.** **Map** p311 1C.
A straight meeting place for Naples' intellectuals, the Intramoenia becomes on summer evenings (from May to September) a catwalk for self-confident gays

to show off their beautiful tans, well-toned bodies and designer clothes. Sit in the open air and relax among beautiful 18th-century buildings and 21st-century bodybuilders.

New Age
Via Atri 36 (081 295 808/338 320 8587).
Metro Dante/bus CD. **Open** 10pm-2am Tue-Sun.
No credit cards. Map p311 1C.
This discobar with darkroom is situated in an underground cavern, right in the Centro storico. After closing time, join the New Age 'ghosts' wandering the Centro. A very mixed crowd is attracted at weekends. You'll have to spend €8 on drinks.

Underground
Troia Assassina, via Santa Maria dell'Aiuto 4 (339 547 7466/338 300 1911/www.theangels.3000.it).
Bus C25. **Open** 10.30pm-2am Sun. **No credit cards. Map** p311 1C.
Near the church of Santa Maria la Nova in the Centro storico, Underground plays revival pop and house music on the lower of two levels. Free pasta is served all evening. There's a fair-sized darkroom. Drinks cost €5 until 11.30pm, €8 thereafter.

Toledo & Sanità

Notting Hill Gallery
Piazza Dante 88A (335 587 0247). Metro Dante/bus CD. **Open** 9pm-4am Sat. Closed late May-late Sept. **No credit cards. Map** p311 1C.
Not exactly a gay nightspot, but a fertile hunting ground. If you're looking for airs and graces, the Gallery is not the place to go. On Saturday nights Naples' alternatives – revolutionary, globalisation-resisting misfits – crowd into this underground hideout. There are those who shun the place, considering it not nearly gay enough, but budding romances and friendships definitely abound. Occasional live music. You must spend a minimum €10 on drinks.

Chiaia to Posillipo

Contatto
Antica Birreria Edenlandia, via Oderico da Pordenone (no number, off viale Kennedy), Fuorigrotta (328 307 1105/vaniajgroup@libero.it).
Metro Piazzale Tecchio/bus C14. **Open** 9.30pm-3am Thur. **No credit cards. Map** p314.
This disco pub with a country American flavour serves pints of beer on wooden tables to a mixed crowd of twentysomethings out for a good laugh. The music is revival pop. There's a terrace in the summer. Drinks cost €5, food from €6.50.

Virgilio Club
Via Tito Lucrezio Caro 6 (081 575 5261). Bus C21, C31. **Open** *Mid June-Sept* midnight-4am Thur-Sat. *Oct-mid June* midnight-4am Sat. **No credit cards. Map** p314.
On hot Neapolitan summer nights, the more sophisticated elite gathers in Posillipo among the heavy

scented pine trees to cool down in the evening breeze. Very classic, very bucolic. You'll have to spend a minimum €10 on drinks.

Elsewhere

Freezer
Via Lauria 6, Centro Direzionale, Isola G6 (081 750 2437/339 210 4142/www.freezerstereo bar.it). Metro Piazza Garibaldi/bus R2. **Open** 11pm-4am Fri. Closed Aug. **No credit cards. Map** p310 2A.
Always packed with extravagant creatures of the night, Freezer is Naples' hippest discobar. Deep in the incongruous Centro Direzionale (*see p103*), it's light years away from the usual Neapolitan baroque: this postmodern club would not look out of place in Berlin or Amsterdam. The minimalist decor and serious-thinking regulars contrast entertainingly with more flamboyant members of the clientele in a typically Neapolitan mixture of extremes. You must spend a minimum €6 on drinks.

Bookshops

Colonnese
Via San Pietro a Maiella 32-33, Centro storico (081 459 858/fax 081 455 420/www.colonnese.it). Metro Dante/bus CD. **Open** 10am-1.30pm, 4-7.30pm Mon-Sat. Closed 1wk Aug. **Credit** AmEx, MC, V. **Map** p311 1C.
In the heart of the Centro storico, next to the Conservatorio (*see p72*), this wood-panelled bookshop exudes mystery and witchcraft. Here you might uncover antiquarian books, modern editions (both new and used), prints, postcards, books on Naples and Campania, and gay and erotic literature – not to mention tried and tested potions for impotence, love and jealousy.

Eva Luna
Piazza Bellini 72, Centro storico (081 292 372/ www.evaluna.it). Metro Dante/bus CD. **Open** 10am-2pm, 5pm-midnight Mon-Sat. Closed 2wks Aug. **Credit** AmEx, MC, V. **Map** p311 1C.
Features mostly women's literature, but also has a large choice of prints and postcards. There's also a public payphone inside.

Mercurio Libri e Riviste
Piazzetta D Salazar 8, Royal (081 240 0371/ www.libreriamercurio.it). Bus C22, C25, R2. **Open** 4-8pm Mon; 10am-1.30pm, 4-8pm Tue-Sat. Closed Aug-mid Sept. **Credit** AmEx, DC, MC, V. **Map** p313 1A.
Located just off piazza del Plebiscito, this is Naples' (indeed, southern Italy's) first proper gay bookshop, stocking a selection of refined books and much more. Gay cult movies, photos, calendars, posters and an internet point are also up for grabs. It's all crammed into a tiny space, but worth a look. Michele, the owner, is very friendly and will be happy to help you find your way around gay Naples.

Gay bookshop **Mercurio**. *See p154.*

Cinemas

There are no gay cinemas as such in Naples;
there are places where male homosexuals
gather to watch male heterosexual movies.
Few see the film though.

Argo
*Via A Poerio 4, Centro storico (081 554 4764).
Metro Piazza Garibaldi/bus CD, CS.* **Open** 9am-
10pm daily. **Admission** €5. **No credit cards.**
Map p310 2B.
The rather sordid atmosphere at this Centro storico
cinema is a turn-on for some. You may find your
long-lost best friend in here during the week. At
weekends it becomes a happy hunting ground for
transsexuals. Not a safe part of town.

Eden
*Via Guglielmo Sanfelice 15, Royal (081 552 2774).
Bus C25, R1, R2.* **Open** 10am-10pm Mon-Sat;
4-10.30pm Sun. **Admission** €5. **No credit cards.**
Map p311 1C.
Eden is situated in an upmarket, central part of
town, and the clientele reflects this.

Events & one-nighters

The following groups organise events and
one-nighters. They have no fixed base, moving
from club to club trailing crowds of adepts,
who wouldn't miss a happening for anything.
The only way to find out what's on the agenda
is to phone and ask.

Angels of the Night
339 547 7466.
The Angels organise gay Sunday events (though the
day may change), popular with the younger set.
Venues change every couple of months.

Other Side Group
335 820 1951/338 345 9007/www.theotherside.it.
This outfit organises Friday and Saturday night gay
parties for younger people.

Gay associations

Arcigay-Circolo Antinoo
*Vico San Geronimo alle Monache 17-20, Centro
storico (081 552 8815/fax 081 268 808/
www.arcigaynapoli.3000.it).* Bus C25, R1, R2. **Open**
5-8pm Mon, Wed, Fri. Closed Aug. **Map** p311 1C.
The Arcigay organisation (www.gay.it), based in
Bologna, is Italy's most serious and most highly
regarded gay lobby. Its Naples offshoot organises
films and events such as poetry readings, often in
collaboration with other cultural associations in
Naples. Welcome sessions are held for new members
on Fridays. The premises house a small bar. Up-to-
the-minute information on bars, clubs and events is
provided. A very young environment.

Arcilesbica-Circolo Le Maree
*Vico San Geronimo alle Monache 17-20, Centro
storico (081 552 8815). Bus C25, R1, R2.* **Open**
5.30-8pm Tue, Thur, Sat. Closed Aug. **Map** p311 1C.
An information point for lesbian events, bars and
clubs in Naples and the surrounding area. Gay and
lesbian library and magazine collection. Small bar.

Saunas

Bar B-Sauna
*Via Giovanni Manna 14, Port & University
(081 287 681). Bus CS, R2.* **Open** 2pm-2am Mon-
Fri, Sun. Closed mid Aug-mid Sept. **Admission** €11.
No credit cards. **Map** p311 1C.
On Saturday Bar B is a steaming disco; during the
week it's a steaming, sensuous paradise. A wander
through the five darkrooms, a session in the jacuzzi,
an exciting massage and a visit to the several private rooms will help you discover your true self.

Blu Angels Sauna
*Via Taddeo Da Sessa, Centro Direzionale, Isola A7
(081 562 5298). Metro Piazza Garibaldi/bus C58,
R2.* **Open** 2pm-midnight daily. **Admission** €11.
No credit cards. **Map** p310 2A.
Naples' first ever sauna, the Blu Angels has a gym,
darkroom labyrinth, two Finnish saunas, a Turkish
bath, a jacuzzi and numerous masseurs spread over
three floors. You'll need to join the Arcigay cultural
association (*see above*; €13 at the door) to get in.

Arts & Entertainment

Nightlife & Music

The scene is small, but you can still party into the small hours.

Given Naples' deep and unquenchable wells of energy, the city has an oddly downbeat club and live music scene. Which doesn't, however, mean that there's nothing happening. On the contrary: look out for posters and flyers around the Centro storico and you'll soon find that though the scene's quiet, it's also quietly thriving.

Rock, roots & jazz

Local musical talent abounds in Naples, and not just among the *posteggiatori* (itinerant musicians) who are likely to come up and inflict a rousing chorus of *O' Sole Mio* on you while you're having an otherwise enjoyable meal in a restaurant. Among the local movers and shakers are **Almamegretta**. They may have a Spanish name, but their music is a heady mixture of traditional Neapolitan melodies with dub and techno sounds. Records like *Sanacore* and *Imaginaria* have impressed the likes of Massive Attack and Leftfield, who have both worked with Almamegretta's charismatic vocalist Raiz.

Other local heroes to watch out for include the **99 Posse**. Having started out as a fairly grim political rap outfit based around the **Officina 99** *centro sociale* squatted space (*see p161*), the Posse have recently lightened up to become a fine pop/hip hop group who retain a fervently left-wing message.

If you're lucky you may catch **Daniele Sepe** performing in one of the centre's bars (or even streets). An unclassifiable saxophonist, Sepe is liable to be found playing traditional Italian music one night, avant jazz the next and Latin American the night after that. His 2001 *Journateri* disc even found him covering an old English sea shanty.

More traditionally based Neapolitan and southern music is best performed by the **Nuova Compagnia di Canzone Popolare** (who have been around for more than 20 years, but are still a heady live experience), **Eugenio Bennato**'s Tarantapower project (rescuing the *tarantella* from being a folk dance and restoring it to the dancefloor) or by **E' Zezi** and their international offshoot **Spaccanapoli** whose 2001 *Anime Perze* recording for the Real World label is a fine introduction to the real sound of Neapolitan music.

LIVE MUSIC VENUES

Sadly, the city suffers from a chronic lack of decent live music spaces. Any reasonably big names who make it this far south will probably end up in the **Palapartenope** (via Barbagallo 115, 081 570 0008/www.palapartenope.it): spacious with a cheap bar, but barn-like and utterly devoid of atmosphere. In summer, keep an eye on programmes for the **Neapolis Rock Festival** (various venues), the **Arenile** (*see p161*) in Bagnoli, or – the best bet – the space beside the Maschio Angioino castle.

For smaller and local groups, check out the club scene: **Notting Hill** (*see p160*), **Velvet Zone** (*see p159*) and **Sanakura** (*see p159*) for rock and dance; **Bourbon Street** (*see p159*), **Around Midnight** (*see p161*) and **Otto Jazz** (*see p161*) for jazz.

TICKETS

Information on – and tickets for – major concerts can be found at **Concerteria** and **Box Office** (for both, *see p142*) or **Libreria Feltrinelli** (*see p131*). It's a good idea to buy tickets for big concerts in advance as there's always a crush for tickets on the door.

Turn up at the advertised times – you never know, miracles sometimes happen in Naples – but be prepared for a long wait before there's any on-stage action.

Nightlife

Everything happens later here. You can digest that big dinner slowly while checking out a nice late-night bar, many of which will be open even after the discos have closed. If you're going to a club, there's not much point in turning up before midnight.

WHERE TO GO

Different areas of the city attract different types of people. Students of all ages, would-be artists, intellectuals and alternative types in general haunt the **Centro storico**, which gets extremely lively on Friday and Saturday nights. Make for the areas around piazza Bellini, piazza del Gesù and via Cisterna dell'Olio, or piazza San Domenico Maggiore and via Paladino. In summer, you won't even need to choose any particular bar: grab a beer anywhere, then wander the streets until you find a congenial flight of steps to perch on and hang out.

Along the bay-front in **Chiaia** and **Mergellina**, Saturday night entertainment is more traditional. What feels like the entire population of Naples and its suburbs take to their cars for a few hours of horn-blowing, minor bumps, scooter-dodging (a necessary skill in Naples) and furious gesticulating. This is usually followed by a 30-minute ice-cream, drink or *passeggiata* (stroll) and then it's back to the cars for the real fun.

If techno and trance is your thing, you'll have to trek out to the Naples–Rome motorway where events – and in particular those organised by the Angels of Love crew (329 163 5445/www.angelsoflove.it) – take place in mega-discos. Be warned: you'll never get there without a car.

GETTING IN
Some bars have small dancefloors where you're welcome to get up and shake your stuff should you feel like it. Sometimes a membership card (*tessera*) is required for admission; there may be a small fee for the card but entry is generally free on subsequent visits.

Most discos charge entrance fees, which may or may not include one drink. In some places you'll be given a card that is stamped for every drink purchased. You are required to spend a minimum amount on drinks before leaving.

Unless otherwise stated, admission to the venues listed below is free.

Royal Naples & Monte Echia

Bars, clubs & discos

Barcadero
Banchina Santa Lucia 2 (333 222 7023).
Bus R3, C28. **Open** *Oct-Apr* 8am-8pm daily.
May-Sept 10am-1am daily (weather permitting: it often closes when it rains). **No credit cards.**
Map p313 2A.
This little bar is on the fishermen's quay by the Castel dell'Ovo; to reach it, turn left down the tiny stairs on the bridge. It's a lovely place to sit on a summer's evening, and particularly popular with less ostentatious seafarers.

Centro storico

Bars, clubs & discos

Intra Moenia
Piazza Bellini 70 (081 290 720/www.intramoenia.it).
Metro Dante/bus 24, R1, R4. **Open** 10am-2am daily.
Credit AmEx, DC, MC, V. **Map** p311 1C.
There's not much to choose between the various bars on this lively piazza, but this one is the largest and also has lots of space inside for the colder

Local hero **Daniele Sepe**. *See p156.*

months. Doubling up as a bookshop and small publisher, Intra Moenia is a great place either for that early morning coffee or that last beer.

Kinky Bar
Via Cisterna dell'Olio 21 (081 552 1571).
Metro Dante/bus 24, R1, R4. **Open** 10.30pm-3am daily. Closed mid June-Sept. **No credit cards.**
Map p312 2A.
Not what its name may seem to promise, this small bar is actually given over to reggae. Neapolitans enjoy their rocksteady and dub, and there's no place better to hear it than here. A DJ-cum-bartender spins the tunes, and there's decent beer and lots of heavily perfumed cigarette smoke. In warmer months the crowd takes over the alleyway outside, much to the discontent of the few drivers crazy enough to attempt to pass. In July, staff organise outdoor reggae concerts and parties on various local beaches.

Party on the streets all night long at **piazza San Domenico Maggiore**

Kukuwaya

Via G Paladino 16 (349 466 1944). Bus CS, E1, R2.
Open 8.30pm-3.30am Wed-Sun. Closed mid July-
mid Sept. **No credit cards. Map** p311 1C.
Kukuwaya is a tiny place on the bar-crowded via
Paladino near the universities, which remarkably
manages to attract dancers as much as drinkers.
There's usually someone grooving away to the
sounds of African music, reggae, funk and drum 'n'
bass on the postage-stamp sized dancefloor. In the
warmer months people spill on to the alleyway outside until the (not so) small hours.

Superfly

*Via Cisterna dell'Olio 12 (347 127 2178). Metro
Dante/bus 24, R1, R4.* **Open** 7pm-3am Tue-Sat;
7pm-3am Sun. Closed July-Sept. **No credit cards.
Map** p312 2A.
There are only half a dozen stools to compete for, so
be prepared to stand in this tiny bar; it's worth it.
The well-coiffed bartender looks after the fine jazz
soundtrack, as well as making sure the drinks and
snacks are of a high quality. Small photographic
exhibitions are held, which are often surprisingly
good. Superfly is a great place to meet up for a drink
before going to the Modernissimo cinema across the
road (*see p152*), the Velvet next door (*see below*), or
for winding up a long evening. In warmer weather,
everyone piles out on to the street outside.

Las Tapas Bar

*Piazzetta del Nilo 36 (333 414 9322). Bus CS, E1,
R2.* **Open** 7pm-2.30am Mon, Wed-Sun. Closed Aug.
No credit cards. Map p311 1C.
There's not much space inside here, but several
tables outside allow mellow drinkers to enjoy the
cool air and the ancient surroundings while Latin-
flavoured music emanates from the interior or the
record shop next door. This is a good place for a
late drink after having eaten somewhere else nearby.
Despite the name, however, there are no tapas to
be had. The statue of the Nile in this little square
is rumoured to whisper indecent suggestions to
lone women at night.

Velvet Zone

*Via Cisterna dell'Olio 11 (347 810 7328/
www.velvetzone.it). Metro Dante/bus 24, E1,
R1, R4.* **Open** 11pm-4am Tue-Thur, Sun; 11pm-
6am Fri, Sat. Closed June-mid Sept. **No credit
cards. Map** p312 2A.
Known to one and all as the Velvet, this warren-like
space is dark, smoky, claustrophobic and atmospheric – and your best bet for a night out dancing in
the Centro storico. Different DJs spin different
sounds (from minimal techno to 1980s revival to
downbeat to rock) every night. Occasionally there's
live music (usually local or Italian dance-oriented
groups). Sit in one of the smaller rooms and chat, or
end up getting sweaty on the packed dancefloor
should you be so moved. The *tessera* (membership
card) is waived for out-of-town visitors, but you'll
be expected to spend about €10 on drinks.

Live music

Sanakura

*Vico Pallonetto a Santa Chiara 5 (339 344 7455).
Metro Dante/bus E1.* **Open** 10.30pm-4am Thur-Sat.
Admission €5 for live music events. **No credit
cards. Map** p311 1C.
A dark, smoky and subterranean place, Sanakura is
popular with the local student population. Despite
murky sound and a tiny stage, it occasionally hosts
good live bands from Italy, as well as Germany and
the UK – particularly from the electronic end of
the musical spectrum.

Toledo

Bars, clubs & discos

Lontano da Dove

*Via Bellini 3 (081 549 4304). Metro Dante/
bus 24, R1, R4.* **Open** 10.30am-1.30pm, 5.30-
8.30pm Mon; 10.30am-1.30pm, 5.30pm-midnight
Tue-Thur; 4pm-1am Fri; 10.30am-1pm, 6pm-1am
Sat; 6pm-1am Sun. Closed Aug. **No credit cards.
Map** p311 1C.
One of several self-styled *caffè letterari* populating
this part of town, the book-lined Lontano da Dove
lives up to its claim with regular poetry readings and
discussions on theatre, art and politics. It's a good
place to head for if you've long since given up rav-
ing for the pleasures of a good book. There's live
music (usually polite jazz) on Fridays and Saturdays.

Sputnik

*Via Santa Teresa degli Scalzi 154 bis (no phone/
www.sputniklub.it). Metro Museo or Piazza Cavour/
bus 24, 110, R4.* **Open** 10pm-3am Tue-Sun.
No credit cards. Map p312 1A.
This is an amiable place with would-be hi-tech decor.
Saturday is dance night; Sunday is more laid-back.
There's food on Tuesdays, and live music on
Thursdays and Fridays. Sputnik also stages exhi-
bitions of work by local artists.

Live music

Bourbon Street

*Via Bellini 52 (328 068 7221/www.bourbonstreet
club.it). Metro Dante/bus 24, R1, R4.* **Open** 9pm-
3am Tue-Sun. Closed July, Aug. **No credit cards.
Map** p311 1C.
Bourbon Street is a largeish centrally located space
dedicated to local jazz, with shows every night. It
usually gets crowded with bright, fashionable
young things. During the club's summer shut-down,
occasional music cruises around the bay are organised; phone for more information.

Murat

*Via Bellini 8 (081 544 5919). Metro Dante/bus 24,
R1, R4.* **Open** 7pm-1.30am Wed-Sun. Closed July,
Aug. **No credit cards. Map** p311 1C.

Arts & Entertainment

This small place attracts a slightly older yet chic and artistic crowd into its fashionable interior. There's live music (mostly local jazz) every weekend.

Notting Hill
Piazza Dante 88A (335 587 0247). Metro Dante/ bus 24, R1, R4. **Open** 10.30pm-4am Tue-Sat. Closed June-Sept. **Admission** €5-€10 depending on event. **No credit cards. Map** p311 1C.

A long, tunnel-shaped club in a cellar on piazza Dante, Notting Hill has recently undergone its umpteenth redecoration and is now thankfully rather more spacious and elegant than before. Bands, however, are still confined to a tiny stage at the far end of the tunnel. If you can't face elbowing your way along to the end, you'll have to settle for an aural, rather than a visual, experience. A long-running fixture on the city's live music scene, Notting Hill hosts everything from local rockers to touring Italian and international musicians. There are also club nights without a band (check out the 'Wednesday Social' for indie sounds, or house and techno on a Saturday).

Port & University

Bars, clubs & discos

Aret' a' Palm
Piazza Santa Maria La Nova 14 (339 848 6949). Metro Montesanto/bus R1, R3. **Open** 10am-2pm Mon-Fri; 6pm-2am Sat, Sun. **No credit cards. Map** p311 1C.

Aret' a' Palm being Neapolitan for 'behind the palm', this small but stylish place is – not surprisingly – located by an incredibly tall palm tree on a quiet square right in the centre of town. Well designed, with a comfortingly long bar, it gets pretty crowded inside at weekends. There's no live music, but DJs spin a soundtrack of jazz and world music so loud that it's audible even if you sit at one of the few tables out on the piazza.

Live music

Vibes
Largo San Giovanni Maggiore 26-27 (081 551 3984/www.vibescafe.com). Bus CD, CS, R2. **Open** 8am-2am Mon-Fri; 7pm-2am Sat. Closed 2wks Aug. **No credit cards. Map** p311 1C.

Situated opposite the Orientale university, the vivacious Vibes is a bar, café, live music venue and restaurant. The interior is attractively designed but very small, though as the tables spill out on to the square, you'll usually manage to find a seat. This is an enjoyable place for a drink at lunchtime or an *aperitivo* before going on to eat elsewhere. On Friday and Saturday evenings, however, it's worth hanging around later on into the night for live music. Daniele Sepe is a regular performer, and there's usually energetic jazz or innovative takes on traditional Neapolitan music.

...and **piazza del Gesù**.

Chiaia to Posillipo

Bars, clubs & discos

Ex-ess
Via Martucci 28/30, Chiaia (081 246 1729/ exesscult@hotmail.com). Metro Piazza Amedeo/ bus C24, C25. **Open** midnight-4am Tue-Fri, Sat; 10.30pm-3am Sun. Closed June-Sept. **Admission** €15. **No credit cards. Map** p313 1B.

Flash, ritzy and chic, Ex-ess advertises itself as a club for Naples' 'elite'. If you want upmarket Italian style (with a house and pumping disco soundtrack), this is where to go, but you'd better dress up first.

S'move
Vico dei Sospiri 10A, Chiaia (081 764 5813/ www.smove-lab.com). Metro Piazza Amedeo/bus C25, R3. **Open** *June, July* 8pm-4am daily. *Sept-May* 2pm-4am Mon; 9am-4am Tue-Sat; 7pm-4am Sun. Closed Aug. **Credit** MC, V. **Map** p311 1A/B.

The smartest place in this part of town, S'move boasts upmarket decor (it's a bit like walking into an extremely posh furniture shop) and a crowded, friendly atmosphere. The area's beautiful young things make up most of the clientele, but it's refreshingly unsnobbish. There's no dancefloor as such, but the careful selection of music ranges from Latin to house to techno, which encourages even the glacially cool to end up shaking a limb or two.

Live music

Otto Jazz

Salita Cariati 23, Chiaia (340 294 1006/). Funicular Centrale to corso Vittorio Emanuele/bus C16. **Open** 11pm-2am Fri-Sun. Closed July, Aug. **No credit cards. Map** p311 1A.

A historical fixture on the city's jazz scene, this is the place if you like your jazz more trad than acid. Musicians are mainly local and always of a good standard, with an enjoyable atmosphere guaranteed. Usually only open at weekends, Otto sometimes stages events during the week, including occasional Tuesday evening jazz lessons.

Vomero

Live music

Around Midnight

Via Bonito 32A (081 558 2834/www.around midnight.it). Funicular Montesanto to San Martino/ metro Vanvitelli/bus V1. **Open** 8.30pm-1am Tue-Sun. **No credit cards. Map** p312 2B.

Around Midnight is dedicated to live jazz; local musicians, along with combos from across Italy, play standards most nights here. The space is small and can be uncomfortable when it gets crowded, but the atmosphere is unpretentious and friendly.

Elsewhere

Arenile di Bagnoli

Via Nuova Bagnoli 10 (081 230 3050). Metro Bagnoli/bus F9. **Open** 9.30pm-5am daily. Closed Oct-May. **Admission** €10. **No credit cards. Map** p314.

Host of regular beach parties and occasional live shows, the Arenile was the first choice for a summer night out for years. It has recently changed ownership, however, and become more commercial, losing some of the spontaneity that made it so attractive.

Officina 99

Via Gianturco 101 (081 734 9091/www.officina 99.org). Metro Gianturco/bus 81, CS. **Open** (live music) *July-Sept* 10pm-3am Fri, Sat; *Oct-June* 10pm-3am Fri-Sun. **Admission** varies; around €4 for live music. **No credit cards. Map** p311 1A.

Naples' most famous *centro sociale* (semi-legally occupied space), the Officina is located in the mean streets south-east of Stazione Centrale in an abandoned factory. Not having spruced itself up like its sibling set-ups the Brancaleone in Rome or the Leonkavallo in Milan, it remains cold, cavernous, raw and edgy. But there's fun to be had here for all who have ever pierced unreasonable parts of their body or walked a mangy dog around on a piece of string. Come along on a Thursday evening if you want to take part in the debate about how the place should be run and/or other pressing topical issues.

Arts & Entertainment

Performing Arts

Naples' strong street theatre tradition is making a comeback.

'There are 56 million actors in Italy,' said Orson Welles, 'and the worst are on the stage.' You'll find this disturbingly true if you're after 'serious' theatre in Naples: few top-rate touring productions get further south than Rome, and the home-grown stuff can be dreadful.

This is strange, given that the *commedia dell'arte* (*see p166* **Pulcinella, Mr Punch and the commedia dell'arte**) was born (or was given its greatest impetus) here in the 16th century, imbuing not only local stages but also streets and squares with a colour and vivacity sadly lacking elsewhere in Italy. Even today it's enough to walk down any Neapolitan street to spot the great stage-less 'actors' Welles had in mind.

But scratch the surface and you'll soon see that Naples' extraordinary theatrical heritage is not entirely lost. Opt for local fare (plus a dollop of what's offered at the Teatro San Carlo; *see p164* **San Carlo**) for a taste of how good Neapolitan theatre can still be. If you can find Luca de Filippo doing a play by his late father Eduardo – considered one of theatre's all-time greats by Laurence Olivier – then you're in for a treat. Naples' most promising theatrical talent, director Mario Martone, recently returned to the city after a period in Rome, but doesn't have a regular gig, preferring to do occasional productions for a selection of theatres.

There's a lot of small, locally based companies, such as those of Enzo Moscato (whose intense, heavily Neapolitan mixtures of mime, music and physical theatre are either brilliant or disastrous) and the Libera Scena Ensemble of Renato Carpentieri (a favourite of film director Nanni Moretti), who uses funds from his mainstream projects to stage experimental productions at theatres in the centre.

The city council recently announced plans to allow fringe groups to stage performances in spaces not traditionally used as theatres. It is to be hoped that this will help bring Neapolitan theatre right back to where it belongs: on the streets.

PRACTICALITIES

Naples boasts a few excellent small musical associations and occasional dynamic, adventurous theatre work. The Naples region also offers some magical summer festivals in stunning settings. Though only premières are likely to be sold out in most venues and for most shows, firm local favourites such as Luca de Filippo and Mario Martone do fill houses, so book early. For ticket agencies, *see p142*. For securing tickets for the San Carlo opera house, *see p164* **San Carlo**.

Small musical companies

Some small local associations put on concerts, often of high quality; check the local press for details. Favourite venues for small-scale performances include the **Goethe Institut** (Riviera di Chiaia 202; 081 411 923), the **Lutheran Church** (via Carlo Poerio 5; 081 663 207) and the **Anglican Church** (via San Pasquale a Chiaia 15; 081 411 842).

Associazione Scarlatti

Piazza dei Martiri 58, Chiaia (081 406 011/ www.napoli.com/assocscarlatti). Metro Piazza Amedeo/bus C24, C25. **Open** *Box office 10am-1pm, 3.30-6pm Mon-Fri. Performances 9pm Thur. Closed June-Sept.* **Tickets** €10-€20.50. **No credit cards.** **Map** p313 1A.

The best of Naples' resident international artists and frequent visitors play at the weekly performances of classical chamber music and occasional jazz staged by the Associazione Scarlatti. The productions are usually held in the Teatro delle Palme (via Vetriera 12; metro Piazza Amedeo, bus C25). The decor's rough – it doubles as a cinema – but the acoustics are good and the tickets fairly priced.

Pietà dei Turchini

Via Santa Caterina da Siena 38, Toledo (081 409 628/www.turchini.it). Funicular Centrale to corso Vittorio Emanuele/bus C16. **Open** *Box office 1hr before performances. Performances Nov-June 9pm (days vary; phone for details).* **Tickets** €9.30-€13. **No credit cards. Map** p313 1A.

In a deconsecrated church, the Pietà dei Turchini group conducted by Antonio Florio puts on a varied and stunningly executed programme of works by 17th- and 18th-century Neapolitan composers. Recently the programme has extended to include small ensembles from different countries, all specialising in early and baroque music.

Venues

Bellini

Via Conte di Ruvo 14-19, Toledo (081 549 9688/ www.teatrobellini.it). Metro Cavour or Museo/bus 24, R1, R4. **Open** *Box office Oct-May 10.30am-1pm, 4.30-6pm Tue-Sat; 10am-1pm Sun. Performances*

Il Baciamano at **Galleria Toledo**.

Oct-May 9pm Tue-Sat; 5.30pm Sun. **Tickets** €10-€30. **Credit** MC, V. **Map** p310 2C.
Sumptuously redecorated, this theatre stages prose, international musicals in English, dance, local musicals and concerts. It has recently become keen on new British drama; if you fancy it, check out Patrick Marber or David Hare in Italian.

Elicantropo
Vico Gerolomini 3, Centro storico (081 296 640/ www.teatroelicantropo.com). Metro Cavour or Museo/bus 149, CD, CS. **Open** *Box office* Oct-May 6-8pm daily. *Performances* Oct-May daily.
Tickets €7-€10. **No credit cards. Map** p311 1C.
With only 40 seats, this tiny space in the Centro storico is certainly intimate, but it's one of the best places to see young companies doing new pieces. Like any fringe theatre, there's always an element of risk. But when it's good, it's worth it.

Galleria Toledo
Via Concezione a Montecalvario 34, Toledo (081 425 824/www.galleriatoledo.com). Metro Montesanto/ bus E2. **Open** *Box office* Sept-May 10.30am-7pm Tue-Sat. *Performances* Oct-May 9.30pm Tue-Sun.
Tickets €10. **No credit cards. Map** p312 2A.

A small modern theatre in the heart of the Quartieri spagnoli (*see p77*) providing a rare forum for new, often challenging theatre by high-standard local and international writers and companies. A favourite hangout of Enzo Moscato, it also runs a good cinema programme (*see p152*).

Mercadante
Piazza Municipio 1, Royal (081 551 3396/081 551 3623/www.caspi.it/mercadante). Bus 24, C22, C25, C57. **Open** *Box office* late Sept-Apr 10.30am-1pm, 5.30-7.30pm Tue-Sun. *Performances* late Sept-Apr 9pm Wed, Fri, Sat; 5.30pm, 9pm Thur; 6pm Sun.
Tickets €12.21-€24.27. **Credit** DC, MC, V.
Map p313 1A.
This beautiful city-owned theatre (with lousy acoustics – the stage was cemented and the sound died) opened in 1779 and, save the occasional hiccup, has been going strong since. It hosts some of the best actors and shows touring Italy and is a regular haunt of Roberto de Simone whose *La Gatta Cenerentola* was a hit in London in 1999. His highly professional, idiosyncratic shows are a unique blend of traditional themes, Stravinskian elaboration, local colour and dialect; some are 30 years old and still going strong.

San Carlo

English Grand Tourist Samuel Sharp visited the original Teatro San Carlo in 1765 and described it as 'almost as remarkable an object as any man sees in his travels'. For Stendhal, entering the Teatro San Carlo was 'like wandering into a Sultan's palace'.

The original 1737 theatre met the sad fate of all too many Italian opera houses: it burned down. Today's velvet-lined, gilt-encrusted theatre was built on the same site in 1816. It has good acoustics; standards of performances range from high to exceptional, making this Italy's second most prestigious opera house (after Milan's La Scala). And if its solidly traditional programming has occasionally left it sticking in the mud, San Carlo continues to hold Neapolitans in thrall, dominating the city's highbrow performing arts sector. Openings at San Carlo are the high-society events of the year (complete with the obligatory crowd of anti-fur protesters).

Great Italian voices and big international names can sometimes be heard in what are routine performances. Vanessa Redgrave was hauled in to do a show in 1999 based on the life of Eleonora de Fonseca Pimentel; Luciano Pavarotti did an *Elisir D'Amore* and Leo Nucci a *Barbiere di Siviglia* in 1998. Big-name conductors drop in, guaranteeing a high standard: Loren Maazel conducted in 1999; Mstislav Rostropovich appears now and then; Gustav Kuhn is good with the German stuff; and when Daniel Oren's on the programme, it's worth going to any length to secure tickets.

Attempts have been made to invigorate the programme. A 2002 *Turandot* was enlivened by David Hockney's direction and stage design. Young local film director Pappi Corsicato directed a *Don Giovanni* in 2001 and Spanish avant-theatre group Fura del Baus livened up Debussy's *Martyrdom of St Sebastian*.

Recent in-house modifications have helped boost San Carlo's standards still further. The orchestra and chorus are still dogged by poor teamwork; however, given the right conditions and conductor, performances can be very good indeed.

San Carlo audiences are opera buffs and, as such, demanding. Extremely warm in their appreciation when a performance merits it, they can be devastatingly cool when it doesn't. It's not enough, either, merely to be famous: however big a name you are, you risk being whistled (the Italian equivalent of booing) off the stage if you don't come up with the goods. Traditionalists at heart, San Carlo-goers give innovative works a rough ride. If it's not a classic, it has to be very good to avoid being rubbished. Still, an ever-increasing number of 20th-century works in recent symphonic seasons has not driven the public away.

The San Carlo ballet company operates year-round, providing an eclectic mixture of traditional and modern works. Standards are improving, and local composers (not to mention local rock band 24 Grana) have been commissioned to write for the company.

THE SEASON AND TICKETS

The opera season runs from January to December, but is suspended in late July and August as the place is simply too hot. Owing to the *abbonamenti* (subscription) system, in which opera-goers reserve their seats for the whole season, most of the theatre is booked out most of the time. What is left over tends to be the dregs: high up, or far off to the left of the stage. Don't despair though: good stall seats can be found (bear in mind that sightlines from many parts of the theatre are not very good, and securing central places will greatly enhance your enjoyment of the performance).

There are no dinner jackets to be seen in a San Carlo audience, but 'casual' here means stylish and elegant; jeans and T-shirts are acceptable in the low-profile top-floor seats, but they might earn you hostile stares in the stalls.

Arts & Entertainment

Le Nuvole

Viale Kennedy 26, Fuorigrotta (081 239 5653/ 081 239 5666/www.lenuvole.com). Metro to Cavalleggeri/Cumana rail to Edenlandia. **Open** *Box office* 30mins before performances. *Performances* Oct-May 11.30am on the 2nd & 4th Sun of the mth. **Tickets** €5.50. **No credit cards. Map** p314.

Specialising in shows for kids, this theatre is inside the Edenlandia amusement park (*see p146*). The Nuvole puts on lots of well-known fairy tales, puppets and some excellent mime. Not just for kids.

Politeama

Via Monte di Dio 80, Royal & Monte Echia (081 764 5001) Bus C22. **Open** *Box office* Oct-May

Bausch, Robert Wilson, Laurie Anderson and Philip Glass) and stages chamber operas and contemporary works for Teatro di San Carlo.

San Carluccio

Via San Pasquale a Chiaia 49, Chiaia (081 405 000). Funicular Chiaia to Amedeo/metro Piazza Amedeo/ bus C24, C25. **Open** *Box office* Oct-May 11am-1pm, 6-9.30pm Tue-Sat; 4.30-6.30pm Sun. *Performances* Oct-May 9.30pm Tue-Sat; 7pm Sun. **Tickets** €6-€11. **No credit cards. Map** p313 1B.
This tiny, friendly space hosts a mixture of cabaret and new local theatre.

Teatro Nuovo

Via Montecalvario 16, Toledo (081 425 958/ 081 406 062/081 542 2272/www.nuovoteatronuovo. com). Metro Montesanto/bus E2. **Open** *Box office* 1hr before shows; phone bookings 9.30am-2pm, 4-7.30pm Mon-Fri. *Performances* Sept-May 9pm Tue-Sat; 7pm Sun. **Tickets** €13; under-25s €7.50. **No credit cards. Map** p312 2A.
The modern Nuovo has been active for around 20 years but it's built on the site of one of the city's oldest theatres. This is one of the few venues in Naples dedicated to new and international theatre; the space is unexciting, but the quality is usually pretty high. There's a rapid turnover of three or four different shows a month: be quick if there's something you want to see.

Totò

Via Frediano Cavara 12E, Sanità (081 564 7525/ www.teatro-toto.com). Metro Piazza Cavour/bus 135, 149, C55. **Open** *Box office* Oct-Apr 10.30am-1pm, 4.30-7.30pm Tue-Sun. *Performances* late Oct-May 9pm Thur, Fri; 5.30pm, 9pm Sat; 6pm Sun. **Tickets** €10.50-€18. **No credit cards. Map** p310 2B.
Named after the famous local comedian, this is a venue for old-style local stand-up comics, cabaret as well as new (though firmly in the traditional music-hall-style) comedies and farces.

Summer music festivals

In the dog days of July and August, when Naples' un-air-conditioned theatres are simply too hot to bear, music strays out of doors (and out of town) to take up residence in some spectacular venues.

The Teatro San Carlo (*see above* **San Carlo**) sponsors touring groups while the opera house is closed in July and August; details of venues and programmes are available from the theatre itself. Performances are often free.

Unquestionably the most spectacular of all the region's outdoor happenings, the **Festival Musicale di Villa Rufolo** takes place from June to August. Events are staged either in the 12th-century villa in Ravello (*see p259*; where Wagner composed parts of *Parsifal* – it's not difficult to see what inspired

If battling for tickets doesn't appeal, or opera's simply not your thing, you should be able to take a guided tour of the theatre instead (*see p61*).

Teatro di San Carlo

Via San Carlo 98F, Royal (081 797 2412/ fax 081 400 902/www.teatrosancarlo.it). Bus 24, C22, C25, C57. **Open** *Box office* Sept-June 10am-3pm Tue-Sun; July 10am-3pm Tue-Fri; 1hr before performances. *Performances* times & days vary.
Tickets €16-€136.50; première & gala performances €181. **Credit** DC, MC, V.
Map p313 1A.

10.30am-1.30pm Mon-Sat; 4.30-7.30pm on performance days. *Performances* 9pm Tue, Wed, Sat, Sun. **Tickets** €15-€30. **No credit cards. Map** p313 1A.
The Politeama is a large modern space that is somewhat characterless, but with good acoustics and sightlines. It hosts international music and dance as much as theatre (recent visitors have included Pina

him) or one of the other lovely venues along the Amalfi Coast (including a surreal, spectacular, specially constructed platform perched above the sea in Ravello). Very occasionally, early risers may be lucky enough to catch a *Concerto all'alba* (dawn concert) when the orchestra welcomes the sunrise in a breathtaking spectacle that begins at 4am. Musical events continue for the rest of the year

in Ravello, including the Concerti di Musica Sinfonica (symphonic concerts) in July, the Settimane Internazionali di Musica da Camera (chamber music) in September and three concerts each week through the winter.

The Fondazione Axel Munthe stages **Concerti al tramonto** (concerts at dusk) at the Swedish doctor/author's Villa San Michele (*see p187*) on the island of Capri most

Pulcinella, Mr Punch and the

Deep in the Centro storico off via Anticaglia are the barely visible remains of a Roman – or possibly even Greek – theatre (*see p72* **Aqueduct**). It's said that Nero himself popped down here when he fancied a laugh. His imperial ribs would have been tickled by one of the *fabula Atellana*: bawdy, burlesque Roman comedies (with antecedents in the more refined Greek comedies of Aristophanes), based around stock characters played by actors wearing masks that indicated their identity. These typically Neapolitan plays became wildly popular among Roman theatre-goers and were

performed in an irreverent mixture of Latin and Oscan, the native language of Campania. But changing fashions around the first century AD swept the *fabula* off the stage, seemingly forever.

The tradition, however, was dormant rather than spent. In the 16th century, an outburst of popular theatre radiated out from Naples to the rest of Italy and went on to influence later European theatre. This was the *commedia dell'arte* (where *arte* means not 'art' but 'trade', to distinguish the professional jugglers and mountebanks who made up its cast from the effete courtiers-turned-thespians who had continued to act out 'serious' Latin drama in courts and cathedrals). Like the *fabula* tradition long before, the *commedia dell'arte* had stock characters, recognisable by their particular outfits and masks, who behaved in stock fashion in wild, part-scripted, part-improvised scenarios.xm

In the *commedia dell'arte*, each character was associated with an Italian city: Harlequin was a faithful but calamity-prone servant from Bergamo, Pantaleone a money-grubbing merchant from Venice, Rugantino an inveterate liar from Rome. Naples supplied the braggart and cowardly Spanish captain Scaramuccia (or Scaramouche) and, more famously, it revived one of the *fabula Atellana*'s best-loved characters – a coarse-tongued, pot-bellied, white-clad clown called Mimus Albus – and transformed him into Pulcinella.

Pulcinella (*pictured*) is carefree and disillusioned, cynical yet optimistic, given to wild dances and uncontrolled laughter followed by fits of the deepest melancholy: all very Neapolitan traits. He is dressed in a voluminous white smock and white trousers, with a white cone-shaped hat, red-and-yellow shoes, and a black mask with a long hooked nose. His main aim in life is to do nothing. He drinks too much and goes hungry, he

Fridays from June to August. Visitors are advised to take a shawl, as it can get chilly in the evenings.

Concerti al tramonto
Fondazione Axel Munthe, Villa San Michele, Anacapri (081 837 1401/fax 081 837 3530/ www.caprionline.com/axelmunthe). **Open** *Box office* June-Aug from 7pm Fri. *Performances* June-Aug 7.30pm Fri. **Tickets** €5. **No credit cards.**

Festival Musicale di Villa Rufolo
Società dei concerti di Ravello, via Trinità 3, Ravello (089 858 149/www.ravello.info). **Open** *Box office* Mar-Oct 9am-1pm Mon-Sat; 4-8pm on performance days. *Performances* Mar 6.30pm Wed. Apr-Oct 9.30pm Mon, Wed, Sat. **Tickets** €20. **Credit** AmEx, DC, MC, V.

Tickets can be booked online with a credit card; the box office is inside the villa.

commedia dell'arte

falls foul of the law and retaliates with devious schemes or simply by beating the local police officer over the head with a big stick. (The stick traditionally had wooden clappers at one end that made a slapping noise when struck, hence 'slapstick comedy'.)

The character probably originated in its modern form in the town of Aversa just outside Naples, as a clown for Carnevale celebrations. His name, inspired by his typical squawking voice, means 'little chicken'; his large nose is a symbol of sexual potency; his hunched back brings good luck to all who touch it (still a common Italian superstition).

Pulcinella is also one of Italy's early emigrants; he turned up in Britain as early as 1662, in puppet form as 'Punchinello'. Samuel Pepys saw a performance in Covent Garden, describing 'an Italian puppet play, that is within the rails there, which is very pretty, the best that I ever saw, and great resort of gallants.' As often happens to emigrants, this manifestation of Pulcinella has since adopted British ways to become the anarchic, violent and disturbingly funny Mr Punch.

Meantime, the Neapolitan Pulcinella became more respectable. By the time he was brought indoors into proper theatres – most notably the San Carlo's cheeky little brother, the San Carlino – Pulcinella had been transformed from its origins as clown into a grass-roots philosopher, a seer of the streets. The hook-nosed mask and white togs were handed down solemnly from generation to generation, from father to son or from *maestro* to protégé; Pulcinella is now a symbol of Naples itself.

Pulcinella masks can be bought on almost any street corner in the Centro storico, and the character is a firm (if somewhat bizarre) fixture in the Christmas *presepe* (nativity scene). A cartoon Pulcinella has been adopted as a mascot by Neapolitan anti-globalisation groups.

Nor has the tradition died in the theatre; Roberto De Simone, Luca De Filippo, Peppe Barra and Enzo Moscato (*see p162*) all work with aspects of the comedy and cruelty of the character. The late, great Massimo Troisi (star of *Il Postino*) was a fine present-day cinematic Pulcinella.

Pulcinella is, all in all, the personification of Naples' contradictions. Like his poor contemporaries in this beautiful, overcrowded, culture-packed, sustenance-starved city, Pulcinella accepts his harsh life with philosophical resignation. The greatest actors who have donned his mask have united his wild, anti-authoritarian hilarity with gut-wrenching pathos. Laughter in Naples is a very serious business.

Arts & Entertainment

Sport & Fitness

Spectators and dressers-up remain blindly faithful, even to Napoli.

Naples has spawned many successful sportsmen and women in recent years. From soccer to water polo and from boxing to rowing and sailing, the city has gained an impressive list of honours, both at professional and amateur levels.

Which is surprising, really, given that the majority of Neapolitan *sportivi* belong to one of two varieties: spectators and dressers-up. The former are generally football devotees (though there has been little to devote themselves to of late locally – *see below* **Calcio and Napoli**).

The latter focus on looking and smelling *sportif* by squandering large sums on designer sports articles, both for the wardrobe and the shower room. Their immaculately groomed offspring grow up believing that wearing the right brand of tennis shoes is far more important than hitting the ball properly.

To show off their impeccable apparel to its greatest advantage, dressers-up operate in private sports clubs (*see p169*). Public sports facilities are few and far between.

But you'll need more than just natty togs to feel at home beside Neapolitan muscle-flexers. A baffling array of quasi-anglicisms is used to entice new customers into the fitness market; being *au fait* with the terminology – *fit-work*, *just-pump*, *life-pump*, *hard gym*, *total-body* and the rest – is essential.

This said, the top Neapolitan sports structures and organisations are very good indeed. The Italian state pays large subsidies to local branches of its Olympic federations to nurture 'minor' sports (in other words anything that isn't football) such as tennis, swimming, hockey and even cricket. A veritable army of scouts sifts assiduously through young talent and does a thorough job, as the recent bumper

Calcio and Napoli

Calcio (football) took off in Naples in 1905, when the crew of a passing English cargo boat was challenged to a match by a team of local dignitaries. Napoli SSC (Società Sportiva Calcio) was founded in 1926; its first manager, an Englishman called Willy Garbutt, kept the team riding high in the first division for many years.

Soccer fortunes mirrored the fate of the badly battered city after World War II, when Napoli dropped to the second division. In the 1980s, a spate of foreign signings (Rudi Krol in 1980, Jose Dirceu in 1983 and, most spectacularly, the Argentinian superstar Diego Armando Maradona in 1984) reversed this run of ill-luck. To the delight of its doggedly faithful fans, Napoli won its first ever *scudetto* (league title) in 1987, its second in 1990 and the UEFA Cup in 1989.

It was all too good to last. Maradona made an ignominious flight from drugs charges and a paternity suit and returned to his native country to dry out at the end of the 1990-91 season (since when he has made more come-backs – all of them destined to utter failure – than George Foreman). The club's finances

worsened, and magistrates delved into the dealings of its chairman, Corrado Ferlaino.

By the end of the 1997-98 season, Napoli was back in Serie B. Promotion to Serie A at the end of the 1999-2000 season prompted scenes of euphoria unseen for a decade. But the joy was short-lived and the club dropped down once more after just one season in the rarefied atmosphere breathed by *i grandi del calcio*.

By the end of the 2001-02 season, it was clear that Serie A was to remain a distant memory. Moreover, the club was in a state of complete turmoil; Ferlaino stepped down to make way for entrepreneur Giorgio Corbelli and a partner. But no sooner had a rescue package been hustled together than Corbelli's own business activities came under extremely close scrutiny by investigating magistrates. Corbelli himself spent a period of detention in a Rome jail. Management of the club's disastrous finances was handed over to an independent financial and legal adviser. And the club announced that it was parting company with its manager Gigi de Canio, though no replacement was named.

crop of Neapolitan representatives on Olympic medal platforms in boxing, swimming, rowing and sailing shows.

Other sports – particularly water sports – facilities can be found on Ischia (*see p191*), Capri (*see p173*) and the Amalfi (*see p240*) and Sorrentine (*see p223*) coasts.

Bowling

Bowling Oltremare

Viale Kennedy 12, Fuorigrotta (081 624 444/ www.bowlingoltremare.it). Cumana rail to Edenlandia/ bus C2, C3, C5. **Open** 9am-2am daily. **Admission** €1.60-€3.70. **No credit cards. Map** p314.

A traditional 20-lane bowling alley next to the Zoo and Edenlandia funfair (*see p146*). There are ping-pong tables for hire too.

Gyms

Athena

Via dei Mille 16, Chiaia (081 407 334/ www.athena.it). Metro Piazza Amedeo/bus C22, C25, C28. **Open** *Oct-Mar* 8am-10.30pm Mon-Fri; 9am-6pm Sat; 9am-noon Sun. *Apr-Sept* 8am-10.30pm Mon-Fri; 9am-4.30pm Sat. **Admission** non-members €8 daily. **Credit** AmEx, DC, MC, V. **Map** p313 1B.

A wide range of facilities for activities including bodybuilding, spinning, aerobics, weights, bicycles, body-sculpt, step and some martial arts. There are also Turkish baths (sauna followed by cold dip), a bar and a squash court (€9 non-members per half hour; the gym hires out rackets).

Bodyguard

Via Torrione San Martino 45, Vomero (081 558 4551). Funicular Montesanto to via Morghen, Centrale to piazzetta Fuga, Chiaia to via Cimarosa/metro Vanvitelli/bus E4, V1. **Open** 10am-11pm Mon-Fri; 11am-7pm Sat. Closed 2wks Aug. **Admission** €8. **Credit** AmEx, DC, MC, V. **Map** p312 2B.

As well as weights, bicycles, a sauna, walking and running machines – along with provision for aerobics and dance – you'll also find a bar here.

Jogging

Although not quite as trendy as during the early 1990s, jogging, skateboarding and roller-blading are still common along the whole stretch of seafront from Castel dell'Ovo (*see p56*) to Mergellina (*see p93*). The upper reaches of via Petrarca and the roads around Capo Posillipo (*see p95*), though more hilly, are also suitable for joggers. The park around the

Reggia at Capodimonte (*see p84*) provides a wonderful backdrop for all improvised sport (though ball games are theoretically *vietati* – banned – so hide that football on the way in).

Swimming pools

Swimming pool opening times change from year to year; phone ahead to check.

Collana

Via Rossini, Vomero (081 560 1988). Metro Quattro Giornate/bus C30, C32. **Open** *July, Aug* 9.30am-2.30pm (last ticket 1.30pm), 3.30-9pm (last ticket 7pm) Mon-Sat; 9am-4pm Sun. Closed Sept-June. **Admission** *Mon-Sat* 9.30am-1.30pm €3.62; 3.30-7pm €4.13; Sun €4.65. **No credit cards. Map** p312 2C.
A city-owned indoor pool measuring 25m x 8m. The admission price includes access to the sundeck and deckchairs. Under-12s pay half-price.

Scandone

Viale dei Giochi del Mediterraneo, Fuorigrotta (081 570 2636/www.comune.napoli.it). Metro Campi Flegrei then bus C3, C5, C14/Cumana rail to Edenlandia. **Open** *July, Aug* 9am-7pm daily. Closed Sept-June. **Admission** Half day (9am-2pm or 2-7pm) €4.13; whole day €6.20. **No credit cards. Map** p314. Under-12s pay half-price.

Tennis

Tennis Club Mostra

Via Terracina, Fuorigrotta (081 239 0444). Cumana rail to Mostra/metro Campi Flegrei/ bus 180, 181, C2, C6, C7, C8, C9, C10, C15. **Open** 8am-8pm daily. **Admission** €5.70 per person per hr. **No credit cards. Map** p314.
Surrounded by orange trees, this tennis club (four clay courts) is a wonderfully peaceful spot in the middle of the Mostra area (*see p104*) in the western suburbs. Turn up any time and the club will usually be able to arrange a partner. There's no need to come equipped: there are rackets available for hire from the club too.

Tennis San Domenico

Via San Domenico 64, Vomero Alto (081 645 660). Bus C36 from piazza Vanvitelli to Tennis San Domenico. **Open** 7am-10pm Mon-Fri; 7am-8pm Sat; 7am-6pm Sun. **Admission** €10.40 per hr per court. **No credit cards. Map** off p312 1C.
The five floodlit clay courts of the San Domenico tennis club are located beneath a (very high) flyover. Rackets can be provided, free of charge. There are also separate gym facilities available (with the full range of physical jerks including bodybuilding, aerobics and the like) at €3.50 daily.

▶ ## Calcio and Napoli (continued)

TICKETS AND MATCHES

Matches are played on alternate Sundays between September and June at the **Stadio San Paolo** in the western suburb of Fuorigrotta. Kick-off can be any time between 2.30pm and 4.30pm; check the time when you buy your ticket.

Entry to games is by ticket only (disgruntled black marketeers ripped out experimental turnstiles in the 1970s).

For the 2001-02 season in Serie B, season ticket prices ranged from €125 for the *curve* (behind the goals) to around the €400 mark for a numbered seat in the *tribuna* (grandstand), but expect a 50 per cent mark-up if the club ever succeeds in clawing its way back to the top flight. Prices for individual matches vary according to who is playing, but currently range from €15 for the *curve* to over €50 for a numbered grandstand seat.

Tickets for important home matches will almost certainly be impossible to procure at the club's main outlet, **Azzurro Service** in Fuorigrotta, unless you are prepared to pay through the nose for a numbered grandstand ticket. If you cannot acquire a ticket honestly, you will have to run the gauntlet of the touts outside the stadium; transactions are out in the open and quite straightforward. To see how it's done (and to gauge the going price) watch a local buy a ticket first. How much more than the official price you pay will depend on who Napoli is playing and what is at stake.

Official club souvenirs are available through the website (www.calcionapoli.it) or by mail order (081 613 3911).

Azzurro Service

Via F Galeota 17, Fuorigrotta (081 593 4001/www.azzuroservice.it/ www.puntazzurro.com). Cumana rail to Mostra or Leopardi/metro Campi Flegrei/ bus 180, 181, C2, C6, C7, C8, C9, C10, C15. **Open** 9am-12.30pm, 4-6.30pm Mon-Fri; 9am-1hr before kick-off for home games Sun. **Credit** DC, MC, V. **Map** p314.

Stadio San Paolo

Piazzale Tecchio, Fuorigrotta (081 593 3223). Cumana rail to Mostra/metro Campi Flegrei/ bus 180, 181, C2, C6, C7, C8, C9, C10, C15. **Map** p314.

Around Naples

Introduction

Tear yourself away from your hotel pool and explore this variegated region.

The province of Naples and the region of Campania of which it is a part fall neatly into separate holiday compartments: there are the islands – **Capri**, **Ischia** and **Procida**; there is **Sorrento** (and the magnificent hinterland of the Sorrentine Peninsula, though few visitors climb the hill to discover it); and there is the **Amalfi Coast** (for all, *see relevant chapters*).

Each has its own particular charm, beauty and facilities; so why bother to wander? Visitors to all tend to make an exception for **Pompeii** (*see p216*): no stay in Campania is complete without a day-trip there (as some two million people prove each year). But however strong the magnetic force of the glistening bit of Mediterranean you find yourself by, Campania deserves a closer look.

Take its archeological sites: Pompeii is staggering but it's only part of the story. Just down the road from Italy's most-visited tourist attraction are the little-known digs and museums at **Herculaneum** (*see p211*), **Stabiae** (*see p220)* and **Boscoreale** (*see p216*). A short train-ride into southern Campania brings you to the dramatic Greek temples at **Paestum** (*see p271*).

Then there are all the imposing reminders of the baroque grandeur of Naples' past. The *palazzi reali* (royal palaces) in **Caserta** (*see p276*) and the **Portici** (*p211*) were the architectural wonders of their age, seriously challenging foreign competition from Versailles and Schönbrunn.

Minor gems are to be found in **Salerno**, where a small museum charts the glorious history of its medieval Medical School (*see p269*), and in **Portici**, where the Pietrarsa railway museum (*see p211*) is an engaging tribute to Italy's first train line.

Then there's the volcanic activity – spurting steam and boiling sulphurous springs – that lurks close to the surface in Ischia and the **Campi Flegrei** (*see p97*).

There are walks too: well-kept, well-marked paths criss-cross the Sorrentine Peninsula and scale the heights of the Amalfi Coast (*see p231* **A piedi**); Capri's mountainous heart is best explored on foot (*see p182* **Capri hikes**); Ischia has tracks wending through forests to the heights of **Monte Epomeo** (*see p199*); **Monte Faito** (*see p220*) and even bubbling

Vesuvius (*see p221*) are a walker's paradise. All this, plus the buzzing, vibrant city of Naples itself, make settling down by the pool with your sunhat pulled firmly over your nose for the entire duration of your holiday look like a missed opportunity.

ACCOMMODATION
Hotel listings are given for most of the destinations covered in the **Around Naples** section after the sightseeing information for individual towns or areas.

GETTING THERE & AROUND
Each chapter in the **Around Naples** section contains exhaustive instructions on getting to the destinations mentioned by car, train, boat and/or bus from Naples (and from Salerno, in the case of the Amalfi Coast and Paestum). For general information on travel in Naples and Campania, *see chapter* **Directory**.

MUSEUMS & GALLERIES
Entrance to all state-owned museums is free for EU citizens of over 65 and under 18 years. Many also have reductions for EU citizens under 26 in full-time education: bring appropriate picture ID. A list of concessions for non-EU citizens whose countries have bilateral cultural agreements with Italy should be posted in each museum.

Capri

The height of Mediterranean chic, plus cliffs and lemon groves.

The essence of Mediterranean holiday chic...

See maps on p174.
Capri is a crag with cafés: a juxtaposition
of soaring cliffs, rambling lemon groves
and high-density tourist tack. In parts this
proud limestone outpost of the Sorrentine
Peninsula is a wilderness of ferns and falcons;
in others it is the very essence of the chic
Mediterranean resort.

It is this contrast that makes Capri so
fascinating, even now that fast hydrofoils
from Naples and Sorrento have opened the
island up to mass invasion by day-trippers.
Between June and September, as many as
50,000 visitors crowd on to the island each day
– that's five for every resident. Every summer,
the mayor makes the ritual announcement
that he is thinking of limiting the number of
daily visitors. And every summer, in time-
honoured *caprese* fashion, he doesn't.

But a combination of rocky topography,
stringent planning regulations and flourishing
small-scale agriculture means that there are
still plenty of quiet corners to explore.

Traditionally Capri town is supposed to be
more chic and urbane, while Anacapri – the
village on the upland side of the escarpment
that slices across the island – is more rural
and down-to-earth. To some extent this is true:
most of the luxury hotels, and their denizens,
cluster around Capri town, while Anacapri has
a small but active population of smallholder-
farmers. But with the big tourist pull of Villa
San Michele (*see p187*), Anacapri gets just as
many visitors as its less elevated rival, and it
has its fair share of souvenir shops and rip-off
restaurants. Capri town, on the other hand, has
the great advantage of being a no-traffic zone.

Much of the credit for the perfect paths, the
litter bins, the ceramic street names and the
regularly repainted church and shopfronts
has to go to the Blue Grotto (*see p188* **Grotta
Azzurra**). The Grotto is undoubtedly a double
blessing for the island: it provides a steady
stream of municipal revenue, and it keeps
visitors off Capri's narrow, crowded streets
for a couple of hours.

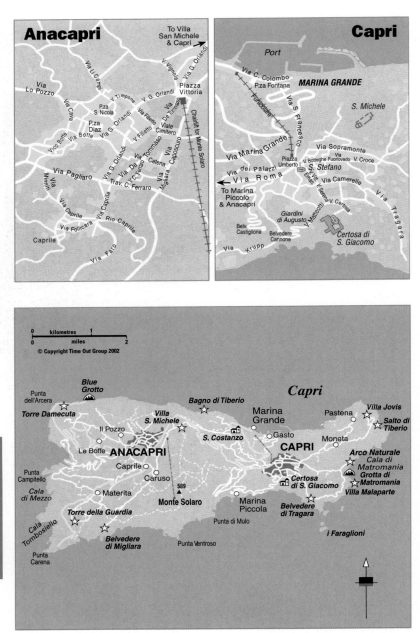

Anacapri

To Villa San Michele & Capri

Via Li Campi

Via Lo Pozzo

Via Cava

Via Boffe

Vico Boffe

V. Timpone

P.za S. Nicola

V. G. Orlandi

Via Filietto

Via Filietto

V. G. Orlandi

Via Vignola

V. G. Orlandi

V. G. Orlandi

Piazza Vittoria

P.za Diaz

Viale Cimitero

Via De Tommaso

Via De Tommaso

Via Migliara

Via Caposcuro

Chairlift for Monte Solaro

Via Mimilu

Via G. Orlandi

Via De Tommaso

Via Catena

Trav. C. Ferraro

V. C. Ferraro

Via Caprile

Via Pagliaro

Via Caprile

Via Rio Caprile

Via Follicara

Via Faio

Caprile

Capri

Port

Via C. Colombo

P.za Fontana

MARINA GRANDE

S. Michele

Funicolare

Via S. Francesco

Via Marina Grande

Via Sopramonte

Via Botteghe Fuoriovado V. Croce

Via Camerelle

Piazza Umberto I

S. Stefano

V. Mitr. Emer.

V. Serena

V. Mattuotti

V. Certosa

Via dei Palazzi

Via Roma

To Marina Piccolo & Anacapri

Giardini di Augusto

Belv. Castiglione

Belvedere Cannone

Via Krupp

Certosa di S. Giacomo

Via Tragara

---

0 — kilometres — 1
0 — miles — 2
© Copyright Time Out Group 2002

Punta dell'Arcera

Blue Grotto

Torre Damecuta

Il Pozzo

Villa S. Michele

Bagno di Tiberio

Marina Grande

Pastena

Villa Jovis

Salto di Tiberio

Capri

Le Boffe **ANACAPRI**

S. Costanzo

Gasto

CAPRI

Moneta

Arco Naturale
Cala di Matromania
Grotta di Matromania
Villa Malaparte

Caprile

Caruso

589

Monte Solaro

Certosa di S. Giacomo

Punta Campitello

Cala di Mezzo

Materita

Marina Piccola

Belvedere di Tragara

Cala Tombosiello

Torre della Guardia

Punta di Mulo

i Faraglioni

Punta Carena

Belvedere di Migliara

Punta Ventroso

To unlock the island's charm, bite the bullet of Capri's inflated hotel prices and stay over. By day, the Piazzetta, social hub of Capri town, is a pedestrian log-jam. In the evening, though, as the lights come on and the last of the day-trippers drift down to the port, it comes into its own as one of the Mediterranean's most elegant open-air living rooms.

If you have a choice, visit out of season – in May or October, say – when the weather is generally cool enough to embark on some of the marvellous walks that the island offers (*see p182* **Capri hikes**), but still warm enough to get a suntan. Between November and mid March, Capri closes down big time; only a fraction of the island's hotels stay open, and even fewer of the restaurants (the tourist offices post weekly bulletins of the survivors). For the adventurous, though – and to see what the island looks like when only the native *capresi* are left – this can be a rewarding time to visit.

GOAT ISLAND

The island's name is the subject of any number of conflicting theories; the most consistent is that it is derived from *Capreae* – a Romano-Italic word meaning 'island of goats'. It has been inhabited since prehistory – first by Neolithic tribes, later by the Greeks of Cumae (Cuma; *see p101*) and Neapolis (Naples). Virgil associated the place with the Teleboans, a legendary race of Greek pirates. For centuries it was more a strategic outpost than a settled community.

It was not until 29 BC that Capri was touched by the mainstream of history, when Octavian – soon to become the Emperor Augustus – first landed on the island. So charmed was he by its beauty that he persuaded the Greeks of Neapolis to take back the already Romanised and much larger island of Ischia and give him Capri instead, for use as a private estate. Though he never lived here, Augustus set about building villas and water cisterns, and seems to have taken an active interest in the island's culture and traditions.

TIBERIUS'S CAPRI

Augustus's successor, Tiberius, ignored the place for the first part of his reign, but while on a tour of southern Italy in AD 27, he stopped off here, and never again returned to Rome. Capri was to be his home for the last ten years of his life, and the reign he established here – absolutist to the point of derangement – has been the subject of much historical embroidery. Suetonius, the scandalmongering author of *De Vita Caesarum* ('Lives of the Caesars') depicted Tiberius as a misanthropist reprobate, who liked to watch as groups of young male and

... perched on a soaring crag.

female servants had sex in front of him; in case they were at a loss, the villa was well furnished with erotic statues, paintings and Egyptian sex manuals. Evidence of torture rooms, prisons and execution chambers in all of Tiberius's Capri villas testify to his other preferred form of entertainment. But Suetonius is practically our only literary source for these final years of the emperor's life, and it has been suggested by many – most notably the British writer Norman Douglas, a long-term resident of Capri – that his account is vindictive and one-sided. For Douglas, Tiberius was no monster but a bitter old recluse, happier in the company of books, works of art and astrological charts than that of human beings.

After the death of Tiberius in AD 37 the island was forgotten once more, and the 12 imperial villas gradually fell into ruin. Capri was used a couple of times as a place of exile for Roman undesirables, then came under the sway first of the Abbey of Montecassino and later of the Republic of Amalfi. Repeated Saracen attacks in the ninth and tenth centuries caused the population to move up from the main settlement of Marina Grande to the more easily defensible sites of Capri town and Anacapri.

Through the Middle Ages the island followed the fortunes of Naples, passing meekly from Anjou then Aragon to Spanish rule. In the 18th century the Bourbons used Capri as a hunting reserve; the bishop of the island was known as the 'bishop of quails', as he had a right to a share of the profits on all sales of the bird.

During the Napoleonic Wars the British occupied Capri as a bastion against the French Kingdom of Naples, but some brilliant decoy tactics by a French invasion force led to the recapture of the island in the space of just two weeks in 1808.

GAY CAPRI

Capri soon became less of a military prize and more of a case study in the history of tourism, after a succession of northern visitors discovered its warm Mediterranean charms and thrilling 'Gothick' scenery. Some of the escapism was of the sexual kind, as the island acquired a reputation as a haven for Greek and Sapphic lovers. An aura of licentiousness still hung around the island where Tiberius had – so the legend went – swung both ways with such perverse dedication. And the pretty, tanned *caprese* boys came from a culture that considered a little innocent masculine tumbling much less reprehensible than heterosexual sex before marriage. Gay Capri's finest years were the first two decades of the 20th century, when wiry writer Norman Douglas (whose *South Wind* is still the definitive Capri novel) and perfumed French aesthete Jacques Fersen helped supply island boys with pocket money.

The gay scene overlapped with the literary scene. Compton Mackenzie and Graham Greene both had houses on the island; the latter's island years are documented in Shirley Hazzard's recent *Greene on Capri*. For a few brief years at the beginning of the 20th century, Capri also hosted an emigré Russian community, centring on the writer Maxim Gorky. Another larger-than-life figure was Curzio Malaparte, a kind of Italian Ernest Hemingway, who was briefly famous in the 1940s and 1950s. His brutalist red house on Punta Massullo is one of the island's more unusual landmarks.

Like any self-respecting tourist destination, Capri has its well-marketed sightseeing and shopping musts. The first is, of course, the Blue Grotto (*see p188* **Grotta Azzurra**), which currently receives over 2,000 visitors a day in high season. The second is *limoncello*, a bright-yellow, sickly-sweet, post-prandial lemon liqueur, most of which is now produced on the mainland in order to meet the demand. You might still come across the occasional home-made version, especially in the more reputable family *trattorie*.

The **Piazzetta**, core of Capri. *See p178*.

One final word: if you want to impress the natives, get the pronunciation right. It's CA-pree, not Ca-PREE.

Getting there

Naples newspaper *Il Mattino* publishes daily updated timetables of all bus, train, sea and air connections to and from Naples. On Capri, the tourist offices give out a free timetable, updated fortnightly, with all the sea crossings; these are also posted on the Capri tourist board website (www.capritourism. com). All the services mentioned below are daily.

By helicopter

Hollywood stars and anyone who is really pressed for time can take a helicopter from Naples Capodichino airport to the heliport at Anacapri – a snip at €862 per one-way flight for up to four people. Details from Cab.air (081 584 4355/www.cabair.it).

By sea from the Amalfi Coast

Services run Apr-Oct only. LMS (Amalfi 089 873 301; Salerno 089 234 892/089 227 979) runs hydrofoils between Salerno, Amalfi, Positano and Capri. From Positano, Consorzio Linee Marittime (089 873 301) runs hydrofoils to Capri; journey time 30mins.

By sea from Ischia

Services run Apr-Oct only. Alilauro (081 991 888) runs one hydrofoil a day from Ischia Porto to Capri; crossing time 40mins. There are two ferries a day on the same route; crossing time 90mins.

By sea from Naples

Caremar (081 551 3882), NLG Linea Jet (081 552 7209) and Snav (081 761 2348) run hydrofoils from the central quay of Molo Beverello (at least hourly in summer). Snav also runs hydrofoils from Mergellina at the western end of the bay (every 2hrs in summer). Crossing time by hydrofoil is around 40mins.

Caremar also runs six daily ferries all year round from Beverello. Three of these are high-speed *traghetti veloci* (50mins); the others take 1hr 20mins. Ferries are cheaper, and they're the only option when the sea is too choppy for the hydrofoils. Note that the last boats from Naples generally leave around 8.30pm in winter, 9.30pm in summer.

By sea from Sorrento

Caremar (081 807 3077) and LMP Alilauro (081 878 1430/081 807 3024) hydrofoils leave from Sorrento's Marina Piccola for the 20mins crossing to Capri (at least hourly in summer). There are also less frequent conventional ferries.

By water taxi

Taxi del Mare (081 877 3600/www.taxidelmare.it) has a fleet of smart yellow 10-seater speedboats available for hire with driver at a rate of €26 per nautical mile (Sorrento–Capri will set you back €208 one way).

Getting around

Beyond the bus terminus on via Roma, Capri town is closed to all forms of motorised traffic except little luggage-bearing electric trolleys, which are also licensed to carry disabled people. If you're staying in an upmarket hotel, you should be met at the quay by a porter, identified by the hotel name on his cap, who will arrange to have your luggage sent up to the hotel. Most upmarket hotels in Anacapri have their own minibuses. Otherwise, the funicular, buses and taxis are all at the end of the quay.

All public transport on the island – including the funicular from Marina Grande to Capri town, but not the Monte Solaro cable car – is covered by the Unico Capri ticket, which comes in three versions: €1.30 for a single trip, €2.10 for 60mins on the whole network (allowing you to change at Anacapri for the Blue Grotto, for example), €6.70 for a day-pass. Tickets should be bought beforehand from the terminus and stamped on the bus. If you get on at an intermediate stop, tickets can be bought from the driver.

By boat

For the Blue Grotto, *see p188* **Grotta Azzurra**. The other popular trip is the complete circuit of the island (*giro dell'isola*) offered by a number of operators in Marina Grande. The standard price is €9 per person.

By bus

The three main services are Marina Grande–Capri (7am-midnight, later in summer), Marina Grande–Anacapri (7am-8pm, sometimes later) and Capri–Anacapri (6.30am-midnight). Other routes, with less frequent services, are Capri–Marina Piccola, Anacapri–Grotta Azzurra (Blue Grotto) and Anacapri–Punta Carena (Faro). Ring SIPPIC (081 837 0420) for information; phone Staiano (081 837 1544) for the Blue Grotto and Punta Carena lines.

By funicular railway

Departures from the station at Marina Grande to Capri town (and vice versa) run every 15mins (6.30am-9pm Oct-Mar; 6.30am-9.30pm Apr, May; 6.30am-12.30am Jun-Sept). Run by SIPPIC (information 081 837 0420).

The *capresi* dumped plague victims over the walls of the **Certosa**. *See p178.*

Around Naples

By scooter

Capri and the Greek island of Mykonos are the
guinea-pigs in an EU-funded, eco-friendly electric
scooter rental initiative. The Capri branch –
imaginatively named Rent an Electric Scooter – is
based at via Roma 68 (081 837 5863), the approach
road to Capri town. Rental of a 50cc scooter costs
€8 per hr, including helmet; a driving licence is
not required. The scooters have a range of 50km
(31 miles; that's a lot on Capri), after which they
have to be returned to base for recharging.

By taxi

Those colourful open-top Capri taxis are fun to ride
in but will not save you much time, given the near-
impossibility of overtaking on the island's narrow
roads. Allow €15 from the port to either Capri town
(can go no further than the taxi rank by the bus
terminus in via Roma) or Anacapri. A complete tour
of the island will set you back around €100.

Capri town & around

Marina Grande is pleasant enough in winter,
when a little bustle is a welcome thing. But
in high season it's a living hell of Blue Grotto
touts and garish souvenir emporia crawling
with *limoncello* addicts. At such times, by
far the best strategy is either to head up the
funicular to Capri town, or catch the little
orange bus to Anacapri.

   The funicular emerges at the far end of via
Roma – Capri town's access road. Above the
funicular station is a terrace with views over the
Marina and the huge bulk of **Monte Solaro**.

   Here, too, is the picturesque bell tower that
separates this antechamber from the **Piazzetta**:
core of the Capri experience, archetype of the
perfect Mediterranean island square, and also
the town's main pedestrian traffic chicane.
There is one route in and out of Capri town that
bypasses the Piazzetta, but it's known only to
locals and habitués who, for whatever reason,
want to slip in or out unnoticed. Most of the
time, the opposite instinct prevails, and the
Piazzetta, with its four rival bars (distinguished
by their colour-coded chairs) is one of the best
places in the world to see and be seen. Grab
a table, order a drink (see it as an investment),
sit back and enjoy the show.

   On the south side of the square, the main
parish church of **Santo Stefano** (open 8am-
8pm daily), with its play of curved roof-arches
corresponding to the chapels inside, sits pretty
at the top of a flight of steps. The present
baroque structure was built on the site of an
earlier church; inside, the intarsia marble
flooring in front of the main altar comes
from the **Villa Jovis** (*see p179*). To see
something of the town's vernacular architecture
– a warren of narrow, sometimes covered
lanes and houses that merge into one another

Lenin lost his chains on Capri jaunts.

in a play of steps and arches – take via Madre
Serafina from the top of the church steps (keep
to the right). This lane eventually becomes the
steep via Castello, at the end of which is the
Belvedere Cannone, with a magnificent view
over **Marina Piccola** (*see p179*) and the
Faraglioni (*see p179*).

   From the Piazzetta, via Vittorio Emanuele III
– the closest Capri comes to a main street –
descends past boutiques and *limoncello* outlets
to the Quisisana (*see p185*), doyen of the island's
luxury hotels. Continue down via Federico
Serena to via Matteotti, a curving balcony lane
that opens on to an unexpectedly rural scene of
olive groves, a medieval monastery and the sea.

   The monastery is the **Certosa di San
Giacomo**, reached by means of a walled
avenue at the eastern end of via Matteotti.
It was established in 1371 by Count Giacomo
Arcucci, powerful secretary to Queen Joan I,
who became a monk here when he suddenly
dropped from favour in 1386. The Carthusian
brotherhood of San Giacomo owned land,
grazing and hunting rights to most of the island
– something that brought it into frequent
conflict with the islanders. When plague broke
out in Capri in 1656, the monks, instead of
tending to the sick, sealed themselves off to
avoid infection; the *capresi* replied by dumping

the corpses of plague victims over the monastery wall. Suppressed by Napoleon in 1808, the monastery was used as a prison and military hospital. Today it is an atmospheric place, partly abandoned, partly given over to municipal uses – including a school, the town library and a museum dedicated to the lugubrious, Gothic-horror canvases of German painter and Capri resident Karl Wilhelm Diefenbach. Other rooms are used to house temporary exhibitions and conferences. The simple church has a fine 14th-century fresco on the façade above the door; among the three praying women to the left of the Virgin is Queen Joan, the monastery's co-founder. In the spring of 2002, a plan to restore the Certosa was given the green light, thanks to a big slice of EU funding – so don't be surprised if parts or all of the complex are *chiuso per restauro*.

At the other end of via Matteotti, past the Hotel Luna Convento, are the **Giardini di Augusto** (open dawn-dusk daily), a panoramic series of terraced gardens. These now form a municipal park, but were once part of the Capri estate of German arms manufacturer Alfred Krupp. Ironically, the gardens now boast a monument to Lenin, who stayed nearby with his friend Maxim Gorky. The **via Krupp** – a hairpin path that winds down the cliff below here to the Marina Piccola – has officially been closed for years due to the danger of rock slides, but the path itself is still in good condition, and locals just slip around the barrier. You, of course, should (not) do the same.

Back up at the Quisisana, via Camerelle heads east past elegant boutiques and bars to via Tragara, lined with upmarket hotels. This is the route of the classic Capri evening *passeggiata* (stroll): just long enough to work up an appetite for dinner, and with a great view at the end from the **Belvedere di Tragara**, which overlooks the three rock-stacks known as the **Faraglioni**. The outermost stack is home to a species of blue lizard found nowhere else in the world.

The paved path that descends from here offers one of the best walks on the island (*see p182* **Capri hikes**), via the mysterious **Grotta Matromania** and the photogenic **Arco Naturale**. But the most classic excursion from Capri town is the easy hike up to Tiberius's **Villa Jovis**. From the Piazzetta, via Botteghe leads to a crossroads just below the island's prettiest church – the tiny chapel of **San Michele** (open Apr-Oct 9am-7pm daily, Nov-Mar 10am-3pm daily), set back from the road in a small garden that cannot have changed much since the 14th century. Beyond here, the path dawdles up past imposing villas and more humble *capresi* dwellings until the

houses thin out and the going gets steep; plentiful signs keep you on the right track. Just before the remains of Tiberius's villa, on the right, is the **Parco Astarita**, an unassuming but scenic patch of grass underneath the pines.

You'll need to take an imaginative leap to see **Villa Jovis** in all its decadent Roman glory, flashing gold and delicate stucco work and swarming with servants. The most impressive remains are those of the huge cisterns in the centre of the complex, which guaranteed the self-sufficiency of what was in effect a miniature town; and the long, straight loggia to the north, which ends in the 330-metre (1,155-foot) Salto di Tiberio, the precipice from which the emperor was supposed to have pitched those who got up his nose. The legend may be mere embroidery, but the stunning view across to Punta della Campanella (*see p238*) on the mainland is real enough.

Head back downhill along via Roma from Capri town and fork left for **Marina Piccola**. There's not much to this place – the nearest Capri comes to a beach resort – except rows of bathing huts in primary colours and a couple of swanky private beach clubs that charge the earth for the pleasure of a swim (the best known is La Canzone al Mare, co-founded by British singer and Capri resident Gracie Fields

The photogenic **Arco Naturale**.

in 1933). But the central bit of beach – around the low rocky outcrop known as the Scoglio delle Sirene – is free, and perfectly feasible for a dip, providing the *scirocco* wind isn't blowing waves and dubious flotsam towards the shore.

Certosa di San Giacomo
Viale Certosa (081 837 6218). **Open** 9am-2pm Tue-Sun. **Admission** free.

Villa Jovis
Via Tiberio (081 837 0634/www.villajovis.it). **Open** 9am-1hr before sunset daily. **Admission** €2. **No credit cards**.

Where to eat

Though Capri has proud culinary traditions – based as much on tomatoes, aubergines, ricotta cheese and herbs as on what the sea has to offer – a constant supply of day-trippers means that there is little incentive to take the sort of risks, or the extra care, that carry restaurants on to a higher plane. One result of this is the sameness of most menus: however delicious *ravioli capresi* (plump ravioli filled with ricotta and herbs) and *spaghetti ai frutti di mare* (seafood spaghetti) may be, one is bound to tire of them eventually; the alternative is pizza. The restaurants listed below, while not always exceptions to this rule, are at least reliable. *See also p182* **Pulalli**.

Most restaurants close for the winter season between November and mid March; from June to September, most are open all week.

Buca di Bacco da Serafina
Via Longano 35 (081 837 0723). **Meals served** noon-3pm, 7pm-midnight Mon, Tue, Thur-Sun. Closed Nov & Wed lunch Aug. **Average** €35. **Credit** AmEx, DC, MC, V.
A warm, bustling trattoria just a whistle away from the Piazzetta, with reliable (though unadventurous) local seafood cooking, good vegetable antipasti and real Neapolitan pizzas. It's also a good place to eat grilled fish without breaking the bank (if it's available, try the *pezzogna* – blue-spotted bream – a local delicacy).

La Cantinella
Viale Matteotti 8 (081 837 0616). **Meals served** *mid Mar-Oct* noon-3.30pm, 7.30pm-midnight Mon, Wed-Sun. Closed Nov-mid Mar. **Average** €55. **Credit** AmEx, DC, MC, V.
The *caprese* offshoot of Giorgio Rosolino's chic Neapolitan eaterie *(see p111)* perches scenically next to the Villa Krupp hotel. The ambience is candlelit and romantic, but this is definitely a restaurant that gives itself airs; Capri habitués and VIPs tend to get better service than the Unknown Tourist, who is liable to be treated in a rather high-handed manner. The cuisine stays faithful to the mother ship, with classic pasta dishes such as *penne alla Cantinella*

Primary colours in **Marina Piccola**. *See p179.*

(pasta with aubergines, tomato and mozzarella); *secondi* are dominated by grilled fish and seafood. Antipasti and desserts are mostly good, but the cooking is neither as special, nor the ambience as unforgettable, as the prices would suggest.

La Capannina
Via Le Botteghe 12 bis (081 837 0732). **Meals served** *Apr-Oct* noon-2pm, 7.30pm-midnight daily. *Mar, Nov* noon-2pm, 7.30pm-midnight Mon, Tue, Thur-Sun. Closed mid Nov-mid Mar. **Average** €50. **Credit** AmEx, DC, MC, V.
One of the most consistently good restaurants on Capri. The light- and plant-filled central dining area and the waiters' pink waistcoats give the place a holiday atmosphere, enhanced by the photos of famous guests that line the walls. This is the place to come for textbook renditions of Capri specialities: the *ravioli capresi* are perfect, as are the *spaghetti alle vongole* and the *linguine allo scorfano* (flat spaghetti with scorpion fish), a house speciality. Prices are on the high side, but that's Capri for you and at least you eat well here. Although closed off-season, the restaurant opens for a week over New Year.

Da Gemma
Via Madre Serafina 6 (081 837 0461). **Meals served** *Aug* noon-3pm, 7.30pm-midnight daily. *Sept-July* noon-3pm, 7.30pm-midnight Tue-Sun. Closed mid Jan-mid Feb. **Average** €30. **Credit** AmEx, DC, MC, V.
This restaurant-pizzeria, in premises that straddle a narrow arched lane a minute's stroll from the

Piazzetta, is a Capri institution. Graham Greene used to eat here when Gemma herself was still around. It's in the same family today, and the pizzas, the pasta with seafood and the *frittura* of mozzarella or fish are reliable, though rarely inspiring. It's just like a decent Neapolitan trattoria, except that, being on Capri, it costs double.

Le Grottelle

Via Arco Naturale 13 (081 837 5719). **Meals served** *July, Aug* noon-3pm, 8-11pm daily. *May, June, Sept* noon-3pm, 8-11pm Mon-Wed, Fri-Sun. *Apr, Oct* noon-3pm Mon-Wed, Fri-Sun. Closed Nov-Mar. **Average** €28. **Credit** MC, V.

One of the best places on Capri for a simple but scenic lunch, this restaurant occupies a cavern on the path to the Arco Naturale; on the other side of the path is a large terrace with views down a steep verdant valley to the sea. The kitchen turns out no-nonsense *primi* such as *ravioli capresi* in tomato and basil sauce, followed by grilled fish, *pezzogna al forno* (oven-baked blue-spotted bream), chicken or rabbit, washed down with a local wine. It's all very basic, but service is friendly and all that nature is great for the digestion.

Da Paolino

Via Palazzo a Mare 11 (081 837 6102). **Meals served** *June-Sept* 8pm-midnight daily. *Oct* 8pm-midnight Mon, Tue, Thur-Sun. *Apr, May* noon-3pm, 8pm-midnight Mon, Tue, Thur-Sun. Closed Nov-Mar. **Average** €35. **Credit** AmEx, DC, MC, V.

If you have time to kill in Marina Grande in the evening – or if you missed the last boat out – this long-established restaurant, five minutes' walk from the first serious bend in the road up to Capri town, offers a safe haven. Set in a lemon grove, with a strong lemon theme throughout (even on the waiters' waistcoats), Da Paolino is justly famed for its antipasti and the final *limoncello*; in order to avoid spoiling the general effect, you might want to skip straight from one to the other.

La Pergola

Via Traversa lo Palazzo 2 (081 837 7414). **Meals served** *June-Sept* 12.30-3pm, 7-11pm daily. *Oct-May* 12.30-3pm, 7-11pm Mon, Tue, Thur-Sun. Closed 3wks Jan (or sometimes Nov). **Average** €35. **Credit** AmEx, DC, MC, V.

This newcomer in a quiet lane just below via Roma has three things going for it: good food, year-round opening and a lovely terrace overlooking the verdant lemon groves that step down the hillside to Marina Grande. The cuisine is firmly in the *caprese* seafood tradition, with good *linguine ai frutti di mare* and *secondi* that depend very much on the day's catch. Friendly and professional service.

La Savardina da Edoardo

Via Lo Capo 8 (081 837 6300). **Meals served** *July, Aug* noon-3pm, 7-11pm daily. *Jan, Mar-June, Sept, Oct, Dec* noon-3pm, 7pm-11pm Mon, Wed-Sun. Closed Nov-22 Dec, 7 Jan-Feb. **Average** €25. **Credit** AmEx, MC, V.

For a change from fish – and to see where real *capresi* live – head for this rustic farm-restaurant, an appetite-building 20-minute walk from the Piazzetta up towards Villa Jovis (*see p179*). In warm weather, tables are arranged outside in an orange grove with views over country villas and smallholdings. Ingredients are almost all home-grown or raised, including the fried courgette flowers that provide such a delicious starter. The ravioli are good, as is rabbit and *parmigiana di melanzane* (aubergines baked with mozzarella). The owner, Edoardo, is liable to burst into song at any moment, and his daughter Angela is a perennial fount of local gossip.

Da Tonino

Via Dentecale 12 (081 837 6718). **Meals served** noon-3pm, 7-11pm daily. Closed mid Jan-mid Mar. **Average** €30. **Credit** AmEx, DC, MC, V.

It's worth seeking out this family-run restaurant hidden away in one of Capri town's most rural corners, off the road that leads to the Arco Naturale. Gennaro Aprea and his dad Tonino offer a creative take on the local tradition in dishes such as *quadrucci di farina, parmigiano e buccia di limone con lupini di mare* (parmesan and lemon-flavoured pasta squares with wedge shells). The cuisine is as much land- as sea-based, with *secondi* such as wild boar, rabbit, frogs, quail and pigeon alongside more familiar marine options. The biggest surprise, though – apart from the reasonable prices – is

The **Piazzetta**: open for cocktails day and night. *See p178.*

Gennaro's wine cellar, hewn out of the solid rock, and stocked with more than 40,000 bottles from all over Italy and further afield. Definitely worth the hike; just make sure you remember the way back.

Cafés, bars & nightlife

On Capri, the most pressing dilemma is which bar to head for in the Piazzetta. Right below the church, **Bar Tiberio** (081 837 0268, closed Wed Nov-Feb & all Nov) attracts most locals and has the best cakes and cocktail nibbles. The **Gran Caffè** (081 837 0388, closed Thur Nov-Feb) has the most restrained sense of elegance and the best-dressed waiters. The **Piccolo Bar** in the corner (081 837 0325, closed Mon Nov-Mar) is good for those who like to watch rather than be watched – especially if you grab one of the tables upstairs by the windows that look on to the square.

An alternative to the Piazzetta flim-flam is **Pulalli** (081 837 4108, closed Tue, mid Nov-mid Dec & Jan-mid Mar), a lofty new wine bar that perches beneath the clocktower (take the stairs by the newsstand and continue up past the public payphones). Pulalli suspends its Tuesday closure in July and August, when it serves lunch only. It offers wines by the glass and by the bottle, as well as a good range of hot and cold dishes for lunch and dinner; prices, though, are on the high side. For cakes and ice-cream, **Buonocore** (via Vittorio Emanuele 35, 081 837 7826, closed Tue Mar-June, Sept, Oct & all Nov-Feb except one week over New Year) is the best one-stop shop: its *caprilù* lemon and almond cakes and *torta caprese* are justly famed. **Sfizi di Pane** (via Le Botteghe 15, 081 837 6180, closed Mon), Capri's best bakery, has slabs of pizza and *torte rustiche* (savoury flans) to take away.

Capri hikes

Few think of the Mediterranean's most stylish island as a trekker's paradise. But although space is limited, there is some fine walking to be had on the island, some of it almost Alpine in character. The following walks, at their best in spring and autumn, are classics: the first, which threads its way above the sea in the spectacular south-eastern corner of the island, is within reach of just about everyone; the second, while not nearly as difficult as it appears from afar, is for more experienced or adventurous walkers. Sunblock, a decent hat and plenty of water are essential.

I Faraglioni, Grotta Matromania & the Arco Naturale

Time 1hr. **Grade** easy.
After the stroll up to Villa Jovis (*see p180*), this classic round-trip is easily the best of the paved walks that depart from Capri town. From the Belvedere di Tragara (*see p179*), take either of the sets of steps that head downwards (they soon meet up). Passing a turn-off on the right to the **Faraglioni** (where there is a small rocky platform of a beach, mostly occupied by the deckchairs of a bar-restaurant), the path continues east around the wooded slopes of Monte Tuoro, with views over the rocky coast and the stunningly located **Villa Malaparte** – house of writer and self-styled man of action Curzio Malaparte. Soon after the villa the path becomes a flight of steps that lead up to the **Grotta**

Matromania, a huge cavern that was long thought to be sacred to the cult of Cybele (the Mater Magna, or Great Mother); the only certain evidence of use, though, is some first-century masonry, a tribute to the Roman mania for turning anything remotely cave-like

Around Naples

Capri nightlife revolves around bars and restaurants. There are a few smooth nightclub-cum-taverns – the most famous of which is the **Taverna Anima e Core** (via Sella Orta 39E, 081 837 6461, closed Mon-Fri in Oct, mid Nov-Mar except one week over New Year, admission €20-€25), but unless toupees and silicon are your thing, it is generally more fun to make your own party around a dry martini in the Piazzetta.

Arts & entertainment

There isn't much. Island cinephiles rely on two cinemas – **L'Isola** in Capri town (via Lo Palazzo 1, 081 837 8898) and the **Apollo** in Anacapri (via Giuseppe Orlandi 103, 081 837 1169, closed Mon-Fri Nov-Mar). Both show first- and second-run commercial films; all non-Italian offerings are dubbed. In summer a series of open-air chamber music concerts,

I Concerti di Capri, take place in the Certosa di San Giacomo. For updated information, ask in the tourist office (see p186).

Shopping

Designer boutiques line via Vittorio Emanuele and via Camerelle: Ferragamo, Gucci, Hogan, Fendi, Alberta Ferretti and others have small, prestige outlets whose aim is more to provide emergency wardrobe supplements than to satisfy a serious hunger for fashion.

The other Capri speciality is, of course, *limoncello*, the 33-per cent proof lemon liqueur that, in the past ten years, has become the statutory Italian restaurant *digestivo*. Opportunities to buy are not lacking on the island, or anywhere else around Naples for that matter; for authenticity and high standards, head for **Limoncello di Capri** (via Roma 79,

into a cute nymphaeum. The steps continue up to a junction by the Le Grottelle bar-restaurant (see p181).

Turn right here and in another couple of minutes you will see the **Arco Naturale**, a limestone arch that was a favourite with Romantic travellers. To head back to Capri town from here, continue straight past Le Grottelle along via Matermania. Smallholdings gradually give way to houses, and soon enough you'll find yourself back in the inevitable Piazzetta.

Monte Solaro via the Passetiello

Time *up* 1hr 30mins; *down* 1hr. **Grade** *up* a tough scramble; *down* moderate. From the panoramic terrace above Capri town's funicular station, the sheer mountain wall that divides Capri town from Anacapri looks impenetrable, aside from the road with its beetling orange buses and the crazy zigzag staircase known as the Scala Fenicia (see p187).

But there is a third way up, all but invisible from down below: the **Passetiello**. Though this is nowhere near as difficult as it looks, it's rather more than a Sunday stroll: the total height gain is 350 metres (1,149 feet) and you should be prepared to put hands on rock in a couple of places. From the Piazzetta, walk down via Roma to the four-way junction known as Due Golfi. Take the road down to Marina Piccola, turning right almost

immediately on to the paved lane that leads up past the side of the island's little-functioning, EU-funded hospital. A little further on, a wooden map-signpost indicates the beginning of the path proper, which is marked with red-and-white flashes (though the colour scheme has changed at least once in the past five years).

Villas and allotments soon give way to a forest of holm oak, and the going becomes steep. Above the tree-line, a tumble of rocks and Mediterranean *macchia* leads to a narrow gully – the **Passetiello** itself, a secret pass in the seemingly impenetrable wall of rock that separates Anacapri from Capri. French soldiers used this route to surprise the English troops quartered down below in 1808.

Once over the pass, one emerges on the ridge of **Monte Santa Maria**, with magnificent views. Follow the waymarked path that heads left (due south), just below the ridge, to the pretty hermitage of **Santa Maria a Cetrella** (erratic opening hours) founded by Dominican hermits in the 14th century.

From here, the clearly visible summit of **Monte Solaro** can be reached by taking the wide path that leads north-west to the pass of La Crocetta, where it joins the path up from Anacapri (see below).

This strenuous walk can be turned into a fairly easy downhill hike by getting the bus up to Anacapri and the chairlift to the top of Monte Solaro.

▶

081 837 5561, www.limoncello.com), which has the rights to the name and the recipe invented around a century ago by the founding father of *limoncello*, Vincenzo Canale.

Other island shop-ops revolve around antiques and ceramics; one of the more unusual pottery workshops is that of **Sara Aprea** (via Le Botteghe 6, 081 837 0165), who makes vases and other objects using the delicate Japanese raku technique; she also sells mosaics, Murano glass and other Italian designer ceramics.

One of the few commercial ventures on the island that is more interested in Capri and the *capresi* than in the day-tripping tourist trade is **La Conchiglia**, a publisher with 70 or so good-looking titles in its catalogue (a few of which are in English translation), all dealing with aspects of the island's history or its literary denizens. It has three bookshop outlets on the island: the main one (via Camerelle 18,

081 837 8199, closed Jan or Feb) has a wide selection of secondhand books about Capri – many in English, by the Brits and Americans who washed up on the island – as well as a good range of antique prints.

For internet access, try **Telecom Italia** (piazza Umberto I, above newsstand, 081 837 5447, open 9am-1pm, 3-8pm daily). Rates are €5 per hour.

Where to stay

Capri's hotel selection is deliberately weighted towards the top end, in order to encourage the 'better' sort of tourist. Booking well in advance is always a good idea – especially in low-budget establishments or small boutique hotels. Most hotels close down between the first week of November and mid March, though some reopen for a week or two over Christmas and New Year.

▶ ## Capri hikes (continued)

Monte Solaro

Time 1hr. **Grade** easy.
The Funivia (chairlift) di Monte Solaro, runs – weather and mechanics permitting – from piazza Vittoria up to the heavily rebuilt English fort on top of **Monte Solaro** (589 metres/2,062 feet). However, away from the hottest days of summer, it is much more pleasant to make the ascent on foot, or to take the chairlift up and walk down. The marked path forks off from via Capo di Monte in Anacapri, halfway between piazza Vittorio and Villa San Michele. It's a steady but not strenuous 300-metre/1,050-foot climb, past vines and through patches of forest, with good views over the western half of the island. Once over the pass of **La Crocetta** – marked by an iron cross – the scenery changes abruptly to reveal a valley of ferns and gorse that seems a continent away from the *beau monde* of the Piazzetta. The views from the summit, where there is a small snack bar, are vertiginous; Gustave Doré used them to make hell seem more realistic in his illustrations to Dante's *Inferno*.

Punta Carena to the Blue Grotto

Time 2hrs each way. **Grade** easy.
A new waymarked footpath, dubbed La Passeggiata dei Fortini ('the fortress walk') has been laid out along the little-visited west coast of the island, connecting Punta Carena with the Blue Grotto by way of three ruined

Napoleonic forts. Bring swimming things, as some of the coves along the way are difficult to resist.

Anacapri to the Blue Grotto

Time 45mins. **Grade** easy.
Away from the summer heat, one of the best ways to visit the **Blue Grotto** (*see p188* **Grotta Azzurra**) from Anacapri is to walk down and take the bus back: from piazza Armando Diaz in Anacapri, via Cava and via Lo Pozzo lead down to a path that continues past orchards and smallholdings to the parking lot above the Blue Grotto, which is also the bus terminus. Stop for a picnic en route at the **Villa Damecuta** (*see p189*).

Anacapri to Migliara

Time 45mins. **Grade** easy.
Another good walk from Anacapri is the flat, contour-hugging stroll to Migliara. Take via Caposcuro, to the left of the Monte Solaro chairlift (*see below*), and continue along it for a couple of kilometres (it soon changes its name to via Migliara), in a landscape that is about as rural as you can get on Capri. At the end of the path, the Belvedere di Migliara affords spectacular views over the cliffs below **Monte Solaro**.

Funivia di Monte Solaro

Via Caposcuro 10 (081 837 1428). **Open** *Mar-Oct* 9.30am-5pm daily. *Nov-Feb* 9.30am-3pm daily. **Tickets** €5.50 return. **No credit cards.**

Punta Carena on the island's wild south-western tip. *See p189.*

Casa Morgano

Via Tragara 6 (081 837 0158/fax 081 837 0681/ www.casamorgano.com). **Closed** Nov-Mar. **Rates** €220-€340 double; €350-€410 junior suite. **Credit** AmEx, DC MC, V.

Under the same ownership as the Quisisana (*see below*) and La Scalinatella (*see p186*), this cheerful hotel, which descends (like at least three others) in a series of bougainvillea-filled terraces from via Tragara, is a Capri classic, offering five-star luxury on a small scale. It has chintzy Mediterranean decor and all the usual comforts, including a good-sized pool. Guests can use the facilities at the Quisisana.

Grand Hotel Quisisana

Via Camerelle 2 (081 837 0788/fax 081 837 6080/ www.quisi.com). **Closed** Nov-mid Mar. **Rates** €190-€230 single; €245-€490 double; €455-€725 suite. **Credit** AmEx, DC, MC, V.

This Capri institution began life in 1845 as a sanatorium set up by a Scottish doctor, but soon transformed itself into the island's top luxury hotel. Behind the cream-and-white neo-classical façade – which has finally been given the balconies envisaged by the original plans – are two swimming pools (one inside, one out), a shady garden, a gym and the Quisi Club health and fitness centre. Service is impeccable, but the decor of the bedrooms can be anonymous, and the air of refined elegance is sometimes disturbed by herds of conference-goers.

Luna

Viale Matteotti 3 (081 837 0433/fax 081 837 7459/ www.lunahotel.com). **Closed** Nov-Mar. **Rates** €108-€142 single; €157-€335 double; €287-€405 suite. **Credit** AmEx, DC, MC, V.

In a spectacular position overlooking the Certosa and the sea, the Luna has a slightly old-fashioned feel about it, but the peaceful setting and magnificent views make up for any design shortcomings. The hotel is approached via a pretty bougainvillea-shaded walk and surrounded by gardens, with an Olympic-sized swimming pool and a restaurant on a rocky balcony above the sea.

Pensione Belsito

Via Matermania 9-11 (081 837 0969/fax 081 837 6622/www.hotelbelsito.com). **Rates** €36-€83 single; €72-€164 double. **Credit** AmEx, MC, V.

This Pompeii-red building stands where the roads to Capri town, Villa Jovis and the Arco Naturale meet. It's a friendly, decently priced, family-run place, open all year, with great views from many of the rooms. The restaurant next door serves up good, unadventurous *capresi* dishes.

Punta Tragara

Via Tragara 57 (081 837 0844/fax 081 837 7790/ www.hoteltragara.com). **Closed** Nov-Mar. **Rates** €300-€434 double; €400-€500 suite. **Credit** AmEx, DC, MC, V.

Designed by Le Corbusier in the 1920s as a private villa, this recently refurbished pink hotel has the best view and the most impressive exterior of any on the island; it also has some of the steepest prices. Most of the 50 rooms are small private suites, each with its own balcony overlooking the Faraglioni. There's nothing inspirational about the room decor, but the terrace bar, with its heated seawater pool, is a great place to watch the sunset.

Around Naples

Relais Maresca

Via provinciale Marina Grande 284 (081 837 9619/fax 081 837 4070/www.relaismaresca.it). **Closed** Jan, Feb. **Rates** €74-€224 single; €99-€249 double. **Credit** AmEx, DC, MC, V.

This new hotel compensates for its location – down in Marina Grande, it offers a fine view of the ferry traffic – with its bright Mediterranean decor (yellow, green or blue, depending on the floor) and reasonable prices. It also works a longer season than most Capri hotels. A pretty fourth-floor breakfast room gives on to a large flowery terrace, and there's an internet workstation off the lobby. It's a good out-of-season choice.

La Scalinatella

Via Tragara 8 (081 837 0633/fax 081 837 8291/www.scalinatella.com). **Closed** Nov-Mar. **Rates** €360-€420 double; €440-€500 suite. **No credit cards.**

This boutique hotel, with its magnificent Moorish-style façade and country-house feel, is a good place for a romantic weekend, if you can afford it. The 28 rooms and suites, most with private terraces, are tastefully decorated, and there's no need to get out of the jacuzzi to make a phone call. The service is professional but occasionally rather haughty – La Scalinatella is a hotel that likes everybody to know how exclusive it is.

La Tosca

Via Birago 5 (tel/fax 081 837 0989/www.capri online. com/latosca). **Closed** mid-Nov-mid Mar. **Rates** €36-€60 single; €62-€100 double. Breakfast €6.50. **Credit** MC, V.

This small one-star hotel, recently refurbished in a spare but elegant white Mediterranean style, is a real bargain. It's family-run and very basic, but the position (in a quiet lane leading down to the Certosa), the small terrace and the friendly welcome make La Tosca a popular choice with travellers shunning the Quisisana. There are only 12 rooms, so make sure you book ahead.

Villa Brunella

Via Tragara 24A (081 837 0122/fax 081 837 0430/www.villabrunella.com). **Closed** Nov-Mar. **Rates** €250-€330 double. Breakfast €10. **Credit** AmEx, DC, MC, V.

From via Tragara, this long, narrow hotel descends the hillside on a series of terraces, with views over Marina Piccola and Monte Solaro. It's bright and friendly, with a pool on the lowest level and terraces outside all the rooms. Service in Capri hotels is often distant and off-hand, but Villa Brunella is a welcome exception: guests are given personal attention, and families are made to feel especially at home.

Villa Krupp

Viale Matteotti 12 (081 837 0362/fax 081 837 6489). **Closed** Nov-Mar. **Rates** €72 single; €103-€134 double. Breakfast €3. **Credit** MC, V.

Perched above the Gardens of Augustus, this white hotel, with breathtaking views, used to be Maxim

Gorky's house. It's one of the best options in this price range, and therefore needs to be booked a fair bit in advance, especially in ever-popular July and August. The rooms are clean and bright, and many have terraces with sea views.

Villa Sarah

Via Tiberio 3A (081 837 7817/081 837 0689/fax 081 837 7215/www.villasarah.it). **Closed** Nov-Mar. **Rates** €93-€124 single; €155-€176 double. **Credit** AmEx, DC, MC, V.

An oasis of peace, near the beginning of the road up to Villa Jovis, this whitewashed villa is set among verdant vines and rural smallholdings. The 20 rooms are simply furnished, the atmosphere is one of a Mediterranean house party where nobody feels the need to party. Ideal for a relaxing long weekend, especially at the beginning or end of the season.

Tourist information

Azienda Autonoma di Cura, Soggiorno e Turismo

Banchina del Porto, Marina Grande (081 837 0634). **Open** *Apr-Sept* 8.30am-8.30pm daily. *Nov-Mar* 9am-3pm Mon-Sat.

In 2001, Capri's tourist board launched Tiberio, an audio-guide available in Italian, English and German from the island's three tourist offices (Marina Grande, Capri town, Anacapri). It's fairly easy to use, though the form of the narration – a dialogue between Tiberius and his wife Julia – sometimes gets in the way of the information. Thirty-two sights

The *anacapresi* strive to be different.

are covered in exhaustive detail, plus more general topics such as the island's flora and the origin of the name Capri. Price is €6.20 per day.

Azienda Autonoma di Cura, Soggiorno e Turismo

Piazza Umberto I, Capri (081 837 0686). **Open** *Apr-Sept* 8.30am-8.30pm daily. *Nov-Mar* 9am-1pm, 3.30-6.45pm Mon-Sat.

Anacapri & around

Until 1877, when a road was finally built, the western part of the island was another country, separated from Capri town and its surrounding area by a solid, impervious wall of cliffs. Anacapri, or 'up-Capri', is the name of the loose-knit cluster of houses on the upland side of this huge seismic fracture. A community of farmers and artisans had already begun to form here in Roman times, but it only condensed into a proper village in the late Middle Ages.

Anacapri's rural vocation and centuries of physical isolation are reflected in the proud, independent character of the *anacapresi*, who preferred to work as ship's caulkers for the king of Naples than have anything to do with the *capresi* down below. The only means of communication between the two centres was the **Scala Fenicia**, a steep flight of steps that leads up from Marina Grande (the island's only proper port, which the *anacapresi* were forced to use even though it was in 'enemy territory')

to the tiny chapel of Sant'Antonio, just below Villa San Michele; the steepest, final stretch was formerly entered through a gate called the Porta della Differencia, designed to safeguard Anacapri's 'difference'. When Swedish doctor Axel Munthe first walked up here in the late 19th century, overtaking the village postwoman (who couldn't read), the hostess of Anacapri's one and only inn told him that she had 'once been down to Capri' – but it hadn't impressed her much. If rural Anacapri today receives as many visitors as swish Capri town, it is largely thanks to Munthe himself. His book *The Story of San Michele* was the *A Year in Provence* of its time, filling Cold Northerners with longing for the Warm South by bringing to life the charming rustic characters of Anacapri. Translated into over 30 languages, Munthe's memoir continues to sell steadily seven decades after its original publication in 1929.

Born in 1857, Munthe first set foot on Anacapri in 1874 as a young medical student. But it was not until 15 years later – after he had become the youngest and most sought-after society doctor in Paris – that he was able to realise his dream of building the **Villa San Michele** on the edge of the Anacapri cliff, on the site of one of Tiberius's 12 Capri villas. Designed in an eclectic style that mixes Romanesque and Renaissance influences with Moorish trills, the villa and its trim gardens are studded with bits of classical statuary.

Some visitors will undoubtedly agree with writer Bruce Chatwin, who wrote in his Munthe-debunking essay *Self-love Among the Ruins* (reprinted in *Anatomy of Restlessness*) that 'in Pasadena or Beverly Hills, Munthe's creation wouldn't get more than a passing glance'.

Nevertheless, the views are spectacular, and the villa and gardens are preserved with Nordic tidiness and attention to detail by a foundation whose members are nominated by the Swedish state. A series of classical music concerts, *Concerti al tramonto*, timed to take make the most of the summer sunset, takes place in the gardens on Friday evenings (*see p166*). The ruined **Castello di Barbarossa** on the crest above – named after the pirate who destroyed it – is part of the same property; it can be visited on a free guided tour each Thursday at 5pm (places are limited, so ring ahead to book). Part of the surrounding hillside, which has a resident population of peregrine falcons, is a **WWF nature reserve**. Guided tours are organised at weekends between May and October; ring 081 837 1325 for details.

Grotta Azzurra

Capri's most famous sight is an important local industry. Like all self-respecting tourist magnets, this one has its discovery legend, involving a Polish poet called Klopisch who swam in here in 1826. The fact that the local fishermen and plenty of other islanders had known about the cave for years is generally overlooked. *Caprese* writer Raffaele la Capria has even suggested that the whole expedition was a practical joke played on the ingenuous Pole by the fisherman and hotel owner who accompanied him, and who told him that 'the cave was inhabited by the devil... and by strange marine creatures'. These legends were of course repeated with po-faced seriousness in the poet's self-glorifying account of his 'discovery'.

Foreigners are still taken for rides to the Grotta Azzurra today, but in a more organised fashion. The quickest route to the Grotto is by motor launch from Marina Grande; the journey can also be made more slowly and only marginally more cheaply by bus (change at Anacapri) to the car park above the cave. All visitors are then decanted into a flotilla of tiny three- or four-seater boats that bob under the low rock lip of the entrance. Each of these three stages – motor launch, rowing boat and actual entrance – has to be paid for; currently, the full experience, with departure from and return to Marina Grande, costs around €14 (around €12.50 by bus). Most of the money goes into the pockets of the cooperatives that run the boat services. Of the entrance fee – in effect a state tax on visitors – 60 per cent is ploughed back into Capri itself, helping the island to keep itself looking clean and well-dressed.

Is it all worth it? Definitely, if you have an hour and a half to spare – especially if you visit out of season, during the lunchtime lull, or towards the end of the day. The iridescent quality of the blue light inside really does need to be seen to be believed. Nineteenth-century traveller Gregorovius summed it up when he wrote that 'the world and the day disappeared; I suddenly found myself in a new element of cerulean light'.

At the back of the Grotto, a small landing stage and rudimentary nymphaeum date back to Roman times (further proof that the 1826 'discovery' was only one of many). Three rock-hewn galleries lead from here into a small chamber – no longer open to visitors – adorned with the signatures of tourists from a less regulated era. The single narrow passage that continues up from this chamber into the side of the mountain gave rise to the legend that the grotto was connected by a secret passageway to Tiberius's Villa Damecuta above. It seems more likely, though, that the cutting was made by Roman engineers looking for a vein of fresh water to add a cascade effect to the nymphaeum.

Note that while it is theoretically possible to swim into the Grotto after having paid only the €4 entrance fee, this is not advisable: firstly because one is likely to be clouted inadvertently by the oars of the boatmen who monopolise access to the cave, secondly because of the strong currents.

Note also that in the event of strong winds and/or rough seas, visits to the Blue Grotto are suspended; this is a common occurrence between November and February.

Grotta Azzurra (Blue Grotto)
Open 9am-1hr before sunset daily.
Admission €4 plus €4.10 rowing boat fee. Access by motor launch from Marina Grande: departures 9.30am-4pm daily; €5-€6 return. **No credit cards.**

Munthe was the first of a steady trickle of discerning foreign residents who preferred Anacapri's quiet charm to the more glitzy delights of Capri town: writers Compton Mackenzie and Graham Greene had houses here, and Queen Victoria of Sweden had a summer villa at Caprile, just south of the town. Today the peace and quiet that attracted these escapees is challenged by the busloads of tourists that come to visit Villa San Michele and offload their euros in a slough of tacky souvenir shops; but away from this thankfully limited outbreak of bad taste – and out of season – Anacapri is a good place to see the other, more rural side of Capri, which, like most Italian islands, has always looked more to the land than to the sea for sustenance.

Gateway to the town, and setting-down point for the regular buses that connect Anacapri with Marina Grande and Capri town, is little piazza Vittoria. Most visitors head straight along the souvenir-lined via Capodimonte to Villa San Michele. From the square, pedestrianised via Giuseppe Orlandi leads west past the tourist office into the centre of the old town. Halfway down on the right is the **Casa Rossa**, an antiquity-encrusted folly built in 1876 by a former Confederate soldier, JC MacKowen, who wrote one of the first guides to Capri.

On the left, via San Nicola leads to piazza San Nicola, dominated by the parish church of **San Michele Arcangelo**. The standard baroque façade presages a standard baroque interior, but the latter is enlivened by a delightful majolica floor dating from 1761. The theme is Earthly Paradise, complete with ostriches, camels and crocodiles: a good opportunity for an impromptu game of I-spy with the kids.

From Anacapri, two bus routes run west (*see p177* for transport information). One route goes to the **Blue Grotto** (*see p188* **Grotta Azzurra**) via the remains of **Villa Damecuta** (ask the bus driver to put you off by the side road to the villa; one of Tiberius's 12 imperial villas, it was devastated first by the volcanic rain of Vesuvius, then by a series of depredations by Bourbon and later French troops, and little is left today, but it's a pretty spot, covered in wild flowers in spring, and ideal for a picnic). The second bus goes to the lighthouse at **Punta Carena**, on the south-western tip of the island. Just before the lighthouse, the rocky beach at **Cala Tombosiello** is one of the less crowded on the island, though it should be avoided when the wind is blowing in from the west.

For walks from Anacapri, and for information on the chairlift to Monte Solaro, *see p182* **Capri hikes**.

Succulent **Da Mamma Giovanni**. *See p190.*

San Michele Arcangelo

Piazza San Nicola (081 837 2396). **Open** *July-Oct* 10am-7pm daily. *Nov-Mar* 9.30am-4pm daily. *Apr-June* 9.30am-5pm daily. **Admission** €1.03. **No credit cards**.

Villa San Michele

Viale Axel Munthe (081 837 1401/www.sanmichele. org). **Open** *May-Sept* 9am-6pm daily. *Apr, Oct* 9.30am-5pm daily. *Nov-Feb* 10.30am-3.30pm daily. *Mar* 9.30am-4pm daily. **Admission** €5. **No credit cards**.

Where to eat

Add'O Riccio

Grotta Azzurra (081 837 1380). **Meals served** *June-mid Sept* noon-3pm Mon-Wed; noon-3pm, 7-10.30pm Thur-Sun. *Mid Mar-May, mid Sept-Oct* noon-3pm daily. Closed Nov-mid Mar. **Average** €35. **Credit** AmEx, DC, MC, V.
Of all Capri's scenic eateries, this long-established restaurant, perching on a cliff just along from the Blue Grotto, has to be the most spectacular. Considering that they could get away with almost anything, the food is very decent: the fish and seafood (as featured in a highly recommended *antipasto di mare*) is squeaky-fresh, pasta dishes such as *linguine ai frutti di mare* are well turned out and the house white wine will help you deal with that view.

Da Mamma Giovanna

Via Boffe 3 (081 837 2057). **Meals served**
Mid June-mid Sept noon-3pm, 7-11pm daily.
Mar-mid June, mid Sept-Nov noon-3pm, 7-11pm
Mon, Tue, Thur-Sun. Closed Dec-Feb. **Average** €25.
Credit AmEx, DC, MC, V.
A good place to take in the more laid-back, villagey
atmosphere of the island's other town, in the company of Mummy Joan and her homely but succulent
cooking. Book ahead to secure one of the four tables
outside, overlooking the pretty square of Santa
Sofia. Order the ravioli with walnut sauce, the *pen-
nette al cartoccio* (oven-baked pasta with seafood,
mushrooms and olives) or the fish with green peppers, and sit back and let Anacapri's quiet charm
wash over you as you watch local kids playing football in front of the church.

Where to stay

Capri Palace Hotel & Spa

*Via Capodimonte 2B (081 978 0111/fax 081 837
3191/www.capri-palace.com).* **Closed** Nov-Mar.
Rates €145-€222 single; €232-€568 double; €413-
€826 double with private pool; €465-€620 junior
suite; €594-€2,014 suite. **Credit** AmEx, DC, MC, V.
Now looking better than ever after a recent
makeover, the Capri Palace has become the island's
luxury hotel of choice. Its tastefully decorated
rooms, urbane and attentive service, and easy access
(via complimentary minibus to and from Marina
Grande) score points for the Palace, as does the
hotel's own Capri Beauty Farm, which is also open
to non-residents, and the good but pricey L'Olivo
restaurant. Four rooms have their own small private
pools; the Megaron suite, on the roof, is a whole
apartment, with a swimming pool, a sliding ceiling
above the double bed for stargazing, and an olive
tree that was winched up by helicopter. Works by
artists-in-residence adorn the hotel.

Il Girasole

*Via Linciano 47 (081 837 2351/fax 081 837 3880/
www.ilgirasole.com).* **Closed** Nov-Mar except 1wk
over New Year. **Rates** €80-€160 double. **Credit**
AmEx, MC, V.
Popular with budget travellers, this hotel is set in a
rural landscape of vines and olives between
Anacapri and Punta Carena (guests can be picked
up at Marina Grande). Rooms are arranged in terraced rows, and give on to terraces bursting with
flowering plants. There is a small swimming pool
and a panoramic dining area under an awning,
where breakfast is served. There are also four iMac
terminals for netsurfing.

San Michele

*Via Giuseppe Orlandi 1/5 (081 837 1427/fax
081 837 1420/www.sanmichele-capri.com).* **Closed**
Nov-Mar. **Rates** €78-€96 single; €135-€170 double.
Credit AmEx, DC, MC, V.
A good choice for families, this large white hotel
on the main road beneath the Villa San Michele has

Capri Palace, luxury hotel of choice.

the island's biggest swimming pool, a huge semi-
Olympic affair perfect for 100m butterfly races.
The decor is extremely chintzy and there is a certain amount of noise from coaches and buses on the
nearby road, but the views are stupendous and the
welcome friendly. The minibus up from or down to
Marina Grande costs €3 extra. The hotel is open
for a week over New Year.

Villa Eva

*Via La Fabbrica 8 (tel/fax 081 837 2040/
www.villaeva.com).* **Closed** Nov-Feb. **Rates** €70-
€90 double (with breakfast). **Credit** MC, V for stays
of 3 or more nights.
Run by a guy who looks like a *caprese* Santa Claus,
this excellent budget option offers a range of
accommodation in extensive, verdant grounds,
from double rooms in the main building to a series
of eclectic, self-contained chalets in the gardens.
There's even a decent-sized swimming pool.
Transport can be arranged to and from Marina
Grande; otherwise, it's a short walk from the Capri–
Blue Grotto road and bus route.

Tourist information

Azienda Autonoma di Cura, Soggiorno e Turismo

Via Giuseppe Orlandi 59 (081 837 1524). **Open**
June-Sept 8.30am-8.30pm Mon-Sat; 9am-3pm Sun.
Oct-May 9am-3pm Mon-Sat.

Ischia

Go southern on this steamy isle of beaches and 103 hot springs.

For map, see p203.

'Out of a Gothic North, the pallid children of a potato, beer-or-whisky guilt culture, we behave like our fathers and come southward into a sunburnt otherwhere of vineyards [and] baroque,' wrote WH Auden, who spent much of his time from 1948 to 1957 on Ischia.

Half a century later, the pallid northerners – and, in particular, middle-aged Germans taking spa cures – are very much in evidence, packing the ugly (though mercifully low-rise) hotels of the island's main towns and villages, eating mediocre food and making do with tatty accommodation. Most will probably never discover that the vineyards and baroque that surrounded Auden (*see p200* **Going southern**) in his home in Forio (*see p198*) are still there. And they will never happen across the island's secret delights: excellent restaurants if you know where to look; some great hotels in hidden corners; the exotic gardens and the verdant forests; not to mention the weird and wonderful antics of imprisoned Typhon.

When Zeus ousted the old gods from heaven, he confined one of them – Typhon – beneath an island in the Mediterranean. There poor Titan remained, occasionally struggling to get out of his prison, but mostly sighing and crying. The island, according to local lore, was Ischia; and though Typhon hasn't tried to shrug the weight off his back since 1883, his sighs of fiery vapour and hot rivers of tears are very much present.

When Greeks from Euboea arrived on the island they called Pithekoussai in the eighth century BC, there were already indigenous peoples living there. Despite the opportunities for gain that were offered by the island's strategic position on one of the Mediterranean's key trade routes, its seismic activity didn't suit the newcomers, most of whom decided to decamp to Cuma on the mainland. Those who remained exploited the local supply of fine clay for pot-making.

Under Roman rule, and renamed Aenaria, the island became famous for its thermal cure treatments. When under Neapolitan rule in the Middle Ages, it suffered badly from attacks by North African Saracens. The first recorded use of the name Ischia (from *insula*, 'island') dates from the ninth century AD.

In 1301, a vast eruption of Monte Arso forced Ischia's inhabitants to leave the island for four years. When they returned, they crowded on to what is now the **Castello Aragonese**, the fortified rocky outcrop off **Ischia Ponte** (*see p192*). The Castello was hotly contended for by Angevins and Aragonese throughout the 14th century and, later refortified, remained a place of refuge from Saracen attack.

In 1495, King Ferdinand II of Spain took Ischia along with Naples and left it under the control of the Dukes of Avalos, who were to rule there until the 18th century.

Saracens continued to threaten the island, their last attack coming as late as 1796. When Ischia supported the Parthenopean Republic in 1799, King Ferdinand's British allies soon overran the place.

The British had more trouble ousting the French who came to occupy Ischia in 1806; the devastation that the British wreaked in their bombardment of the Castello Aragonese can still be seen today.

OPENING HOURS

The opening hours of Ischia's many churches are often dependent on the whims of their priests. Most of the buildings can be visited from around 7am to 11am and from 5pm or 6pm to 7pm or 8pm. To be sure of getting in, go immediately before or after the mass times (which are posted on the door).

Take note, also, that the churches on the island are, in many cases, known by several different names – confusion can often result.

The best | Beaches

The *spiaggia libera* (open access) stretch of any beach is often (though not always) confined to the rocky, seaweedy bits at the edges. Hiring an umbrella and a couple of deckchairs on a privately run beach should cost between €14 and €18 per day. If you don't mind congestion, the town beaches in **Forio** and **Ischia Porto** are long, sandy, and perfectly acceptable. For something more out of the way, try:

San Montano *See p197.*
Sorgeto *See p199.*
Spiaggia dei Maronti *See p201.*
Spiaggia dei Pescatori *See p192.*

BOOKING A HOTEL

Be prepared for hotel proprietors to refuse to reserve rooms on a bed-and-breakfast basis. Many hotels offer only half board, especially during the summer months. But ask firmly for *camera con colazione* and most will reluctantly quote you a price. You'll also find that single supplements are common.

Most of Ischia's hotels close for the whole of the winter. But a growing number of them are now opening up for a couple of weeks around Christmas and the New Year. If you fancy taking a Yuletide break, it is worth phoning to see whether the hotel of your choice has decided to follow this trend.

Getting there

By boat

For general boat transport information, *see chapter Directory: Getting around*.

Caremar (081 551 3882/www.caremar.gestelnet.it), Lauro (081 551 3352/www.lauro.it) and Traghetti Pozzuoli (081 526 7736) run regular hydrofoil and car ferry services between Ischia (Porto and Casamicciola) and the mainland (Naples and Pozzuoli), plus less frequent ones between Ischia Porto and Capri, Sorrento and Procida. Naples to Ischia takes about 1hr 35mins by ferry (around €7, depending on the company) and 45mins by hydrofoil (around €11); none of the ferry companies accepts credit cards. There's a booking charge for advance hydrofoil tickets, but this is worth paying on crowded summer Sundays.

Getting around

By boat

Sogema (081 985 080/www.ischiasogema.it) organises boat trips that travel around the island (tickets cost €12), in addition to day trips to neighbouring Capri (€21).

By bus

Sepsa (081 991 828) runs a highly efficient, if crowded, bus service around the island. The main routes are the **Circolare sinistra**, which circles the island anticlockwise, stopping at Ischia Porto, Casamicciola, Lacco Ameno, Forio, Serrara, Fontana, Barano, returning to Ischia Porto; and the **Circolare destra**, which covers the same route in a clockwise direction. The services run every 30mins, with buses every 15mins during rush hours. There are also services from Ischia Porto to Sant'Angelo (every 15mins), Giardini Poseidon at Citara (every 30mins) and spiaggia dei Maronti via Testaccio (every 20mins). In addition, minibus services operate within Ischia Porto and Ponte, and in Forio. Tickets must be purchased before boarding; get them at the terminus in Ischia Porto (where bus maps and timetables are available), in any *tabacchi* or at newsstands. Tickets cost 93¢ (single trip), €1.65 (half-day), €2.74 (24hr), €11.88 (weekly) and €16.53 (fortnightly).

Ischia Porto & Ponte

Once two separate towns called Villa dei Bagni and Borgo Celsi, Ischia Porto and Ischia Ponte are now one long, colourful, hotel-, shop- and tree-filled agglomeration stretching from the ferry port to the Castello Aragonese.

The deft manoeuvring of ferries and hydrofoils inside the little port can distract attention from the uniqueness of the harbour itself. Until 1854, this was an inland lake in an extinct volcanic crater; then King Ferdinand II, sickened by the smell of its brackish waters when he stayed in his Ischian villa, ordered an opening to be made to the sea.

Overlooking the port, the church of **Santa Maria di Portosalvo** was another of Ferdinand's good works, also built in 1854. The former royal palace – now a spa treatment centre for the military – is situated east of the church, along a driveway guarded by imposing faux-Egyptian lions on the gateposts. Across the road, the **Antiche Terme Comunali** no longer functions as a spa, but houses town council offices and hosts the occasional (and often fairly dreadful) art exhibition.

On the eastern shore of the port, via Porto leads past restaurants and bars galore out to the point at Punta San Pietro, which is dominated by its dark-red underwater research station (not open to the public).

Ischia's main drag – via Roma, which becomes corso Vittoria Colonna – has been pedestrianised and is usually hopping with people. Lanes running north of via Roma lead to the town's main beach. Where corso Colonna meets via Gigante, the church of **San Pietro** (aka Madonna delle Grazie, or Purgatorio) is a baroque extravaganza with a curving façade and stucco whirls inside.

Just beyond the junction with via D'Avalos, a gate off the main road leads to the unkempt but beautifully shady gardens of the **Villa Nenzi Bozzi** (open 7am-8pm daily). Looking uphill from here, the stone pines – those that haven't been sacrificed to creeping construction – are all that remains of the woods that were planted in the mid 19th century on the great lava flow from Monte Arso; beneath them lies the village of Geronda, which was buried in the devastating eruption of 1301. The little chapel of **San Girolamo dell'Arso** (aka Madonna della Pace) commemorates the disaster; a church has stood here since the 16th century.

The eastern end of corso Colonna, and via Pontano, run along the **spiaggia dei Pescatori**, where fishing boats are still pulled

Castello Aragonese: an impregnable fortress and cultural magnet.

up among the bathers along an expanse of dark sand, and where there's an unimpeded view across to the Castello. The church of **Santa Maria delle Grazie e Sant'Antonio**, at the top of a flight of steps off corso Colonna, was constructed in the 18th century to replace the 14th-century original.

Via Seminario is home to the **Palazzo del Vescovado** (Bishop's Palace, open 3-5pm Mon, 9.30am-noon Wed, Fri) where sarcophagi from the fourth to the 14th century are on display. Opposite, Vicolo Marina leads to **Palazzo Malcoviti** where much of *The Talented Mr Ripley* was shot; stark and forbidding as you approach, the *palazzo* hides a pretty flower-filled courtyard behind.

On via Mazzella, the 17th-century church of **Santo Spirito** (aka San Giovan Giuseppe) has a fine 18th-century marble altar. Across the road from here, the **Assunta** (aka Santa Maria della Scala) became Ischia's cathedral after its predecessor in the Castello Aragonese (*see p194*) was bombed by the British in 1809. The original 13th-century church was replaced in the 17th and 18th centuries, but the 14th-century baptismal font managed to survive the reworkings, as did the Romanesque wooden crucifix, and the 14th-century painting of the Madonna in the right-hand end of the nave.

Facing the cathedral you'll find the Palazzo dell'Orologio, home to the engaging **Museo del Mare**; nets, tackle, photos, stamps, plus a few classic posters of films shot on the island chart Ischia's relationship with the sea. Via Mazzella continues to the **Ponte Aragonese** bridge, built in 1432 by the Aragonese King Alfonso, leading to the **Castello**.

Castello Aragonese

The rocky outcrop on which the Castello is sited was fortified in the fifth century BC by Greeks from Siracusa in Sicily, then it was used as a stronghold or lookout by Romans, Goths, Arabs and just about every other tribe that ruled or aimed to rule the Naples area. When Monte Arso erupted in 1301, locals took refuge here.

Alfonso of Aragon refortified the crumbling rock in the mid 15th century, adding the bridge but making the Castello into an impregnable fortress where the island's inhabitants could hole up during Saracen attacks. In the 16th century, it was home to a brilliant court centred around Vittoria Colonna, wife of Ischia's feudal chief Ferrante D'Avalos. Beautiful, devout and very learned, Vittoria made her rocky outcrop in the Mediterranean into a cultural magnet. Her verses were praised by the poet Ludovico Ariosto and her learning by the humanist philosopher Pietro Bembo. But it was Vittoria's profound and touchingly platonic relationship with Michelangelo (who may have lived in the tower that bears his name opposite the castle) that ensured her lasting fame.

Around Naples

'Nature, that never made so fair a face, remained ashamed, and tears were in all eyes,' wrote Michelangelo in 1574 after watching over Vittoria on her death bed.

By the 18th century, the Castello held 2,000 families, 13 churches, and a few Poor Clare (*Clarisse*) nuns. A hundred years later, with the Saracen threat a thing of the past, the families had moved out and the place was going to rack and ruin. What time didn't destroy, the British did when they bombarded the island in 1809 in a bid to oust its French occupiers. The crippled fortress was later used as a prison.

There's a lift up to the high ground of the castle, but if you're feeling energetic, take the magnificent tunnel hewn through the solid rock by King Alfonso. Paths to the *castello*'s various churches and viewpoints are clearly signposted.

The 18th-century church of the Immacolata has a stark white interior built to a Greek cross plan and hosts temporary exhibitions. The convent of **Santa Maria della Consolazione** was a convenient place for families with more titles than funds to park their dowry-less younger daughters. When the nuns died, their corpses were placed sitting upright on macabre thrones in the *cimitero* beneath the convent. The living visited their decomposing sisters daily in a grim reminder of the less dignified side of death. The nuns remained ensconced in their convent until 1809.

The **Cattedrale dell'Assunta** was erected after the 1301 eruption but, like so many of the region's churches, it was given a heavy baroque reworking in the early 18th century. What remains of the stucco decorations after the

British bombardment are eerily lovely. In the cathedral crypt are fragments of 14th-century frescos, created by followers of Giotto. The elegant, grey-and-white hexagonal church of **San Pietro a Pantaniello** was constructed in the mid 16th century.

The Castello is now in private ownership; the former ruler's residence at the top of the building is closed to the public.

Ischia's own private Atlantis, the Roman town of Aenaria, may lie immediately to the east of the *ponte*. According to contemporary records, this thriving settlement sank beneath the waves some time during the second century AD. Underwater explorers have come up with a sufficient number of ancient artefacts from the zone to lend some credence to the legend.

Around the Bay of Cartaromana, the 16th-century chapel of **Sant'Anna** overlooks rocks thrusting out of the sea. Brightly lit decorated fishing boats and rafts from all over Ischia and Procida compete for a trophy in the bay on 26 July each year in a multicoloured celebration and spectacular firework display that looks age-old but, in fact, was invented in the 1930s. Nearby, the solid, square **Torre Michelangelo** (open occasionally in summer for concerts) may or may not be where the great Renaissance artist stayed when attracted to Ischia by Vittoria Colonna and her court (*see p193*).

Castello Aragonese

(081 992 834). **Open** *Mar-Nov* 9.30am-1hr before sunset daily; also 10 days over Christmas. **Admission** €8 (includes weapons museum). **No credit cards**.

Museo del Mare

Via Giovanni da Procida 2 (081 981 124). **Open** *Nov-Jan, Mar* 10.30am-12.30pm daily; *Apr-June, Sept, Oct* 10am-12.30pm, 5-8pm daily; *July, Aug* 10.30am-12.30pm, 6.30-10pm daily. Closed Feb. **Admission** €2.58. **No credit cards**.

Where to eat & drink

Alberto a Mare

Via Cristoforo Colombo 8 (081 981 259). **Meals served** noon-3pm, 7-11pm daily. Closed Nov-mid Mar. **Average** €35. **Credit** AmEx, MC, V.
Restful blue interior on a platform jutting into a blue sea. Alberto serves imaginative takes on local favourites; the pasta with *spigola* (sea bass), almonds and tomato is excellent.

Bar Calise

Piazza degli Eroi 69 (081 991 270). **Open** *Nov-Mar* 7am-2am Mon, Tue, Thur-Sun. *Apr-Oct* 7am-2am daily. **Credit** MC, V.
The jungle at the centre of this traffic roundabout conceals one of the island's best bars, where the ice-cream's good and the cakes are great.

The best Spas

True aficionados choose a spa with the right mineral content for their particular complaint; taking the waters is purely medicinal. But even in such a dedicatedly *curativo* resort as Ischia, there's no shortage of hedonists – there for the sheer joy of the warm water experience. Ischia has 103 hot springs, most of which are funnelled into *stabilimenti termali*, many of which are full-fledged hotels with treatments for hotel guests only. Others are open to all; here are some of the best.
Giardini Poseidon See *p199*.
Negombo See *p198*.
Parco Termale Aphrodite Apollon See *p202*.
Terme Belliazzi See *p198*.
Terme di Cava Scura See *p202*.
Terme della Regina Isabella See *p198*.

View from **Castello Aragonese**. *See p193*.

This wine bar serves hearty bruschette (from €5), salads, *salumeria* (charcuterie) and cheeses from all over the place. There's an excellent *menu degustazione* (taster menu) for €18.

Pane & Vino
Via Porto 24 (081 991 046). **Open** *Nov-mid Jan, Mar* 10am-1pm, 4.30-9.30pm Mon, Tue, Thur-Sun. *Apr-Oct* 10am-2am daily. Closed mid Jan-Feb. **Credit** MC, V.
The *pane* (bread) served in what is primarily a wine shop is extraordinarily good, as are the cheeses, cold meats and a few hot dishes that change daily. Wash it all down with something from their fine range of *vino* which you can order by the glass or bottle at little more than off-the-shelf prices.

Sport

Captain Cook – Ischia Diving
Via Iasolino 116 (081 982 090/335 636 2630/cook_ischia@hotmail.com). **Open** *Easter-Oct* 8.30am-1pm, 3-7.30pm daily. *Nov-Easter* by appointment only. **Credit** MC, V.
Captain Cook organises night dives and marine nature dives for experienced divers between Ischia and Procida. A double dive costs from €62 and courses at all levels can be arranged.

Tennis Lido
Via Cristoforo Colombo 2 (081 985 245). **Open** 8am-1pm, 3-9pm daily. **Admission** €9.30-€12.40 per court per hr. **No credit cards.**
These well-kept tennis courts are in a recently revamped park by Ischia Ponte's beach.

Where to stay

Miramare e Castello
Via Pontano 5 (081 991 333/fax 081 984 572/www.miramareecastello.it). **Closed** mid Oct-mid Apr. **Rates** €114-€186 single; €176-€434 double. **Credit** AmEx, DC, MC, V.
Literally on the beach, and eyeball-to-eyeball with the Castello (*see p193*), the Miramare is tastefully furnished in shades of blue. Rates rise for rooms with a sea view and/or a balcony overlooking the sea. The spa centre offers special weekly pampering packages from €184.

Il Monastero
Castello Aragonese 3 (tel/fax 081 992 435/www.castelloaragonese.it). **Closed** mid Oct-Mar. **Rates** €54.70-€65 single; €108.40 double. **Credit** AmEx, DC, MC, V.
Situated inside the Castello Aragonese (*see p193*), Il Monastero has what must rank as one of the finest views anywhere in the world, and by Ischian standards it's cheap. Former management succeeded in making the place ghastly, force-feeding guests unspeakable food; the new owners look like a definite improvement, though the rooms could do with a facelift and there's no spa pampering. Bed and breakfast only.

Da Ciccio
Piazza Antica Reggia 5 (081 991 314). **Open** *Nov-Mar* 7am-midnight Tue-Sun. *Apr-Oct* 7am-2am daily. **No credit cards.**
Ciccio makes arguably the best ice-cream on the island. The coffee's good too, and there's an enormous selection of truly mouth-watering cakes.

Cocò
Piazzale Aragonese (081 981 823). **Meals served** *Mar, Apr, Oct-Dec* 12.30-3pm, 7.30-11pm Mon, Tue, Thur-Sun. *May-Sept* 12.30-3pm, 7.30-11pm daily. Closed Jan, Feb. **Average** €20. **Credit** AmEx, DC, MC, V.
Right at the 'mainland' end of the Ponte Aragonese, Cocò is frequented by locals who appreciate the simple, well-priced seafood pasta and fish.

Damiano
Via Variante Esterna SS270 7 (081 983 032). **Meals served** 8pm-midnight Mon-Sat; noon-3pm, 8pm-midnight Sun. Closed Nov-Mar. **Average** €40. **Credit** DC, MC, V.
Slightly overpriced, and resting on its laurels, Damiano will have to work hard to keep its place among Ischia's top restaurants. But the fish is fresh and the view is lovely. Note there's no Sunday lunch opening from June to August.

Oh! X Bacco
Via Luigi Mazzella 20 (081 991 354). **Open** *Jan, Feb* 6pm-midnight Mon, Wed-Sun; *Mar, Dec* 10am-1pm, 5pm-midnight Mon, Wed-Sun. *Apr-Oct* 11am-3pm, 7pm-2am Mon, Wed-Sun. Closed 3wks Nov. **Credit** DC, MC, V.

Il Moresco
Via E Gianturco 16 (081 981 355/fax 081 992 338).
Closed Nov-Mar. **Rates** €125-€165 single; €158-€350
double; €560-€620 suite. **Credit** AmEx, DC, MC, V.
Part of a group that also includes the newly restored
Grand Hotel Excelsior across the road, the Moresco
lives up to its name with low white Moorish-style
arches and wrought-iron gratings. The gardens are
delightful, it's a stone's throw from the sea, there's
a thermal pool in a rocky cave, and the staff are
delightful and very, very informative.

La Villarosa
*Via G Gigante 5 (081 991 316/fax 081 992 425/
www.lavillarosa.it).* **Closed** Nov-Mar. **Rates** €80-
€103.20 single; €134-€180.40 double. **Credit** AmEx,
DC, MC, V.
Immersed in a jungly garden, the Villarosa is a
homely place with comfortable nooks in hidden corners and a fourth-floor dining room with a great
view over town. There are chalets in among the
greenery, plus all the usual spa treatments.

Car & scooter hire

Autonoleggio PA.AN
Via Iasolino 76 (081 982 332). **Open** *Apr-Oct*
8am-8pm daily. **Credit** MC, V.
Scooters from €21 per day, cars from €31.

M Balestrieri
Via Iasolino 35 (081 985 691). **Open** *Apr, May,
Oct* 8am-1.30pm, 3.30-8pm daily. *June-Sept* 8am-8pm
daily. *Nov-Mar* 8am-1.30pm, 3.30-8pm Mon-Sat.
Credit MC, V.
Scooters cost from €21 a day, cars from €31. Staff
can deliver rented vehicles straight to your hotel.

Tourist information

Azienda Autonoma di Cura
Soggiorno e Turismo
*Corso Vittoria Colonna 108 (081 507 4231/
www.ischiaonline.it/tourism).* **Open** 9am-1.30pm,
3-7.30pm Mon-Sat.
Ischia's extraordinarily unhelpful tourist office also
has a branch by the Ischia Porto hydrofoil dock in
piazzale Trieste. Opening times are erratic.

The North Coast

Casamicciola Terme

Ischia's second port, Casamicciola, added Terme
(thermal spring) to its name in 1956. In the first
century AD, however, Pliny the Elder described
the town's Gurgitello spring, in which water
bubbles out of the earth at 80°F (27°C). Hundreds
of years later, Casamicciola spawned the idea
of coupling thermal treatment for medical
conditions with luxurious accommodation.

By 1883, when the town was razed by an
earthquake (2,300 died, including 600 Britons),
a stopover at Casamicciola was an essential
part of any Grand Tour. And though a decrease
in demand for spa cures has now driven many
centres – including the largest of them all, the
Pio Monte della Misericordia – to shut up shop,
there's still plenty of scope here for wallowing,
sweating and inhaling. It may have ancient
roots, but today's Casamicciola dates almost
entirely from after the 1883 earthquake.

The main seafront drag is crowded with
bars offering beer from the tap. The desolate
shell of the once-glorious **Pio Monte della
Misericordia** dominates the central stretch;
down a lane to the left of the hotel, a market
(6am-3pm Mon-Fri) sells tacky clothes and
some fresh produce inside the remains.

One block back from the congested coast
road is a warren of narrow streets with gaily
painted houses. East of the Pio Monte, roads
striking inland lead to corso Vittorio Emanuele,
which winds uphill. Via Cretaio (left at the T-
junction) heads up towards Monte Rotaro. Two
kilometres along this road, on the left, there's a
green metal bar across a track that leads into a
volcanic crater. Verdant with myrtle and huge
holm oak trees, and criss-crossed by well-made
walking paths, this strange depression looks
pure sylvan glade. The idyll is only skin deep.
If you stumble across anything looking like a
rabbit hole, put your hand inside: there's a good
chance it will be belching steam.

Corso Vittorio Emanuele continues to piazza
dei Bagni. Below the **Terme Belliazzi** (*see
p198*) is Casamicciola's main Gurgitello spring,
complete with pools built by ancient Romans
so that they could wallow in its waters. Further
uphill, via Paradisiello leads to the huge red
municipio (town hall) building that dominates
the town (also reachable by steps from the town
centre). The view from the square in front is
stunning. The town council has also occupied
Villa Bellavista, where a *museo civico*
contains old photos, maps and press cuttings
about the area. Further up still, Casamicciola's
parish church, the **Sacro Cuore** (aka Santa
Maria Maddalena) dates from 1898.

Museo Civico Villa Bellavista
*Via Principessa Margherita, Casamicciola Terme
(081 507 2522).* **Open** 9am-1pm Mon, Wed, Fri;
9am-1pm, 3-6pm Tue, Thur. **Guided tours** *mid
June-Oct* 7-9pm Sat, Sun. **Admission** free.

Lacco Ameno

Piazza **Santa Restituta** and the candy-pink
and white 19th-century church of the same
name are the heart of this seaside town, site of
the Greek settlement of Pithekoussai (*see p191*).

Taste the grape at the **Pietratorcia winery**. *See p200.*

The body of Tunisian virgin-martyr Restituta arrived, borne by lilies, on nearby San Montano beach (*see below*) in the fourth century; this event provided the theme for many of the church's artworks. Below, in the crypt/**Area archeologica**, are the remains of a fourth-century Christian basilica and burial site, of a second-century BC Roman town and of much older Greek pottery kilns. The little museum has fascinating painted thank-you notes dedicated to Santa Restituta, written by seamen delivered from storms.

Uphill from the piazza, the 18th-century Villa Arbusto is home to the **Museo Archeologico di Pithecusae** containing a beautifully arranged collection of artefacts from ancient Ischia. One of the prize possessions of the museum is 'Nestor's Cup', which is inscribed with probably the oldest writing – and the oldest transcription of a Homeric verse – in existence. The garden, and its view, are a delight to behold.

Lacco Ameno's best-known landmark is the **fungo** (mushroom), sitting in the water off the seafront promenade. This piece of volcanic rock reaches about ten metres (33 feet) out of the water; it is thought to have been catapulted here thousands of years ago by a rumbling Mount Epomeo (*see p199*).

Heading west out of town, the **Baia di San Montano** has one of the island's most pleasant beaches. Follow the signs to the Negombo spa (*see p198*) to reach this long crescent of sand. There's a public end, a section for guests at the Hotel della Baia (*see below*) and another for those who have paid for a session at the spa.

Area Archeologica di Santa Restituta

Piazza Santa Restituta, Lacco Ameno (081 980 538). **Open** 9.30am-12.30pm, 3.30-6pm Mon-Sat; 9.30am-12.30pm Sun. Closed mid Oct-Mar. **Admission** €3. **No credit cards**.

Museo Archeologico di Pithecusae

Villa Arbusto, corso Angelo Rizzoli 210, Lacco Ameno (081 900 356/www.pithecusae.it). **Open** 9.30am-12.30pm, 3-7pm Tue-Sun. **Admission** €5. **No credit cards**.

Where to stay & eat

You'll need your own transport to reach the best restaurant in Casamicciola, **Il Focolare** (via Cretaio 68, 081 980 604, closed Wed Oct-Apr, lunch Mon-Fri & 3wks Dec, average €25), where members of the D'Ambra family use mountain resources – rabbit, snails and herbs – to create wonderful earthy dishes.

Lacco Ameno's **Albergo Regina Isabella & Royal Sporting** (piazza San Restituta 1, 081 994 322, www.reginaisabella.it, closed Nov-Mar, double room €186-€476) is a grand hotel whose grandeur is somewhat faded but which manages to be elegant nonetheless, with a pool overhanging the beach, and a glorious spa treatment centre. The **Villa Angelica** (via IV Novembre 28, 081 994 524, www.villa angelica.it, closed Nov-Mar, double room €104-€124) is a beautiful, palm-filled hotel with a thermal pool and massage treatments.

Off the road between Lacco and Forio, the **Hotel della Baia** (via San Montano, 081 995 453, closed mid Oct-mid Apr, double room

Around Naples

Lady Susana Walton's luxurious gardens, **La Mortella**. *See p199.*

€104-€134) is silent, comfortable, and on one of Ischia's loveliest beaches. Further up the road, down a secluded lane, the stately **Grand Hotel Mezzatorre** (via Mezzatorre 23, 081 986 111, www.mezzatorre.it, closed Nov-Mar, double room €220-€440) has pastel rooms with neo-classical paintings. It also provides a huge selection of spa treatments, and has one of the finest hotel views on the island.

Spas

Negombo
Via Baia di San Montano, Lacco Ameno (081 986 152/www.negombo.it). **Open** 8.30am-7pm daily. Closed mid Oct-mid Apr. **Rates** €23-€26 per day. **Credit** AmEx, DC, MC, V.
In a beautiful garden with more than 500 exotic plant species, the Negombo has thermal and sports facilities, plus access to – and deckchairs on – the pretty San Montano beach (*see p197*).

Terme Belliazzi
Piazza Bagni 134, Casamicciola (081 994 580). **Open** *May-Oct* 7am-noon, 5-6.30pm Mon-Sat. Closed Nov-Apr. **Credit** MC, V.
A neo-classical temple to the healthy body in the upper part of Casamicciola, Belliazzi is built over (visitable) ancient Roman pools and offers various kinds of massage (€20-€32), a dip in the heated pool and whirlpool bath (€19) and mud treatments (€28).

Terme della Regina Isabella
Piazza San Restituta, Lacco Ameno (081 994 322/ www.reginaisabella.it). **Open** 8am-12.15pm, 5-7.30pm Mon-Sat; 8am-12.15pm Sun. Closed Nov-Mar. **Credit** AmEx, DC, MC, V.

Attached to the hotel of the same name (*see p197*), this spa is decidedly in the grand style, with various massages ranging from €25.82 to €72.30, a host of skin treatments and personal gym programmes.

Car & scooter hire

Giuseppe di Meglio
Via Tommaso Morgera 4, Casamicciola (081 980 312). **Open** *Mar-Oct* 8am-1pm, 2-8pm daily. *Nov-Feb* 8am-1pm, 2-8pm Mon-Sat. **Credit** AmEx, DC, MC, V. Situated right opposite the ferry port, this outlet rents scooters from €20 per day, Mini-Mokes for €33 and other cars from €30.

Tourist information

See p196.

Forio & the West Coast

Forio

The largest town on Ischia, with about 20,000 residents, Forio has some of the island's best restaurants and worst traffic jams. Its exposed position left it prey to attacks by Saracen pirates. A total of 12 watchtowers were built along this stretch of the coast. **Il Torrione**, dating from 1480 (open for exhibitions), which dominates the town centre with its craggy crenellations is the most prominent survivor.

There are 17 churches in and around Forio, most of which were heavily reworked during the 18th century, and none of which contains outstanding artworks. All open at highly erratic times. Standing apart from the town on its headland (where Forio's youth congregates of an evening), the stark, white **Santuario della Madonna del Soccorso** would not look out of place in Spain; there are pretty majolica stations of the cross around the steps outside the church. In corso Umberto, a church has stood on the site of **Santa Maria di Loreto** since the 14th century; in piazza del Municipio (from where there's a great sea view) much of the **convento di San Francesco** is now occupied by council offices but the church is visitable, as is the neighbouring **Santa Maria della Grazie** (aka Visitapovere) where alms were dispensed to the poor in the 17th century; in the piazza of the same name, **San Vito** is Forio's parish church.

Just north of Forio, along the road to Lacco Ameno, a sign points left to **La Mortella** and another green world.

In this garden, initially designed by renowned British landscapist Russell Page but lovingly completed by Lady Susana Walton – widow of composer Sir William Walton – New Zealand tree ferns unfurl with a prehistoric languor, while the heavily scented flower of the Amazon water lily contemplates its once-in-a-lifetime sex change.

Having arrived on the island at the end of the 1940s in search of sun, quiet and inspiration, Walton and his young Argentinian wife set about turning a wild plot of land – described by their friend Laurence Olivier as 'nothing but a quarry' – into one of southern Italy's most luxurious gardens.

La Mortella is not only a garden, but headquarters of the William Walton Trust, dedicated to the life and work of the composer who died here in 1983. The Trust provides accommodation and coaching for young musicians, and organises classical music concerts (included in the price of admission) on weekends between April and June, and again in September and October. There is also a tea house where – in true 'some corner of a foreign field' spirit – Fortnum & Mason tea is served. To get there, take a bus from Lacco Ameno to Forio, or vice versa, and ask the driver to set you down at La Mortella.

Monte Epomeo & the South-west

Looming over Forio to the east, Monte Epomeo – Ischia's highest point at 787 metres (2,582 feet) – can be ascended by following via

Monterone or via Bocca to one of the badly marked paths that lead through the glorious Falanga forest to the summit (*see also p201*).

If Forio's long town beaches don't appeal, **spiaggia di Citara** to the south has another long stretch of sand, although much of it has been monopolised by the **Giardini Poseidon**. **Sorgeto**, another beach treat, can be reached from the nearby village of Panza; watch out in the village for flaking, half-hidden signs to Sorgeto. A series of hairpin bends, then some long flights of stairs, lead down to a rocky cove. In the eastern corner, a spring gushes up between the rocks and into the sea at about 90°F (32°C). Alternate your cold-water antics with hot rock-pool luxuriating.

La Mortella
*Via F Calise 35, Forio (081 986 220/www.ischia.it/ mortella). **Open** Apr-mid Nov 9am-7pm Tue, Thur, Sat, Sun.* **Concerts** *Apr, June, Sept, Oct 5pm Sat, Sun; arrive at least 30mins before to be sure of a seat.* **Admission €8. No credit cards.**

Where to stay & eat

Inexpensive beds can be found in the Forio area at the busy youth hostel **Il Gabbiano** (via Provinciale Panza 182, 081 909 422, closed Nov-Mar, rates €16 per person) right above Citara beach, and at the pretty farm **Il Vitigno**

Efficient **Giardini Poseidon**.

Going southern

Ischia in the 1940s was renowned as a haven for British and American homosexuals who were seeking sun and sex. WH Auden first visited the island in 1948 with his long-term partner Chester Kallman and found his own Eden in the poor and then-primitive fishing village of Forio, 'one of the loveliest spots on earth'. After a few weeks, he had taken out a long-term let on a villa there.

For Auden, the island was the kind of liberal playground undreamt of in the repressed north: 'the sex situation in Forio is from my point of view exactly what it ought to be. Very few of the men and boys are queer... but all of them like a *divertimento* now and then, for which it is considered polite to give 35 cents or a package of cigarettes, as a friendly gesture. It's so nice to be with people who are never shocked, or psychologically insecure, though half of them don't get enough to eat.'

Though self-avowedly 'outstandingly non-aboriginal', Auden settled down into a routine of summers in Ischia spent writing, gardening, swimming and, in the evenings, holding court with dry humour and despotic authority over other expat writers, artists and musicians in Maria's café in the centre of town. So

much a feature of the landscape was he, that Tennessee Williams wryly advised writers who were intending to visit Ischia in search of Parnassus to address their visa applications straight to Auden.

Auden engaged a handsome local boy with artistic aspirations named Giocondo to look after the house. But clouds started to gather over his domestic bliss. British homosexuals flocked in ever greater numbers to Ischia, much to Auden's annoyance. And Chester's remorseless promiscuity was causing 'a spot of bother with the local parish priest'.

The storm broke in 1956 over a public row with Giocondo, who tried to cash an enormous cheque Auden had mistakenly given him. The boy claimed it was a gesture of gratitude for 'favours' rendered. In the feud that followed, the whole village split between Giocondo's family and Auden's friends. A disgusted and embittered Auden fled the island in 1957 for Austria, never to return. 'I don't like sunshine,' he grumbled. 'I would like Mediterranean life in a northern climate.'

In his farewell poem to Ischia, Auden warns northerners: 'If we try to "go southern", we spoil in no time, we grow flabby, dingily, lecherous, and forget to pay bills.'

(via Bocca 31, 081 998 307, open all year, rates €44-€50 per person, half-board only) where the restaurant (average €18) serves delicious meals of home-grown produce to non-residents too, but only if they book. Well south of town, the **Hotel Punta Chiarito** (via Sorgeto 51, 081 908 102, www.puntachiarito.it, closed Nov-Apr, double €124-€176) is another attractive option. It perches on a spectacular peninsula protruding into the sea between Sorgeto beach (*see p199*) and Sant'Angelo (*see p201*); the rooms are pleasant, and there's a beautifully landscaped garden with thermal pool; some self-catering rooms are available all year round.

If good hotels are a rarity in Forio, not so restaurants. Beneath the Soccorso church, **Umberto a Mare** (via Soccorso 2, 081 997 171, www.umbertoamare.it, closed Jan, Feb and Mon, Tue in Nov, Dec, Mar, average €35) has delicate pasta with squid and asparagus, or *al profumo di mare*, the freshest of fish, and a great orange sorbet; there are ten bright rooms too (double room €80-€140). The central **Bar Stany & Elio** (via Castellaccio 77, 081 997 668, closed Nov-Feb, Tue in Mar, Apr) serves some of the best ice-cream on Ischia.

Off the coast road heading south, Ischia's only Michelin-star restaurant **Il Melograno** (via G Mazzella 110, 081 998 450, closed Jan-mid Mar, Mon, Tue in Nov, Dec, average €39) does excellent raw fish antipasti and also delicious *orecchiette* pasta with clams, mussels, broccoli and chilli; the fish is fresh off the boat, and the outside patio is charming. Miles up a tortuous road leading to Monte Epomeo, **Da Peppina di Renato** (via Montecorvo 42, 081 998 312, closed Dec-mid Mar, Wed in Apr-June, Oct, open evenings only, average €25) has great pizza and good fish. Above the beach at Citara, neon signs make **Grusoni** (via Provinciale Panza, Località Cuotto, 081 907 272, closed mid Nov-mid Mar, lunch in July, Aug, average €40) look like the worst of tourist traps. In fact, it may provide the best eating experience on the island; the pasta dishes are exquisite, the grilled fish is out of this world. Accompany your meal with one of over 200 wines.

Pietratorcia (via Provinciale Panza 267, 081 907 277, closed mid Nov-Mar, lunch mid June-mid Sept) is one of Ischia's leading wine producers; taste the grape on a sunny terrace where *assaggi* of three different wines and a big plate of cheese and cold meats cost €12; the chef will cook full meals in the summer evenings, but only if you order in advance; open until late evening in summer.

Spas

Giardini Poseidon

Via Mazzella, spiaggia di Citara (081 907 122/ www.giardiniposeidon.it). **Open** *May-Oct* 8.30am-7pm daily. *Apr* 9am-6.30pm daily. Closed Nov-Mar. **Rates** €25 per day. **Credit** AmEx, MC, V.
A complex comprising saunas, 21 pools, jacuzzis and a long private beach – all run with Teutonic efficiency. Credit cards accepted for massages and health treatments only.

Tourist information

See p196.

The South

Sant'Angelo & Maronti

The pretty (ex-)fishing village of Sant'Angelo is the one place on the island where slim, bronzed and nattily dressed Italian folk are likely to outnumber the German tourists. They'll be lounging in the dockside cafés, or just strolling insouciantly along the isthmus that joins the jumble of white and blue houses to the *scoglio* (rock) opposite. Here the remains of an old watchtower can be seen. Reaching Sant'Angelo is a traffic nightmare.

From the village, a cliff-top footpath hugs the south coast, above the **spiaggia dei Maronti**. Once a two-kilometre stretch of unbroken sand, Maronti has been eaten away of late by the sea and storms. Of what remains, the eastern end is family fun, and best reached by bus from Barano (*see p192*); for the western end, where steam belches out from blow-holes between rocks below the **Terme Apollon** (*see p202*), take the path leading east out of Sant'Angelo. For the deserted coves stranded between the two ends, take a boat-taxi from Sant'Angelo. Between Sant'Angelo and Maronti, signs point up a steep valley to the extraordinary **Cava Scura** spring (*see p202*).

The southern villages

From Sant'Angelo, the road (SS270) meanders inland, taking a tortuous route among the leafy, craggy hills, to Serrara, Fontana, Barano d'Ischia and then back to Ischia Porto. Though architecturally uninspiring, the southern villages offer glorious views both over the sea

and up to **Monte Epomeo**. In **Fontana**, don't be deterred by a steep road marked *strada militare* and *vietato l'ingresso* (no entry). It is in fact the perfectly legitimate route (*see also p199*) up to the path for the summit of Epomeo; motor vehicles can be driven as far as the bar-restaurant immediately before the military zone really begins with a metal bar across the road.

The path to the left of the bar leads up to the eyrie-like rock formation at the top (the walk will take you about 40 minutes), from where the 360° view over the island is absolutely breathtaking. Below is the hermitage and the newly restored chapel of San Nicola di Bari, which was hewn out of the rock in the 15th century and remained occupied until World War II (erratic opening, mornings only, key with the local priest in Fontana).

From **Barano**, a narrow road plunges down through delightful verdant countryside to **Testaccio** and on towards the eastern end of the **spiaggia dei Maronti**.

Shortly before the SS270 enters Ischia town, a turn-off to the left leads to **Campagnano**, where the church of **San Domenico** has some

The **spiaggia dei Maronti**.

Haunt of slim, bronzed, nattily dressed Italians: **Sant'Angelo**. *See p201.*

striking 19th-century majolica decorations on its façade; the view from the village down to the Castello Aragonese (*see p193*) is glorious.

Where to stay, eat & drink

In Sant'Angelo, the elegant **Park Hotel Miramare** (via Maddalena 29, 081 999 219, www.hotelmiramare.it, closed Nov-Easter, double room €211-€503) is the flagship of a group that has colonised the whole headland; its **Casa Apollon** (same phone number) next door costs slightly less (a double room is €164) and allows free entrance to the Parco Termale Aphrodite (*see below*). The **Hotel Celestino** (via Chiaia di Rose, 081 999 213, closed Nov-Apr, double room €92-€118) is a reliable option in the village centre.

Lo Scoglio (via Cava Ruffano 58, 081 999 529, closed mid Nov-mid Dec, Jan-Mar, average €25) perches on a cliff overlooking Sant'Angelo, with fresh sea spray on the windows, and fresh seafood on its plates.

On the port, there's **La Tavernetta del Pirata** (via Sant'Angelo 77, 081 999 251, closed Nov-Feb, mid Nov-26 Dec, 10 Jan-Mar). This is Sant'Angelo's hippest bar, and remains a good place to sink an *aperitivo* or a seafood snack (served all day, average €18). When you can't face any more seafood, **Da Pasquale** (via Sant'Angelo 79, 081 904 208, closed Nov-Apr) will provide you with good cheap pizzas; its staff will also sell you a beer, to be drunk alongside noisy crowds on long pine benches.

Spas

Parco Termale Aphrodite Apollon

Via Petrelle, Sant'Angelo (081 999 219/ www.aphrodite.it). **Open** *Apr-Oct* 8.30am-6pm daily. **Admission** €21 all day; €16 after 1pm. **Credit** AmEx, DC, MC, V.

Rambling over the headland east of Sant'Angelo, the Aphrodite offers 12 pools, saunas, gym classes and a free boat-taxi from Sant'Angelo port in its admission fee. There's a nude bathing area. Massages (from €27) and medical treatment are extra.

Terme di Cava Scura

Via Cava Scura, spiaggia dei Maronti, Serrara Fontana (081 905 564). **Open** 8.30am-1.30pm, 2.30-6pm daily. Closed Nov-mid Apr. **No credit cards.**

Squeezed between (and hewn out of) tall cliffs at the end of a long coast walk, this is a spa for devotees. There's a natural sauna in a dingy cave, grave-like baths with steaming sulphurous water (€24), plus massages (€19) and thermal and beauty treatments.

Sport

Roja Diving Center

Hotel Conte, via Nazario Sauro 54, Sant'Angelo (081 999 214/338 762 0145/fax 081 999 076/ www.ischiadiving.it). **Open** Easter-Oct; Nov-Easter by appointment only. **No credit cards.**

Roja does single dives from €27 and runs courses.

Tourist information

See p196.

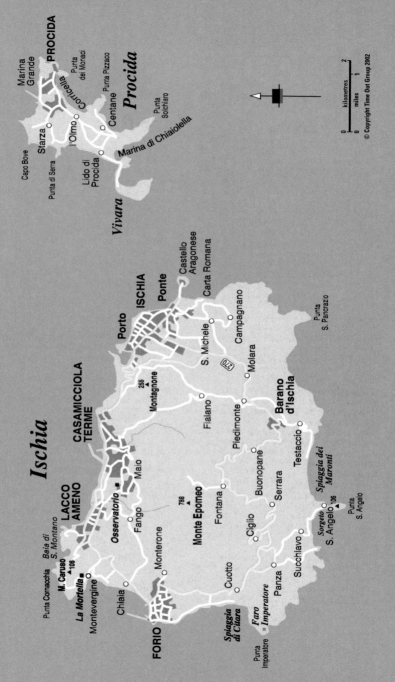

Procida

A charming, little-visited island, ideal for boat-lovers.

Procida, according to Dionysius of
Halicarnassus, was named after Aeneas's wet
nurse Prochyta who died here. Formed by four
volcanic craters, this smallest dot of land in the
Gulf of Naples is the most densely inhabited
island in the Med. It covers less than four
square kilometres (one-and-a-half square miles),
but its population explodes from a low-season
11,000 to 20,000 in August. And yet the island
has its own very particular charm.

In the past, the local economy revolved
around the sea. Procida has produced
generations of fishermen or sailors for the
world's merchant navies. Today, it's tourism
that fills the coffers: smart cafés and
restaurants line the harbours, and there's a
spanking new yacht marina in Marina Grande.
On the downside, jerry-built holiday homes
have sprouted in the old orchards, and August
heaves with daytrippers. But even in high
summer you can still stroll through lemon
groves, savour a freshly made *granita di limone*
(lemon ice) or watch the day's catch being
unloaded from boats: a perfect way to spend a
few days' break away from the hustle of Naples.

The island was first inhabited by Greeks
from Cuma (*see p101*). Small fishing
communities grew up around its natural
coves, but frequent Saracen attacks in the
Middle Ages forced the villagers to flee to the
highest point of the island, the Terra Murata.
The characteristic local architecture with its
steep staircases, arches and loggias, dates
back to this period.

The island began to develop from the 16th
century, despite continuing attacks by pirates.
(In 1544, according to local legend, Barbarossa
the barbarian fled the island after a miraculous
vision of St Michael in the Terra Murata, but
not before he indulged in a little rape and
pillage.) Medieval Terra Murata was refortified
after 1520, but the defence mentality was
already fading. Prosperous families from the
mainland built summer homes on the island,
shipbuilders constructed their family *palazzi*
and the population ventured outside the walls
to make Marina Grande the centre of the fishing
industry. Sailing ships were built next to the
port until the end of the 19th century.

Procida was a favourite haunt of the Bourbon
kings who, in 1744, bought the Castello
d'Avalos and did the island the dubious honour

of turning the whole place into a royal hunting
reserve. Locals caught hunting – or even
keeping cats that might upset the pheasants –
were subject to heavy fines and imprisonment.

Procida's Good Friday *Processione dei
Misteri* is a little bit of folklore definitely worth
catching. In what was once a procession of
flagellants, a life-size wooden sculpture (dating
from 1754) of the dead Christ is carried by
fishermen from the Abbazia di San Michele
Arcangelo to Marina Grande under a black
veil. It is followed by the other *misteri* –
handmade wooden models representing
religious scenes – carried by members of
the Turchini confraternity, dressed in white
habits and turquoise capes, and children
wearing medieval costume.

The best way to see Procida is to walk;
a complete circuit of the island will take the
fit around four hours.

Approaching Procida by ferry, the view is
dominated by the formidable former prison,
Castello d'Avalos – an Italian Alcatraz
until 1986 – surrounded by the gently faded
colours of the traditional fishermen's houses,
with their arches and loggias.

Ferries dock in the **Marina Grande**, among
the traditional fishing boats moored in front of
modern cafés and restaurants. Old men sit on
the edge of the wharf mending their nets. The
fishmongers – all run by fishermen – open in
the afternoon (Mon-Fri). They sell only that
day's catch from the Canale di Procida: prawns,
red mullet and squid, as well as the traditional
misto di paranza (small fish and seafood
caught in the fishermen's nets) for frying.

Towards the eastern end of the Marina
Grande, by the church of **Santa Maria della
Pietà** (1760), the steep via Vittorio Emanuele
leads off to the right up into the centre of the
island. Some 100 metres (350 feet) further on
the left, via Principe Umberto, with its old
houses and courtyards, leads to piazza dei
Martiri. From here catch the view of the castle
and the **Terra Murata** above, with the
enchanting fishing village of Corricella below.

The road continues steeply past the forlorn,
abandoned Castello d'Avalos. Built in the
mid 16th century, the castle belonged to the
D'Avalos family until it was bought by the
Bourbon kings in 1744. In 1818 it became a
prison; it's now locked up and derelict. The

Approaching Procida's **Marina Grande**, with the Terra Murata above. *See p204.*

Porta di Mezz'omo (1563) leads into the medieval Terra Murata walled village. There are breathtaking views over Naples and Capri from via Borgo at the top of the hill, where the **Abbazia di San Michele Arcangelo** is built on the edge of the sheer rock. Dating from the 11th century, but remodelled in the 17th-19th centuries, the abbey has a painting (1699) by Luca Giordano of the archangel Michael on its coffered ceiling. Inside the building is an 8,000-strong religious manuscript library, a museum containing religious thank-you pictures from sailors, an 18th-century nativity scene, and a maze of catacombs (once the local cemetery) leading to a secret chapel. The ruins of the 16th-century church of **Santa Margherita Nuova** stand on the Punta dei Monaci.

From piazza dei Martiri, the little harbour at **Corricella** is reached down the Scalinata Scura steps. On the way you'll pass tiny houses massed on the rock with their communicating arches and communal entrances (some of them have now been renovated into chic homes for weekenders). The bay, exposed to African winds, has a microclimate so mild that bananas grow here.

From the western end of Corricella, steps lead up to via Scotti, where 18th-century buildings have vaulted entrances leading to flowery gardens, lemon groves and terraces overlooking the sea. As you pick up via Vittorio Emanuele again, the road (unpleasant at this point, with cars and scooters screaming by with their usual disregard for pedestrians) leads to the southernmost part of the island.

From piazza Olmo, via Pizzaco leads to **Pizzaco**, where a stunning nature walk rounds a sadly crumbling promontory that has fantastic views across to Corricella and Terra Murata. The beach below – **la Chiaja** – is reached from the piazza by about 180 steps. Flagging spirits can be revived at the excellent beach trattoria **La Conchiglia** (*see p206*).

Via Giovanni da Procida leads from piazza Olmo to **Chiaiolella**, a small yacht marina, its port enclosed by two promontories. On the western side of the island, the kilometre of sand stretching from Chiaiolella to **Ciriaccio** is Procida's most fashionable (and most crowded) beach, the **Lido**. At the southern tip of the Lido, a lane leads to a bridge connecting Procida to the nature reserve of **Vivara** (*see p206*).

For something more off the beaten track, even in high season, the north-east of Procida between the lighthouse on Punta di Pioppeto and Punta Serra has lanes meandering through lemon groves and fantastic sea views. From piazza Olmo, via Flavio Gioia leads to a belvedere with an outstanding view over Chiaiolella, Vivara and Ischia. A short path hugs the promontory of Punta Serra, overlooking the sea. Via Flavio Gioia continues to the old cemetery and, below, quiet **Pozzo Vecchio** beach, made famous by the film

Il Postino. The road (at this point called via Cesare Battisti) passes a restored 16th-century tower and hamlet, now a restaurant. Via Rinaldi (left) rambles past isolated farmhouses and woodlands (taking in yet more views) to the lighthouse, from where via Faro leads back to the main road.

Off Procida's south-western tip and reachable by footbridge, the tiny isle of **Vivara** was inhabited even before Procida: traces of neolithic remains have been found. Vivara was once a hunting reserve for the Bourbon kings, but today is one of the most beautiful and unspoilt nature reserves in Italy. More than 150 different species of birds live or migrate through here. Besides Vivara rabbits, you may be lucky enough to spot the island's rare rat walking on its hind legs. In spring, iris and wild asparagus abound.

The path from Vivara's gatehouse leads up through woodland with tantalising glimpses of the sea. An overgrown path to the right winds down to the ruins of a hamlet beside the coast. In the centre of the island is an abandoned manor house with a loggia, and an old olive press in the cellar. The path continues down to a lookout point, with views stretching to Naples, Capri and Ischia, as well as of Procida itself. Narrow paths veer off, some scrambling down to rocks and the sea. On the way back to the gatehouse, a path to the right of the manor house skirts the coast overlooking Procida, before rejoining the main path.

At the time of this guide going to press, Vivara was still closed to the public as storm damage to the bridge had not been repaired. (This does not, needless to say, deter locals from ducking through the fence.)

Abbazia di San Michele Arcangelo
Via Terra Murata 89 (081 896 7612). **Open** 9.45am-12.45pm, 3-5pm Mon-Sat; 9.45am-12.45pm Sun. **Admission** *Church* free. *Museum, library & catacombs* €2. **No credit cards**.

Riserva Naturale di Vivara
No phone. **Open** 8.30am-noon Mon-Sat; last entry 10am. **Admission** free.

Santa Maria della Pietà
081 896 7005. **Open** 8.30am-noon, 5-8pm Sun; and whenever the lady with the keys has nothing more pressing to do.

Where to eat & drink

Among the many restaurants on the Marina Grande harbour, **L'Approdo** (via Roma 76, 081 896 9930, average €25) serves enormous portions of *linguine agli scampi e zucca* (pasta with prawns and marrow) or *astice e zucchini* (lobster and courgettes), as well as

an unbeatable *fritto misto* just off the boat. Alternatively, try squid stuffed with artichoke, or one of the excellent pizzas (€6).

La Medusa (via Roma 116, 081 896 7481, closed Jan, Feb & Tue in Oct-May, average €25) will tempt you with a really fresh fish antipasto and *zuppa di pesce* (fish soup).

The **Bar Roma** (via Roma 163, 081 896 7460, closed Tue Oct-Apr), tucked away next to the church of Santa Maria della Pietà, may be short on atmosphere but has great cakes. Or rub elbows with yachting types and Neapolitan intellectuals as you quaff the cocktails at **Bar del Cavaliere** (via Roma 42-3, 081 810 1074, closed Mon Oct-May). Wait for the boat or just hang out at friendly **Bar Capriccio** (via Roma 99, 081 896 9506, closed Thur Oct-May).

And for a romantic evening, take a private boat ride from Corricella to family-run **La Conchiglia** on Chiaia beach (no car access, steps from via Pizzaco 10, piazza Olmo, 081 896 7602, closed mid Nov-Mar, average €25, booking necessary for boat ride). Enjoy scrumptious antipasti, pasta with seafood, local veg and fish fresh off the boat.

For home-cooking on the beach, lunch at **Grotte Blu** (via Roma 153, 081 896 0345, average €20), on the right of the port in Marina Grande. The Procida-style rabbit is delicious; there are takeaway snacks too.

Sport & leisure

Procida Diving Centre
Lungomare Cristoforo Colombo 6, Lido di Procida (081 896 8385/www.vacanzeaprocida.it). **Open** 9am-8pm daily. **Credit** MC, V.
Diving courses and trips with expert instructors, and diving equipment hire. A single dive costs €30, including equipment.

Where to stay

Hotel accommodation is scarce so it's a good move to book well ahead for Easter, summer weekends and August.

Overlooking Corricella and under the Terra Murata is the charming **La Casa sul Mare** (salita Castello 13, 081 896 8799, www.lacasasulmare.it, double room €88-€155) in an 18th-century palazzo with sunny, air-conditioned rooms and fabulous terraces overlooking the bay. Situated right on the harbour at Chiaiolella, the **Hotel Crescenzo** (via Marina Chiaiolella 33, 081 896 7255, double rooms €62-€93) is convenient for the sandy beach; its fish restaurant is usually crowded with yachting types. To get away from it all, try enchanting **Casa Gentile** (Marina

Messing about in boats

Whether it's a traditional wooden *gozzo* or a modern yacht, chartering a boat can be a highlight of a visit here. Procida's new yacht marina – the largest in Campania – has yet to be opened officially, and services are literally limited to a petrol pump. In addition, Chiaiolella harbour is jam-packed in summer. Nevertheless, Procida is one of the best bases in Italy for a sailing holiday, be it a long weekend to Capri, Ischia and the Amalfi Coast or a holiday to Sicily or Sardinia. The following outfits rent boats.

Bluebone – Graziella Travel

Via Roma 117 (081 896 9594/fax 081 896 9190/www.isoladiprocida.it/bluebone). **Open** 9.30am-1pm, 4.30-8pm Mon-Sat. **Rates** €2,550-€4,130 per week. **No credit cards**. Rent a ten-berth 13m (43ft) yacht.

Ippocampo

Lato ponente (west side), Marina Chiaiolella (081 810 1437/amedeoippocampo@
tisca linet.it).* **Open** 9am-7pm daily. Closed mid Oct-Mar. **No credit cards**. Ippocampo rents typical fishing *gozzi* (from €62 per day excluding fuel – no prior experience is required) and also runs a taxi-boat service to Ischia. A two-hour island boat trip with a handsome sailor costs €62 for a group of ten.

Sailitalia Procida

Via Roma 10, Marina Grande (081 896 9962/www.sailitalia.com). **Open** 9.30am-1pm, 3-7pm Mon-Fri. **Rates** from €992 per week in low season for 2+2 berth to €6,803 per week for 8+4 berth in high season. Skipper €1,000 per week; hostess €670 per week. **No credit cards**. This long-established company rents a wide range of modern yachts with from two to 12 berths. No sailing licence is required for yachts under 10m (33ft) used within 12 miles (19km) of the coast. Airport transfers can also be arranged.

Corricella 88, 081 896 7799, closed Nov-1wk before Easter, double room €70-€100) in the pedestrian-only Corricella fishing village (access by steep steps). The suite has a wonderful terrace on the bay and there's a boat service to a nearby beach in the summer.

Getting there

From Naples-Beverello

Caremar (081 551 3882) runs ferries (1hr; €4.29) and hydrofoils (35mins; €7.49).

From Naples-Mergellina/Beverello

Snav (081 761 2348) runs hydrofoils (35mins; €8.80).

From Pozzuoli

Caremar (081 526 2711) runs ferries (35mins; €2.43); Procida Lines 2000 (081 896 0328) runs car ferries. (35mins; rates vary according to size of vehicle).

Getting around

Note that during the summer there are heavy restrictions on private cars and scooters.

By bus

Buses run to all parts of the island with very frequent services in July and August. Line 1 runs all year from Marina Grande to the Marina di Chiaiolella; this service operates all night July and Aug. Tickets cost 93¢ and should be bought in advance from *tabacchi*.

By taxi

Marina di Chiaiolella or Marina Grande (081 896 8785); a tour around the island costs €35-€40. Taxis can also be booked on 339 485 0303.

Scooter hire

Antonio

Via Roma 137 (081 896 0319/360 306 450). **Open** 9am-1pm, 2-8pm daily. Closed Nov-Mar. **Rates** €25 per day. **No credit cards**. A scooter is a good way to get around the island.

Tourist information

Azienda Autonoma di Cura Soggiorno e Turismo

Next to Caremar ticket office, Marina Grande (081 810 1968). **Open** (in theory, but in effect often closed) *May-Sept* 9.30am-1pm, 3.30-7pm Mon-Sat. *Oct-Apr* 9.30am-1pm Mon-Sat.

Graziella Travel

Via Roma 117 (081 896 9594/fax 081 896 9190/ www.isoladiprocida.it). **Open** *Apr-Sept* 9.30am-1pm, 4.30-8pm Mon-Sat. *Oct-Mar* 9.30am-1pm, 4.30-8pm Mon-Fri; 9.30am-1pm Sat. **Credit** (airline tickets only) AmEx, DC, MC, V. This is a better bet than the unpredictable tourist office for information (get your map of the island here), accommodation in fishermen's cottages or villas, and yacht charters.

Around Naples

Pompeii & Vesuvius

Archaeological wonders await amid urban horrors.

In among the urban sprawl of the *comuni vesuviani* – the towns around Vesuvius – lies a veritable feast of Roman sites and 18th-century villas, all set against the backdrop of the quiescent volcano. The contrasts are striking: lava fields from the 1944 eruption stand wild and deserted just a few miles from the busy remains of streets and houses buried in a bigger blow two millennia earlier; sumptuous Roman villas set in quiet countryside overlook ugly urban agglomerations with some of Europe's highest unemployment rates.

The sprawl is a 20th-century blight and can (with a massive effort of the imagination) be overlooked. Vesuvius rising out of its plain, with the Sorrentine Peninsula to the south and Naples to the north, is a scene that has held both inhabitants and visitors spellbound throughout history.

The Greeks, Oscans and then Romans occupied the lower slopes of Vesuvius with a variety of settlements: towns such as **Pompeii** (*see p216*) and **Herculaneum** (*see p211*),

The grand **Reggia** in Portici. *See p211.*

farmsteads as in **Boscoreale** (*see p216*), and sumptuous villas as at **Oplontis** (*see p215*) and **Stabiae** (*see p220*). In the 18th century, the Bourbon monarchs had the **Reggia** (royal palace; *see p211*) built in Portici; the rich and noble followed their example, building more than 120 villas between Portici and Torre del Greco in an area that became known as the *Miglio d'Oro* ('golden mile').

For Europe's titled or moneyed youths on their Grand Tour, a visit to this bit of the Bay of Naples was considered a desirable part of a well-rounded classical education (the somewhat hazardous climb up Vesuvius was optional). The area became even more popular after the Roman town of Herculaneum was discovered in about 1710, and Pompeii a few decades later.

DIGGING DEEP

Using digging styles that make modern archaeologists shudder in horror, the Bourbons carted off statues and frescos to be exhibited in the nearby Reggia. Many more works of art were damaged during excavations, or ended up being smuggled out to private collections abroad. The sites still bear the scars of the cavalier excavation techniques; ancient villa walls had tunnels bored through them in attempts to reach the treasure troves within. When describing a visit to Herculaneum in the 18th century, the poet Thomas Gray wrote to his mother how 'the passage they have made with all their turnings and windings is now more than a mile long'.

With large injections of European Union funds and private sponsorship deals, the normally cash-strapped Italian cultural heritage ministry has been busy capitalising on the immense archaeological resources in the area: grandiose plans are afoot to divert some of the tourist traffic (1.5 million paying visitors pass through Pompeii each year) to lesser-known sites such as Stabiae; several key services at archaeological sites have been privatised (long-awaited audio-guides were introduced in 2001); and new areas at Pompeii were opened to a restricted public in 2002.

Some things, though, are here to stay. Ancient Herculaneum, for example, is buried beneath the modern town of Ercolano and will never be brought to light. Stray dogs still roam the main site in Pompeii, while at the entrance the old-style tour guides still tout persistently

for custom. In the streets of the modern *comuni vesuviani*, environmental quality is poor. If Roman satirist Juvenal complained in the second century AD of 'the swearing of drovers on narrow, winding streets', today's visitors are plagued by scooters tearing round the area like chainsaws on wheels.

The five key archaeological sites of the *area vesuviana* (Pompeii, Herculaneum, Oplontis, Stabiae and Boscoreale) can be visited on a **cumulative ticket**, which costs €13.50, is valid for three days and is available at any of the sites. Unlike the smaller sites, both Pompeii and Herculaneum now have snack-bar facilities.

Getting there

By bus

SITA (081 552 2176) runs frequent services from via Pisanelli (near piazza Municipio) in Naples to **Pompei**. ANM (www.anm.it) bus 157 from piazza Municipio or 255 from piazza Carlo III go to **Ercolano**. But given the traffic hell, the train is a far better bet. For **Vesuvius**, *see p222*.

By car

Most sites are fairly close to the nerve-tingling A3 Naples–Salerno motorway.

For **Herculaneum**, take the Ercolano exit and follow the signs to Scavi di Ercolano. For **Oplontis**, exit at Torre Annunziata Sud, turning right when you hit the first main road. Follow signs to Scavi di Oplontis. For **Pompeii**, take the Pompei exit from the A3 motorway. Ancient Pompeii is beside this exit. For **Vesuvius**, *see p222*.

For **Boscoreale**, exit as for Pompeii and follow signs from that site to the Antiquarium (or get directions from the helpful information office at Porta Marina, Pompeii).

For **Stabiae**, take the Castellammare di Stabia exit from the A3 and follow the signs to Sorrento (not Castellammare). Take the first exit (Gragnano) from the Sorrento road; the Passeggiata Archeologica starts at the junction (opposite) where the exit road meets the main Gragnano–Castellammare road.

At both Herculaneum and Pompeii you'll have to pay to park, while Stabiae and Boscoreale have free parking facilities on site.

By train

The major sites are served by the Circumvesuviana railway (081 772 2444/www.vesuviana.it). Note that for ancient **Pompeii**, if coming from Naples you should take the Naples–Sorrento line and get off at Pompei Scavi-Villa dei Misteri. The other Pompei station lies on a different Circumvesuviana line and is closer to the amphitheatre entrance.

Boscoreale (Boscoreale station) requires a considerable amount of legwork and is very poorly signposted, while for **Stabiae** (Via Nocera station, Castellammare) you need to take the Linea Azzurra bus from near the station.

Fares depend on distance: a day pass (*biglietto giornaliero*) covering Fascia 3 (Zone 3) between

Ancient fast-food stall at **Herculaneum**. *See p212.*

Naples and Pompei (including travel within Naples itself) is €4.03, and is equivalent to two singles. This will enable you to hop on almost all buses and trains throughout the area. Portici is in Fascia 1 (€2.58 for a day pass), and Ercolano in Fascia 2 (€3.10). along with Torre del Greco and Torre Annunziata.

Tourist information

Azienda Autonoma di Cura, Soggiorno e Turismo

Via Sacra 1, Pompei (081 850 7255/fax 081 863 2401/www.uniplan.it/pompei/azienda). **Open** *Apr-Oct* 8.30am-7pm Mon-Fri; 8.30am-3pm Sat. *Nov-Mar* 8am-3.30pm Mon-Fri; 8.30am-3pm Sat.

Ufficio di Informazione e di Accoglienza Turistica

Via IV Novembre 82, Ercolano (tel/fax 081 788 1243). **Open** 9am-2pm Mon-Sat.
The Ercolano office will also give information on neighbouring Portici.

Ufficio di Informazione e di Accoglienza Turistica

At the Porta Marina entrance to the archaeological site, by the main ticket office (081 536 5154/ www.pompeiisites.org). **Open** *Apr-Oct* 8.30am-6pm daily. *Nov-Mar* 8.30am-3.30pm daily.
The tourist offices at Pompeii provide information on Torre del Greco, Torre Annunziata and Castellammare di Stabia.

Around Naples

Portici

With the dubious distinction of being the most densely populated town in Europe – though the other *comuni vesuviani* can't be far behind – Portici was devastated when Vesuvius erupted in 1631. So it was little more than a wasteland when King Charles III, Naples' first Bourbon king, gave orders for a palace to be built here. The palace and its grounds, now besieged by concrete on all sides, give you an idea of what the whole area would have looked like 200 years ago. The town was also the terminus for the first railway line built in Italy (the terminus now houses the excellent **Museo Ferroviario** railway museum) and the site of over 30 villas along the *Miglio d'Oro*.

Museo Ferroviario di Pietrarsa

Via Pietrarsa, Portici (081 472 003/ www.microsys.it/pietrarsa). **Open** Closed for restoration as this guide went to press, due to reopen Sept 2002. **Admission** free.

The first railway on the Italian peninsula was a modest 7.4km (4.5-mile) stretch between Naples and Portici, inaugurated with much fanfare by Naples' King Ferdinand II in 1839. The following year, a railway factory and workshops were installed in an area close to Portici called Pietrarsa ('burnt stone'), aptly enough given its proximity to Vesuvius; they continued to operate there until 1975. To celebrate 150 years of rail travel in Italy, the workshop area was opened to the public as a museum in 1989.

The biggest – and arguably the best – railway museum in Europe, the Museo Ferroviario di Pietrarsa is a joy, even for non-railway buffs. The buildings housing the original workshops and lathes have been minimally, and tastefully, restored. Pavilion A has a wondrous display of steam locomotives, including a faithful reconstruction of the royal train used for the inaugural trip on the Portici railway in 1839. Across the gardens, Pavilion C has the full gamut of 20th-century rolling stock, and the immaculately preserved royal carriage built in 1928. Raised walkways around the carriage allow a good view of the plush upholstery and gilded ceilings.

Beautifully located, the museum grounds are washed by the Bay of Naples. The central courtyard has been made into a Mediterranean garden, incorporating an open-air theatre used for summer concerts. Detailed information in English can be obtained at the museum reception.

To find the museum, take the Portici exit from the A3 motorway and head down to the coast road (SS145), turning right towards Naples; the easily missed Museo Ferroviario sign is on the seaward side of the main road in the area called Croce del Lagno. Alternatively, take a mainline train from Naples' Stazione Centrale (information 848 888 088) to Pietrarsa-San Giorgio a Cremano.

Reggia di Portici & Orto Botanico

Via Università 100 (081 775 5135/Orto 081 775 4850/www.agraria.unina.it). **Open** *Reggia Sept-July* 8.30am-7pm Mon-Fri. *Orto* 9am-12.30pm Mon-Fri. **Admission** free.

Designed by Antonio Medrano, the Reggia di Portici is the greatest of all the Vesuvian villas. Ferdinando Fuga worked on it, as did Luigi Vanvitelli. The Reggia's vast façade looks out across what was once its own private terraced gardens, cascading down towards the seashore. The lower of the Reggia's two buildings is separated by a square – crossed by the Strada reale delle Calabrie, the former main road joining Naples to the south – from the upper wing, which looks out towards Vesuvius. Charles and his son Ferdinand had the spoils from digs at Pompeii and Herculaneum brought here, creating a royal antiquarium of incomparable richness (most of the former contents can now be seen at the Museo Nazionale Archeologico; *see p79*). Since 1873, the Reggia has been home to Naples University's Faculty of Agriculture: to visit, wander in student-like. On the Vesuvius side of the main road is the Orto botanico (botanical garden), an impressive collection of over 500 species of both native and exotic plants, abutting the large holm oak wood where the royals used to go hunting.

Ercolano & Herculaneum

Rivalling Portici for urban squalor, traffic noise and poor visitor facilities, Ercolano also has some sumptuous 18th-century villas and a spectacular ancient site, **Herculaneum**.

You could drive through the post-war construction catastrophe of the south-of-Naples sprawl and never notice the splendour. But as you hurry through Ercolano erase, in your mind's eye, everything built since 1945. You're left with some fishermen's huts near the shore, a once-smart late 19th-century main street, and *ville* – crumbling, dilapidated, concealed behind locked rusting gates and beneath runaway gardens.

The Reggia at Portici was home to the Bourbon court for several months each year. Wealthy court hangers-on from all over the Kingdom of the Two Sicilies – anxious to be on hand when honours or cash rewards were being distributed – summoned the leading architects of the time to build luxurious homes along that stretch of coast between Naples and Torre del Greco that became known as the *Miglio d'Oro* ('golden mile').

With the absorption of Naples into the united Kingdom of Italy in 1860, the frivolous, worldly *ville* of the *Miglio d'Oro* became obsolete; their owners sold them to nouveau riche Neapolitan property speculators or left them to collapse. Many were divided up long ago into flats. Others – such as the spectacular

Around Naples

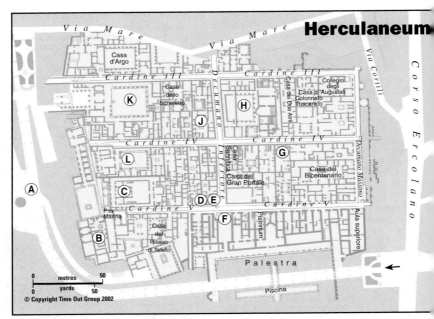

Herculaneum

HERCULANEUM – KEY

A Original shoreline
B Terme Suburbane
C Casa dei Cervi
D Taberna di Priapo
E Thermopolia
F Palaestra
G Casa di Nettuno e Anfitrite
H Terme del Foro
J Casa del Tramezzo di Legno
K Casa dell'Albergo
L Casa dell'Atrio a Mosaico

Villa Favorita – were boarded up and
abandoned by their owners for generations.
A tiny handful have been salvaged by the *Ente
per le Ville Vesuviane* (Vesuvian Villas Board)
and are open to the public. If the Villa Favorita
itself – designed by Fernando Fuga – has
escaped the Ente's benevolent clutches, not so
its spruced-up lower park and the restored
annexe, the **Palazzina del Mosaico**, which
reopened in early 2002.

In Ercolano, the Ente Ville has its
headquarters in the stupendous **Villa
Campolieto**. Also in Ercolano, the Ente has
given a new lease of life to the **Villa Ruggiero**.

Herculaneum (Scavi di Ercolano)

Corso Resina 6 (081 739 0963). **Open** *Apr-Oct*
8.30am-7.30pm daily; ticket office closes 6pm. *Nov-
Mar* 8.30am-5pm daily; ticket office closes 3.30pm.
Admission 8.50 *(see also p210).* **No credit cards.**
Letters in the text refer to map above.
Described by the ancients as being situated *inter
duos fluvios infra Vesuvium* ('between two rivers
below Vesuvius'), the topography around Herculaneum has changed beyond all recognition. The rivers
have disappeared, the present-day shoreline is 1km
(0.6 miles) to the west, and that part of Herculaneum
that has not been excavated lies as much as 25m
(80ft) below the modern town of Ercolano.
Descending from Ercolano, emerging from newly
built tunnels leading into the site, and strolling
through the ancient town of Herculaneum, is like
entering a time capsule.

The town was founded most probably by Greek
settlers of undocumented provenance some time in
the fourth century BC – although Dionysius of
Halicarnassus rather implausibly attributes the
foundation to Hercules on his return from Iberia.
Most of what is visible today dates back no further
than the second century BC. The town had a grid
layout similar to its neighbour Neapolis; at the time
of its destruction in AD 79, it would have had around
5,000 inhabitants. Buried swiftly in an airtight
layer of solidified volcanic mud (unlike Pompeii,
where volcanic ash took a while to settle and

Around Naples

become compressed), Herculaneum has yielded organic remains allowing insights into aspects of everyday life, such as diet, clothing and furniture.

Access to the site is via an impressive ramp offering fine overviews of the Roman town; from here, a tunnel leading down to the original **shoreline [A]** is the best place to admire the thick volcanic deposits towering up around. It was near here that 250 skeletons were discovered in the 1980s (most still in situ): inhabitants overwhelmed by the surge cloud from Vesuvius while hoping, vainly, to be rescued by sea. Most of the interesting and best-preserved houses (with many upper storeys still intact) are to be found either side of Cardo IV and Cardo V, running perpendicular to the two *decumani* (main roads).

Near the seaward end of Cardo V, an altar and a statue base stand outside the **Terme Suburbane** (Suburban Baths) **[B]**; the statue, dedicated to local dignitary Nonius Balbus, is now in Naples' Museo Nazionale Archeologico (*see p79*).

In Insula IV, the **Casa dei Cervi** (House of the Stags) **[C]** was a villa with a prime seafront location and gazebo. It is named after the two sculptures of deer attacked by hunting dogs found in the garden; the ones here now are replicas. Excavated systematically in the early 20th century, Casa dei Cervi suffered less and preserved more of its upper storeys than the houses in Insula II on the northwestern side of the site, excavated 100 years before. Nearby are two shops **[D & E]**, identifiable by their fronts, which were broad to allow space for folding wooden screens to partition off the shop from the street. The first **[D]** is the **Taberna di**

Priapo (Priapus's Tavern), complete with waiting room, a rather tired-looking fresco in the entrance and private inner chambers. On the street corner, with amphorae set into marble counters, is one of the town's **thermopolia [E]**; these were the fast-food outlets of the ancient world, where passers-by might have bought *garum*, a fish-based sauce, reputedly the Viagra of Roman times.

Where Cardo V meets the lower *decumanus* (one of the two main roads of a Roman town) there are two columns marking the entrance to the large **palaestra** (Insula Orientalis) **[F]**, where a variety of ball games and wrestling matches would have been staged. Two sides of its rectangular peristyle are still largely buried under impressive volcanic deposits. Within this leisure complex were two *piscinae* (swimming pools or fishponds): one at the centre of the peristyle, tunnelled out of the rock, with a replica of the original monumental bronze hydra fountain in the middle; and the other (a more recognisable pool) on the northern side, with amphorae set in its sides for fish-farming purposes.

The houses in Herculaneum are virtually all named after archaeological finds or architectural peculiarities. The **Casa di Nettuno e Anfitrite** (House of Neptune and Amphitrite, Insula V) **[G]** on Cardo IV is no exception, taking its name from the beautifully preserved mosaic adorning the wall of the secluded *nymphaeum* at the back of the house. In the days when bridal consent was not a prime consideration among Olympians, Neptune sees Amphitrite dancing with the Nereids on the island of Naxos, and spirits her away to marry him.

Buried swiftly under volcanic mud, **Herculaneum** is remarkably intact.

Just opposite are the **Terme del Foro** (Forum Baths, Insula VI) **[H]**, with separate sections for men and women. The women's baths have the more attractive and better-preserved mosaic flooring; the male section is larger and contains an exercise area and a round *frigidarium*, in addition to the mandatory *apodyterium* (changing room), *tepidarium* and *calidarium* found in the female section next door. Note the *apodyteria* with partitioned shelves for depositing togas, and the low podia to use as seating space while queuing.

The **Casa del Tramezzo di Legno** (House of the Wooden Partition, Insula III) **[J]** unusually has two atria, which suggest that there were originally two houses here, joined together in the first century AD when one of the emerging class of *mercatores* (traders) perhaps bought out the patrician owner. Note the carbonised wooden screen beyond the marble *impluvium*, separating the atrium from the *tablinum*, where the *patronus*, or master of the house, used to do business with his clients.

Further down Cardo IV is the **Casa dell'Albergo** (House of the Hotel, Insula III) **[K]**. One of the largest buildings in Herculaneum, it was undergoing restoration from previous earthquake damage when overwhelmed by the AD 79 eruption. Note the small private baths area just to the right of the main entrance, with the wall decorations in the second Pompeian style. Beyond the atrium is an impressive peristyle, enclosing a sunken garden. The trunk of a pear tree was found here, suggesting the garden may have been an orchard in antiquity. The pear trees have been replanted in an attempt to recreate the original vegetation.

Opposite the Casa dell'Albergo is the **Casa dell'Atrio a Mosaico** (House of the Mosaic Atrium, Insula IV) **[L]**, with geometrically patterned flooring in the *vestibulum* leading into a black and white chequerboard pattern in the atrium, and the *tablinum* in the background. The *tablinum* is unusually elaborate, with its three aisles separated by two rows of pillars topped by Corinthian capitals, conforming to the design described by Roman architect Vitruvius as *oecus aegyptius*. Like many other houses both in Herculaneum and Pompeii, this has suffered considerable wear and tear in modern times and will most probably be locked, though peeking is feasible through the bars of the gate.

Note that only part of Herculaneum is visitable at any given time, and much of the site is screened off by some rather unsightly red plastic fencing. A list of the buildings open to the public is posted in the ticket office on corso Resina.

Villa Campolieto

Corso Resina 283, Ercolano (081 732 2134/ www.villevesuviane.net). **Open** *Ente per le Ville Vesuviane office* 9am-2pm Mon-Fri. *Villa* 10am-1pm Tue-Sun. **Admission** free.
Designed by Luigi and Carlo Vanvitelli, the Villa Campolieto was built between 1760 and 1775. The circular portico – where a summer concert season is held (check the Ente's website for details) – has a sweeping view over Ercolano and down to the sea. On the first floor, a few rooms have been restored to their original state and are open to the public; even more are on view during the Villa's frequent exhibitions. For information and a list of the *ville* in the area, call in at the Ente's office on the ground floor.

Villa Favorita

House: corso Resina 291, Ercolano. Park: via Gabriele D'Annunzio. **Open** *Park only* 10am-1pm Tue-Sun. **Admission** free.
Dotted with pavilions and teahouses, the villa's lower park sweeps down to the sea and a jetty – all that remains of a Bourbon construction that was the nearest thing Italy had to Brighton Pier. On the seaward side of the park is the recently restored Palazzina del Mosaico, which is now used for conferences and ceremonies.

Villa Ruggiero

Via A Rossi 40, Ercolano (081 732 2134). **Open** 10am-1pm Tue-Sun. **Admission** free.
Set slightly back from the main road, the villa was built in the mid-18th century for the baronial Petti family; an extra floor was added at a later stage. Currently only the elegant courtyard is on show.

Torre del Greco

Displaying much of the urban blight common to all the *comuni vesuviani*, Torre del Greco has experienced both the ravages of 'build-em-high' post-war development and Vesuvius's eruptions over the centuries. In the heart of the volcano's red-alert area, its 110,000 inhabitants continue their business pretty much as usual. Besides floriculture, a major source of income is the manufacture of coral and cameos that are still highly prized items on East Asian markets.

Some of the world's best artists and trainees can be seen at work at the privately owned **APA Coral & Cameo Factory** conveniently close to the Torre del Greco motorway exit. This is a fairly slick marketing operation, but if you can negotiate your way in between large Japanese tour groups, the quality of the artistry and factory displays may persuade you to part with some of your holiday euros.

The **Museo del Corallo** has some fine 18th-century pieces from the Trapanese school and attractive cameos on malleable lavic stone. The museum is on the first floor of the Istituto Statale d'Arte technical college; when not too busy with school duties, a member of staff will show you round the locked museum hall.

APA Coral & Cameo Factory

Via De Nicola 1 (081 881 1155/fax 081 849 2383/ www.giovanniapa.com). **Open** 8.30am-6.30pm daily. **Credit** AmEx, DC, MC, V.

Discover superb wall paintings in the Roman villa at **Oplontis**.

Museo del Corallo

Piazza Luigi Palomba 6 (081 881 1360/fax 081 881 1741). **Open** 9am-noon Mon-Fri. **Admission** free.

Where to stay & eat

The **Hotel Marad** (via San Sebastiano 24, 081 849 2168/fax 081 882 8716, www.hotelmarad.it, double room €81-€114) is lodged between the major archaeological sites and Vesuvius; best reached by car, this quiet, comfy hotel also has two excellent restaurants (average €23, €41).

Torre Annunziata & Oplontis

Once a thriving town where Neapolitans spent their summer holidays lazing on black volcanic beaches, Torre Annunziata has long lost its allure as a resort; instead it specialises in providing material for the *cronaca nera* (crime news) pages of local papers.

The wondrous archaeological site of **Oplontis** is its saving grace.

Oplontis

Via Sepolcri 1 (081 862 1755). **Open** *Apr-Oct* 8.30am-7.30pm daily; ticket office closes 6pm. *Nov-Mar* 8.30am-5pm daily; ticket office closes 3.30pm. **Admission** €5 *(see also p210)*. **No credit cards**.
Thought – on the basis of an inscription on an amphora – to have belonged to Nero's second wife, Sabina Poppaea, the prosaically named Villa A of Oplontis has some of the finest examples of the Pompeian Style II of wall painting. If Poppaea really

lived here and indulged in her asses' milk baths within its finely frescoed walls, she would have done better to stay put with her husband, Marcus Otho, than take up with Nero, who arranged for hubby to be posted as governor of the far-flung province of Lusitania (central Portugal). Poppaea eventually became imperial wife number two in AD 62 before – if Tacitus is to be believed – she received a fatal kick from Nero while pregnant three years later.

This delightful, under-visited site amply merits a ramble through the villa. The west wing is right up against the main road; much more lies unexplored beneath. West of the reconstructed main atrium (room 5 – the numbers are over the doors), the walls of the *triclinium* (room 14) contain some stunning illusionist motifs. The *calidarium* in the adjoining baths complex (room 8) has a delicate miniature landscape scene surmounted by a peacock in a niche at the far end; the adjacent *tepidarium* (room 18) gives an insight into Roman heating systems and bath design. The floor is raised by *suspensurae*, brick pilasters enabling warm air to pass beneath.

Off the portico on the southern side of the site is an *oecus* or living room (room 23) with some spectacular still-life frescos in Pompeian Style II; the *cubicula* nearby (rooms 25 and 38) have frescos in the finer, less brash Style III. As you leave the warren of *cubicula*, the spaces become more grandiose, culminating at the eastern end with a large *piscina* (swimming pool) fringed in Roman times by plane, oleander and lemon trees. The ancient atmosphere of relaxation and contemplation lingers on, making Oplontis a pleasant antidote to what the Latin poet Horace would have called the *profanum vulgus* down the road in urban Pompeii.

Around Naples

The site is strategically close to both the Circumvesuviana railway station and the motorway exit for Torre Annunziata, making a visit to the area relatively swift, painless and rewarding.

Pompei & Pompeii

To many Italians, Pompei is a place of pilgrimage. People flock here from all over the south to pay their respects to the Madonna in the large, early 20th-century **Santuario** on the main square (piazza Bartolo Longo), praying for the kind of miracle that healed a girl suffering from acute epilepsy in 1876. Others bring their new cars to have them blessed and secure divine protection; given local driving standards and roads, this seems a wise precaution.

The enormous throughput of religious and cultural tourists caught modern Pompei by surprise. For a long time it reaped the benefits of mass tourism and gave little in return. Things are gradually changing. Seedy lodgings have given way to well-appointed hotels, and eating out is no longer a hit-and-miss affair, especially if you stray from the archaeological site towards the centre of town.

About 3 kilometres (2 miles) to the north is the **Antiquarium di Boscoreale**, opened in the 1990s as a permanent exhibition on Pompeii and its environment 2,000 years ago. Reconstructions show idyllic scenes of wildlife along the nearby river Sarno, now sadly one of the most polluted watercourses in Italy.

Antiquarium di Boscoreale

Villa Regina, via Settetermini 15 (081 536 8796). **Open** *Apr-Oct* 8.30am-7.30pm daily; ticket office closes 6pm. *Nov-Mar* 8.30am-5pm daily; ticket office closes 3.30pm. **Admission** €3 (*see also p210*). **No credit cards.**
Set rather incongruously in the middle of a 1960s housing estate, the Antiquarium documents daily life, environment and technology in Roman times. Disparate finds ranging from fishing tackle to cages for rearing dormice (a favourite with Roman gourmets) are displayed alongside life-size photos of original mosaics and frescos from other sites and museums. In the grounds of the museum is Villa Regina, an ancient farmstead with storage capacity for 10,000 litres (2,200 gallons) of wine. The ancient vineyard around the villa has been replanted along the same rows as in antiquity. The Porta Marina tourist office (*see p210*) will give directions to this out-of-the-way site.

Scavi di Pompeii

Via Villa dei Misteri 2 (081 536 5154). **Open** *Apr-Oct* 8.30am-7.30pm daily; ticket office closes 6pm. *Nov-Mar* 8.30am-5pm daily; ticket office closes 3.30pm. **Admission** €8.50 (*see also p210*). **No credit cards.**
Letters in the text refer to map on p217.

POMPEII – KEY

A	Porta Marina
B	Basilica
C	Forum
D	Tempio di Giove
E	Macellum
F	Terme del Foro
G	Casa del Fauno
H	Porta Ercolana
I	Villa dei Misteri
J	Terme Stabiane
K	Teatro Grande
L	Odeion
M	Casa dei Casti Amanti
N	Palaestra
O	Vineyards
P	Anfiteatro

Unlike Rome, where ancient monuments have suffered millennia of weathering, reuse and pillaging, Pompeii had the great fortune (for posterity at any rate) of being overwhelmed by the AD 79 eruption of Vesuvius. The ancient street plan is intact, the town still has its full complement of civic buildings, the houses have preserved their frescoed walls and – thanks to painstaking work by generations of archaeologists – we have a fairly clear picture of what life was like here 2,000 years ago.

The picture is still being completed: emergency digs during roadworks on the Naples–Salerno motorway in 2000 revealed the full extent of a frescoed leisure complex close to the Sarno river; within the site, archaeologists are still working on the Casa dei Casti Amanti (House of the Chaste Lovers); palaeobotanists, anthropologists and vulcanologists are gradually piecing together the mosaic of knowledge gleaned from latest finds.

Allow at least two hours for visiting Pompeii; it will take longer if you intend to see both the amphitheatre and the Villa dei Misteri, a good 25 minutes' hike apart. Audio-guides offer two-, four- or six-hour itineraries – times that are probably underestimates if you choose to listen to optional in-depth information supplied. On Saturday and Sunday mornings, there is the added bonus of three extra buildings on display: the Terme Suburbane (Suburban Baths; *see also p218* **Tempora mutantur?**) by Porta Marina; Casa di Giulio Polibio (House of Julius Polybius) on via dell'Abbondanza; and Casa del Menandro (House of Menander) near the theatre. For access to these houses you have to ask for (free) coupons at the main ticket office when you buy your ticket. You will be assigned a time at each house. The Casa dei Vettii, on the other hand, was closed for restoration as this guide went to press.

There is little shade, so take the obvious precautions against the sun, and stock up with drinking water. Afternoon visits pay dividends when the crowds start to thin out. Ask for the site map from

Pompeii

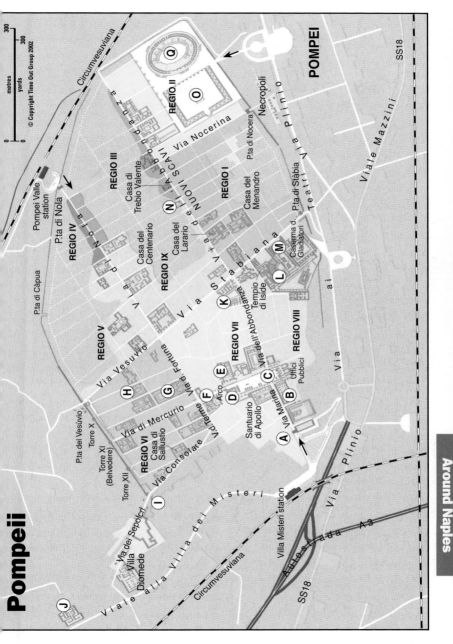

POMPEI

REGIO II

Q

O

Via Nocerina

Necropoli

P.ta di Nocera

P.ta di Stàbia

Viale Mazzini

SS18

Circumvesuviana

Pompei Valle station

P.ta di Nola

REGIO IV

P.ta di Capua

REGIO III

Casa di Trebio Valente

N

REGIO IX

Casa del Centenario

REGIO I

Casa del Menandro

Casa del Larario

REGIO V

Via Stabiana

Caserma d. Gladiatori

M

P.ta del Vesuvio Torre X

Via Vesuvio

Via d. Fortuna

K

Tempio di Iside

L

Via Teatri

Via Plinio

Torre XI (Belvedere)

REGIO VI

Via di Mercurio

G

H

Via d. Terme

F

Arco

E

D

REGIO VII

Via dell'Abbondanza

C

Uffici Pubblici

Via

Torre XII

Casa di Sallustio

Via Consolare

Santuario di Apollo

B

A

Via Marina

REGIO VIII

Via dei Sepolcri

Villa Diomede

I

Villa alla Villa dei Misteri

Villa Misteri station

Via Plinio

Autostrada A3

J

Viale alla Villa dei Misteri

Circumvesuviana

SS18

metres 300
yards 300
© Copyright Time Out Group 2002

Tempora mutantur?

In 1980, a massive earthquake shook to the ground thousands of buildings in the Campania region surrounding Naples, prompting a building spree that – critics say – caused more devastation than the quake itself. With utter disregard for planning permission, historic towns were transformed beyond recognition, two-storey cottages suddenly became four-storey apartment blocks and fortunes were all too easily made, many of them with hastily pocketed central government funding.

But, as archaeologists and historians will tell you, there's nothing particularly 20th-century about *abusivismo edilizio* (construction without permission) in Campania. Pompeii's newly opened **Terme Suburbane** (Suburban Baths; *see p216*), for example, were put up illegally at least in part during a building free-for-all that got under way after an earthquake in AD 62. A combination of epigraphic and literary sources tells us that an increasingly infuriated Emperor Vespasian was eventually forced to send a tribune by the name of T Suedius Clemens to enforce zoning laws. On this occasion, several buildings appear to have been demolished, and boundary stones delimiting public areas were set in place bearing the inscription LPP, probably standing for *Locus Publicus Pompeianorum* ('public place of the Pompeians').

If little has changed in the construction field over the millennia, entertainment, too, suggests some interesting parallels. When a riot took place in Pompeii's amphitheatre in AD 59 between local supporters and those from nearby Nucera (Nocera), Nero banned all shows from Pompeii's arena for ten years.

the information office or from the audio-guide kiosk at Porta Marina. The Circumvesuviana railway station Pompei Scavi-Villa dei Misteri is opposite the main Porta Marina entrance to the site; just inside, the forum is a good place to get your bearings.

The **Porta Marina** **[A]**, with its separate entrances for pedestrians (on the left) and animals and light vehicles (right), is near the original harbour, hence the name. (The shoreline is now much further away than in antiquity, when a canal is thought to have provided access from the sea to the town.) This gate provided the quickest way of getting to that hub of Roman life, the forum, but as the route was also the steepest, most vehicles at the time would have chosen one of the other seven gates leading into town.

On the right is the **basilica [B]**, Pompeii's law court and stock exchange. These rectangular buildings ending in semicircular apses were the model for early Christian churches.

The nearby **forum [C]** is a rectangular area with a colonnade surmounted by a loggia running along three sides. Plinths at the southern end indicate that there was a row of large statues, perhaps equestrian. At the northern end is what remains of the second-century BC **Tempio di Giove** (Temple of Jupiter) **[D]** with the cone of Vesuvius behind. As Jupiter was head of the Roman pantheon, it was standard practice to dedicate a temple to him (together with Juno and Minerva) at the centre of town. The temple had already suffered severe damage in an earthquake before AD 79.

The elegant three-columned portico on the eastern side of the forum marks the entrance to the **macellum [E]**, the covered meat and fish market built in early imperial times.

The **Terme del Foro** (Forum Baths) **[F]** are relatively small as Roman baths go, but retain much of the original stucco decoration. Within the *calidarium* is a well-preserved marble *labrum* (fountain) with an inscription in bronze letters around the rim, recording the names of the officials (C Melissaeus Aper and M Staius Rufus) who installed it in AD 3-4, as well as its cost (5,420 sesterces). Sexes were segregated in all Roman baths; women would probably have had the morning shift and men the afternoon.

Close to the baths on via della Fortuna is the **Casa del Fauno** (House of the Faun) **[G]**, named after the small bronze statue in the middle of the marble *impluvium* (the original is in the Museo Nazionale Archeologico; *see p79*). One of the largest and most sophisticated houses in Pompeii, it includes a front section arranged around two atria rather than the usual one; behind is a peristyle with a portico of Ionic columns. Found in the *exedra* (discussion hall) at the far end of the first peristyle, flanked by two *triclinia*, was a million-tesserae mosaic (also in the Museo Nazionale Archeologico) thought to depict the Battle of Issus in 330 BC between Alexander the Great and the Persian emperor Darius III.

Situated about 300 metres (330 yards) outside the city walls through the attractive **Porta Ercolano [H]**, leading towards Herculaneum and Neapolis, the **Villa dei Misteri** (Villa of Mysteries) **[I]** has frescos in the *triclinium* depicting – experts believe – a young woman's initiation into the cult of Dionysus. There are ten scenes of vivid intensity, thought to have been copied by a local artist from a fourth- or third-century BC Hellenistic original. The villa was a working farm for much of its existence; the wine-making area is still visible at the northern end.

Stroll down the main street (via dell'Abbondanza) from the forum towards the amphitheatre, and the town begins to take on a different feel. The shops along here can be identified by their much broader entrances for easy access from the street. Private houses, on the other hand, had *fauces* (narrow passages); security was a problem in ancient Pompeii, and inhabitants went to great lengths to protect themselves and their property.

The **Terme Stabiane** (Stabian Baths) **[J]** are a much larger complex than the forum baths, with the exercise area in the middle surrounded by the male and female sections. The stuccoed vault in the men's *apodyterium* (changing room), with its images of nymphs and cupids, is particularly well preserved.

To the south is the theatre complex. The **Teatro Grande [K]** seats about 5,000 and – like so many theatres in the ancient world – enjoyed a stunning backdrop, in this case the Sarno river plain in the foreground and the heights of the *Mons Lactarius* (Monti Lattari) behind. This second-century BC theatre underwent much restoration in antiquity, unlike the adjoining smaller **Odeion** or **Theatrum Tectum [L]**. The semicircular *cavea* (seating area) was truncated at both ends to facilitate the building of a permanent roof, offering welcome shade to Pompeii's concert-goers in the main summer season.

North of via dell'Abbondanza, excavations continue around the **Casa dei Casti Amanti** (House of the Chaste Lovers) **[M]**. Not open to the public as this guide went to press, the house has revealed important evidence about life immediately prior to the eruption that challenges previously accepted facts. Earthquake damage from AD 62 had been repaired long before, and the inhabitants were trying to patch up cracks from recent tremors perhaps days before the AD 79 eruption; the rooms were being replastered and painted by teams of master craftsmen at the very moment Vesuvius erupted. In the rapid getaway, tools were downed, plaster abandoned and walls left unfinished. The unlucky donkeys – for turning the grindstone and milling wheat in the adjoining bakery – were left to their fiery fate.

The **Anfiteatro** at Pompeii, where the gladiators fought.

West of the large **palaestra** [N] – the rectangular porticoed exercise area dating back to Augustan times – are recently planted **vineyards** [O] that use varieties and training systems thought to have been employed in ancient times. The first grapes were harvested in 1999 and wine produced, though the thick, scented nose of ancient Roman wine (drunk diluted) is unlikely to appeal to modern palates.

By Roman standards, Pompeii's **Anfiteatro** (amphitheatre) [P] was fairly small, seating only about 20,000. Entertainment would probably have been limited to gladiatorial combat, with only occasional *venationes* (contests with wild animals) or *naumachiae* (mock sea-battles). Though gladiators had fairly short life expectancies – it was considered an occupation for slaves and social outcasts – records exist of the odd volunteer signing on for combat and creating quite a stir. The amphitheatre preserves a fair amount of its seating area, visibly divided into three sections of seats, with a series of *vomitoria* (entrances) near the top.

Where to stay & eat

Located close to the amphitheatre entrance of the Pompeii archaeological zone, the **Hotel Amleto** (via B Longo 10, 081 863 1004, www.hotelamleto.it, double room €85-€120) has themed rooms with decor ranging from 19th-century Neapolitan to Venetian styles; the *trompe l'oeil* wall painting of the House of the Vettii in the breakfast room is guaranteed to mesmerise you. The newly opened youth hostel, **Casa del Pellegrino** (via Duca D'Aosta 4, 081 850 8644, www.hostels-aig.org; rates €13 per person in dorms, €15.50 per person in family room) is in a low-rise Spanish-style ex-convent just off Pompeii's main square, with rooms and dormitories opening on to a peaceful inner courtyard.

Il Principe (piazza B Longo 8, 081 850 5566; closed Sun, Mon dinner Nov-Mar & 3wks Aug; average €60) is one of Campania's finest restaurants, serving ancient specialities gleaned from classical authors; if you make it to dessert, try the exquisite *cassata Oplontis*, made with honey and goat's milk ricotta cheese.

Castellammare di Stabia & Stabiae

Famed for its spa, its shipyards and its *biscottifici* (biscuit factories), Castellammare has not only been bypassed by the coast road but has also suffered gradual industrial decline over the past 30 years. The town has recently started to exploit its archaeological heritage; the site at ancient **Stabiae** is now considered a potential economic mainstay. Castellammare is

The crater of **Vesuvius**. *See p222.*

well served by rail, and has the added bonus of hydrofoil and ferry services to Capri, as well as a cable-car (*funivia*) service up **Monte Faito**.

Funivia & Monte Faito

Stazione Circumvesuviana, Castellammare di Stabia (081 879 3097/081 772 2646/www.vesuviana.it). **Open** *Apr-mid June, Sept, Oct* 9.25am-4.25pm daily. *Mid June-Aug* 7.25am-7.15pm daily. Closed Nov-Mar. **Tickets** €4.65 one way; €6.71 (€7.23 in July & Aug) return. **No credit cards.**

With pleasant walks set among shady beech woods, Monte Faito provides the perfect panacea for an excess of Mediterranean heat during steamy summer months. An eight-minute ride on the *funivia* (cable car; leaves every 23-30mins) from the main Castellammare di Stabia Circumvesuviana station whisks you up into Apennine-type woodland, affording nerve-tingling vistas over the Bay of Naples.

Robins retreat up here in summer from the coastal *maquis*; the distinctive calls of nuthatches can be heard as they flit from tree to tree. Plants tend to flower much later here than down on the coast; for late spring orchids, look in the clearings and in the more exposed areas below the cable-car station.

The upper *funivia* station is the start of some hiking trails across to Positano (*see p244*; allow five to six hours, take good maps and water, and be prepared for lots of ups and downs), but there are also low-key circular routes through the beech forest. The path from the *funivia* to the chapel of San Michele (1,278m/4,193ft above sea level) about 3km (2 miles) away, for example, climbs just 170m (595ft) and you get good views of the bay for your efforts. Stock up with water and picnic fare in Castellammare.

Stabiae (Scavi di Castellammare)

Via Passeggiata Archeologica (081 871 4541).
Open *Apr-Oct* 8.30am-7.30pm daily; ticket office
closes 6pm. *Nov-Mar* 8.30am-5pm daily; ticket office
closes 3.30pm. **Admission** free.

'Ash was already falling, hotter and thicker as the
ships drew near, followed by bits of pumice and
blackened stones, charred and cracked by flames:
then suddenly they were in shallow water, and the
shore was blocked by debris from the mountain.
For a moment my uncle wondered whether to turn
back, but when the helmsman advised this he
refused, telling him that Fortune stood by the
courageous and they must make for Pomponianus
at Stabiae.'

So reads Pliny the Younger's account of his uncle's
ill-fated attempt to rescue Pomponianus, a friend
living 5km (3 miles) south of Pompeii at Stabiae,
modern-day Castellammare di Stabia. Pliny would
be more than surprised to see today's coastline,
which extends much further out to sea than it did in
AD 79. Nowadays, decidedly unlovely post-war
urban development rises where his uncle would
have encountered shallow water, while the seaside
settlement where Pomponianus may have lived is
perched on the bluff of a hill called Varano, almost
1km (0.6 miles) inland.

Partially explored and plundered by the Bourbons
over 200 years ago – some of the original Roman
wall paintings were deliberately defaced in situ to
enhance the value of artworks removed to adorn the
king's palaces – the archaeological site of Stabiae
fell into decay when financial and human resources
were siphoned off to unearth Pompeii in the late 18th

and 19th centuries. It was only in the 1950s, when
excavations began, that the site started to recover
from centuries of neglect. Damage from the 1980
earthquake set the work back.

Two villa complexes can now be visited: Villa
Arianna and Villa San Marco, both of which can be
reached from the Passeggiata Archeologica, the road
skirting the south-eastern side of Castellammare.
The ground plans of the two villas are complex, not
only because of the additions and extensions carried out in antiquity, but also because they were
designed to fit the lie of the land.

Named after a fresco depicting King Minos's
daughter Ariadne, who helped Theseus out of the
labyrinth after he killed the Minotaur, Villa Arianna
is the oldest structure on the hill (first century BC)
although it was renovated and extended in the first
century AD. There's a variety of decorative styles
still in situ, and a (disheartening) opportunity to
compare the opulence and taste of such top-notch
ancient real estate (note the summer and winter
dining rooms) with the 1960s housing development
on the seaward side 50m (159ft) below.

Although the frescoed decorations are less spectacular in Villa San Marco, this would have made
for a secluded summer retreat for some Roman magnate, away from the imperial intrigues on the other
side of the Bay of Naples in Baiae (*see p99*), and yet
reasonably close to main thoroughfares linking large
urban centres like Pompeii and Nuceria (now
Nocera). With its 30m (98ft) *natatio* (swimming pool)
flanked by four rows of plane trees enclosed on three
sides by a peristyle, this was a place for enjoying
otium (relaxation) to the full.

Around Naples

Where to stay

Set in luxuriant gardens, the **Grand Hotel La Medusa** (via Passeggiata Archeologica 5, 081 872 3383, www.lamedusahotel.com; double room €150-€206) is a recently renovated fin-de-siècle villa providing the perfect antidote for the hustle down in the *comuni vesuviani*.

Vesuvius

The question experts ask about Vesuvius is not whether it will erupt but when. According to the Osservatorio Vesuviano, the institute that has monitored its activity since 1841, this could be any time between 20 and 200 years hence, and the longer the period of quiescence (the last eruption was in 1944), the greater the risk. Any bleeps on the sensors that could point to an imminent eruption are constantly monitored. When the volcano does blow, scientists believe, it will not be ash fallout or lava flows that pose the greatest danger, but a possible surge cloud of the kind that rolled down the mountain in AD 79 at an estimated 65-80 kilometres (40-50 miles) per hour and produced the ultimate open-air *calidarium*, reaching 400°C.

In the 13 *comuni vesuviani* around the base and on the lower slopes of the 1,281-metre (4,203-foot) high volcano, 700,000 residents opt to be as blissfully unaware of this threat as their counterparts 2,000 years ago. Life's too good here to entertain the idea of abandoning the area. The volcanic soils are fertile; the slopes are still producing wine (Lacryma Christi, which is beginning to shake off its downmarket reputation thanks to some state-of-the-art wineries), and the small cherry tomatoes or *pomodorini* (delightful on pasta) are earning tidy profits for local farmers.

Besides, there are no visible reminders of volcanic hazards such as Sicily's volcanos produce. Vesuvius does not spew lava like Etna or eject ash like Stromboli. It lost its *pennacchio*, or plume of smoke, in 1944, and the lava fields created by previous eruptions are being gradually colonised by vegetation, giving the volcano a deceptively benign appearance.

Vesuvius is now a national park and a UNESCO Biosphere Reserve. But of the almost 200,000 visitors a year who trek up to the rim of its cone and peer down into the depths of the crater 200 metres (700 feet) below, few stay to enjoy the wilder side of the volcano. The park authority has begun to mark out footpaths (one of the best goes from the town of San Sebastiano al Vesuvio up to the Bourbon observatory), although much of the park is fenced off for security reasons: forest fires (started deliberately to free up land for building

purposes) have wrought considerable damage in recent years, and access to many areas is only granted for scientific purposes.

Vesuvius is at its best in May or June when the upper slopes are awash with colour (especially the leggy Mount Etna broom and red valerian) and nightingales, whitethroats and blue rock thrushes are marking out their territory with prolific song. Start first thing in the morning and avoid windy days when conditions on the exposed rim can be critical.

The standard 30-minute route to the cone zigzags along a well-kept path that begins at the 'Quota 1,000' car park, situated at the end of the road up the mountain's western flank. Although the inside of the crater itself is off-limits, there's a good view of steaming fumaroles and stratified pyroclastic deposits on the other side of the crater rim. Fight your acrophobia and peer down into the crater; pioneer plants have moved in, and with them several interesting bird species.

Also located on the road up the western slope of the volcano, the **Museo dell'Osservatorio Vesuviano** offers a broad overview of the geology of the volcano and the threats it poses, as well as some Heath-Robinsonesque seismographs from the 19th century. It's housed in the old Bourbon observatory, a distinctive Pompeian red building that has survived the ravages of at least seven eruptions.

Cratere del Vesuvio

081 777 5720/337 942 249/fax 081 739 1123.
Open 9am-2hrs before sunset daily. **Admission** (including guide) €6. **No credit cards.**
Trips to the volcano's crater are suspended during bad weather and/or fog.

Museo dell'Osservatorio Vesuviano

081 777 7149/www.ov.ingv.it. **Open** 10am-1pm Sat, Sun. **Admission** free.
Look for signs to the Osservatorio at 600m (2,000ft) above sea level, just behind the Eremo Hotel.

Getting there

By bus

Trasporti Vesuviani (081 559 2582/081 559 3173) runs regular services up Vesuvius. The bus starts from piazza Anfiteatro in Pompei, stops at piazza Esedra near the motorway toll booth, and at Ercolano train station, and then winds up past the Osservatorio and the old chairlift station, stopping in the large car park 1,000m (3,280ft) up. One-way from Pompei costs €3, from Ercolano €1.70. Check return times with driver and say if you need to stop at the Museo dell'Osservatorio.

By car

From Torre del Greco or Ercolano, follow signs to Parco Nazionale del Vesuvio.

Sorrento & Around

Rocky crags and wild walks surround a classic holiday spot.

Viewed from Naples, the Sorrentine Peninsula resembles an outstretched arm: a long, straight sweep of land reaching towards Capri, closing off the southern end of the bay. Visit it, however, and you'll find that its apparent smoothness dissolves into an endless labyrinth of rocky crags and jagged cliffs covered with lush citrus orchards, olive groves and frequent, tiny towns and villages, criss-crossed with a dense web of well-kept paths leading to views of indescribable beauty. The town of Sorrento itself, a mecca for Grand Tourists in the 18th and 19th centuries, and still on the map for the mass tourists of the 21st century, is the area's hub. But though many visitors fail to venture beyond it, it's far from the whole story.

The only thing that's missing from this earthly paradise is, oddly, the sea. Its deep, dazzling blue provides a frame for all the views from the peninsula, but the sea is oddly divorced from many of the towns and villages, which have a decidedly mountainous, countryside feel to them. The narrow, winding roads leading down to the few tiny fishing villages and ports in pebbly coves are rarely even signposted. If it's a watery holiday you're after here, make sure your hotel has a swimming pool… or be prepared to walk.

The area around Sorrento has been inhabited since prehistoric times, as the remains on display in museums in **Vico Equense** and **Piano di Sorrento** (for both, *see p233*) show. Etruscans who moved in from the north in the sixth century BC found Greek settlers there. So important was it for the Greeks that Homer allowed his hero Ulysses to be sorely tempted by the siren songs of the peninsula's mermaids in the *Odyssey*.

View of **Sorrento**.

Around Naples

Sorrento

0 metres 200
0 yards 200
© Copyright Time Out Group 2002

Bay of Naples

Belvedere

Marina Piccola
Port

Marina Grande

Museo Correale

Piazza Gargiulo

Via Califano

Via Capasso

Via Nizza

S. Anna

Via Marina Grande

Villa Comunale

S. Francesco

Piazza d. Vittoria

Via Vitt. Veneto

Via L. De Maio

Via Correale

Piazza A. Lauro

Carmine

Via Capasso

Via del Mare

S. Paolo

Via Tasso

Via Giuliani

Piazza S. Antonino

Corso Italia

Railway + bus station

NAPLES

Vico San Nicola

Via S. Cesareo

Piazza Tasso

Sedile Dominova

Via S. M. d. Pietà

Via Marziale

Via degli Aranci

Via Fuoro

Piazza Veniero

Corso Italia

Duomo

Arco Romano

Via degli Aranci

Via Capo

Via degli Aranci

When the Romans routed the Greeks and the local Samnite tribes in the late fourth century BC, they made the peninsula a sought-after holiday venue, building luxury villas all along the coast from **Castellammare di Stabia** (*see p220*) out to **Punta della Campanella** (*see p238*), and, incidentally, sparking a trend that remains to this day: building houses on the most scenic stretches, and roads where the view is obscured.

As the Roman Empire in the west wavered and fell, the Goths stampeded along the peninsula, razing many of its smaller towns. Sorrento, on the other hand, passed formally under the control of the eastern Roman Empire, ruled from Byzantium (Constantinople).

Harried by Lombards, who had set up their southern Italian headquarters in nearby Benevento (*see p273*) around 570, by power-hungry Amalfi (*see p251*) on the other side of the peninsula, and later by marauding Saracen pirates from north Africa, the Sorrentines fought hard to maintain some independence. They were often successful. However, the Normans who arrived in the 12th century were too powerful for them. The towns of the peninsula were absorbed into the southern Italian kingdom, their fate inextricably linked to that of Naples.

Getting there

From Naples airport

Autolinee Curreri Service (081 801 5420) runs six coaches in each direction daily between Naples airport and Sorrento (also stopping at Vico Equense, Piano, Meta and Sant'Agnello); one-way tickets cost €5.20 and are available on the bus.

By boat

Linee Marittime Partenopee (081 807 1812/fax 081 532 9071) and Alilauro (081 807 3024/fax 807 3782) run frequent hydrofoil services between Naples (Molo Beverello) and Sorrento. Services run all year (weather permitting). Linee Marittime Partenopee €7 single (35mins); Alilauro €8.50 single (20mins).

By bus

SITA (081 871 4020) covers routes from Sorrento across the peninsula to the Amalfi Coast (*see p240*) and Salerno (*see p268*). Note that services are curtailed on Sundays and public holidays (last bus at 7pm). Ticket prices vary according to distance, ranging between 93¢ and €2.12. There are hourly services from around 6.35am to 8.05pm along the Sorrento–Meta di Sorrento–Positano–Amalfi route.

The smaller inland towns aren't so well connected. There are hourly services from around 6am to 11pm on the Sorrento–Massa Lubrense–Sant'Agata sui Due Golfi route, but only a few continue to Nerano, Marina di Cantone and Marina di Lobra.

By car

Head south along the busy SS18 coast road or the A3 motorway to its end at Castellammare di Stabia. From the end of the motorway the SS145 (a continuation of the SS18) goes south-east around the peninsula; it's tortuous and slow, but it's the only way.

Take the SS142 to pass through Vico Equense, Piano and Meta or stay on the SS145 as it swings inland for Sant'Agata sui Due Golfi. An unnumbered road forks east along the peninsula through Massa to Termini, before rejoining the SS145 at Sant'Agata.

Inland roads on the peninsula vary greatly in quality; all have hair-raising hairpin bends (sound your horn before going round them). All of these roads can get horribly traffic-filled on Sundays and during the holiday season.

By train

Sorrento is the terminus of the Circumvesuviana railway (information 081 772 2444), which runs from Naples; services every 30mins in both directions. The train also stops at Vico Equense and Sant'Agnello. The last Sorrento–Naples train leaves at 11.26pm; if you miss it there's a bus at 12.15am. A Naples–Sorrento ticket costs €2.84 and is valid for 180mins on any form of public transport between the two towns.

Sorrento

Sorrento only partly deserves its recently earned reputation as Eastbourne-on-the-Med. It is true that the blue-rinse brigade can often be spotted wandering up and down the main streets and haunting *diners-dansants* at the priceless **Circolo dei forestieri** (Foreigners' Club – *see p229*). And the lager-and-tattoos brigade can be found crowded around Sky TV in the numerous English pubs.

But it doesn't take much effort to leave the bussed-in package tourists behind. Sorrento's central location, facilities and decent transport links make it a good base from which to explore the peninsula; its peaceful atmosphere makes a refreshing change for anyone fazed by decidedly more chaotic Naples.

The regular grid plan of the streets stretching west from piazza Tasso is about all that is left of Greek and Roman Surrentum. The Normans destroyed much of the Roman fortifications. What remains of the town's 15th-century walls can still be seen along the traffic-clogged via degli Aranci ringroad or on piazza delle Mure Vecchie. As late as the 16th century these defences were fundamental for the town, subject as it (and the whole peninsula) was to attacks by Saracen pirates from across the Mediterranean. On 13 June 1558, these North African marauders sacked Sorrento, after which a chain of lookout towers, many of which are still standing, was built along the coast. A more complete picture of how the city and its

surrounding area looked until quite recently can be found at the **Museo Correale di Terranova**, where 18th- and 19th-century paintings show rustic scenes around crumbling town gates, and along wild unspoilt coasts.

While Sorrentine youths congregate in the soulless modern area around piazza Lauro, older citizens and the endless hordes of visitors gather in **piazza Tasso**. Bar tables cluster on the pavements, and the evening *struscio* (stroll) begins and ends here when the surrounding streets of the centro storico are closed to traffic between 8pm and midnight daily.

A balcony on the northern side of the square offers views down the dark ravine that leads to **Marina Piccola**, the port from where ferries depart for Capri and Naples. Stairs lead down from the piazza towards the dock, which is also served by the local bus company (*see p232*).

Sorrento's most famous literary son, Torquato Tasso (1544-95), author of the ponderous epic poem *Gerusalemme liberata* ('Jerusalem Deliver'd'), lends his name to the square; his statue looks over it. Leading out of the south-western corner, the narrow via Pietà

Souvenir hub: **via San Cesareo**. *See p227*.

contains **Palazzo Correale** (No.24), an early 15th-century building with an impressive door and arched windows upstairs (go into the florist's shop in the courtyard to admire the 18th-century majolica-tiled wall), and the 13th-century **Palazzo Veniero** (No.14) with windows framed with geometric designs in pretty coloured stone.

Via Pietà emerges on to corso Italia by the **Duomo** (cathedral), which is surrounded by a bishop's palace now occupied by Church offices. Beyond the Duomo, via Sersale leads to the remains of the Roman southern town gate, and to a stretch of 15th-century wall. Corso Italia heads on, lined by smart shops, past the small park and art gallery **Villa Fiorentino** (No.53) and quiet piazza Veniero before leading round the cliff towards Capo (*see p236*).

Turn right down via Tasso to reach the narrow, souvenir-shop-packed **via San Cesareo**. This is the place to pick up examples of the marquetry for which Sorrento was famous in the 18th century (though then its renown rested on inlaid furniture, rather than the music boxes and coasters now on sale) and bottles of the tangy local brew, *limoncello*.

One block east, where via Cesareo intersects with via Giuliani, the arched **Sedile Dominova**, with its fading frescos, was one of two open-air meeting places where the local aristocracy discussed local policy in the 15th century; their coats of arms can be seen around the walls. In an ironic twist of fate, the Sedile is now the front porch of a working men's club; local OAPs gather there to play cards and argue volubly about nothing in particular.

Parallel to via Cesareo, via Santa Maria delle Grazie changes name several times as it runs west towards the **Museobottega della Tarsialignea**, a museum dedicated to the local craft of marquetry.

Several blocks to the north-east, via Veneto gives on to the **Villa Comunale**, a small but leafy park with splendid views over the Bay of Naples to Vesuvius.

By the entrance, the church of **San Francesco** stands beside a small 14th-century cloister (open 8am-1pm, 2-8pm daily; ring the bell if the gate is closed) with pretty ogival arches. The nearby piazza Sant'Antonino is named after Sorrento's patron saint, whose tomb can be admired in the 18th-century crypt of the basilica of **Sant'Antonino** (open 9am-noon, 5-7pm daily). Though heavily baroque-ified, the basilica has stood here since the 14th century, and probably occupies the site of an even earlier church. There's an 11th-century door surrounded by bits and pieces of Roman remains on the right side of the building, and an impressive Nativity scene inside.

Via Marina Grande or narrow via Sopra le Mura lead down to the confusingly named **Marina Grande** (it's smaller than the Marina Piccola). This was the old fishing village of Sorrento – until the natural deep-water harbour of the Marina Piccola made it more convenient for ferries to dock there (thus shifting the entire focus of the town). Paint is peeling off the walls of Marina Grande's tall grey stone houses, stray dogs sleep under the seafront benches, stray cats raids bins for fishy leftovers, kids play football in front of the tiny church of Sant'Anna and fishermen leisurely mend their nets. A couple of big restaurants have tried to make the place more like the rest of Sorrento; fortunately, however, it remains amiably down at heel.

If you want beaches in Sorrento, avoid the dark, volcanic sand beach of Marina Grande. Instead, head for a private beach (such as Bagni Salvatore, via Spiaggia San Francesco, 081 878 1214, open daily in summer) or Bagni della Regina Giovanna (*see p236*) where there's clean water and good snorkelling. Otherwise, ask one of the local boatmen to drop you off in some secluded bay and pick you up later; they'll usually do this for a handsome tip of about €25.

Duomo (Santi Filippo e Giacomo)

Corso Italia (081 878 2248). **Open** 7.40am-noon, 4.30-8.30pm daily.
The original Romanesque cathedral was largely rebuilt in the 15th century. Despite its Gothic appearance, the Duomo's façade is fairly modern, though the door with the Aragonese coat of arms on the right dates from the late 15th century. The three-aisled interior has 16th- and 17th-century paintings in its chapels and on the ceiling. The bishop's throne (1573) is a jigsaw of ancient marble fragments; the choir stalls are adorned with fine examples of local *intarsio* (wooden inlay) work.

Museobottega della Tarsialignea

Via San Nicola 28 (081 877 1942/ www.alessandrofiorentinocollection.it). **Open** *Apr-Oct* 9.30am-1pm, 4-8pm Tue-Sun. *Nov-Mar* 9.30am-1pm, 3-7pm Tue-Sun. **Admission** €8. **Credit** AmEx, DC, MC, V.
From the mid 18th century, Sorrento became famous for its delicate *intarsio* furniture, which was avidly collected both by the Neapolitan royal family and by Grand Tourists. The beautifully restored 18th-century Palazzo Pomarici Santomasi contains a private collection of *intarsio*, both local and from further afield, plus old paintings and photographs of Sorrento. The ground-floor shop sells contemporary interpretations of marquetry furniture that are a world away from the quaint knick-knacks you'll find in Sorrento's souvenir shops.

Museo Correale di Terranova

Via Correale 50 (081 878 1846). **Open** 9am-2pm Mon, Wed-Sun. **Admission** €6. **No credit cards.**

San Francesco has a 14th-century cloister. *See p227.*

Brothers Alfredo and Pompeo Correale, the last male heirs to the title of Count of Terranova, left their 18th-century family villa and its fascinating collection of local art and artefacts to the town in the 1920s. The museum has an archaeological section with finds from around the town on the ground floor; upstairs are views galore of 18th- and 19th-century Sorrento and its environs, plus examples of wooden inlay furniture. A long path through a garden full of camellias and birdsong leads to a lookout with a view across the bay to Sorrento town centre.

Villa Fiorentino

Corso Italia 53 (081 533 5111). **Open** 9am-1pm, 4-7pm daily.
Run by the local council, this late 19th-century villa has a small but pleasant public garden. The villa is open occasionally when it hosts exhibitions by local artists or on local history.

Where to eat & drink

While much of the food served in Sorrento tends to be undistinguished and undemanding, standards have recently risen somewhat. Locals still head for the surrounding hills when they fancy a good meal, but decent food can be found in the centre – at a price. Places offering simple dishes or pizza (preferably with menus translated into the minimum number of languages) do exist. Bars proudly advertising 'English beer' are best avoided.

Bar Ercolano

Piazza Tasso (081 807 2951). **Open** *Apr-Sept* 6am-1.30am Mon, Wed-Sun. *Oct-Mar* 6am-10.30pm Mon, Wed-Sun. Closed 3wks Jan-Feb. **No credit cards.**
The Ercolano is an elegant kiosk with matching tables from which to observe evening strollers. Good ice-cream, slow waiters.

Bar Primavera

Via Fuorimura 20 (081 878 3375). **Open** *July-Sept* 24hrs daily. *Apr-June* 6am-midnight daily. *Oct-Mar* 7am-10.30pm daily. **No credit cards.**
Not only possibly the best cakes in Sorrento (check out the *delizie al limone*), but also hot chocolate with chilli pepper, and hot white chocolate.

Bar Villa Comunale

Villa Comunale (081 807 4090). **Open** *Mar-June, Sept, Oct* 9am-9pm daily; *July, Aug* 9am-midnight daily. Closed Nov-Feb. **No credit cards.**
With tables beneath the palms and pines of the Villa Comunale park, this otherwise unmemorable bar is the perfect place to savour a traffic-free rest while appreciating the sea view from the cliff-top.

Il Buco

Seconda Rampa, Marina Piccola 5 (081 878 2354). **Meals served** noon-3pm, 7pm-midnight Mon, Tue, Thur-Sun. Closed Jan. **Average** €50.
Credit AmEx, MC, V.
The unpromisingly named Il Buco ('the hole') is just off piazza Sant'Antonino in the cellars of an old convent, but there are also tables on the steps outside

during the summer. The food is *nouvelle* Italian (the portions may look small, but they are filling and beautifully presented) and mostly fish-based. Service is swift and courteous, and if the food is slightly overpriced, the extensive and reasonable wine list about balances it out.

Circolo dei forestieri (Foreigners' Club)
Via Luigi di Maio 35 (081 877 3263/fax 081 877 3012). **Open** *Bar* 9.30am-midnight daily. *Restaurant* 11.30am-3pm, 7pm-midnight daily. Closed Dec-Feb. **Credit** AmEx, DC, MC, V.
Inside the tourist office building, the Foreigners' Club is, as the name implies, the preserve of that kind of visitor who comes to Sorrento for its reassuringly non-Italian facilities. Live music, restaurant and bar in a slightly surreal expat atmosphere.

Da Emilia
Via Marina Grande 62 (081 807 2720). **Meals served** *July, Aug* 12.30-3pm, 7.30-11pm daily. *Apr-June, Sept, Oct* 12.30-3pm, 7.30-11pm Mon, Wed-Sun. *Nov-Mar* 'for lunch when the weather's fine'. **Average** €18. **No credit cards.**
Still run by the redoubtable Signora Emilia herself, this unassuming restaurant has wooden tables, checked tablecloths and old-style food and service that make it an essential stop. Grab a table outside and imagine young Sophia Loren sashaying past.

Ristorante Vittoria
Grand Hotel Excelsior Vittoria, piazza Tasso 34 (081 807 1044). **Meals served** 12.30-2pm, 7.30-10pm daily. **Average** €50. **Credit** AmEx, DC, MC, V.
For the ultimate Grand Tour dining experience, head for the grandiose frescoed and mirrored dining room at the Excelsior Vittoria Hotel, where grave white-jacketed waiters whisk silver cloches off food that is trying hard – and with some degree of success – to reach standards a notch above usual hotel fare. Chef Giancarlo Schettini does good things with seafood, but he also branches out into pasta dishes that make use of other regional produce such as capers, olives and mozzarella.

Sant'Antonino
Via Santa Maria delle Grazie 6 (081 877 1200). **Meals served** *May-Oct* noon-3pm, 7-11.30pm daily. *Dec-Apr* noon-3pm, 7-10.30pm Tue-Sun. Closed Nov. **Average** €20. **Credit** AmEx, MC, V.
This unassuming trattoria serves pizza at lunch and dinner, and does a good fish barbecue on its terrace beneath the orange trees.

Shopping

Corso Italia is packed with clothes shops: the cheaper stores are east of piazza Tasso; the more upmarket boutiques are to the west. Via Cesareo and its continuation via Fuoro are the places for souvenirs: *limoncello*, a digestivo liqueur made from lemons (if you want to see

the stuff being produced on the premises, try **Limonoro**, via San Cesareo 51, 081 807 2782, www.cosedisorrento.com); local produce (**Fattoria Terranova**, piazza Tasso 16, 081 878 1263, www.massalubrense.it/terranova); and marquetry. For the latter, try **Salvatore Gargiulo** (via Fuoro 33, 081 878 2420, www.gargiuloinlaid.it), a well-established workshop where objects are made on the premises. For an interesting alternative to the proliferation of mass-produced tiles, plates and cups, visit **Primo Piano Oggetti** (corso Italia 161, 081 807 2927).

Arts & entertainment

Sorrento's largely tourist-centred economy fairly rules out a truly vibrant cultural scene, and most night-time entertainment consists of strolling up and down the traffic-liberated via Cesareo, or relaxing in bars (*see p228* **Where to eat & drink**) and watching others strolling.

Artis Domus
Via San Nicola 56 (081 877 2073/www.artisdomus.com). **Open** *Sept-June* 11pm-3am Sat. **No credit cards.**
A small stone doorway leads into the garden of a sumptuous villa where Sorrento's arty types congregate of a Saturday, when there's either live music or a disco, as well as food. A decided change from the rest of the nightlife to be found in Sorrento.

Teatro Tasso
Piazza Sant'Antonino, 25 (081 807 5525/www.teatrotasso.it). **Open** *Box office* 9am-1pm, 4.30-9.30pm on performance days. **Shows** *Theatre* Apr-Oct 9.30pm daily. **Tickets** *Theatre* €21; *Cinema* €6.20. **Credit** AmEx, DC, MC, V.
A cinema during the winter and a theatre in the summer months, Teatro Tasso has a live programme heavily slanted towards the kind of *folkloristico* musical variety shows that require no knowledge of Italian. Watch out for the season of summer shows, entitled *Sorrento Musical.*

Where to stay

The best of Sorrento's grand hotels are truly grand, as befits this classic resort, and if your bank account is up to splashing out for the Grand Tourist experience, this is definitely the place to do it.

The mid-range hotels, on the other hand, tend to be very mediocre, however, and cheap places are virtually non-existent. Unless otherwise stated, breakfast is included.

Campsites include the **Nube d'Argento** (via Capo 21, 081 878 1344, www.nubedargento.com, rates per person €7-€9; tent site €8.26-€11.88) and, slightly further out of town, the **Santa Fortunata** (via Capo 39, 081 807 3579, www.santafortunata.com, rates per person €5.20-€8.30; tent site €4.15-€6.20). You'll need your own transport to reach the latter.

Agriturismo Marecoccola
Via Malacoccola 10 (081 533 0151/ www.fattoriamarecoccola.com). **Rates** €80-€150 double. **No credit cards.**
An old stone farmhouse above Sorrento with sublime views. All meals use the farm's own produce. The owners also organise hiking expeditions.

Bellevue Syrene
Via Marina Grande 1 (081 878 1024/fax 081 878 3963/www.bellevue.it). **Rates** €165-€205 single; €205-€255 double; €290-€335 suite. **Credit** AmEx, DC, MC, V.
Elegant, light, airy and decorated in a tasteful if slightly bland style, the Bellevue is built on the site of a second-century BC villa. It has been a hotel since 1820, hosting royalty, writers and many generations

Marina Grande: amiably down at heel. *See p227.*

of the world's rich and famous. Rooms with a sea view cost more, but are worth it – waking up to a pure blue view of sea and Mount Vesuvius is a wonderful experience. The Lord Astor restaurant is a faithful replica of a Roman villa; the 'Roman bath' looks suspiciously like a jacuzzi.

Grand Hotel Excelsior Vittoria
Piazza Tasso 34 (081 807 1044/fax 081 877 1206/ www.excelsiorvittoria.com). **Rates** €230-€256 single; €296-€420 double; €525-€1,690 suite. **Credit** AmEx, DC, MC, V.
The grandest of Sorrento's grand hotels, the Vittoria has been in the hands of the Fiorentino family since the 1830s. The cool Pompeii-meets-art-deco corridors are in restful pastels; the rooms (not all of which have been recently decorated, with some falling below the standards you'd expect of a hotel in this category) have period furniture and delightful terraces overlooking the sea or the lush five-hectare (12½ acre) garden. The bathrooms, though small, have an abundance of white marble. There's a pool and a children's playground. Low-season deals can be found on the hotel website.

Hotel Regina
Via Marina Grande 10 (081 878 2722/fax 081 878 2721/www.belmare-travel.com). **Closed** Nov-Mar. **Rates** (half-board obligatory) €95.60 per person double room; €113.70 per person single room. **Credit** AmEx, DC, MC, V.
The view from the Regina's rooftop restaurant goes some way towards compensating for the dubious colour schemes of its rooms. Clean, functional and with balconies outside almost every room, it's about as much as you can expect in Sorrento at these moderate prices.

Imperial Hotel Tramontano
Via Veneto 1 (081 878 1940/fax 081 807 2344/ www.tramontano.com). **Rates** €155 single; €250 double; €360-€440 suite. **Credit** AmEx, MC, V.
One of Sorrento's classic hotels, the elegant cliff-top Tramontano has hosted Shelley, Byron, Goethe and Ibsen (a plaque rather incongruously notes the fact that it was here, while 'meditating on human misery', that the Norwegian playwright was moved to write *Ghosts*) – as well as royalty galore. It's situated on top of a Roman villa, and includes part of the house where the 16th-century Sorrentine poet Torquato Tasso was born. It was in this hotel that GB de Curtis penned the town's classic weepy ditty (*see p236* **Turna a Surriento**), which you'll hear ad nauseam all over town. There's a pool, a lift down to the beach and a superb garden.

La Neffola
Via Capo 21 (081 878 1344/fax 081 807 3450/ www.nubedargento.com). **Rates** €620-€878 per wk for four people. **Credit** AmEx, DC, MC, V.
In the same location as the Nube d'Argento campsite, La Neffola offers classy self-catering apartments: a good alternative for those who don't fancy holidays under canvas. There's a huge garden.

A piedi

Viewed from car or train, the dramatic cliff faces, rocky hillsides and lush gardens of the Sorrentine Peninsula may look inaccessible. But a network of reasonably well-kept footpaths criss-crosses the entire area, from **Castellammare di Stabia** (see p220) to **Amalfi** (see p251) to **Punta della Campanella** (see p238).

Many of these are maintained by the Club Alpino Italiano (CAI) which marks routes with coloured paint flashes on rocks, walls, lamp posts or whatever else comes to hand en route. Paths vary dramatically in difficulty; the further you go from habitation, the less well defined they become. But given the paint marks and the simple maps available from most tourist information offices, you shouldn't have much difficulty exploring the peninsula's wilder side.

Heading west from Sorrento, there are a few easy, pleasant walks winding down to the **Villa di Pollio Felice** (see p236) or up to the **Deserto** (see p240) in Sant'Agata sui Due Golfi (where you should stop in the Bar Orlando and ask about the legendary smoking cat). These can be easily done in a morning.

Slightly more strenuous are walks to **Punta della Campanella** and the **Baia di Jeranto**, or the **Sentieri degli Dei** ('Pathway of the Gods') that follows the ridge from **Ravello** (see p259) down to Sorrento. These have little shade – if you attempt them in summer, be sure to take a hat, sunscreen and lots of drinking water – but are rewarding not only for breathtaking views, but also for the pleasure of pulling off your sweaty boots and diving into the sea when you reach your destination.

Be aware, also, of the Italian farmers' habit of leaving large, aggressive dogs to roam freely around what they perceive to be their

land. Though they may bark, however, they rarely bite. For more information about walks, contact the local branch of the **World Wide Fund for Nature** (WWF, corso Italia 67, Sorrento, 081 807 2533, www.digilander.iol.it/wwfsorrento, open 9.30am-1pm, 3-7pm Mon-Fri; 9.30am-1pm Sat) or the **Ente Parco Punta della Campanella** (viale Filangieri 40, Massa Lubrense, 081 808 9877, www.punta campanella.org, open 9am-1pm, 3.30-7pm Mon-Fri).

Ostello delle Sirene (Youth Hostel)

Via degli Aranci 160 (081 807 2925/fax 081 877 1371/info@hostel.it). **Rates** €14 per person in dorm without bathroom; €16 per person in dorm with bathroom; €42-€52 double. **No credit cards.** Open all year, the youth hostel offers unquestionably the cheapest bed in town.

Parco dei Principi

Via Rota 1 (081 878 4644/fax 081 878 3786/ www.grandhotelparcodeiprincipi.com). **Closed** Nov-Mar. **Rates** €153-€170 single; €198-€270 double. **Credit** AmEx, DC, MC, V.
Somewhat to the east of the town centre, the Parco dei Principi was designed – building, furniture,

fittings and all – in shades of blue and white by architect Giò Ponti in the 1960s. The result is charmingly dated. There's a seawater pool, a sauna, a lift down the cliff to the private beach, and a lush private botanical garden packed with rare tropical species covering 27 hectares (67 acres).

Car & scooter hire

Avis

Viale Nizza 53 (081 878 2459). **Open** *Apr-Oct* 9am-1pm, 4-8pm Mon-Sat; 9am-12.30pm Sun. *Nov-Mar* 9am-1pm, 4-8pm Mon-Fri; 9am-1pm Sat. **Credit** AmEx, DC, MC, V.

Pompeii meets art deco at the **Grand Hotel Excelsior Vittoria**. *See p230.*

Hertz
Via degli Aranci 9A (081 807 1646/fax 081 807 2521). **Open** *Mar-Oct* 8.30am-12.30pm, 2.30-7.30pm Mon-Sat; 9-11.30am Sun. *Nov-Feb* 8.30am-12.30pm, 3.30-7pm Mon-Sat. **Credit** AmEx, DC, MC, V.

Sorrento Rent a Car/ Rent a Scooter
Corso Italia 210A (081 878 1386/fax 081 878 5039). **Open** 8am-1pm, 4-8.30pm daily. Closed 2wks Feb. **Credit** AmEx, DC, MC, V.

Church services

Duomo
Corso Italia (081 878 2248).
Anglican services (in English, logically) at 5pm on Sun in Apr-July, Sept, Oct.

San Francesco
Piazza Saverio Gargiulo 8 (081 878 1269).
Mass in English at 6pm daily and 10am Sun in July-Sept; confession in English half an hour before mass, or whenever the English-speaking priest is around.

Communications

Phone exchange/Internet point
Piazza Tasso 37 (081 878 2400). **Open** *Nov-Apr* 9am-1.30pm, 4-9pm daily. *May-Oct* 9am-1.30pm, 4-10pm daily.

Calls are metered and then paid for when you've finished in this telephone exchange, from where you can also send faxes or check your email for 10¢ for every 70 seconds.

Getting around

For **Getting there**, *see p224.*
Four orange bus lines serve the Sorrento area, running from 5.30am to midnight. Line A goes from Meta to Capo di Sorrento, B from the port at Marina Piccola to the centre, C from the port at Marina Piccola to Sant'Agnello, and D between Marina Grande and the centre. Tickets cost €1.50 from most newsstands and *tabacchi* shops. The bus terminus is in front of the railway station in piazza GB De Curtis.

Tourist information

Latest events are featured in the bi-monthly magazine *Surrentum*, parts of which are in English; it's distributed free at the tourist office and in hotels.

Azienda Autonoma di Cura Soggiorno e Turismo
Via Luigi di Maio 35 (081 807 4033/fax 081 877 3397/www.sorrentotourism.it). **Open** 8.30am-7pm Mon-Sat.
English-speaking staff will provide information on local events and maps.

Around Naples

East from Sorrento

Since the building and tourism boom of the 1950s and 1960s, what was once a collection of fishing and farming villages punctuated by the occasional stately holiday villa has become one urban sprawl… albeit an extremely pretty kind of urban sprawl. It's a long, low, whitewashed conurbation containing dozens of hotels that mop up the Sorrento overflow. Many of these have pretty gardens and sports facilities that town hotels don't have the space to offer; but if you're on a package tour and want to be in Sorrento itself, check the small print to avoid ending up out here.

Sant'Agnello is, administratively speaking, part of Sorrento, and its traffic-clogged main street is little more than a funnel into and out of town; as you drive through, you may not even realise it exists. More pleasant (and less congested) is the almost-coast road, which cuts past beautiful villas – many of them converted into hotels – and their flower-filled gardens just a block back from the sea.

Piano di Sorrento still retains the feel of a separate town. In the 18th-century Villa Fondi on the coast road, the **Museo Archeologico Georges Vallet** contains archaeological finds from all over the Sorrentine Peninsula: pre-Roman pottery, artefacts from necropoli, arrowheads galore and a scale model of the Roman villa at Capo di Sorrento (*see p236*) – all beautifully laid out, but with labels in Italian only. A tortuous track leads down to the little harbour – **Marina di Cassano** – where the beach is encroached upon by boats from one of the peninsula's few remaining economically significant fishing fleets.

Meta di Sorrento, in turn, boasts the area's longest stretch of sand, the **spiaggia** (beach) **di Alimuri**. Until a century ago, Meta's marina moored one of Italy's largest shipping tonnages, but it is now another bustling modern suburb, with more Sorrento overflow hotels, and cafés with tables out in sunny *piazze*. In a square on the main road, the **Madonna del Lauro** basilica (open 7am-noon, 4-7pm daily), with its low, tiled dome and neo-classical façade, was rebuilt in the 18th century but is believed to stand on the site of a temple to Minerva.

With fishing and shipping now largely just a memory, the area's economic mainstay – after tourism – is lemons, which were probably introduced by Saracen invaders.

All over the area you'll see the groves of lemon trees, branches heavy all year round with the often enormous fruit, sheltered from the occasionally bitter, salty sea-winds by high black or green nets suspended on frames made from wooden poles.

After Meta, there is a slight lull in the conurbation before the village of **Seiano**, where the 16th-century chapel of **Santa Maria delle Grazie** (closed to the public) has a medieval fresco over its front door. You'll also see the 18th-century church of **San Marco** (opening times vary according to Mass), which has the highest dome on the peninsula. Both coast road and railway line then cross the breathtaking, and somewhat frightening, viaduct over the Murrano river to Vico Equense.

VICO EQUENSE

Aequana was probably founded by the Romans, who found its steep, sunny slopes perfect for cultivating grapes before the Goths descended upon and razed it in the fifth century. (The area's wine production has since moved further up the hill to **Gragnano**, where a tasty, slightly fizzy red is still produced today.) The town of Vico Equense was resurrected in the 13th century by Naples' King Charles II of Anjou.

The privately owned **Castello Giusso** (not open to the public) looms unmissably over the town, its folly-like crenellations added in a 19th-century addition to the original 1284-9 medieval construction. The (crenellated) Renaissance section above was added in the mid 16th century.

Santissima Annunziata. *See p234.*

I Casali

From Vico Equense (*see p233*), the circular via Raffaele Bosco wends its way up (and back down) the slopes of the Sorrentine peninsula, passing through woods and fields and the tiny villages – known as *i casali* – where the everyday, non-tourist-trade life of the area goes placidly on, unnoticed by visitors to the coastal resorts.

Setting out from Vico's main square, piazza Umberto I, via Roma soon becomes via Bosco, and climbs through the outskirts of town. A well-marked turn-off (via Cimitero) to the left leads to the church of **San Francesco** (opening hours erratic), a scruffy baroque affair full of plaster saints with staring eyes. Opposite the church, a path leads past Stations of the Cross set into the wall, to a vine-clad belvedere with an extraordinary view along the peninsula to Capri. On the sharp bend by the cemetery before the final climb to the church, a verdant track leads off to the sorgente di Sperlonga (Sperlonga spring, 30 minutes' easy walk). Until the coast road was built in the early 19th century, this was the only road from Castellammare di Stabia (*see p220*) to the Sorrentine Peninsula.

Back on via Bosco, the road climbs to **Massaquano**, the unlikely location of what is perhaps the peninsula's greatest artwork. Creating a bottleneck in the main road on the right as you drive through, the chapel of **Santa Lucia** was built in 1385 and frescoed by followers of Giotto soon after. (To visit the chapel, distract the denizens of the Circolo San Luigi Gonzaga pool hall across the road from their game, and get them to locate the foot-long 14th-century key.)

Saved from imminent ruin in a recent restoration, the chapel's haunting frescos (behind the altar) show scenes from an apocryphal gospel story in which Christ returns his dead mother's soul to her (in the shape of a baby) before taking her, body and soul, into heaven; the archangel Michael slices the hands off a sacrilegious onlooker who tries to overturn Mary's bier, while saints Lucy (with the lantern) and Catherine of Alexandria (with the original catherine wheel, on which she was martyred) watch the scene from the bottom left.

On the right wall are scenes from the passion of Christ. The left wall once had a detailed cycle on the life of St Lucy but much of this has disappeared over the centuries. The apparition of St Agatha to Lucy and the saint's intercession to stem Lucy's mother's haemorrhage are still visible.

Via Bosco continues to climb to **Moiano**, from where a hiking trail (N38) departs for Monte Faito (around 2.5 hours; *see p220*).

To the south, in via Puntamare, the church of the **Santissima Annunziata** (open 9-10.30am Mon-Sat; 9am-12.30pm Sun) sits atop a dramatic drop to the sea, making it an essential photo opportunity. The Annunziata was Vico's cathedral until the bishopric was abolished in 1799 when the last incumbent, Michel Natale, was hanged for his over-enthusiastic support of the Parthenopean Republic (*see p16*). His portrait is missing from the medallions of former bishops in the sacristy: instead, there's a painting showing an angel with its finger raised to its lips, inviting onlookers to draw a veil of silence over Natale's unwise choice. Some Gothic arches from the original 14th-century church can be seen in the side aisles.

Along viale Rimembranza, the baroque church of **San Ciro** (open 8.30am-noon, 4.30-7.30pm daily) has a pretty tiled dome. Nearby, in via San Ciro, the **Museo Mineralogico Campano** has a collection of some 5,000 bits of rock from all over the world, including fluorescent ones that glow under ultraviolet light; there are a few chunks of meteorite and some fossils, too. Inside the town hall, a collection of seventh- to fifth-century BC artefacts from a local necropolis are on display in the **Antiquarium**.

Below the town centre to the east, **Marina di Vico** (occasional buses run from Vico station) has a short pebbly beach with a handful of restaurants. To the west, on the other hand, the harbour at **Marina di Equa** allows access to long stretches of sun-worshipping space at the *spiagge* (beaches) of Pezzolo (where ruins of a first-century AD villa are visible) and Vescovado to the east, and Calcare to the west. The imposing ruin at the far end of Calcare beach was part of a lime quarry that operated for hundreds of years, closing down in the late 19th century. There's a Saracen watchtower and lots of bars in pretty Marina di Equa, as well as one of the best restaurants in the area, the **Torre del Saraceno** (*see p235*). (Finding Marina di Equa can be a problem: head out of Vico on the SS145; just beyond the far end of the railway viaduct, there's a small sign marked 'Marina di Equa', but don't blink or you'll miss it.)

Beyond the village centre, a road on the left leads to the hamlet and church of **Santa Maria del Castello** (three kilometres/two miles). In the church are marble statues and paintings of saints made in Naples in the 16th and 17th centuries (the family in the house at the foot of the stairs has the key).

From the church, perched 685 metres (2,397 feet) above sea level on the crest of the peninsula, the hills fall away south to the Amalfi Coast (see p240) and north to Sorrento. The view is simply breathtaking. There's a hiking trail (N33; two hours) from Santa Maria del Castello to Positano (see p244).

Back on via Bosco (either of the descents from Santa Maria del Castello will do), past the village of **Arola**, a steep, narrow road to the left leads to the remains of the 17th-century **convento dei Camaldolesi**, from where there's another superlative view down to the sea. Via Bosco then drops sharply back to reach the coast at **Seiano**.

Fairly frequent guided walks around some of the *casali* are organised by local groups. Check www.massalubrense.it or the tourist information offices in Sorrento or Vico for more information.

Antiquarium

Casa Municipale, via Filangieri 98, Vico Equense (081 801 9228). **Open** by appointment only 8.30am-12.30pm Mon, Wed, Fri; 8.30am-12.30pm, 4-6pm Tue, Thur. **Admission** free.

Museo Archeologico Georges Vallet

Via Ripa di Cassano 14, Piano di Sorrento (081 534 1050). **Open** 9am-1pm, 4-7pm Tue-Sun. **Admission** €4.13. **No credit cards.**

Museo Mineralogico Campano

Via San Ciro 2, Vico Equense (081 801 5668). **Open** *Mar-Sept* 9am-1pm, 5-8pm Tue-Sat; 9am-1pm Sun. *Oct-Feb* 9am-1pm, 4-7pm Tue-Sat; 9am-1pm Sun. **Admission** €1.60. **No credit cards.**

Where to eat & drink

In Piano di Sorrento, the **Bar Villa Fondi** (via Ripa di Cassano 14, 081 534 1050, closed Mon) is an airy pavilion in a lovely cliff-top garden surrounding the town's Museo Georges Vallet (see above) overlooking the sea.

Vico Equense calls itself 'the home of pizza by the metre', thanks solely to the endeavours of **Gigino Pizza al Metro** (via Nicotera 15, 081 879 8426, average €12), a great barn of a place, popular with busloads of tourists and large Neapolitan families. Stretch-pizzas of all imaginable varieties are served here; order slices of a length to match your appetite.

In Marina di Equa, the **Torre del Saraceno** (via Torretta 9, 081 802 8555, closed dinner Sun Sept-June, Mon, average €50) more than deserves its Michelin star. Chef Gennaro Esposito creates some of the best food on this (or any) coast: the seafood antipasti consist of a mouth-watering selection ranging from caviar to sea urchins; the pasta for the exquisite, delicate first courses is strictly home-made, and the fish tastes as if it has only recently left the sea. And these delicacies can all be consumed on a beautiful patio beneath the Saracen watchtower after which the place is named.

Where to stay

Down a sharp drop off the coast road east of Vico Equense, the **Hotel Capo La Gala** (via Luigi Serio 8, 081 801 5758, www.capolagala.com, closed Nov-Mar, double room €156) is a big cut above the generally mediocre accommodation on offer in town. Tastefully decorated rooms with balconies overhang waves crashing on to rocks below; the pool is filled with mineral-rich water from the nearby Scraio spring.

Perched miles above Vico in Santa Maria del Castello, off via Bosco (see p234 I **Casali**), the family-run **Agriturismo La Ginestra** (via Tessa 2, 081 802 3211, www.laginestra.org, double room €72.30-€80.05 half-board, €87.80-€98.13 full-board) has simple, bright rooms in a farmhouse with spectacular views down the green slopes of the peninsula to the sea in the distance. The farm's own organically grown produce is used in the restaurant (average €18), where non-residents are welcome as long as they book.

Getting there & getting around

See p224 and p232.

Tourist information

Azienda Autonoma di Cura Soggiorno e Turismo

Via San Ciro 16, Vico Equense (081 801 5752/ fax 081 879 9351/www.vicoturismo.it). **Open** *July-Sept* 8am-8pm Mon-Sat. *Oct-June* 8am-5pm Mon-Sat. Keeps a good supply of maps, including walking maps, of the area.

Around Naples

Heading west from Sorrento is a very good idea: ribbon development and heavy-duty tourism have yet to reach this area. Towns are hemmed in by lemon groves, and the air in spring and summer is full of the pungent perfumes of wild garlic and gorse.

The first stop out of Sorrento is the small village of **Capo di Sorrento**, where a plaque on the front wall of the Villa Il Sorito commemorates Maxim Gorky's stay there from 1924 to 1933. A little further on, a high-walled path leads off the coast road to the right (north). It is edged by impossibly romantic fields of lemon trees and asphodels, and goes down to what is known locally as the **bagni della Regina Giovanna** (baths of Queen Joan). In fact, the medieval Joan (*see p12*) had little to do with what was a sumptuous Roman villa, possibly built by one Pollio Felice. The ruins that ramble across the headland,

surrounding a deep, man-made seawater inlet, are much easier to interpret after a pre-emptive visit to the **Museo Archeologico Georges Vallet** in Piano di Sorrento (*see p233*), where there's a scale model of the villa. The outcrops of brick are a good place to sit and contemplate the view up the sweep of coast to Sorrento.

Beyond Capo, a pretty road drops down to the tiny **Marina di Puolo** where there's a little sandy beach (a long walk down from the car park). More citrus orchards and olive groves (nets to collect the falling fruit are stretched out between the trees from October to December, then rolled up and left between the trees in multicoloured swathes) line the winding stretch of coast road from here to the lively town of Massa Lubrense.

MASSA LUBRENSE

Probably founded in its current position by the Lombards – Massa comes from the Lombard word for settlement, *mansa* – this area was also

Turna a Surriento

It's odds-on that even before you've emerged from Sorrento's railway station you'll have heard the strains of an overwrought romantic song called *Turna a Surriento* ('Come Back to Sorrento' in Neapolitan dialect).

Recently given its umpteenth lease of life by Andrea Bocelli and Luciano Pavarotti (though purists sneer: both of them being northerners, they'll never get it right...), this is one of many popular ditties dating from Naples' late 19th- and early 20th-century music hall and *café-chantant* tradition, with little to do with authentic Neapolitan roots music (*Funiculì, Funiculà, O' Sole Mio* and *Santa Lucia* are others).

Strangely, this particular classic weepy is in fact a political protest song.

According to local lore, painter and decorator Giambattista De Curtis was hard at work on the Imperial Tramontano hotel (*see p230*) in 1902 during a visit by Prime Minister Giuseppe Zanardelli. To urge the government chief to come back and do something about Sorrento's then disastrous economy, transport links, collapsing buildings and non-existent sewerage systems, De Curtis dashed off the song in a couple of hours, tugging at his heartstrings as much as at his purse strings. Hence the lines:

E tu dice: "I' parto, addio!".
T'alluntane da stu core...
Da la terra de l'ammore...

Tiene 'o core 'e nun turna'?
Ma nun me lassa',
Nun darme stu turmiento!
Turna a Surriento,
Famme campa'!
(And you say 'I'm leaving, farewell!'/Far from this heart/From the land of love.../Can you have a heart and not return?/Don't leave me here/Don't torment me like this!/Come back to Sorrento/Let me live!)

The song was originally popularised by the great tenor Enrico Caruso when he introduced the practice of singing popular Neapolitan songs as an encore after a triumphant operatic performance.

Caruso was Neapolitan by birth, but had a troubled relationship with his native city, where – already a phenomenon in opera houses round the world – he was booed off the stage and rubbished by critics after his debut at San Carlo (*see p61*) in 1905. In a fury, he vowed never to return, preferring to stay in Sorrento when in Italy.

Many bars and restaurants in the town still have pictures of the bulky dandy: two-tone shoes and a carnation in his lapel, staring moodily towards Naples across the bay from the terrace of one of Sorrento's hotels. It was not until he realised he was dying that Caruso returned not to Sorrento but to Naples to breathe his last in the Albergo Vesuvio (*see p47*) on 2 August 1921.

Around Naples

Contemplate the coast at
Capo di Sorrento. *See p236.*

known in ancient times. Lubrense comes from
the Latin word *delubrum*, 'temple', two of which
are known to have existed in the vicinity.

There's a great view across to Capri from the
belvedere in largo Vescovado. On the other side
of the square there's the haunting, crumbling
façade of the former cathedral of **Santa Maria
delle Grazie** (open 7am-noon, 4.30-8pm daily),
which dates from the early 16th century, though
it was reworked in 1769. The chapel of
Sant'Erasmo, to the left of the main altar, may
stand above a temple to Hercules. Directly
opposite the church, a road leads down to the
pretty village and beach of **Marina di Lobra**
(take a scenic shortcut down the first flight of
steps heading down right from the road; you
may, however, want to hitch a lift or wait for
the infrequent bus on the way back up).

Halfway down the road, the church of **Santa
Maria di Lobra** (open 6.30-8am, 5-8pm daily)
has a pretty yellow-and-green tiled dome, a
'miraculous' 16th-century *Madonna and Child*
over the altar, and a cool, homely cloister with a

tiled well-head (there's a door from the cloister
into the church that is generally open when the
church is officially shut). There was a temple
here, too, probably dedicated to Minerva. The
whole place has a charmingly lived-in feel to it,
though only two old Franciscan monks remain
in the adjoining monastery; if you feel moved to
join them for a while, the Piccolo Paradiso Hotel
(*see p238*) takes bookings for a handful of very
simple rooms in the monastery.

From Massa's main square, a road north-west
(soon swinging south) heads to the villages of
Santa Maria and **Annunziata**, this latter
little more than a handful of houses around a
rarely open church of the same name, and the
ruins of the 14th-century castello di Massa.
A well-marked walking trail goes from Massa
to Annunziata, worth taking not only for the
walk itself, but also to see the **Villa Rossi**
where Joaquin Murat (*see p18* **King Joaquin**)
holed up after the Battle of Capri and signed
the capitulation that put an ignominious end
to French rule in Naples.

Around Naples

BEYOND MASSA

The coast road out of Massa swings past the church and cemetery of **San Liberatore** (open *Apr-Sept* 8am-12.30pm, 4-6pm Mon, Tue, Thur-Sat; 8.30am-noon Sun; *Oct-May* 8.30am-12.30pm, 2.30-5pm Mon, Tue, Thur-Sat; 8.30am-noon Sun), a final resting place of incredible beauty on the edge of a cliff with Capri tantalisingly close across the bay. The little whitewashed chapel was originally built in 1420, though it has been heavily restored since.

In ancient times, the coast road continued as far as the temple to Minerva on Punta della Campanella. Nowadays, it curves inland a couple of kilometres short of the point, to the town of **Termini**.

A nondescript place with a spectacular view, Termini is the starting point for walks (*see also p231* **A piedi**) galore around Punta della Campanella, down to the Amalfi Coast (*see p240*) and along the crests of the peninsula. The paths are colour-coded and, in general, quite easy to follow; the tourist information office in Massa Lubrense (*see below*) has a good selection of town and walking maps.

The lane that heads south opposite the church leads to one such track (look for the green and red stripes... though colour coding can change) to the chapel of **San Costanzo**; the walk takes around 40 minutes. The chapel is a stark white construction, rarely open; the view down towards the very tip of the peninsula at Punta della Campanella and the Baia di Jeranto immediately to the north is awe-inspiring.

From the same departure point, another path (grey and green stripes; 90 minutes) follows the headland out to the Saracen watchtower on Punta della Campanella; there are remains of a Roman villa too. The path for Punta Penna, with access to Jeranto Bay, begins in Nerano (*see p242*).

Punta della Campanella was formally established in 2000 as a marine reserve – aimed mostly at protecting the date shell mollusc (*dattero del mare*) from being fished and eaten out of existence by humans who care more about their delicacies than their environment – despite strong opposition from powerboat fiends and property developers.

Where to stay & eat

Accommodation is low-key in Massa Lubrense, and the family-run **Hotel La Primavera** (via IV Novembre 3G, 081 878 9125, double room €67-€72) is no exception, but it's clean, most of the rooms have balconies, and the restaurant serves excellent, unpretentious seafood (average €25). The **Antico Francischiello da Peppino** (via Partenope 27, 081 533 9780,

closed Wed Nov-Mar, average €40) is Massa's premier restaurant, serving wonderful local cheeses as well as good, fresh, traditional seafood dishes. The staff will even come and pick you up if you're staying in Sorrento. **Il Tritone** (via Massa Turro 2/A, 081 808 9046, closed Jan & Wed, average €20) is a good alternative if you don't fancy splashing out and want something simple; try the own-made *scialatielli* pasta with clams and mussels.

In Marina di Lobra, the **Piccolo Paradiso** (piazza Madonna della Lobra 5, 081 808 9534, closed mid Nov-mid Mar, double room per person €38.73-€43.90) is a more upmarket accommodation option with a swimming pool and watersports (including scuba diving, which is arranged on request). It also handles the very simple monks' cells for rent (€24 per person B&B) at the monastery opposite (*see p237* **Santa Maria di Lobra**).

Diving centres

While descending to the sea isn't always easy, it's worth it. Experienced divers will appreciate the area around Punta della Campanella and the islets of Vervece and Vetara. But a mask and snorkel are all you really need to enjoy underwater activity.

Boa Diving

Via Marina di Praia, Praiano (089 813 034/fax 089 813 1084/www.laboa.com). **Open** 8am-8.30pm daily. **Credit** MC, V.
Open all year, this centre arranges two diving trips daily and night dives on request. Trips start at €33 per person.

TGI Diving Sorrento

Via Marina di Puolo, Massa Lubrense (081 877 2034/www.divingtour.it/tgidiving.com). **Open** 9am-1pm, 4-8pm daily. **No credit cards.**
A dive with air tanks begins at €30; hire of wetsuit and other equipment costs more. The diving centre is open all year, but has no permit for 'Zone A' restricted areas. To avoid disappointment when you turn up, you can book your dive at Mondo a Strisce (via Capo 2, Massa Lubrense).

Getting there & getting around

See p224 and p232.

Tourist information

Ufficio Turistico Comunale

Viale Filangieri 11, Massa Lubrense (081 808 9856/ fax 081 808 9571/www.massalubrense.it).
Open *May-Oct* 8am-2pm, 4-7pm Mon, Wed, Fri; 8am-2pm, 3.30-6.30pm Tue, Thur; 9am-noon Sat, Sun. *Nov-Apr* 8am-2pm Mon, Wed, Fri; 8am-2pm, 3.30-6.30pm Tue, Thur.

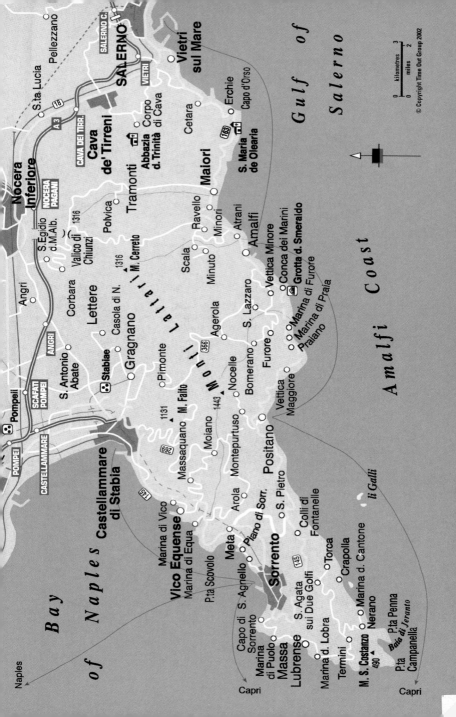

The Amalfi Coast

It's official: paradise is vertical.

What is it about earthly paradises? The inhabitants of Capri say that the calcareous rocks make them depressed; Amalfi Coast residents, on the other hand, are always grumbling about the lack of parking spaces and the winter cold. But this is really just a smokescreen: deep down, they know they have it good – otherwise, why would so many tourists keep telling them so?

For many centuries, though, life along this sheer, rocky stretch of coastline was as hard as anywhere in Italy. The Amalfitan Republic may have had a florid Byzantine heyday, but for the rest of the time pirate raids, floods, landslides and isolation meant that to live on the Amalfi Coast was, in more ways than one, to live on the edge.

The cultured northern European traveller's discovery of the area's spectacular views and romantically crumbling *palazzi* in the 19th century coincided with the mass emigration of many of the inhabitants, especially to the United States; it was only after World War II that tourism became a reliable source of income. For many visitors, it is the thrilling contrast between the coast's intractable geology and the *dolce vita* of Positano or Ravello that makes the Amalfi Coast such an unforgettable experience.

Come early or late in the season to see it at its best – but not too early or late, as facilities really wind down between November and February. April and October are marvellous months to visit – the former to see the coast opening up into a profusion of flowers, the latter (if you're lucky with the weather) for beach-lounging without the sardine effect. Bring a car only if you have quick reflexes, a head for heights and enough spare cash to pay

for the few non-resident parking spaces, which average €20 per day in high season. If you do drive, get used to glancing in the mirrors that are set up at every sharp corner. You'll have a far cheaper and less stressful holiday if you trust your life to the expert local bus drivers or, better still, take boats between the main towns. Best of all, in spring or autumn, walk: a well-signposted network of paths extends along the whole coast, from short village-to-village strolls to a spectacular long-distance footpath, the Alta Via dei Lattari, that follows the ridge dividing the Amalfi Coast from the Bay of Naples. So vertical is the topography of the coast that walking between two points – for example, the short hop from Ravello to Minori or Atrani – is often quicker than taking the bus, at least if you're going down. The footpath numbers in the text refer to the official CAI (Club Alpino Italiano) numbers, and should be written on markers along the way. The CAI's excellent Monti Lattari map and walking guide can be found in book and newspaper shops all over the Amalfi Coast.

The best way to approach the Amalfi Coast is from Sorrento (*see p225*), via Sant'Agata sui Due Golfi (*see p242*) along the Nastro Azzurro road, which drops immediately into the most spectacular part of the coast. It is this west-to-east direction that has been followed in this chapter.

West of Positano

For many visitors, Positano is the western limit of the Amalfi experience. The steep, rocky, spectacular stretch of coastline further west has few hotels or historical sites; administratively part of the province of Naples, it possesses only a sprinkling of tiny villages, most of them built well back from the shoreline, which until relatively recently was only accessible by boat. Even today the road descends to the sea in only one place, the **Marina di Cantone**.

But it is this very remoteness that makes the coast between **Punta della Campanella** (*see p238*) and Positano worth exploring, as this is what the Amalfi Coast proper must have looked like before it was discovered by mass tourism in the 1950s. The lack of roads is the walker's gain: there are some spectacular paths down to hidden coves and wild headlands, and the

Trust your life to expert local bus drivers.

western section of the Alta Via dei Lattari – for serious walkers only – traverses the whole coast. Perhaps unexpectedly, this stretch also boasts some of the best restaurants on the Costiera Amalfitana.

Sant'Agata sui Due Golfi, set in a dip on the ridge dividing Sorrento from the sheer southern coast, was a favourite summer resort for well-off Neapolitan families in the 18th and 19th centuries. It doesn't look like much today, with cars vying with agricultural equipment for parking places outside the 17th-century church of **Santa Maria delle Grazie** (open 8am-1pm, 5-7pm daily), with its monumental multicoloured inlaid marble altar.

But there are two very good reasons for a stopover. One is the Michelin-starred restaurant **Don Alfonso** (*see p243*); the other is the convent of **Il Deserto**, situated a kilometre (just under a mile) north-west of town along a (badly) signposted road.

A forbidding bunker built by the Carmelite order in 1679 and now occupied by a very recalcitrant closed order of Benedictine nuns, Il Deserto (081 878 0199) has a roof terrace with a view across the peninsula that defies description. It is ostensibly open 3-6pm daily; in fact, it's open when the nuns feel like it, and when they're prepared to slide the huge key out

Pretty, lemon-fringed **Amalfi**. *See p251.*

through the revolving barrel in their visitors' room, in exchange for a small contribution towards the upkeep of the convent.

From Sant'Agata, via Torricella leads south-east to **Torca**, a tiny village with terrific views down over the coast. From Torca, a marked footpath (No.37) leads steeply down to the **Marina di Crapolla**. Don't let the name (a corruption of the Latin for goat) put you off: this picturesque, pebbly fishing cove is well worth the scramble down and the slow climb back. On the headland to the west are the remains of a 12th-century abbey; on the beach is a ruined Roman villa. The islet of **Isca**, just offshore, was owned by the Neapolitan actor and playwright Eduardo de Filippo.

The road from Sant'Agata west to **Termini**, jumping-off point for Punta della Campanella (*see p238*), is frustratingly viewless. Beyond the hamlet of **Caso**, a side road on the left winds down to the pretty village of **Nerano** and the seaside resort of **Marina di Cantone**, which has one of the longest beaches on the southern side of the peninsula. This is not necessarily a blessing, as Cantone seems to have gone from nothing to resort without passing through the limbo of planning permission, but it's still small-scale – the topography sees to that – and has a certain low-key family charm that contrasts with the sometimes excessive refinement – and often excessive prices – of resorts such as Positano.

Cantone has an excellent diving centre, **Diving Nettuno** (via Vespucci 39, 081 808 1051, www.villaggionettuno.it, closed Nov-Mar), and makes a good springboard for the breathtaking natural beauty of the **Baia di Jeranto** (*see also p231* **A piedi**) to the west. This untouched sandy bay is reachable either by boat (shop around on Cantone beach) or by marked footpath (No.39) from the church in Nerano. East of Cantone, Torca can be reached in three hours along a spectacular – and strenuous – cliff-hugging section of the Alta Via dei Lattari long-distance footpath.

East of Sant'Agata, the Nastro Azzurro road leads, in 14 nail-biting kilometres (nine miles) to Positano. Off the coast are three small islands that the ancients believed to be the home of the Sirens, who lured mariners on to the rocks with their song; once known as Le Sirenuse, they now have the more prosaic name of **Li Galli** – the cockerels. In 1925, the villa on the largest of the islands was bought by dancer and choreographer Léonide Massine; Stravinsky and Picasso were among his guests.

Over the pass of San Pietro, where the road across from Sorrento joins the Nastro Azzurro, the Amalfi Coast proper comes into view – but if you're driving, you won't be looking at the

Slim pickings for the fashion-conscious in **Positano**. *See p244.*

view. Even passengers may have a hard time: in 1953, John Steinbeck and his wife 'lay clutched in each other's arms, weeping hysterically', while their driver, Signor Bassani, expounded happily on the region's 'molto lot old heestory'.

Where to stay & eat

In Sant'Agata sui Due Golfi, the chintzy decor of **Don Alfonso 1890** (corso Sant'Agata 13, 081 878 0026, closed mid Jan-Feb, Mon & Tue lunch June-Sept, Mon & Tue Oct-May, average €95) may not be to everyone's taste, but there's no denying that Alfonso Iaccarino's exquisite cuisine deserves its two Michelin stars. The seasonally changing sculptures that appear include an unbelievably light soufflé of marrow with mozzarella and anchovy sauce, the classic oyster-stuffed potato with lentils and raw prawns, and a *boccadoro* (bream) that tastes as if it had leaped straight out of the sea and into the lemon leaves it was cooked inside. All the garden produce comes from the Iaccarino family's organic farm. The wonderful desserts and the petits fours and chocolates presented at the end of the meal are the only things that could make you wish you hadn't eaten so much. Don Alfonso also has five pretty apartments (double room €175 for bed and breakfast – and what a breakfast!).

In Marina di Cantone, the **Taverna del Capitano** (piazza delle Sirene 10, 081 808 1028, www.tavernadelcapitano.it, closed Jan, Feb, Mon Oct-May, average €55), housed in a nondescript white building on the seafront, proves that appearances can be deceptive. Inside, on the ground floor, is an elegant restaurant presided over by young chef Alfonso Caputo, who does succulent things with seafood and local garden produce. Trademark dishes include baby cuttlefish in balsamic vinegar and *tagliolini bianchi e neri* (white and black tagliolini) with baby octopus, potatoes and broad beans – but on any given day, the menu depends very much on what was fished that morning. The desserts are equally worthwhile, and the selection of wines is extensive. Upstairs are 15 bright, airy, reasonably priced rooms (double €90-€130).

Cantone's other hot culinary contender is **Quattro Passi** (via Vespucci 13N, 081 808 2800, closed Tue dinner, Wed, 6 Nov-26 Dec, open daily mid June-mid Sept, average €60), which lies a little way back up the approach road in extensive grounds. It's an elegant place with the heart of a family restaurant and a real vocation for fine food. The daily changing menu includes gourmet mouthfuls such as large ravioli with angler fish, local Furore tomatoes and organic olive oil, or *pezzogna* (blue-headed bream) bundles with spiky lettuce and pine nuts. The cellar – which extends under the road – is a cave of oenological wonders, and desserts such as the wild berry bavarois in raspberry sauce are no let-down. There are also six simple double rooms (€85) and three suites (€135), which look on to terraces of olive trees.

Characteristically coloured dome of **Santa Maria Assunta**. *See p245.*

Getting there

See page 248.

Tourist information

See page 248.

Positano

Positano is not so much a town as a cliff with houses on. Unlike its neighbour Amalfi, it had no long, narrow river valley to expand up and shelter in; here, life is vertical and exposed. Perhaps this explains why the town has little history on show: more vulnerable to pirate raids and without the watermills that made Amalfi an industrial as well as a naval power, it kept things small and rebuildable. In the 12th and 13th centuries, Positano's merchant fleet rivalled Amalfi's, but thereafter the town declined, coming under the control of a succession of Neapolitan overlords. In the 19th century, three-quarters of the population emigrated to the United States; even today, Columbus Avenue in New York has more *positanesi* than Positano.

When John Steinbeck came here in 1953 to write an article for *Harper's Bazaar*, Positano was a secret closely guarded by the few Italian writers and painters who had discovered it. But its *dolce vita* star rose rapidly; in the mid 1960s, it was briefly more fashionable than Capri. Traces of this high tide are visible everywhere – in hotel decor, 1960s seaside postcards and above all in the town's much-touted 'fashion' shops, where the truly fashion-conscious will find slim pickings.

As so often, the dramatic topography that made life in Positano so difficult is what makes it such a tourist attraction today. It's endlessly photogenic, with stacks of colourful houses clinging to every inch of the steep terrain. To the joy of local hoteliers, Positano's vertical layout means that almost every house has a clear view over the top of the one in front; to their despair, this means decent-sized swimming pools are out of the question – at least until someone invents a vertical one.

Like Capri, Positano has deliberately priced itself out of the package-tour range: of its 30 hotels, more than two-thirds are three star or above, and in high season it's well nigh impossible to find a double room for less than €100 a night, unless you have booked weeks or even months in advance.

Tourist income is used to keep the place looking spruce and clean, though the cleanliness is skin-deep, as Positano still does not have an efficient sewage treatment system: in high summer, the smell emanating from the conduit that runs down through town and under the main beach is far from pleasant, and the sea can be distinctly murky.

Directions in Positano are either up or down, unless you're in a car, in which case they're round and round for hours. The SS163 coast road hugs the contours in the upper part of town, where it goes by the name of via Marconi. From the town hall to the west, one-way viale Pasitea winds down in a series of curves to piazza dei Mulini, then changes its name to via Cristoforo Colombo and climbs again to rejoin the coast road on the eastern edge of town. These are the only roads open to traffic; in summer, the lower one is permanently clogged with cars hunting for parking spaces. A strong pair of legs will get you almost anywhere in town more quickly than a set of wheels, though if you can't face the climb there is a regular circular bus service.

From piazza dei Mulini, narrow, shop-lined via dei Mulini runs down to the beach past the parish church of **Santa Maria Assunta** (open 8am-noon, 3.30-7pm daily), with its characteristic brightly coloured majolica dome; there's a 13th-century burnished gold *Madonna and Child* above the main altar.

The main beach, **Marina Grande**, consists of a neat stretch of fine grey pebbles with colourful fishing boats pulled up in serried ranks; to the right looking seawards is the quay for boats to Capri, Amalfi and Salerno, to the left a private section of beach. Above the quay, steps lead up to a path that winds around the side of the cliff, past the **'O Guarracino** restaurant (*see p245*) to the smaller, rockier, but very popular beach of **Fornillo**, in a small bay guarded by two ancient watchtowers.

Above Positano lie the tiny perched villages of **Montepertuso** and **Nocella**. Until very few years ago, the road (and bus) up from Positano ended at Montepertuso. The inhabitants of Nocella either took the mule track from here, or walked straight up the 1,700 steps from Positano. Road access seems not to have spoiled Nocella, which is still a charming scatter of rustic houses with breathtaking views. And the fact that the bus now stops here (check the timetables down in piazza dei Mulini in Positano) means that one of the Amalfi Coast's great hikes is that much more accessible.

The Sentiero degli Dei – 'Path of the Gods' – winds up the side of a sheer cliff to the pass of Colle di Serra, from where there is an easy descent to **Bomerano** and **Agerola** (with buses to Amalfi). This spectacular hike is not particularly difficult, though some walking experience, a good head for heights and plenty of water and sunblock are essential. Allow two-and-a-half hours for the ascent to Colle di Serra.

Where to eat

La Cambusa

Piazza Vespucci 4 (089 875 432). **Meals served** noon-4pm, 7pm-midnight Mon, Wed-Sun. Closed 3wks Jan. **Average** €40. **Credit** AmEx, DC, MC, V.
Of the handful of long-established tourist restaurants down by the beach, this is one of the most reliable. It's not a bargain by any means, and service can be rather unctuous, but it offers decent seafood, and the few outside tables on a balcony above the main beach offer a prime people-watching position.

Il Capitano

Via Pasitea 119 (089 811 351). **Meals served** noon-3pm, 7.30-10.30pm Mon,Tue, Thur-Sun; 7.30-10.30pm Wed. Closed Nov-Mar. **Average** €50. **Credit** AmEx, DC, MC, V.
Positano's best restaurant prepares classic versions of local dishes such as *totani con le patate* (baby octopus with potatoes) as well as more creative fare such as *ravioli di astice* (ravioli filled with lobster) and excellent grilled fish *secondi*. The seafood antipasti are delectable, the desserts traditional but good; and there is a fine view over the coast from the terrace, where tables are set out under a flower-decked pergola. The professional service and extensive, reasonably priced wine list give this place an edge. It pays to book, especially if you want an outside table.

Donna Rosa

Via Montepertuso 97/99 (089 811 806). **Meals served** *Aug* 7pm-midnight daily. *July, Sept, Oct* 7pm-midnight Mon, Tue; noon-4pm, 7pm-midnight Wed-Sun. *Apr-June, Nov, Dec* noon-4pm, 7-11pm Mon, Wed-Sun. Closed Jan-Mar. **Average** €35. **Credit** AmEx, DC, MC, V.
Perched in the village of Montepertuso, this once-simple trattoria with views over the main village square and the football pitch is now an elegant, romantic restaurant. Smart *positanesi* drive up here of an evening because they know that the food is better than just about anywhere down on the coast. The pasta that goes into *primi* such as *tagliatelle verdi ai frutti di mare* (green pasta with seafood) is all home-made, and main courses include a great *tortino di alici* (anchovy pie). The desserts are good too. Lunchtimes are generally quiet, but if you're planning to eat here on a summer evening, book at least a day in advance.

'O Guarracino

Via Positanesi d'America 12 (089 875 794). **Meals served** *mid June-Sept* 12.30-3pm, 7pm-midnight daily. *Apr-mid June, Oct* 12.30-3pm, 7pm-midnight Mon, Wed-Sun. Closed Nov-Mar. **Average** €35. **Credit** AmEx, DC, MC, V.
The position is splendid – a long scenic veranda on the footpath that leads around the cliff to Fornillo beach. The decor and service are ostentatiously no-frills; so too the menu, which offers basic classics such as *linguine alla puttanesca* (pasta with olives, capers and tomatoes) or simply grilled sea bass,

Around Naples

swordfish and seafood. There's also pizza. On summer evenings it's always packed with locals and second-homers – so book ahead.

Il Ritrovo

Via Montepertuso 77 (089 812 005/ www.ilritrovo.com). **Meals served** *May-Oct* 12.30-3pm, 7pm-midnight daily. *Feb-Apr, Nov, Dec* 12.30-3pm, 7pm-midnight Mon, Tue, Thur-Sun. Closed Jan, 1wk Feb. **Average** €28. **Credit** AmEx, DC, MC, V.
Just off the main square of Montepertuso, Il Ritrovo provides a more rustic alternative to its close neighbour, Donna Rosa (*see p245*). Strings of local Furore cherry tomatoes hang from wooden beams and, when winter sets in, a fire roars in the grate. In summer, tables fill a large wooden terrace with views back down the valley to the sea. The vegetable antipasti – all made from home-grown produce – are excellent; the pasta is mostly home-made, and there is also a good range of non-marine *secondi,* such as grilled chicken or rabbit. Ring ahead to arrange free transport from Positano in the restaurant's minibus.

Bars & nightlife

La Zagara (via dei Mulini 6, 089 875 964, closed Nov-mid Mar) has a scenic patio with lemon trees coming up through a garish red floor and an inner *salotto* with a fireplace for cold winter days. It's utterly touristy, but the cakes, pastries and fruit sorbets are delicious. At the eastern end of the main beach, the scenic **Music on the Rocks** nightclub (Grotta dell'Incanto 51, 089 875 874/335 422 856, closed Oct-Mar, open Fri & Sat only in Apr & May) purveys smooth piano-bar music and safe disco to the likes of Franco Zeffirelli.

Far and away the best disco on the *Costiera* (not that there's much competition) is the **Africana**, just west of Marina di Praia, between Positano and Amalfi (089 874 042, closed Oct-May). Hidden in its very own rocky cove, the Africana has a dancefloor inside a grotto done out in wild Mondo Bongo style; in the cove below, fishermen hunt for *totani* (baby octopus) undisturbed by the driving beat. An access road leads down between the 21-kilometre and 22-kilometre milestones on the main road; otherwise, walk from Marina di Praia. When it's open, boats run to here from Salerno, Maiori, Minori, Amalfi and Positano; for details ring 089 811 171 (for boats from Positano), 333 795 4404 (from Amalfi) and 338 253 3308 (from Minori).

Shopping

La Libreria (via Colombo 165, 089 811 077), a brand-new bookshop near the top of via Colombo, has a good selection of guidebooks, some in English; they also organise literary

soirées. If you need to check your email, the **Brigantino** bar/pizzeria (via del Saracino 35, 089 811 055) on the main pedestrian lane to the beach has a number of Internet workstations; rates €6 per hour.

Scuba diving

Scuba divers should head to **Centro Sub Costiera Amalfitana** (via Fornillo, 089 812 148/347 378 7372), which rents out equipment and runs courses.

Where to stay

Casa Albertina

Via della Tavolozza 3 (089 875 143/fax 089 811 540/www.casalbertina.it). **Rates** (half-board) €137-€157 per person in double. **Credit** AmEx, DC, MC, V.
Casa Albertina occupies a 12th-century building in a narrow, stepped lane about halfway up the daunting stack of houses to the west of the main beach. It offers a cool refuge from the summer heat and bustle with its white walls, ornate decorative details and old-fashioned blue- or red-themed rooms with a view. The panoramas from the restaurant terrace where breakfast and dinner are served, the relaxed atmosphere and the helpfulness of the Cinque family, who own and run the hotel, justify the climb. However, the high-season half-board only policy is a bind, especially as the restaurant is by no means one of Positano's best. Low season rates are significantly lower (call and haggle; you may be pleasantly surprised), and allow one to eat around. The hotel sometimes closes during January and February. Parking is €20 per day extra.

La Fenice

Via Marconi 4 (089 875 513/fax 089 811 309). **Rates** €115 double. **No credit cards.**
A sort of low-budget San Pietro (*see p247*), this charming B&B sprawls up a series of verdant terraces on either side of the main coast road, on the Amalfi edge of town. There are six rooms in the main villa above, with a terrace with a lovely view where breakfast is served and a caged mynah bird says *buon giorno* in the voice of Kevin Spacey. Another six rooms occupy a series of little *villette* below, near the pretty swimming pool (open June-Oct). From this lower section, a path descends to a small semi-private beach. Which is not at all bad for €115 a night – though you'll need to bring wads of cash to cope with the Phoenix's 'no credit cards' policy. Between April and October, a three-night minimum stay is required.

Maria Luisa

Via Fornillo 42 (tel/fax 089 875 023). **Closed** Dec-Feb. **Rates** €57-€62 double. **No credit cards.**
In Positano, you get what you pay for, and this is the cheapest hotel in town. So don't expect any frills,

Positano: a cliff with houses on it.

just a simple *pensione* with bright, sea-facing rooms, on the lane down to Fornillo beach. The panoramic balcony rooms are worth the small extra outlay.

Palazzo Murat

Via dei Mulini 23 (089 875 177/fax 089 811 419/ www.palazzomurat.it). **Closed** Mar. **Rates** €181-€233 single; €207-€380 double. **Credit** AmEx, DC, MC, V.

This characterful 18th-century palazzo, right in the centre of the old town, once belonged to Joachim Murat, King of Naples and Napoleon's brother-in-law (*see p18* **King Joaquin**). Get a room in the old wing, if you can, which extends around two sides of a palm- and bougainvillea-filled courtyard, where classical concerts take place in late summer. The rooms here are furnished with antiques and have tiny decorative iron balconies overlooking the court-yard. In the adjacent modern wing, rooms are more mod-Med in style, but also significantly cheaper; some have balconies with sea views. In summer, breakfast is served under the arches of the entrance patio; free boat trips are also on offer. All in all, a perfect refuge for the latter-day Grand Tourist – especially now that the hotel restaurant, Al Palazzo, is making a bid for more serious consideration.

Poseidon

Viale Pasitea 148 (089 811 111/fax 089 875 833/ www.hotelposeidonpositano.it). **Closed** Jan-Mar. **Rates** €181-€263 double; €253-€439 suite. **Credit** AmEx, DC, MC, V.

The most health-and-fitness-oriented of the town's hotels, with its own independently run Laura Elos Beauty Center, the Poseidon is set in a pretty garden just off viale Pasitea. Rooms have panoramic balconies where breakfast is served; the restaurant gives on to a large terrace, which manages to fit in a heated swimming pool and solarium. There is also a gym, a sauna and a hydromassage room; alternatively, you could just try walking up and down all those steps to the beach a couple of times. The rates are competitive for a Positano four-star. Parking costs €21 extra per day.

San Pietro

Via Laurito 2 (089 875 455/fax 089 811 449/ www.ilsanpietro.it). **Closed** Nov-Mar. **Rates** €375-€425 single; €385-€435 double. **Credit** AmEx, DC, MC, V.

One of the most exclusive hotels anywhere in Italy, the five-star 'L' (one better than five-star) San Pietro is based around a private villa that the hotel's founder, Carlo Cinque, built on (and into) a rocky promontory 2km (1.4 miles) east of Positano. Over the years, more rooms were added, and gradually the idea of turning this remarkable feat of engi-neering into a hotel took shape. From the road, the only evidence of the hotel is a discreet sign and a tiny chapel surrounded by parked cars; a lift plunges down to the bright lobby, which opens out on to a hibiscus-strewn terrace. The rooms – decorated with Mediterranean tiles and friezes, and each with a jacuzzi and private balcony – spill down the hillside on 20 separate rock-hewn terraces, connected by a warren of stairways. A second lift plunges down through the cliff to the private beach, bar and what must be one of the world's most dramatically placed tennis courts. Service is attentive and professional, and breakfast sumptuous.

Le Sirenuse
Via Cristoforo Colombo 30 (089 875 066/fax 089 811 798/www.sirenuse.it). **Rates** €231-€616 single; €253-€638 double. **Credit** AmEx, DC, MC, V.

The Sirenuse has almost as many fans among the international jet set as the San Pietro (*see p247*) – and it's certainly better placed for Positano shopping, dining and nightlife. Everything about the former private villa of the Marchesi Sersale is tastefully and thoughtfully done, from the majolica-covered panoramic terrace (with its pocket-sized swimming pool) to the lived-in elegance of the antique-filled rooms. There is also a well-equipped gym, and one of the few hotel restaurants in Positano – La Sponda – impressive enough to attract diners from outside.

Villa Franca
Viale Pasitea 318 (089 875 655/fax 089 875 735/ www.villafrancahotel.it). **Closed** Nov-Mar. **Rates** €176-€290 single; €196-€310 double. **Credit** AmEx, DC, MC, V.

Right above the sea at the point where viale Pasitea comes closest to the cliff edge, Villa Franca is an extremely elegant, well-run hotel with bright Mediterranean decor and a profusion of plants and flowers; the pretty rooms have cream bedspreads and curtains, frescoed details and panoramic balconies. The hotel also has one of the nicest of Positano's rooftop swimming pools, with a truly magnificent view over the coast, and a new *centro benessere* (fitness centre). If you can't face the walk down or up, there is a free minibus service. Parking is €16-€18 per day extra.

Getting there

From Naples airport
Take the Curreri (081 801 5420) bus to Sorrento (four daily) and change for SITA services (*see below*).

By car
Take the A3 motorway to Castellammare di Stabia, and follow signs to Sorrento. At Meta, 4km (2.5 miles) east of Sorrento, take the SS163; alternatively, take the slower but more scenic SS145 Nastro Azzurro route across the peninsula from the western edge of Sorrento, passing through Sant'Agata dei Due Golfi. From Salerno, take the SS163, which runs the length of the Amalfi Coast.

By bus
SITA (www.sita-on-line.it/Naples 081 552 2176/ Amalfi 089 871 016) runs one morning bus between Naples and Positano from Monday to Saturday, returning in the early evening. The rest of the time,

take the Circumvesuviana railway from Naples and change at Meta, just before Sorrento, for the Sorrento-Positano-Amalfi bus. Buses to Amalfi and Sorrento from Positano stop at the top of via Colombo and at the top of viale Pasitea, outside the Bar Internazionale. Tickets can be bought from the Bar Internazionale (via Marconi 164) or the Bar-Tabacchi Collina (via Colombo 3-5).

By boat
Hydrofoils run between Salerno, Amalfi, Positano and Capri: there are one to four per day, depending on the time of year. Amalfi-Positano shuttle services are more frequent. Between June and September, there is a direct hydrofoil link to Naples' Mergellina dock, run by Consorzio Linee Marittime (089 873 301). It is also possible to hop from Positano to Naples via Capri – though this is only really worth it if you want to spend some time on the island.

Getting around

By bus
A local bus service departs from piazza dei Mulini and does the anticlockwise circuit of via Colombo, via Marconi and viale Pasitea every 15 minutes between 8am and 10pm (winter) or midnight (summer). A less frequent service (roughly every 2hrs) serves the perched villages of Montepertuso and Nocella. Tickets for both of these routes cost 80¢ and can be bought on the bus.

By boat
From a booth on the quay to the right of Positano's main beach, Gennaro and Salvatore (089 875 211) run boat trips to Capri, the Grotta dello Smeraldo (*see p251*) and the Li Galli islets, inclusive of meals; they also organise night fishing trips on request. The Lucibello brothers (089 875 032/www.lucibello.it) run similar excursions from a nearby booth; they also have boats, canoes and pedalos for hire.

Tourist information
You can pick up guidebooks from **La Libreria** bookshop (*see p246*).

Azienda Autonoma di Soggiorno e Turismo
Via del Saracino 4 (089 875 067/fax 089 875 760). **Open** *June-Sept* 8am-2pm, 3-8pm Mon-Sat. *Oct-May* 8am-2pm Mon-Sat.

From Positano to Amalfi

Until 1853, most Amalfi Coast settlements were accessible only by sea or by tortuous mountain tracks from the other side of the Sorrentine peninsula. In that year, Ferdinand II of Naples inaugurated the Strada Amalfitana, the rock-blasted coast road that connects Positano with Vietri and Salerno. Built to accommodate horse-drawn traffic, this narrow perched road is used today by lorries, buses, tourist coaches and swarms of private cars; it's hardly surprising that the Amalfi Coast suffers from some of Italy's worst summer traffic jams.

East out of Positano, the road winds around steep gullies towards **Vettica Maggiore** and **Praiano**, which merge into one another on either side of the Capo Sottile promontory. Neither place has much of a centre, and both are often lumped together as Praiano. Vettica has a small beach and one of the coast's more worthwhile churches, **San Gennaro** (erratic opening hours), with colourful tiles on both dome and bell tower. The square outside the church affords good views back along the coast to Positano and beyond. Praiano proper, on the eastern side of the promontory, is a viable low-key alternative to Positano. It has a charming seaward extension to the east – tiny **Marina di Praia**, a fishing cove consisting of a scrap of beach pinched between two high rock walls, with just enough room for a few boats, a handful of houses, a couple of bar-restaurants and a diving centre, **La Boa** (089 813 034/335 345 739, www.laboa.com). A path around the cliff to the right leads to the seriously groovy Africana disco (*see p246*).

The jagged coastline between here and Conca dei Marini is the wildest stretch of the *Costiera* – nowhere more so than at the **Vallone di**

It's a tight squeeze at **Marina di Furore**.

Furore, a deep gully two kilometres beyond Marina di Praia. Such an unrepentantly steep river valley is called an *orrido*, or 'horrid', in Italian; its seaward opening is the nearest Italy comes to a fjord. From the viaduct over the valley – where it is virtually impossible to park – a steep footpath descends to **Marina di Furore**, an even tighter squeeze than Marina di Praia, with a few rock-hewn fishermen's huts and a scatter of boats on the narrow beach. The buildings were recently restored with funds from the Campania region, and include a bar-restaurant (*see p251*), a herbarium, a cinema archive, a cultural centre dedicated to Italy's 'painted villages' and a museum of paper-making inside an old paper mill at the head of the beach. All these bits go under the rather grand name of the **Ecomuseo**; there's no fixed timetable, so finding them open can be a problem. For information, call 089 830 4711.

Back on the coast road, just before Conca dei Marini, is the big tourist pull of this stretch: the **Grotta dello Smeraldo**. There is a car park on the road above, with a lift that plunges down to the cave, where visitors are decanted into box-like rowing boats; alternatively, various operators offer boat trips from Positano and Amalfi. Every self-respecting Mediterranean tourist destination needs its Blue (or in this case Emerald) Grotto; this one was discovered in 1932, ending Capri's 100-year monopoly. Cave buffs will tell you that it is but a pale imitation of that island's Blue Grotto (*see p188* **Grotta Azzurra**), but the translucent sapphire-blue light that filters into the cave from an underwater crevice is pretty enough, and it's a lot cheaper than its rival. The main attractions are the crazed boatmen, who cajole their passengers into seeing Mussolini's profile in the shadow of a stalagmite.

Beyond the headland of Capo di Conca, the bay of Amalfi appears at last in all its glory. The sprawl of houses on the hillside to the left is **Conca dei Marini**, which once had a merchant fleet to rival those of its more muscular neighbours, Positano and Amalfi.

The upper part of the town is accessible from the Agerola road, which forks off sharply to the left just past the random collection of houses that call themselves (confusingly) **Vettica Minore**, a couple of kilometres before Amalfi. If you've had enough of the glitz and crowds of the *Costiera*, this road offers a worthwhile detour – though it's not a short one, and unless you want to press on to Naples, the only way out is back the same way. It begins by heading back west, passing by the long, barrel-vaulted profile of the **Convento di Santa Rosa**. This was formerly a house of Augustine nuns, famous as the inventors of the *torta di Santa*

Amalfi: for centuries a glorious maritime republic. *See p251.*

Rosa, a flaky pastry, blancmange and dried fruit concoction traditionally eaten on 30 August, Santa Rosa's feast day. Nowadays the abandoned convent is used as an evocative backdrop for the classical concerts of the Festival di Ravello (*see p260*).

Rising gently up through the contour lines, the road continues around the upper part of the Vallone del Furore to **Furore** itself, a rugged village that – like so many around these parts – lacks a centre. But it does have some unexpected bits of modern sculpture and murals – part of a laudable municipal attempt to make the place known for something other than being isolated – and it produces the Amalfi Coast's best wine. To sample it, head for the **Gran Furor-Divina Costiera winery** (via GB Lama 14, 089 830 348, www.granfuror.it, open 8am-6pm daily by appointment), which also goes under the name of its owner, Marisa

Cuomo. From precarious vineyards on beetling slopes come the grapes that go into the six wines produced here, the best of which are the white Furore Fiord'uva cru, and the red Furore Riserva. Furore also does a small trade in prickly pears – *fichi d'india* in Italian – and tiny cherry tomatoes (*pomodorini a piennolo*) sold in bunches on their stalks.

Beyond Furore, the road snakes up to the ridge in a series of intestinal curves before spilling out into the upland plain of **Agerola**, an entirely unexpected collection of agricultural settlements, cut off by the rugged terrain both from the *Costiera* below and from the Vesuvian plain beyond. Though the coast sells itself as a fertile Garden of Eden, it is Agerola that actually produces most of the fruit, vegetables, cheese and meat that end up in swanky Amalfi restaurants; the local mozzarella is especially famous. Its small-scale textile workshops also act as sweatshops for Positano's 'glamorous' boutiques. The only visitors that Agerola usually sees are elderly Neapolitans, who come here for the summer cool, and the occasional walker (the Alta Via dei Lattari passes along the ridge that closes the plain to the north).

Grotta dello Smeraldo

1km west of Conca dei Marini on the main coast road (information from APT Amalfi 089 871 107). **Open** *Apr-Oct* 9am-4pm daily. *Nov-Mar* 10am-3pm daily. **Admission** €5. **No credit cards.**

Where to stay & eat

Hidden away off a quiet lane below the coast road in Praiano, the **Hotel Le Sirene** (via San Nicola 10, 089 874 013, www.lesirene.com, closed Nov-mid Mar, double room €80-€95) is a simple, pretty white hotel with stone-flagged courtyard (complete with ping-pong table) in front and views behind over olive trees and kitchen gardens to the sea. The rooftop terrace-solarium and the friendliness of the owners are two other bonuses.

On the main road out of town towards Amalfi the **Hotel Continental** and **Villaggio Turistico La Tranquillità** (via Roma 21, 089 874 084, closed mid Nov-mid Mar, double room €90, bungalow €90, camping pitch €35 for two people) is a multi-purpose accommodation option that is very popular with budget travellers. As well as providing scenic camping pitches under the olives for those with canvas, it also offers more conventional rooms, plus a series of bungalows immersed in greenery on a terrace above the sea, which is accessible via a rock-hewn staircase. It's also handily placed for the Africana disco (*see p246*).

Back in Praiano's 'main' street, the scenic **La Brace** (via Gennaro Capriglione 146, 089 874 226, closed Wed mid Oct-mid Mar, all Nov, average €35) does good, simple seafood dishes such as spaghetti with clams and excellent Neapolitan pizzas, cooked in a wood-fired oven.

In Marina di Praia, **Alfonso al Mare** (089 874 166, www.alfonsoamare.it, closed Nov-Mar, average €35) has a huge, covered terrace on the beach and offers simple but competent seafood cooking.

Marina di Furore's tiny bar-restaurant **Al Monazeno** (368 451 542, closed Nov-May), run by an engineer from Watford, is one of the more unusual places to dine on the *Costiera*: at the foot of a cliff, overlooking an inlet, it offers bar snacks and a few more substantial dishes in the classic Amalfi tradition. On the road above, towards Positano, **La Locanda del Fiordo** (via Trasita 9/13, 089 874 813, www.lalocanda delfiordo.it, double room €80-€205) is a stylish new luxury B&B with an entrance at road level

and rooms (each named after an Italian screen diva) on two rock-hewn terraces below, from where steps descend to the sea.

In Vettica, **Vettica House** (via Maestra dei Villaggi 92, 089 871 814, vetticahousehostel@ amalficoast.it) offers some of the best budget accommodation on the entire *Costiera*. Run by the same family that owns A' Scalinatella in Atrani (*see p258*), it consists of a series of white chalets perched on a terrace above a working lemon farm. Various accommodation options are available, from hostel-style beds (from €18.50 per person) to double rooms with private bathrooms (€52-€62). Be warned though – it's a stiff climb up 270 steps from the nearest bus stop on the Furore/Agerola road, about 200 metres (700 feet) before the Convento di Santa Rosa (ring ahead for precise instructions on how to get here). The view from the top, though, amply repays the exertion.

In Furore, **Hostaria da Bacco** (via GB Lama 9, 089 830 360, closed Fri Nov-Feb, average €30), which is run by the energetic mayor of this airy sprawl of a village, draws plenty of customers up from the coast with its refined home cooking. Local produce (as much land- as sea-based) goes into trademark creations such as *ferrazzuoli alla Nannarella* – spiral pasta with swordfish, capers and pine nuts, a dish dedicated to actress Anna Magnani, who briefly owned a house down in the Marina. Succulent Agerola cheeses are on offer, and one of the more unusual local harvests can be sampled in the form of *cicale di Furore* – little almond and prickly pear cakes. The ambience is rustic, the local wine extremely drinkable and, if that's not enough, there's a huge selection of grappas and other spirits to finish the meal on a high note. If you can't face the cliff-hugging drive back, there are also 18 simple rooms (double €62-€72).

Getting there

The villages covered in this section can be reached by bus or car from Positano or Amalfi. See *p244* and *below* respectively.

Tourist information

See p259 **Amalfi** and *p248* **Positano**.

Amalfi & Atrani

Amalfi oozes history. Today it is a pretty, lemon-fringed tourist resort, partly spilling over on to the coast, but mostly facing inwards – lining both sides of the steep and fertile Valle dei Mulini. Between the ninth and the 12th centuries, though, this was a glorious maritime

The real Duchess of Malfi

Generations of students have thrilled to university productions of John Webster's dark Jacobean tragedy *The Duchess of Malfi*, a macabre story crawling with spies, murder, psychosis, torture and implied incest. Written around 1613, Webster's play – set in Amalfi, Ancona and Milan – was based on a tale in William Painter's *Palace of Pleasure*, which in turn was plagiarised from a popular collection by 16th-century Italian raconteur Matteo Bandello. In the introduction, Bandello claims to have had the tale straight from the mouth of one of the main players; and other sources confirm that Webster's gorefest is a not-too-distant echo of a true story.

The duchess in question was Giovanna d'Aragona (Joan of Aragon), a scion of the soon-to-be-ousted rulers of Naples, who in 1490 – at the age of 12 – was married off to Alfonso Piccolomini, son and heir of the first Duke of Amalfi. Alfonso died of gout eight years later, and at the age of 20, pregnant with her second child, Giovanna was left a widow. It wasn't long before she had fallen passionately in love with her steward, a certain Antonio Bologna. Fearful that her brothers – Lodovico, a cardinal, and Carlo, Marquis of Gerace in Calabria (who becomes 'Francesco' in Webster's version) – would be enraged by her marriage to a commoner, she kept it secret. The couple even managed to have two children before palace spies in the pay of the brothers gave the game away.

Antonio fled with the kids to Ancona; Giovanna, pregnant once more, followed him a few months later, declaring her intention to renounce her rank and live humbly with her family. But her cardinal brother managed to put pressure on the legate of Ancona to have Antonio banished. In Webster, the *grand guignol* strangling of the Duchess by men in the pay of her brothers follows fast on Antonio's departure; in reality, though, the couple moved around Italy for another year before being finally separated by a promise of safe conduct for Antonio and their eldest son, who ended up in Milan. Giovanna returned to Amalfi with her two younger children, and was never heard of again. Antonio survived for another year, until October 1513, when he was stabbed in a Milanese street by four hired assassins.

Prime *Duchess* location is the Torre dello Zirro (*see p255*), the ruined molar of a watchtower that perches on the ridge between Amalfi and Atrani. Here, legend has it, Giovanna and her younger children were murdered. In reality, if it happened at all, the deed was probably done further up the same ridge, in the Norman castle that was the residence of the Dukes of Amalfi until they, and it, were dismantled in 1583. The ruins of the castle and the Torre dello Zirro can be visited in an easy one-hour walk from the village of Pontone, connected to Amalfi by bus; ask locally for directions.

republic, precursor and later rival of Pisa and Genoa. In its prime, it had 70,000 inhabitants, and many more lived abroad, in merchant colonies scattered around the Mediterranean from Tunis to Constantinople to Beirut. As in Venice, souvenirs of Byzantium were brought back to embellish private houses and municipal buildings; the most famous example are the great bronze doors of the Duomo, cast in Constantinople in around 1066.

On land, Amalfi's dominion extended over the whole of the Sorrentine peninsula and beyond; at sea, it had few rivals, and its navies were used not only to protect the republic's own independence but also to win battles for allies such as the Lombards and the Duchy of Naples. It was almost certainly Amalfitan sailors who introduced the compass to the Christian West from Muslim Africa at the end of the 12th century, and it was Amalfitan merchants who founded the hospice of St John in Jerusalem in 1020, which became the headquarters of the Knights Hospitallers of St John, later the Knights of Malta.

The republic survived at least nominally from 839 until the devastating Pisan raids of 1135 and 1137, though for its last 100 years it was subject to repeated periods of Norman domination. Gradually, a Venetian-style system of government was adopted, led by a doge elected by a council consisting of the male members of the town's most important families. Amalfi coined its own money and made its own laws; its maritime code, the *Tavole Amalfitane* was recognised in the Mediterranean until well into the 16th century.

Mercantile prosperity continued even after the end of the republic; in the early 14th century Boccaccio wrote that Amalfi was 'full of little cities, gardens and fountains, and rich men'. But an earthquake in 1343 destroyed most of the old town, which now lies under the sea.

The Arab-Norman **Duomo**.

The **Chiostro del Paradiso**. See p254.

Amalfi never really recovered – at least not until the 19th century, when its spectacular setting and aura of former glories began to attract literary and artistic travellers from northern Europe. A reminder of the town's golden age is the **Palio delle Quattro Repubbliche Marinare**, a ceremonial boat race between Amalfi, Pisa, Genoa and Venice held on the first Sunday in June. The towns take it in turn to host the race; Amalfi's next opportunity comes in June 2005.

On its coast side, the town has a brief chance for bustle, with port, bus terminus and a number of bars and restaurants all making the most of the available space. To the east, the grey shingle beach gets packed in summer; cleaner water can be found in a series of coves to the west, served by a regular circular ferry service (marked *Spiagge*) from the main quay. Dominating the hillside to the west is a Capuchin convent founded in 1212, now the **Hotel Cappuccini Convento** (*see p258*). Along corso delle Repubbliche Marinare to the east are the post office and the tourist office; just around the corner, in a palm-shaded piazza, stands the Municipio, or town hall, where – in a room grandly referred to as the **Museo Civico** – a late manuscript draft of Amalfi's maritime code, the *Tavole Amalfitane*, is on display. The sweep of the bay beyond ends in a medieval watchtower that now houses the restaurant of the **Luna Convento** (*see p258*); the hotel itself occupies a former Franciscan convent on the other side of the road.

From sea-facing piazza Flavio Gioia – dominated by a statue of Flavio himself, a man who not only didn't invent the compass, as the plaque at his feet claims, but may never even have existed – the Porta Marinara gate leads into the centre of town. Before you go under it, have a look at all that remains of Amalfi's shipyard, the Arsenale della Repubblica, beneath an arch to the left of the gate. This was the engine room of the republic, where huge galleys with over 100 oars were built by teams of shipwrights.

Piazza del Duomo is dominated by Amalfi's colourful **Duomo**, a masterpiece of the Arab-Norman style, at the top of a steep staircase. The lively façade you see today is a doubtful reconstruction of the early 13th-century original, carried out after part of the church collapsed in 1861. The pretty, free-standing *campanile*, from 1276, is more the real thing, having been tampered with very little in the course of the centuries. Underneath a lofty porch, the central bronze doors of the Duomo were cast some time before 1066 by a Syrian master; an inscription records that they were donated to the republic by Pantaleone di Mauro

Piazza del Duomo's squirty-titted nymph.

Comite, head of the Amalfitan colony in
Constantinople. The cathedral interior, recently
restored to reduce some of its baroque excess,
is nevertheless a disappointment in comparison
with the clean, Romanesque simplicity of its
close cousin in Ravello (*see p262*). Remnants
of the original church furniture include the
two reassembled *amboni* (pulpits) on either
side of the main altar, some ancient columns
and a beautiful mother-of-pearl cross – another
piece of Crusader loot.

More worthwhile is the delightful **Chiostro
del Paradiso**, entered (for a small fee) through
a door at the left end of the porch in front of the
Duomo. Built in 1266 as a burial ground for the
members of Amalfi's aristocracy, this cloister,
with its Moorish-style arches and central
garden, is as close as one comes on the *Costiera*
to the cosmopolitan spirit of the glory days of
the maritime republic.

A door leads from the cloister into the
Cappella del Crocefisso, the only part of
the church to have survived more or less intact
from the 12th century (at least now that its
baroque additions have been stripped off).
Glass cases hold treasures belonging to the
diocese, including a lovely 15th-century marble
bas-relief known as *La Madonna della Neve*,
and a bejewelled mitre made for the Anjou court
of Naples in 1297.

From the chapel, which also has some faded
14th-century frescos, stairs lead down to the
crypt, dedicated to St Andrew, whose mortal
remains were looted from Constantinople in
1206. The sarcophagus that contains the saintly
body oozes a miraculous fluid, known as
manna, which is said to have restorative
properties (the truly pious drink it neat).

With its bars and cafés, piazza del Duomo
is a good place to rest, refuel and contemplate
the squirty-titted nymph who graces the central
fountain. To the north, via Genova and via
Capuano lead up through an increasingly quiet
residential part of town where the sound of fast-
flowing water can be heard everywhere, even at
the height of summer.

This deep valley – the **Valle dei Mulini** –
was the site of some of Europe's first paper-
making factories, powered by a series of
watermills; one, at Palazzo Pagliara, has been
turned into the **Museo della Carta**, with
photos illustrating the history and techniques
of this ancient industry. Downstairs, the
original vats and machinery are preserved.
A small amount of high-quality paper is still
produced in Amalfi by the Cartiera Amatruda.

The wild upper part of the Valle dei Mulini
(take the road that skirts the eastern side of the
valley) is well worth exploring.

In its Alpine upper reaches, the valley
becomes the **Vallone delle Ferriere**, named
after the ironworks (*ferro* means iron) that –
like the papermills downstream – drew their
power from the abundant, fast-moving water
of the torrent.

Marked path No.25 follows the valley floor
beneath high rock walls, past a riot of botany
(including the rare fern *Woodwardia radicans*,
whose only European sites are here and on the
island of Ischia), to the entrance of the WWF
riserva naturale, which occupies the high part
of the valley; from here a circuit of the valley
head can be made on a scenic footpath that
ends up in the village of **Pontone**, on the ridge
between Amalfi and Atrani. A shorter but
equally vertical path heads up a mere thousand

Pulp fact: Amalfi produced some of Europe's first paper. *See p254* **Museo della Carta**.

or so steps from Amalfi to the village and castle of **Pogerola**, with a splendid view down over the Gulf of Amalfi.

In the days of the republic, **Atrani** – located less than a kilometre east along the coast and reachable on foot via the confusing web of staircases that straggle across the hill – was the upmarket residential quarter of Amalfi. It was razed to the ground by the Pisans in 1187 and today feels, if anything, more workaday than its neighbour. It has a busy fishing port and some good examples of vernacular Amalfitan architecture, with a maze of arches, long pedestrian tunnels, staircases and barrel-vaulted houses on different levels. Space is so tight here that the main coast road sweeps right across the centre on a viaduct whose arches separate the port from the main square, piazza Umberto I. As you walk around, keep an eye out for the full bottles of water that stand on the thresholds of the village houses: ostensibly there to keep cats from pissing on the tiles and plants, they have a more ancient pedigree as chasers-away of malignant spirits.

The little church of **San Salvatore de' Bireto**, perched at the top of a flight of steps on the opposite side of the piazza, was where the investiture of Amalfi's doges took place; its name derives from the *berretto*, or ducal cap. The church has been *in restauro* for years; its bronze doors – a gift, in 1087, from the same Amalfitan merchant in Constantinople who commissioned the doors of Amalfi's Duomo – can now be seen in the parish church of **Santa Maria Maddalena** (open Sun mornings for mass), which rises high above the road to the east. The dome is a classically colourful example of the Amalfitan style; inside, the original Romanesque was swept aside in a baroque makeover. However, there are some marvellous wooden statues of roasting sinners on the wall to the right of the main door. High above the town to the west, the 13th-century church of **Santa Maria del Bando** (open only in September; ask at the town hall in via dei Dogi) perches on a narrow ledge halfway up a vertical cliff below the **Torre dello Zirro**, a medieval watchtower.

The **Duomo**'s façade is a doubtful reconstruction.

Duomo di Amalfi
(Cattedrale di Sant'Andrea)

Piazza del Duomo (089 871 059). **Open** *Apr-June, 2wks around Christmas* 9am-7pm daily. *July-Sept* 9am-9pm daily. *Oct, Mar* 9.30am-5.15pm daily. *Nov-Feb* 10am-1pm, 2.30-4.30pm daily. **Admission** *Cathedral* free. *Chiostro del Paradiso* €2.50. **No credit cards**.

Museo Civico

Piazza del Municipio 6 (information from tourist office 089 871 107). **Open** 8.30am-1.30pm Mon-Fri. **Admission** free.

Museo della Carta

Palazzo Pagliara, via delle Cartiere 23 (089 830 4561/www.museodellacarta.it). **Open** *Nov-Mar* 10am-3pm Tue-Sun. *Apr-June, Oct* 10am-6pm daily. *July-Sept* 10am-8pm daily. **Admission** €3.40 (includes guided tour in English). **No credit cards**.

Where to eat

Cantina San Nicola

Salita Marino Sebaste 8 (089 830 4549). **Meals served** noon-3pm, 6pm-1am Mon, Wed-Sun. Closed 3wks Jan-Feb. **Average** €20. **Credit** AmEx, DC, MC, V.

It's well worth exploring the quiet side streets that run parallel to Amalfi's tourist-infested main drag. Not only do they reveal a lesser-known, more vernacular side of the town, they also harbour some unexpected surprises, such as this new wine bar, housed in the chapel of a former monastery. It fills an important niche, providing high-quality fare for those who don't necessarily want a full meal. There is a good cheese selection, including delicious *mozzarella di bufala* from the Sele plain (*see p271*) and *scamorza* (grilled cheese) wrapped in lemon leaves. Hot dishes range from *caponata* (a sort of

Sicilian ratatouille) to chickpea soup. The cellar is especially strong on Campanian wines (*see p108* **Selecting local wine**).

La Caravella

Via Matteo Camera 12 (089 871 029/ www.ristorantelacaravella.it). **Meals served** noon-2.30pm, 7.30-10.30pm Mon, Wed-Sun. Closed mid Nov-Dec. **Average** €65. **Credit** AmEx, MC, V.

Easily Amalfi's best restaurant, the Caravella resists the quick-fix-for-tourists formula of so many other local eateries, concentrating all its energies on hitting the culinary peaks. Sandwiched between the main road and the remains of the old Arsenale, in two rooms without a view decorated with marine murals and paintings, it offers excellent seafood cooking, attentive service and an extensive wine list. Don't miss the *stuzzichini della Caravella*, a selection of mouth-watering seafood antipasti. Pasta dishes such as *tagliata di pasta allo zafferano con zucca e crostacei* (pasta strips with saffron, marrow and crustaceans) are equally fine, and *secondi* such as *totano ripieno di zucchine* (flying squid stuffed with courgettes) pull out all the stops. The desserts are one step down from all this splendour; but it's a small step. There is also a good selection of local cheeses, served with home-made preserves. Though it's not cheap, prices are fair for what is a really special gourmet meal – all the more so if you opt for the €57 taster menu.

Da Gemma

Via Fra' Gerardo Sasso 10 (089 871 345). **Meals served** *Aug* 7.30-10.30pm Mon, Tue, Thur-Sun. *Mid Feb-July, Sept-mid Jan* 12.30-2.30pm, 7.30-10.30pm Mon, Tue, Thur-Sun. Closed mid Jan-mid Feb. **Average** €45. **Credit** AmEx, DC, MC, V.

The setting of this historic and ever-popular Amalfi restaurant is hard to beat: a rooftop terrace high above the bustle of the main street, with views across to piazza del Duomo. Mario Grimaldi continues the tradition of good local cooking begun here by his mother Gemma, which looks mostly to the sea but also includes a few dishes from the hinterland, such as *fettuccine alla genovese* (fettuccine in a mincemeat and onion sauce). Lovers of *zuppa di pesce* (fish soup) will find Gemma's hard to beat. The home-made desserts include *melanzane in salsa di cioccolato* (aubergines in chocolate), a local speciality that harks back to Amalfi's days of trade with Turkey and the Middle East. Book well in advance in summer.

Da Maria

Via Lorenzo d'Amalfi 14 (089 871 880). **Meals served** noon-3pm, 7-11.30pm Tue-Sun. Closed Nov. **Average** €25. **Credit** AmEx, DC, MC, V.
There are plenty of cheap *trattorie* and *pizzerie* in Amalfi. This one, just up from the piazza on the main street, is a notch above the average, with affable (not to say extravagant) service and reliable home cooking. Don't be put off by the menu in four languages; even with their simple starters such as *sauté frutti di mare* (mixed seafood sautée), the standards are generally high. The seafood pasta dishes are tasty and filling, and the excellent pizzas, cooked in a real wood oven, are the authentic Neapolitan variety. The €2.50 cover charge includes a basket of garlic bread.

'A Paranza

Traversa Dragone 2 (089 871 840). **Meals served** *Aug* 12.30-3pm, 7.30pm-midnight daily. *Sept-July* 12.30-3pm, 7.30pm-midnight Mon, Wed-Sun. Closed 3wks Dec. **Average** €35. **Credit** AmEx, DC, MC, V.
The Proto brothers certainly know one end of an octopus from another. On the road that leads inland from Atrani's pretty main square, their friendly, relaxed seafood trattoria spreads over two plain barrel-vaulted rooms done out in white and orange (so dress accordingly). Antipasti such as *alici marinati* (anchovies marinated in oil and lemon – simple but exquisite) are a prelude to delicious home-made pasta (the *scialatielli 'A Paranza* – thick, hand-made spaghetti with seafood – is especially good). Go for simple *secondi* like the *grigliata mista locale* (mixed seafood grill) or the grilled swordfish, which tastes as if it's come straight off the boat (it has). Desserts are home-made; the lemon sorbet is particularly good. The house white wine is a very drinkable Ravello DOC.

Bars & nightlife

Opposite the Duomo in Amalfi, the **Bar Francese** (piazza Duomo 20, 089 871 049, closed Thur Oct-May) is a good place to sit and muse on the passing of empires over a cappuccino and a copy of the *Duchess of Malfi* (*see p252* **The real Duchess of Malfi**). In Atrani, **Bar Risacca** (piazza Umberto I 16, 089 872 866, closed Mon Oct-May) in the main

square is the locals' favourite lounging spot; have breakfast here before heading under the arches to the beach, munch on a bruschetta at lunchtime, or enjoy the evening cool over a campari soda. In Amalfi, the only disco of note is **RoccoCò** (via delle Cartiere 98, 089 873 080, open Fri & Sat only Nov-Mar), a rather cheesy place some way up the valley, which hosts the occasional guest DJ. Alternatively, jump on a boat to the **Africana** disco (*see p246*).

Shopping

Food is the big draw in Amalfi – especially anything to do with lemons. In piazza del Duomo, **Pasticceria Andrea Pansa 1830** (piazza del Duomo 40, 089 871 065, closed Tue) uses the local fruit in any number of inventive ways: candied lemon rind, *frolla* (a ricotta-filled pastry dome) and the sticky *delizia al limone* cakes are especially good. Almond lovers will also appreciate the delicate *paste di mandorla*.

For more intoxicating treats, head for the tiny corner outlet of **Antichi Sapori d'Amalfi** (piazza Duomo 39, 089 872 062), by the cathedral steps, which makes its own *limoncello* and fruit liqueurs (a rarity in this neck of the woods, where most come from huge factories inland).

Paper is the other traditional industry; the best place to view and buy some of the high-quality paper still made hereabouts – mainly by Cartiera Amatruda – is **La Scuderia del Duca** (largo Cesareo Console 8, 089 872 976, www.delucaedizioni.it), a cave of wonders that is a cut above most of the tourist emporia on the *Costiera*. They also have a good selection of books on Amalfi and the surrounding area, some of them in English.

L'Altra Costiera (via Lorenzo d'Amalfi 34, 089 873 6082/www.altracostiera.com, closed Sun Nov-Mar) has a few internet workstations for rent at €5.20 per hour.

Where to stay

Amalfi

Vico dei Pastai 3 (089 872 440/fax 089 872 250/ www.starnet.it/amalfi). **Rates** €52-€88 single; €72-€120 double. **Credit** AmEx, DC, MC, V.
The town's best three-star, the Amalfi gives on to a quiet lane in the old town, up a flight of steps from the main street. Though occasionally overwhelmed by British tour groups, it is affably and efficiently run. There is a panoramic rooftop terrace where breakfast and other meals are served, and a pretty garden around the back, accessible from the third floor. All rooms have phones and satellite TVs, and some have balconies. It's good value, especially out of high season.

Cappuccini Convento

Via Annunziatella 46 (089 871 877/fax 089 871 886/www.hotelcappuccini.it). **Rates** €88-€114 single; €156-€198 double. **Credit** AmEx, DC, MC, V.

An alarmingly exposed cliffside lift of green girders beams guests up to this unique hotel, which is grafted on to a 12th-century Franciscan monastery. The position is breathtaking; surrounded by lemon groves, the hotel extends along a mountain terrace, ending in a shady monks' walk with spectacular views. The hotel was founded in 1821 and has always been in the same family; Wagner stayed here, as did any number of forgotten stage divas who simper from dusty photographs on the wall. Faded gentility is the keyword: don't expect cutting-edge design in the rooms – formerly the monks' cells – which house an apparently random collection of old furniture. But for atmosphere, this place is hard to beat.

Luna Convento

Via P Comite 33 (089 871 002/fax 089 871 333/www.lunahotel.it). **Rates** €151-€202 single; €166-€217 double; €233-€518 suite. **Credit** AmEx, DC, MC, V.

Another monastery hotel, the Luna is a little more tastefully designed and a little more upmarket than the Cappuccini. It too has had its share of famous guests, including Wagner (again), Ibsen, Mussolini and Tennessee Williams. Focal point of the hotel is a delightful Byzantine cloister where breakfast is served in summer. The pool is carved out of the rocks beneath the Saracen tower opposite, which houses the hotel restaurant. Rooms are bright and comfortable, and the desk staff are helpful. Half-board is obligatory between June and September.

Santa Caterina

Via Nazionale 9 (089 871 012/fax 089 871 351/www.hotelsantacaterina.it). **Rates** €245-€515 double; €415-€830 suite. **Credit** AmEx, DC, MC, V.

Location, location and location are the three best things about the Santa Caterina, which has a whole section of the coast to itself a kilometre west of central Amalfi, on the Positano road. Now looking better than ever after a makeover in the winter of 2001-2, this is not at all a bad option for a luxury cocoon holiday – if you can afford it. All rooms have terraces with sweeping views, and the hotel is surrounded by its own terraced park, verdant with lemon trees and bougainvillea, where two self-contained suites hide out – including the spectacular Romeo and Juliet suite (rates €620-€985). From the spacious hall, a lift takes guests down to the private beach, pool and one of the hotel's two restaurants; there is also a fitness club. The original structure was destroyed by a landslide in 1902, but don't worry – the replacement was built on safer rocks.

A' Scalinatella

Piazza Umberto I 5/6, Atrani (tel/fax 089 871 492/www.amalficoast.it/hotel/scalinatella). **Rates** hostel €13-€21 per person; €37-€83 double room. **No credit cards**.

The charming, laid-back village of Atrani has no hotel as such, but it does have this budget operation, consisting of a couple of cheap hostel-style dormitories in a house off to the right of the main street, plus double rooms and mini-apartments spread all over the village, at rates that come closer to the Amalfi Coast norm. Breakfast is served from April to September at the Scalinatella bar in the main square, which is also where new arrivals should check in (before 2pm if possible). Open all year round, A' Scalinatella acts as a meeting point for backpackers and independent student travellers, who are otherwise poorly served on the *Costiera*.

Left luggage

Divina Costiera

Piazza Flavio Gioia 3 (089 872 467). **Open** *Apr-Oct, 2wks over Christmas* 8am-1pm, 2.30-8pm daily. **Rates** €3 per day per bag. **No credit cards**.

You can also buy bus and boat tickets, and staff can make bookings for Amalfi hotels.

Getting there

From Naples airport

Take the Curreri bus (*see p248*) to Sorrento (four daily) and change for the SITA bus to Amalfi.

By car

From Naples, leave the A3 motorway at the Angri exit, just past Pompeii, and follow signs through the urban blight to the Valico di Chiunzi pass and Ravello. Equally scenic, but a good deal longer, is the SS366 route which crosses over from Castellammare di Stabia via Gragnano, Agerola and Furore, to emerge on the coast road 2km west of Amalfi. From Salerno, take the SS136 road along the Amalfi Coast.

By train

There is no Amalfi Coast line; the nearest station is Vietri, at the eastern limit of the *Costiera*, which is served by only a few very slow trains; it's better to go to Salerno station (40mins from Naples) and continue either by boat or SITA bus.

By bus

There are regular buses between Amalfi and Salerno. For Naples, there are three main options: via Positano (one daily), via Agerola (15 daily) or via Vietri (four daily). Alternatively, take the Circumvesuviana train from Naples and change at Meta for the Sorrento–Amalfi bus. For times and information: SITA 089 871 016/www.sita-on-line.it. Note that Sunday services on all these lines are much less frequent.

By boat

It is possible (Apr-Oct) to hop to Amalfi from Naples via Capri (*see p173*), but unless you want to spend some time on the island, it is cheaper and quicker to get the regular boat from Salerno.TraVelMar (089 873 190/www.coopsantandrea.it) run ferries (Apr-Oct only) from the Molo Manfredi quay in Salerno

Location, location, location at the **Hotel Santa Caterina**. *See p258.*

to Amalfi via Maiori; most then continue to Positano and Capri. LMS (Amalfi 089 873 301, Salerno 089 227 979) covers the same route by faster hydrofoils, some of which continue to Naples.

Getting around

By bus

Amalfi's bus terminus is in piazza Gioia on the waterfront. Local services run to Ravello and Scala and Pogerola. Tickets can be bought from the SITA outlet in largo Scoppetta, next to the bus terminus.

By boat

The main quay behind the bus terminus is the hopping off point for regular boats to the western beaches (marked *Spiagge*), which leave at least every hour 9am-5pm daily from June to September. A return ticket costs €3.

Tourist information

Azienda Autonoma di Soggiorno e Turismo

Corso delle Repubbliche Marinare 27 (089 871 107/ www.azienturismoamalfi.com). **Open** 8.30am-1.30pm, 3-5.12pm Mon-Fri, 8.30am-1pm Sat.

Ravello

Ravello is the aristocrat of the Amalfi Coast. Down there are the chattering sunburned masses, the traffic jams, the long queues for

ice-cream. Up here, on a long stone raft high above the sea, all is shade, gardens and serenity. Even in high season, when coach parties hit Ravello to troop dutifully around **Villa Rufolo** and **Villa Cimbrone**, it takes very little to leave them behind: the turn of a corner in the old town or, in the gardens themselves, a visit timed for the early evening.

Subject through most of its early history to its more muscular neighbour Amalfi, Ravello grew rich on trade. But if Ravello's golden age was almost as florid as Amalfi's – in the 13th century it counted as many as 36,000 inhabitants – its fall was more complete. With the end of its mercantile empire, Amalfi took to other trades: fishing, paper-making and iron foundries. Continued activity meant that its medieval centre was overlaid by new buildings. In Ravello, on the other hand, decline to its present population of around 2,500 was so swift that parts of the town look like a medieval Pompeii, frozen one day in the 14th century.

Traces of the town's 15 minutes of fame are everywhere: in its delightful, treasure-packed **Duomo**, in the doorways of its *palazzi*, flanked by ancient columns, in the Sicilian-Moorish exoticism of **Villa Rufolo**'s cloisters. The romantic, nobly decayed ambience of the place has attracted scores of writers, artists and musicians, among them Wagner, Liszt, André Gide, Virginia Woolf and most of the Bloomsbury group, and DH Lawrence, who

Festival Musicale di Ravello

Ravello's musical vocation was determined by two northern composers who found inspiration in its romantic gardens and warm southern breezes: Wagner and Grieg. Crumbling Byzantine arches, palms and scented climbing plants ended up, transformed, in both *Parsifal* and *Peer Gynt*. Today, they act as the backdrop for a series of live classical concerts, plus the occasional ballet, organised by the efficient and professional Ravello Concert Society.

Though collected under the Festival di Ravello umbrella, these performances, by prestigious Italian and international musicians and orchestras, are not so much a concentrated festival as a long season of open-air concerts, predominantly of chamber music, running from March until the beginning of November.

There are also various associated sub-festivals during the year, including the Concerti di Musica Sinfonica (symphonic concerts) in July and the Settimane Internazionali di Musica da Camera (Chamber Music Week) in September.

The gardens of **Villa Rufolo** (*see p261*) – where a regionally funded Piano High School is based – are the main venue. Recently, two other venues have been added: the **Convento di Santa Rosa** in Conca dei Marini (*see p249*) and the bay of **Marina di Praia** (*see p249*). Most concerts start at 9.30pm (6.30pm in March and November). Full details can be found on the Ravello Concert Society website, and you can also book online.

Ravello Concert Society

Via Trinità (089 858 149/fax 089 858 249/ www.ravelloarts.org). **Box office** 9am-1pm Mon-Sat; 4-8pm on concert days. **Credit** *Box office* AmEx, DC, MC, V. *By phone or online* MC, V.
Numbered seats cost €20 each; they can be reserved by phone, fax or email, and collected on the evening of the concert. Tickets are also sometimes available on the same day (but phone ahead to check). There is a special bus after each concert from Ravello or Conca dei Marini to all main Amalfi Coast towns and Sorrento.

---

wrote parts of *Lady Chatterley's Lover* at the now-defunct Hotel Rufolo. Graham Greene stayed in Ravello while writing *The Third Man* and Gore Vidal still lives here. The town's musical vocation is celebrated in a top-notch summer classical festival (*see above* **Festival Musicale di Ravello**).

Staying overnight is the best way to tune in to Ravello's quiet, contemplative atmosphere, which is at its most limpid in the early morning or around sunset. There are some renowned luxury hotels, but also one or two mid-range and budget gems. One drawback is parking: the main non-residents' car park, just beneath piazza Duomo, is expensive, even with a 50 per cent reduction for guests of any of the town's hotels; and other spaces are hard to come by, unless you're staying in one of the few more upmarket hotels that have their own garages. There are frequent buses from Amalfi; alternatively, Ravello is an appetite-building walk up a long tunnel, enters the main from the coast at Amalfi, Atrani or Minori.

From Atrani, the Ravello road winds up the **Valle del Dragone** and, doubling back on itself just before a long tunnel, enters the main part of town at the church of **Santa Maria a Gradillo** (open 9am-1pm, 3-6pm daily; if closed enquire at the Duomo), a pretty 12th-century

Romanesque structure whose bell tower is a good example of the Arab-Sicilian style, and whose charming interior has been stripped of distracting ornament. The lanes that skirt the church on the right and left both end up in piazza del Duomo, the civic heart of Ravello.

The **Duomo** was founded in 1086; little remains of its original façade, which was reworked in the 16th century. The real interest begins when you ascend the steps that lead up to the central bronze doors, divided into 54 bas-relief panels with stories of the saints and the Passion. Barisano da Trani, who designed them in 1179, was undoubtedly influenced by the Oriental Greek style of the earlier doors at Amalfi and Atrani.

The light-filled interior was redone in the baroque style in 1786; in the early 1980s, the courageous decision was taken to rip it all down and restore the church to something close to the state it had reached by the late 13th century.

Halfway down the central aisle are two exquisite pulpits, arranged face to face as if for a preachers' duel. The *pergamo* (high pulpit) on the right was commissioned by a scion of the local Rufolo family in 1272; six doggish lions support six spiral columns that hold up the pulpit itself, richly decorated with Cosmatesque mosaics. The simple *ambone* (low pulpit) opposite was donated by Costantino Rogadeo, the second bishop of Ravello, in 1130; its two cute mosaics of Jonah being swallowed (on the right) and regurgitated (on the left, with a little wave for all his fans) by an improbable whale are symbols of the Resurrection.

To the left of the main altar is the chapel of San Pantaleone, Ravello's patron saint, with an ampoule of his blood, which is supposed to liquefy on 27 July each year and stay liquid until mid-September (*see p70* **Bloody miracles**; in Naples, San Pantaleone is less obliging). The crypt contains the **Museo del Duomo**, a better-than-average collection of late imperial and medieval architectural and sculptural fragments, including a delicate marble portrait bust of Sichelgaita della Marra – wife of the Nicola Rufolo who paid for the *pergamo* upstairs.

Both of Ravello's famous villas are historical assemblages, the work of expatriate Britons who came, saw, and did a bit of gardening.

Villa Rufolo, entered via the 14th-century tower to the right of the Duomo, is named after its original 13th-century owners, the Rufolo family, who amassed a fortune acting as bankers for, among others, Charles of Anjou, and are mentioned in Bocaccio's *Decameron*. By the time Scotsman Francis Reid bought the place in 1851, the villa and its surrounding garden were little more than tangled ruins. The house was reborn as an eclectic melange, though certain parts – especially the charming double-tiered Moorish cloister – were not tampered with too much.

But it is the gardens, above all, that draw people here: scenic parterres studded with geometric flowerbeds amid the romantic ruins. When Wagner saw them in 1880, he knew that he had found the magic garden of Klingsor, the setting for the second act of his opera *Parsifal* (though he could hardly have guessed that one day the Pasticceria Klingsor, in piazza Duomo, would rise from the mystic mists to celebrate his discovery). In Wagner's honour, a world-class series of classical concerts is held here in the summer (*see p260* **Festival Musicale di Ravello**).

The town's other garden estate, **Villa Cimbrone**, is a fair walk from the centre along via San Francesco, which climbs up past the reworked Gothic church and monastery of the same name, and via Santa Chiara, which does the same. But it is an enchanting place, one of the real highlights of the Amalfi Coast, and well worth the trek. If the architectural part of Villa Rufolo is a reshuffle of pre-existing antique elements, that of Villa Cimbrone is an out-and-out fake, built (with the incorporation of a few old bits and pieces) at the beginning

of the 20th century by Lord Grimthorpe, whose other big claim to designer-fame is Big Ben. It hosted most of the Bloomsbury group in the 1920s; later, the reclusive Greta Garbo and conductor Leopold Stokowski used it briefly as their love nest.

To see the inside of the villa, you'll need to check in to the **Hotel Villa Cimbrone** (*see p263*), but the gardens can be admired by all. Roses, camellias and exotic plants line the lawns and walks, which are less formal than those of Villa Rufolo. There is a pretty faux-Moorish tea room and – one of the high points of the visit – a scenic viewpoint, the **Belvedere Cimbrone**, lined with classical busts; the view stretches along the coast from Atrani to the plain of Paestum (*see p271*).

Back in piazza del Duomo, the stepped lane by the side of the tourist office leads up to via dell'Episcopio; veering to the left, this becomes via San Giovanni del Toro, where Ravello's most upmarket hotels are situated, and where the **Belvedere Principessa di Piemonte** provides a great (free) view over Minori and the coast to the east. Further along on the left, opposite the Hotel Caruso (closed for refurbishment as this guide went to press), the church of **San Giovanni del Toro** (erratic opening hours; information from the tourist office 089 857 096) conserves much of its original 12th-century appearance. Its mosaic-encrusted pulpit, built for the local Bovio family, rivals the two on show in the Duomo, with another Jonah-eating whale and deep blue-green plates of Arab workmanship embedded in the centre of the mosaic circles. In a niche in the sacristy, there is a rare 12th-century stucco statue of Santa Caterina, with traces of the original paintwork.

If you can't take the pace in Ravello, head up to **Scala**, a village perched on the opposite side of the Dragone valley. Older than either Amalfi or Ravello, and once almost as prosperous, Scala is now the sort of place where the arrival of the grocery truck is a major event. It has a fine **Duomo** (open 8am-noon, 5-7pm daily) dedicated to San Lorenzo, with a good 12th-century portal and an interior that conceals a few gems beneath its baroque facelift. The wooden crucifix over the main altar dates from 1260; to the left is the Gothic tomb of the Coppola family. Note among the figures on the canopy above the tomb that of the rabbi who – according to an apocryphal gospel – had his hands lopped off when he gave the Virgin Mary's coffin a shove.

Scala is a good starting point for a number of walks. The most ambitious (No.51) leads in around two hours via the peak of Il Castello to **Casa Santa Maria dei Monti**, with a magnificent view over both sides of the Sorrentine peninsula. An easier option is to continue past the Duomo to the aptly named hamlet of **Minuto** ('tiny') – also served by six buses a day from Amalfi and Ravello – where the road ends just above the pretty 12th-century **Chiesa dell'Annunziata** (open Sunday morning for mass; otherwise knock on the first door on your left down the steps from the road and ask the custodian for the key). Inside are ten ancient granite columns and some very fine Byzantine frescos in the crypt. In the square in front of the church is a drinking fountain; behind this, a well-made stepped path descends in about 40 minutes to Amalfi via the little medieval village of Pontone.

Duomo di Ravello (Cattedrale di San Pantaleone)

Piazza del Duomo (089 858 311). **Open** *Church* 8.30am-1pm, 3-8pm daily. *Museum* Apr-Oct 9.30am-1pm, 3-7pm daily. Nov-Mar 9.30am-1pm, 3-7pm Sat, Sun. **Admission** €1.50. **No credit cards.**

Villa Cimbrone

Via Santa Chiara 26 (089 857 459). **Open** 9am-30mins before sunset daily. **Admission** €4.50. **No credit cards.**

Villa Rufolo

Piazza del Duomo (information from tourist office 089 857 096). **Open** 9am-30mins before sunset daily (closes 5pm on concert days). **Admission** €4. **No credit cards.**

Where to eat

Cumpà Cosimo

Via Roma 46 (089 857 156). **Meals served** *Mar-Oct* 12.30-3pm, 7.30-11pm daily. *Nov-Feb* 12.30-3pm, 7.30-11pm Tue-Sun. **Average** €30. **Credit** AmEx, DC, MC, V.
The decor and dishes are those of a simple trattoria, but the prices are in the restaurant league. But it's a seller's market in Ravello, and Cousin Cosimo can be relied on to deliver reliable pasta courses (with mushrooms in the autumn) and – a speciality of the house – excellent meat-based *secondi* such as *salsiccia al finocchietto in mantello di provola* (fennel-flavoured sausage in a cheese jacket). The ambience is unassuming but friendly, the wine drinkable.

Palazzo della Marra

Via della Marra 7-9 (089 858 302). **Meals served** *Apr-Oct* 12.30-2.30pm, 7-10pm daily. *Nov-mid Jan, Mar* noon-3pm, 7-10pm Mon, Wed-Sun. Closed 2wks Nov, mid Jan-Feb. **Average** €40. **Credit** AmEx, DC, MC, V.
Housed in a 12th-century palazzo, which has been carefully restored so as to keep the original vaults and arches intact, this upmarket restaurant produces creative Mediterranean cuisine. Some dishes – such as *tagliolini* with prawns, courgette flowers

and saffron – don't quite achieve their aim, but overall Palazzo della Marra makes a good (and fairly priced) attempt to go a little beyond the standard Amalfi Coast seafood experience. Much use is made of local produce, including cheeses from Agerola, and there is a good selection of fairly priced Campanian wines. There are two taster menus, priced at €32 and €48.

Rossellinis

Hotel Palazzo Sasso, via San Giovanni del Toro 28 (089 818 181). **Meals served** 7.30pm-10.30pm daily. Closed Nov-Feb. **Average** €80. **Credit** AmEx, DC, MC, V.
'Never eat in a hotel restaurant' is generally a sound rule; Rossellinis is an exception. Until this restaurant opened in 1997, Ravello was a blank on the gourmet map of the Amalfi Coast. Then the Virgin group poached young chef Antonio Genovese from the Enoteca Pinchiorri in Florence, and set him loose in the kitchens of its Palazzo Sasso hotel. Though Genovese has since moved on to Rome, his former assistant, Pino Lavarra, continues to push the gourmet boat out. On a typical evening in spring, the seasonally changing menu might include an *antipasto* of scallop carpaccio with caviar, sundried tomatoes, asparagus tips and lime ice, followed by tarragon-scented *garganelli* (a local pasta) tossed in a sauce of veal fillet, cannellini beans and crispy bacon. Seconds are evenly divided between fish and game or meat, and desserts are suitably theatrical. Add the charms of candlelit tables on the panoramic terrace, the professional service and excellent wines – some also available by the glass – and the chance of touching all bases with the taster menu (€80) and you have what some would consider the best meal this side of Don Alfonso (*see p243*).

Shopping

Limoncello opportunities abound; two of the more reliable are **I Giardini di Ravello** (via Civita 14, 089 872 264), which also makes its own extra virgin olive oil, and **Ravello Gusti & Delizie** (via Roma 28-30, 089 857 716), a tiny shop that also has a good selection of wine and deli treats. Ceramics are the best bet for serious shoppers, though don't expect rock-bottom prices.

Where to stay

Marmorata

Strada Statale S163, località Marmorata (between 32km and 33km milestones) (089 877 777/fax 089 851 189/www.marmorata.it). **Rates** €185-€310 double. **Credit** AmEx, DC, MC, V.
Marmorata, Ravello's seaside offshoot, is no more than a scatter of houses and is much closer by road to Minori than to Ravello itself. Now part of the Best Western group, the hotel of the same name occupies a former paper factory perched right above the sea

View from the **Belvedere**. *See p261.*

If you want lived-in luxury, then it's got to be the Palumbo. A degree more atmospheric than its upstart neighbour, Palazzo Sasso, this hotel has been run by the Swiss family Vuilleumier since 1875. It has switched premises twice, moving into its present home, the 12th-century Palazzo Gonfalone, in 1978. The tone is set as soon as you walk into the elegant hall, with its ancient marble columns, traditional tiled floor and profusion of plants and antique furniture. An inner courtyard has Moorish pointed arches, and the garden terrace where breakfast and other meals are served in summer is delightful. Each of the 18 rooms and three suites is individually decorated with antiques. The annexe across the road is cheaper (€195 per person half-board for two sharing a double), but has a lot less atmosphere. The summer half-board requirement is a bit of a bind, especially as the Palumbo restaurant (closed Nov-Mar) relies too much on its captive audience. The hotel also makes its own wine, bottled under the Episcopio label (the cellars are just across the road, beneath the annexe).

Villa Amore

Via dei Fusco 5 (tel/fax 089 857 135). **Rates** €44-€50 single; €67-€73 double. **Credit** DC, MC, V.
Ravello's best budget option, this hotel is on a quiet, stepped lane near Villa Cimbrone. Twelve clean, bright rooms, a garden with views down to the sea, and a friendly welcome from the two elderly ladies and the mynah bird that run the place add up to a real bargain. In among the threadbare sofas and pine panels are ancient columns and biforate windows. If you come with a car, there are free parking spaces to be found occasionally at the bottom of via dei Fusco on via della Repubblica – but be warned, it's a steep climb up.

Villa Cimbrone

Via Santa Chiara 26 (089 857 459/fax 089 857 777/www.villacimbrone.it). **Closed** Nov-Mar. **Rates** €155-€170 single; €222-€274 double; €310-€362 suite. **Credit** AmEx, MC, V.
For a sense of privilege, it's hard to beat the Hotel Villa Cimbrone, which occupies the historic main building of Ravello's famous garden. A stay here gives you the chance to stroll around the garden before and after the paying visitors are allowed in; and the villa itself is hardly less special. Many of the rooms (all recently refurbished) are museum pieces in their own right, with frescoed ceilings and antique furniture, and the library, with its huge stone fireplace, enters right into the country house spirit of the place. It's not for everyone – given the lack of car access – but if you're travelling light and are with that special person, there are few more romantic hideaways on the *Costiera*.

Villa Maria

Via Santa Chiara 2 (089 857 255/fax 089 857 071/www.villamaria.it). **Rates** €132-€152 single; €160-€253 double; €367-€408 suites. **Credit** AmEx, DC, MC, V.

in a small cove. A nautical theme runs through the decor, up to and including the beds, which have wooden borders like sailors' bunks. The terrace in front of the hotel has great views along the coast; as well as a small pool, there is a private swimming platform off the rocks. Marmorata is ideal for those with cars, or who want to combine some seaside cocooning with the occasional boat tour, which the hotel can arrange.

Palazzo Sasso

Via San Giovanni del Toro 28 (089 818 181/fax 089 858 900/www.palazzosasso.com). **Closed** Nov-Feb. **Rates** €181-€568 double; €491-€1,291 suite. **Credit** AmEx, DC, MC, V.
The Virgin group shook up the top end of the local tourist market when it opened this luxury hotel in 1997 in a 13th-century palazzo with views over the valley and the coast to the east. The cream and white façade is almost over-restored, but inside the mix of Moorish details with Empire-style furniture works convincingly, in an airbrushed international luxury sort of way. The hotel has 44 air-conditioned rooms and suites, most of them with jacuzzis. The staff are professional and friendly, and the hotel also has a pool, on a terrace below the hotel. One final incentive is the hotel's Rossellinis restaurant (*see p262*). Note that all rooms are doubles, and there is no reduction for single occupancy.

Palumbo

Via San Giovanni del Toro 16 (089 857 244/ fax 089 858 133/www.hotelpalumbo.it). **Rates** *Apr-Oct* (half-board only) €550 per person in single room; €360 per person for two in double room. *Nov-Mar* €310 single; €360 double; €440-€890 suite. **Credit** AmEx, DC, MC, V.

San Giovanni del Toro preserves its 12th-century appearance. *See p261.*

Definitely the best hotel in its price range, the Villa Maria is located in a converted villa on the lane that leads to Villa Cimbrone (*see p263*). In the shady garden, where meals are served in summer, tables and chairs are arranged to make the most of the view across the spectacular Dragone valley and down to the coast. The restaurant has a good reputation, and attracts clients from outside the hotel. The rooms are light and mostly spacious, and all are furnished with brass bedsteads and antique furniture. Room three is a huge suite with a panoramic terrace, the perfect lodging for modern-day Grand Tourists. Friendly, hands-on owner Vincenzo Palumbo also runs the nearby Hotel Giordano (via Santissima Trinità 14), a modern and less atmospheric (but also cheaper) option. Guests of the Villa Maria can take advantage of the Giordano's free car park and heated outdoor swimming pool.

Villa San Michele

SS163, Castiglione di Ravello (tel/fax 089 872 237/ www.amalficoast.it/smichele). **Closed** Jan-mid Feb. **Rates** €98-€140 double. **Credit** AmEx, DC, MC, V. For those wanting to combine proximity to Ravello with beach access without spending the earth, the San Michele is a good option. Located just below the turn-off for Ravello on the main coast road, the hotel occupies a pretty white villa with blue shutters set among terraced gardens ablaze with hibiscus and bougainvillea. The rooms are pretty and light-filled, and all face the sea. Steps descend from the garden to a stone diving platform with deckchairs and beach umbrellas.

Getting there

Ravello is best approached from Amalfi by public transport (*see p258*) and on the signposted road leading off from the coast road.

Getting around

A blue SITA bus runs at least hourly (less frequently on Sundays) from piazza Flavio Gioia in Amalfi to Ravello between 7am and 10pm; the journey takes around 25mins. In Ravello, the bus sets down and turns around just before a short road tunnel; walk through this to Villa Rufolo and piazza Duomo. The bus then stops (and turns around again) in front of the church of Santa Maria a Gradillo, and continues to Scala, on the other side of the valley, before making the return journey to Amalfi. Some services stop at Scala before Ravello; six buses a day continue up the crest of the hill beyond Scala to the hamlets of San Pietro and Minuto.

Tourist information

Azienda Autonoma di Soggiorno e Turismo

Piazza Duomo 10 (089 857 096/fax 089 857 977/ www.ravello.it/aziendaturismo). **Open** *May-Sept* 8am-8pm Mon-Sat. *Oct-Apr* 8am-7pm Mon-Sat.

East of Atrani

This stretch of coast is often seen simply as the inevitable traffic jam between Amalfi and Salerno, but if you have the time, it has its rewards – especially in the village of **Cetara**, the only truly authentic fishing port on the *Costiera*.

Minori, three kilometres (two miles) east of Atrani (or a pleasant hour's hike from Ravello down an ancient staircase) is by no means picturesque in the Positano sense, but it is a pleasant enough place with a certain low-key charm – and a restaurant, **L'Arsenale** (*see p266*), that justifies a stopover. If you're heading east, this is also the first of the Amalfi resorts to have a relatively flat town centre – you could almost fit two decent-sized football pitches between the high valley walls. Nestling in the middle of the warren of houses that make the most of this rare luxury is the **Villa Romana**, the only visitable archaeological site on the *Costiera*.

Excavations began in 1951, but were held up by a catastrophic flood in 1954 that buried not only the villa but much of Minori and neighbouring Maiori. Arranged around a large *viridarium*, or courtyard garden, the property belonged to a rich nobleman, as is evident from the dimensions of the villa and the traces of frescos on the walls of many of the rooms, whose style dates the building to the beginning of the first century AD. Upstairs, an antiquarium contains material found here and in two other nearby sites.

Around the next headland is **Maiori**, nestling in a flood plain that has been a continual source of danger to its inhabitants – but also given them the space to expand. In the 11th century the town was girded round with walls and towers by its overlord, Amalfi, and used as a shipbuilding centre for the republic. Today, it is the *Costiera*'s only example of a nondescript tourist resort, packed with modern hotels that sprang up on the new flat building land created by the 1954 flood. But it does have the Amalfi Coast's longest beach and one unexpected, historic gem of a hotel, **Casa Raffaele Conforti** (*see p266*).

From Maiori, a side road ascends the Valle di Tramonti to the **Valico di Chiunzi**, a 665-metre (2,327-foot) high pass (also accessible from Ravello) with amazing views across the construction-plagued Sarno plain to the menacing bulk of Vesuvius. Like Agerola (*see p250*), **Tramonti** itself is not a single village but a series of communities scattered over a fertile upland plain; it is known for its farm produce, cheese, honey and baskets woven from branches of the chestnut trees that grow hereabouts. A cold north wind that Amalfi mariners called the *tramontana* howls out of the mountains that encircle the plain; the word has now become standard Italian for a biting northerly.

The coast road east of Maiori negotiates the great massif of **Monte dell'Avvocata**, providing spectacular views back along the coast. A short distance beyond the 39-kilometre milepost, a path on the left leads up to the rock-hewn chapel of **Santa Maria de Olearia**

(339 580 3486/fax 089 852 205, open by appointment only), also known as the Catacombe di Badia, one of the more unusual holy sites on the *Costiera*, and well worth a visit if you can find a place wide enough to leave the car or persuade the bus driver to set you down. Two hermits were the first to occupy this site in 973; their shrine became a Benedictine abbey, squeezed between the towering rocks, which still has some atmospheric faded frescos from the 11th century.

Beyond the little fishing cove of **Erchie**, with a pretty beach watched over by a Saracen tower (look for the access road on the eastern side of the valley, after the main road has joined the coast again), the coast road winds along to **Cetara**, a fishing village with the by-now familiar Amalfi Coast layout: long, thin and up the valley. Historically, this was the eastern limit of the Amalfitan Republic, and the place still has a salty, frontier town feel to it. Of all the towns along the coast, this is the one with the most active fishing fleet, which roams the whole Mediterranean in search of shoals, with the help of two spotter planes.

Forget *limoncello*: the best Amalfi Coast souvenir is a small pot of salted anchovies or an even smaller pot of *colatura di alici*, a close relative of the Roman fish sauce known as *garum*, whose recipe survives here and nowhere else. With its small beach – overlooked by yet another medieval watchtower – and the honest, unprettified houses that line the single street, Cetara is a good place to stop to get some of the flavour of what life must have been like along this coast before the tourist industry moved in; another incentive are its two excellent restaurants (*see p267*).

East of Cetara, the road sticks close to the sea, passing by what is left of the massive hotel at Punta Fuenti. For years, this illegally built blot on the landscape was at the centre of a struggle between environmental pressure groups and local politicians, who feared a domino effect (and the end of lucrative backhanders) if it were shown that what went up could indeed come down. Finally, in 2000, the bulldozers moved in. In 2002, however, rumours abounded of equally unsightly projects in the pipeline for the area, dreamt up by the former hotel's owners.

Further east, on the site of the Etruscan town of Marcina, **Vietri sul Mare** is the capital of southern Italy's handcrafted ceramics industry, and the town centre is clogged with shops selling the ubiquitous wares. Though pottery had been made here since Roman times, the locals had lost their touch by the early 20th century. It was at this point that German ceramicists moved into the area and got

Around Naples

Casa Raffaele Conforti: historic gem of a hotel. *See p267*.

the industry going again. The history of the town's relationship with ceramics is documented in the **Museo Provinciale della Ceramica** in the village of **Raito**, just before Vietri on the road from Amalfi.

Ceramiche Solimene produces some of the area's brightest and best ceramics; the factory, a multicoloured tile-and-glass extravaganza hanging off a rock a short distance from the centre, is a sight in itself. It's a good place to see the clay being worked and developed into finished products, and to pick up some lovely ceramics at reasonable prices.

There are pretty examples of the local line in tiles on the dome of the 18th-century church of **San Giovanni Battista** (open 7.30-9.30am, 5.30-8.30pm daily).

The beach at **Marina di Vietri**, with its seaside bars and *gelaterie*, is a popular summer hangout for residents of Salerno (*see p268*).

Ceramiche Solimene
Via Madonna degli Angeli 7, Vietri sul Mare (089 210 243/www.solimene.com). **Open** 8am-6pm Mon-Fri; 8am-1pm, 3-6.30pm Sat. Closed 3wks Aug. **Credit** AmEx, DC, MC, V.

Museo Provinciale della Ceramica
Torretta di Villa Guariglia, Raito (089 211 835). **Open** *May-Sept* 9am-1pm, 4-7pm Tue-Sun. *Oct-Apr* 9am-1pm, 3-6pm Tue-Sun. **Admission** free.

Villa Romana and Antiquarium
Via Capodipiazza 28, Minori (089 852 893). **Open** 9am-1hr before sunset daily. **Admission** free.

Where to eat, drink & stay

In Minori, **L'Arsenale** (via San Giovanni a Mare 20, 089 851 418, closed 3wks Jan-Feb, Thur Oct-Mar, average €35) offers good-value seafood cooking. Space is tight, so book ahead, especially if you want to eat at one of the few outdoor tables. Alongside local favourites such as *scialatielli ai frutti di mare* (pasta with seafood) and *totani con le patate* (flying squid with potatoes), the friendly Proto brothers do one or two more creative dishes, such as fish tortellini with prawns and *funghi porcini* (boletus mushrooms). Minori also has the best bar on the Amalfi Coast, **Bar de Riso** (piazza Cantilena 1, 089 853 618, closed Wed Sept-June), which sits on a corner between the main square and the traffic-bound Lungomare. The coffee is excellent, as are the local cakes (*sfogliatelle, babà*) and home-made ice-cream. Grab a seat outside and eat a *granita di caffè* ostentatiously while those caught in the inevitable traffic jam look on with envy.

It's not obvious from the cement-lined waterfront, but Maiori too has a historic centre, though floods and other catastrophes have pared it back a little. Just off pedestrianised corso della Regina stands a glorious remnant of a more elegant past: the **Casa Raffaele Conforti** (via Casa Mannini 10, 089 853 547, www.casaraffaeleconforti.it, double room €85-€135, closed Nov & Jan), a small, nine-room hotel that occupies the second floor of a 19th-century townhouse. Frescoed ceilings, antique furniture and large gilded mirrors set the design tone that's guaranteed to make one feel as if one has stepped out of package resort land and into a Grand Tour.

In Cetara, the **Acqua Pazza** (corso Garibaldi 38, 089 261 606, closed Mon, 3wks Jan, average €30) is one of those restaurants Amalfi habitués like to keep quiet about. Not that the place is a snooty temple of *haute cuisine*, far from it; it's the freshness of the fishy ingredients (here you can be sure they are straight off the boat), the bravura of the chef at combining them in tasty but simple ways, the friendliness of owner and frontman Gennaro Castiello and the extremely honest prices that keep the clientele loyal. The never-ending antipasti are delicious (some dishes – based on raw tuna – are close to sushi) and a meal in themselves. The local speciality goes into the *linguine con colatura di alici*; and the home-made desserts look and taste sumptuous. Book well ahead, and don't show up too early for dinner: you're likely to find that the tables in this relaxed eaterie aren't even laid until well after 8pm. Some years the annual closure shifts to November.

Back up in the main square, **San Pietro** (piazzetta San Francesco 2, 089 261 091, closed Tue & late Jan-Feb, average €30) is Cetara's other cut-price gourmet fish temple. The *antipasti misti caldi* are well worth nodding yes to: dishes such as *farro* (spelt or emmer wheat) with *colatura di alici*, courgettes with clams and prawns, follow in a seemingly endless progression. Try to leave room for excellent pasta dishes such as *tubatoni con pescatrice* (pasta with anglerfish) and make the heroic effort to swallow at least one *secondo* – perhaps the *neonati* (whitebait) in a garlic and parsley broth. Finish up with a delicious home-made dessert and a mandarin liqueur. It's a little more upmarket and formal than Acqua Pazza, but all done to an equally high standard; and the piazzetta is a lovely place to sit outside of a summer's evening.

If you would rather take away the local goodies and try it yourself, head for **Sapori Cetaresi** (corso Garibaldi 44, 089 262 010), where you can invest in small jars of *colatura di alici* (anchovy sauce) or – to really ingratiate yourself with the rest of the people on your flight home – huge earthenware pots of salted anchovies.

Getting there

By car
Take the Vietri exit from the A3 motorway; from here, the SS163 coast road winds its way west along the coast.

By train
The station at Vietri sul Mare is served by only a very few very slow trains. Most of the time it's quicker to go straight to Salerno station (40mins from Naples) and continue by SITA bus.

By bus
The regular Amalfi–Salerno bus stops in all the localities mentioned here, and plenty more besides. Ring SITA (089 871 016) for timetable information.

By boat
TraVelMar (089 873 190) runs frequent summer ferry services between Maiori, Amalfi and Positano.

Tourist information

Associazione Autonoma di Soggiorno e Turismo
Corso Regina 73, Maiori (089 877 452/fax 089 853 672/www.aziendaturismo.maiori.it). **Open** 8.30am-1.30pm, 3-5pm Mon-Fri.

Circolo Turistico ACLI
Piazza Matteotti, Vietri sul Mare (tel/fax 089 211 285/www.comune.vietri-sul-mare.sa.it/cta). **Open** *Oct-May* 10am-1pm Mon-Fri. *June-Sept* 9am-1pm, 5-8pm Mon-Fri; 9am-1pm Sat.

Frontman Gennaro at the **Acqua Pazza**.

Around Naples

Further Afield

History and geography make Naples' neighbours worlds apart.

As so often happens in southern Italy, geography and history have combined to give each of Naples' neighbouring provinces a very different feel: the province of **Caserta** stretches from flat coastal plains high up into the craggy Apennines, **Benevento** is dominated by huge expanses of rolling farmland, while **Salerno** and its surrounding area is a scenic mix of landscapes and cultures, epitomised by the Greco-Roman site of **Paestum**.

Salerno

The crescent-shaped Gulf of Salerno stretches from Punta della Campanella to Punta Licosa, its northern and southernmost edges laced with rocky cliffs and beautiful coves, its central part low and flat. At the northern end of this plain lies **Salerno**.

Archaeological evidence shows that the area was settled by Etruscans as early as the sixth century BC. Its official history kicks off, however, in 194 BC, when the Romans founded a colony called Salernum. Fought over and occupied down the centuries by Goths and Byzantines, it came firmly under the thumb of the Germanic Lombards in 646. Despite internal power struggles and constant harrying by Saracens, the city flourished. It was the Lombard Prince Arechi, local lore relates, who founded the city's illustrious Medical School.

But it took the Normans, who conquered Salerno in 1076, to fulfil the city's real potential. The first capital of what was to become the kingdom of southern Italy (Palermo succeeded it in 1127), Salerno's Norman court was legendary, and its Medical School drew patients and students from all over the known world. Following centuries of fluctuating fortunes, Salerno became an increasingly insignificant backwater as Naples' star rose under the Angevins and Aragonese. Only after Italian Unification in 1870 – as Naples declined – did Salerno begin to regain some of its lost vitality. On 8 September 1943 Allied troops landed just south of the city, forcing the Germans to withdraw north; for five months in 1944, Salerno was the seat of the Italian government.

Today, it is a buzzing industrial city, and its port is one of the most important on the Tyrrhenian Sea. The seafront area, badly bombed during World War II, is decidedly

Salerno's Norman **Duomo** celebrates victory over the Lombards. *See p269.*

post-war functional; the medieval heart of the old town has recently undergone extensive – though controversial – restoration, much of it at the hands of Catalan Oriol Bohigas, the architect responsible for Barcelona's makeover. Whether or not his flourishes appeal, there's no denying that the decline of the historic centre has been halted and some of the city's original splendour restored.

Dominating the old centre, Salerno's **Duomo** – dedicated to the city's patron saint Matthew – was begun by the Norman conqueror Robert de Hauteville (known as *le Guiscard*, 'the Crafty') in 1077, in thanks for his victory over the Lombards. It was heavily baroque-ified in post-earthquake restoration in the 18th century, though subsequent facelifts have revealed large sections of the glorious Romanesque original.

At the base of the imposing gateway leading into the Duomo are a sculpted lion and a lioness feeding her cub, symbols of the power and charity of the Church. The church proper is preceded by a porticoed courtyard with columns filched from ancient buildings and an ancient granite basin at its centre, a spectacular 12th-century bell tower and a room off to the right that may have been the lecture theatre of the Medical School.

Inside, through vast bronze doors cast in Constantinople in 1099, the Latin cross-plan church has three naves; in the central nave are two carved and inlaid pulpits, the one on the right (with matching paschal – Easter – candlesticks) dating from the early 13th century and the one on the left from the late 12th. The 16th-century wooden choir stalls are preceded by sections of the 1175 mosaic-encrusted iconostasis (screen). Beside the stalls in the left aisle, the statue of Margaret of Durres, mother of Naples' Angevin King Ladislas, dates from 1435. In the transept and choir are sections of the Duomo's original, spectacular Byzantine-inspired floor. In the cavernous baroque crypt, columns wind around to form interlacing curves. Beneath the main altar lie the remains of St Matthew.

East of the Duomo, via San Michele leads to the **Museo Archeologico Provinciale**. Housed in the former abbey of San Benedetto (one of 36 religious institutions in the city), the museum's collection testifies to the extensive Etruscan influence in their southernmost outpost, as well as displaying an interesting chance find – a first-century bronze head of Apollo fished out of the Gulf of Salerno in 1930.

Bustling with boutiques (most of the city's smart shops are here) and lined with medieval buildings, via dei Mercanti is the picturesque main thoroughfare of the old town. The **Museo della Scuola Medica Salernitana** is housed

Filched ancient columns in the **Duomo**.

in the deconsecrated church of San Gregorio and illustrates the activities of Salerno's illustrious Medical School. Manuscripts, documents and illustrations are organised in eight sections, each dedicated to a branch of medieval medical knowledge, and chart the school's activities during its heyday in the 11th to 13th centuries and beyond.

Rising above the centre on Colle Bonadies, the **Castello di Arechi** (bus 19 from piazza XIV Maggio or via Ligea; alternatively, it's a tiring, poorly marked 40-minute haul on a network of footpaths leading uphill from the Duomo) was part of a great Lombard defence system, with walls extending from the castle to the sea surrounding the wedge-shaped town. The castle now houses a museum (currently closed for restoration) containing ceramics and other artefacts that were found within the castle. The view over the city and gulf is spectacular.

Duomo (Cattedrale di San Matteo)
Piazza Alfano 1 (089 231 387).
Open 7.30am-8pm daily.

Museo Archeologico Provinciale
Via San Benedetto 28 (089 231 135).
Open 9am-7.30pm Mon-Sat; 9am-1.30pm Sun.
Admission free.

Museo della Scuola Medica Salernitana
Via dei Mercanti 72 (089 257 3111/089 257 3220).
Open 9am-2.30pm Mon-Sat. **Admission** free.

Around Naples

Where to stay & eat

Situated right on the beach, the **Jolly Hotel** (Lungomare Trieste 1, 089 225 222,www. jollyhotels.it, double room 134) is within walking distance of the old town. On the traffic-free main drag you'll find two comfortable and well situated hotels: the **Hotel Montestella** (corso Vittorio Emanuele 156, 089 225 122, www.montestella.it, double room 78) and **Hotel Plaza** (piazza Vittorio Veneto 42, 089 224 477, www.plazasalerno.it, double room 80).

For good seafood, try **Portovecchio** (Molo Manfredi 38, 089 255 222, closed Mon, 2wks Dec, average 25). In the old town, the **Pizzeria Vicolo della Neve** (vicolo della Neve 24, 089 225 705, closed lunch, Wed, average 15) serves great pizzas and delicious pasta and beans, as well as its famous *cianfotta* (a dish made with potatoes, peppers, courgettes, bacon and tomato).

Between the Duomo and the Villa Comunale park, **Portacatena** (via Portacatena 28-34, 089 235 899, closed Mon, dinner Sun, average 27) occupies an atmospheric vaulted cellar and has an inventive vegetable-based cuisine. It's closed for two weeks in August.

Getting there

By car
Salerno is 55km (34 miles) south of Naples on the A3 motorway.

By train
There are regular services from Naples' Stazione Centrale on the Naples–Reggio–Calabria line.

By bus
SITA (089 405 145/www.sita-on-line.it) runs regular services from piazza Municipio in Naples.

Getting around

CSTP (089 252 228/089 487 286/toll-free 800 016 659) operates bus services around Salerno and surrounding areas. Tickets cost 70¢ for one hour's travel, 1.30 for 24 hours.

Tourist information

Ente Provinciali per il Turismo (EPT)
Piazza V Veneto 1 (tel/fax 089 231 432/toll-free 800 213 289/www.salernocity.com). **Open** 9am-2pm, 3-8pm Mon-Sat.
The website is in Italian only.

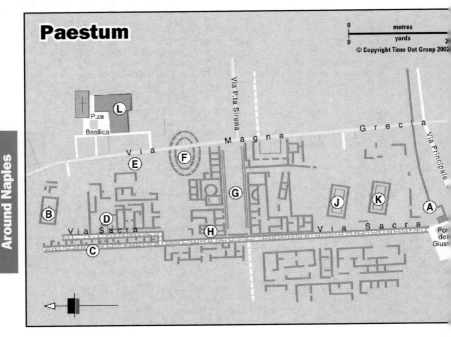

Paestum

metres

yards

© Copyright Time Out Group 2002

Around Naples

Paestum

Letters in bold in the text refer to the map on p270.

The flat, straight coast road out of Salerno skirts wide sandy beaches where locals flock in summer. There are pine and eucalyptus trees, and fields full of artichokes or strawberries, depending on the season. River buffalo, whose milk is used to produce mozzarella cheese, graze on land that was once a malarial swamp around the mouth of the River Sele. It was across this fertile plain that the Allies battled the Germans in September 1943, fighting for 20 bloody days before capturing Salerno and forcing the Germans to withdraw north.

Paestum's ancient territory starts on the southern bank of the River Sele. The **Santuario di Hera Argiva** (accessible from both the coast road and the SS18) was built by the Greeks around 600 BC, at the same time as the city of Poseidonia-Paestum. It was a temple to Hera, goddess of women and marriage. Although the actual site consists of little more than temple foundations, a state-of-the-art learning centre, formidably called the **Museo Narrante del Santuario di Hera Argiva**, gives useful insights (with English panels) into the cult of Hera, while displaying replicas of original finds now housed in the **Museo Archeologico Nazionale** (see p272) in Paestum. The Museo Narrante opened in late 2001 and occupies an imaginatively converted farmhouse on land adjacent to the temple site.

Paestum itself – ten kilometres (six miles) south of the Santuario – is best known for its three standing Greek temples, though there are traces of continued occupation throughout ancient times, including extensive Roman building works down to the second century AD.

The town – originally named Poseidonia – was founded most probably in the early sixth century BC by Greeks from Sybaris, a Greek colony on Italy's south-eastern coast. Like almost all the other settlements in Greece and Magna Graecia (southern Italy), the colony had the basic trappings of a Greek *polis*: places of worship, a civic centre (the *agorà*), an assembly area for all male citizens (*ekklesiasterion*), and an area for exercise and games (*gymnasion*). In about 400 BC, the city appears to have been overrun by a local tribe, the Lucanians; they unwisely backed Pyrrhus, king of Epirus, in his struggle against the Romans and were eventually trounced.

In 273 BC Poseidonia became a Roman colony, and the tangible signs of Greek civic life were gradually removed: the *ekklesiasterion* was filled in and replaced by the Roman *comitium* (assembly area) to the south; the

temples were left standing (the pious Romans would never have dismantled them), but were probably rededicated to other divinities; and the Roman forum replaced the Greek *agorà*, again further to the south. At some stage, the name of the town was adapted to a more Italic pronunciation, ending up as Paestum. This overlapping of civilisations can make Paestum a confusing site to visit.

To see it at its best, tour Paestum first thing in the morning or late in the afternoon after the tour buses have left. After passing through the impressive ancient **city walls [A]** – almost five kilometres (three miles) long and rising from five metres (16.5 feet) to 15 metres (49 feet) high – head for the main road (SS18), which offers easy access to both the site and the museum.

At the northern end of the site lies what was previously called the **Temple of Ceres [B]**, dedicated – as archaeologists subsequently discovered from the temple's votive offerings – to the goddess Athena. This Athenaion, built in about 500 BC, was a Doric temple with some Ionic features: there was an inner colonnade with Ionic capitals, two of which are now on display in the site museum. The temple was used as a burial site in early Christian times and then succumbed to the same fate as many other Greek temples throughout the Mediterranean, being converted into a church in medieval times.

From the Athenaion a well-preserved **Roman road [C]** leads south through the site, passing the curious half-buried sixth-century shrine (**heroon**) **[D]** to Poseidon's founder in which archaeologists unearthed some finely worked bronze vases (*hydria*) now given pride of place in the museum. Although much of the rest of the Greek area was built over in Roman times, the **ekklesiasterion [E]**, a small circular building where meetings of the *ekklesia* (adult male assembly) were held, is the one part of the Greek *agorà* that is now recognisable; most of the limestone seating is lost. Fifty metres (55 yards) further south, past Roman residential areas, the Roman civic area begins; close by stand the partially rebuilt arches of the **amphitheatre [F]**.

Begun during the first century BC, the amphitheatre was substantially enlarged in early imperial times when an outer colonnade was added (only stubs of brick pillars are left standing). With an estimated capacity of 2,000, the amphitheatre is pint-size compared to those in Pompeii (see p216), Capua (see p278) and Pozzuoli (see p98), and is unlikely to have been able to offer the whole bloodthirsty gamut of Roman entertainment. Much of it – including the Porta Libitinensis through which the hapless losers were hauled out – lies under the main road hacked through the site in the 18th century.

Around Naples

Temples rise like mirages from the **Paestum** plain.

Close by stand the remnants of other civic buildings from Roman times, all of which were within easy reach of the Roman **forum [G]**, the hub of urban life from the third century BC onwards. The centrepiece of the *campus*, the ancient sports and leisure centre, is the third-century BC **piscina [H]** or swimming pool, which evokes the memorable diving scene in the frescoed Tomb of the Diver on display in Paestum's museum, although the tomb itself predates the *piscina* by as much as 200 years. The purpose of the sunken network of limestone pillars remains a mystery.

The architectural jewel of the site, 100 metres (110 yards) south of the Roman forum, is the remarkably preserved (but misnamed) **Tempio of Neptune [J]**, which was undergoing conservation work as this guide went to press. Dedicated perhaps to Poseidon or – according to a recent theory – Apollo, the temple was built in the mid fifth century BC when the Greek colony was enjoying a period of prosperity. It employs similar techniques to those used in other contemporary Doric temples (curvature of the horizontal lines, slightly convex columns or entasis). Like the other temples in Paestum this was built with local limestone rather than the more usual marble.

The columns were originally faced with white stucco to imitate marble and perhaps mask the defects of the stone. Together with the sixth-century basilica – more accurately called the **Temple of Hera [K]** – to the south, it rises out of the Paestum plain like a mirage and continues to throw even the world-weariest of visitors into raptures.

The **museum [L]** has some excellent displays of archaic Greek sculptures (from the Santuario di Hera Argiva temple (*see p271*), interesting

finds from local necropolises complete with the paraphernalia for the afterlife, an extensive collection of frescoed tombs and a recently opened Roman section on the top floor.

In summer, concerts and theatrical performances (information 0828 811 016) are held close by the temples.

Museo Archeologico Nazionale

Via Magna Grecia (0828 811 023). **Open** *Site* 9am-1hr before sunset daily. *Museum* 8.45am-7pm daily. Closed 1st & 3rd Mon of the mth. **Admission** *Site or museum* €4. *Both* €6.50. **No credit cards**.

Museo Narrante del Santuario di Hera Argiva

Masseria Procuriali, Capaccio (0828 861 440). **Open** 9am-3pm Tue-Sat. **Admission** free.

Where to stay & eat

About two kilometres north of Paestum on the road to Capaccio Scalo, the **Azienda Agricola Seliano** (via Seliano, 0828 723 634, www.agriturismoseliano.it, half-board €50-€70 per person) occupies two remodelled 19th-century farmhouses. There's riding, a pool and cooking lessons, too. It's closed from November to February, except over New Year.

In Paestum's archaeological zone, there is the **Villa Rita** (via Nettuno 5, Zona Archeologica, 0828 811 081, www.hotel villarita.it, closed Nov-mid Feb, double room €73-€83) and the Hotel **Helios** (via Principe di Piemonte, Zona Archeologica, 0828 811 451, www.hotelheliospaestum.com, double €70-€83). Both have quiet gardens.

In the midst of a welter of restaurants serving fairly dreadful tourist fare, **Nonna Scepa** (via Laura 53, Paestum, 0828 851 064, closed Thur Oct-May, average €27) stands out a mile with excellent seafood and good pizzas.

Getting there

By car

The SS18 follows the coast south of Salerno. If coming direct from Naples, take the Battipaglia exit off the Salerno–Reggio–Calabria motorway.

By train

There are frequent services to Paestum on the Naples–Salerno–Reggio–Calabria line. Paestum town's main station is called Capaccio Scalo, from where infrequent buses run to the ruins; a few trains each day stop at the smaller Paestum station, which is a 10mins walk from the archaeological site.

By bus

CSTP (089 252 228/089 487 286/toll-free 800 016 659) runs hourly services from piazza della Concordia in Salerno to Paestum.

Tourist information

Azienda Autonoma Soggiorno e Turismo (AAST)

Via Magna Grecia 889 (0828 811 016/fax 0828 722 322/www.paestumtourism.it). **Open** 9am-1pm, 3-5pm Mon-Sat; 9am-1pm Sun.

Benevento

Despite appearances – unattractive late 20th-century development straddles hillsides and valleys around – Benevento conceals unexpected nuggets from its long, distinguished history. In early Roman times the area was occupied by the Oscan-speaking Samnites, a fearsome Italic hill tribe. But by the beginning of the fourth century BC the Samnites were out on a limb, and a peace treaty with Rome was finally concluded in 290 BC. The settlement where Benevento now stands was renamed Beneventum and became a Roman colony in 268 BC, reaping considerable benefits from its strategic position along the main north–south Appian Way and from its later status as a *municipium*, formally subject to Rome but governed by its own laws.

In the turbulent centuries that followed the fall of the Roman Empire, Benevento emerged as a Lombard capital whose influence extended throughout most of southern Italy. Caught in a tug of war between the Normans and the Papacy in the 11th century, it remained a papal stronghold for two centuries before it was sacked (twice) by the Swabian Frederick II. Its subsequent history is marked by a lengthy period of papal dominion until 1799 when it was occupied by French troops who indulged in their usual pastime of purloining local artworks. Extensive damage was done during World War II when an estimated 65 per cent of the city was turned to rubble.

Today, its plush shop windows and shiny new fleet of cars show that Benevento has resisted the urban blight often found in other towns in Campania. Landmarks are well kept, traffic is heavy but fairly well disciplined, and the surrounding countryside is generally well tended and conserved.

The major sites in the city are clustered either side of the main shopping thoroughfare, corso Garibaldi. Evidence of Benevento's early Roman heritage can be seen at the **Museo del Sannio**, tucked in behind the church of Santa Sofia. The museum has several galleries filled with Roman sculptures and fine marble sarcophagi from ancient settlements in the province, while the covered courtyard contains finds from the first-century Temple of Isis, one of several Egyptian deities worshipped in the area. Statues of Thoth, Horus and Anubis may seem out of place in an Italian hilltown, but eastern cults enjoyed

Benevento's real jewel: the **Arco di Traiano**. *See p275.*

considerable popularity at home as Rome's empire expanded and assimilated new religions. With the arrival of the Lombards in the sixth century, all traces of pagan worship were eliminated: the magic powers of Isis were demonised, perhaps giving rise to the area's reputation for witchcraft, a reputation that survives to the present day.

The museum extends into the delightful 11th-century cloister of the church of **Santa Sofia**, with elaborately sculpted column capitals reminiscent – in style and quality – of medieval masterpieces such as Monreale in Sicily.

The church of Santa Sofia was founded by the Lombard Duke Arechi II in 762 AD; though restored in the 12th century, the innovative original plan – an inner hexagon of columns surrounded by a decagon of pillars – has survived intact. In two of the three apses behind the altar there are traces of an eighth-century fresco cycle depicting locally born St Zacharias on the left and a New Testament scene on the right.

But Benevento's real jewel – recently unveiled after a lengthy facelift – is the **Arco di Traiano**, a triumphal arch erected in 114 to celebrate the achievements of Roman emperor Trajan. Described as *optimo* in the inscription surmounting the arch, Trajan had restored a measure of peace and prosperity to the Empire with his military campaigns in Germany and the Danube area. Despite its location – the busy inner-city ring road passes to one side of it – the arch's sculpted friezes depicting the emperor performing various civic duties have weathered the millennia remarkably well. Floodlit at night, this must rank as one of Campania's finest Roman monuments.

At the western end of the town beyond the Duomo is the **Teatro Romano**, probably built during the reign of Commodus at the end of the second century. While much of the arcaded superstructure has been lost, other parts of the theatre have been extensively restored. With the distant backdrop of the Taburno mountain range, the theatre is an atmospheric venue for summer concerts and plays – contact the local tourist office for information.

Museo del Sannio

Piazza Santa Sofia (0824 21 818). **Open** 9am-1pm Tue-Sun. **Admission** €2.58. **No credit cards**.

Santa Sofia

Piazza Santa Sofia (0824 21 206). **Open** 7am-noon, 4-8pm daily.

Teatro Romano

Piazza Caio Ponzio Telesino (0824 47 213). **Open** 9am-1hr before sunset daily. **Admission** €2. **No credit cards**.

Where to stay & eat

The obvious choice in town is the well-appointed **Hotel President** (via GB Perasso 1, 0824 316 716, www.hotelpresident.8m.com, double room €67-€97), conveniently close to the museum. For budget accommodation, opt for one of two historic farmsteads six kilometres (four miles) north-east of Benevento on the road to Pietralcina: **Agriturismo Le Camerelle** (contrada Camerelle, 0824 776 134, p.barricelli@tin.it, double €45-€55) or **Agriturismo La Francesca** (contrada La Francesca, same contact details and rates), both owned by the Barricelli family. La Francesca also operates a thriving restaurant (average €15) serving local produce within its pleasingly restored 17th-century farmhouse.

In Benevento itself, make for the **Teatro Gastronomico** (via Traiano 65, 0824 54605, closed Mon, dinner Sun, average €25) decorated exotically with stage scenery and located conveniently close to Trajan's arch.

Getting there

By car
From Naples take the A1 motorway to Caserta Sud, then the traffic-laden SS7 to Benevento; or take the relatively stress-free A16 Naples–Bari motorway to the Benevento exit.

By train
There are few direct trains from Naples; you'll have to change in Caserta. To avoid long waits check connections carefully. Benevento station is a good 30mins walk from the major sites, though bus 1 runs frequently between the station and the centre.

By bus
On weekdays SITA (081 552 2176/www.sita-on-line.it) does six daily runs from Naples (piazza Garibaldi) to Benevento, where the bus station is a 5mins walk from piazza Santa Sofia.

Tourist information

Ente Provinciale per il Turismo (EPT)
Piazza Roma 11 (0824 319 938/fax 0824 312 309/ www.eptbenevento.it). **Open** 8.30am-1.45pm, 3-6pm Mon-Fri; 9am-1pm Sat.

Caserta

Situated 20 kilometres (12 miles) north of Naples, Caserta began life in the 12th century as the village of La Torre, inhabited by the overflow from crowded **Casertavecchia** (*see p277*). It remained a quiet backwater until the 1750s, when the first Bourbon king Charles

Around Naples

(see p15) selected it as a peaceful residence where he could indulge his passion for hunting and at the same time avoid Naples' twin dangers of eruptions from Vesuvius and marauding Saracens. Aiming at the opulence of the Palace of Versailles, he commissioned leading Neapolitan architect Luigi Vanvitelli (see p35) to build the **Reggia**, one of Italy's largest palaces. The royal project sparked a baroque property boom as trade and industry flocked to cash in on the town's new status.

In the 19th century, Caserta was an important military base. The key encounter of Italian Unification – when Giuseppe Garibaldi met King Victor Emanuel II and agreed to hand over his southern Italian conquests to the crown (see p19) – took place at nearby Teano in 1860. Although the economy of the town is primarily agricultural and its industry operates at little more than craft level, modern Caserta is comfortably off by southern Italian standards, and is a lively backdrop to the stately Reggia.

Begun by Vanvitelli in 1752 and finished by his son Carlo in 1774, the Reggia is perhaps the finest example of the Neapolitan baroque. Though construction work set off at a great rate under the enthusiastic Charles III (1731-59), it almost ground to a halt in 1759 when he returned to his native Spain to assume the crown there. It was not until the 1770s, in fact, that Charles's son Ferdinand I (1759-1825) began pushing for the work to be completed, after which his court spent the spring and autumn seasons there.

The palace is built around four courtyards, has 1,200 sumptuous rooms (only a fraction are open to the public; many, controversially, are occupied by the air force), 1,790 windows and cost around six million ducats to build.

The **Scala d'Onore** (main staircase), with 117 steps carved from one stone block, leads up to the royal apartments. Beyond the upper octagonal hall, the **Salone degli Alabardieri** (halberd bearers) has busts of various queens, while the **Salone delle Guardie di Corpo** (bodyguards) has scenes from the lives of the Farnese family, dukes of Parma, a title that passed to King Charles through his mother Elizabetta Farnese. The bust of Ferdinand I on a mantelpiece is attributed to Antonio Canova. The next room (Sala di Alessandro) gets its name from the fresco depicting Alexander the Great's marriage to Roxana; the porch outside was used by the monarchs and their families for royal waves.

To the left of this room lies the suite of rooms called the **Appartamento Vecchio**, the first in the Reggia to be occupied. The first four rooms are dedicated to the seasons: *primavera* (spring) with paintings by Antonio Dominici;

estate (summer) with works by Fedele Fischetti, walls covered in San Leucio silk and a Murano glass chandelier; a dining room dedicated to *autunno* (autumn) with frescos of Bacchus and Ariadne; and *inverno* (winter).

In the private study of Ferdinand II (1830-59) the clock and vases are French and the lacquered furniture is German, but the overall effect is oriental. Behind the mirror, a private door leads to the king's bedchamber via a narrow passageway. Since this king died of a contagious disease, the contents of his bedchamber were destroyed; the furniture now on display dates from Ferdinand I's reign. Next to the bedchamber is the queen's dressing room, followed by the spacious **Sala di Ricevimento**, where the sovereigns received their guests. Beyond two large reading rooms is the **Biblioteca** (library), where a collection of more than 10,000 volumes is distributed over several rooms. The adjoining room contains a nativity scene with 1,200 figures crafted by 18th-century artisans and dressed in clothes made by the queen and her ladies-in-waiting; the glass display cases occupy the place where a small stage used to be, before the palace theatre was built.

To the right of the Sala di Alessandro is the suite of rooms called the **Appartamento Nuovo**. This suite was not completed until 1845. The first two rooms were probably used by court officials for routine palace business. The **Sala del trono** (throne room) was where the king received ambassadors and where balls were held; it is lit by 14 Bohemian glass and bronze lamps, and the throne is of carved and gilded wood. The private part of the suite begins with Ferdinand II's bedchamber, which contains a very early example of a roll-top desk. The adjoining bathroom and study belonged to the private apartment of Napoleon's brother-in-law Joaquin Murat, Naples' king from 1808 to 1816 (see p18 **King Joaquin**). His bedchamber is in the French Empire style, with mahogany and bronze inlay furniture and Murat's initials ostentatiously carved into the chairs. The Royal Chapel has a barrel-vaulted ceiling reminiscent of the one at Versailles.

Within the palace complex is the **Museo dell'Opera**, which contains documents and plans tracing the history of its construction.

Also designed by Luigi Vanvitelli, and modified by his son Carlo, the 120-hectare (296-acre) gardens – **Il Parco** – surrounding the royal palace are a vast expanse of manicured green, traversed by spectacular fountains and pools. Some 700 metres (765 yards) from the palace exit stands the **Fontana di Margherita**, followed by a series of long ponds, at the head of which is the **Fontana**

dei Delfini (dolphin fountain). The **Fontana di Eolo** (Aeolus, god of the winds) has six tiered waterfalls; it should have been adorned with 54 statues, but only 29 were completed. At its far end lies the **Fontana di Ceres** (goddess of fertility). The final fountain, composed of 12 mini-waterfalls, has statues of Venus and Adonis.

Beyond, the **Grande Cascata** crashes down over greenery from a height of 78 metres (255 feet), flanked by statues of Diana, and of Actaeon being turned into a stag for daring to observe the bathing goddess. The stairs on either side of the waterfall lead to the grotto, where water brought from the surrounding hills by the **Acquedotto Carolino** arrives to feed the garden's fountains; stretching for 40 kilometres (25 miles), passing through five mountains and over three bridges, the aqueduct was an amazing feat of hydraulic engineering by Vanvitelli.

Reggia di Caserta (Palazzo Reale)

Via Douet 2 (Reggia 0823 321 400/0823 447 147/ Museo dell'Opera 0823 332 1400). **Open** *Reggia* 8.30am-7.30pm Tue-Sun. *Museo* 9am-1pm Tue-Sun. *Parco* 9am-1hr before sunset Tue-Sun. **Admission** *Reggia & Museo* €6. *Parco* €2.10. **No credit cards.**

Where to stay & eat

Caserta is not spoilt for well-appointed accommodation. Of the budget places, the **Hotel Baby** (via Verdi 41-3, 0823 328 311, double room €43-€52) is one of the more acceptable. Opposite the Reggia is the newly renovated **Hotel Jolly** (viale Vittorio Veneto 9, 0823 325 222, www.jollyhotels.it, double €110-€150), which also has disabled facilities.

Surprisingly, the self-service cafeteria in the **Reggia** (just by the entrance to the palace gardens) offers reasonable food at highly competitive prices (average €15). Of the surrounding towns, Casertavecchia offers the best chance of finding a good, atmospheric eatery. A ten-minute drive north of the centre, **Leucio** (strada Panoramica, San Leucio, 0823 301 241, closed Mon, dinner Sun, average €25) serves outstanding food with a heavy fish bias, home-made pasta and has excellent service.

Getting there

By car

From Naples take the A1 motorway and exit at Caserta Sud.

By train

There are frequent services from Naples' Stazione Centrale (journey time 30mins). The station in Caserta is a 5mins walk from the Reggia.

By bus

CTP (081 504 8150) runs frequent services from piazza Garibaldi in Naples to Caserta and Capua; the buses marked *per autostrada* take the motorway and get there faster.

Tourist information

Ente Provinciali per il Turismo (EPT)

Via Douet 2 (inside the Reggia) (0823 322 233/ fax 0823 326 300/www.casertaturismo.com). **Open** 8.30am-5.30pm Mon-Sat.

<h1 style="background:black;color:white">Around Caserta</h1>

Probably founded in the eighth century, **Casertavecchia** (Old Caserta) is self-consciously picturesque, with medieval alleyways and a ruined castle; it was the seat of the counts of Caserta until the 16th century, when they moved to the plains below. Deserted during the day, the place bursts into life as its many *trattorie* open up in the evening. The 12th-century cathedral of **San Michele Arcangelo** in piazza del Duomo (though the entrance is round the corner) is one of the finest examples of Romanesque architecture in the region, with an outstanding bell tower of Arabic and French influence, and an Arab-looking eight-sided dome. Ancient columns with Corinthian capitals added to compensate for height differences divide the Latin-cross interior into three aisles. The tiny Gothic church of the **Annunziata** dates from the late 13th century.

Every September, Casertavecchia is home to the extremely popular **Settembre al Borgo** festival (information 0823 273 268/0823 322 233) with high-quality music, dance, open-air theatre and exhibitions.

Nearby is the quiet, old town of **Santa Maria Capua Vetere**; with its crumbling *palazzi*, medieval cobbles and new money, it is hard to imagine it was once the apple of the Roman imperial eye, gateway to the south and to the wealth of oriental sea trade making its way through Naples.

Inhabited since the ninth century BC, it flourished under the Etruscans, resisted the Greeks but fell to the Samnites. When the Romans got down to building the Appian Way – their first major long-distance highway – in 312 BC, it led to old Capua, now Santa Maria Capua Vetere. The city supported Hannibal during the second Punic War (218-210 BC) but Roman rule was heavy-handedly reinstated after his defeat and an attempted uprising.

By that time, its trade and agricultural sectors were flourishing and its Seplasia forum (today's piazza Mazzini) was world-famous for perfume. In the first century BC, Livy described old Capua as the biggest and richest city in Italy; for Cicero it was 'a second Rome'.

In AD 465, the city was sacked by the Vandals and in 841 the Saracens arrived to finish off the job. The population took to the hills, to where modern Capua now stands. The destruction of the old city was completed by the citizens themselves, who freely pillaged building material from the ruins until as late as the 19th century. Even archaeologists happily plundered the site and sold off their booty to the highest bidder. This may explain why it took so long for the delightful **Museo Antica Capua** to claw back some of its heritage. It opened in 1995.

In piazza Matteotti, the **Duomo** (Basilica di Santa Maria Maggiore; open 8-11.30am, 5-7pm daily) was founded in 432 on the site of first-century catacombs; it was heavily remodelled in the 17th and 18th centuries.

The **Anfiteatro** is across town. There was probably an arena here in Etruscan times, and there was certainly a gladiator school in 73 BC, when Spartacus and 30 other gladiators broke down its doors in a bid for freedom, sparking off the two-year Slave Revolt. The gladiators gained and trained 50,000 supporters, and conducted guerrilla warfare from hideouts on Vesuvius. Six thousand of them later decorated crosses along the Appian Way.

Successive emperors extended the amphitheatre until it was second only to Rome's Colosseum in size and crowd capacity. It featured heavily in the Empire's bread-and-circuses policy for whipping up political support and camouflaging social problems. Crowds (Cicero says 100,000 but experts would downsize that by 50 per cent) were issued tickets with gate numbers (there were around 80 entrances). Elevators brought gladiators, animals and scenery into the arena from the underground passages that you can walk through today. Part of the outer wall still stands. It originally consisted of four tiers of arches with Doric half-columns and busts of the gods set in the keystones. The marble facing was stripped and recycled long ago; the traces of mosaic and the curving passages are littered with fragments and ornaments.

Such an important city attracted the full gamut of religions. The ancient Persian cult of Mithras, known to the Greeks from the fifth century BC, was probably brought to the town by the gladiators, who frequently came from the east. The religion divided everything into good and evil; its all-male adherents (it was very popular among Roman soldiers) swore to combat evil. Membership was secret and there was an initiation ceremony, depicted on the walls of the **Mithraeum**; note that some of the

novices are blindfolded. The Tauroctonia, which forms the centre panel on the back wall, shows Mithras slaying a bull, the symbol of brute force and vitality. According to the Mithraic creation myth, all life forms sprang from the blood spilt when Mithras killed the bull, the only other living creature on a barren earth. The channel that runs from the altar collected the blood spilt in animal sacrifices.

On the Caserta–Santa Maria Capua Vetere road is one of the best wine and gourmet shops in Campania, **Enoteca La Botte** (Via Nazionale Appia 168-180, 0823 494 040, www.enotecalabotte.it, open 4-8pm Mon, 9am-1pm, 4.30-7.30pm Tue-Sat).

Anfiteatro
Piazza 1 Ottobre, Santa Maria Capua Vetere (0823 798 864). **Open** 9am-1hr before sunset. **Admission** *Amphitheatre, Mithraeum & museum* €2.50. **No credit cards**.

Duomo (San Michele Arcangelo)
Piazza Vescovado, Casertavecchia (0823 371 318). **Open** *May-Sept* 8.30am-8pm daily. *Oct-Apr* 9am-1pm, 3.30-6pm daily.

Mithraeum
Via Morelli, Santa Maria Capua Vetere. **Open** by request 9am-4pm Tue-Sun; ask at the amphitheatre or the museum.

Museo Antica Capua
Via Roberto D'Angiò 48, Santa Maria Capua Vetere (0823 844 206). **Open** 9am-7pm Tue-Sun. **Admission** *Amphitheatre, Mithraeum & museum* €2.50. **No credit cards**.

Where to eat

In Casertavecchia, **La Castellana** (via Torre 4, 0823 371 230, closed Thur Oct-Mar, average €20) has good home-made pasta (try the *tris*, a taster of three different types) and game.

Getting there

By car
For Casertavecchia take the Caserta Nord exit from the A1 motorway; 2km north-east of town on minor road (signposted). For Santa Maria Capua Vetere, leave the A1 motorway at Caserta Nord; SS7 (via Appia) from Caserta (4.5km/3 miles).

By train
For Santa Maria Capua Vetere, there's an infrequent service from Caserta.

By bus
See p277 **Caserta**.

Tourist information

See p277 **Caserta**.

Directory

Features

Directory

Getting Around

By air

Capodichino Airport

The Aereoporto Internazionale di Napoli (Capodichino) is located 8km (5 miles) or 5-10mins from Stazione Centrale rail station and 20mins from the ferry and hydrofoil ports.

GESAC

081 789 6259/www.gesac.it. **Open** 5.30am-midnight daily. Flight and transport information.

Alisud

081 789 6272/081 789 6642. **Open** 9am-8pm daily. **Credit** AmEx, DC, MC, V. Bookings for all airlines using Capodichino.

AIRLINES
Alitalia

Information 848 865 643/domestic flights 848 865 641/international flights 848 865 642/www.alitalia.it. **Open** *Booking service* 24hrs daily. **Credit** AmEx, DC, V.

British Airways

Bookings & information 199 712 266/www.britishairways.it. **Open** 8am-8pm Mon-Fri; 9am-5pm Sat. **Credit** (cards with Italian billing address only) AmEx, DC, MC, V.

Go

848 887766/www.go-fly.com. **Open** *Booking service* 8am-8pm Mon-Sat. **Credit** AmEx, DC, MC, V.

ON FROM THE AIRPORT

See also **Getting there** in **Around Naples** section.

To Naples centre

CLP (081 5311 706/www.clpbus. com) runs blue buses from outside the airport's Arrivals lounge to Stazione Centrale (piazza Garibaldi) and piazza Municipio (near the ferry port) approximately every 40mins, from around 6am to 11pm daily. **Tickets** €1.55.

Local **orange bus** number 3S runs from outside Arrivals to piazza Garibaldi and the ferry port, leaving every 5mins or so throughout the day

when landings are scheduled. Buy tickets (77¢) at any *tabacchi* (see *p291*) and stamp them on board.

A *taxi* from the airport to central Naples should cost €15-€20. There's a surcharge of €2.58 for airport runs; for other extras, *see p282*.

To Sorrento & around

Autolinee Curreri (081 801 5420) runs six buses daily from outside Arrivals. **Tickets** €5.20.

To the islands & Sorrento/Amalfi Coast

Hydrofoils (*aliscafi*) and ferries (*traghetti*) leave from Molo Beverello port (*see below*).

By bus

Most long-distance buses operate from piazza Garibaldi. SITA buses serving destinations around Naples operate from the main Naples port area, piazzale dell'Immacolatella.

By train

Some late-night long-distance rail services terminate at Stazione Campi Flegrei in the eastern suburbs. For rail information, *see p282*.

The www.campaniatrasporti.it website provides information on transport in and around Naples. For public transport in the city, *see also p54* **Public transport** and *p104* **Useful bus routes**.

By bus

The bus service in Naples is run by ANM (tollfree 800 639 525/081 763 2177/www.anm.it). **Open** *Phone information* 8am-6pm Mon-Fri.

There is no central bus station in the city. Many services operate from piazza Garibaldi, others from piazza Municipio or nearby in via Pisanelli.

By boat

Timetables for water transport around the Bay of Naples are published daily in *Il Mattino*. There are two ports in Naples.

Molo Beverello

Map p311 2C.
Ferry and hydrofoil services to the islands, Sorrento and the Amalfi Coast are run by:
Alilauro (081 551 3236/www. alilauro.it); **Caremar** (081 551 3882/ www.caremar.it); **Linee Lauro** (081 552 2838/www.lineelauro.it); **Navigazione Libera del Golfo (NLG)** (081 552 7209/www.navlib. it); and **SNAV** (081 761 2348/ www.snavali.com).

Ferry services to Sicily (daily), the Aeolian Islands (2-3 times weekly) and Sardinia (twice weekly) are run by **Tirrenia** (199 123 199/www. tirrenia.it). **SNAV** runs a hydrofoil service to Palermo (Apr-Oct daily).

Mergellina

Map p313 2C.
Hydrofoil services only to Capri, Ischia and Procida are run by **SNAV** and **Alilauro** (081 761 4909).

Pozzuoli

Car ferries also leave for Procida and Ischia from Pozzuoli, 12km (8 miles) north-west of Naples. **Traghetti Pozzuoli** (081 526 7736/www. traghettipozzuoli.it) and **Caremar** (081 551 3882/www.caremar.it).

Taxi del Mare

Via degli Aranci 180, Sorrento (tollfree 800 547 500/081 877 3600/ fax 081 877 3672/ www.taxidelmare.it). **Open** 24hrs daily. **Credit** AmEx, DC, MC, V. Ten-person water taxis anywhere around the Bay of Naples. Sample prices: Capri–Ischia (one way) €494; Capri–Positano–Capri €832.

By car & motorbike

EU visitors can drive on their home licences; an international licence is advisable for non-EU citizens. When driving, bear in mind the following rules, written and unwritten:
● The law requires you to wear a seat belt and to carry a hazard triangle in your car; motorcyclists and scooter-riders must wear helmets.
● Keep your driving licence, insurance documents, vehicle registration and photo-ID documents on you at all times; if you are stopped by the police, you may be fined if you can't produce them all on the spot.

● Flashing your lights means that you will **not** slow down/give way.
● Neapolitans often ignore red lights, so approach any junction with caution. If traffic lights flash amber, stop and give way to the right.
● Watch out for death-defying scooters and pedestrians; the latter fully expect you to stop if they step out in front of you.
● Be patient, be flexible, maintain your cool and stay calm at all times; be prepared for anything.

TRAFFIC INFORMATION

Phone 166 664 477 for 24hr traffic information with English-speaking operators (61¢ per min). For a less expensive service (Italian only) call 1518. Isoradio (103.3FM) also provides regular traffic updates (Italian only).

REASONS NOT TO DRIVE

There's nothing car-friendly about Naples and its surrounding area. Far from giving you the freedom to explore, motoring is more likely to give you a serious headache. Remember:
● Only vehicles with catalytic converters are allowed to circulate in the city between 8.30am and 6.30pm Mon, Wed and Fri. There's an Area Azzurra (Blue Zone) in the centre where only residents can circulate between 7.30am and 6.30pm Mon-Fri. On many Sundays (usually the first of the month) all vehicles are banned.
● In summer, traffic in and around Sorrento and on the Amalfi Coast is horrific, as tour buses wind their way along narrow coastal roads. Local day-trippers worsen the situation at weekends: if you must drive here, stick to weekdays.
● On the islands, roads are packed in the summer. You can't take cars to Capri; you're better off using public transport or walking on Procida. Car rental companies on Ischia charge better rates than on the mainland, but roads can be jammed and you cannot take the car off the island.
● Car theft is always a potential hazard, which you can minimise by taking precautions: park in authorised car parks; always use an anti-theft device on the car (a visible steering-wheel lock or pedal block can deter would-be thieves); do not leave bags or packages visible.

BREAKDOWN SERVICES

National motoring groups (Britain's AA or RAC and the AAA in the US) have reciprocal arrangements with the Automobile Club d'Italia (ACI), which offers breakdown assistance.
If you require extensive repairs, go to a manufacturer's official dealer. Dealers are listed in the Yellow Pages under *Auto*; specialists are

listed under *Gommista* (tyre repairs), *Marmitte* (exhaust repairs) and *Carrozzerie* (bodywork and windscreen repairs). The *English Yellow Pages* (*see p288*) lists garages where English is spoken.

ACI

Piazzale Tecchio 49D, Fuorigrotta (24hr emergency service 800 116 800/081 239 4511/www.aci.it). Metro Campi Flegrei/Cumana rail to Piazzale Tecchio/bus 180, 181, C2, C6, C7, C8, C9, C10, C15, CU. **Open** 8.40am-2.30pm, 3.30-5.30pm Mon-Fri; 8.40am-11.30am Sat. **No credit cards. Map** p314.

Touring Club Italia

Via C Battisti 11, Toledo (081 420 3485/fax 081 420 3477/www. touringclub.it). Bus 24, 149, C57, CS, E3, R1, R3, R4. **Open** 9am-7pm Mon-Fri; 9am-1pm Sat. **Credit** AmEx, DC, MC, V. **Map** p312 2A. Specialised bookshop for maps and guides, with a travel agency.

RENTALS

The minimum age for renting an economy car is 21; you must be 25 years old to rent a larger-cylinder car. Most rental companies require you to be covered for both theft and collision-damage: if they don't, you should. (And you should consider using a different hire-car firm.) If you're adventurous, a scooter is a great way to get around Ischia, the Sorrento area and the Amalfi Coast.

Avis

Airport (199 100 133/081 780 5790/fax 081 751 7544/ www.avisautonoleggio.it). **Open** 7.30am-11.30pm daily. **Credit** AmEx, DC, MC, V.
Branch: *Hotel Terminus, corso Lucci 203, Port & University (081 284 041).* **Open** 8.30am-7.30pm Mon-Fri; 8.30am-1pm, 4-6pm Sat; 9am-1pm Sun. **Map** p311 1B.

Europcar

Airport (tollfree 800 014 410/081 780 5643/www.europcar.it). **Open** 8am-10.20pm daily. **Credit** AmEx, DC, MC, V.

Hertz

Airport (081 780 2971). **Open** 8am-10.20pm daily. **Credit** AmEx, DC, MC, V.
Branch: *Stazione Centrale (199 112 211/081 206 228/www.hertz.it).* **Open** 8am-1pm, 2-7pm Mon-Fri; 8am-noon Sat. **Map** p310 2B.

Maggiore-Budget

Airport (848 867 067/081 780 3011/ fax 081 599 1233/www.maggiore. it). **Open** 7.30am-11.30pm daily. **Credit** AmEx, DC, MC, V.

Branch: *Stazione Centrale (081 287 858).* **Open** 8am-1pm, 3-7pm Mon-Fri; 8am-1.30pm Sat. **Map** p310 2B.

Thrifty

Airport (081 780 5702/fax 081 751 5013/www.italybycar.it). **Open** 8am-10pm Mon-Fri; 8am-8pm Sat, Sun. **Credit** AmEx, DC, MC, V.

PARKING

Blue lines on the road mean residents park free and visitors pay. The cost per hour varies from €1.02 to €1.55; pay at the pay-and-display ticket dispensers, or buy a scratch card or parking debit card from *tabacchi* (*see p291*) or *edicole* (newsstands).
Elsewhere, anything resembling a parking place is up for grabs, with some exceptions: watch out for signs saying *passo carrabile* (access at all times), *sosta vietata* (no parking) and disabled parking spaces (yellow lines). The sign *zona rimozione* (tow-away area) means no parking, and is valid for the length of the street, or until the next tow-away sign with a red line through it. If a street or square has no cars parked in it, you can assume it's a no-parking zone. Illegal parking attendants operate in many areas – they will 'look after' your car for about €1. The safest solution is to use a pay car park; there is a full list in the *Yellow Pages* under *autorimesse e parcheggi* or at www.radiotaxinapoli.it/garage.htm.

Via Brin Parking

Via B Brin, Port & University (081 763 2855). Bus 194, 195, C81, C82, C89, CS/tram 1, 29. **Open** 24hrs daily. **Rates** €1.02 for first 4hrs, 26¢ per successive hr; €15.46 for 70hrs; €25.82 for 100hrs. **No credit cards. Map** p311 1A.
A 850-car facility located between Stazione Centrale and the port (take

On foot

Naples is covered easily on foot. Neapolitan pedestrians don't, on the whole, bother with crossings, and will cross the road wherever and whenever they want. Cars (almost) invariably give them a wide berth. Watch how the locals do it – ensure approaching cars have enough space to slow down, and cross with conviction.

the Porto exit from the ring road or motorway). Shuttle buses for the ferry port at Molo Beverello leave every 10mins. You can leave a car here for free if you rent an electric car: €12.91 refundable deposit, €12.91 as a down-payment on car hire, at €1.55 per hour.

By helicopter

Cab.air

Airport (tel/fax 081 584 4355/ www.cabair.it). **Open** *Oct-Apr* 8.30am-6pm daily. *May-Sept* 8am-8pm daily. **Rates** Naples to Capri or Sorrento €826; Naples to Ischia €930. **Credit** AmEx, MC, V.

By taxi

Taxis in Naples

Authorised white taxis have the city's emblem on the front doors and rear licence plate, and a meter. Steer clear of any unauthorised 'taxi'.

As you set off, the meter should read €2.58. There's a €4.13 minimum charge per trip. Extra charges include: €1.55 on Sundays or holidays; €2.07 from 10pm to 7am; 52¢ per piece of luggage in the boot; 77¢ for a radio taxi call; and an additional €2.58 to or from the airport. For some of the more distant suburbs a supplement of €1.03 is added, while outside the city limits the amount on the meter is doubled for the return trip.

Taxis can be found at ranks around the city or 'cruising'.

Most Neapolitan taxi drivers fight hard to disprove their reputation for questionable standards of honesty. If, however, you suspect you are being ripped off, make a note of the driver's name and number from the photo ID in the cab. The more ostentatiously you do this, the more it's likely that the fare will drop to its proper level. Complaints can be lodged with the drivers' co-operative (the phone number of which is written outside the car) or with the police.

You can phone for a taxi at the numbers listed below. You'll be given a code-name (always a geographic location followed by a number) and a time, as in *Bahama 69, in tre minuti* ('Bahamas 69, arriving in three minutes'). The driver should put the meter on as you get into the taxi; a call supplement of 77¢ will be added. Taxis accept cash only.
Consortaxi 081 552 5252/ www.consortaxi.it.
Cotana 081 570 7070.
Free Taxi 081 551 5151.
Napoli 081 556 4444/ www.radiotaxinapoli.it.
Partenope 081 556 0202.

Taxis outside Naples

Many of Capri's taxis are vintage cars; Ischia has three-wheeled 'micro taxis'; Sorrento has horse-drawn carriages. There are fare structures, though they are not always respected by operators: be prepared to bargain. Some of the taxi companies listed above run fixed-rate one-way or return trips to Pompeii, Vesuvius, the Amalfi Coast, and the Campi Flegrei, among other places. Many of the drivers speak English, making the trip into a guided tour. Naples–Pompeii–Naples, including two hours to visit Pompeii, costs €72.30; Naples–Positano costs €93; Naples–Lago di Averno–Cuma–Naples costs €62.

By train

Main-line trains

All Italian stations now have the same phone number for information: 848 888 088; operates 7am-9pm daily. To talk to an operator – who may speak basic English – rather than coping with a recorded message in Italian, say 'no' very clearly after the initial recorded instructions. From 9pm to 7am there are automatic recordings of train schedules.

The website **www.trenitalia.com** gives complete schedule information (in English). Tickets can be booked through the website by credit card and picked up from machines in stations; in practice, it doesn't always work.

There are three main-line Ferrovie dello Stato-Trenitalia (FS, State Railways) stations in Naples, the main one being the Stazione Centrale in piazza Garibaldi. Most FS trains come and go from here, including the very fast (Eurostar, InterCity) and very slow (local trains). Below the street-level main station there are two lower levels. On the first lower level is the ticket counter for the Circumvesuviana line (*see below*). Piazza Garibaldi station is on the second level down; it is used by regional metro lines and long-distance services, some of which also stop at Naples' other big stations, Mergellina and Campi Flegrei.

Tickets for main-line train services can be bought at stations or travel agents with the Ferrovie dello Stato-Trenitalia (FS) logo. At main stations there are automatic ticket machines; these accept all major credit cards. Most trains are equipped for wheelchair access (*see also p284*), though it's best to check.

In the station, check that the ticket window you are queuing for is the right one: some sell ordinary tickets, Eurostar tickets and high-speed supplements (*supplementi rapidi*); some also do bookings; and some

only do bookings. There is a separate window for international trains. The staff in the information office at Stazione Centrale speak English.

Ticket prices are directly related to distance travelled. The slower trains (the *diretti*, *espressi*, *regionali* and *interregionali*) are much cheaper than in northern Europe, but a system of supplements means that the faster trains – InterCity (IC), EuroCity (EC), and Eurostar Italia (ES) – are closer to the European norm.

Seat bookings are obligatory (and free) on ES trains on Fridays and Sundays and all week at certain peak times of year. An R inside a square on train timetables indicates this; check when purchasing your ticket. Booking a seat on IC and internal EC routes costs only €3 and is well worth it, even when it is not obligatory, especially on Friday and Sunday evenings. If your ES, IC or EC train arrives more than 30mins late and you have a seat booking, you can claim a refund (at the booth marked *rimborsi*) of part of the cost of the ticket (30% of IC and EC, 50% of ES). Note that many ES and IC trains do not run on Sundays or public holidays.

You must stamp your ticket – and any supplement – in the yellow machines at the head of each platform before boarding the train. Failure to do this can result in a fine. Looking contrite and sounding foreign might persuade the ticket inspectors to let you off, but not necessarily. If you forget to stamp your ticket, find the inspector as soon as possible after boarding the train and have it clipped.

Local railways

Naples and its province is covered by a complex system of underground and overground railways (information tollfree 800 568 866).

Metro Linea 1 runs from piazza Dante to piazza Vanvitelli and the hospital zone in the north-eastern suburbs (6.30am-10.58pm).

Metro Linea 2 (the underground service of the state railway) operates from piazza Garibaldi (beneath Stazione Centrale), skirting the Centro storico, to the Mergellina main-line station and the Campi Flegrei (5.38am-11.52pm).

The **Ferrovia Cumana** (081 551 3328/www.sepsa.it) runs services from piazza Montesanto to Campi Flegrei (5.21am-9.41pm). Note that the station at Cuma is closed; get out at Fusaro station and take the bus.

The **Ferrovia Circumvesuviana** (081 772 2444/www.vesuviana.it) leaves from its own terminus in corso Garibaldi, south of (and accessible from) Stazione Centrale. Trains run south-east to Pompeii, Herculaneum and Sorrento (dawn-10.30pm).

Resources A-Z

Accommodation

Accommodation in the Naples region includes some of the world's finest hotels and some of the worst. Hotels are classified on a star system (one star for simple *pensioni*, five for top-end luxury) – but stars do not always reflect what you'll really find.

Prices are fixed annually and should be posted in the reception and behind each bedroom door. They may vary from high to low season; they may or may not include breakfast; they may vary according to whether or not there's a sea view and/or balcony. In some hotels (especially on the islands and other package-tour destinations) you may be required to pay for half-board (breakfast and one meal). It is always worth asking the receptionist exactly how much your stay is going to cost. In very cheap accommodation, you will avoid unpleasant (and sometimes unsanitary) surprises if you ask to see the room before checking in.

SEASONS

High season on the islands and coastal areas around Naples begins at Easter and continues well into September. Many hotels, especially in Ischia, Capri, Sorrento and the Amalfi Coast, will close from October to Easter, opening, if at all, for a few days over Christmas. In 2002 the regional council announced initiatives to persuade these hotels to remain open year-round. Naples itself is a year-round city.

EXTRAS

In areas such as the Amalfi Coast and the heart of Naples, where parking spaces are like gold dust, expect to pay extra for parking. Most hotels will put a cot or fold-up bed in your room for children, charging you anything up to 35% extra. A double room used as a single should be charged at the top rate for a single room, or a maximum of 70% of the usual double rate for that room.

Hotel booking

The **Associazione Albergatori** (hoteliers' association) has listings for many of the area's hotels on its website www.campaniahotels.com. For hotels in Naples see *p38*; for hotels outside Naples see listings in **Around Naples** chapters.

The following agency will arrange accommodation anywhere in Naples or the surrounding region:

Prom Hotels

Airport (081 789 6716/fax 081 789 6717/www.girandonapoli.it). **Open** 9am-11.30pm daily. **Credit** AmEx, DC, MC, V.
Branch: *Stazione Centrale (081 266 908/fax 081 264 818). Metro Piazza Garibaldi/bus 14, 15, 110, 125, 135, 191, 192, 194, 195, C30, C40, C55, C58, CD, CS, OF, R2/tram 1, 29.* **Open** 9am-7.30pm Mon-Sat; 9am-2pm Sun. **Map** p310 2B.

Age restrictions

Cigarettes and alcohol cannot legally be sold to under-16s. Beer and wine can be consumed at bars from the age of 16, spirits from 18. Anyone aged 14 or over can ride a moped or scooter of 50cc; no licence is required. You must be over 18 to drive and over 21 to hire a car.

Business

The commercial sector of your embassy (*see p284*) may be able to provide you with some important information and contacts, as well as trade publications, marketing reports and databases. Both the UK and US consulates have lists (not necessarily up to date) of lawyers, translators and interpreters.

The **Unione Industriale** (piazza dei Martiri 58, Chiaia; 081 583 6111/ www.unindustria.na.it; open 8.30am-12.45pm, 3.30-7pm Mon-Fri) oversees an increasing number of Naples' industries. The active **British Chamber of Commerce** has its headquarters at St Peter's School of English (Riviera di Chiaia 124, Chiaia; 081 683 468; open 9am-7pm Mon-Fri; closed Aug). It provides support services for British businesses, as well as trading, legal and taxation information.

Conferences

Naples and the surrounding area abounds with potential conference sites. Most of the major hotels can cater for events of all sizes. If you don't wish to handle the details yourself, **GP Relazioni Pubbliche** (via San Pasquale a Chiaia 55, Chiaia; 081 401 201/081 412 835/ fax 081 404 036/gpcongress@napoli. com) will smooth the way for you.

Couriers

Reliable couriers include **DHL** (199 199 345/www.dhl.it); **Federal**

Express (toll-free 800 123 800/ www.fedex.com); **Freccia Azzurra** (081 552 1520/www.frecciaazzurra.it); **Tartaruga Service** (081 202 027/ www.paginegialle.it/tartaruga service); **TNT** (toll-free 800 803 868/ www.tntitaly.it); and **UPS** (toll-free 800 877 877/www.ups.com).

Mail Boxes, etc

Via Bracco 57/59, Port & University (081 580 0256). Bus 24, 149, C11, C25, C57, C82, CS, E3, R1, R2, R3, R4/tram 1, 29. **Open** 9.30am-6.30pm Mon-Fri; 10am-1pm Sat. Closed 1wk Aug. **Map** p313 1A.
This is a one-stop centre for local couriers, photocopies and postbox. Fax, packing and shipping, UPS and Western Union services are also offered.

Interpreters

Outfits include: **AIT Coop** (via Depretis 88, Port & University; 081 551 3507/aittrad@tin.it) and **GIC'90** (via Monte di Dio 66, Royal; tel/fax 081 764 7427/www.gic90.com).

Customs

EU citizens do not have to declare goods brought into or out of Italy for their personal use, as long as they arrive from another EU country. For non-EU citizens, the following limits apply:
● 200 cigarettes or 100 small cigars or 50 cigars or 250g of tobacco.
● 1l of spirits (over 22% alcohol) or 2l of fortified wine (under 22% alcohol); 50g perfume.
There are no restrictions on the import of cameras, watches or electrical goods for personal use. Visitors are allowed to carry up to €10,330 in cash.

Disabled travellers

You won't see many people in wheelchairs around Naples, and those you do see are nearly always accompanied. Narrow streets make life difficult for those who can't flatten themselves against a wall to let passing vehicles by. Picturesque cobblestones turn even wheelchairs with excellent suspension into bone-rattlers. Where they exist, wheelchair/pram ramps from street to pavement are likely to be blocked by a parked car or motorbike.

Once off the streets, you're faced with the problems of old buildings with narrow corridors, lifts that (if there at all) are too small for a

Directory

wheelchair, and toilets at the top or bottom of impossibly steep stairs. However, things are getting better. Lifts, ramps and special toilets are being installed in museums, restaurants, stations and public offices, and although willingness has not always been matched by careful thinking (you may be expected to levitate up a couple of steps to reach that brand-new toilet or lift), these days you're more likely to be treated like a human being rather than some noble victim of fate.

Surprisingly, Capri is one of the most wheelchair-friendly places around. A craggy island of steep cliffs and picturesque stairways it may be, but the town of Capri is car-free, and the only way to get supplies, luggage and often people up and down is by small electric cart. The main paths may be steep slopes, but they have no stairs. Getting up to the town from the port will, however, involve help up the few steps to the funicular. Capri buses are decidedly not disabled-friendly.

Information

Comune di Napoli, Uffico H

Galleria Principe di Napoli 33, Toledo & Sanità (081 544 0970/081 544 3761/www.comune.napoli.it). Metro Piazza Cavour, Dante or Museo/ bus 24, 47, 110, 135, 137, 149, CD, CS, E1, R1, R4. **Open** 9am-1pm Mon-Fri. **Map** p312 1A.

Naples city council's disabled office provides limited information on the area's disabled-friendly hotels, restaurants, sites and landmarks. In 2000 it created the helpful site www.pp2000.it, although it has not been updated since then.

Italia Per Tutti

www.italiapertutti.it.
A useful website, with an English section, that selects accessible sites throughout Italy based on your needs.

SuperAbile

Toll-free 800 810 810/ www.superabile.it. **Open** *Phone enquiries* 9am-7pm Mon-Sat.
Provides information on hotels, restaurants and job opportunities for the disabled throughout Italy.

Transport

By boat

Caremar *(081 551 3882/ www.caremar.it)* runs several wheelchair-friendly ferries between Naples and Ischia, and between Sorrento and Capri, and occasionally on various other routes. If you

book ahead, the other hydrofoil/ ferry lines will have staff available to help you board.

By bus

Naples has some city buses – C12, C16, C18, C25, R1, R2, R3, R4 – equipped with extra-large central doors and an access ramp; inside, there's a space where a wheelchair can be secured. These buses are identifiable by the wheelchair symbol on the front of the bus and beside the bus number at bus stops. They serve the downtown area, especially between the Museo Nazionale Archeologico, piazza Trieste e Trento and the ports. Outside the city, the situation varies from town to town; contact local tourist offices or bus companies for information.

By train

For rail travel, the Stazione Centrale has a *Direzione Servizi alla Clientela* (customer services office, near platform five; also accessible from outside the station by car). This provides information for disabled travellers (081 567 2991; open 7am-9pm daily), takes reservations (book at least 24 hours prior to departure) and provides wheelchair assistance and access to most, but not all, trains. It will also arrange for staff to meet incoming wheelchair-bound passengers. Departing passengers must be at the *Direzione Servizi alla Clientela* at least 45mins before the train departs.

Hotels & restaurants

More upmarket hotels in well-established tourist resorts cater best to special needs. Cheaper hotels and *pensioni*, often on the upper floors of old *palazzi*, can be a problem. If you have special needs, make them known when you book. Ask specific, detailed questions about the facilities; Neapolitans have a tendency to look on the bright side of life, ignoring the 'minor' barriers that could make your stay a misery.

Local by-laws now require restaurants to have disabled access and toilets, though in practice few have made the necessary alterations. However, if you phone ahead and ask for an appropriate table, most will do their best to help. In summer, the range of restaurants with outdoor or pavement tables makes life easier.

Wheelchair hire

Ortopedia Morelli

Via Costantinopoli 28/29, Toledo (081 444 281/www.ortopedia morelli.inwind.it). **Open** 9am-1.30pm,

4-7.30pm Mon-Fri; 9am-1.30pm Sat. **No credit cards**.
Wheelchairs cost €2.50 a day and can be delivered free of charge all over the Naples area. Book at least one week in advance.

Sanitas Rosy

Vico Secondo Fuoro 9, Sorrento (081 807 3858/333 352 2046). **Open** 9am-1pm, 5-9pm Mon-Sat; 10am-1pm Sun. **No credit cards**.
This orthopaedic shop rents wheelchairs (€6 per day), and sells orthopaedic equipment.

Drugs

It is an offence to buy or sell drugs, or even to give them away. If you are caught in possession of illegal drugs of any type, you will be taken before a magistrate. If you can convince him or her that the tiny quantity you were carrying was for purely personal use, then you will be let off with a fine or ordered to leave the country. Habitual offenders will be offered rehab. Anything more than a tiny amount will push you into the criminal category; couriering or dealing can land you in prison for up to 20 years. Sniffer dogs are a fixture at most ports of entry into Italy; customs police will take a dim view of visitors entering with even the smallest quantities of narcotics, and are likely to allow them to stay no longer than it takes a magistrate to expel them from the country.

Electricity

Most wiring systems in the Naples area work on 220V. Two-pin adapter plugs can be bought at electrical shops (look for *Casalinghi* or *Elettricità*).

Embassies & consulates

All countries with official missions to Italy have embassies in Rome; Naples has many consulates, which will provide essential documents (such as birth and death certificates) and emergency help (such as replacement passports). A full list of consulates and embassies can be found in the phone book under *Ambasciati/consolati*.

Consulates in Naples

Britain

Via dei Mille 40, Chiaia (081 423 8911/fax 081 422 434/ www.ukinitalia.it). Metro Piazza

Emergencies

Thefts or losses should be reported immediately at the nearest police station, either the Polizia di Stato or the Carabinieri. Report the loss of your passport to your consulate or embassy (*see p284*). Lost or stolen credit cards or travellers' cheques should be immediately reported to your credit card company (*see p289*).

National emergency numbers (toll-free)

Polizia di Stato (police) **113**
Carabinieri (police) **112**
Fire brigade **115**

Ambulance **118**
Car breakdown (Automobile Club d'Italia) **803 116**
Coastguard **1530**
Guardia forestale (forest rangers and mountain rescue) **1515**

Domestic emergencies

Phone these emergency lines to report a malfunction in any of the main services.
Electricity (ENEL) toll-free **800 900 800**
Gas toll-free (from Naples only) **800 553 000**
Telephone (Telecom Italia) **188**
Water (ARIN) **081 451 317/081 451 557**

Amedeo/bus C24, C25, C27, C28.
Open 9am-12.30pm, 2-4pm Mon-Fri.
Map p313 1B.

Canada

Via G Carducci 29, Chiaia (081 401 338/fax 081 410 4210). Metro Piazza Amedeo/bus C24, C25, C27, C28. **Open** 9am-1pm Mon-Fri. **Map** p313 1B.
After 1pm phone 081 407 825.

United States

Piazza della Repubblica, Mergellina (081 583 8111/fax 081 761 1869/www.usembassy.it). Metro Mergellina/bus 140, C12, C18, C19, C24, C25, C28, R3. **Open** 8am-1pm, 2-5pm Mon-Fri. **Map** p313 2C.

Embassies in Rome

Australia 06 852 721.
Ireland 06 697 9121.
New Zealand 06 441 7171.
South Africa 06 852 541.

Gay & lesbian

Southern Italians, on average, are slow to accept novelty – be it body-piercing, dark-skinned immigrants or same-sex couples. Many have a deep-rooted attachment to the 'norm', having difficulty in imagining that anything outside it can be as valid as their own way of doing things. That said, what at first might seem like intolerance towards 'exceptions' will, in most cases, soon reveal itself to be no more than mild surprise at anyone's wishing to do things differently. Visiting gays are unlikely to meet hostility from anyone but members of the unpleasant conservative fringe that exists everywhere. For more info on gay and lesbian life in Naples, *see p153*.

EnolaGay

Vico San Domenico Maggiore 12, Centro storico (081 211 0824/ fax 081 211 0840/www.enolagay tour.com). Metro Dante/bus 24, 137, 149, C57, C86, CD, CS, E1, R1. **Open** 9am-1pm, 4-6.30pm Mon-Fri; by appointment Sat. **Map** p311 1C. This specialised travel agency organises tours of Naples, as well as worldwide jaunts.

Health

Emergency health care is available for all travellers through the Italian national health system and, by law, hospital casualty departments must treat all emergency cases for free. However, to avoid hassle if you're only visiting for a short time, it's worth taking out private health insurance (*see p286*).

If you require regular medication during your stay in Italy, bring adequate supplies of your drugs with you. Also, ask your GP for the chemical rather than the brand name of your medicines; they may only be available in Italy under a different name.

Both the UK and US consulates (*see p284*) have lists of English-speaking doctors.

Accident & emergency

The following hospitals provide 24hr casualty (*pronto soccorso*) services:

Naples

Cardarelli: *Via Cardarelli 9, Vomero Alto (081 747 1111). Metro Colli Aminei/bus 135, C38, C39, C40, C41, C43, C44, C76, OF, R4.*

Southern Italy's largest hospital, with an ever-busy casualty department. Not luxurious, but staff get the job done.
Santobono: *Via M Fiore 6, Vomero (081 220 5797). Metro Piazza Medaglie D'Oro/bus 181, C34, C39, C41, C44, R1.* **Map** p312 2B. The city's main paediatric hospital, serving all emergencies from new-borns to puberty.

Capri

Ospedale Capilupi: *Via Provinciale Anacapri, Due Golfi (081 838 1205/081 838 1111).*

Ischia

Ospedale Anna Rizzoli: *Via Fundara, Lacco Ameno (081 507 9267/081 507 9111).*

Sorrento

Ospedale Civico: *Corso Italia (081 533 1111).*

Guardie mediche

Public emergency doctors operate 8pm-8am daily, and from 10am on Saturday to 8am on Monday, giving medical advice over the phone or ordering ambulances if necessary.
Central Naples 081 254 2424.
Naples from Posillipo to Chiaia 081 761 3466.
Ischia 081 983 292.
Pozzuoli 081 526 6954.
Vomero 081 578 0760.

Contraception & abortion

Condoms are on sale near the check-out in supermarkets or over the counter at chemists. They're expensive. The contraceptive pill is

Directory

freely available on prescription at any pharmacy. Abortions are legal only if performed in public hospitals; health or financial hardship criteria need to be met to qualify.

Dentists

In the case of serious dental emergencies, make for the hospital casualty departments (*see p285*). For non-emergency treatment, the *English Yellow Pages* (*see p288*) has a list of English-speaking dentists in the Naples area.

Health hazards

Do not underestimate the strength of the sun in southern Italy; there's little shade at archeological sites such as Pompeii and Paestum, and sea breezes on beaches on the coast can hide the damage that is being done. Bring, and use, a hat, strong sunscreen and lots of common sense. Carry water with you at all times to stave off dehydration.

In spring, the Mediterranean flora explodes, especially parietaria, a common weed that grows everywhere in the Naples region. This, and the year-round pollution that besets the city itself, can make life difficult for those who suffer from allergies or asthma.

Helplines

AIDS Helpline
Toll-free 800 019 254. **Open** 24hrs Mon-Sat; 8am-2pm Sun. Information on tests and prevention advice. Italian only.

Alcoholics Anonymous
Via San Pasquale a Chiaia 15, Chiaia (0823 765 837/335 210 914/ www.naplesaa.8k.com). Metro Piazza Amedeo/bus 140, C12, C18, C19, C24, C25, C27, C28, R3. **Sessions** 3.30-4.30pm Sat. **Map** p313 1B. An English-speaking support group meets at the Anglican/Episcopal Christ Church.

Drogatel
840 002 244. **Open** 9am-8pm daily. A government-run drug helpline. Italian only.

Salvation Army
Tel/fax 081 281 202. **Open** 9am-5pm daily.

Hospitals

Southern Italian hospitals or clinics may not be as pristine as you are used to, and not everyone will speak

English. But if conditions and non-medical staff sometimes leave something to be desired, you are likely to find top-rate doctors. As a general rule, a public hospital will provide care and treatment that is as good as, or better than, any costly private establishment.

Pharmacies

Pharmacies (*farmacia*, identified by a large red or green cross) will give informal medical advice for simple ailments, and will make up prescriptions from a doctor. Over-the-counter drugs such as aspirin are more expensive in Italy than in the UK or US.

Chemists' standard opening hours are 8.30am-1pm, 4-8pm Mon-Fri; 8.30am-1pm Sat. During closing times, a duty rota system is operated. A list by the door of any pharmacy, or in the local papers, indicates the nearest ones that are open outside normal hours. In some duty pharmacies there may be a surcharge of €2.58 per client (but not per item) when the main shop is shut and only the special-duty counter is open – which is usually between midnight and 8.30am.

Most pharmacies sell homeopathic and veterinary medicines, as well as products and equipment for babies and the elderly. All will check your height/weight/blood pressure.

For pharmacies in the city of Naples, *see p142*.

ID

You are required by law to carry photo ID at all times. However, you will only be asked to show it on rare occasions, such as cashing traveller's cheques. Hotels will ask for photo ID when you check in and may wish to keep it until you check out; you are, however, quite entitled to ask for your document back at any time, and should do so if that is the only photo ID you have.

Insurance

EU nationals are entitled to medical care in Italy, provided they have an E111 form. Using an E111 involves having to deal with the intricacies of the Italian health bureaucracy, and for short-term visitors it's better to take out health cover under private travel insurance. Non-EU citizens should take out private medical insurance before leaving home.

Note that emergencies are treated free in *pronto soccorso* – casualty – departments of public hospitals; *see p285*.

Visitors should also take out adequate property insurance. If you rent a vehicle, motorcycle or moped, make sure you pay the extra charge for full insurance cover, and sign the collision damage waiver when hiring a car.

Internet & email

Italian providers offering free internet access include **Caltanet** (www.caltanet.it), **Libero** (www.libero.it), **Tiscali** (www.tiscalinet.it), **Kataweb** (www.kataweb.com) and **Fastweb** (www.fastweb.it).

There's a growing number of internet points in Naples (three are listed below). Most small towns in the provinces and on the islands will have, at best, a dedicated internet centre or, at worst, a bar with a computer. Ask in any computer store (listed in the Yellow Pages under *Personal computers e informatica*) for the nearest.

Most Italian phone lines now have sockets for RJ11 jacks. Older lines will have sockets for large three-pin plugs. If you're lucky, you'll find there's a removable RJ11 going into the old three-pin model. If not, you may have to scour supermarkets, phone and electricity shops for an adaptor.

Clic Net
Via Toledo 393, Toledo (081 552 9370/www.clicnet.it). Metro Montesanto/bus CS, E2, R1, R4. **Open** 9.30am-9.30pm Mon-Sat. **Rates** €3 for 1hr; €5 for 2hrs; €7 for 3hrs; €25 for 15hrs. **No credit cards. Map** p312 2A.

Internet Bar
Piazza Bellini, Centro storico (081 295 237/www.internetbarnapoli.it). Metro Dante or Museo/bus 24, 137, 149, C57, C86, CD, CS, E1, R1. **Open** 9am-2am Mon-Sat; 8pm-2am Sun. **Rates** €2.50 per hr. **No credit cards. Map** p311 1C.

Multimedia Napoli
Via Sapienza 43, Centro storico (081 298 412/www.viasapienza43.com). Metro Museo/bus 24, 47, 110, 135, 137, 149, C57, C86, CD, CS, E1, R1. **Open** 9.30am-9.30pm daily. **Rates** €1.55 per hr. **No credit cards. Map** p311 1C.

Left luggage

The left luggage office at Naples' **Stazione Centrale** (081 567 2181) is open 8am-8pm daily for leaving luggage, which can be collected at any time; €3.87 per item for 24 hours. There is no service at Mergellina or Campi Flegrei stations.

At **Ischia Porto**, the left luggage office (081 982 061) is at the *Centro servizi turistici* by the ferry port; it is open 9am-9pm daily in Apr-Sept, 9am-1pm, 4-8pm daily in Oct, Jan-Mar and is closed Nov, Dec. It charges €2.58 per item.

In **Capri** the left luggage office (081 837 0700) is operated by the Caremar ferry company, and is located at the port in Marina Grande. It's open 6am-8pm daily in the summer, 6-11am, 1-6.30pm in winter, and costs €1.55 per item.

In **Sorrento**, the tourist office (*see p232*) may watch your bag during opening hours.

There is no left luggage office at Naples' **Capodichino** airport.

Legal advice

If you're in need of legal advice, your first stop should always be your consulate or embassy (*see p284*).

Libraries

If you intend to use Naples' libraries for research, be prepared for red tape, restricted hours and patchy organisation. All the libraries listed below are open to the public. Other specialist libraries can be found in the phone book under *Biblioteche*.

Archivio di Stato

Piazzetta del Grande Archivio 5, University (081 563 8111/ www.archivi.beniculturali.it/ASNA). Bus C55, C58, CD, CS, E1, R2. **Open** 8am-6.45pm Mon-Fri; 8am-1.30pm Sat. Closed 2wks Aug. **Map** p311 1C.
Located in a former Benedictine monastery with fourth- and fifth-century frescos, the Archivio houses those state archives not destroyed in 1943 by retreating German forces, as well as some new donations such as documents from the Bourbon era. Accessible for consultation to all aged over 18 with ID.

Biblioteca Caprense Ignazio Cerio

Piazzetta Cerio 8, Capri (081 837 6681/www.centrocaprense.it). **Open** 4.30-8pm Tue, Thur, Fri; 9.30am-1pm Wed, Sat.
Contains anything written on or about Capri, with many first editions. No ID needed. Reference only.

Biblioteca Nazionale

Palazzo Reale, piazza del Plebiscito, Royal (081 781 9111/www.bnn online.it/www.sbn.it). Bus 110, 140, C22, C25, E3, R2, R3. **Open** 8.30am-7.30pm Mon-Fri; 8.30am-1.30pm Sat. Closed 2wks Aug. **Map** p313 1A.

The National Library contains possibly the largest collection anywhere of works on southern Italian history, as well as many other collections. These include the Officina dei Papiri Ercolanese, with papyruses dating back to the ninth century BC, and the JFK American section, a lending library containing mostly American literature (both North and South) as well as many reference books. It also organises seminars and reading groups. Library users and borrowers must be 16 or over and have valid ID.

Biblioteca San Francesco

Via San Francesco 13, Ravello (089 857 727). **Open** 9am-1pm, 4-6pm Mon, Wed, Fri; outside of these times, knock on the convent door at via San Francesco 9.
A vast, eclectic collection of books in myriad languages, including the library left by long-term Capri resident Gracie Fields.

Biblioteca Universitaria

Via Paladino 39, University (081 551 7025/www.bun.unina.it). Metro Dante or Museo/bus 24, 137, 149, C57, C86, CD, CS, E1, R1. **Open** Sept-July 8am-6.45pm Mon-Fri; 9am-1.45pm Sat. Aug 8am-1.45pm Mon-Sat. **Map** p311 1C.
The university library is open to anyone with valid ID. There's an international database exchange facility too.

British Council Library

Via Morghen 31, Vomero (081 558 5817/www.britishcouncil.it). Funicular Montesanto to via Morghen/bus C28, C31, C32, C36, E4, V1. **Open** Sept-July 11.30am-1pm, 3-7.30pm Mon-Fri; 10am-2pm Sat. Closed Aug, Sat July. **Map** p312 2B.
Mostly multimedia with some reference books. There's a video club for members; annual membership costs €104.

Istituto Universitario Orientale

Palazzo Giusso, piazza San Giovanni Maggiore, University (081 690 9916/www.iuo.it). Bus CD, CS, C25, C55, C58, E1, R1, R2, R4. **Open** 9am-5pm Mon-Thur; 9am-1.30pm Fri. Closed 3wks Aug. **Map** p311 1C.
A decent English-language section focuses on North American literature; there are also works on and in Chinese, Japanese, Arabic, Finnish, Bulgarian and other languages. Anyone can consult; only registered students can borrow.

Lost property

If you lose anything valuable – or suspect it has been stolen – go immediately to the nearest police station (*see p291* **Safety & security** and *p285* **Emergencies**) and make a *denuncia* (statement).

If you leave anything on a train, go to the *ufficio oggetti rivenuti* (081 567 4700) at desk 13 of the ticket office at Stazione Centrale. (As this guide was going to press, plans were afoot to move the office.) If you leave anything on municipal transport in Naples, go to the *capolinea* (terminus) of the route you were travelling and ask there. Failing that, try phoning the very helpful helpline (800 639 525 from Naples only/081 763 2177). For items left on SITA buses, call 081 552 2176.

The lost property office at Capodichino Airport is open 7am-11pm daily (information 081 789 6237/081 789 6765).

Maps

Various basic maps for Naples and surrounding areas are available free from hotels, and from city or local tourist offices. Tourist office maps vary from excellent (Sorrento, Massa Lubrense) to hardly worth having (Ischia). Newsstands and *tabacchi* near stations, ports or tourist sites will sell a better-quality map. Detailed transport maps for Naples are sometimes available at funicular and train stations.

For serious hikers, green **Touring Club Italia** (TCI) maps are reliable; **Kompass** 1:15,000 maps are good for the islands; and the **Club Alpino Italiano** (CAI) 1:30,000 map of the Monti Lattari is a must for exploring the Amalfi Coast and area above Sorrento on foot.

Media

Italian newspapers can be a frustrating read. Stories tend to be long and indigestible, and very little background is provided. On the plus side, they are delightfully unsnobbish and happily blend serious news with well-written, often surreal, crime and human-interest stories.

Though most Italian papers look like national affairs, the printed press is traditionally local or regional. Naples' major daily is *Il Mattino*; the Rome-based *La Repubblica* and Milan's *Corriere della Sera* have Neapolitan sections. Sports coverage in the dailies is generally extensive, but if you're not sated try the sports rags *Corriere dello Sport*, *La Gazzetta dello Sport* and *Tuttosport*.

Directory

Corriere della Sera

www.corriere.it.
To the centre of centre-left, this solid, serious but often dull Milan-based daily is good on crime and foreign news. Its Neapolitan insert, 'Corriere del Mezzogiorno', is worth reading, with good local entertainment listings.

Il Manifesto

www.ilmanifesto.it.
A reminder that, although the Berlin Wall is a distant memory, there is still some corner of Rome where hearts beat Red.

Il Mattino

www.ilmattino.it
The epitome of moderation, *Il Mattino* is, politically, firmly seated on the fence. National news is thoroughly covered, but there's only superficial coverage of international affairs. Most of what it reports could be overheard (with more dramatic flair) eavesdropping on bus stop or café conversations.

La Repubblica

www.repubblica.it
The centre-ish, left-ish *La Repubblica* is good on the Mafia and the Vatican, and comes up with the occasional major scoop on its business pages. It contains a fairly exhaustive Naples section.

La Stampa

www.lastampa.it
Part of the empire of Turin's Agnelli family (Fiat is another), *La Stampa* has good (though, inevitably, pro-Agnelli) business reporting.

Foreign press

Foreign newspapers and magazines aren't always available at newsstands in Naples, though the situation is improving. Editions may, however, take up to two days to arrive at the kiosks. You can find British broadsheets, tabloids and magazines, as well as the **Herald Tribune**, which includes the four-page supplement 'Italy Daily', at kiosks in the Stazione Centrale in piazza Garibaldi, in piazza Municipio facing the port, and in via Calabritto off piazza dei Martiri.

British dailies are generally available on the day of issue in major tourist destinations during high season.

Magazines

With the naked female form blazoned across their covers most weeks, Italy's serious news magazines are not always distinguishable from the soft porn among which they are lodged on newsstands. But **Panorama** and **Espresso** provide a high-standard round-up of the week's news. For tabloid-style scandal, try **Gente**, **Oggi** or the execrable **Novella 2000** and **Cronaca Vera**. The biggest-selling magazine of all is **Famiglia Cristiana** – everything a Christian family would want to know about current affairs and much, much more.

Local, listings & small ads

Bric-a-Brac, Fiera Città

Bric-a-Brac (www.bricabrac.it) is a thrice-weekly rag (Mon, Wed, Fri) packed with miscellaneous items for sale. It's a great source of information for flat hunters and buyers. Fiera Città is similar, but issued on Mon and Thur.

English Yellow Pages

www.intoitaly.it.
The handy EYP directory lists English-speaking professionals, services, organisations and businesses in major cities in Italy. It is aimed at foreign residents but is also useful to tourists, and the information is updated annually. Can be consulted at consulates and hotels, or purchased at major bookstores for €8.

Leggo, City

Published Mon-Fri, these informative newspapers are distributed free in metro and train stations throughout the city.

Il Mattone, Quattro Mura

www.ilmattoneonline.it.
Both these titles deal exclusively with property, for sale or for rent, and are issued on Sat.

Le Pagine dell'Ozio

www.gruppoelianto.it.
A monthly guide to what's going on in the city, with day-by-day listings for bars, cinemas, theatres and exhibitions, with a section in English.

Panorama

www.nsa.naples.navy.mil/panorama/panorama.htm.
This 16-page newspaper, published each Fri, gives a fascinating insight into US military life. An authorised publication of the US Naval Support Activity, intended for US service families based in and around Naples, it has engrossing stories on military activities (nothing secret) and a classified section advertising anything from Turkish carpets to babysitters. Pick up a copy from shops near the Agnano navy base or the Capodichino base near the international airport.

Qui Napoli

Issued by the Naples Tourist Board, this monthly bilingual booklet is a dry read, but is a mine of useful facts – from underground tours to ferry timetables. Available free from tourist offices (*see p293*).

Television

Italy has six major networks: three owned by the state broadcaster **RAI** (www.rai.it) and three (www.mediasetonline.com) belonging to Prime Minister Silvio Berlusconi. When the soaps, interminable game shows or political chat shows have bored you, there's any number of dreadful local stations to provide hours of channel-zapping fun.

The standard of television news and current affairs programmes varies from channel to channel; all, however, offer a breadth of international coverage that makes British equivalents look remarkably like parish magazines. For local news, catch the regional programme after the 7pm and 10.30pm news broadcasts on RAI-3.

La 7 (www.la7.virgilio.it) broadcasts *Fox News* from 1.20am-5.25am. **MTV** (www.mtv.it) and **Viva** (www.vivaretea.it) pump out 24hr music videos.

Radio

There are three state-owned stations: **RAI-1** (89.3 and 94.1 MHz FM stereo and 1332 KHz AM); **RAI-2** (91.3 and 96.1 MHz FM stereo and 846 KHz AM); and **RAI-3** (93.3 and 98.1 MHz FM). They play classical and light music, with news bulletins once an hour.

AFN

www.afneurope.army.mil.
If southern Italy gets too much for you, the American Forces Network radio programme will shoot you straight into Smalltown, USA. On 106.0FM (Z-FM) there are locally produced programmes and news, and music ranging from American contemporary and pop to country. On 107.0FM (Power Network) there are talk shows and National Public Radio news bulletins.

Radio Capital

www.capital.it.
On 88.05 and 104.75 MHz FM. Classics and hits from the UK and US with lots of home-grown goodies thrown in. Based in Rome.

Radio Club 91

www.radioclub91.it.
On 90.75 and 93.0 MHz FM.
Broadcasting to the Naples area since
1976, playing chart hits from home
and abroad, with regular traffic
updates. Club 91 also sponsors
events and concerts in the city.

Radio Kiss Kiss Napoli

www.kisskissnapoli.it.
On 99.25 and 103.0 MHz FM. This
music station broadcasts Naples'
football games live, and can be
heard from many windows, buses
and bars on a Sunday afternoon
throughout the season.

Money

The lira ceased to be legal tender
in February 2002, giving way to
the euro. The changeover was
chaotic in Naples, with locals
continuing to spend lira until the
end. They still think in lira, but have
also embraced the new currency;
Italy's first counterfeit euro coin
was found in Naples just five weeks
after the euro's introduction. A euro
is worth L1,936.27. Euro coins and
notes from any Eurozone country
are legal tender in Italy.

By law, you must be given a till
receipt (*scontrino fiscale*) for any
transaction. Some places may try to
avoid giving you a receipt for tax
reasons, in which case it is your right
(and according to the *guardia di
finanza*, also your duty) to ask for
one. In the unlikely event of your
being accosted by a police officer as
you exit a shop, you, as well as the
shopkeeper, are liable for a fine if
you do not have proof of payment
for any goods purchased.

Most banks are open 8.20am-
1.20pm, 2.45-3.45pm Mon-Fri. All
are closed on public holidays, and
work reduced hours the day before a
holiday, usually closing around noon.

ATMs

Most banks, even in the smallest
towns, have cash machines
(*Bancomat*) that allow you to
withdraw cash with cards bearing
the Eurocard/Maestro/Cirrus/Visa
symbols; most have a limit of €250
per day. Don't count on ATMs
always working: in more out-of-the-
way places, they may occasionally be
switched off at night and weekends.

Credit cards

Italians still harbour a great affection
for cash, though the Bancomat cash/
debit card is fast gaining favour, and
far outstripping the credit card.

Nearly all hotels of two stars and
above accept at least some of the
major credit cards, as do most shops.

If you lose a credit or charge card,
phone one of the emergency numbers
listed below. All lines are freephone
numbers, have English-speaking
staff and are open 24 hours a day.

American Express
800 864 046/800 874 333.
To speak to an operator dial 0 after
the recorded message.
Diner's Club 800 864 064.
Wait after the recorded message to
speak to an operator.
Mastercard 800 870 866.
Visa 800 819 014.

Foreign exchange

Banks usually have better exchange
rates than the private bureaux de
change (*cambio*). It's a good idea to
take a passport or other ID whenever
you're dealing with money, and you
will definitely need ID if you want
to change travellers' cheques or
withdraw money on a credit card
(other than through an automatic
machine).

Commission rates vary
considerably: you can pay from
nothing to €5-plus for each
transaction. Watch out for 'no
commission' signs, as the rate of
exchange in these places will almost
certainly be terrible.

Some city-centre branches have
automatic exchange machines that
will change bank notes (provided
they are in good condition) from most
major currencies. Most banks will
also give cash advances against a
credit card, but this varies according
to the bank, and increasing numbers
refuse to do so if you do not have a
PIN number.

Exchange offices are plentiful
at the airport, around the Stazione
Centrale area, on the port side
of piazza Municipio, and near all
major tourist sites. Their rates
may not be the best, but they are
conveniently located and open much
later than banks.

Main post offices have exchange
bureaux. Commission is €2.58 plus
1.5% for all cash transactions;
traveller's cheques are not accepted.

If you need to have money sent to
Italy, the best method is via Thomas
Cook or Western Union (for both, *see
below*). When this guide went to
press there was no American
Express office in Naples.

Banco di Napoli

*Via Toledo 177/178, Toledo
(exchange 081 792 4567). Bus
CS, E2, R1, R4.* **Open** 8.10am-
1.20pm, 2.40-3.30pm Mon-Fri.
Map p313 1A.

Thomas Cook

*Airport (toll-free 800 004 488/
departure lounge 081 780 1825/
arrival lounge 081 780 9107).*
Open *Departures* 5.30am-9.30pm
daily. *Arrivals* 8am-10.30pm daily.
There is a €3 minimum charge up
to €85, then 3.5% commission is
charged on all transactions. Money
can be transferred to the Naples
offices from any Thomas Cook or
MoneyGram branch in the world.

Western Union Money Transfer

*c/o Espresso Service, piazza Garibaldi
69, Port & University (081 207 597).
Metro Piazza Garibaldi/bus 14, 15,
110, 125, 135, 191, 192, 194, 195,
C30, C40, C55, C58, CD, CS, OF,
R2/tram 1, 29.* **Open** 9am-1pm,
3-7pm Mon-Fri; 9am-1pm Sat, Sun.
Closed 2wks Aug. **Map** p310 2B.
Money sent from/to Western Union
should arrive within the hour.
Commission is paid by the sender.

Postal services

For postal information of any kind,
phone the freephone central
information office on 160 (8am-8pm
Mon-Sat). After the recorded
message, say *'informazione'* if you
want to talk to an operator.

Concrete improvements have
been made recently in Italy's
notoriously unreliable postal services
(www.poste.it), and you can now be
more or less sure that your letters
will arrive in reasonable time (though
in some southern Italian backwaters,
'reasonable' will be interpreted in a
very loose fashion).

Most post-boxes are red and have
two slots, *per la città* (for the city)
and *tutte le altre destinazioni* (for
everywhere else). Some have a gold
sticker on front for *posta prioritaria*
and should, in theory, be used only
for that.

Queues in post offices can be huge;
if you require stamps only and are
sure your letter doesn't exceed 20g,
you are better off going to a *tabacchi*
(*see p291*).

Delivery services

Italy's equivalent to first-class
post, *posta prioritaria*, generally
works very well. It promises delivery
within 24hrs in Italy, three days
for EU countries, and longer for
the rest of the world; more often
than not, it delivers. A letter of 20g
or less to Italy or any EU country
costs 62¢ by *posta prioritaria*; rates
go up in 62¢ stages. Special *posta
prioritaria* stamps can be bought
at post offices and *tabacchi* (*see
p291*) and letters can be posted in

Directory

any box, though there's more chance of them arriving within the stipulated time if they're placed in the special boxes in post offices.

Regular post, too, has improved of late, but it can still take a week or more for letters (and especially postcards, which are treated as utterly unimportant by sorters) to reach EU destinations. A 20g letter to Italy or Europe costs 41¢, and to elsewhere 52¢.

Also available is the more expensive *Postacelere*, which also promises 24hr delivery to major cities in Italy and two- to three-day delivery abroad, again to larger cities. It is available from main post offices only, and offers the advantage of being able to track the progress of your letter or parcel through the website or freephone number.

Registered mail (*raccomandata*) costs €2.58 above the ordinary price for your letter or parcel, which may assure delivery but is no guarantee of speed. Private couriers (*see p283*) are quicker but considerably more expensive.

Post office

Palazzo Centrale della Posta
Piazza Matteotti, Toledo (081 551 1456). Bus 24, 149, C57, E2, E3, R1, R3, R4. **Open** 8.15am-7pm Mon-Fri; 8.15am-noon Sat. **Map** p312 2A.
Naples' main post office.

Faxes

Main post offices will send faxes for an exorbitant fee. Many photocopy shops (*fotocopie*), some stationery stores (*cartoleria*) and some *tabacchi* (*see p291*) also have fax services. Shop around to avoid rip-offs. Some do-it-yourself fax/phones can be found at Naples Airport and at the Stazione Centrale.

Telegrams & telexes

These can be sent from the main post offices. Telegrams can also be dictated over the phone. Dial 186 from a private phone and a message in Italian will tell you to dial the number of the phone you're calling from (which will be billed for the charges). You'll then be passed to a telephonist who will take your message. For a telegram with text in English, make sure you print clearly on the post office form, or speak clearly on the phone, and hope the final version will be close to your original.

Queuing

Italians, and southern Italians especially, tend to have an inherent me-first attitude when driving, boarding a bus or approaching a ticket counter. If you're too polite you may just have to catch the next bus. Despite the apparent chaos, in slow lengthy lines, queue-jumpers are usually given short shrift. Hanging back deferentially, on the other hand, is taken as a clear sign of stupidity and if you're not careful the tide will sweep contemptuously past you. In busy shops and bars, be aware of who is in front of you and behind you and when it's your turn, assert your rights emphatically.

Religion

None of Naples' Catholic churches has mass in English, though confession is heard in several languages, including English, at the Duomo (*see p73*) and the churches of Gesù Nuovo (*see p68*) and Santa Chiara (*see p69*), at times that change frequently. (*See also p232* **Sorrento**.) The following non-Catholic churches are all in Naples.

Anglican/Episcopal
Christ Church, via San Pasquale a Chiaia 15, Chiaia (081 411 842). Metro Piazza Amedeo/bus 140, C12, C18, C19, C24, C25, C27, C28, R3. **Services** 10am Sun. **Map** p313 1B.
A hub for Naples' English-speaking community. The Church Hall is also used for Commonwealth Club meetings (081 640 755), Pot Luck Club (monthly brunch get-togethers, 081 762 8767), American Women's Club meetings (081 560 4483), and English-speaking meetings of Alcoholics Anonymous (0823 765 837/335 210 914). The Reverend Murray Grant also celebrates the Eucharist in Sorrento.

Baptist
Via Foria 93, Sanità (081 287 650). Metro Piazza Cavour/bus 12, 47, 110, 135, 149, 182, C51, C52, C83, CD. **Services** 7pm Thur, 11am Sun. **Map** p310 2C.
There's a bilingual Italian-English service on Sundays, and on Thursdays by request.

Jewish
Via Santa Maria a Cappella Vecchia 31, Chiaia (081 764 3480). Metro Piazza Amedeo/bus 140, C12, C18, C19, C22, C24, C25, C27, C28, R3/tram 1, 4. **Services** 9.30am Sat. Closed 3wks Aug. **Map** p313 1A.
For information on times and events, call the above number from 10am to noon, on Mon, Wed or Fri.

Lutheran

Via Carlo Poerio 5, Chiaia (081 663 207). Bus 140, C12, C18, C19, C24, C25, C28, R3/tram 1, 4. **Map** p313 1B.
German-language services are held here at 10.30am on the first Sunday of the month, Sept-June. Services are also held in Ischia, Capri and Sorrento; phone for details. The church in Naples hosts a fine programme of Wednesday evening classical musical concerts in autumn and spring.

Relocation

Naples and its surrounding region is a wonderful place to live in and enjoy, especially if you don't work. Trying to earn a living here can bring many problems, both in adjusting to southern Italian attitudes and in practical terms. If you intend staying here, you'll need to prove to the police that you can support yourself, or that you're in full-time education, in order to get a *permesso di soggiorno* (*see p291*).

English-language schools and translation agencies (of a very wide range of standards) have sprung up all over the area; the better your qualifications and experience, the more you'll be able to pick and choose among them. A lot of money can be made giving private English lessons, although finding students in the first place is a challenge.

Local classified ads papers (*see p288*) have some job advertisements; you can also place a free ad there yourself. Temping is a new phenomenon in Italy, and only those with fluent Italian are likely to find jobs, but the occasional position for a native English speaker does arise.

Employment agencies

Adecco
Via F Crispi 52, Chiaia (081 761 8829/www.adecco.it). Metro Piazza Amedeo/bus C24, C25, C27, C28. **Open** 9am-7pm Mon-Fri. **Map** p313 1B.

Manpower
Via Pessina 90, Toledo (081 564 0790/www.manpower.it). Metro Dante or Museo/bus 24, 47, 110, 135, 137, 149, CD, CS, E1, R1, R4. **Open** 9am-6pm Mon-Fri. **Map** p311 1C.

Quandoccorre
Centro Direzionale Isola E1 (081 562 8443/www.quandoccorreinterinale. com). Bus 191, C30, C40, C58, C61, C81. **Open** 9.30am-12.30pm Mon-Fri. **Map** p310 2A.

Documents

Having a proper job involves obtaining certain essential documents. Private agencies specialise in getting all kinds of documents if you can't face going through all the procedures yourself (look under *Pratiche e certificati – agenzie* in the phone book).

EU citizens employed in Italy must have the following:

Permesso di soggiorno (permit to stay)

Visitors should theoretically get their *permesso* after eight working days in Italy; few do. You need to take your passport, three passport photos and, for non-EU citizens, a €10.33 *marca da bollo* (a tax stamp, available from *tabacchi; see p291*) and a letter from your employer/university or college/spouse with the right to reside in Italy to the *ufficio stranieri* (foreigners' department) of the nearest *questura* (police station).

Codice fiscale (tax code)

This credit card-sized piece of plastic bears a number that you'll need for things as varied as opening a bank account and signing a contract with the electricity board. Take your passport to the nearest offshoot of the Ministero delle Finanze (for the office closest to you look for *Agenzia delle Entrate* under *Uffici Finanziari* in the phone book). It should be issued immediately. For (a limited amount of) further information consult the ministry's website at www.finanze.it.

Permesso di lavoro (work permit)

In addition to the documents listed above, you should (though in fact you may find you'll never need one) have a *permesso di lavoro* (work permit). This can be obtained by going to the *Direzione Provinciale del Lavoro*. You'll need a letter from your employer, your passport and your *permesso di soggiorno* (with photocopies). Non-EU citizens coming to Italy to take up a prearranged job should apply for a working visa from the nearest Italian consulate before arriving.

Certificato di residenza (residence certificate)

Necessary if you want to buy a car or import your belongings without paying customs duties, the *certificato di residenza* can cause diplomatic rows with your landlord. To get it, the tax on rubbish collection (*nettezza urbana*) must be paid for the property you reside in – which means that either you have to volunteer to pay it (and landlords renting out property but not paying taxes on the income run the risk of being discovered), or you have to persuade the owner to. You need to go to your local *ufficio anagrafe* (look under *Municipio* in the phone book) with photocopies of your documents.

Carta d'identità (ID card)

Not strictly necessary for foreigners who can use their own national IDs and passports as a means of identification. Anyone with a *certificato di residenza* can get one, obtainable from your local *ufficio anagrafe* (look under *Municipio* in the phone book). It costs €5.16 and you'll need to take your passport (with photocopies), three photos and your *permesso di soggiorno*.

Partita IVA (VAT number)

Company owners and some freelancers will need a VAT number for invoicing. This is free and available by bringing a valid document (with photocopy) to the nearest offshoot of the Ministero delle Finanze (for the office closest to you look for *Agenzia delle Entrate* under *Uffici Finanziari* in the phone directory). Your Partita IVA should be issued immediately. Don't forget to cancel it when you no longer need it, or you may receive demands for IVA payments years later.

Safety & security

Naples has a reputation for being a dangerous city. It's true that pickpockets and bag-snatchers (including children operating singly or in gangs) are particularly active in the main tourist areas of the city and in much-frequented sites in the surrounding region. However, you are highly unlikely to experience violence or assault, which occur mainly in the context of gangland activities in areas visitors are unlikely to stray into.

If you are a victim of any crime, go immediately to the nearest police station to report a *scippo*. A *denuncia* (written statement) of the incident will be made by or for you. You will need the *denuncia* for making an insurance claim.

Take the following precautions:
● Attitude is crucial. Look as if you know what you're doing and where you're going.
● Don't carry wallets in back pockets, particularly on buses. If you have a bag or camera with a long strap, wear it across your chest and not dangling from one shoulder.

● Keep bags closed, with your hand on them. If you stop at a pavement café or restaurant, do not leave bags or coats on the ground or the back of a chair where you cannot see them.
● When walking down a street, hold cameras and bags on the side away from the street, so you're less likely to become the prey of a motorbike thief, or *scippatore*.
● Don't pull out large wads of cash to pay for things at street stalls or in busy bars. Keep some small bills and change easily accessible.
● Don't wear expensive jewellery.
● Avoid groups of noisy children. Walk past as quickly as possible, keeping a hold on your valuables. Insistent, touchy women with babies at their breast may also be after more than a coin or two.
● Crowds offer easy camouflage for pickpockets. Be especially careful when boarding buses and boats, and when entering museums.
● You will almost certainly be offered a mobile phone, video or digital camera at a very attractive price – stay away from these bargains, as you will invariably be sold a plastic toy or a block of wood.

OCCUPATIONAL HAZARDS

Old habits die hard and some unenlightened restaurateurs and taxi drivers will pad out their bills. Don't feel offended: locals suffer the same treatment. An angry reaction will inevitably get you into deeper water; smile and point out the unintentional slip-up, and the total will, as a rule, return to its correct level. Never take unauthorised taxis.

Smoking

Smoking is theoretically not permitted in public offices, bars, restaurants, on public transport or in taxis. The law has, for the most part, gone unregarded, but times are changing and the once-arrogant smoker will probably put his cigarette out if you diplomatically point out the *vietato fumare* (no smoking) sign.

Tabacchi

Tabacchi or *tabaccherie*, identified by signs with a white T on a black or blue background, are the only places where you can legally buy tobacco products. They also sell stamps, phone cards, tickets for public transport, lottery tickets and the stationery that's required for dealing with Italian bureaucracy. Most *tabacchi* keep shop hours, but many are attached to bars and stay open later. Many *tabacchi* have cigarette machines for when the shop is shut.

In Naples, black-market cigarettes can be bought on many street corners for less than you'll pay in a *tabacchi*. Buying them is against the law; moreover, you are contributing to the organised crime outfits that run the contraband market. However, many families depend on this illegal trade for their livelihood: consult your conscience before buying.

Study

Naples' universities are the **Università Federico II** (www. unina.it), founded in 1224; the modern **Seconda Università di Napoli** (www.unina2.it); and the **Istituto Universitario Orientale** (www. iuo.it). EU citizens have the same right to study at Italian universities as Italian nationals. You will need to have your school diplomas translated and authenticated at the Italian consulate in your own country before presenting them to the *ufficio studenti stranieri* (foreign students' department) of any university.

Centro Turistico Studentesco (CTS)

Via Mezzocannone 25, University (081 552 7960/fax 081 552 7975/www.cts.it). Bus C25, C55, C58, CD, CS, E1, R1, R2, R4. **Open** 9.30am-1.30pm, 2.30-6pm Mon-Fri. **Credit** MC, V. **Map** p311 1C. The CTS Student Travel Centre arranges discount travel tickets for students and non-students.

Erasmus Student Network Napoli (ESN)

Università Federico II, Facoltà di Giurisprudenza, Aula studenti, via Porta di Massa 32, University (328 202 8906/www.esn.it). Bus C55, C58, CD, CS, E1, R2. **Meetings** 11.30am-1.30pm Mon. **Map** p311 1C. The ESN offers informal orientation and support activities – including help through university bureaucracy, language lessons and introductory parties – for foreign students living and studying in Naples as part of the Erasmus exchange programme.

Italian courses

Centro Italiano

Vico Santa Maria dell'Aiuto 17, Centro storico (081 552 4331/ fax 081 552 3023/www.centro italiano.it). Bus 24, 149, C57, CD, CS, E1, E2, E3, R1, R3, R4. **Open** 9am-5pm Mon-Fri. **Map** p311 1C. A lively language school that also offers cultural, musical and literary events, and video screenings. The school helps foreign students find temporary accommodation in Naples.

Telephones

Phone numbers

All Italian phone numbers must be dialled with their area codes, even if you are phoning from within the area. All numbers in **Naples** and its province begin **081**; this includes **Pozzuoli**, **Ischia**, **Capri**, **Sorrento** and **Pompeii**. It does not include **Positano** and **Amalfi**, which are in the province of Salerno, area code **089**. Numbers in Caserta begin 0823 and Benevento 0824.

Phone numbers in the Naples area usually have seven digits; some of the older numbers may have six digits. If you have difficulties, check the directory (*elenco telefonico*) or ring directory enquiries (12; remain silent through the recorded message and eventually a human being will talk to you).

All numbers beginning with 800 are toll-free lines. For numbers starting 840 and 848 you'll be charged one unit only, and two units for those beginning 199, regardless of where you're calling from or how long the call lasts. These numbers can only be called from within Italy; some only function within one phone district.

Mobile phone numbers begin with 3; until recently they began with 03 and may still be written thus.

Rates

Italy's once-exorbitant telephone company, Telecom Italia (www.telecomitalia.it), is edging its rates down towards those of other European companies.

The minimum charge for a local call from a private phone is about 7¢. The normal rate for the first minute to northern Europe and the US is 49¢ (23¢ per successive minute); 98¢ to Australia and New Zealand (72¢ per successive minute). In all cases the rate is higher if you're using a public phone. To keep costs down, phone off-peak (6.30pm-8am Mon-Fri; all day Sat, Sun). Phones in hotels may carry extortionate surcharges.

Public phones

Public phones in Naples tend to be clustered in areas where the traffic makes it almost impossible to hear. However, as locals are addicted to their mobile phones, telephone kiosks are rarely occupied. The minimum charge for a local call is 10¢. Most public phones now only accept phone-cards (*schede telefoniche*). A few also accept major credit cards (especially at the airport or train stations).

Telecom Italia phones are silver (older ones are orange); cards costing a variety of amounts are sold from *tabacchi* (*see p291*), some newsstands and some bars. Phonecards have expiry dates, after which, no matter how much credit you have, you won't be able to use them.

Green public phones require Infostrada (Telecom's chief competitor) phonecards, also sold at some *tabacchi*, newsstands and bars.

International calls

To make an international call from Italy, dial 00, then the appropriate country code, area code (for calls to the UK or Ireland, omit the initial zero of the area code) and the individual number.

To phone Naples from abroad, dial the international code, then 39 for Italy and 081 for Naples, followed by the individual number.

To make a reverse-charge (collect) call, dial 170 for the international operator in Italy. If you are placing a reverse-charge (collect) call from a phone box, you will need to insert a coin or card, which will be refunded after your call.

Phonecards with a greater number of units for international calls can be found in newspaper stands and *tabacchi*, especially in or near stations or ports or tourist sites. These may be issued by Telecom Italia, or by competitors such as Xenia or Planet Communications. The cards can be used from any phone, public or private: dial the phone number specified on the card, then punch in the card's PIN number. Units are subtracted as you talk.

Operator services

These services operate 24hrs daily.

Italian directory enquiries 12.
International operator 170.
International directory enquiries 176.
Telegrams 186.
Wake-up calls 114.
An automatic message will ask you to dial in the time you want your call, with four figures on a 24hr clock, followed by your phone number.

Mobile phones

Owners of GSM phones can use them on both 900 and 1800 bands, though reception can be patchy in some areas of Naples and in smaller towns in mountainous areas; British, Australian and New Zealand mobiles work without problems. US cell phones cannot be used in Italy.

Tourist information

Local tourist-board offices in and around Naples will provide maps and information specific to their area. For areas outside Naples, see under **Tourist information** in individual chapters in **Around Naples**.

ASST

Via San Carlo 9, Royal (081 402 394/ www.aziendaturismonapoli.com/www. presidituristici.campania.it). Bus 24, 149, C25, C82, E3, R2, R3. **Open** *9am-7.30pm Mon-Sat; 9am-3pm Sun.* **Map** *p313 1A.* **Branch**: *Piazza del Gesù, Centro storico (081 552 3328/081 551 2701). Bus 24, 140, 149, C57, CD, E1, R1, R4.* **Open** *9am-8pm Mon-Sat; 9am-3pm Sun.* **Map** *p311 1C.*

Ente Provinciale del Turismo (EPT)

Piazza dei Martiri 58, Chiaia (081 405 311/ fax 081 401 961/www.ept.napoli.it). Bus 140, C12, C18, C19, C24, C25, C28, R3/ tram 1, 4. **Open** *8am-3.30pm Mon-Fri.* **Map** *p313 1A.* **Branches**: *Mergellina rail station (081 761 2102). Bus 140, C16, C24, R3.* **Open**

8am-8pm Mon-Sat. **Map** *p313 2C. Stazione Centrale (081 268 779). Bus 14, 15, 110, 125, 135, 191, 192, 194, 195, C30, C40, C55, C58, CD, CS, OF, R2/tram 1, 29.* **Open** *9am-7pm Mon-Sat; 9am-1pm Sun.* **Map** *p310 2B.*

Hello Napoli

Toll-free 800 251 396/www.hellonapoli.org. **Open** *Phone enquiries 9.30am-1pm, 2.30-6.30pm Mon-Fri.*
Operated by the Chamber of Commerce, this extremely helpful and efficient call centre provides information on events and practical hints in several languages. The Chamber of Commerce has also created the useful website www.guidatour.it.

Osservatorio Turistico-Culturale

Piazza del Plebiscito, Royal (081 247 1123/ www.comune.napoli.it). Bus 110, 140, C22, C25, E3, R2, R3. **Open** *9am-7pm Mon-Fri; 9am-2pm Sat.* **Map** *p313 1A.*
Tourist, cultural and practical information, including free maps.

Time

Italy is one hour ahead of GMT, six hours ahead of New York, and nine hours behind Sydney. The clocks are moved forward one hour in spring (*ora legale*) and back one hour (*ora solare*) in autumn, in line with all other EU countries.

Tipping

In Naples, as in the rest of Italy, tipping is discretionary, and you are quite justified in leaving nothing for service that merited nothing. However, a tip – rarely over 12% – is appreciated everywhere (and in more expensive, sophisticated eateries, it's expected). Most locals leave 5¢ or 10¢ on the counter when buying a coffee or a drink standing at a bar. The price will be much higher if you sit down at a café table and order the same thing – and your tip is expected to be proportionately higher.

Restaurants may add a service charge of 10%-15% to the bill; don't feel obliged to leave anything over this. It's better to tip in cash than by credit card.

Rounding your fare up to the nearest euro will make a taxi driver happy; in summer beach resorts,

where maids, porters and waiters only work seasonally, tips are especially welcome.

Toilets

There are few public toilets in the city or outside it, and those you do find are likely to be closed. The easiest thing is to go to a bar. Fast-food joints and some department stores can also come in handy. There are modern lavatories at or near most of the major tourist sites; most have attendants and require a nominal fee.

Visas

Citizens of the EU, the US, Australia, New Zealand and Canada do not need visas for stays of up to three months, after which they must apply for a *permesso di soggiorno* (see *p291*).

Water & drinking

The tap water in the city of Naples is pure spring water from the mountains and entirely safe to drink. Most resorts around Naples also have drinkable tap water. For locals, there's no stigma attached to having

acqua non potabile (non-drinking water); if you are in a country area, they will advise you whether or not to stick to bottled water.

When to go

Climate

The Naples area can sizzle at 30°-40°C (85°-105°F) in July and August, and humidity levels can also be high. On the islands and coast, sea breezes make the heat more bearable.

Spring and autumn are almost always warm and pleasant, although there may be occasional heavy showers, particularly in March, April and September. They never last long, however, and you're rewarded with clean, crisp air and crystal-clear visibility afterwards. March and October can be wonderful times to visit the islands; they will be extremely quiet, and you stand a chance of finding freak summer temperatures.

Between November and February, the Naples area is usually blessed with crisp, bright and often pleasantly warm sunshine, though you may be unlucky enough to run into one of its rare spells of cloudy,

Directory

dreary weather, or rain. But the lack of tourists will prove some compensation for less than perfect weather. In December and January temperatures can fall to around zero, and there's a dusting of snow on the top of Vesuvius. The biting air is then dramatically clear and visibility spectacular.

Public holidays

On public holidays (giorni festivi) public offices, banks and post offices are closed. So, in theory but not always in practice, are shops – phone ahead to check. How severely public transport is curtailed depends on the whims of councils and transport authorities. Christmas Day, New Year's Day, Easter Monday and 1 May are favourite days for cancelling buses.

Public holidays that fall on a Tuesday or Thursday are welcomed as a chance to have a long weekend (known as il ponte, 'the bridge').

National public holidays are:
1 Jan New Year's Day (Capodanno); **6 Jan** Epiphany (La Befana); **Easter Mon** (Pasquetta); **25 Apr** Liberation Day (Festa della Liberazione); **1 May** Labour Day (Festa del Lavoro); **15 Aug** Feast of the Assumption (Ferragosto); **1 Nov** All Saints' Day (Tuttisanti); **8 Dec** Feast of the Immaculate Conception (L'Immacolata); **25 Dec** Christmas Day (Natale); **26 Dec** Boxing Day (Santo Stefano).

Naples and the surrounding area also shuts down on 19 Sept, the feast of the city's patron saint, San Gennaro.

School & family holidays

Italian schoolchildren have short (around ten-day) breaks at Easter and Christmas, and no half-term breaks at all. Schools break up in mid June and don't resume until mid September, so beaches and pools are packed with local youth in late June and July.

August is the holiday month and there are interminable queues on roads to holiday resorts. Many businesses, shops and restaurants in Naples will close down partly or totally for August, which can prove one of the quietest (and one of the hottest) times to visit the city.

Resorts outside Naples remain crowded throughout the summer, especially over weekends from June to September. It's best to avoid travelling to the islands or driving around the Amalfi Coast and Sorrento on summer weekends, if you possibly can.

Seasonal events

NAPLES
February
Galassia Gutenberg
Mostra d'Oltremare, Fuorigrotta (081 410 7807/www.galassia.org). **Map** p314.
Largest book fair in southern Italy.
Carnevale
081 247 1123.
Children get to show off their fancy-dress costumes.

March
Benvenuta Primavera
081 247 1123.
Guided tours and theatrical 'happenings' in the squares and gardens of central Naples.
Napoli Marathon
081 873 1955/ www.napolimarathon.it.
Full marathon, 5km fun-run and a more leisurely walk.

April
Settimana per la cultura (Culture Week)
www.beniculturali.it.
All Naples' (in fact, all Italy's) publicly owned museums are free and many open until late for one week in spring.

May
Maggio dei Monumenti
081 247 1123.
A vast calendar of free events: from guided walks to guided scuba dives, access to sites that have been locked for decades, concerts and exhibitions. Programmes available from tourist offices (see p293).

June
'O Curt
Casina del Boschetto, Villa Comunale (081 456 425/www.comune.napoli.it/ santasofia). **Map** p313 2B.
Short, Naples-related films.

June-September
Estate a Napoli (Summer in Naples)
081 247 1123.
Open-air films, theatre and music around central Naples.

July
Neapolis Festival
Ex-Italsider (former steelworks), Bagnoli (www.neapolis.it). **Map** p314.
Local and international rock groups for the largest musical event in southern Italy.
Santa Maria del Carmine
Map p311 1B.
The bell-tower of this church (see p66), the tallest in Naples, is 'blown up' with fireworks on 16 July.

August
Ferragosto
The Feast of the Assumption (Ferragosto, 15 Aug) is celebrated all over the city and surrounding region; in Pozzuoli (see p98) there's a competition involving shinning up a slippery pole.

September
Pizzafest
www.pizzafest.net.
The city celebrates its most famous dish with pizza chefs from all over Italy doing their stuff, open-air concerts and other events.
Festival di Piedigrotta
081 247 1123. **Map** p314.
Once this was a spectacular song and theatre festival in the Piedigrotta district (see p93). Attempts are afoot to revive theatrical improvisations and the firework display traditionally held on 8 Sept. Some street parties are held.
Feast of San Gennaro
The blood of Naples' patron saint liquefies (if all goes to plan) amid frantic praying in the Duomo (see p73) on 19 Sept.

December
Natale a Napoli (Christmas in Naples)
081 247 1123.
Concerts of sacred music in churches around the city.
Natale (Christmas)
Shopping frenzy in the streets around San Gregorio Armeno (see p75), where Neapolitans stock up on figures for their traditional Nativity scenes. Few churches are without a Christmas crib; the 18th-century examples in San Martino (see p89) and the Palazzo Reale (see p60) are particularly fine.
Capodanno (New Year's Eve)
Piazza del Plebiscito. **Map** p313 1A.
Packed concert of classical, traditional and rock music that lasts well into the morning, punctuated by fireworks over Castel dell'Ovo.

January
La Befana
Piazza del Plebiscito. **Map** p313 1A.
The old hag who brings gifts to good children and leaves charcoal in the shoes of bad ones descends from the sky to distribute presents in piazza del Plebiscito.

AROUND NAPLES
Capri
14 May: Capri
A statue of the town's patron, San Costanzo, is carried to the sea, where procession participants are blessed.
May-Aug: Anacapri
Concerti al tramonto classical music concert season in the Villa San Michele.

Directory

13 June: Anacapri
Statue of the town's patron saint,
Antonio di Padova, is processed
around the town.
Sept: Marina Grande
Statue of Santa Maria della Libera
is carried to the sea on the Sun after
8 Sept.

Ischia

Good Friday: Forio
Easter procession around town
(can halt traffic for miles around).
16-18 May: Lacco Ameno
Procession and fireworks for the
feast of the town's patron saint,
Restituta.
26 July: Ischia Ponte
Fireworks and torchlit procession
of boats for the feast of St Anne
(www.festadisantanna.it) around
the *scogli* (rocks) di Sant' Anna.
Sept: Ischia Ponte The feast of the
island's saint, Giovan Giuseppe della
Croce (www.settembresulsagrato.
ischia.it), is celebrated with a sea-
borne procession of a statue of the
saint from Porto to Ponte and four
days of *feste* and fireworks around
the first Sun of the month.

Procida

Good Friday: Marina Grande
Hooded penitents carry a veiled
statue of Christ through the town,
accompanied by Roman centurions
and hosts of little angels.

Area Vesuviana

Easter Monday:
Madonna dell'Arco
A fresco of the Virgin Mary was hit
by a stray cannon-ball in the 16th
century and bled, since when bare-
footed blue-scarfed *fujenti* ('flee-ers';
devotees of Madonna dell'Arco)
have gone around begging.
Decorated floats.
July: Ercolano
Festival delle Ville Vesuviane (081
732 2134/www.villevesuviane.net).
Classical concerts are held in neo-
classical villas.
22 Oct: Torre Annunziata
Procession for the feast of the town's
patron saint, the Madonna della Neve
(Our Lady of the Snow).

Sorrento & around

Good Friday: Massa Lubrense
Easter procession with hooded
penitents.
Holy Week: Sorrento
Processions in costume throughout
the week leading up to Easter.
July-Aug: Sorrento
Classical music concert season in
the cloister of the church of San
Francesco.
Oct: Sorrento
Incontri Internazionali del Cinema,
a festival of feature and made-for-TV
films, and cartoons.

Amalfi Coast

Apr: Positano
Cartoons on the Bay (06 3749 8423/
www.cartoonsbay.com), an animated
film festival.
June: Amalfi
Every four years the town hosts
the Regata Storica delle Antiche
Repubbliche Marinare (first Sun
of the month). The next Regata is
in 2005.
25-27 June: Amalfi
Processions and fireworks for the
feast of Sant'Andrea; a statue of the
saint and Amalfi's fishing fleet are
blessed by local priests.
June-Sept: Ravello
Concerti a Villa Rufolo offers a
series of classical concerts in a
spectacular setting.
July-Aug: Minori
Jazz on the Coast (089 877087), a
series of open-air jazz concerts.
15 Aug: Positano
Procession and fireworks for the
feast of the Assumption.
24 Dec, 6 Jan: Amalfi
A shining 'star' descends from
Mount Tabor above the town into
the main square.

Salerno & around

May: Salerno
Salerno Porte Aperte (089 231 432).
Long-closed churches, *palazzi* and
collections are open to the public.
July: Giffoni Valle Piana
Giffoni Film Festival (www.
giffoniff.it). Cinema for and by
children.
July & Aug: Paestum
Theatre, music and dance around
the Greek temples (0828 811 016).
Nov: Salerno
Festival Internazionale del Cinema
(089 231 953/www.cinefestival
salerno.it).

Caserta & around

Sept: Casertavecchia
Settembre al Borgo festival (0823 322
233). Music, dance, open-air theatre
and exhibitions.
Sept: Caserta
Antiques fair in the grounds of the
Reggia during the last two weeks
of the month.
Christmas: Sant'Angelo
in Formis
Locals transform their village into
a living Nativity scene.

Benevento & around

July-Sept: Benevento
Sannio Estate (0824 319 938)
provides music and theatre in the
Teatro Romano.
Sept: Torrecuso
VinEstate, a week of wine tasting
(0824 872 222).
Oct: Fragneto Monforte
Hot Air Balloon festival (0824 993
649/www.fragneto.com).

The *maschilista* (macho) southern
Italian male can be daunting for the
foreign female traveller, but he is,
as a rule, a lot more bark than bite.
A bit of common sense and a lot of
attitude will get you out of all but the
very rare worst-case scenarios.

Avoid lodging or lingering in the
area around Stazione Centrale/piazza
Garibaldi; it's bad in the day but
horrible at night. You are perfectly
safe in the Centro storico – piazza
San Domenico with its strollers and
strummers, and piazza Bellini with
its intellectual crowd present no
greater threat than the occasional
druggie. At tourist sites, there's a
good chance that would-be Romeos
will approach women without male
companions. Perfect the art of saying
'no'. A joking tone will be much
more effective than reacting in an
aggressive, hurt or upset fashion.

Taxi Rosa

Consortaxi (081 552 5252/
www.consortaxi.it) provides a
service for single women. Call
between 10pm and 6am and you will
not be charged the usual 77¢ for the
radio call. Your driver will see you
to your door.

Health

Each district has a *Consultorio
familiare* (family-planning clinic),
run by the local health authority.
EU citizens with an E111 form are
entitled to use them, paying the same
low charges as locals. Ask in any
chemist's for the address of the
nearest one. Queues can be
interminable, but you will eventually
get any advice and help you need
on contraception, abortion and
gynaecological problems.

The pill is available on prescription.
Abortions are legal when performed
in state-run hospitals. For
gynaecological emergencies, head
for the *pronto soccorso* at your
nearest hospital (*see p285*).

AIED

*Via Cimarosa 186, Vomero (081
578 2142). Funicular Montesanto to
via Morghen, Centrale to piazzetta
Fuga or Chiaia to via Cimarosa/bus
C28, C31, C32, C36, E4, V1.* **Open**
9.30am-6.30pm Mon, Wed, Fri;
9.30am-12.30pm, 3.30-6.30pm Tue,
Thur; 9.30am-12.30pm Sat. Closed
2wks Aug. **Map** p312 2B.
This private clinic offers medical
care, check-ups, contraceptive advice,
menopause counselling and smear
tests. With a membership card (€8
for one year), check-ups cost €34
and smear tests €13.

Directory

Further Reference

Books

The Ancients
Massie, Allan *Augustus, Tiberius, Caesar*
Popular rewrites of history.
Suetonius *De Vita Caesarum* (Lives of the Caesars)
Ancient muck-raking by a highly biased Roman historian.
Virgil *Georgics*
Written during his stay in Naples.

Art & history
Acton, Harold *The Bourbons of Naples*
A lively historical romp focusing on the reign of Ferdinand I.
Behan, Tom *See Naples and Die: The Camorra and Organized Crime*
A vivid account of the Camorra, the criminal organisation whose influence today is as strong as ever.
Cutler, Bruce *Seeing the Darkness: Naples, 1943-1945*
An account of the liberation of the city during World War II.
Ginsborg, Paul *A History of Contemporary Italy*
Excellent introduction to the complex goings-on in post-war Italy.
Grant, Michael *Eros in Pompeii: The Erotic Art Collection of the Museum of Naples (with photographs by Antonia Mulas)*
A history of ancient Pompeii, examining all aspects of the city and its people, with emphasis on erotic imagery.
Lefkovich, Mary & Fant, Maureen *Women's Life in Greece and Rome*
A riveting collection of extracts, covering everything from ancient gynaecology to choosing a wet nurse.
Mazzoleni, Donatella *Palaces of Naples (with photographs by Mark E Smith)*
A look inside 30 of the city's estates and palaces.
Norwich, John Julius *The Normans of the South*
A colourful account of the other Norman conquest.
Palescandolo, Frank J (Translator) *The Naples of Salvatore Di Giacomo: Poems and a Play*
A collection of this Neapolitan poet's works.
Wittkower, Rudolf *Art and Architecture in Italy 1600-1750*
All you ever wanted to know about the Italian baroque.

Cuisine
Schwartz, Arthur *Naples at Table: Cooking in Campania*
A gastronomic trip through the Campania region.

Sheldon Johns, Pamela *Pizza Napoletana!*
A history of pizza, plus authentic recipes from ten of the city's pizzerias.

Fiction
Dibdin, Michael *Cosi Fan Tutti: An Aurelio Zen Mystery*
Suspense and mystery in this thriller set on the dark side of Naples.
Douglas, Norman *South Wind*
Celebration of Bacchic Mediterranean goings-on.
Sontag, Susan *The Volcano Lover*
A postmodern bodice-ripper centring on the Nelson-Hamilton trio.

Travel & biography
Casanova di Seingalt, Giacomo *The Story of My Life*
The libertine's highly coloured autobiography includes adventures in 18th-century Naples.
Goethe, Johann Wolfgang *Italian Journey*
The German poet's 18th-century travel diary; the translation by WH Auden and Elizabeth Mayer is best.
Hazzard, Shirley *Greene on Capri*
Memoirs of a post-war Capri resident's meetings with the writer.
Lewis, Norman *Naples '44*
Experiences of an intelligence officer in wartime Naples.
Munthe, Axel *The Story of San Michele*
A whimsical, self-glorifying account of the Swedish doctor's life, times and love affair with Anacapri.
Tullio, Paolo *North of Naples, South of Rome*
Life in the Comino Valley.
Walton, Susana *Behind the Façade*
Bloomsbury moves to Ischia.

Films

Il Decameron (dir Pier Paolo Pasolini, 1970).
Pasolini used Neapolitan locations and dialects for his adaptation.
Napoli D'Altri Tempi (dir Amleto Palermi, 1938).
Composer renounces fame and fortune for his anonymity in Naples; starring Vittorio De Sica.
L'Oro di Napoli (dir Vittorio De Sica, 1954).
Featuring Sophia Loren, Eduardo de Filippo and Totò; anthology of tales depicting aspects of Neapolitan life.
Polvere Di Napoli (dir Antonio Capuano, 1998).
Update of *L'Oro di Napoli*.
Il Postino (dir Michael Radford, 1994).
Oscar-winning drama based on the life of Chilean poet Pablo Neruda.

Le Quattro Giornate di Napoli (dir Nanni Loy, 1962).
Oscar-nominated war drama.
Totò, Peppino e La... Malafemmina (dir Camillo Mastrocinque, 1956).
Classic comedy.

Music

Almamegretta *Sanacore*
Dub and techno.
Bennato, Edoardo *Non farti cadere le braccia*
Still produces hits after 30 years.
Bennato, Eugenio *Taranta Power*
Folk songs from southern Italy.
Daniele, Pino *Terra Mia*
Melodic blues.
99 Posse *Curre curre guaglio'*
Politics, rap and hip hop.
Nuova Compagnia di Canto Popolare *Lo guarracino*
Folk outfit.
Pavarotti, Luciano *Favourite Neapolitan Songs* Includes *O' Sole Mio* and other Neapolitan classics.
Sepe, Daniele *Spiritus Mundi*
Eclectic saxophonist.
Spaccanapoli *Lost Souls*
Traditional tarantella style.

Websites

Culture, museums & events
www.aziendaturismonapoli.com
www.beniculturali.it
Culture Ministry site (Italian only).
www.comune.napoli.it
The Naples City Council's site.
www.ept.napoli.it
Local tourist board's excellent site.
www.guidatour.it
The Chamber of Commerce's site.
www.icampiflegrei.it
www.italia.ms/campania/napoli

Popular culture
www.antoniodecurtis.com
All about comic actor Totò.
www.calcionapolinet.com
News of the city's football team.
www.matrimonianapoli.it;
www.napolisposi.it
How to organise your wedding in Naples.
www.napolisworld.it/napoli gentile/index.htm
Information on the city's parks.

Listings
http://napoli.lanetro.it
http://napolinews.too.it
www.napolichespettacolo.it
www.napoli.com
www.nottambulando.it
www.touchnapoli.com

Glossary

Amphitheatre (*ancient*) oval open-air theatre

Apse large recess at the high-altar end of a church; adj **apsidal**

Ashlar large square-cut stones, usually used to face a building (*see also below* Rustication)

Atrium (*ancient*) courtyard

Baldacchino canopy supported by columns

Balustrade series of vertical posts and a handrail, usually as protection on the open side of a flight of stairs

Baptistry building – often eight-sided – outside church used for baptisms

Baroque artistic period from the 17th to 18th centuries, in which the decorative element became increasingly florid, culminating in Rococo (*qv*)

Barrel vault a ceiling with arches shaped like half-barrels

Basilica ancient Roman rectangular public building; rectangular Christian church

Bas-relief carving on a flat or curved surface where the figures stand out from the plane

Brunelleschi considered the first Renaissance architect, Filippo Brunelleschi (1377-1446) applied his discoveries in the field of perspective to his classical-style architectural designs

Byzantine artistic and architectural style drawing on ancient models developed in the fourth century in the Eastern empire and developed through the Middle Ages

Campanile bell tower

Capital the decorated head of a column (*see below* Orders)

Cardine (*ancient*) secondary street, usually running north–south

Caryatid supporting pillar carved in the shape of a woman

Castellated (building) decorated with battlements or turrets (*see also* Crenellations)

Cavea semicircular step-like seating area in an amphitheatre (*qv*) or theatre (*qv*)

Chapter room room in monastery where monks met for discussions

Chiaroscuro painting or drawing technique using no colours, but shades of black, white and grey

Choir area of church, usually behind the high altar, with stalls for those singing sung mass

Cippus (*ancient*) cylindrical stone or marble block standing on one end, usually as a milestone or funerary monument

Coffered (ceiling) with sunken square decorations

Colonnade row of columns supporting an entablature (*qv*) or arches

Confessio crypt (*qv*) beneath a raised altar

Crenellations battlements and/or archery holes on top of building or tower

Cupola dome-shaped roof or ceiling

Crypt vault beneath the main floor of a church

Cryptoporticus underground corridor

Decumanus (*ancient*) main road, usually running east–west

Domus (*ancient*) Roman city house

Embrasure a recess around the interior of a door or window; a hole in a wall for shooting through

Entablature section above a column or row of columns including the frieze and cornice

Ex-voto an offering given to fulfil a vow; often a small model in silver of the limb/organ/loved one to be cured as a result of prayer

Fresco painting technique in which pigment is applied to wet plaster

Gothic architectural and artistic style of the late Middle Ages (from the 12th century), using soaring, pointed arches

Greek cross (church) in the shape of a cross with arms of equal length

Hypogeum (*ancient*) underground room

Impluvium (*ancient*) cistern in the middle of a courtyard to gather rainwater funnelled into it by a sloping roof with a hole in the middle

Insula (*ancient*) city block

Intarsio technique by which patterns or pictures are made in wooden surfaces by inlaying pieces of different-coloured wood

Latin cross (church) in the shape of a cross with one arm longer than the other

Loggia gallery open on one side

Mannerism High Renaissance style of the late 16th century; characterised in painting by elongated, contorted human figures

Marquetry wooden inlay work, also known as intarsio (*qv*)

Mullioned windows made up of small panes divided by vertical bars

Narthex enclosed porch in front of a church

Nave main body of a church; the longest section of a Latin-cross church (*qv*)

Necropolis (*ancient*) literally 'city of the dead'; graveyard

Nymphaeum (*ancient*) grotto with pool and fountain dedicated to the Nymphs, female water deities; name given to ornate fountains with grottos in Renaissance architecture

Ogival (of arches, windows and so on) curving in to a point at the top

Orders classical styles of decoration for columns, the most common being

the very simple Doric, the curlicued Ionic and the leafy, frondy Corinthian

Palaestra (*ancient*) wrestling school

Palazzo large and/or important building (not necessarily a palace)

Parlatorio a convent or monastery's reception room or room for conversation

Pendentives four concave triangular sections on top of piers supporting a dome

Peristyle (*ancient*) temple or court surrounded by columns

Piazza (or **largo**) square

Pilaster square column, often with its rear side attached to a wall

Portal imposing door

Portico open space in front of a church or other building, with a roof resting on columns

Presbytery the part of a church containing the high altar

Pronaos (*ancient*) roofed temple vestibule (*qv*) with closed sides and columns in its open front

Proscenium (*ancient*) stage; arch dividing stage from audience

Reggia royal palace

Reliquary receptacle – often highly ornate – for holding and displaying relics of saints

Rococo highly decorative style fashionable in the 18th century

Romanesque architectural style of the early Middle Ages (c500-1200), drawing on Roman and Byzantine influences

Rustication large masonry blocks, often roughly cut, with deep joints, used to face buildings (*see also above* Ashlar)

Sacristy room in church, usually off choir (*qv*), where vestments are stored

Sarcophagus (*ancient*) stone or marble coffin

Spandrel near-triangular space between the top of two adjoining arches and the ceiling or architectural feature resting above them

Stucco plaster

Succorpo similar to a crypt (*qv*), underground space beneath the apse (*qv*) of a church

Tablinium (*ancient*) private study

Tessera small piece of stone or glass used to make mosaic

Theatre (*ancient*) semicircular open-air theatre

Transept shorter arms of a Latin-cross church (*qv*)

Triclinium (*ancient*) dining room

Triumphal arch arch in front of an apse (*qv*), usually over the high altar

Trompe l'oeil decorative painting effect to make surface appear three-dimensional

Tufa volcanic stone widely used in building

Vestibule entrance hall

Vocabulary

Though hotel and restaurant staff in resorts around Naples will have some grasp of English, don't expect anyone in shops or bars to manage any more than prices in anything but Italian. In Naples itself, foreign-language speakers are even thinner on the ground. The exceptions to this rule are Sorrento, which is practically a British colony, and Ischia, where you can use any language you like as long as it's German.

Any attempt on your part at spoken Italian, no matter how atrocious, will be appreciated.

Italian

Italian is spelled as it is pronounced, and vice versa: learn. Grammar books will tell you that the stress falls on the penultimate syllable, but this is not a fail-safe rule: pronunciation must be learnt by trial and error.

There are two forms of address in the second person singular: *lei*, which is formal, and *tu*, which is informal. Older southern Italians will use *voi* for both.

PRONUNCIATION
VOWELS
a – as in *ask*
e – like *a* in *age* (closed e) or *e* in *sell* (open e)
i – like *ea* in *east*
o – as in *hotel* (closed o) or *hot* (open o)
u – as in *boot*

CONSONANTS
c and *g* both go soft in front of *e* and *i* (becoming like *ch* and *g* in *check* and *giraffe* respectively).

Before a vowel, *h* is silent. An *h* after *c* or *g* makes them hard, no matter what vowel follows.
gl – like *lli* in *million*
gn – like *ny* in *canyon*
qu – as in *quick*
r – always rolled
s – either as in *soap* or in *rose*
sc – like *sh* in *shame*
sch – like *sc* in *scout*
z – can be *ds* or *tz*

Neapolitan

If your hard-learned Italian is proving inexplicably useless, don't despair: what you're hearing is probably Neapolitan dialect. It's something more than an accent but less than a language, spoken habitually between Neapolitans of all ages and classes: even other Italians don't understand a word of it.

PRONUNCIATION
Neapolitans tend to...
...leave off the ends of words, or put an English *er* sound: *buona ser'* (*buona sera*) or *librer* (*libro*, book).
...replace some *e* sounds by *ie*: *tiemp'* (*tempo*, time/weather) or *apiert'* (in Italian *aperto*, open).
...replace some words beginning *pi* by a very hard *ki* sound: *cchiu* (in Italian *più*, more).
...replace a hard *sc* (like *sk* in English) by a soft, English-style *sh*: *scusate* (excuse me) becomes a drunken-sounding *shcusate*.
...make *a* sounds longer than other Italians: *Napule* (Neapolitan for Naples) is *Naapuler*.
... turn *v* into *b*: *che volete?* (what do you want?) becomes *che bullite?*
... turn *d* into *r*: *domenica* (Sunday) becomes *rumenica*.

OTHER HINTS
Bene (well) becomes *buono* (good). Indefinite articles: *un/uno* (a/n, masculine) become *nu*; *una* (a/n, feminine) becomes *na*: *nu gelaate* (*un gelato*, an ice-cream). Definite articles: *il/lo* (the, masculine) become *'o*; *la* (the, feminine) becomes *'a*: *'o gelaate* (*il gelato*, ice-cream).

ENGLISH/ITALIAN/ NEAPOLITAN
BASICS
hello/goodbye (informal) ciao
hello (informal) salve
good morning buon giorno
good evening buona sera
good night buona notte
please per favore, per piacere
thank you grazie
you're welcome prego
excuse me, sorry mi scusi (formal), scusa (informal); *shcusate* (formal and informal)
I'm sorry mi dispiace; *dishpiasher*
I don't speak Italian (very well) non parlo (molto bene) l'italiano; *non parl' buon' l'italian'*
I don't/didn't understand non capisco/non ho capito; *n'aggio capit'*
how much is (it)? quando costa?/quanto viene?
open aperto; *apierto*
closed chiuso
entrance entrata
exit uscita
where is? dov'è?; *a ro'sta?*

TRANSPORT
bus autobus
coach pullman
train treno
underground railway metropolitana (metro)
platform binario
ticket/s biglietto/biglietti

a ticket for... un biglietto per...
one way sola andata
return andata e ritorno
right destra
left sinistra

COMMUNICATIONS
phone telefono
email posta elettronica
fax fax
stamp/s francobollo/francobolli
letter lettera
postcard cartolina

EAT, SHOP, SLEEP
See also p120 **The menu**.
a reservation, booking una prenotazione
I'd like to book a table for four at eight vorrei prenotare una tavola per quattro persone alle otto
breakfast/lunch/dinner colazione/pranzo/cena
the bill il conto
is service included? è compreso il servizio?
that was poor/good/(really) delicious era mediocre/buono/(davvero) ottimo
I think there's a mistake in this bill credo che il conto sia sbagliato
100g/300g/1kg/5kg of... un etto/tre etti/un kilo (or *chilo*)/cinque chili di...
more/less ancora/di meno
shoe/clothes size numero/taglia
a single/twin/double room una camera singola/doppia/matrimoniale
a room with a (sea) view una camera con vista (sul mare)

DAYS & NIGHTS
Monday lunedì
Tuesday martedì
Wednesday mercoledì
Thursday giovedì
Friday venerdì; *viernari*
Saturday sabato
Sunday domenica; *rumenica*
today oggi
tomorrow domani; *rimane*
see you tomorrow! a domani!
morning mattina
afternoon pomeriggio
evening sera
night notte
weekend fine settimana, weekend

NUMBERS
0 zero, 1 uno, 2 due, 3 tre, 4 quattro, 5 cinque, 6 sei, 7 sette, 8 otto, 9 nove, 10 dieci, 11 undici, 12 dodici, 13 tredici, 14 quattordici, 15 quindici, 16 sedici, 17 diciassette, 18 diciotto, 19 diciannove, 20 venti, 30 trenta, 40 quaranta, 50 cinquanta, 60 sessanta, 70 settanta, 80 ottanta, 90 novanta, 100 cento, 200 duecento, 1,000 mille, 2,000 duemila, 200,000 duecentomila, 1,000,000 un milione.

Index

Numbers in **bold** indicate key information on a topic; *italics* indicate photographs.

Advertisers' Index

Please refer to the relevant pages for
addresses and telephone numbers

Place of interest	....
Railway station	....
Park	....
Metro station	.... Ⓜ Ⓜ
Metro route	.... — —
Archaeological site	.... ⊡
Area name	.... **VOMERO**

Maps

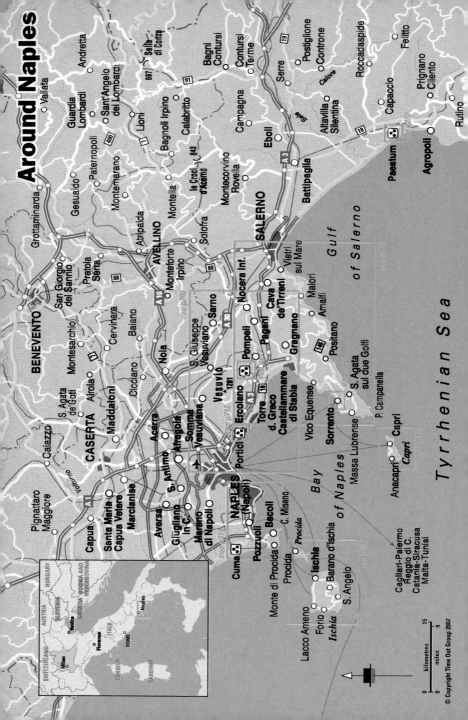

Naples Overview

SAN ROCCO

VIA SAN ROCCO

VIA MIANO

CORSO SECONDIGLIANO

Parco di
Capodimonte

CAPODICHINO

see p310-311

Galleria
Capodimonte

CAPODIMONTE

PIAZZA
CARLO III

see p312-313

VIA FORIA

VIA CASANOVA

TOLEDO &
SANITÀ

Museo Naz.
Archeologico

C.SO G. GARIBALDI

Castel
Capuano

Stazione
Centrale F.S.

PIAZZA
MEDAGLIE
D'ORO

*Quartieri
Spagnoli*

Duomo

VIA DUOMO

PIAZZA
GARIBALDI

VIA L. GIORDANO

VIA TOLEDO

CENTRO
STORICO

C.SO UMBERTO I

Stazione
Circumvesuviana

VOMERO

Stazione
Cumana

Università

PORT & UNIVERSITY

Castello
S. Elmo

Certosa di
San Martino

VIA TOLEDO

Castel Nuovo

Palazzo Reale

CHIAIA

ROYAL NAPLES &
MONTE ECHIA

PIAZZA DELLA
REPUBBLICA

VIA F. CARRACCIOLO

Stazione F.S.
Mergellina

MERGELLINA

Castel
dell'Ovo

POSILLIPPO

B a y

o f   N a p l e s

T y r r h e n i a n   S e a

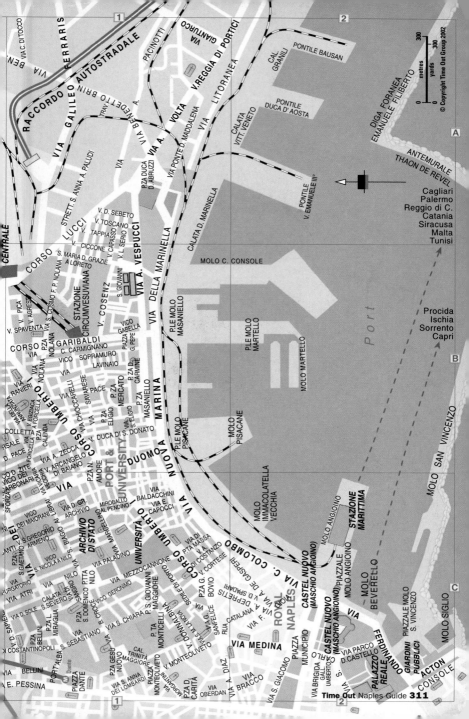

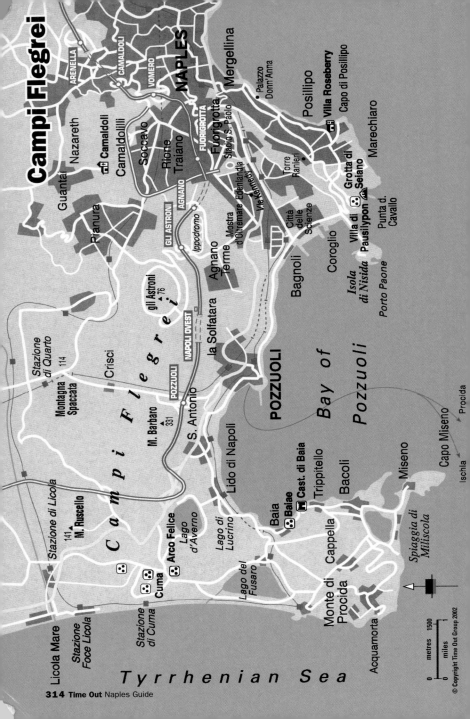

Campi Flegrei

NAPLES

ARENELLA

CAMALDOLI

VOMERO

Mergellina

Posillipo

Palazzo Donn'Anna

Villa Roseberry

Capo di Posillipo

Camaldoli

Camaldolilli

Soccavo

Rione Traiano

Fuorigrotta

FUORIGROTTA

Stadio S. Paolo

Marechiaro

Guantai

Nazareth

Guantai

Pianura

AGNANO

Mostra d'Oltremare

Via Kennedy

Edenlandia

Torre Ranieri

Grotta di Seiano

Villa di Pausilypon

Punta d. Cavallo

GLI ASTRONI

Ippodromo

Città delle Scienze

Coroglio

Isola di Nisida

Porto Paone

gli Astroni
▲ 76

Agnano Terme

la Solfatara

Bagnoli

Bay of Pozzuoli

NAPOLI OVEST

Stazione di Quarto

Crisci

114

POZZUOLI

POZZUOLI

Montagna Spaccata

M. Barbaro
▲ 331

S. Antonio

S. Antonio

Capo Miseno

Procida

Ischia

Stazione di Licola

M. Ruscello
141 ▲

Lido di Napoli

Cast. di Baia

Trippitello

Bacoli

Miseno

Arco Felice

Lago d'Averno

Lago di Lucrino

Baia

Baiae

Cappella

Monte di Procida

Spiaggia di Miliscola

Licola Mare

Stazione Foce Licola

Stazione di Cuma

Cuma

Lago del Fusaro

Acquamorta

metres 1500
miles 1

© Copyright Time Out Group 2002

T y r r h e n i a n   S e a

C a m p i   F l e g r e i

Street Index